Register Now f[...]   s
to You[...]

SPRINGER PUBLISHING COMPANY
CONNECT™

Your print purchase of *Operations Management in Healthcare* **includes online access to the contents of your book**—increasing accessibility, portability, and searchability!

Access today at:

**http://connect.springerpub.com/content/book/978-0-8261-2653-5
or scan the QR code at the right with your smartphone
and enter the access code below.**

RJW9VKVC

*Scan here for
quick access.*

SPRINGER PUBLISHING COMPANY
View all our products at springerpub.com

Operations Management in Healthcare
Strategy and Practice

Corinne M. Karuppan PhD, CPIM
Nancy E. Dunlap MD, PhD, MBA
Michael R. Waldrum MD, MSc, MBA

Resources for Students:

- Video tutorials on how to use tools covered in the book
- Excel data sets for statistical process control and queuing simulation
- ExtendSim® files for models used in the book
- Excel files for problems posed in the book

Resources for Instructors:

Access to the student resources above
- Instructor's Manual
- PowerPoints
- Test Bank

Instructions for Downloading ExtendSim® Student:

The models discussed in this book have been implemented in the simulation application **ExtendSim®**. To view, run, and experiment with the models, download a Student version of the ExtendSim software. The Student version will also allow you to save changes you make to the models, build small models on your own, and print those models. List price of ExtendSim Student is $100. However, *Operations Management in Healthcare: Strategy and Practice* readers can download it for just $10 by following these instructions:

1. Go to **ExtendSimStore.com**.

2. Click the **Academic icon**, then click **ExtendSim Student**. This takes you to the product page where you can learn about the software.

3. Add ExtendSim Student to your Shopping Cart.

4. In the Shopping Cart, click "Have a discount coupon?" on the bottom right. Enter the code **OMH-75CK1264XG**, then click Redeem. Your order total will drop to $10 indicating coupon acceptance!

5. Go to Checkout to finalize your order.

Your invoice will contain a unique link to download an installer for ExtendSim Student plus a serial number to activate your software.

Once you've installed the software, save the installer file you downloaded on an external device for safekeeping.

© 1987–2016 ExtendSim is a registered trademark of Imagine That Incorporated in the United States and/or other countries.

SPRINGER
PUBLISHING COMPANY

Student Resources available at this url: **springerpub.com/karuppan**
Instructor Resources available by e-mailing **textbook@springerpub.com**

OPERATIONS MANAGEMENT IN HEALTHCARE

Corinne M. Karuppan, PhD, CPIM, is professor of operations management at Missouri State University, Springfield, Missouri. Her teaching responsibilities include areas such as quality measurement and management in healthcare, business process management, and management science. Her work has been published in the *Journal of Operations Management, Production and Operations Management, International Journal of Operations and Production Management, European Journal of Information Systems, Journal of Healthcare Management, The Health Care Manager,* and *Journal of Communication in Healthcare.* Corinne is currently one of the area editors of *Operations Management Research.* She holds a PhD in business administration from the University of Nebraska—Lincoln and is certified in production and inventory management by the Association for Operations Management (APICS).

Nancy E. Dunlap, MD, PhD, MBA, is physician-in-residence with the National Governors Association Center for Best Practices in Washington, DC, and professor of medicine, nursing, and public health at the University of Virginia. She has practiced medicine in the field of pulmonary critical care for over 25 years and held executive positions in two academic medical centers, most recently as dean of the School of Medicine at the University of Virginia. She served as the medical director for the Alabama Department of Public Health and vice president of the University of Alabama at Birmingham Health System. Throughout her career, she has worked to improve healthcare quality and outcomes through more efficient patient care delivery processes and information technology. Nancy holds an MD from Duke University School of Medicine, a PhD in microbiology from the University of Alabama at Birmingham, and an MBA from the University of Michigan.

Michael R. Waldrum, MD, MSc, MBA, currently serves as chief executive officer (CEO) of Vidant Health, an eight-hospital integrated system affiliated with East Carolina University in Greenville, North Carolina. Prior to his current role, Dr. Waldrum served as president and CEO of the University of Arizona Health Network (UAHN). He also served as CEO of the University of Alabama Hospital (UAB), and chief information officer for the UAB Health System. He was a member of the medical staff of the UAB School of Medicine and the University of Arizona College of Medicine. Dr. Waldrum received a master's degree in epidemiology from Harvard School of Public Health and an MBA from the University of Michigan. He is a specialist in critical care medicine and in pulmonology.

OPERATIONS MANAGEMENT IN HEALTHCARE

STRATEGY AND PRACTICE

Corinne M. Karuppan, PhD, CPIM

Nancy E. Dunlap, MD, PhD, MBA

Michael R. Waldrum, MD, MSc, MBA

SPRINGER PUBLISHING COMPANY
NEW YORK

Springer Publishing Company, LLC
11 West 42nd Street
New York, NY 10036
www.springerpub.com

Acquisitions Editor: Sheri W. Sussman
Composition: Exeter Premedia Services Pvt Ltd.

ISBN: 978-0-8261-2652-8
e-book ISBN: 978-0-8261-2653-5

Student Supplements are available from springerpub.com/karuppan
Student Resources: 978-08261-5998-4

Instructor's Materials: Qualified instructors may request supplements by emailing textbook@springerpub.com
Instructor's Resources: 978-0-8261-5997-7

The author and the publisher of this Work have made every effort to use sources believed to be reliable to provide information that is accurate and compatible with the standards generally accepted at the time of publication. The author and publisher shall not be liable for any special, consequential, or exemplary damages resulting, in whole or in part, from the readers' use of, or reliance on, the information contained in this book. The publisher has no responsibility for the persistence or accuracy of URLs for external or third-party Internet websites referred to in this publication and does not guarantee that any content on such websites is, or will remain, accurate or appropriate.

Library of Congress Cataloging-in-Publication Data

Names: Karuppan, Corinne M., author. | Dunlap, Nancy E., author. | Waldrum, Michael R., author.
Title: Operations management in healthcare : strategy and practice / Corinne M. Karuppan, Nancy E. Dunlap, Michael R. Waldrum.
Description: New York, NY: Springer Publishing Company, [2016] | Includes bibliographical references and index.
Identifiers: LCCN 2016007628 | ISBN 9780826126528 | ISBN 9780826126535 (e-book)
Subjects: | MESH: Health Planning—methods | Health Services Administration | Quality Control
Classification: LCC RA971 | NLM W 84.1 | DDC 362.1068—dc23
LC record available at http://lccn.loc.gov/2016007628

Special discounts on bulk quantities of our books are available to corporations, professional associations, pharmaceutical companies, health care organizations, and other qualifying groups. If you are interested in a custom book, including chapters from more than one of our titles, we can provide that service as well.

For details, please contact:
Special Sales Department, Springer Publishing Company, LLC
11 West 42nd Street, 15th Floor, New York, NY 10036-8002
Phone: 877-687-7476 or 212-431-4370; Fax: 212-941-7842
E-mail: sales@springerpub.com

We dedicate this book to our families for their patience and loving support, and to the many outstanding healthcare professionals with whom we have had the honor of working and who continue to inspire.

CONTENTS

FOREWORD

Some say that healthcare used to be simple and ineffective and relatively safe, but now it is complex, effective, and potentially dangerous. But, that doesn't mean that today's healthcare professionals—clinicians and administrators—are left without levers for success. Corinne Karuppan, Nancy Dunlap, and Michael Waldrum, in this artfully accessible textbook, provide a comprehensive and diverse conceptual overview of these levers and reinforce key foundational concepts with an interesting variety of examples, vignettes, and practical problems. Few textbooks give readers both timely thinking about healthcare operations skills and competencies and ideas about how to successfully enact these practices in healthcare delivery organizations (HDOs). Even fewer textbooks are written in such an engaging and readable way so as to provide insight to a wide range of healthcare delivery professionals ranging from executives, leaders, and administrators to clinicians and others on the front lines of care. It is rare to find thought leaders who have studied these issues first hand and have successfully put these ideas into practice. It is rare to find thought leaders who deeply understand the intricacies of healthcare operations and who are committed to making it better. Quality, efficiency, effectiveness, and reliability are no longer elusive goals that HDOs aspire to—they are essential in today's competitive healthcare environments.

CHANGE NEVER STARTS BECAUSE IT NEVER STOPS

One of this book's most important contributions is to highlight that although healthcare is undergoing rapid change, the potential for unexpected surprises and untoward consequences remains constant. HDOs are complex systems—inherently and unavoidably hazardous by their own nature. Healthcare, relatively speaking, is a low-reliability industry and is undergoing tremendous social pressure for improvement. In fact, one of the more troubling facts about medical harm is that most mishaps and errors are an indigenous feature of a dynamic, uncertain, and oftentimes vague unfolding work process. Pursuing excellence in healthcare delivery requires the ability to develop sound operations and manage for unexpected surprises. Highly reliable performance, performance that is both safe and high quality, should be the goal. Highly reliable organizations are sensitive to and constantly adjust to small cues or mishaps that, if left unaddressed, could accumulate and interact with other parts of the system, resulting in larger problems. By constantly adapting, tweaking, and solving small problems as they crop up throughout the system, organizations prevent more widespread failures.

ANTICIPATION AND RESILIENCE

The authors' perspective early on in the book is that developing a highly reliable organization that can deliver on the promise of quality care necessarily requires a clear strategy and excellent operations. Strategy plays a key role in coloring and shaping how HDOs view and attempt to enact their futures. Excellent operations require a clear understanding of the nature of the work and how it is accomplished; they also require that organizational members use the tools of science and technology to anticipate and identify the events and occurrences that must not happen, identify all possible causal precursor events or conditions that may lead to them, and then create means for avoiding them. Repeated high performance then is achieved by a lack of unwanted variance in performance (e.g., by doing things just this way through a set of strategies, operating procedures, and routines). The most highly reliable HDOs are obsessed with a logic of anticipation—as demonstrated throughout this textbook—using the most up-to-date analytical tools and methodologies to better anticipate and control the behavior of organizational members to perform effectively and efficiently. Anticipation removes uncertainty and reduces the amount of information that people have to process. It also decreases the chances of memory lapses, judgment errors, or other biases that can contribute to mishaps and failures, provides a pretext for learning, protects individuals against blame, discourages idiosyncratic informal modifications that are not widely disseminated, and provides a focus for any changes and updates in procedures. Anticipation is crucial. But as the authors point out, existing procedures cannot handle what they don't anticipate. Anticipation is only part of the story. To be truly reliable in the face of unexpected surprises, in addition to their focus on efficient and effective practices, the most highly reliable organizations go a step further. They develop their capabilities for resilience.

Resilience is a capability to respond flexibly in real time, reorganizing resources and taking actions to maintain functioning despite unforeseen surprises, variations, or peripheral failures. It requires organizational mindfulness, a concept discussed in the final chapter of the book. Mindfulness is the capability to become alert and aware of emerging details (such as errors, mishaps, discrepancies) and the associated capability to act swiftly and wisely in response to those details. As the authors carefully highlight in the last chapter, these abilities are generally traced to dynamic organizing around a set of five principles. The hallmark of a highly reliable organization is not that it is error-free but that errors don't disable it.

BUILDING A CULTURE OF QUALITY AND RELIABILITY

You often hear people in healthcare say: "If we only had a better culture, care around here would be safer and of higher quality." It is hard to judge the validity of these claims because they are often vague and they rarely point to one specific thing that is wrong. Changing culture is a long, hard road. And as scholars of organizational culture know, you never start with the idea of changing culture. You start with the issue the organization is facing. You dig down to better understand the problems. What are people doing that you do not want them to do? What are they not doing that you want them to do? Why is this the case? To change culture you have to start by solving the operational problems in front of you. When you get people behaving in new ways, a new culture begins to emerge. The culture takes the form of a new set of expectations and standards (norms) and a new urgency that people live up to them. People act their way into new values, beliefs, attitudes, and habits. Broadly speaking, effective cultures are enabled by organizational leaders through their actions and the operating management systems they create; they are enacted by organizational members when they use existing tools and technologies and put the organization's operational policies and procedures into practice; and they are continually elaborated, made stronger, and more effective over time as people reflect on performance and other feedback indicative of how things are going. The beauty of this book is that it shows what it takes to build a culture of quality and high reliability, and it also shows how to do it. The guidance provided by Karuppan, Dunlap, and Waldrum on how to accomplish this is invaluable.

Kathleen M. Sutcliffe, PhD
Bloomberg Distinguished Professor of Business and Medicine
Johns Hopkins University
Baltimore, Maryland

PREFACE

Healthcare organizations are the most complex form of human organization we have ever attempted to manage.

—Peter Drucker

The speed of change in healthcare is unprecedented. New technologies, genetic therapies, and scientific discoveries are transforming the way we care for patients. At the same time, care processes in the exceedingly complex world of healthcare are being reworked. More than ever, those working in this field need to develop the skills to manage operations, acquire the ability to adapt, and the agility to navigate in the new environment. This book is written for anyone working, or aspiring to work, in a healthcare organization. As a result, it addresses the learning needs of a very diverse market: business students enrolled in curricula that emphasize healthcare (undergraduate and graduate levels), healthcare administration/public health students (undergraduate and graduate levels), nursing students (undergraduate and graduate levels), medical students and clinicians, allied health professionals, and administrators.

WHAT IS THE PURPOSE OF THIS BOOK?

Facing pressures to rein in their costs, improve quality, and sustain revenue streams, healthcare organizations have had to rethink the *way* they deliver care. This is where operations management (OM)—the art and science of making products or providing services—plays an important role. It imparts the knowledge and skills to create *value* along the care continuum. This book is therefore about **how** to manage healthcare operations. It combines clinicians' and administrators' viewpoints to provide a common platform and framework for building competitive advantage through superior operations.

A strategic perspective is taken by achieving excellence in the four competitive priorities of an operations strategy: quality, cost, on-time and fast delivery, and flexibility. The competitive priorities should not be pursued in isolation. They are indeed interrelated, with excellent quality laying the foundation for performance in the other competitive priorities, and with targeted improvement initiatives having synergistic effects. After reading this book, you will have developed a conceptual mental model of healthcare operations in which all concepts and tools fit together. You will recognize the dangers of pursuing local optimization and appreciate the benefits of aligning the entire operations system with the business strategy. To bring the cultural context to life, we engage you with a series of short stories showcasing the struggles of a fictitious healthcare organization, Bradley Park Hospital (BPH), as it embarks on its journey to becoming a *highly reliable organization*.

WHAT IS UNIQUE ABOUT THIS BOOK?

The approach taken in this book is very *"hands-on."* Not only should you learn the concepts and tools, but you should also be able to apply them in a variety of contexts. As a result, the tools are presented using step-by-step instructions and are fully integrated with the chapter materials. Most of our students have felt that they were able to use these decision aids on the job right away.

To promote learning and reflection on important topics, the book includes the following features:

- **Mind mapping** to integrate all concepts along the competitive priorities. Mind maps are used throughout the book. An example of a mind map is shown here:

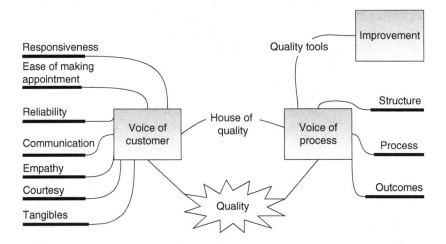

- Use of **icons** to represent the competitive priorities and tool coverage. These icons are placed in the margins to highlight concepts/tools that support competitive priorities.

- Development of an extensive **tool kit,** which is summarized as a table at the end of several chapters and displayed in its entirety in the last chapter.

- Emphasis on measurement and tracking progress by constructing **dashboards** for each competitive priority.

- **Interactive short stories** that involve Bradford Park Hospital are included. Each chapter begins with a performance problem that gets resolved as the protagonists learn to use the chapter material to make the right decisions. The chapter material and the story are intermixed, and the reader is asked to reflect on the issues confronting the characters in the story and propose solutions.

- **Frequently asked questions:** In several chapters, we present boxed features (LET'S TALK!) with our answers to frequently asked questions.

- **Boxed features** (OM in practice!) with real-world implementations of the various concepts and tools covered in the book.

- **Definitions of key terms appear in margins.**

- Different types of **problems/exercises**:

  - *WHAT DO YOU REMEMBER?* This section includes basic questions about the material covered in the chapter.

  - *SOLVE BPH'S PROBLEMS.* Discuss/solve various problems faced by BPH. These types of exercises are conducive to group/class discussions. Numerous problems involving quantitative decision making are provided in this section. Several data sets similar to those found in an actual hospital are provided in an electronic format to facilitate analysis.

  - *THINK OUTSIDE THE BOOK!* This section includes high-level exercises, such as literature reviews, research, essays, field work, projects, team collaboration ideas, and so on.

HOW IS THIS BOOK ORGANIZED?

The book is organized in six parts, with a special emphasis on the competitive priorities:

1. **Getting Organized to Pursue Excellence in Healthcare Delivery**

   This part covers a brief history of healthcare, the challenges it faces today, and the role of operations in overcoming these challenges. It describes the process of strategy development and functional strategy alignment with the business strategy. As the journey to operations excellence proposed in this book requires launching a series of improvement projects, the concepts and techniques of project management are also addressed here.

2. **Competing on Quality**

   In this section, we cover methodologies, tools, and techniques central to quality improvement. Quality is defined by the customer. Although there are several different customers in healthcare, the ultimate customer is the patient. Patients' perceptions of quality (the "voice of the customer") are translated into objective process metrics (the "voice of the process") using a framework called the "house of quality." Total quality management, Lean, and Six Sigma principles are described along with tools and statistical process control techniques to uncover problems, direct improvements, and monitor performance.

3. **Competing on Delivery**

   In this section, we build on the quality gains made by a healthcare organization to develop the capabilities necessary to be responsive to patients' needs. As delays can be life threatening, timeliness is of paramount importance in healthcare. Process analysis and design principles pave the way for a smooth flow of patients, supplies, and information along the care continuum. Techniques to determine optimal capacity levels and to formulate patient-centric schedules are presented.

4. **Competing on Cost**

   As organizations start to provide the right service at the right time, they learn to purge costly waste and expand their efficiencies outside the organization, along the supply chain. This part begins with the tools and techniques to develop accurate forecasts of demand. These forecasts help determine the correct quantity and timing of orders to avoid shortages and excess inventories of critical supplies, both of which can be costly. The importance of selecting the right supplier(s) and establishing mutually beneficial relationships with them is emphasized. A review of cost-accounting principles is provided, and the operations professionals' influence on cost containment is explained.

5. **Competing on Flexibility**

   The business environment constantly changes. So does the patient mix. Healthcare organizations must be agile enough to respond to change (and even anticipate it!) with little or no penalty in terms of cost, time, and quality. This section explores the multiple facets of flexibility and its drivers. It also highlights the role of technology in facilitating the flow of consistent information about different patients and their care across different providers and organizations.

6. **Connecting the Concepts and Reaping the Rewards**

   The final section covers the completion of a successful journey to operations excellence. It mentions the merits of accreditation, but urges organizations to go beyond meeting the standards to become a *highly reliable organization*. The Malcolm Baldrige National Quality Award framework is described, and all the concepts of this book are mapped onto the framework. We connect all the concepts covered in the book, culminating with the development of a comprehensive mind map.

WHAT SUPPLEMENTAL MATERIALS ARE INCLUDED?

- Instructor's manual (teaching tips, answers to end-of-chapter questions and problems, answers to discussion questions at the end of Bradley Park Hospital short stories, several project ideas and team assignments, and recommended cases to complement the chapters)

- Test bank (true–false and multiple-choice questions, short answers and problems)

- PowerPoint presentations

- Video tutorials for some of the tools

- Excel files for most problems covered in the chapter materials

- The ExtendSim simulation software is used in two chapters of the book (see inside cover for coupon code to obtain ExtendSim Student version for 10% of list price). ExtendSim models used in this book are available in electronic format.

- Data sets for statistical process control and queuing simulation

Qualified instructors can obtain all supplemental materials by e-mailing textbook@springerpub.com.

Your concerns and opinions matter to us! Please contact Corinne Karuppan (ckaruppan@missouristate.edu) to let her know how we can serve you better.

OPERATIONS MANAGEMENT
IN HEALTHCARE

PART

I

Getting Organized to Pursue Excellence in Healthcare Delivery

CHAPTER 1

HEALTHCARE: PAST, PRESENT, AND FUTURE

INTRODUCTION AND LEARNING OBJECTIVES

The desire to reform healthcare in the United States is nothing new. Since the early 1900s, the issues of rising medical costs, insufficient health insurance coverage, and disparity in quality care have been the subjects of countless debates. The purpose of this book is certainly not to delve into the politics of healthcare reform, but rather to provide a constructive framework to improve patients' health through better healthcare operations. To improve, it is necessary to take stock of where we are now and how we got here. This chapter, therefore, covers a short history of healthcare in the United States and presents the challenges of today and tomorrow. It provides an overview of the field of operations management and of its unique contributions to overcoming these challenges.

Finally, this first chapter introduces you to a fictional hospital, Bradley Park Hospital (BPH), whose journey from predicament to success will highlight the lessons of failure, the dynamics of decision making, and the rewards of teamwork. After reading this chapter, you will be able to:

1. **List the main events that have shaped healthcare reform over the past century**
2. **Identify the challenges healthcare faces today**
3. **Describe operations management and a productive system**
4. **Identify the inputs and outputs of a healthcare productive system**
5. **Identify the decisions that operations management professionals make**
6. **Explain key terms**
7. **Understand how this textbook is organized**

THE PAST: EARLY 20TH CENTURY TO PRESENT

Much has been written about the ills of healthcare organizations, but before we embark on our journey to treat them, we need to understand the events that shaped the environment in which providers operate today. Until the beginning of the 20th century, healthcare was essentially primitive, and medical remedies were quite eccentric: goat glands, electromagnetic bathing fluids, snake oil liniments, and other potions that cured nothing (Box 1.1). Fortunately, this type of care was cheap. In 1900, the cost of healthcare for the average resident in the United States was $5.00 a year, which is equivalent to about $135 today. Medical colleges did exist, but clinical instruction was provided in under-equipped facilities, was limited in scope, and largely ignored scientific research. By the end of the century, science had taken over, modern medicine was born, and organization for a better healthcare system began. A brief history of the U.S. healthcare system is presented in Table 1.1.

⊕ BOX 1.1 – DID YOU KNOW?

Vin Mariani—Coca Wine

Angelo Mariani, a French chemist, read a paper on the effects of coca and started marketing a "tonic" made from red wine laced with coca extract. To export his wine and compete with other coca drinks sold in the United States, Mariani increased the coca content from 6 mg per fluid ounce to 7.2 milligrams. The elixir was claimed to boost one's health and vitality. Queen Victoria, Popes Leo XIII and Saint Pius X, Thomas Edison, and Ulysses Grant drank the beverage and publicly endorsed it (Vin Mariani Winery, 2007–2008).

TABLE 1.1 – Brief History of the U.S. Healthcare System

Milestone	Time	Events
Founding of the American Medical Association (AMA)	1847	• Pushed for medical scientific research and improvement of medical education
Birth of modern medicine	Early 1900s	• Standards for medical licensure • Standards for hospitals • Government regulation of pharmaceuticals
Birth of health insurance	1920–1939	• The Baylor Plan: prepaid program similar to health insurance • Farmers' Union Cooperative Health Association is the first health maintenance organization • No national health insurance program, but private plans gain popularity

(continued)

TABLE 1.1 – Brief History of the U.S. Healthcare System (*continued*)

Milestone	Time	Events
Growth and progress	1940–1969	• Numerous medical and technological breakthroughs: widespread use of penicillin, polio vaccine, pacemakers, first heart transplant, electronic medical records (EMRs) • Expansion of private insurance • Creation of Medicare and Medicaid programs providing healthcare coverage for the elderly and for the poor, blind, and disabled
Looming crisis and rise of HMOs	1970–1989	• New diseases emerge • Fragmented, inefficient system • Rising costs create serious concerns • Expansion of HMOs and changes in payment systems to control costs
Toward universal healthcare	1990s–to date	• Pharmaceutical companies' direct-to-consumer advertising, greater use of expensive technologies, and higher demand for drugs and medical services contribute to unsustainable cost increases • Significant proportion of U.S. population cannot afford health insurance • Sustainability of Medicare program is questioned • Quality of care is questioned • Enactment of the Patient Protection and Affordable Care Act (PPACA): Everyone must be insured or pay a penalty; measures to control costs and improve quality are enforced

Early 1900s: The Establishment of Standards and Regulations

BOX 1.2 – WORDS OF WISDOM

"Medical ethics, as a branch of general ethics, must rest on the basis of religion and morality" (Code of Medical Ethics, AMA, 1847, p. 83).

Nathan Smith Davis established the AMA in 1847 for the purpose of improving medical education in the United States. AMA's ambitious goals included the advancement of the science of medicine, the improvement of standards for medical education, the development of a program of medical ethics, and the improvement of the public's health (Box 1.2). The founding meeting welcomed 250 delegates from 28 states (AMA, 2010). In the early 1900s, the AMA became a dominant national force with about 70,000 physician members, marking the beginning of "organized medicine." It created the Council on Medical Education to develop standards for medical licensure. Concurrently, Abraham Flexner, an expert on educational practices, wrote a report that prompted the elimination of proprietary schools and established the biomedical model as the gold standard of medical training (Flexner, 1910). The American College of Surgeons was also active in setting standards for quality care. In 1917, it developed the Minimum Standard for Hospitals and started on-site inspections the next year. This program was the precursor of hospital accreditation. It is thus no wonder that U.S. hospitals began to modernize and use the latest scientific breakthroughs to improve the quality of care (Silverman & Danner, 2000).

The early 1900s also saw the beginning of government regulation of pharmaceutical companies. In 1906, the Pure Food and Drug Act required them to be truthful in their product labeling, and Congress authorized the random sampling of specimens for misbranding and adulteration (Swann, 2001).

To gain the political support of the working class, governments in other developed countries had enacted some sort of social insurance program protecting individuals against the loss of wages during sickness. Progressive reformers in the United States also called for similar protection, but their efforts were thwarted by influential interest groups (physicians, labor, insurance companies, and businesses), fragmented support for social legislation, and the entry of the United States into World War I (Palmer, 1999; Public Broadcasting Service, 2010).

1920-1939: Birth of Health Insurance

The war and improved quality in healthcare increased the demand for services, resulting in higher costs and heightened interest in medical insurance. In 1929, the surge in unpaid medical bills led Baylor Hospital in Dallas, Texas, to institute a prepaid program considered to be the first example of health insurance in the United States. Shortly thereafter, the Farmers' Union Cooperative Health Association was formed. This pioneering **health maintenance organization** offered its members comprehensive healthcare. All members paid a flat fee irrespective of their use of the program (Goodridge & Arnquist, 2009). The Great Depression of the 1930s encouraged many other hospitals to follow suit, resulting in more widespread use of prepaid health plans. Not only did these plans protect individuals, but they also gave providers a stable source of income during these difficult economic times (Zhou, 2009). As the healthcare debate shifted toward the cost of medical care, the Committee on the Cost of Medical Care—funded by philanthropic organizations—recommended the creation of community medical centers and the expansion of voluntary, as opposed to compulsory, insurance schemes. The AMA condemned the report for its endorsement of socialized medicine (Box 1.3); (Palmer, 1999; Public Broadcasting Service, 2010).

Health Maintenance Organization (HMO)

A type of insurance plan that limits coverage to care from doctors contracting with the HMO.

⚙ BOX 1.3 – WORDS OF WISDOM

"SOCIALIZED MEDICINE IS URGED IN SURVEY: Wilbur Committee Advocates Community Centers to Treat and Prevent Illness" (*New York Times* Editors, 1932).

In this atmosphere, the national health insurance program, which was initially proposed for inclusion in the Social Security Act of 1935, was never seriously discussed for fear that it would threaten the passage of the entire legislation. The proposed National Health Act of 1939 failed to pass as well, but private hospital insurance plans gained popularity (Goodridge & Arnquist, 2009; Public Broadcasting Service, 2010). Around the same time, Congress required that drugs be certified as safe by the Food and Drug Administration before they could be marketed (Swann, 2001).

1940–1969: Growth and Progress

The 1940s witnessed several important developments in healthcare. During World War II, penicillin became available in quantities sufficient to treat Allied soldiers and significantly reduce the incidence and severity of infections (Oatman, 2005). At the end of the war, mass production and lower costs increased its availability to the public (Grossman, 2008).

At the same time, Congress expanded access to healthcare through widespread hospital construction, especially in rural areas, and prohibited discrimination based on race, religion, or nationality. Competing for a limited supply of workers, American employers started offering health benefits, which could be part of collective bargaining. In the early 1950s, it was estimated that 77 million Americans had some form of private insurance (Goodridge & Arnquist, 2009).

In the 1950s and 1960s, important medical advances in illness treatment and prevention took place: the polio vaccine (1952), the cardiac pacemaker (1952), coronary angiography (1958), artificial placenta (1961), the measles vaccine (1964), and the first heart transplant (1967), to name a few. In 1951, the American College of Physicians, the American Hospital Association, the AMA, and the Canadian Medical Association joined the American College of Surgeons to create **the Joint Commission on Accreditation of Hospitals (JCAH),** whose main purpose was to provide voluntary accreditation. Another breakthrough was the advent of electronic medical records. In the early 1960s, Dr. Lawrence L. Weed described the concept of an automated system to store and organize patient medical records. He believed the system would facilitate retrieval of patient information for prompt and accurate decision making, as well as sharing of information among specialists, ultimately resulting in more effective care. A team of physicians and information technology experts at the University of Vermont worked on this concept and delivered the Problem-Oriented Medical Record (POMR) system to the Medical Center Hospital of Vermont in 1970. During the same time period, the Mayo Clinic was also pursuing the development of EMRs (Gungor, 2011).

The Joint Commission (TJC; formerly JCAH and JCAHO) A U.S.-based nonprofit organization that accredits healthcare organizations and programs in the United States. It evaluates their compliance with federal regulations.

Although quality improved, spiraling hospital costs made it difficult for the unemployed and the elderly to afford insurance, ultimately leading to the Social Security Amendments of 1965 and the creation of the Medicare and Medicaid programs (Centers for Medicare & Medicaid Services, 2009). Medicare provided healthcare coverage for people aged

Fee-for-Service (FFS)

A payment system in which providers are paid separately for each service (office visit, test, or procedure) they perform.

65 years and older, and Medicaid was designed to care for the most vulnerable citizens—long-term care for the aged, and healthcare for the blind, disabled, and poor mothers and children. These programs were designed to be "**fee-for-service**," which means that each visit or test is paid for separately from a fee schedule. Only hospitals accredited by the JCAH were "deemed" to be in compliance with the Medicare Conditions of Participation and could participate in the Medicare and Medicaid programs.

At the end of the 1960s, growing pains surfaced. The proportion of physician specialists had increased to 69%, intensifying a primary care physician (PCP) shortage (Public Broadcasting Service, 2010). Other areas of concern included the increasing number of unnecessary and expensive tests, disparities of healthcare quality across the United States, a demand for healthcare outstripping supply, greater burden on taxpayers, and inefficiency in hospital administration and facility utilization (Schmeck, 1968).

1970–1989: Looming Crisis and Rise of HMOs

During the 1970s, increases in the number of medical schools and their enrollments assuaged the problem of physician shortages. However, the ratio of specialists to PCPs remained high. Although this ratio was unequally distributed across the country, some saw the abundance of qualified specialists as necessary to deal with the ills of a changing society: increase in venereal diseases and drug addiction, as well as emergence of new diseases, such as Legionnaires' disease and AIDS.

Coverage of these issues in the media kept the population interested in health issues. Boosted by inflation in the economy and growing hospital expenses and profits, the average healthcare expenditures per American more than doubled over the decade. In the search for solutions, the organization of the healthcare system emerged as a culprit. The conglomeration of vast hospital systems, pharmaceutical companies, insurers, and government programs was uncoordinated. This fragmentation engendered a myriad of inefficiencies, such as duplication of technologies, paperwork, and services. Despite agreement that access to affordable healthcare was jeopardized, neither President Nixon's nor Senator Ted Kennedy's plans for national health insurance mustered enough political support to get passed. However, federal support for pilot HMO projects and regulation of benefit (including health) plans offered by employers (Employee Retirement Income Security Act—ERISA) were passed into law.

Diagnosis-Related Group (DRG)

A system that classifies hospital cases into groups (e.g., appendectomy) and sets payment rates based on the diagnosis.

In the 1980s, further expansions of healthcare protection included the compulsory screening and stabilization of all emergency room patients, and under the Consolidated Omnibus Budget Reconciliation Act (COBRA) of 1985, employees who lost their jobs had the option to keep their group health plan for up to 18 months. Healthcare became increasingly privatized as corporations started integrating decentralized healthcare units into a system. As costs continued their uncontrollable ascent, Medicare adopted the **diagnosis-related group** system, which reimburses hospitals a set amount for treatment of a disease or condition, as insurance companies started denouncing excesses in the FFS method of payment to doctors (Goodridge & Arnquist, 2009; Public Broadcasting Service, 2010; Rosenthal, Berndt, Donohue, Frank, & Epstein, 2002). Many physicians started joining HMOs and were paid salaries. To control costs, these HMOs directed patients away from hospitals and to physicians' offices and ambulatory care centers for an expanding number of services (Coombs, 2005). Although the concept of HMOs capping payments was good in that it incentivized providers to care for patients in the most cost-effective ways, quality issues and denial of some procedures by the HMOs caused concern in some patients, who feared they were getting inferior medical care. Many HMOs ceased to exist.

1990s–to Present: Moving to Comprehensive Reform

⚙ BOX 1.4 – WORDS OF WISDOM

"Economic goods that can be valued in monetary terms are not the only kinds of good that we value having. Providing certain important goods like healthcare to all members of society has its own value" (Institute of Medicine [IOM], 2003, p. 11).

In the 1990s, President Bill Clinton proposed to reform the U.S. healthcare system with universal healthcare funded through expanded competition among private insurers in a regulated market. Partisan politics, concerns about the cost of the program, a lack of transparency by the administration, and an influential lobby put an end to the effort. During the decade, with new drugs available to treat more conditions, pharmaceutical companies' spending on direct-to-consumer advertising and promotion to healthcare professionals surged, leading to a dissemination of more information, as well as an increase in demand, and therefore in health expenditures. The growing use of more expensive technology became another source of rising costs. For example, the use of MRI procedures increased by more than 50% between 1993 and 1999. At the end of the 20th century, the number of uninsured Americans had reached 44 million, or 16% of the population. In addition, the spectrum of the baby boomers' upcoming retirement had started looming, causing individuals to question the sustainability of the Medicare program. To make matters worse, the high costs of healthcare were not commensurate with its quality. In 1999, the IOM sent shockwaves when it released a report placing the number of annual deaths resulting from preventable medical errors between 44,000 and 98,000 (IOM, 1999). A 2000 report by the WHO supported these findings by ranking the U.S. healthcare system 37th out of 191 national healthcare systems (WHO, 2000).

The growth of healthcare costs accelerated during the 2000s, with an increase from 13% of gross domestic product (GDP) in 2000 to 17.9% in 2010. During the Great Recession of 2008–2009, the dismal economy and high rate of job losses contributed to individuals losing their healthcare

Affordable Care Act (ACA)

A law that requires all citizens to be covered by health insurance and obligates insurance companies to cover all applicants, regardless of preexisting conditions.

coverage. By 2009, the number of uninsured Americans was 49 million (U.S. Census Bureau, 2011). These conditions, along with a Congress slightly more favorable to reform, paved the way for President Obama to sign the Patient Protection and Affordable Care Act—shortened to the **Affordable Care Act**—into law on March 23, 2010. It was the largest expansion of healthcare regulation and coverage since the implementation of Medicare and Medicaid in 1965. The law required all citizens to be covered by health insurance (private or government programs), obligated insurance companies to cover all applicants (regardless of preexisting conditions), and provided assistance for the purchase of health insurance through tax subsidies for eligible participants. Provisions within the ACA included inducements for the states to expand Medicaid to all Americans under the age of 65 years with incomes at or below 133% of the federal poverty level. Initially, the law put federal funding at risk for states opting to forgo Medicaid expansion. In 2012, the U.S. Supreme Court ruled that this practice would be illegal, which made Medicaid expansion optional for each state (Hansen, 2014). Nevertheless, by early 2015, the rate of uninsured U.S. adults had dropped to a historic low of 12.9%, and 16.9 million people had gained coverage (Carman, Eibner, & Paddock, 2015; J. Levy, 2015).

The law also included measures designed to improve the quality and delivery of care: free prevention services, better coordination of patient care through transition programs for seniors and bundled payments, quality reporting, payments based on value and not volume, and so forth. The Congressional Budget Office projected that the ACA would decrease future governmental healthcare expenditures, but the ACA's budgetary effects are dependent on a myriad of factors (e.g., new regulations, state of the economy, changes in the tax code), making it impossible to assess the net effect of the law over an extended period of time (Congressional Budget Office, 2014). It is also fair to say that the ACA introduced a new series of regulations in one of the industries that was already highly regulated (Box 1.5). Since the ACA was signed into law, there have been ongoing political and legal battles to overturn or revise it. As of 2015, none of these activities has been successful in bringing about substantive change to the law. Despite the battles, there is general consensus that transformation of the U.S. healthcare industry is needed. This consensus is driven by acceptance that the U.S. healthcare system has challenges that make the status quo unacceptable and unsustainable.

⊕ BOX 1.5 – DID YOU KNOW?

The Rise of Regulations

For more than a century, federal and local governments have enacted laws and regulations covering all aspects of the complex and fragmented components of the healthcare industry. These regulations govern issues such as how patients are treated and transferred (Emergency Medical Treatment and Active Labor Act [EMTALA]), how hospitals

(continued)

⊕ BOX 1.5 – DID YOU KNOW? (*continued*)

interact with their physicians (Stark law), how health information is protected (Health Insurance Portability and Accountability Act [HIPAA]), how delivery organizations provide care and are reimbursed (Centers for Medicare & Medicaid Services [CMS], ACA), how information technology is overseen (Health Information Technology for Economic and Clinical Health Act [HITECH Act]), and so forth. The Joint Commission has expanded its survey process to non–hospital-based services. Many payers now require accreditation as a condition for reimbursement.

Despite the legitimate justification for reforms and regulations, reform is significantly modified by the political process. This has led to a piecemeal approach, fragmentation of efforts, and increased complexity. The growth in regulations has been likened by some to a hidden tax that costs billions (Conover, 2004). In this environment, it is largely incumbent on the individual communities to persuade state and local policymakers to provide some regulatory flexibility allowing creative solutions to be implemented. For example, the Arkansas state legislature passed exemptions from legal and financial requirements for collaboratives developing community-based health plans (The National Policy Consensus Center, 2004).

THE PRESENT: CHALLENGES

❖❖ BOX 1.6 – WORDS OF WISDOM

"The U.S. Health Care system is on a dangerous path, with a toxic combination of high costs, uneven quality, frequent errors, and limited access" (Porter & Teisberg, 2006, p. 1).

How "toxic" is the combination mentioned by Porter and Teisberg in Box 1.6? How high are the costs? How inconsistent is the quality? How untimely and limited is access to services? These are legitimate questions that need to be answered before offering solutions.

How High Are the Costs?

At approximately $9,000 per capita, the United States spends more on healthcare than any other industrialized country (Figure 1.1). Total healthcare expenditure reached $2.9 trillion in 2013, or 17.4% of the GDP (Centers for Disease Control and Prevention, 2015). These numbers are projected to increase to $4.6 trillion and 19.8%, respectively, by 2020 (CMS, 2012a, 2013). The growth in expenditures is driven by several factors, including the greater use of expensive healthcare technologies, trauma and injuries in young people, the aging of overweight Americans, rising drug costs, and waste.

FIGURE 1.1 –
Per capita health
expenditure in
Organization
for Economic
Cooperation and
Development (OECD)
countries for the year
2012.

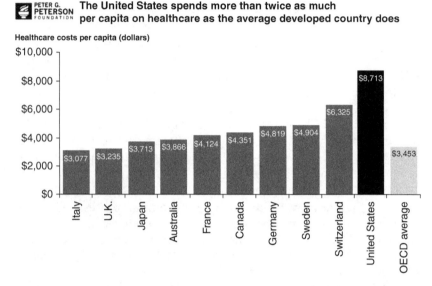

PETER G. PETERSON FOUNDATION **The United States spends more than twice as much per capita on healthcare as the average developed country does**

Healthcare costs per capita (dollars)

Italy	$3,077
U.K.	$3,235
Japan	$3,713
Australia	$3,866
France	$4,124
Canada	$4,351
Germany	$4,819
Sweden	$4,904
Switzerland	$6,325
United States	$8,713
OECD average	$3,453

Note: Per capita health expenditures are for 2013, except Australia for which 2012 data are the latest available. Chart uses purchasing power parities to convert data into U.S. dollars.

Source: Organization for Economic Cooperation and Development (2015). Copyright by Peter G. Peterson Foundation. Used with permission.

Healthcare Technologies

The United States is a wealthy nation that can afford to spend money (and it does!) on healthcare technologies (Kaiser Family Foundation, 2012b). Several healthcare economists have claimed that the use of new medical technologies and increased use of older ones contribute between 40% to 50% of the increase in healthcare costs. If so, technology would be a primary target for cost containment (Smith, Newhouse, & Freeland, 2009). This is a difficult argument to make. Technological innovation has been heralded as a source of pride for the United States for decades. Patients want it, doctors acquire the skills to use it, and the industry that produces it posts enviable earnings. On the political side, both conservatives and liberals oppose controlling these costs, either because they see it as a threat to market freedom or because they value boundless scientific progress (Callahan, 2008).

Expenditures in health information technology have increased at a fast pace as well. In 2009, the Health Information Technology for Economic and Clinical Health Act provided incentive payments to adopt electronic health records and achieve "**meaningful use.**" This intent was strengthened in the ACA of 2010. As a result, providers, payers, and physician groups are investing billions of dollars in healthcare information technology (HIT). Early cost–benefit analyses suggested that HIT was having a positive impact on effectiveness and efficiency (Buntin, Burke, Hoaglin, & Blumenthal, 2011). More recent studies show a more disappointing performance of health IT as a result of sluggish adoption of health IT systems coupled with

Meaningful Use
A set of standards defined by the CMS that regulates the use of electronic health records and allows providers to earn incentives by meeting preestablished criteria.

the incompatibility of these systems (Kellerman & Jones, 2013). In a nutshell, advances in both medical technology and health IT have obvious benefits but are plagued by implementation problems and are costly.

Trauma and Injuries in Young People

A study by the IOM and the National Research Council found that deaths before the age of 50 years account for approximately two thirds of the difference in life expectancy between males in the United States and males in 16 other developed countries, and about one third of the difference for females. The countries in the analysis included Canada, Japan, Australia, France, Germany, and Spain. Car accidents, gun violence, and drug overdoses were major contributors to years of life lost by Americans younger than age 50 years. Traumatic brain injury is a leading cause of death and lifelong disability among this age group. For a survivor, the lifetime cost can reach $4 million (Brain Injury Alliance of Utah, 2016).

Aging of Overweight Americans

The first wave of baby boomers turned 65 in 2010. Along with older Americans, they account for the greatest proportion in healthcare spending. With age comes a greater number of diseases and therefore a growing demand for healthcare services. Some of the most common health issues among the elderly are heart disease, diabetes, arthritis, dementia, and respiratory problems. These are chronic conditions that require long-term care and are therefore costly to treat. However, an aging demographic by itself does not explain the vast differences in healthcare spending between the United States and other industrialized countries. In fact, the U.S. population is relatively young compared to those in the industrialized countries listed in Figure 1.1. In Germany and Japan, more than 20% of the population was 65 years and over in 2009, compared to only 13% in the United States (Squires, 2012). The higher spending for older adults in the United States can be attributed to the higher prevalence of obesity among this group. About 35% of adults aged 65 years and over are obese (Fakhouri, Ogden, Carroll, Kit, & Flegal, 2012). Healthcare costs for overweight elderly are 6% to 17% higher than for those within a normal weight range (Yang & Hall, 2008). Medical progress has enabled the system to treat many of the chronically ill who might have otherwise died years ago, but this progress will not solve Medicare's troubles unless similar leaps are made on the prevention of chronic diseases in the first place (Kaiser Family Foundation, 2012b; S. Levy, 2013; Pittman, 2012).

Rising Drug Costs

In 2009, drug manufacturers started raising their prices at the fastest rate seen in years in order to boost their profits before Congress passed the ACA as a means of curbing spending (Wilson, 2009). In reality, prices have been rising ever since. In 2012, drug prices rose at twice the inflation rate, both as a result of high research and development costs and advertising expenses. These steep increases have offset the savings associated with the greater use of generic drugs (Cauchon, 2013). With increased demand from the newly insured post-ACA, spending growth is expected to intensify to 8.8%, and then to 6.6% per year from 2015 to 2021 (CMS, 2012a).

Waste

It is estimated that about 20% of the total health expenditures originate from various inefficiencies such as unnecessary treatments, poor care coordination, administrative complexity (Box 1.7), and fraud and abuse. Unnecessary treatments and tests—**overuse**—are the major culprits in wasteful spending and have prompted the creation of the Choosing Wisely® initiative to reduce overuse. Leading medical societies participated in this effort and released lists of tests and procedures that are sometimes unnecessary.

Overuse

The provision of healthcare services given without medical justification.

Chronic medical conditions often involve multiple illnesses with multiple needs across care delivery sites. Poor coordination of patient transfers may have cost between $25 billion and $45 billion in unnecessary spending in 2011 as a result of avoidable readmissions, complications, and test duplications. Differences in computer systems, lack of accountability for failing to send inpatient records to outpatient physicians upon discharge, and payment policies that do not encourage team collaboration for patient care are mainly to blame. The ACA has several provisions to alleviate these problems: increased Medicare reimbursements for performance measures addressing discharge, 1% reimbursement penalties to hospitals with high readmission rates, and increased use of EMRs to facilitate care coordination among providers (Health Policy Brief, 2012a).

✥ BOX 1.7 – WORDS OF WISDOM

"On an average day in 1968, U.S. hospitals employed 435,100 managers and clerks to assist the care of 1,378,000 inpatients. By 1990, the number of patients had fallen to 853,000, while the number of administrators has risen to 1,221,600" (Hurley, 1993, p. 58).

The administrative complexity of the U.S. healthcare system further exacerbates the inefficiencies discussed earlier. It is rooted in (Ivey, 2006):

- A mix of multiple payers and quasicustomized insurance products with different coverage structures, deductibles, and copayments. For a provider, negotiating a contract with an insurer or plan sponsor consumes an average of 5.5 hours. For a large medical group handling more than 100 contracts, this could result in several hundred million dollars in annual costs.

- A plurality of payment mechanisms making it difficult for the provider to standardize its claim filing procedures: capitation (monthly payment allocated to patient), FFS (number of services performed), DRG (payment based on a set of services associated with a diagnosis), per diem payment (payment made by payer for each day patient spends at the hospital) schemes, and so forth.

- The coexistence of multiple standards for coding, prescribing medicine, credentialing, quality metrics, and so on. Not only does this create confusion, but it also results in errors and duplication of work.

- Federal and state regulations which create a complex and costly administrative burden that costs billions (Conover, 2004).

Fraud involves deceit and misrepresentation to obtain something of value without being entitled to it. Examples include knowingly billing for services or supplies not provided, altering claims, and kickbacks. **Abuse** occurs when providers or suppliers follow improper practices that result in unnecessary costs or payments, such as misusing codes on claims, overcharging for services or supplies, and billing for medically unnecessary treatments or procedures (see "overuse" discussed earlier; CMS, 2012b). No one knows how much fraud and abuse in healthcare actually cost. In 2011, fraud and abuse resulted in Medicare and Medicaid payments in excess of $98 billion (Berwick & Hackbarth, 2012). Both programs process millions of claims each day and strive for rapid reimbursements at the expense of claim inspection. This situation makes them easy prey to fraud and abuse. Under the ACA, CMS is better equipped to prevent fraud from both providers and enrollees: One automated system detects dubious claims, another screens out ineligible providers or suppliers before they are enrolled or validated, and a bidding program for suppliers of medical equipment establishes a higher standard for entry (Health Policy Brief, 2012b).

Fraud
Refers to deceit and misrepresentation intended to obtain something of value.

Abuse
Refers to improper practices that result in unnecessary costs or payments.

We often say that we get what we pay for, implying that there is a positive correlation between costs and quality. As the United States ranks on top as far as healthcare costs are concerned, you would therefore expect the same for quality. Unfortunately, the facts paint a different picture, as explained in the next section.

How Inadequate Is the Quality?

Despite the large expenditures for healthcare, there is wide recognition of a "quality crisis." In 2006–2007, the United States had the highest mortality rate amenable to healthcare among 16 high-income nations (Doe, 2009; Nolte & McKee, 2011). The Commonwealth Fund's national scorecard (2011) indicated that in the area of quality, the United States scored an average of 75 compared to 100, the benchmark set by top performers domestically and abroad. Notable quality indicators used in this report were effectiveness, safety, coordination, and patient centeredness (Figure 1.2).

FIGURE 1.2 –
National scorecard
on U.S. health system
performance.

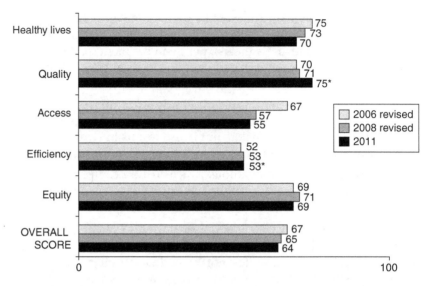

*Includes indicator(s) not available in earlier years.

Source: The Commonwealth Fund (2011). Used with permission.

Effectiveness

The provision of services based on scientific knowledge to all who could benefit; doing it right the first time.

Effectiveness

With an emphasis on public reporting, the country has made progress in the control of chronic conditions, such as blood pressure, in hospitals' use of evidence-based treatments for heart conditions and pneumonia, and in the prevention of surgical infections. Unfortunately, there remain deficiencies in the areas of primary and mental care. In 2008, too few adult Americans received the proper immunizations, cancer screenings, and blood pressure and cholesterol tests. In some states, only 40% of young children received all recommended immunizations against transmittable diseases (The Commonwealth Fund, 2011). As for mental health, more than one third of adults and 40% of children did not receive the care they needed. The lack of mental health services has even resulted in prisons sometimes being used as the largest mental health providers in their states (O'Shea, 2012). The ACA attempted to remedy some of these problems by requiring that, in 2010, new insurance plans cover 16 preventive services for adults, 22 specifically for women, and 27 for children without requiring copayments or deductibles (HealthCare. gov, 2010). By forbidding the exclusion of people with preexisting conditions and allowing young people to remain on their parents' health insurance, it also allowed access to mental health services that might have otherwise been denied (Friedman, 2012).

Disparities in effectiveness often follow racial and ethnic lines. In general, minorities receive lower quality care and experience worse outcomes than do their White counterparts, even after controlling for factors such as insurance coverage, socioeconomic status, and comorbidities (IOM, 2002). The reasons for these disparities are multifaceted, but limited English proficiency, lack of access to care in general and to minority healthcare providers in particular, and prevalence of chronic conditions appear to be big contributors. Further disparities are observed with respect to income, age, location, gender, disability status, and sexual orientation. Not only do disparities in healthcare end up costing the economy an excess of $300 billion annually (LaVeist, Gaskin, & Richard, 2009), but they also impede improvements in overall healthcare quality and population health. As our society becomes more diverse, it is imperative that disparities be addressed seriously. Provisions of the ACA target disparity problems by expanding vulnerable populations' access to care, promoting cultural competence in healthcare settings, and funding disparity research efforts (Kaiser Family Foundation, 2012a).

Safety

Safety
Refers to avoiding harm to patients.

Since the IOM's (1999) report, *To Err Is Human*, patient safety has been a priority in healthcare. Nevertheless, the incidence of medical errors remains high, with an updated estimate placing the annual number of deaths associated with preventable harm in hospitals between 210,000 and 400,000 (James, 2013). Pressure ulcers, postoperative infections, and persistent pain following back or leg surgeries are associated with the most frequent errors and are among the costliest to treat (Van Den Bos et al., 2011). Also common are adverse drug events (prescription of contraindicated drugs and/or poor monitoring) and the unwarranted use of antibiotics. Yet, of all the adverse medical events, almost one half are preventable (de Vries, Ramrattan, Smorenburg, Gouma, & Boermeester, 2008).

Given the stakes and the potential for improvement, there have been several initiatives to increase patient safety. Most notably, the Institute for Healthcare Improvement (IHI) launched The 100,000 Lives Campaign in 2005 with the ambitious goal to prevent 100,000 avoidable inpatient deaths over an 18-month period. Hundreds of healthcare organizations joined the effort, and the results beat expectations with approximately 122,300 lives saved (Box 1.8). The success of the initiative prompted the IHI to follow up with The 5 Million Lives Campaign (Institute for Healthcare Improvement, 2006). Whether the campaign reached its objective of saving 5 million lives remains unclear. What is certain, however, is that it provided a blueprint for ongoing improvements in reducing harm to patients.

> **⟐ BOX 1.8 – WORDS OF WISDOM**
>
> "The names of the patients whose lives we save can never be known. Our contribution will be what did not happen to them" (Donald M. Berwick, MD, MPP; Institute for Healthcare Improvement [n.d., p. 1]).

Coordination

Coordination
Communication and cooperation among providers as patients move through different facilities and settings.

Care coordination is not a measure of quality per se, but it is a determinant of quality. Earlier, we mentioned that poor care coordination resulted in costly inefficiencies. It also has detrimental effects on quality. The fragmented care delivery system, the lack of communication among providers across and within sites, and payment structures unfavorable to coordinated care cause complications, treatment delays, drug overdoses or interactions, and lack of follow-ups, discharge plans, and medication reviews (California Healthcare Foundation, 2007). There have been several initiatives to improve care coordination. Most rest on the strengthening of primary care, whereby a physician, physician assistant, or nurse practitioner provides ongoing care to patients and coordinates their care according to a preestablished service plan (Craig, Eby, & Whittington, 2011).

Patient Centeredness

Patient Centeredness

Care that is respectful of patients' preferences, needs, and values.

Patient centeredness "encompasses qualities of compassion, empathy, and responsiveness to the needs, values, and expressed preferences of the individual patient" (IOM, 2001, p. 48). A major component of patient centeredness is clear communication. It is vital that the provider understands and addresses the patient's needs and that the patient understands the provider's diagnosis and recommendations for treatment. According to The Commonwealth Fund's report (2011), U.S. providers' performance on listening to patients, communicating with them, and respecting their opinions was 25% lower than the benchmark. Differences in language, culture, and levels of patients' health literacy, which are prominent in a melting pot like the United States, may explain the score gap. Nevertheless, convincing evidence that patient centeredness improves patients' health status and reduces costs by minimizing the overuse of medical care makes progress in this area an imperative (Berry, Seiders, & Wilder, 2003; Stewart et al., 2000). As a result, the ACA established the Patient-Centered Outcomes Research Institute (PCORI) to sponsor clinical effectiveness research with a patient-centeredness perspective (Selby, Beal, & Frank, 2012). Its purpose is to study treatments, outcome preferences, and information needs for different patient populations.

In the next decade, multiple initiatives will seek progress on effectiveness, safety, coordination, and patient centeredness. Their success will be linked to patients' timely access to care itself.

How Untimely Is Access?

We all think of timeliness in terms of time spent waiting in a doctor's office or in the emergency department of a hospital as not being too long. However, timeliness also means that the intervals between the identification of a medical problem and the specific tests or treatment needed are done promptly. In an international survey of patients and PCPs in seven industrialized countries, the U.S. healthcare system ranked fifth overall in timeliness of care, behind the Netherlands, Germany, New Zealand, and the United Kingdom (Davis, Schoen, & Stremikis, 2010). Although insured patients have rapid access to specialists, they—as well as the uninsured—have more difficulty getting timely appointments with PCPs, especially after hours.

Timeliness of care is so closely related to quality of care that the IOM included it in its list of six objectives for quality improvement (IOM, 2001). Indeed, timeliness of care determines many health outcomes.

The mortality and long-term disability from a stroke is influenced by the time from the onset of symptoms to implementation of successful therapy (Schellinger & Warach, 2004). Similarly, the time to care for patients with heart attacks, trauma, and severe infections may determine whether the patient lives or dies (Houck & Bratzler, 2005). Even timeliness of outpatient care may govern the outcome from many chronic conditions. A popular model of access to care (Penchansky & Thomas, 1981) identifies five primary dimensions of access: availability, acceptability, affordability, accommodation, and accessibility.

Availability

Availability refers to the supply of providers in relation to the demand for their services. Shortages of providers certainly limit access. Health professionals shortage areas (HPSAs) are "designated as having shortages of primary medical care, dental or mental health providers" (Health Resources and Services Administration, 2013; http://datawarehouse.hrsa.gov/tools/analyzers/hpsafind.aspx). In 2013, there were approximately 5,900 primary care HPSAs, 4,600 dental HPSAs, and 3,800 mental HPSAs across the United States. The shortage/access problem is especially persistent in rural counties, where the supply of healthcare providers is the lowest, with less than half the number of PCPs per 100,000 people than in urban areas. By expanding coverage to millions of new American patients, the ACA may well exacerbate the impact of the shortage, at least in the short run. The Act includes legislation to improve access to oral care for children and to mental health services, to expand primary care residency programs, to add a significant number of new providers, and to increase the number of community health centers. It also promotes the use of nurse practitioners, physician assistants, and dental therapists for basic services. However, given the long time span needed to train new healthcare professionals, the imbalance between demand and supply is likely to increase before slowly subsiding (Childress, 2012; Cullen, Ranji, & Salganicoff, 2011).

Availability
The supply of providers in relation to demand for their services.

Acceptability

According to Dillip et al. (2012), acceptability is the neglected dimension of access to healthcare. **Acceptability** represents "the relationship of clients' attitudes about personal and practice characteristics of providers to the actual characteristics of existing providers, as well as to provider attitudes about acceptable personal characteristics of clients" (Penchansky & Thomas, 1981, p. 129). As such, it captures the notion of fit between patients and providers. It could involve insurance acceptability issues and/or negative perceptions related to the patient–provider interaction. Many factors affect these perceptions: gender, ethnicity, values, healthcare facility type or neighborhood, and so on. Lack of acceptability is a prevalent barrier to access among some racial minority groups as well as sicker, low-income individuals between the ages of 26 and 54 (Kullgren, McLaughlin, Mitra, & Armstrong, 2012). The ACA attempts to remedy this issue by requiring that healthcare facilities and providers be consistent with medical ethics and various cultural traditions (Gable, 2011). It funds projects aimed at improving

Acceptability
The patients' and providers' attitudes about each other's characteristics.

quality of care and outcomes through an integration of race, culture, and language into the health system structure. It also introduces incentives for improving diversity among healthcare professionals and developing cultural competence within the workforce (Andrulis, Siddiqui, Purtle, & Duchon, 2010).

Affordability

Affordability

The patients' ability to pay for healthcare services.

Affordability refers to patients' ability to pay for healthcare services, which is tied to their insurance status. Lack of insurance or high out-of-pocket expenses are often cited as the most important reasons for untimely access to care. Even insured patients may find their access to services constrained by the design of their insurance plan. The cost of coverage is commensurate with the cost of healthcare. In other words, it is extremely high. As a result, plans with limited benefits as well as high deductibles and copayments have become commonplace. Patients covered by such plans are known as "underinsured" and, to a lesser extent, face similar barriers to access as do the uninsured.

This is true for both patients with private or public coverage. In fact, compared to individuals with private insurance, Medicaid beneficiaries face more barriers to timely primary care and use the emergency department more often for routine care. This is partly the result of PCPs' reluctance to see Medicaid patients because the program used to reimburse them about 59% of the amount paid for Medicare patients. Provisions of the ACA mandated an increase in Medicaid payments to Medicare levels. The match was to incentivize PCPs to accept the millions of new patients the Act would add to the Medicaid program. However, the success of this rate increase is far from certain. First, the program's provision sunset in 2015, which created uncertainty about future reimbursement levels. Second, it excluded nurse practitioners, whose presence in primary care delivery is expected to increase significantly. Whether nurse practitioners will be willing to treat more Medicaid patients at the low rate cannot be taken for granted (Cheung, Wiler, Lowe, & Ginde, 2012).

Accommodation and Accessibility

Accommodation

The patients' perceptions of the ease with which they can obtain care on a timely basis and at their convenience.

Accessibility

Refers to the proximity of healthcare facility and easy access by transportation.

Accommodation involves patients' perceptions of the ease with which they can schedule and obtain care on a timely basis and at their convenience. **Accessibility** refers to the geographical proximity of the healthcare facility and easy access by transportation. Long waiting times, lack of transportation to get to a doctor's appointment, difficulty in making appointments and/or taking time off work, and other responsibilities are all major hindrances to getting timely care. These issues were highlighted in a report from the Centers for Disease Control and Prevention (CDC; Gindi, Cohen, & Kirzinger, 2012), which indicated that 79% of the adults aged 18 to 64 had visited the emergency room because of lack of access to other providers. The main reasons were (a) the doctor's office was not open, (b) there was no other place to go where they lived, (c) the emergency room was the closest provider, and (d) they thought only a hospital could help them. As mentioned before, the ACA attempts to increase the supply of providers in medically underserved areas, but it will take time for these provisions to have an impact on accessibility. As for accommodation, much of the improvement depends on the management of the providers' facilities. The average patient's wait time to see a provider is 22 minutes, and patient satisfaction decreases substantially for each 5 minutes of waiting time. Solutions include better scheduling through (a) the addition of "catch-up slots," (b) leaving a large portion of the schedule open for same-day appointments rather than overbooking far in advance, (c) studying the volume of patients throughout the year to identify patterns, (d) measuring the time elapsed between patient arrival and departure to identify bottlenecks, (e) conducting follow-ups via phone, e-mail, or video chat, and (f) preregistering on the phone or online, rather than at the provider's facility (Beck, 2010).

The current crisis faced by the U.S. healthcare system requires sweeping solutions from its major stakeholders. Patients must be more actively involved in their health and well-being. Policymakers must create an environment favorable to the pursuit of uniform quality and cost control. Providers must reevaluate their ways of delivering care and strive for both effectiveness (doing it right the first time) and efficiency (doing it with minimum waste of time and resources). Insurers must acknowledge and support providers' performance. Change will not happen overnight. In fact, it might be overly optimistic to believe that all parties will synchronize their efforts and develop congruent plans in the near future. Currently, the best hopes for improvement lie with providers because they are the best positioned to critically analyze their operations and steer them on the path to excellence. What does it take to get there? And what do we mean by *operations*? These questions are the basic premises of this book.

WHAT IS OPERATIONS MANAGEMENT?

Operations, in general, represent the core activities of an organization. They are what the business is essentially about. What is the first thing that comes to your mind when you hear "General Motors"? They make cars. The post office? It delivers mail and packages. A hospital? It provides healthcare to patients. Of course, these different organizations provide a variety of other services. For example, General Motors is involved in parts service and sales as well as financing. These are support services that complement the core activities. They enhance the core offering and make it a more attractive "package" to customers. Similarly, a health system may offer health plans, provide education, and fund research and development projects. Again, these are complementary services that enrich the core of healthcare delivery.

Without demand (sales) and its fulfillment (operations), there would simply be no business. Therefore, sales and operations are considered the "life lines" of the business. This paramount role played by operations in a business organization makes the quality of their management a prerequisite to survival and competitiveness.

So, what does managing operations entail? **Operations management (OM)** is the practice of designing, running, and controlling the most

Operations
The core activities of an organization; what the business is about.

Operations Management
The practice of designing, running, and controlling the most effective and efficient transformation processes resulting in the production of goods or services.

Efficiency
Involves producing the desired output with a minimal amount of resources or waste.

Productive System
The transformation of inputs into outputs.

effective and **efficient** systems for the production of products or provision of services. A **productive system** involves the transformation of inputs into outputs of greater value (Figure 1.3). An efficient transformation is achieved when the output is produced with the least amount of resources and waste. In a way, operations management is the "black box"—or management of the transformation process—that can unlock excellence in care delivery. Nevertheless, the use of OM is still a novelty in the healthcare industry (Box 1.9).

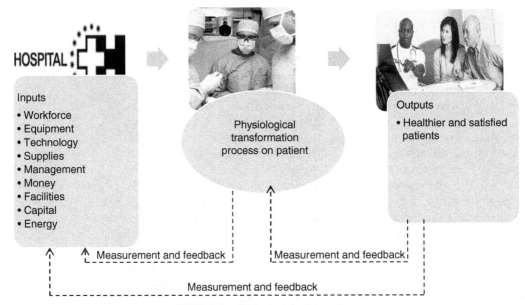

FIGURE 1.3 – Clinical productive system.

✪ BOX 1.9 – WORDS OF WISDOM

"I was very much surprised that probably the biggest industry in the world does not apply the operation management tools that every single other industry is applying." (Eugene Litvak, industrial efficiency expert, and president and CEO of the Institute for Healthcare Optimization; Restructuring the ER, 2005; http://www.pbs.org/newshour/bb/health-jan-june05-er_6-07)

The operations manager is the professional who understands and applies the knowledge and tools of operations management to transform inputs into outputs. This is a vital and important discipline with high stakes. For example, no one disputes that Toyota had established itself as a leader in automotive quality in the 1980s and 1990s. Toyota had well-trained employees, the latest equipment, a reputation for managerial excellence, extensive capital, and so on. Yet, several of its vehicles produced in 2007–2009 were subject to one of the biggest car recalls in automotive history because of faulty window switches. The source of the problem: an operations decision to share components on a wide range of vehicles for greater economies of scale. The same pertains to healthcare. At Johns Hopkins Hospital, one of the most renowned hospitals in the world with the best trained clinicians and state-of-the art medical technologies, the 10-day rate of central line infections used to be 11%. It remained high until Dr. Peter Pronovost, one of the intensive care unit physicians, created new operational procedures. He developed a checklist that included all steps to prevent infections and granted nurses the authority to intervene if physicians missed a step on the checklist. The rate dropped to zero (Gawande, 2007).

To ensure that the transformation processes are carried out to produce the desired outputs, data collection at various stages of the healthcare delivery process should take place. These measurements (feedback) should be gauged against preestablished standards to determine whether corrective action is needed at the input and/or transformation process levels (Figure 1.3). For example, patients' complaints about long wait times in the emergency department may lead to changes in triage procedures and reallocation of resources. Similarly, poor utilization of hospitalists' time during their rounds may result in floor redesign to minimize steps between patient rooms.

The Ubiquity of Operations Management

The physiological transformation process involving the care of a sick patient is supported by a myriad of other transformation processes throughout the healthcare organization: registering patients, ordering medical supplies and storing them, billing, filing insurance claims, training employees, preparing financial statements, archiving medical records, housekeeping, and so on (Figure 1.4). Every activity in a business organization is part of a process, which should be designed and managed to deliver value to its customer. Therefore, whether or not you plan to work in the field of operations management, there is a compelling reason to learn more about it. Because it permeates all

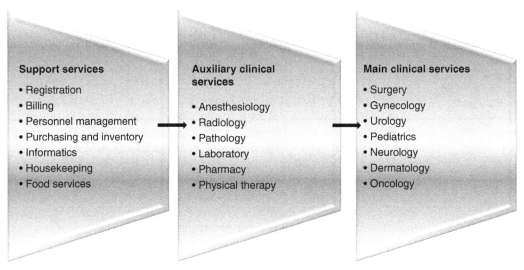

FIGURE 1.4 – Processes in a hospital.
Adapted from Amberg and Graber (1996).

areas of a business, operations management can be the key to reducing fragmentation among the various parts of a business and offering a unified "way of doing things" that is both customer focused and efficiency driven. Therefore, knowledge of operations management provides a broad perspective of the organization that facilitates collaboration and cooperation. For example, rifts between physicians and administrators are quite common as physicians often view administrators' cost-cutting initiatives as threats to the quality of care. The modern operations management approach called "Lean" (covered in Chapter 6) has been a catalyst as it positions error reduction (better quality) and smarter process design as major drivers of cost reduction. This approach brings both groups together. As highlighted in Box 1.10, physicians subscribe to it when they see that it provides opportunities for better patient care; administrators appreciate its emphasis on waste elimination.

✛ BOX 1.10 – OM IN PRACTICE!

The Virginia Mason Production System

In 2001, Virginia Mason Medical Center (VMMC) in Seattle, Washington, formed a physician compact listing the physicians' and organization's new goals: becoming the quality leader through patient-centered care and evidence-based practice, emphasizing teamwork, and embracing change. To achieve these goals, they turned to the Toyota Production System (TPS). Toyota and VMMC essentially wanted the same things: a customer focus, the pursuit of perfection, and a dedication to good employee relations.

After seeing TPS in action in Japan, they began envisioning the Virginia Mason Production System (VMPS) modeled after Toyota's. To encourage the staff to participate in process improvements, they guaranteed that **no layoffs** would occur as a result of newly found efficiencies. They implemented **value-stream mapping** to chart various processes and identify waste. This was the first step undertaken in the **rapid process improvement workshops** geared toward eliminating waste, improving processes, increasing efficiency, and improving productivity in a given unit. They organized the workplace according to the **5S system** (sort, simplify, sweep, standardize, and self-discipline) to "unclutter" the system and improve the visibility of potential problems. They implemented the **3P system** (production, preparation, process) to redesign the layout according to flow. All employees were encouraged to participate in the "**every day Lean** idea system" to reduce waste in their jobs and create value for the patient. The **patient safety alert (PSA) system** was inspired by Toyota's *andon* cords to stop the line when a serious mistake had occurred. Similarly, PSA empowered front-line employees to signal when a mistake had occurred or a safety problem had emerged, leading to the resolution of the problem onsite. Finally, they instituted the use of **bundles** or **checklists** to prevent infections or improve care.

The adaptation of TPS into VMPS was heralded as a success in terms of cost savings and quality improvement. Now legendary, VMMC's practices have been copied by hospitals across the country.

Decision Making in Operations Management

At the highest level, a vice president of operations is concerned with scanning the environment, developing an operations strategy (the long-term direction of the operations function), and monitoring the operations function's performance in achieving its strategic goals. At the lower levels, OM professionals make decisions directly related to the production of goods or the provision of services (Slack, Chambers, & Johnston, 2010). These decisions involve:

- WHAT needs to be done?
- WHY does it need to be done?
- WHO needs to do it?
- WHEN does it need to be done? How often? In what sequence?
- WHERE should it be done?
- HOW should it be done? What are the best methods to deliver the service(s)? What equipment should be used?
- HOW MUCH does it cost? What is the amount of resources needed?

Several alternatives are available for these decisions, and none emerge as the clear choice in all situations. Rather, the OM professional has to consider the internal constraints in the organization, as well as the repercussions that one informed decision has on another. For instance, deciding to use robot-like hydrogen peroxide vaporizers to disinfect hospital rooms would help destroy superbugs, but the devices cost more than $40,000 (Johns Hopkins Medicine, 2012), which limits their adoption rate across the country. Table 1.2 displays a vast range of decisions, from strategic to tactical, that vice presidents of operations and OM professionals make to ensure the competitiveness of a healthcare organization.

TABLE 1.2 – Operations Decisions	
Examples of Operations Management Decisions	**Operations Management Topics**
How do healthcare organizations use operations to build a competitive advantage?	Healthcare operations strategy
How does one plan major changes in "the way of doing things"? Who should be involved? How do we prevent failure?	Project management
How do we measure quality? When and how do we conduct inspections? What tools do we use to monitor quality performance? What do we do when we detect problems?	Quality management and statistical process control
How do we know that our processes can meet our objectives? How do we reduce variation in performance? Where can we eliminate waste?	Six Sigma and Lean

(continued)

TABLE 1.2 – Operations Decisions (*continued*)

Examples of Operations Management Decisions	Operations Management Topics
How do we measure costs? How do we compute value? How do we control costs without affecting quality?	Cost management
What is the demand for healthcare services? How do we make sure that supplies are available to cover the demand without inflating costs? Which suppliers are we going to select?	Managing the supply chain
How do we design processes that add value and ensure a smooth flow? Do we need to change the layout of our facility? What are the cost savings?	Process analysis and design
How much workforce do we need to meet the demand for our services? How much will it cost?	Balancing demand and capacity
When and how do we schedule work? How about patients?	Scheduling
How do we adapt to expected or even sudden changes? What are the limitations?	Designing flexible systems
How can IT improve healthcare operations? Will it support decision making effectively? What are the costs versus benefits?	IT/operations integration

PURPOSE AND FOCUS OF THIS BOOK

It is hoped that you now have a better glimpse of the issues faced by the U.S. healthcare system: spiraling costs, disappointing overall quality performance, limited access, a complex regulatory environment, unfavorable population demographics, and shortages of PCPs and nurses. If you are in the healthcare field, you must deal with these seemingly insurmountable problems and contribute to the solution. The rest of this book is devoted to equipping you with the knowledge and tools necessary to use operations as a strategic competitive weapon. An operations strategy is based on four competitive priorities: quality, cost, fast or on-time delivery, and flexibility. The main modules of this book cover these four competitive priorities. Whenever we discuss them, you will see their respective icons in the margins. You first learn the importance of setting quality as an initial priority in designing an operations system for a healthcare organization. Based on the customer's perceptions of healthcare quality, you develop internal quality indicators that will be used to assess performance. In order to improve, you must be able to measure processes and outcomes and use performance metrics to show progress over time. And as performance is never perfect, you will learn various methods and techniques to improve it. You will be surprised to find out that as you strive to improve customers' satisfaction, you can also make operations more efficient: less waste, better layout, and fewer delays! Many concepts are interconnected—quality affects cost, cost affects flexibility, and so forth. In order to show that a concept or tool discussed in a given chapter impacts a concept discussed in another chapter, we use visuals called "mind maps." A **mind map** is a diagram used to represent ideas or concepts and shows how they relate to each other (Buzan, Griffiths, & Harrison, 2012). You will see that approaching problems in operations management is not a linear process. Instead, solutions must draw on many different concepts simultaneously. The mind maps illustrate how concepts and tools are linked together. Some of the concepts covered in the book may seem abstract at first. We thought that they would make more sense if they were presented in a work context. Meet the employees of Bradley Park Hospital! Because operations management depends on working with people, the personal and cultural challenges that you will face must be anticipated. The story about the trials and successes of a fictional hospital (Bradley Park Hospital) introduces you to some common situations that you will encounter. You will see how the employees use chapter materials to solve problems day after day. We did not want you to believe that their achievements were purely fictional. In every chapter, you will also discover how healthcare organizations in the real world have implemented OM solutions.

Mind Map

A diagram used to represent ideas or concepts to show how they are related.

BRADLEY PARK HOSPITAL 1.1

Mike Chambers had been an effective leader in the city of Bradley Park. He had been highly active in community activities and had recently retired from running a successful manufacturing plant. Under his leadership, the auto parts manufacturing plant had grown significantly. He was well respected by many, including the board members of the Bradley Park Hospital (BPH). Mike had served on the board of the hospital for the last 5 years and was committed to his role in the governance of this important institution. He had the calling to help the hospital after supporting his brother through his battle with cancer 10 years earlier. His brother had not survived, but he saw how special the caring of healthcare providers could be to patients and family. He deeply respected the doctors and nurses and sought to help BPH be a valued resource in the community.

BPH was the first hospital in the area, but 3 years ago Madison Hospital was built down the road. Madison had newer facilities and was known for innovative care. BPH had started to struggle, particularly after the pipe manufacturing plant closed last year. In this town of 300,000 people, the unemployment rate had increased to 12%, and all of the industries were pushing to move to managed care to reduce their healthcare costs.

It all seemed to be happening so fast. Just last week at the BPH board meeting, Tom, the chief executive officer (CEO), had acted normally and given a number of reports. There were no indications of any problems, and the reports seemed to be generally favorable. So when Mike got the call that Tom had suddenly resigned along with the chief financial officer (CFO) and that they had left town, Mike was very confused and concerned.

In the emergency board meeting that Friday afternoon, there were few answers and a lot of speculation. What was known was that Francine Sutton, the respected chief nursing officer, was running the hospital and needed help. It was also clear that BPH needed an executive with leadership experience. There was no time to waste, for the staff would soon learn of Tom's sudden departure, and uncertainty would permeate the organization. They needed someone to quickly step in, sort things out, prioritize issues, and build the plan for the future. Mike was asked to take the lead.

Mike was flattered, but uncertain and perplexed. He had the leadership experience, maturity, and dedication. That was clear to everyone. In addition to that, he had been on the BPH board of directors for 5 years and had also served on their finance committee. He had some knowledge of the organization. Surely he could run a 450-bed community hospital and associated clinics that had revenues that were half those of the company he recently ran. What could be that different from running a manufacturing company? After much discussion, it was reasoned that with his business skills matched to Francine's understanding of care delivery, Mike could be successful in helping BPH move forward.

Mike became convinced. Why not? he reasoned. He had the calling to help, was respected, had Francine's and the board's support, and had the time. Could healthcare be that different anyway? He agreed to assume the CEO position starting Monday. What could go wrong?

SUMMARY

This chapter reviewed the history of healthcare and healthcare reform in the United States. This reform was driven primarily by quality, costs, and access concerns. These concerns were multifactorial and complex, but you learned that OM professionals can be instrumental in improving healthcare. Their expertise enables them to design processes for better, faster, and more cost-effective care delivery. Finally, you were given an overview of this book's organization and were introduced to Bradley Park Hospital.

KEY TERMS

Health maintenance organization (HMO)	Abuse	Accommodation
The Joint Commission (TJC)	Effectiveness	Accessibility
Fee-for-service (FFS)	Safety	Operations
Diagnosis-related group (DRG)	Coordination	Operations management
Affordable Care Act (ACA), The Act	Patient centeredness	Efficiency
Meaningful use	Availability	Productive system
Overuse	Acceptability	Mind map
Fraud	Affordability	

WHAT DO YOU REMEMBER?

1. Over the years, what have been the largest obstacles to healthcare reform? Explain.

2. Select five major events that shaped healthcare in the 20th century and describe them.

3. What are the major challenges for U.S. healthcare today?

4. What are the main factors responsible for high costs today?

5. What are the roots of the administrative complexity of the U.S. healthcare system?

6. How is the performance of the U.S. healthcare system in terms of effectiveness, safety, coordination, and patient centeredness? How do the ACA and other initiatives propose to alleviate some of these problems?

7. What do we mean by *operations*? What is operations management?

8. Operations strategy is based on four competitive priorities. What are they?

9. Give examples of inputs in healthcare. What are the three common types of processes? What are the outputs?

10. What are the decisions typically made by OM professionals?

11. When looking at the issues that have contributed to the increase in healthcare costs in the United States, list the one(s) that is (are) under the influence of operations management.

THINK OUTSIDE THE BOOK!

1. The term *socialized medicine* has been overused and misused. Research the term and provide some needed clarification about its meaning. Do you know of any industrialized country that provides *socialized medicine*?

2. Select a piece of healthcare legislation that was passed in the last 10 years. What are its benefits to society? What are its unintended drawbacks?

3. Go to www.YouTube.com. Select an interesting video (e.g., NEJM Roundtable: The Cost of Healthcare, Part 1) on one of the topics covered in this chapter. Analyze the strengths and weaknesses of the main arguments.

4. Look at the timeline for healthcare reform provided in *The New York Times*: www.nytimes.com/interactive/2009/07/19/us/politics/20090717_HEALTH_TIMELINE.html?_r=1&. Explore the history of a healthcare topic (e.g., regulation of pharmaceuticals, medical informatics, or healthcare litigation) and develop an online timeline with text, pictures, and articles such as the one presented in *The New York Times*.

5. Read Box 1.5. In your opinion, what are the pros and cons of healthcare regulation?

6. Read Box 1.9. To what extent do you think OM tools and concepts are appropriate for healthcare? Are there limitations?

7. Read this editorial by Drs. Boyer and Pronovost:
    Boyer, K., & Pronovost, P. (2010). What medicine can teach operations: What operations can teach medicine. *Journal of Operations Management, 28*, 367–371.
    What do they believe operations management can contribute to healthcare? Do you agree or disagree? Support your answers.

REFERENCES

Amberg, M., & Graber, S. (1996). Specifying information systems using business process modeling. In J. Brender, J. P. Christensen, J.-R. Scherrer, & P. McNair (Eds.), *Medical informatics Europe '96* (pp. 1037–1041). Amsterdam, Netherlands: IOS Press.

American Medical Association. (1847). *Code of Medical Ethics*. Chicago, IL: American Medical Association Press.

American Medical Association (AMA). (2010). Our history. Retrieved from http://www.ama-assn.org/ama/pub/about-ama/our-history.shtml

Andrulis, D. P., Siddiqui, N. J., Purtle, J. P., & Duchon, L. (2010). *Patient protection and Affordable Care Act of 2010: Advancing health equity for racially and ethnically diverse populations*. Washington, DC: Jint Center for Political and Economic Studies.

Beck, M. (2010, October 18). The doctor will see you eventually. *The Wall Street Journal*. Retrieved from http://online.wsj.com/article/SB10001424052702304410504575560081847852618.html

Berry, L. L., Seiders, K., & Wilder, S. S. (2003). Innovations in access to care: A patient-centered approach. *Annals of Internal Medicine, 139*(7), 568–574.

Berwick, D. M., & Hackbarth, A. D. (2012). Eliminating waste in US health care. *Journal of the American Medical Association, 307*(14), 1513–1516. doi:10.1001/jama.2012.362

Brain Injury Alliance of Utah. (2016). *Facts about brain injury*. Retrieved from http://biau.org/facts-about-brain-injury

Buntin, M. B., Burke, M. F., Hoaglin, M. C., & Blumenthal, D. (2011). The benefits of health information technology: A review of the recent literature shows predominantly positive results. *Health Affairs, 30*(3), 464–471.

Buzan, T., Griffiths, C., & Harrison, J. (2012). *Modern mind mapping for smarter thinking*. Cardiff Bay, UK: Proactive Press.

California Healthcare Foundation. (2007). *Uncoordinated care: A survey of physician and patient experience*. Oakland, CA: Author.

Callahan, D. (2008). Health care costs and medical technology. In M. Crowley (Ed.), *From birth to death and bench to clinic: The Hastings Center bioethics briefing book for journalists, policymakers, and campaigns* (pp. 79–82). Garrison, NY: The Hastings Center.

Carman, K. G., Eibner, C., & Paddock, S. M. (2015). Trends in health insurance enrollment, 2013–2015. *Health Affairs, 34*(6), 1–5.

Cauchon, D. (2013, February 13). Drug prices jump again while other health costs decline. *USA Today*. Retrieved from http://www.usatoday.com/story/news/nation/2013/02/13/price-of-a-prescription-rising-again/1918099

Centers for Disease Control and Prevention. (2015). Health expenditures. Retrieved from http://www.cdc.gov/nchs/fastats/health-expenditures.htm

Centers for Medicare & Medicaid Services. (2009, November 13). Key milestones in CMS programs. Baltimore, MD: Author. Retrieved from https://www.cms.gov/About-CMS/Agency-Information/History/index.html?redirect=/History

Centers for Medicare & Medicaid Services. (2012a). *National health expenditure projections 2010–2020*. Baltimore, MD: Author. Retrieved from https://www.openminds.com/wp-content/uploads/indres071511stratnhe2020.pdf

Centers for Medicare & Medicaid Services. (2012b). Medicare fraud & abuse: Prevention, detection, and reporting. Baltimore, MD: Author. Retrieved from https://www.cms.gov/About-CMS/Agency-Information/History/index.html?redirect=/History

Centers for Medicare & Medicaid Services. (2013). *National health expenditures 2011 highlights*. Baltimore, MD: Author.

Cheung, P. T., Wiler, J. L., Lowe, R. A., & Ginde, A. A. (2012). National study of barriers to timely primary care and emergency department utilization among Medicaid beneficiaries. *Annals of Emergency Medicine, 60*(7), 4–10e12.

Childress, S. (2012, June 28). How the Supreme Court's ruling affects dental care. *Frontline—Dollars and dentists*. Retrieved from http://www.pbs.org/wgbh/frontline/article/how-the-supreme-courts-ruling-affects-dental-care

The Commonwealth Fund. (2011). *Why not the best? Results from the national scorecard on U.S. health system performance*. New York, NY: Author.

Congressional Budget Office. (2014). *Updated estimates of the effects of the insurance coverage provisions of the affordable care act (45231)*. Washington, DC: Author.

Conover, C. J. (2004). *Health care regulation: A $169 billion hidden tax*. Washington, DC: CATO Institute.

Coombs, J. G. (2005). *The rise and fall of HMOs: An American health care revolution*. Madison, WI: University of Wisconsin Press.

Craig, C., Eby, D., & Whittington, J. (2011). *Care coordination model: Better care at lower cost for people with multiple health and social needs (IHI innovation)*. Cambridge, MA: Institute for Healthcare Improvement.

Cullen, E., Ranji, U., & Salganicoff, A. (2011). *Primary care shortage (Background brief)*. Menlo Park, CA: The Henry J. Kaiser Family Foundation.

Davis, K., Schoen, C., & Stremikis, K. (2010). *Mirror, mirror on the wall: How the performance of the U.S. health care system compares internationally—2010 update*. Washington, DC: The Commonwealth Fund.

de Vries, E. N., Ramrattan, M. A., Smorenburg, S. M., Gouma, D. J., & Boermeester, M. A. (2008). The incidence and nature of in-hospital adverse events: A systematic review. *Quality & Safety in Health Care, 17*(3), 216–223.

Dillip, A., Alba, S., Mshana, C., Hetzel, M. W., Lengeler, C., Mayumana, I., . . . Obrist, B. (2012). Acceptability—A neglected dimension of access to health care: Findings from a study on childhood convulsions in rural Tanzania. *BMC Health Services Research, 12*(113), 1–11.

Doe, J. (2009). *WHO Statistical Information System (WHOSIS)*. Geneva, Switzerland: World Health Organization.

Fakhouri, T. H., Ogden, C. L., Carroll, M. D., Kit, B. K., & Flegal, K. M. (2012). *Prevalence of obesity among older adults in the United States, 2007–2010 (NCHS data brief)*. Hyattsville, MD: National Center for Health Statistics.

Flexner, A. (1910). *Medical education in the United States and Canada* (Bulletin Number 4). New York, NY: The Carnegie Foundation for the Advancement of Teaching.

Friedman, R. A. (2012, July 10). Good news for mental illness in health law. *The New York Times*. Retrieved from http://www.nytimes.com/2012/07/10/health/policy/health-care-law-offers-wider-benefits-for-treating-mental-illness.html

Gable, L. (2011). The Patient Protection and Affordable Care Act, public health, and the elusive target of human rights. *Journal of Law, Medicine & Ethics, 39*(3), 340–354. doi:10.1111/j.1748-720X.2011.00604.x

Gawande, A. (2007, December 10). The checklist. *The New Yorker*. Retrieved from http://www.newyorker.com/magazine/2007/12/10/the-checklist

Gindi, R., Cohen, R., & Kirzinger, W. (2012, May). *Emergency room use among adults aged 18–64: Early release of estimates from the National Health Interview Survey, January–June 2011*. Atlanta, GA: National Center for Health Statistics. Retrieved from http://www.cdc.gov/nchs/data/nhis/earlyrelease/emergency_room_use_january-june_2011.pdf

Goodridge, E., & Arnquist, S. (2009, July 19). A history of overhauling health care. *The New York Times*. Retrieved from http://www.nytimes.com/interactive/2009/07/19/us/politics/20090717_HEALTH_TIMELINE.html?_r=0

Grossman, C. M. (2008). The first use of penicillin in the United States. *Annals of Internal Medicine, 149*(2), 135–136.

Gungor, F. (2011). History of electronic medical records. Retrieved from http://www.onesourcedoc.com/blog/bid/71537/History-of-Electronic-Medical-Records

Hansen, M. (2014). Affordable Care Act Medicaid expansion. Retrieved from http://www.ncsl.org/research/health/affordable-care-act-expansion.aspx

Health Policy Brief. (2012a, September 13). Improving care transitions. Better coordination of patients among care sites and the community could save money and improve the quality of care. *Health Affairs.* Retrieved from http://healthaffairs.org/healthpolicybriefs/brief_pdfs/healthpolicybrief_76.pdf

Health Policy Brief. (2012b, July 31). Eliminating fraud and abuse. New tools to reduce Medicare and Medicaid payments promise savings. But many implementation challenges remain. *Health Affairs.* Retrieved from http://healthaffairs.org/healthpolicybriefs/brief_pdfs/healthpolicybrief_72.pdf

Health Resources and Services Administration. (2013). Find shortage areas: HPSA by state & county. Retrieved from http://hpsafind.hrsa.gov

HealthCare.gov. (2010, September 27). *Preventive services covered under the Affordable Care Act.* Retrieved from http://www.healthcare.gov/news/factsheets/2010/07/preventive-services-list.html

Houck, P. M., & Bratzler, D. W. (2005). Administration of first hospital antibiotics for community-acquired pneumonia: Does timeliness affect outcomes? *Current Opinions in Infectious Diseases, 18*(2), 151–156.

Hurley, D. (1993). Administration: 25% of hospital spending hospital administrative costs. *Medical World News, 34*(9), 58.

Institute for Healthcare Improvement. (n.d.). *Overview of the 100,000 Lives Campaign.* Cambridge, MA: Author. Retrieved from https://www.ihi.org/Engage/Initiatives/Completed/5MillionLives Campaign/Documents/Overview%20of%20the%20100K%20Campaign.pdf

Institute for Healthcare Improvement. (2006). *5 million lives campaign.* Cambridge, MA: Author.

Institute of Medicine (IOM). (1999). *To err is human.* Washington, DC: National Academies Press.

Institute of Medicine (IOM). (2001). *Crossing the quality chasm: A new health system for the 21st century.* Washington, DC: National Academies Press.

Institute of Medicine (IOM). (2002). *Unequal treatment: Confronting racial and ethnic disparities in health care.* Washington, DC: National Academies Press.

Institute of Medicine (IOM). (2003). *Hidden costs: Value lost: Uninsurance in America*. Washington, DC: National Academies Press.

Ivey, J. L. (2006). The effect of administrative complexity on the cost of health care in the United States. Retrieved from http://digitalcommons.law.msu.edu/king/75

James, J. T. (2013). A new, evidence-based estimate of patient harms associated with hospital care. *Journal of Patient Safety, 9*(3), 122–128.

Johns Hopkins Medicine. (2012). Hydrogen peroxyde vapor enhances hospital disinfection of superbugs. Retrieved from http://www.hopkinsmedicine.org/news/media/releases/hydrogen_peroxide_vapor_enhances_hospital_disinfection_of_superbugs

Kaiser Family Foundation. (2012a). *Focus on health care disparities: Key facts*. Menlo Park, CA: Author.

Kaiser Family Foundation. (2012b). *Healthcare costs: A primer—Key information on health care costs and their impact*. Menlo Park, CA: Author.

Kellerman, A. L., & Jones, S. S. (2013). What it will take to achieve the as-yet-unfulfilled promises of health information technology. *Health Affairs, 32*(1), 63–68.

Kullgren, J. T., McLaughlin, C. G., Mitra, N., & Armstrong, K. (2012). Nonfinancial barriers and access to care for U.S. adults. *Health Services Research, 47*(1, pt. 2), 462–485.

LaVeist, T. A., Gaskin, D. J., & Richard, P. (2009). *The economic burden of health inequalities in the United States*. Washington, DC: Joint Center for Political and Economic Studies.

Levy, J. (2015). In U.S., uninsured rate sinks to 12.9%. Retrieved from http://www.gallup.com/poll/180425/uninsured-rate-sinks.aspx

Levy, S. (2013). The most common issues of aging. Retrieved from http://www.agingcare.com/Articles/common-issues-of-aging-102224.htm

The National Policy Consensus Center. (2004). *Improving health care access: Finding solutions in a time of crisis*. Portland, OR: Portland State University.

New York Times Editors. (1932, November 30). Socialized medicine is urged in survey. *The New York Times*, p. A1.

Nolte, E., & McKee, M. (2011). Variations in amenable mortality—Trends in 16 high-income nations. *Health Policy, 103*(1), 47–52.

Oatman, E. (2005). The drug that changed the world. *P&S: The College of Physicians and Surgeons of Columbia University, 25*(1). Retrieved from http://www.cumc.columbia.edu/psjournal/archive/winter-2005/drug.html

Organization for Economic Cooperation and Development, OECD Health Statistics 2015. (2015, November). Compiled by PGPF. Retrieved from http://www.pgpf.org/chart-archive/0006_health-care-oecd

O'Shea, B. (2012, February 19). Psychiatric patients with no place to go but jail. *The New York Times*, p. A25A. Retrieved from http://www.nytimes.com/2012/02/19/health/in-chicago-mental-health-patients-have-no-place-to-go.html?pagewanted=all&_r=0

Palmer, K. S. (1999). A brief history: Universal health care efforts in the US. Retrieved from http://www.pnhp.org/facts/a_brief_history_universal_health_care_efforts_in_the_us.php

The Patient Protection and Affordable Care Act, Public Law 111-148 C.F.R. (2010).

Penchansky, R., & Thomas, J. W. (1981). The concept of access: definition and relationship to consumer satisfaction. *Medical Care, 19*(2), 127–140.

Peter G. Peterson Foundation. (2015). The United States spends more than twice as much per capita as the average developed country does. Retrieved from http://pgpf.org/Chart-Archive/0006_health-care-oecd

Pittman, D. (2012, December 13). Chronic disease key to cutting Medicare costs, analyst says. *Medpage Today*. Retrieved from http://www.medpagetoday.com/PublicHealthPolicy/Medicare/36453

Porter, M. E., & Teisberg, E. O. (2006). *Redefining health care: Creating value-based competition on results*. Brighton, MA: Harvard Business Review Press.

Pure Food and Drug Act of 1906, Pub. L. No. 59-384, 34 Stat. 768.

Restructuring the ER. (2005, June 7). *PBS NewsHour*. Arlington, VA: Public Broadcasting Service. Retrieved from http://www.pbs.org/newshour/bb/health-jan-june05-er_6-07

Rosenthal, M. B., Berndt, E. R., Donohue, J. M., Frank, R. G., & Epstein, A. M. (2002). Promotion of prescription drugs to consumers. *New England Journal of Medicine, 346*(7), 498–505.

Schellinger, P. D., & Warach, S. (2004). Therapeutic time window of thrombolytic therapy following stroke. *Current Atherosclerosis Reports, 6*(4), 288–294.

Schmeck, H. M., Jr. (1968, April 28). Spiraling medical costs reflect deficiencies in U.S. health care. *The New York Times*. Retrieved from http://www.nytimes.com/packages/flash/health/HEALTHCARE_TIMELINE/1968_health_costs.pdf

Selby, J. V., Beal, A. C., & Frank, L. (2012). The Patient-Centered Outcomes Research Institute (PCORI) national priorities for research and initial research agenda. *Journal of the American Medical Association, 307*(15), 1583–1584.

Silverman, F. (Producer, Director, Writer), & Danner, B. (Narrator). (2000, November 3). Healthcare timeline (Classroom Materials). *Healthcare Crisis: Who's at Risk?* Arlington, VA: Public Broadcasting Service. Retrieved from http://www.pbs.org/healthcarecrisis/history.htm

Slack, N., Chambers, S., & Johnston, R. (2010). *Operations management* (6th ed.). Upper Saddle River, NJ: Prentice-Hall.

Smith, S., Newhouse, J. P., & Freeland, M. S. (2009). Income, insurance, and technology: Why does health spending outpace economic growth? *Health Affairs, 28*(5), 1276–1284.

Squires, D. A. (2012). *Explaining high health care spending in the United States: An international comparison of supply, utilization, prices, and quality (Issues in international health policy).* Washington, DC: The Commonwealth Fund.

Stewart, M., Brown, J. B., Donner, A., McWhinney, I. R., Oates, J., Weston, W. W., & Jordan, J. (2000). The impact of patient-centered care on outcomes. *Journal of Family Practice, 49*(9), 796–804.

Swann, J. P. (2001). Pharmaceutical industry. In P. S. Boyer (Ed.), *The Oxford companion to United States history.* New York, NY: Oxford University Press.

U.S. Census Bureau. (2011). Highlights: 2010. Retrieved from http://www.census.gov/hhes/www/hlthins/data/incpovhlth/2010/highlights.html

Van Den Bos, J., Rustagi, K., Gray, T., Halford, M., Ziemkiewicz, E., & Shreve, J. (2011). The $17.1 billion problem: The annual cost of measurable medical errors. *Health Affairs, 30*(4), 596–603.

Vin Mariani Winery. (2007–2008). The history behind the wine. Retrieved from http://www.cocanaturally.com

Wilson, D. (2009, November 15). Drug makers raise prices in face of health care reform. *The New York Times.* Retrieved from http://www.nytimes.com/2009/11/16/business/16drugprices.html?pagewanted=all&_r=0

World Health Organization (WHO). (2000). The world health report 2000—Health systems: Improving performance. Retrieved from http://www.who.int/whr/2000/en/whr00_en.pdf

Yang, Z., & Hall, A. G. (2008). The financial burden of overweight and obesity among elderly Americans: The dynamics of weight, longevity, and health care cost. *Health Services Research, 43*(3), 849–868.

Zhou, K. (2009). The history of medical insurance in the United States. *Yale Journal of Medicine & Law, 6*(1), 38–39.

CHAPTER 2

STRATEGY

BRADLEY PARK HOSPITAL 2.1

Brent Greg, the new chief financial officer of Bradley Park Hospital knocked on the door. "Come in," said a voice.

Brent walked in. "Wow, you look rough! Have you been here all night?" Brent asked. "No, couldn't sleep very well and came in early." Mike Chambers, the chief executive officer, was wearing a rumpled shirt and sitting at his desk, which was cluttered with papers and empty coffee cups. "These numbers that you gave me yesterday look terrible. Our financial condition is bad enough, but look at patient satisfaction. It is the worst in the state! And this quality report. . . I am just embarrassed." Brent's brow furrowed. "What can we do? The payers are starting to pay based on quality and when these patient satisfaction scores get out, who will come to us when they can go to Madison Hospital down the street? Our weak financial condition means we cannot invest in fancy technology or new facilities. What are we going to do?"

"I am not sure yet," Mike replied. "But I can tell you one thing. We are not giving up! We need a plan. And we need it fast!"

 How should Mike Chambers approach this problem? What would you do first?

INTRODUCTION AND LEARNING OBJECTIVES

Corporate strategy is typically concerned with (a) the various types of business units in which the corporation or health system decides to operate, (b) the allocation of resources among those business units, and (c) the coordination of the various business strategies to achieve overall cohesiveness (Grant, 2009; Box 2.1). The business units under the umbrella of the health system are hospitals, clinics, hospices, pharmacies, and so on. They develop their own strategies—business strategies— which describe their long-term plans to compete in an industry, or business line, in accordance with the direction set by the corporate strategy. Concurrently, the various functions (i.e., marketing, operations, finance, information technology [IT], and human resources [HR]) of the business units formulate strategies that are aligned with the business strategy (Figure 2.1).

Corporate Strategy
A long-term plan that establishes where the health system will compete, how it will win, and how it will maximize value. It requires the coordination of the strategies of the individual business units.

> ### ⚙ BOX 2.1 – WORDS OF WISDOM
>
> "Strategy is the result of choices executives make, on where to play and how to win, to maximize long-term value" (Favaro, Rangan, & Hirsh, 2012; http://www.strategy-business.com/article/cs00002).

FIGURE 2.1 –
Strategy levels.

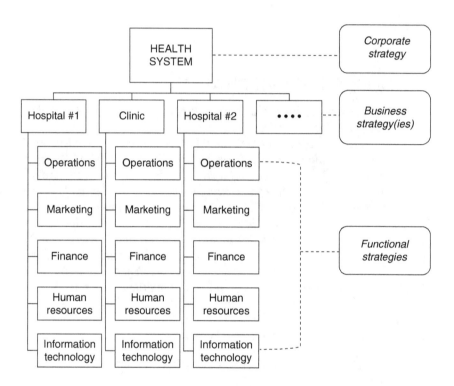

Because the focus of this book is on the operations function, the scope of this chapter is limited to the development of the operations function's strategies that are consistent with the business strategy. After reading this chapter, you will:

1. **Understand the process of developing a business strategy**
2. **Be able to identify the factors that influence business strategy development and to perform a SWOT analysis**
3. **Know the role of the different functional areas within an organization**
4. **Understand how functional areas interrelate**
5. **See how the operations function's strategy supports the business strategy and contributes to creating a competitive advantage**
6. **Know the four competitive priorities and understand the importance of each one**

7. **Know how to evaluate an operations strategy**
8. **Distinguish between order winners and qualifiers**

HOW ARE BUSINESS STRATEGIES FORMULATED?

A **business strategy** focuses on *what* business units need to do to compete in the marketplace (Vadarajan & Clark, 1994). It specifies the game plan the business has selected to maximize its long-term value to customers, and it outlines the resource deployments necessary to "win the game." Executives do not select the courses of action articulated in the strategy in a vacuum. They are derived from a rigorous process; a full discussion of strategy development is beyond the scope of this text. However, it is important to understand the basic framework used to develop strategies. It usually starts with a deep understanding of the organization and the environment in which it conducts business. This process is known as a SWOT analysis (Humphrey, 2005).

SWOT Analysis

A **SWOT analysis** identifies the business's internal strengths (S) and weaknesses (W) and evaluates the environmental opportunities (O) and threats (T; Figure 2.2 offers some examples). Its objective is to leverage the business's internal capabilities and to benefit from market opportunities while mitigating external threats. This matching procedure helps the firm evaluate the viability of various strategies and position itself favorably in the marketplace. An **internal audit** of the firm helps identify its capabilities and deficiencies in terms of facilities, workforce, technology, managerial talent, culture, and so on. This assessment spans all the functional areas of the firm and requires a great deal of objectivity. The internal assessment culminates with a clear understanding of the organizational strengths and weaknesses (the S and W). An **environmental scan** helps the firm gauge external forces over which it has no or limited control. The intent of this scan is to identify opportunities (the O) to gain competitive advantage and identify threats (the T) that should be mitigated (see some examples in Figure 2.2). These external forces are (a) the customers, (b) the legal/political environment, (c) the economy, (d) societal trends, (e) the competition, and (f) suppliers of goods and knowledge services. Let us look at the environment in more detail.

The Customers

For a healthcare provider, the customers include patients (the people accessing health services) and payers (the entities that pay for or reimburse the cost of health services, i.e., public and private insurers, third-party administrators, health plan sponsors, and self-paying patients).

Patients. Patients' characteristics, such as demographics (age, ethnicity, gender, past illnesses, marital status, socioeconomic status, geographic

Business Strategy
A long-term plan that focuses on *what* business units need to do to compete in the marketplace. It specifies the game plan the business has selected to maximize its long-term value to customers, and it outlines the resource deployments necessary to "win the game."

SWOT Analysis
Identifies the business's internal strengths (S) and weaknesses (W) and evaluates the environmental opportunities (O) and threats (T) to leverage the business's internal capabilities and to benefit from market opportunities while mitigating external threats.

Internal Audit
Helps identify the business unit's strengths and weaknesses in terms of facilities, workforce, technology, managerial talent, culture, and so on.

Environmental Scan
Helps identify external forces over which the business unit has no or limited control. The intent of this scan is to identify opportunities and threats.

location, etc.) and psychographics (personal beliefs, values, knowledge about disease, attitudes toward health services, etc.) influence their healthcare needs and therefore shape the demand for services (Andersen & Newman, 2005). For example, consider a market with a large proportion of low-income patients. These people may have more restricted access to care and therefore resort to the use of more expensive resources for care (e.g., emergency room). This leads to higher costs and lower revenue for the provider.

Payer Mix

The share of revenue that comes from public insurers, private insurers, and self-paying individuals.

Payers. The **payer mix** is essentially the share of revenue that comes from public insurers, private insurers, and self-paying individuals (Wall, 2010). Public and private insurers account for the majority of payers. The payers' relative strengths and the number of insured within each insurance program dictate the reimbursement for services rendered. For over a decade, the largest private health insurers have engaged in the fierce acquisition of their smaller counterparts. This sustained consolidation has undermined competition and created numerous geographic pockets of payer dominance. Dominant payers are in excellent negotiating positions and therefore able to demand substantial discounts from providers. Dominant employers and/or their unions have also put pressure on providers to give considerable discounts for services (PHCS Savility, 2008). Finally, Medicare and Medicaid reimbursements have shrunk, further eroding providers' revenue streams. When fully implemented under the Affordable Care Act (ACA), the health insurance exchanges will further intensify competition among payers with the offering of a variety of competing health plans.

The Legal/Political Environment

Legal/political factors include the laws and regulations at the national and local levels that govern healthcare. At the national level, the Centers for Medicare & Medicaid Services (CMS) impose data submission requirements from all providers treating Medicare and Medicaid patients. Some states may mandate approval of facility projects (i.e., Certificate of Need). In those instances, providers must justify the need for planned facilities and gain state approval. This process can be politically contentious and lead to delays and increased costs for executing the strategy. An example of local regulation would be the Health Care Security Ordinance in San Francisco, which provides greater access to the city's uninsured residents. It requires that large- and medium-sized employers contribute a minimum amount per hour to healthcare for their employees (San Francisco Department of Public Health, 2015).

The Economy

Economic forces deal with the supply and demand for labor, the unemployment rate, inflation, interest rates, and so on. These forces influence the volume and type of services rendered, as well as their cost and the revenue they generate. For instance, the persistently weak economy during the Great Recession contributed to the loss of jobs and health insurance coverage. According to the Gallup–Healthways Well-Being Index, the percentage of U.S. citizens without health insurance coverage increased to 17.7% in 2011 (Mendes, 2012). Some of the repercussions included a drop in the use of routine medical care and elective procedures, the elimination of community-based public health programs, including prevention services by cash-strapped states, and an increase in the demand for psychiatric and public hospital emergency care by patients with little or no ability to pay (Abramson, 2009). These conditions strained the resources of many safety net providers and therefore restricted their strategic choices as they struggled to make the investments necessary for future growth. Another example of economic forces influencing strategic choices would involve the ability to access needed capital. In times of economic prosperity, capital markets often loosen their restrictions, making it easier to borrow the capital needed to execute a strategy.

Societal Trends

Societal forces can have a significant impact on healthcare. Rapid growth of the fast food industry, aging of the population, greater public awareness of mental health issues, evolving attitudes toward plastic surgery, increased availability of healthcare-related information on the Internet, and so on, influence the growth—and decline—of some healthcare services and require providers to adapt quickly. For instance, if a hospital serves a region known to be "retirement friendly," its strategy may emphasize the expansion of geriatric care services. Likewise, cell phones' ever greater role in people's lives may lead a hospital to emphasize easy access to medical records via mobile devices.

The Competition

The competitive landscape is determined by the type and number of care providers who serve the same market. Competition among providers is sometimes viewed as an opportunity for improving quality while controlling costs (Porter & Teisberg, 2004). Others argue that competition may result in overcare or in the underutilization of resources, both of which contribute to increasing costs. Basically, no one knows how much competition is appropriate in the healthcare sector and to what extent it is a threat or opportunity (Dash & Meredith, 2010). Threats and opportunities are contingent upon market size and type. In a small community, the market entry of a new provider of specialized services for which demand is low (e.g., bariatric surgery) will constitute a major threat for the existing provider(s). On the other hand, it may have little or no impact in a large city with a significant obese population. As a general rule, a competitive analysis would uncover competitors' strengths and weaknesses. Competitors' weaknesses can then be exploited to secure a market advantage, whereas their strengths signal the need to improve or look for another market niche.

Suppliers of Goods and Knowledge Services

New drugs, new technologies, new equipment, new medical supplies and devices, and new therapies present new opportunities for improved diagnoses and treatments, improved coordination of care, increased revenue, and lower cost. The opposite is also true. New drugs may be less effective than older ones (Vastag, 2012), new devices may present risks of injury and are recalled (Villaraga, Guerin, & Wood, 2009), and new technologies may actually increase costs while not improving revenue. The financial impact of investing in new technologies is highly dependent on the technology and the payer environment in which the organization operates. There is no consensus on the impact of new products and supplies on healthcare costs and quality. What is certain is that the American public strongly equates innovation and technology with progress and often creates the demand for new products they have seen advertised on TV or on the Internet. Providers, therefore, face the dilemma of balancing the dual pressures of (a) patients and vendors urging them to be on the cutting edge and (b) payers forcing them to remain conservative by placing limits on reimbursements.

FIGURE 2.2 – Examples of strengths, weaknesses, opportunities, and threats.

INTERNAL	
Strengths	**Weaknesses**
• People's diverse skills and abilities • Culture conducive to innovation • Modern and modular facilities • Abundant financial resources • Strong and growing customer base • Up-to-date equipment • Latest technologies • Solid reputation • Managerial expertise • Strong leadership	• Lack of skills • Resistance to change • Outdated facilities • Lack of financial resources • Dwindling customer base • Outdated equipment • Obsolete technologies • Poor reputation • Incompetent management • Weak leadership
Opportunities	**Threats**
• Population growth in geographic area • Availability of government grants • Competition's weaknesses • Availability of better supply networks • Untapped market niches	• Weak economy • New regulations limiting revenue • Weak labor supply • New, expensive technologies • Political uncertainty
EXTERNAL	

POSITIVE (left margin) — NEGATIVE (right margin)

BRADLEY PARK HOSPITAL 2.2

"That was a great meeting, Mike," said Francine Sutton, chief nurse of Bradley Park Hospital, turning to Mike Chambers as she was leaving the strategic planning meeting with her nursing supervisors. "The SWOT analysis helped me understand what challenges we are facing, both internally and externally, but it also supported my belief that we have real strengths and opportunities. If we all work toward the common goal, we can make Bradley Park a truly great hospital!"

BPH SWOT Analysis		
	INTERNAL	
	Strengths • Strong primary care network coordinated with clinicians in 20 specialties • Close proximity of clinics and hospital • Lab and advanced imaging onsite • Talented administrative leaders • New CEO with fresh ideas • Comprehensive IT infrastructure	**Weaknesses** • Long wait times in the emergency department • Scheduling access problems • Inadequate parking when clinic busy • Outdated facilities • Low staff morale • Poor funding for personnel • Poor statewide reputation for quality care • Cost overruns
P O S I T I V E	**Opportunities** • Partnerships with outside physicians • Governmental pressures for new care models requiring multispecialty clinicians • Cutbacks at smaller hospitals and physician groups	**Threats** • Weak economy • New government regulations, including penalties for poor quality • Large Medicare patient population • Weak labor supply • New payment models • Difficulty recruiting physicians • Innovative competitor	N E G A T I V E
	EXTERNAL	

Generic Business Strategies

After conducting a SWOT analysis, the organization must take a more focused look at the competition, exploit its own strengths, determine which weaknesses can be overcome, formulate its vision, and maneuver for a competitive position. This exercise leads to the formulation of feasible business strategies that improve the chances of gaining and/or sustaining market dominance and assuring financial success.

All strategic choices determine the position of the business unit relative to its competitors. There are several classification schemes used to describe these positioning strategies. The two most common typologies are discussed here.

Miles and Snow (1978) and Porter (1980) have proposed typologies of business-level strategies that are now well established in practice and in the literature. Porter focuses on the goal of the organization and the actions it takes to produce value greater than that offered by the competition. **Value** is the health outcome achieved per dollar spent (Porter & Lee, 2015). Miles and Snow focus on the internal capabilities (structure, processes, and resources) management intends to use to achieve a particular strategy. In order to capitalize on their respective strengths and create a more comprehensive framework, these two approaches have been combined (Olson, Slater, & Hult, 2005; Walker & Ruekert, 1987). The ensuing hybrid typology comprises four positioning strategies:

Value
The health outcome achieved per dollar spent.

1. Prospectors
2. Analyzers
3. Low-cost defenders
4. Differentiated defenders

Prospectors
Prospectors tend to be innovators focusing on early market entry.

1. **Prospectors.** Prospectors focus on innovation and early market entry. These are typically decentralized organizations that rely on the creativity of numerous specialists in the organization to produce breakthroughs.

Analyzers
Analyzers promptly release improved or cheaper versions of the product/services introduced by prospectors.

2. **Analyzers.** Analyzers are prompt to release improved or cheaper versions of the product/services introduced by prospectors. They also defend their established position in existing markets.

Low-Cost Defenders
Low-cost defenders try to achieve quality at the lowest possible cost.

3. **Low-Cost Defenders.** Low-cost defenders must achieve high quality at the lowest overall costs. They rely on centralized decision making to achieve efficiency through standardized practices and cost control.

Differentiated Defenders
Differentiated defenders emphasize premium services to customers willing to pay higher prices.

4. **Differentiated Defenders.** Differentiated defenders concentrate on premium services or products to appeal to customers who are willing to pay higher prices. They are usually decentralized organizations that empower decision making at the customer interface.

It is important to note that few organizations adopt a strictly pure strategy. Many times, there will be "spillovers" from one to the other. For instance, some services in an organization primarily described as a low-cost defender may innovate, whereas some of the services offered by a differentiated defender may be of low cost and high quality. In Table 2.1, we provide examples of healthcare organizations and the markets they might serve.

TABLE 2.1 – Business Strategies for Selected Healthcare Organizations

Business Strategy	Healthcare Organization	Market
Prospector	Cleveland Clinic	In 2000, the Cleveland Clinic founded Cleveland Clinic Innovations. This organization's use of the health system's research in medical technology to create new companies has earned it a top spot in the entrepreneurial field. Examples of projects include the development of new ophthalmology diagnostic technology and the expansion of technology for orthopedic surgery. It has filed for more than 1,600 patents (Tribble, 2012).
Analyzer	Geisinger Health System	Geisinger cardiac surgeons identified practices from nationally published guidelines for patients undergoing cardiopulmonary bypass surgery. They standardized this practice, achieved a lower cost, and provided a 90-day "warranty" on the service (Abelson, 2007).
Low-Cost Defender	Denver Health	Denver Health serves a very large population of Medicaid patients. In 2005, it adopted the Lean strategy for reducing waste and continuous improvement as it redesigned patient care. Denver Health has reaped financial benefit while achieving high quality scores (Auge, 2010).
Differentiated Defender	Mayo Clinic	Mayo Clinic offers busy executives an efficient, cost-effective way to manage their health. Thousands of executives from around the world come to the clinic to have a comprehensive evaluation and thorough screening in a luxurious setting (Mayo Foundation for Medical Education and Research, 2012).

✛ BOX 2.2 – OM IN PRACTICE!

Bumrungrad International Hospital: Prospector, low-cost defender, or differentiated defender?

Bumrungrad is a 554-bed hospital with over 30 specialty centers and 55 subspecialties in Bangkok, Thailand. It cares for over 1 million patients annually, including 400,000 international patients from 190 countries. Its vision is simple and appealing: "World Class Medicine; World Class Service." To achieve this vision, Bumrungrad employs over 1,200 full-time and consultant physicians, many of whom are board certified in the United Kingdom, Australia, Singapore, Japan, Germany, and the United States. Nurses are recertified every five years. Many of the staff members speak English, and there are over 58 interpreters to assist patients. It boasts the latest technologies (fully integrated health system, pharmacy robot, online medical imaging, lab automation, etc.) in state-of-the-art facilities. By hospital standards, inpatient accommodations look more like luxury hotel suites, or extended-stay residences, than hospital rooms. Their families are offered a wide range of international dining options. Bumrungrad is accredited by The Joint Commission International, the international branch of The Joint Commission here in the United States. Based on the 2009 reader survey of the Asian *Wall Street Journal*, it is the sixth most admired Thai company overall and the second most admired in terms of quality. In 2009, it received a Thailand's Top 10 Most Innovative Companies award. Its decentralized management structure encourages training and development for various categories of staff, leading to their awards for Best Practice Workplace on Labor Relations

(continued)

> **⊕ BOX 2.2 – OM IN PRACTICE!** (*continued*)
>
> and Labor Welfare. Bumrungrad has been featured on *60 Minutes* and in *Time* magazine, *Newsweek*, *AARP Bulletin*, and *The Wall Street Journal*, to name a few media outlets (Bumrungrad International Hospital, 2016).
>
> How much does it cost? A total bill (surgical fees, lab fees, doctor's fees, room fees, etc.) for a heart bypass surgery costs approximately $19,027. According to the Healthcare Blue Book (2016), a fair price for such a procedure in the United States would be $49,947. To an uninsured or underinsured U.S. patient, or to a self-insured U.S. employer, this would be a good deal. For a Thai citizen, it would be a matter of getting high quality services at a premium price.
>
> So, does Bumrungrad position itself as a prospector (innovative and decentralized), low cost defender (very affordable to Western patients), or differentiated defender (quality superiority)?

BRADLEY PARK HOSPITAL 2.3

Mike smiled and turned toward Brent Greg. "We made a lot of progress today. It really became clear through the discussion that the best business strategy is to be the low-cost defender. But to do that, we need to get our house in order, improve our quality, and lower our costs. Our advantage over our competition is that we have a large number of physicians' offices located close to the hospital and we have an integrated IT system. This will allow us to make decisions more rapidly and push our plans more effectively. Madison Hospital is a strong innovator, so we don't want to go there. We do not have the financial resources to modernize drastically and compete with them. Until we streamline our processes, we can't even take their innovations and implement them here in a cost-effective way."

"We now need to get down to the specific details. As soon as our strategic plan is fleshed out, we will get the board involved. Change this significant is going to be tough. There will be physicians who resist some of the changes, and in this community, they wield a lot of power. I need to be sure that the board is behind me as we develop a plan. We must also be sure that the physicians give input and clearly understand what we are doing and why."

 Based on its SWOT analysis, is BPH's decision to position itself as a low-cost defender the right one? What other information would be required to make that decision? Would your analysis change if Madison Hospital were not in the area?

FUNCTIONAL STRATEGIES

In the previous section, you learned about the development of a business strategy. The question now is, "How do you execute the business strategy?" All strategic choices involve decisions about resource allocation and initiatives. This section tackles these resource issues by showing the importance of engaging the various functional areas of the organization (operations, finance, marketing, HR, and IT) in the successful implementation of the business strategy.

BOX 2.3 – WORDS OF WISDOM

"Functional strategies [describe] how the different functions of the business support the corporate and business strategies" (Ritson, 2008, p. 19).

Functional strategies are designed to support the business strategy (see Figure 2.1; Box 2.3). Although the business strategy specifies WHAT to do to beat the competition, the functional strategies focus on HOW to do so. For example, to implement its business strategy successfully (see Box 2.2), Bumrungrad Hospital needs to have the appropriate functional strategies in place to finance its projects, to recruit competent personnel from chefs to surgeons who are board certified in Western countries, to establish protocols for safety and superior customer service, to maintain electronic medical records to facilitate postoperative care in the patient's country of residence, and to advertise its services through a network of medical facilitators around the world. A lack of fit between the WHAT and the HOW will hinder the implementation of the business strategy and will potentially cripple performance, resulting in organizational failure (White, 1986). Indeed, the various functions within an organization play a vital role in executing the business strategy. These roles are defined here.

Operations

The **operations function** represents the core essence of the business. In a healthcare organization, the core activities of the business involve the treatment of patients. Successfully managed operations transform inputs into outputs that have value for these customers. Managing these transformations is the job of the operations manager. The operations manager makes decisions in the following areas: design of the processes needed to create services (Chapter 7), quality improvement and assurance (Chapters 4, 5, and 6), facility layout and expansion (Chapters 7 and 13), supply chain management (Chapter 11), resource utilization (Chapter 8), and scheduling (Chapter 9). Decisions must be coordinated across these domains of operations to ensure that the transformation of inputs into outputs is both effective and efficient. Many of the decisions are made in collaboration with the managers of the other functions. Let us take a quick look at the roles of these other functions.

Operations Function
A process that involves the core essence of the business.

Finance

In the healthcare industry, the **finance function** typically covers accounting and financial management. Traditional accounting activities include tracking revenue and expenses tied to the operations, resources, and financing of the organization in order to produce statements (income statement, balance sheet, statement of cash flows) about the organization's financial performance. Financial management focuses on this financial information to make decisions regarding the procurement of capital and its effective use (Gapenski, 2009). OM professionals interact extensively with the finance function. They provide data regarding resource utilization, purchasing, and inventory; they also

Finance Function
A department that is responsible for accounting and financial management.

submit capital budgeting requests, as well as capacity expansion plans. The finance function supplies Operations with budgets, cost analyses, and capital investment decisions (Russell & Taylor, 2014). As we have discussed, one of the primary objectives of operations management is efficiency, a goal that makes it imperative for the operations and finance functions to interact effectively and support one another.

Marketing

Marketing
A process that focuses on creating, communicating, delivering, and exchanging offerings that have value for customers, clients, partners, and society at large.

According to the American Marketing Association (2007), "**Marketing** is the activity, set of institutions, and processes for creating, communicating, delivering, and exchanging offerings that have value for customers, clients, partners, and society at large." These endeavors are realized through the 4 Ps: product, price, place, and promotion. The creation of value is achieved by providing the right *product* (or service) at the right *price*. The delivery of value deals with the *place* where the service is delivered. Communication manages the *promotion* of the service (Kotler, Shalowitz, & Stevens, 2008). The concepts of value creation and delivery underscore the tight linkages between Operations and Marketing. Marketing provides Operations with an assessment of customers' perceptions, unmet needs in the market, and demand forecasts for various services. Customers' requirements will serve as Operations' blueprint for the design of value-added processes. In turn, Operations will inform Marketing of its operating capabilities, output rates, and capacity so that Marketing can promote services effectively and develop its own strategies. Therefore, ongoing interaction between Operations and Marketing is vital.

Human Resources

HR
A department that plays a major role in the recruitment, selection, training and development, retention, and compensation of the workforce.

HR balances the needs of the organization and those of its employees. This department plays a major role in the recruitment, selection, training and development, retention, and compensation of the workforce. HR works closely with Operations to acquire and/or develop a pool of employees whose skill set matches Operations' requirements for performing value-added processes. Furthermore, HR ensures that the organization is managing its human resources in a way that complies with federal and state laws. HR further supports Operations by communicating organizational goals, values, policies, and procedures to employees. Compliance can be achieved through incentives such as financial reward and recognition. Finally, HR provides Operations with cost (training and hiring/layoff) information and labor market trends so that human resources can be deployed and managed effectively.

Information Technology

IT
A department that manages the applications and their associated databases, security protocols, and the various information technologies used to run the business of healthcare.

IT is responsible for managing the data and technology infrastructure. Usually, this includes managing the applications and their associated databases, security protocols, and the various information technologies used to run the business of healthcare. The IT function must ensure that providers have timely and accurate information to accomplish their work. The role of IT in healthcare has been elevated in the ACA, with several provisions emphasizing the importance of a close IT–Operations collaboration: Use of healthcare data to improve quality, efficiency, and outcomes (Lipowicz, 2010).

STRATEGY ALIGNMENT

As you can see from the earlier discussion, there needs to be coordination among the functional areas in order to set and execute functional strategies. Additionally, business and functional strategies must be aligned. Ideally, the alignment of a business strategy and functional strategies is the result of both a top-down and a bottom-up approach. Developing a business strategy with no timely concern for its functional support will either doom its implementation or, at the very least, delay it significantly. For example, if the business strategy involves the acquisition of a new patient registration system, IT's involvement should be sought to ensure that the new system is compatible with the existing IT infrastructure. Similarly, establishing functional priorities that do not promote the business strategy will have limited impact. For instance, if the vice president of clinical excellence commits significant resources to improving patient flow in the hospital's oncology department while ignoring the plan to host the department in a new cancer center currently under construction, then time, effort, and money will be wasted. Both top-down and bottom-up approaches are required simultaneously, and their effective fusion depends on transparent communication and coordination.

Figure 2.3 summarizes the business strategy development process we have described so far. The healthcare business unit performs a

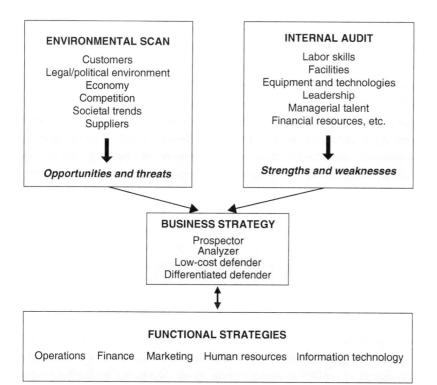

FIGURE 2.3 – Strategy development process.

SWOT analysis to help identify prospective strategies. The potential courses of action are further evaluated through the ability of the various functional resources to support them. Top management (CEO and other senior-level executives) eventually selects the strategy that provides the best fit between the opportunities in the environment and the organization's strengths and functional support. Clearly, all functional strategies are equally important. However, as our focus is on operations, the rest of this chapter deals with operations strategy only.

OPERATIONS STRATEGY

Operational

Refers to routine, short-term activities that occur where services are rendered.

You may wonder whether the term *operations strategy* is actually an oxymoron. After all, how can healthcare operations, which involve the day-to-day activities related to the creation of healthcare services, be strategic? This apparent contradiction stems from the association between two words that are phonetically similar, yet semantically different: **operations** and **operational** (Slack, Chambers, & Johnston, 2010). As mentioned in Chapter 1 and in this chapter, operations are really what the business is about. Their scope spans all the areas of a healthcare organization involved in the design, control, and improvement of the business processes associated with care delivery. These areas include quality management, resource allocation, layout design, supply-chain management, and so on, which are critical to the success of the business strategy and require long-term, high-level decision making. On the other hand, the term *operational* often denotes routine, short-term activities that occur where services are rendered. All the business functions—finance, marketing, HR, IT, and operations—develop and implement strategic plans. They also perform operational tasks.

Remember that the purpose of the business strategy is to pursue a successful differentiation of its products or services from its competitors'. It is therefore market driven. An operations strategy supports the business strategy. It specifies HOW the operations function plans to align its resources (facilities, people, equipment, technology, and supply networks) with the demands of the business strategy (Waters, 2006). In short, it is the blueprint for achieving competitiveness through superior operations.

Evaluation of an Operations Strategy

Consistency of Operations Strategy

Involves the operations strategy's ability to fit (a) the business strategy, (b) the other functional strategies, and (c) itself.

We evaluate an operations strategy in terms of its *consistency* and its *contribution* to creating a competitive advantage (Hayes, Pisano, Upton, & Wheelwright, 2005). **Consistency** relates to an operations strategy's ability to fit (a) the business strategy, (b) the other functional strategies, and (c) itself! As we saw earlier, in addition to supporting the business strategy, the operations strategy must conform to the strategies formulated by the other core functions of the organization and be coherent. For instance, if there is a freeze on training (HR), there is no point in Operations' launching a Six Sigma program, which will require extensive staff development. In the same vein, it may not be prudent for Operations' goals to contradict themselves, for example, by targeting substantially lower lab turnaround times while decreasing staffing levels in the lab.

In order to be effective, an operations strategy must also produce a distinctive competitive advantage. Using Hill's (2000) conceptualization of operations strategy, we can view it as a set of operations-oriented strategic priorities (competitive priorities) that help increase market share by "winning orders." In a healthcare environment, "winning orders" means attracting patients and health insurers to consume your services instead of your competitors'. The **competitive priorities** are: quality, cost, delivery, and flexibility (Figure 2.4).

- **Quality**: Competing on quality means accomplishing better patient outcomes (clinical and experiential) than those produced by your competition.

- **Cost**: Competing on cost refers to the ability to offer services at lower prices than those charged by the competition.

- **Delivery**: Competing on delivery refers to the ability to provide services on time (on-time delivery) or to deliver the services faster (fast delivery) than the competition.

- **Flexibility**: Competing on flexibility refers to the ability to respond to changes with minimal penalties and uniform outcomes for services.

The importance of these concepts will be explored further in the following sections.

Competitive Priorities
The strategic priorities that help increase market share.

Competing on Quality
Refers to accomplishing better patient outcomes (clinical and experiential) than those produced by your competition.

Competing on Cost
Refers to offering services at lower prices than those charged by the competition.

Competing on Delivery
Refers to providing services on time (on-time delivery) or delivering the services faster (fast delivery) than the competition.

Competing on Flexibility
Refers to the ability to respond to changes with minimal penalties and uniform outcomes for services.

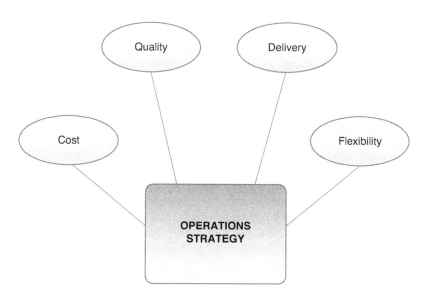

FIGURE 2.4 – Competitive priorities in operations strategy.

COMPETING ON QUALITY
Facts

In Chapter 1, we mentioned the high incidence of medical errors. How can they possibly occur in a country where the best-trained health professionals, the most sophisticated technologies, and the most up-to-date facilities are available? The unfortunate death of 18-month-old Josie King may help us answer this question. Josie was admitted at Johns Hopkins Hospital after suffering first- and second-degree burns. She recovered promptly and her burns healed well. Two days before her release from the hospital, she died of severe dehydration. What happened? In the first episode of "Remaking American Medicine" (Christopher, Eisen, & Shaffer, 2006), Josie's poignant story highlights a lack of communication between nurses and physicians, a disregard for her parents' involvement in her care, and uncoordinated processes. All these errors were preventable and yet they occurred in one of the best hospitals in the world. After Josie's death, her mother launched a crusade to improve patient safety and collaborated with Johns Hopkins and other hospitals to find solutions (Box 2.4).

 BOX 2.4 – OM IN PRACTICE!

Josie King Foundation Programs at Johns Hopkins

Patient Safety Program
- Staff is educated in the science of safety.
- Front-line caregivers are encouraged to detect problems and raise their concerns freely.
- Senior management must provide rapid and meaningful feedback.
- Staff is engaged in problem solving and makes recommendations regarding the allocation of resources necessary to solve the problems.
- Accountability is increased to prevent harm.

Pediatric Rapid Response Teams
- Creation of a Pediatric Rapid Response Team that arrives at the patient's bedside within minutes
- Regular review of causes, management, outcomes, and prevention of cardiopulmonary arrests of children treated at Johns Hopkins
- Ongoing data collection to assess cardiopulmonary arrests
- System in place to report assessment results to Pediatric Advisory Cardiopulmonary Resuscitation committee and to the Children's Center Pediatrician-in-Chief and Physician Advisor
- Parent-initiated Pediatric Rapid Response Team calls, that is, parents have the ability to "pull the cord" when they feel the patient is not receiving proper attention or are concerned about his or her condition (i.e., Condition Help, also known as "Condition H").

OM Initiatives

Patient safety and effective care are definitely within the scope of operations strategy. To improve patient safety, the Institute of Medicine (1999, p. 2) suggests the design of a health system that "makes it harder . . . to do something wrong and easier . . . to do something right." This statement suggests that process redesign or reengineering might be the key to ensuring a care delivery process that minimizes medical errors and optimizes clinical outcomes. Such a process often minimizes handoffs, that is, the number of steps in the process. Why? At each step of a process, there is an opportunity to make an error. The lower the number of steps, the fewer the opportunities for error.

Competitiveness

Excellent performance in clinical care in general, and patient safety in particular, boosts a healthcare organization's reputation and improves its standing relative to its competitors. Other quality attributes, such as well-designed and maintained facilities, prompt service, responsive staff, and effective communication, shape the patient's experience. A first-class experience drives patient loyalty, which in turn improves competitiveness through repeat business. Finally, the ability of a healthcare provider to produce excellent patient outcomes—clinical and experiential—may increase reimbursement.

Porter's perspective (Box 2.5) is strongly anchored in the OM tradition, which views quality as a means to decrease the costs associated with poor performance, such as rework, retesting, scrapped supplies, litigation, lower reimbursements from Medicare, and so on. Ultimately, superior value wins orders and leads to greater competitiveness. Besides improving quality, are there other ways to reduce costs? The answer is provided in the next section.

▶ **BOX 2.5 – LET'S TALK!**

Your words	. . . and ours
"Is healthcare quality expensive?"	"Well, let us try to answer this question with another. What attributes do you consider when you shop?"
"I try to balance the quality of the product with its cost."	"Exactly! You search for VALUE. Remember that in our discussion on business strategies, Porter stressed customer *value*. The notion of value actually captures the relationship between cost and quality: $$Value = \frac{Quality}{Cost}$$ Value = Health outcome per \$ spent (Porter's definition) To improve value, you can increase quality, or decrease cost, or do both. Porter recommends doing both. He argues that the best way to decrease costs is to drive quality up!"

COMPETING ON COST

Facts

According to the 2014 *National Survey of Employer-Sponsored Health Plans* (Mercer, 2014), the average health benefit cost per employee was $11,204 in 2011. Rising healthcare costs have put tremendous pressure on employers to shop for competitive healthcare plans. Mercy Hospital in Springfield, MO, has been able to meet their needs. Mercy contracts either with insurers or directly with self-insured, large employers. In the latter case, the annual cost of health benefits per employee has remained very stable. Over the years, costs for three of the major employers have remained rather stable and well below the national average. Although several market forces influence healthcare costs, Mercy attributes some of its success to its care management and various operations programs.

OM Initiatives

Mercy strives to achieve efficiency at multiple levels of the care delivery process. Through its Nurse-on-Call program, patients call and describe their symptoms to a nurse who will direct them to the emergency department (ED), refer them to an urgent care facility, or simply schedule an appointment with a physician. This early triage reduces the incidence of costly ED visits. Mercy also works with employers to emphasize preventive care not only to improve patient health, but also to intervene before conditions become serious and require expensive procedures and treatments. Furthermore, the deployment of process improvement projects to improve the quality of care has contributed to a reduction in waste (errors, complications, rework, transfers, etc.), which has the dual benefit of improving Mercy's operational efficiency and controlling healthcare costs for patients and their employers. Finally, Mercy's supply chain division, "Resource Optimization and Innovation (ROi)," has helped streamline and integrate the supply chain for all Mercy hospitals by eliminating non–value-added steps along the supply chain; consolidating purchasing, inventory management, and distribution; negotiating directly with manufacturers and eliminating third-party distributors; revamping and continuously improving medication administration processes; and repackaging pharmaceuticals and supplies (e.g., 20 pairs of gloves out of a box of 200) to deliver exactly what is needed while taking advantage of volume purchasing. All these initiatives are guided by a unifying principle: improve patient care (Moore, 2009).

Competitiveness

What are the benefits? Because of their lower costs, efficient care providers improve their financial position in several ways. They can increase their profit margins even when their prices are on par with their competitors. They can also increase their market share by attracting third-party payers with reduced prices. Finally, they are less threatened by the lower Medicare reimbursements for a growing elderly population because they have a better understanding and mastery of cost-control mechanisms (Arnst, 2010). In Mercy's case, its visibility and reputation were enhanced when ROi was ranked the number 2 global supply chain in the Gartner Healthcare Supply Chain Top 25 (Blake et al., 2011) listing. More important, it was able to market a lower utilization of high-cost services to employers and insurers while ensuring quality care. Its reputation for high quality combined with attractive pricing has contributed to its designation as one of the six centers of excellence where Wal-Mart employees can undergo some procedures away from home, with no co-pays or deductibles (American Medical News, 2012).

COMPETING ON DELIVERY

On-Time Delivery

On-time delivery is simply the ability to keep your promise to deliver a product or service on time. Setting an appointment carries the tacit understanding that all parties involved are responsible for showing up on time. The basic expectation is just adherence to an agreed-upon time.

Facts

Disruptions in delivery reliability lead to higher costs and a decrease in customer satisfaction, which can lead to a decline in revenue. Failure to serve the customer can undermine the viability of the business enterprise as a whole. This is what happened at the University of Alabama (UAB) Hospital in 2004 after moving into a state-of-the-art facility with 40 new operating rooms (ORs). The facility came with new capacity and technology, but the procedures to schedule cases, educate staff, and assure that specific instruments were available prior to opening the new ORs were deficient. These problems led to high error rates for instrument trays, delays in first-case starts, increased time between cases, and extension of operating schedules into the night. In addition, there was decreased employee satisfaction, high turnover, and lower patient satisfaction. This threatened the viability of the OR operations as a whole. Can you imagine being scheduled for a needed surgery and thinking that it would take place somewhere around 9 a.m. and then waiting much of the day to enter at 5 p.m.?

OM Initiatives

In order to improve the delivery reliability of the ORs, a number of management interventions were simultaneously implemented at UAB. These included an improved scheduling process, the launch of an OR block release policy, mandatory staff training, central sterile process improvements with reengineering of case-cart management, the mandatory implementation of the National Patient Safety Goals, and the establishment of defined performance measurements and reporting processes. In addition, a new role was defined, "Surgeon of the Day," for someone who works to resolve conflicts and assure that patient needs are met in a timely fashion throughout the day.

Competitiveness

Once the issues that threatened the reliability of UAB's ORs were addressed, first-case start time improved from 23% to 63% compliance, turnover time improved (adding 27 hours of OR capacity a month), and the number of cases extending to after hours decreased. Additionally, nursing turnover decreased, the vacancy rate went from around 40% to less than 10%, and instrument tray errors plummeted. All these improvements in on-time delivery enabled a significant growth in services, improved financial performance, and better safety and customer satisfaction (Heslin et al., 2008).

Just like a kept promise, on-time delivery is pretty much expected from the concerned parties. Therefore, delivery reliability may not necessarily improve a provider's competitive advantage, but it can certainly make its business uncompetitive when it is lacking!

FAST DELIVERY

Facts

Esmin Green had been in the waiting room of the psychiatric emergency department of Kings County Hospital Center for almost 24 hours before she collapsed and died on the floor. An autopsy revealed that the cause of death was pulmonary embolism, which often results from a blood clot forming in the legs and traveling to the lung (Meisel & Pines, 2008).

Unfortunately, Esmin Green is not alone. According to research from Press Ganey, almost 400,000 patients waited for 24 hours or longer in the ED in 2009 (Rice, 2011). Patients who wait for long periods of time may die in the ED or, exasperated by the long wait, may leave before seeing a physician and die at home or have their condition worsen.

OM Initiatives

Many emergency rooms have taken steps to reduce wait times in the ED and speed up delivery. These steps often include process redesign (triage and split flow), simplification (fewer steps), facility redesign (separating patients based on acuity), and better match between capacity and demand (avoiding boarding practices, i.e., leaving admitted patients in the ED until inpatient beds become available), which all lead to a smoother patient flow and lower lead times.

Competitiveness

In many cases, such as emergencies, fast delivery or the ability to deliver the service promptly (ideally faster than the competition) improves the competitive position. Scottsdale Healthcare in Arizona gained competitive advantage by updating the estimated times at its four emergency departments every 3 minutes. These estimates are posted on an electronic billboard outside each hospital and on their Web sites (Yoshino, 2009). Such improvements not only have the potential to save lives and increase patient satisfaction, but they also boost revenue by reducing the number of patients who will leave if they have to wait too long.

COMPETING ON FLEXIBILITY

Facts

Healthcare operates in a highly dynamic environment. Technologies, clinical procedures, and the demand for services change at a quick pace. Internally, patient conditions are in flux as well. A patient may require general care one day and intensive care the next. To accommodate these changes, the universal bed care delivery model has become increasingly popular. It allows patients to stay in one room irrespective of their changing needs during their entire hospital stay. This means that the room must be designed for a multitude of options ranging from critical care to family visitation. In these acuity-adaptable rooms, there must be space for medical equipment, caregivers, patient ambulation, and visitors. In some hospitals, the nursing staff is cross-trained to provide both intensive care and recovery care (Brown, 2007). Providence Regional Medical Center designed the Cyambaluk Medical Tower with flexibility in mind. Two floors are dedicated to invasive procedures with rooms that can be used as ORs, cath labs, or interventional radiology. Every other wing has acuity-adaptable patient rooms, and some of these rooms can be converted from private to semiprivate, and vice versa (Simmons, 2011).

OM Initiatives

A strategically flexible business unit must be supported by flexible organizational functions, such as operations. In turn, Operations needs to develop the capabilities to cater to a diverse patient and case mix (mix flexibility); to handle fluctuating volumes of patients (volume flexibility); and to pioneer treatments, procedures, or processes (innovation flexibility). Instrumental to these capabilities are the ability to change processes (process flexibility) and the acquisition of flexible resources (labor, equipment, facility flexibility) that can handle a variety of situations (see Chapter 13).

The case of Providence Regional Medical Center demonstrates that an innovative facility redesign with flexible resources enables a rapid adjustment to different types of patients. This design enables the provider to meet a variety of patient needs in a single facility without incurring the costs of building multiple wards, wings, or even facilities for specific conditions or treatments. By eliminating multiple handoffs, these designs also have the potential to simplify patient flow and improve the continuity of care and the comfort of patients whose evolving needs require prompt adjustments to new levels and types of care. The business units investing in such flexible facilities organize their resources around the patient rather than processes. They believe that their patient-centered focus will increase their competitive advantage on multiple fronts: costs, outcomes, speed, and satisfaction.

Competitiveness

As emphasized in the SWOT analysis section, the environment in which a business operates is dynamic, and businesses that can quickly accommodate, or even anticipate, change are better positioned to improve or maintain their competitiveness. The adaptive response should be quick, inexpensive, and have little or no impact on the quality of outcomes. In other words, a flexible business unit must accommodate a wide variety of patients with unique needs, but without compromising efficiency and effectiveness. This challenge will place even more pressure on the operations function to continually manage its processes for optimal quality, timely delivery, and cost. The implication is that excellent performance on all competitive priorities is expected. Is it plausible? Let us explore this issue in the next section.

THE CUMULATIVE MODEL

In operations, there was a long-held belief of trade-offs among the competitive priorities (Skinner, 1966). This is especially true in healthcare. Cost cutting is often seen as a threat to the quality of clinical outcomes. In fact, many healthcare professionals claim that the U.S. healthcare system is costly because it is "the best in the world." There is a sound logic behind the high-cost–high-quality paradigm. Employing surgeons with outstanding track records, using the latest and most sophisticated equipment and technologies, acquiring premium supplies, continuously developing the skills of the nursing and support staff, and so on, should, in theory, yield the best possible outcomes. By the same token, cost savings that threaten the quality of these inputs would likely jeopardize the quality of the outputs.

Now, let us reflect for a while. When discussing quality as a competitive priority, we said that improving quality could actually lower the costs of rework, inventory, litigation, poor resource utilization, and so on. The Institute of Medicine's (2012) report, *Best Care at Lower Cost: The Path to Continuously Learning Health Care in America*, further supports this relationship. It explores the potential to attack the higher costs associated with increasingly complex medical care. Opportunities resulting from increased computational power, connectivity allowing for improved dissemination of information, progress in organizational capabilities, and patient empowerment are now present to help improve the quality of care while reining in the costs.

We also said that improving quality through a simplification of processes with fewer handoffs improved patient flow and rapid response to evolving needs (on-time and fast delivery). Then we discussed that the businesses with excellent performance on cost, quality, and delivery were best positioned to adapt to the rapid changes required by a dynamic environment (flexibility). There appears to be a synergistic effect among all the competitive priorities. This was first noticed by Nakane (1986), who realized that world-class manufacturers excelled in all competitive priorities. He also established a sequence. World-class companies should first devote their efforts to achieving excellence in quality, then to delivery, cost, and flexibility. Others (Ferdows & De Meyer, 1990; Noble, 1995) came up with a different sequence, but there was a consensus that quality was the building block of outstanding performance in all dimensions. Therefore, improving quality in order to decrease costs made sense, but not vice versa. This practice of pursuing all competitive priorities, starting with quality, is known as the **cumulative model.**

Nevertheless, the companies that excelled at everything also distinguished themselves by "beating the competition" or differentiating themselves on one or several dimensions. Hill (2000) captured this phenomenon in his distinction between "order winners" and "order qualifiers." **Order winners** are literally the competencies that enable the business to *win* orders or customers, that is, the competencies on which a particular business's performance outclasses that of the competition. On the other hand, **order qualifiers** merely *qualify* the business to be competitive in the marketplace, that is, performance on these competencies is on par with that of the competition. Let us take fast delivery, for example. If the ER's average wait is 3 hours at Hospital X, and this wait is comparable to the wait in the other ER departments in town, fast delivery is a qualifier for Hospital X. If its average waiting time is only 2 hours compared to the competition's 3 hours, then it is an order winner. Now, let's say that Hospital X averages wait times of 4 hours or more, then it no longer meets the threshold for competitiveness and risks losing—as opposed to winning—some market share to its competitors. For this reason, you should never underestimate the significance of order qualifiers.

It is therefore very important for a care provider to continuously monitor its performance on the various competitive priorities in order to take quick action if needed. The balanced scorecard and dashboards assume this tracking task.

HOW ARE WE DOING? MEASURING PERFORMANCE

Balanced Scorecard

In order to assess whether the organization is on track to meet its strategic objectives, the organization must have an effective performance measurement system. The **balanced scorecard** provides a balanced view of organizational performance (Box 2.6). It allows for monitoring of different performance metrics—often called key performance indicators—simultaneously from four different angles: the organization's ability to (a) create value for its customers, (b) manage its internal processes to meet customers' expectations, (c) innovate and improve, and (d) generate financial growth and strength (Kaplan & Norton, 1992, 1996). Note that the balanced

Cumulative Model
The practice of pursuing all competitive priorities, starting with quality.

Order Winners
The competencies that enable the business to win orders or customers; that is, the competencies on which a particular business's performance outclasses that of the competition.

Order Qualifiers
The competencies that qualify the business to be competitive in the marketplace. Performance on these competencies is on par with that of the competition.

Balanced Scorecard
A visual display mechanism that conveys critical information on key performance indicators in finance, marketing, operations, and HR at a glance.

scorecard reflects the collaboration of all functional areas on overall performance. For example, creating value for customers requires Marketing's input regarding patients' wants and needs. Likewise, HR promotes a culture of innovation and improvement through employee selection, training, and development. Operations relies on Marketing's and HR's contributions to design, manage, and control the processes that enable the creation of value and lead to financial performance (Figure 2.5). In a sense, Operations measures take precedence in a balanced scorecard because they focus on the "doable," and are therefore action oriented. The scorecard brings people together to understand what is strategically important and, therefore, connects the business strategy with the functional strategies.

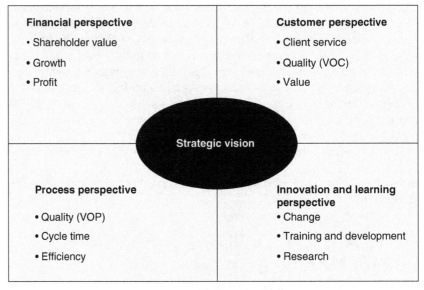

FIGURE 2.5 – Balanced scorecard.
VOC, voice of the customer; VOP, voice of the process.

The balanced scorecard has evolved over the past few decades and has seen significant adoption within the healthcare industry. At a minimum, it is used as a monitoring system to track progress and watch areas that need improvement. It can even be linked to a personnel performance review system and tied to pay or incentives. In its fullest form, the balanced scorecard is a strategy management tool used for mapping functional activities and resources to the business strategy.

Scorecards/Dashboards

The balanced scorecard emphasizes the multifunctional nature of strategy deployment. It involves a collection of scorecards, also called strategic dashboards, from each functional area. The terms "scorecard" and "dashboard" tend to be used interchangeably. To maintain a consistent and unified strategy at various levels of the organization, dashboards or scorecards cascade down from strategic to operational performance (Eckerson, 2006).

1. Strategic dashboards monitor the achievement of strategic objectives in each functional area (e.g., readmission rate for *quality*; average cost per discharge for *cost*). They emphasize performance management and the actions necessary to accomplish long-term goals through coordination and collaboration.

2. Tactical dashboards track specific departmental measures (e.g., survival rate for hip fractures, same-day breast cancer surgery cancellation rate). They focus more on analysis (time series, segmentation, prediction, forecasting, modeling, etc.) than on performance management.

3. Operational dashboards track real-time data in specific processes (e.g., lab turnaround time, current ED occupancy). They emphasize monitoring and signal alerts for quick intervention.

There are hundreds of measurements that determine your car's functioning and performance. Nevertheless, only a few critical gauges are displayed: speedometer, tachometer, fuel, temperature, and oil pressure. The same is true for a scorecard or dashboard: it only displays the "vital few" measurements that are the strongest indicators of performance. Table 2.2 depicts a strategic dashboard for Operations (process perspective). As we cover the competitive priorities in more detail throughout the rest of the book, we disaggregate the dashboard to the tactical and operational levels.

BRADLEY PARK HOSPITAL 2.4

"Let's get down to business," Mike Chambers stated at the quarterly meeting of the board. "Bradley Park could be in trouble if we don't start to do things differently. Since coming to Bradley Park, the management team has analyzed our business based on the four competitive priorities—cost, quality, timeliness, and flexibility. We want to excel in all of these areas, but we are currently not doing well in any.

"In addition, we just got the details of how the government is going to start paying us for quality and value. The private insurers are following suit. We analyzed our patient satisfaction and quality measurements and if we don't improve, and improve quickly, our revenue will be cut by millions of dollars. We can't handle that!"

TABLE 2.2 – Strategic Dashboard for Operations								
Measures	FYTD Actual	FY Target	Jan	Feb	Mar	Apr	May	Jun	Jul
QUALITY									
Mortality index	1.07	0.95	1.21	1.32	0.95	0.87	1.02	1.12	1.00
Patient satisfaction	3.5	4.5	3.9	3.7	3.5	3.6	3.2	3.2	3.1
Hospital-acquired conditions per 1,000 discharges	141	135	145	143	140	138	142	138	140
All-cause, 30-day readmission rate	11.4%	< 11%	12	12	11	9	12	13	11
COST									
Cost per adjusted patient/ day ($)	18,123	18,000	18,290	18,380	18,140	18,090	18,059	18,000	17,900
Productivity index (%)	90	97	87	88	90	92	95	89	90
Occupancy rate (%)	68	85	72	67	58	62	69	73	72
Supply cost per adjusted patient day ($)	2646	2500	2821	2721	2528	2562	2762	2621	2508
Inventory turns	3.4	6	3	3	4	5	3	3	3
DELIVERY									
Average length of stay (ALOS)—inpatient	3.8	3.7	3.8	4.4	4.1	3.9	3.6	3.9	3.1
Extended stay of more than 5 days	113	85	105	107	115	131	108	100	123
Extended stay of more than 20 days	14	12	8	19	15	12	16	15	15
FLEXIBILITY									
Cross-trained nurses (%)	14.3	20	10	10	10	15	15	20	20
Bed turnover rate admit/discharge/transfer percentage (%)	78	80	76	75	77	77	78	80	80
2-hour discharge rate (%)	34	75	30	34	40	36	28	32	37

▨ RED FLAG! Needs improvement.

FYTD, fiscal year to date.

The board members were quiet as they looked over the spreadsheet that had been handed out. Finally, John McManus, a long-time board member and community leader, spoke up. "This is concerning. Mike, I thought we were doing well financially and taking good care of our patients. What is going on?"

"John, the world is changing. Healthcare costs too much, and consumers are demanding more convenience. Patients now have a choice as to where they can go, and Madison Hospital, down the road, has a billboard touting their quality.

We are starting to lose patients and doctors. Bradley Park Hospital is stuck in an old model where the focus is on our convenience, not the patient's. When our revenues are dependent on patient satisfaction and quality measures, we won't be in business if things don't change. That is the reason I am scheduling a board retreat to talk about healthcare quality."

Joanne Frank, a new board member, spoke up. "Mike, I certainly don't want to be argumentative, but don't you think we need to focus on our finances, and not quality? I know quality is important, but as I read this spreadsheet, you need money first. And what does the board know about quality?"

"Joanne, if we can improve our quality, I know that that our revenue will improve," Mike responded. "In this environment, the reverse won't work. And I need the board to hold us all accountable for improving our quality. Our hospital needs the institutional will to execute big changes. I need to have us all on the same page and I need you to support our initiatives. Some physicians or community members may not like some of the changes we make. We may need you to help run interference for me!"

 Why do you think that by addressing quality issues, you can positively impact the financial situation at Bradley Park Hospital? Why is Mike Chambers not attacking the other competitive priorities?

SUMMARY

In this chapter, you have learned about the development of a business and operations strategy. The development of a business strategy rests on a careful assessment of a business's strengths (S) and weaknesses (W) in order to respond to the opportunities (O) and the threats (T) presented by the environment. Based on this SWOT analysis, the business or healthcare organization elects one of the following strategic paths: being (a) a prospector, (b) an analyzer, (c) a cost defender, or (d) a differentiated defender. Another factor to this selection process is the feasibility of the functional strategies necessary to support the strategic choice. In order to ensure the success of a business strategy, the marketing, operations, finance, HR, and IT functions must be able to support the strategic direction of the firm. For operations, building a strategic advantage means developing superior operations in terms of their ability to compete on the bases of quality, cost, on-time or fast delivery, and flexibility. World-class healthcare organizations are able to compete on all four competitive priorities (Figure 2.6). However, research has shown that achieving quality first paves the way for excellence on cost, delivery, and flexibility. In other words, quality is the building block for overall superiority. Developing and tracking performance metrics in the four competitive priorities is vital to the effective execution of the operations strategy.

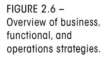
FIGURE 2.6 –
Overview of business,
functional, and
operations strategies.

KEY TERMS

Corporate strategy	Low-cost defenders	Competitive priorities
Business strategy	Differentiated defenders	Competing on quality
SWOT analysis	Operations function	Competing on cost
Internal audit	Finance function	Competing on delivery
Environmental scan	Marketing function	Competing on flexibility
Payer mix	HR function	Cumulative model
Value	IT function	Order winners
Prospectors	Operational	Order qualifiers
Analyzers	Consistency of operations strategy	Balanced scorecard

TOOLS USED IN THIS CHAPTER

TOOL	PURPOSE
SWOT analysis	Approach used to identify the business's internal strengths (S) and weaknesses (W) and to evaluate the environmental opportunities (O) and threats (T). Its objective is to leverage the business's internal capabilities and to benefit from market opportunities while mitigating external threats.

TOOL	PURPOSE
Balanced scorecard	Visual tool that provides a balanced view of organizational performance with key performance indicators.

WHAT DO YOU REMEMBER?

1. What is a SWOT analysis? Give examples of S, W, O, and T.
2. What are the external forces that impact a healthcare business unit? Explain how they help shape a business strategy.
3. Describe the four generic business strategies mentioned in this chapter.
4. What are an organization's functional areas?
5. Why are the various functions important in the formulation of a business strategy?
6. Describe the strategy development process.
7. Explain the interface between Finance and Operations, Marketing and Operations, HR and Operations, and IT and Operations.
8. What are the four competitive priorities that help an organization compete through superior operations? Briefly explain each one.
9. What is the difference between on-time and fast delivery?
10. Describe the cumulative model.
11. Discuss the difference between an order winner and an order qualifier. Use an example for illustration.
12. What is a balanced scorecard and why is it important?
13. What are the three types of dashboards?

THINK OUTSIDE THE BOOK!

1. Select a major hospital in your city/region. Identify the external forces impacting this hospital's strategy and performance.
2. Research three hospitals in your region. What are their respective business strategies? Justify.
3. Based on its prospectus, Bumrungrad's strategy is to compete as a differentiated defender. Do you agree? (bh.listedcompany .com/misc/DEBENTURE/20120124-BH-prospectusNo01-2011-EN.pdf)
4. Go to these two Web sites: (a) video.hbs.edu/videotools/ play?clip=rhc_faq073 and (b) video.hbs.edu/videotools/ play?clip=rhc_faq071. Do you agree that increasing quality is the best way to decrease cost?

5. Watch the following PBS video: "Money and medicine" (http://www.pbs.org/video/2283573727). Describe how Intermountain Healthcare and the UCLA Medical Center tried to improve quality while cutting costs.

6. Develop more Key Performance Indicators to include in the strategic dashboard presented in Figure 2.6.

REFERENCES

Abelson, R. (2007, May 17). In bid for better care, surgery with a warranty. *The New York Times*, p. A1. Retrieved from http://www.nytimes.com/2007/05/17/business/17quality.html?ref=healthplans

Abramson, S. S. (2009). *Holes in the Net: Surveying the impact of the current economic recession on the health care safety net*. Washington, DC: American Public Health Association. Retrieved from https://www.apha.org/~/media/files/pdf/factsheets/1safetynet.ashx

American Marketing Association. (2007). Definition of marketing. Retrieved from http://www.marketingpower.com/AboutAMA/Pages/DefinitionofMarketing.aspx

American Medical News. (2012, October 29). Wal-Mart gives major boost to domestic medical tourism movement. Chicago, IL: American Medical Association. Retrieved from http://www.amednews.com/article/20121029/business/310299966/4

Andersen, R., & Newman, J. F. (2005). Societal and individual determinants of medical care utilization in the United States. *Milbank Quarterly, 83*(4), 1–28.

Arnst, C. (2010, January 18). Radical surgery. *BusinessWeek*, pp. 40–45.

Auge, K. (2010, July 29). Denver health saves millions using Toyota efficiency principles. *The Denver Post*. Retrieved from http://www.denverpost.com/news/ci_15627406

Blake, B., O'Daffer, E., Elvy, C., Hofman, D., Applebaum, T., & O'Brien, D. (2011). *The healthcare supply chain top 25 for 2011*. Stamford, CT: Gartner.

Brown, K. K. (2007). The universal bed care delivery model. *Patient Safety & Quality Healthcare, March/April*. Retrieved from http://psqh.com/marapr07/caredelivery.html

Bumrungrad International Hospital. (2016). Bumrungrad International Hospital. Retrieved from http://www.bumrungrad.com/investor/investor.html

Christopher, F., Eisen, M., & Shaffer, M. (Writers and Producers). (2006). Silent killer [Program 1; Television series episode]. In *Remaking American Medicine a Crosskeys Media production*. Arlington, VA: Public Broadcasting Service.

Dash, P., & Meredith, D. (2010, November). When and how provider competition can improve health care delivery. *McKinsey Quarterly, 10*, 30–41.

Eckerson, W. W. (2006). *Deploying dashboards and scorecards*. Seattle, WA: The Data Warehouse Institute.

Favaro, K., Rangan, K., & Hirsh, E. (2012, May 29). Strategy: An executive's definition. *Strategy+Business, Issue 67*. Retrieved from http://www.strategy-business.com/article/cs00002

Ferdows, K., & De Meyer, A. (1990). Lasting improvements in manufacturing performance. *Journal of Operations Management, 9*(2), 168–184.

Gapenski, L. C. (2009). *Fundamentals of healthcare finance*. Chicago, IL: Health Administration Press.

Grant, R. M. (2009). *Contemporary strategy analysis* (7th ed.). Hoboken, NJ: John Wiley & Sons.

Hayes, R., Pisano, G., Upton, D., & Wheelwright, S. (2005). *Operations, strategy, and technology: Pursuing the competitive edge*. Hoboken, NJ: John Wiley & Sons.

Healthcare Blue Book. (2016). Coronary Artery Bypass Grafting. Retrieved from http://healthcarebluebook.com/page_Results.aspx?id=29&dataset=hosp

Heslin, M. J., Doster, B. E., Daily, S. L., Waldrum, M. R., Boudreaux, A. M., Blair Smith, A., . . . Rue, L. H. (2008). Durable improvements in efficiency, safety, and satisfaction in the operating room. *Journal of the American College of Surgeons, 206*(5), 1083–1089.

Hill, T. (2000). *Manufacturing strategy: Text and cases* (3rd ed.). New York, NY: McGraw-Hill.

Humphrey, A. S. (2005). SWOT analysis. Retrieved from http://www.businessballs.com/swotanalysisfreetemplate.htm

Institute of Medicine. (1999). *To err is human*. Washington, DC: National Academies Press.

Institute of Medicine. (2012). *Best care at lower cost: The path to continuously learning health care in America*. Washington, DC: National Academies Press.

Kaplan, R. S., & Norton, D. P. (1992). The balanced scorecard—Measures that drive performance. *Harvard Business Review, 70*(1), 71–79.

Kaplan, R. S., & Norton, D. P. (1996). Using the balanced scorecard as a strategic management system. *Harvard Business Review, 74*(1), 75–85.

Kotler, P., Shalowitz, J., & Stevens, R. J. (2008). *Strategic marketing for health care organizations: Building a customer-driven health system*. Hoboken, NJ: Jossey-Bass.

Lipowicz, A. (2010, March 23). IT plays critical role in health care reform. *Federal Computer Week*. Retrieved from https://fcw.com/articles/2010/03/23/health-it-provisions-health-care-reform-legislation.aspx

Mayo Foundation for Medical Education and Research. (2012). Executive health program. Retrieved from http://www.mayoclinic.org/departments-centers/executive-health-program/overview

Meisel, Z., & Pines, J. (2008, July 24). Waiting Doom. *Slate*. Retrieved from http://www.slate.com/articles/health_and_science/medical_examiner/2008/07/waiting_doom.html

Mendes, E. (2012, January 24). More Americans uninsured in 2011. *GALLUP Wellbeing*. Retrieved from http://www.gallup.com/poll/152162/americans-uninsured-2011.aspx

Mercer. (2014, November 19). Modest health benefit cost growth continues as consumerism kicks into high gear. New York, NY: Marsh & McLennan Companies. Retrieved from http://www.mercer.com/newsroom/modest-health-benefit-cost-growth-continues-as-consumerism-kicks-into-high-gear.html

Miles, R. E., & Snow, C. C. (1978). *Organizational strategy, structure, and process*. New York, NY: McGraw-Hill.

Moore, V. (2009). *Dangerously good medicine: The infectious impact of innovation, success, and recognition* (Vol. 6, pp. 1–16). Lombard, IL: Council of Supply Chain Management Professionals.

Nakane, J. (1986). *Manufacturing futures survey in Japan, a comparative survey 1983–1986*. Tokyo, Japan: Waseda University, System Science Institute.

Noble, M. A. (1995). Manufacturing strategy: Testing the cumulative model in a multiple country context. *Decision Sciences, 26*(5), 693–721.

Olson, E. M., Slater, S. F., & Hult, G. T. M. (2005). The performance implications of fit among business strategy, marketing organization structure, and strategic behavior. *Journal of Marketing, 69*(3), 49–65.

PHCS Savility. (2008). *Payer consolidation and its impact on provider revenue: Strategies to ensure negotiating power, healthier cash flow and a competitive market* [White paper]. Retrieved from http://www.phcssavility.com/userpdfs/whitepaper.pdf

Porter, M. E. (1980). *Competitive strategy*. New York, NY: Free Press.

Porter, M. E., & Lee, T. H. (2015). Why strategy matters now. *New England Journal of Medicine, 372*(18), 1681–1684.

Porter, M. E., & Teisberg, E. O. (2004). Redefining competition in health care. *Harvard Business Review, 82*(6), 65–76.

Rice, S. (2011, January 13). Don't die waiting in the ER. *The Empowered Patient, CNN Health*. Retrieved from http://www.cnn.com/2011/HEALTH/01/13/emergency.room.ep

Ritson, N. (2008). *Strategic Management*. New York, NY: Neil Ritson & Ventus Publishing ApS.

Russell, R. S., & Taylor, B. W. (2014). *Operations and supply chain management* (8th ed.). Hoboken, NJ: John Wiley & Sons.

San Francisco Department of Public Health. (2015). Health Care Security Ordinance (HCSO) compliance. Retrieved from http://sfgov.org/olse/health-care-security-ordinance-hcso

Simmons, T. M. (2011). Providence health and services: Scott Anderson: Vice president of construction project management. Retrieved from http://www.healthcareix.com/2011/05/providence-health-and-services-scott-anderson-vice-president-of-construction-project-management/#

Skinner, W. (1966). Production under pressure. *Harvard Business Review, 44*(6), 139–146.

Slack, N., Chambers, S., & Johnston, R. (2010). *Operations management* (6th ed.). Upper Saddle River, NJ: Prentice-Hall.

Tribble, S. J. (2012, September 12). Cleveland clinic innovations earns top spot. Cleveland, OH: Cleveland Plain Dealer. Retrieved from http://www.cleveland.com/healthfit/index.ssf/2012/09/cleveland_clinic_innovations_e.html

Vadarajan, P. R., & Clark, T. (1994). Delineating the scope of corporate, business, and marketing strategy. *Journal of Business Research, 31*(2–3), 93–105.

Vastag, B. (2012, March 21). Hidden data show that antipsychotic drugs are less effective than advertised. *The Washington Post*. Retrieved from http://www.washingtonpost.com/blogs/the-checkup/post/hidden-data-show-that-antipsychotic-drugs-are-less-effective-than-advertised/2012/03/20/gIQAXX4IQS_blog.html

Villaraga, M. L., Guerin, H. L., & Wood, J. M. (2009). Five year review of class I medical device recalls: 2004–2008. *Food and Drug Law Journal, 64*(4), 663–676.

Walker, O. C., & Ruekert, R. W. (1987). Marketing's role in the implementation of business strategies: A critical review and conceptual framework. *Journal of Marketing, 51*(3), 15–33.

Wall, J. K. (2010, October 20). "Payer mix" playing role in hospital merger. *Indianapolis Business Journal*. Retrieved from http://www.ibj.com/articles/22925-payer-mix-playing-role-in-hospital-merger

Waters, D. (2006). *Operations strategy*. Handover, UK: Cengage Learning.

White, R. E. (1986). Generic business strategies, organizational context and performance: An empirical organization. *Strategic Management Journal, 7*(3), 217–231.New reference:

Yoshino, K. (2009, December 21). Emergency room wait times in Southern California. *Los Angeles Times*, pp. E1, E4. Retrieved from http://articles.latimes.com/2009/dec/21/health/la-he-er-wait-times-socal21-2009dec21

CHAPTER 3

PROJECT MANAGEMENT

BRADLEY PARK HOSPITAL 3.1

The environment at Bradley Park Hospital was tense. Francine Sutton, chief nursing officer, called Jennifer Lawson into her office. Jennifer had just taken on the position of quality director. While working as a young nurse at the hospital for 4 years, she had taken night classes at the local university. The hard work had paid off, and she now had a master's degree in healthcare administration. She had been so excited and felt that this new opportunity was her big break. Right around the same time, the top brass at Bradley began fretting about the financial future of the hospital. Competition was getting tougher and the third-party payers were about to change the way the hospital was reimbursed based on quality and value. Yesterday, the chief executive officer of Bradley Park Hospital made a speech to all the staff saying that from now on, things were going to be done differently. At the meeting, the other nurses were looking around, not knowing what he meant. Jennifer was thinking, "What does that mean to me? Why did I take this position just when everything is going to change? Could I get fired?"

"Come in Jennifer," Francine said cheerfully. "Mr. Chambers asked us to remodel the geriatrics unit. It will now be called the acute care for the elderly, or ACE unit. Mr. Chambers and the board decided that we need to focus on improving the efficiency of care for our largest group of patients while increasing the quality of care that we deliver." Jennifer was stunned. "You mean, . . . uh . . . you mean I am not fired?" she stammered. "No!" Francine said laughing. "I think your job just got more important! And we all have a lot of work to do."

Francine looked thoughtfully at Jennifer. "We need to develop a project plan for the ACE unit over the next month. This is a complex project, and the stakes are high. Don Nguyen, the chief operating officer is taking the lead, but I need you to be his second in command. This is a very important project for our hospital and we cannot fail!"

Think of a project in which you have been involved. What was the hardest part for you to do well? Have you ever worked on a project that failed? Why did it fail?

INTRODUCTION AND LEARNING OBJECTIVES

Project

A set of team activities designed to produce a unique product or service. Its basic characteristics include a large number of activities, a long time frame, and a high cost.

Chapter 2 provided a framework for us to think about the business strategy—determining *what* direction an organization will follow. But how do you move from knowing what needs to be done to actually doing it? That is where project management comes in. Although the term *project* is often used loosely, in this chapter, a **project** denotes a set of team activities designed to produce a one-of-a-kind product or service. These types of projects are not routine, or part of ongoing business operations. Examples include launching a rocket, building a bridge, implementing a hospital information system, or developing a new drug. Such endeavors involve a large number of activities and require resources (people, money, or equipment) over an extended period of time. As such, they tend to be complex and costly, and must be managed carefully.

Projects require that many people from different departments, and even different organizations collaborate closely. All parties involved assume specific roles and responsibilities necessary for the successful completion of the project. Because projects have many moving parts and may be active over time, specific tools and techniques have been developed to help you stay on track. Some of these tools include the work breakdown structure, the Gantt chart, program evaluation and review technique (PERT), and the critical path method (CPM). In this chapter, you will learn how to:

1. **Define the scope of projects**
2. **Describe a project charter**
3. **Define the roles and responsibilities of individuals involved in projects**
4. **Identify the various phases of project management**
5. **Develop work breakdown structures**
6. **Draw network diagrams**
7. **Schedule projects with deterministic times**
8. **Schedule projects with probabilistic times**
9. **Crash activity times**
10. **Discuss the advantages and disadvantages of PERT/CPM**
11. **Understand the major causes of project failure**

WHAT IS PROJECT MANAGEMENT?

Project Management

A systematic approach to planning and steering the project processes to achieve the specific project goals.

Project management is a systematic approach to planning and steering the project processes to achieve the specific project goals. Project management is difficult because it must be balanced with constraints. There is never enough time, money, or people to do everything that an organization would like to accomplish. Therefore, choices need to be made to define the scope of a project so that it can be completed on time

FIGURE 3.1 – The triple constraint.

and within budget. These competing constraints are sometimes called the **triple constraint** (Haughey, 2011; Figure 3.1):

- Projects must meet performance specifications (quality, scope, standards).
- Projects must be within cost (people, materials, supplies, contracts, etc.).
- Projects must be delivered on time.

Projects come in all sizes. For our purposes, we focus on projects that require significant resources across a number of departmental units or organizations. These types of projects are usually led by a trained project manager and involve individuals working together outside their normal job roles. For example, if different physician groups decide to come together and combine their financial systems with a hospital's to form an accountable care organization, finance specialists from each entity will work together on this project. If a hospital board decides to build a new diagnostic and treatment center, a project team will be chosen from various functional areas to work on the planning and construction of the new facility.

BRADLEY PARK HOSPITAL 3.2

Don Nguyen was sitting at his desk when Jennifer entered his office. "Come in. You must be Jennifer Lawson. I am Don Nguyen. Have a seat. I understand that you are our new quality director, and we will be managing a project together."

"Thank you." Jennifer sensed that Don was a warm and highly capable person. "I hope you know that I have not done this before. I really want to do this, and will work hard, but I do not even know where to start!"

Don smiled. "Everyone has to begin somewhere. So let's get going. First off, do you know what project management is?"

Jennifer looked nervous, "I read that project management is an approach to planning and steering a project to be sure that the goals are met. I know there are certain tools that are used, but it all sounds very technical."

"Have you ever planned a big party or moved to a new apartment?" Don asked.

"Yes, of course."

"Well, then you have experience in project management! The approach to planning a big event and planning an ACE unit is similar. You need to balance the cost, the scope of the project, and the time available. The tools that you will learn just help to keep things on track as the project gets more complicated. That is the easy part."

Jennifer asked, *"What do you mean?"*

"Project management can be tough because, unlike small projects, such as planning a party, large projects require that you work with other people to get things done. Therefore, two of the most important skills that a project manager must develop in big organizations are effective communication and conflict resolution."

"But don't people understand that the projects are important and go along?"

"It is not that simple. Sometimes people block the project because they are busy and have other priorities. There are times when the project's objective is to change what members of the team are doing and they don't want that to happen. Sometimes, people who are not on the project team block it because they were not included. Our job is to be sure that we do what we can to make this project a success! We need to be sure that we plan all phases of the project well, that the team members know what their roles are, and that we get buy-in from them. Moreover, we must secure top management's commitment to support the project and intervene when necessary.

"Meet me here Monday morning and we will start defining the goals of the project and start thinking who we need on our project team. In the meantime, start learning what you can about ACE units."

"I will. Have a great weekend and I will see you Monday." Jennifer left Don's office. Wow, she thought. This is a big deal!

On Monday, Jennifer arrived at Don's office at 8 a.m. sharp. Don was already at his desk shuffling some papers. *"Jennifer, come in. I have started outlining the tasks we need to do prior to kicking off this project and I am listing possible team members. I want to get your thoughts."*

Jennifer pulled a chair up to Don's desk so she could see the lists and charts. She saw several names listed on a sheet of paper. Don had included individuals from finance, nursing, facility planning, and human resources. Many names she did not recognize, but one, Sue Hawkins, her manager, stood out. *"Excuse me, Don. But is Ms. Hawkins a member of the project team?"*

"I think she should be. She is over at hospital quality and has a vested interest in the success of this project."

"But won't that be awkward since I report to her? What if I have to tell her what to do?"

"Jennifer, your role as assistant project manager is different from your role as quality director. You report to Sue as a quality director, but in this role, you report to me. That is one thing that members of a project team need to keep in mind. When you are on a project team, your loyalty and focus are on the team. I can certainly help you maneuver through any difficulties with your relationship this time. But I expect, you will become the project manager on future assignments, so I hope you can learn how to manage different roles."

"I guess I do have a lot to learn!"

"Our first step is to produce a plan for the overall project," Don continued. We need to get our selected team members together. We must have all the

necessary players at the table to address the project-related issues and specify our objectives clearly. We can then develop a plan and sell it to the other executives of the hospital. If they agree with the goals and the approach, they will be likely to fund it."

Why is it important to get the right people on the team? What happens if an important area is not represented? Can you recover from that oversight? How?

PROJECT CHARTER AND ROLES
The Project Charter

A **project charter** serves as a road map for the project. It is a document that clearly states why the project is being pursued, what the expected benefits are, who the team members are and the roles they will play, and the timeline for completion. This document is used as a communication tool for all members of the team. It includes:

Project Charter
A document that clearly states why the project is being pursued, what the expected benefits are, who the team members are and the roles they play, and the timeline for completion of the project.

- A business case—reason for doing the project and the financial impact

- A problem statement—clear articulation of the problem that you are trying to solve

- A goal statement—the desired outcome and measures of success

- The project scope—the boundaries of the project (*only* the work required to complete the project successfully)

- A list of team members and their roles

- Milestones and deliverables—project activities, who will do them, and by what date

A project leader is generally responsible for drafting the project charter with input from the other team members. The business case needs to clearly state why the project is important to the organization, why it is imperative that the project be executed at a particular time, and what the cost of inaction might be. The problem should be described in terms of (a) what it is, (b) how long it has been present, and (c) the impact it has on the organization and customer(s). The group then needs to determine the desired outcomes and actions to take. The roles of participants, boundaries of the project, and timelines are important to delineate because projects tend to have a way of expanding beyond what is initially conceived. This situation, called "**scope creep**," can result in cost overruns and project failure.

Scope Creep
Expansion of the project scope beyond what was initially intended.

The Project Manager

The role of the **project manager** is one of great responsibility. It is the project manager's job to direct, supervise, and control the project from beginning to end. Because of the complexity of many projects and the technical skills needed to lead them successfully,

Project Manager
The project manager directs, supervises, and controls the project from beginning to end.

certification programs have been developed to train individuals in project management. Project management software is available to help managers keep track of tasks and timelines. Some programs also support collaborative interactions among team members. Organizations with multiple, simultaneous projects may require several project managers. These project managers may be located at the function unit level (e.g., marketing or finance) within the organization. However, larger organizations may pursue a pure project management organizational structure with a **project management office**, which involves a separate entity with its own staff and administration dedicated to project management. The type of organizational structure selected by the institution depends on the nature of the projects being pursued and the goals of the overall organization (Bobera, 2008).

Project managers manage multiple relationships at the same time. They must be able to work with the project team, heads of functional areas within the organization, senior management, and external stakeholders. As these people are likely to hold different views, project managers must help them talk through their differences and come to an acceptable solution (Kerzner, 2013). Moreover, project managers should not carry out project tasks because they must keep their eyes on the bigger picture. In addition to verifying that the project is defined and planned accurately, and that resources are available, they must ensure that all stakeholders are kept informed, conflict is managed, and all issues are addressed. No project ever goes exactly as planned, so the project manager must be able to adapt to and manage change. Project managers get to know the organization from the ground up. This knowledge provides them with excellent opportunities to contribute in a meaningful way and prepares them for higher level management positions. In other words, if you can get involved in a project, do not pass up the chance!

Project Management Office (PMO)
A separate entity with its own staff and administration that is dedicated to project management.

The Project Team

Project Team
A temporary organizational structure designed to harness expertise from many groups throughout the organization and to carefully define the scope and specific objectives of the project. The team is also responsible for executing tasks and producing deliverables as outlined in the project plan.

Essentially, the **project team** gets the necessary work done to achieve the goal. The team is a temporary organizational structure designed to harness expertise from many groups throughout the organization, and to carefully define the scope and specific objectives of the project. The team is also responsible for executing tasks and producing deliverables as outlined in the project plan. However, project teams usually work with many outside contributors who have the needed expertise (e.g., information technology [IT consultants]) or are invested one way or the other in the outcome of the project. It is important that the project team reaches out to these parties who may have information or insights to contribute. This improves the chances that the overall project will be successful.

Being a project team member is a major responsibility. You must commit to the project goals and communicate honestly, particularly if you have concerns. You must also understand your work assignments and complete them on time to the best of your ability.

Characteristics of a Good Project Team

Some people are much better at working in teams than others. They tend to be constructive and positive people who are interested in giving and seeking information to solve the problem. They find areas of common ground within the group and work to build consensus. Other people can be destructive when working in teams. The negativity of these individuals can end up lengthening the time frame of the project and degrade the team's morale. But, in all fairness, many individuals who appear difficult may have valuable perspectives that are important to the quality of the project. Teams should have a balance of personality types—those who are detail oriented and those who are more visionary. Diversity of types ensures that teams have people focusing on the specifics and the big picture simultaneously and can execute tasks while remaining creative (Tate, 2015).

Employees in Functional Areas

As we mentioned earlier, the team is responsible for getting the project completed, but often this work must be done by employees in specific functional areas. Because these employees do not directly report to the project team, it may be challenging to get them to commit to the team's needs. This is why it is very important to secure the support of the employees' supervisors for the project. The team must ensure that supervisors agree with employees performing project-related tasks, that the timeline is in line with the supervisor's priorities, and that good lines of communication are maintained with the functional areas. If timelines shift or project constraints change, all involved, including supervisors, need to be informed.

Executives

By now, you realize that project support at the highest levels of the organization is critical. Executives need to shepherd the project forward, secure the needed resources, and resolve conflicts. They have the responsibility to make effective and timely decisions to keep the project on track. Although executives may help with setting priorities and defining the projects' objectives, they do not need to lead them. Project sponsorship may be pushed down to middle-level management or committees. However, when there are differences in priorities, executives must clarify what activities take precedence.

Project Champions

It is sometimes helpful to have someone within the organization to proclaim the benefits of the project and work with different stakeholder groups to explain its importance. This **project champion** is often the one who came up with the idea in the first place. Project champions can often gain support for the project more effectively than someone on the project team. As such, they should be kept apprised of progress and challenges.

Project Champion
Someone within the organization who proclaims the benefits of the project and works with different stakeholder groups so that everyone understands why the project is important for the organization.

PHASES OF A PROJECT

Now that you understand the roles of the individuals involved in a project and the importance of effective communication, we turn to the five phases through which a project must pass (Weiss & Wsocki, 1992):

1. Definition
2. Planning
3. Execution
4. Control
5. Closure

Definition

This phase comprises multiple steps:

- Project goals are defined and objectives are delineated (Box 3.1).
- Critical success factors are explicitly described.
- Everything that needs to happen before the project begins is outlined.
- Stakeholders for the project are identified.
- A project team, with the necessary expertise, is assigned.
- All foreseeable barriers to the project are identified and understood.

🌐 BOX 3.1 – WORDS OF WISDOM

"If you don't know where you are going, you will probably end up somewhere else" (Peter & Hull, 1969, p. 125).

When defining the goals of a project, be sure to take the business strategy into account. First, ask where the organization wants to be in 1 year and 5 years. Then, identify the barriers keeping the organization from getting to where it wants to be. Will the project get the organization closer to that point? If not, a discussion with the project sponsor is warranted. When the project is large and complex, the organization may want to formally perform a SWOT (strengths, weaknesses, opportunities, threats) analysis (see Chapter 2).

Planning

Planning involves preparing detailed outlines of how the work will be carried out, including people, roles, and other resource estimates. The project manager is key to successful planning (Box 3.2). This is a rigorous process that must be systematic but flexible enough to handle unique situations. The project team members must thoroughly understand what is being asked of them and they must be capable of handling inputs from diverse groups.

> ### ◈ BOX 3.2 – WORDS OF WISDOM
>
> "By failing to prepare, you are preparing to fail" (Benjamin Franklin, n.d.).

Planning begins with a clear understanding of the underlying objective. The assumptions being made should be documented at the beginning of the project and revalidated at intervals. These assumptions include the external conditions that can affect the project, changing requirements, use of technology, and even government regulations. Planning also involves operational issues such as establishing budgets, setting timelines with major milestones, making decisions regarding personnel involvement and resource allocations, and setting performance expectations. All these issues are typically addressed in a kickoff meeting involving the major stakeholders of the project.

The project plan is a road map intended to communicate to all concerned parties within the organization what is going to happen and when. It attempts to eliminate crises by preventing issues from falling through the cracks, and it decreases conflict by showing participants what changes need to be made. If there is disagreement regarding the project plan, it is best to settle matters before the project begins.

Execution

> ### ◈ BOX 3.3 – WORDS OF WISDOM
>
> "Vision without execution is hallucination" (Thomas Edison, n.d.).

This phase involves doing the work to deliver the product or desired outcome, and it is the hard part (Box 3.3). One of the most common mistakes that project managers make at this stage is letting the project goals shift (i.e., scope creep). When scope creep is allowed to happen, the outputs of the definition and planning phases are no longer relevant, and these must be reworked. Effective communication is crucial during execution.

Control

This phase is focused on systematic monitoring and ensuring that the project stays on track. If problems develop, troubleshooting can help determine where the project went off track. Are people not being held accountable for their tasks? Are the project's assumptions still in line? Have circumstances changed that require a change in the project plan? When assessing the triple constraint—cost, time, and scope—it is important to determine whether the actual work schedule, resource requirements, or cost vary from the planning document. A **variance** is any deviation (schedule, technical performance, cost, etc.) from the project plan. Early identification of variances can allow the plan to get back on track through schedule revision and/or reallocation of resources.

Variance
Any schedule, technical performance, or cost deviation from the project plan.

The very act of measuring progress and communicating it to stakeholders motivates team members to focus on results. It is human nature to complete tasks when monitored. The question to be asked is, "Are we on track to complete the project as planned? If not, why? What do we need to do to get back on course?"

Closure

Projects must come to an end. This is the time to reflect and learn from what happened during the project. "What did we do right? What could have been done better? Did we achieve the desired quality result? Did we achieve our goal within the time frame and with the resources allocated?" In other words, did we achieve our goals within the "triple constraint?" Incorporating a process of intentional and disciplined project review will impact the success of later projects as project managers and team members will want to improve their performance in the future.

 BOX 3.4 – OM IN PRACTICE!

VA Hospital in Denver

On April 15, 2015, KTAR News reported that the construction of the Veterans Administration Hospital in Denver, CO, had extreme cost overruns. The hospital, initially projected to cost $630 million and be complete by 2015, would actually cost an additional $1.73 billion and would not open until 2017. According to the report, delays and cost overruns occurred because plans were not finalized before construction began. The design had some extravagant features, including an outsized atrium that was difficult to harmonize with other construction features. Also cited were construction cost increases and premiums paid to compensate ontractors for the risks associated with the project (Elliott, 2015).

You must have heard of countless projects that were late and well over budget. This is often the result of poor planning, scheduling, and control (Box 3.4). Fortunately, there are a variety of tools available to facilitate a project manager's job during those phases. They are presented in the following sections.

 # PLANNING TOOL: WORK BREAKDOWN STRUCTURE

Work Breakdown Structure (WBS)
The hierarchical organization of a project's components at various levels of detail.

Because typical projects are large in scope, planners break down the project into identifiable, manageable parts. The **work breakdown structure** is a hierarchical organization of a project's components at various levels of detail. The first step in developing a WBS is to identify the main modules of the project (Figure 3.2, Level 2). Next, these modules are divided into the major activities that need to be carried out to finish the module (Level 3). In turn, these major activities are subdivided into the activities (Level 4) required to complete them. Further breakdowns at higher levels of detail can also be performed if deemed necessary.

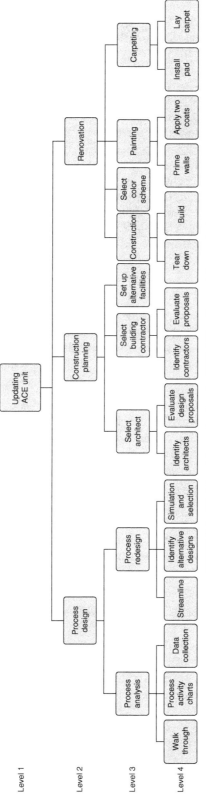

FIGURE 3.2 – Work breakdown structure for BPH's ACE unit remodeling project.

This method helps the planner to identify all the work requirements of a project and to organize them in a logical fashion. A good WBS provides the framework to plan for resources and to estimate the time and cost of the project.

 # SCHEDULING AND CONTROL TOOLS

Once all activities have been identified, it is important to establish their sequence and estimate their individual completion times. In doing so, managers list all the resources (people, materials, and supplies) that are needed. In the planning phase, these tasks enable the development of accurate schedules and budgets, which then constitute a common frame of reference as well as a benchmark during the execution phase. During the control phase, if variances surface, the original schedule and budget may need to be updated. The most common tools used for scheduling, controlling, and reallocating resources are the Gantt chart, PERT/CPM, and crashing.

The Gantt Chart

Gantt Chart
A horizontal bar graph, with each bar corresponding to a specific activity. The length of the bar indicates the duration of the activity.

Visual tools can be developed to chart the scheduling of activities and/or resources. One popular tool is the Gantt chart. A **Gantt chart** is a horizontal bar graph. Each bar corresponds to a specific activity, and its length indicates the duration of the activity. The Gantt chart displays important information, which includes (Russell & Taylor, 2009; Stevenson, 2012):

1. **The activities to be performed**. In the Gantt chart shown in Figure 3.3, we chose to display the major activities (Level 3 on WBS), but we could elect to show a greater level of detail with Level 4 activities.

2. **The order in which they must be performed**. You will note that some activities must be completed sequentially, whereas others can be performed in parallel, that is, at the same time. For example, the construction work can only start after the selection of a building contractor and setting up alternative facilities, but process analysis can start at the same time as the selection of an architect.

3. **Their expected durations**. In our example, process redesign is expected to last 2 weeks, whereas the selection of the color scheme should take only 1 week.

4. **The estimated date of project completion**. Because certain activities can be performed in parallel, the project's duration is not equal to the sum of all the activity times. Rather, the project is expected to take 10 weeks to complete.

Project managers can use Gantt charts to monitor the progress of each activity by comparing planned progress to actual progress and react accordingly. They can incorporate "traffic light" flagging systems to keep everyone aware of what is happening and what problems may be developing (Figure 3.3).

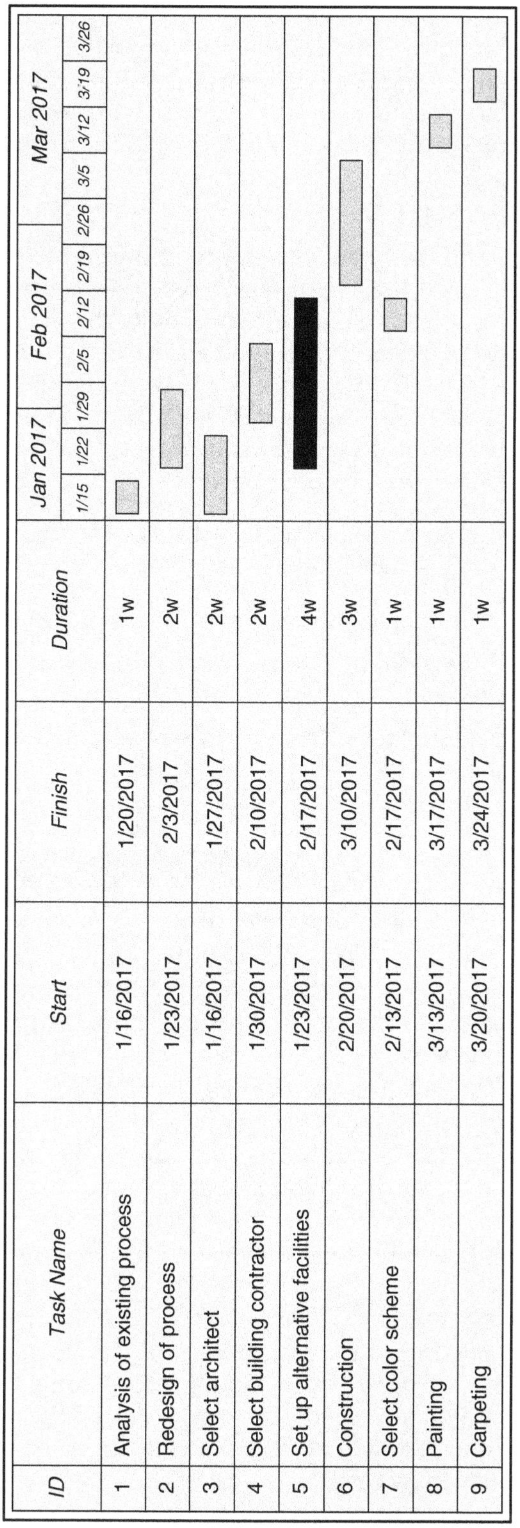

ID	Task Name	Start	Finish	Duration	Jan 2017			Feb 2017				Mar 2017			
					1/15	1/22	1/29	2/5	2/12	2/19	2/26	3/5	3/12	3/19	3/26
1	Analysis of existing process	1/16/2017	1/20/2017	1w											
2	Redesign of process	1/23/2017	2/3/2017	2w											
3	Select architect	1/16/2017	1/27/2017	2w											
4	Select building contractor	1/30/2017	2/10/2017	2w											
5	Set up alternative facilities	1/23/2017	2/17/2017	4w											
6	Construction	2/20/2017	3/10/2017	3w											
7	Select color scheme	2/13/2017	2/17/2017	1w											
8	Painting	3/13/2017	3/17/2017	1w											
9	Carpeting	3/20/2017	3/24/2017	1w											

FIGURE 3.3 – Gantt chart for BPH's ACE unit remodeling project.

■ A risk of being delayed!

Although appropriate for displaying simple projects with a relatively small number of activities, Gantt charts are, however, quite limited in their ability to capture the interrelationships among activities that can arise in more complex projects. In such situations, the powerful project management techniques of PERT and CPM are preferred.

PERT and CPM

PERT and CPM were developed independently during the 1950s (Box 3.5). As the Polaris Missile Project was a completely new endeavor, PERT was based on uncertain activity times. Conversely, DuPont had prior experience with the construction of chemical plants, and, therefore, the activity times in CPM were assumed to be fairly certain. Although they were developed separately, both techniques shared a lot of common features, leading many users to "merge" the two techniques. Used together, the techniques provide (Heizer & Render, 2011):

1. A graphic display of all activities and their interrelationships

2. An activity schedule

3. An estimate of the duration of the project

4. A list of the activities critical to the timely completion of the project

5. An estimate of the time by which an activity can be delayed without delaying the entire project

---

⊕ BOX 3.5 – DID YOU KNOW?

CPM and PERT History: Complex Projects Lead to Modern Methods

During the mid-twentieth century, complex projects, such as the Manhattan Project of World War II and the Polaris submarine weapons system, necessitated the need for better methods to plan, manage, and evaluate projects.

DuPont, one of the contractors, developed practices to help manage the Manhattan Project. This work was the precursor to the Critical Path Method (CPM). In the 1950s, Morgan Walker of DuPont and James Kelley of Remington Rand started developing project scheduling algorithms at DuPont. They used plant shutdowns as pilot projects. In their first paper, they explained the need for rigorous tools to manage project complexity, which separated the functions of planning and scheduling (Kelley & Walker, 1959).

At about the same time, work on the Polaris missile project by Lockheed, the U.S. Navy, and the consulting firm of Booz, Allen, and Hamilton led to the development of the Program Evaluation and Review Technique (PERT) to plan complex, unique projects with uncertain activity times.

PERT and CPM filled an important need and set the foundation for creating project management as a discipline.

The Network Diagram

The graphic display of the project is known as the **network diagram** or precedence diagram. It depicts the project activities and their precedence relationships. Two different conventions can be used to draw the network diagram: activity-on-the-arrow (AOA) and activity-on the-node (AON). Both use arrows (⟶) and nodes (○). In the AOA network, arrows depict activities and nodes represent their beginning and ending points. In the AON network, the nodes represent the activities that are connected by arrows. Activities take time and consume resources. Both conventions are illustrated in Figure 3.4.

The last two AOA network sections displayed in Figure 3.4, (e) and (f), include an additional activity called a *dummy* activity. The sole purpose of the dummy activity is to clarify the nature of the relationships between the activities. As such, it consumes neither time nor resources.

Network Diagram
A diagram that depicts the project activities and their precedence relationships.

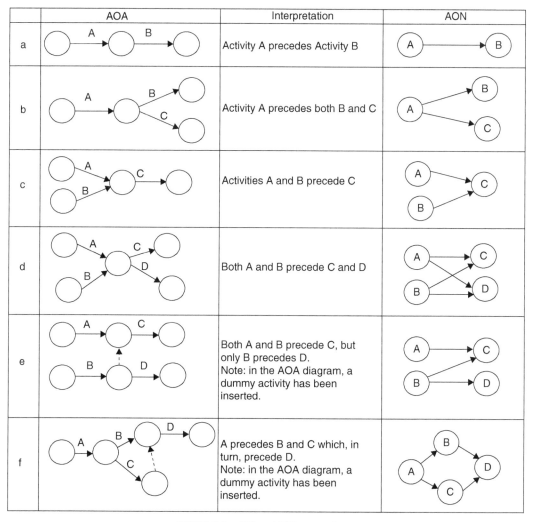

FIGURE 3.4 – AOA and AON conventions.

In (e), the dummy activity is used to preserve the integrity of the relationships between immediate predecessors and followers: both A and B are immediate predecessors of C, but only B is the immediate predecessor of D. In (f), the dummy activity is used to maintain the identity of the two relationships by preventing two activities (here B and C) from having the same starting and ending nodes.

Based on the relationships depicted in the Gantt chart (Figure 3.3) and specified more explicitly in Table 3.1, the two network diagrams shown in Figure 3.5 were developed. For all practical purposes, a network has one starting node and one ending node. With the AON convention, this can be easily achieved by adding a START node at the beginning and a FINISH node at the end.

TABLE 3.1 – Precedence Relationships for ACE Unit Remodeling Project

Activity	Description	Immediate Predecessor(s)	Estimated duration (weeks)
A	Analyze existing process	—	1
B	Redesign process	A	2
C	Select architect	—	2
D	Select building contractor	C	2
E	Set up alternative facilities	A	4
F	Construction	E, D	3
G	Select color scheme	D	1
H	Painting	F, G	1
I	Carpeting	H	1

FIGURE 3.5 – Network diagram.

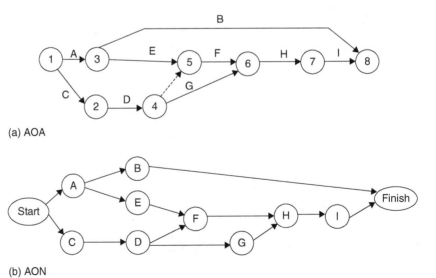

(a) AOA

(b) AON

Although both conventions convey the same information, the AON's simplicity makes it intuitively appealing. Moreover, it is the convention of choice in some of the popular project management software packages such as Microsoft Project. Accordingly, we will use the AON convention in the remainder of this chapter.

Critical Path

There are multiple paths in a typical network diagram. A **path** is a sequence of activities from the starting node to the ending node. In Figure 3.5, there are four paths:

1. A-B
2. A-E-F-H-I
3. C-D-F-H-I
4. C-D-G-H-I

The duration of a path is determined by summing the expected times of the activities on that path. Delaying one activity on a path will prolong the duration of the path. The longest path on a network is of special relevance because it determines the entire project's duration. Delays on this path would delay the entire project. Because the longest path is critical to on-time project completion, it is appropriately called the **critical path**, and the activities along the path are **critical activities**. Shorter paths can experience some delays and not affect the on-time completion of the project as long as their final completion times do not exceed that of the critical path. The amount of time by which an activity can be delayed without delaying the entire project is referred to as **slack**. Critical activities have no slack as they cannot be delayed (Box 3.6).

- Path A-B: 1 + 2 = 3 weeks
- Path A-E-F-H-I = 1 + 4 + 3 + 1 + 1 = 10 weeks*
- Path C-D-F-H-I = 2 + 2 + 3 + 1 + 1 = 9 weeks
- Path C-D-G-H-I = 2 + 2 + 1 + 1 + 1 = 7 weeks

Because path A-E-F-H-I is the longest, it is the critical path. Remodeling the ACE unit is expected to take 10 weeks at a minimum. Path A-B can be delayed by up to 7 weeks, path C-D-F-H-I by no more than 1 week, and path C-D-G-H-I by up to 3 weeks, without affecting the duration of the project.

The network displayed in Figure 3.5 is quite simple and includes only nine activities. Real projects may involve dozens of paths with hundreds or even thousands of activities. In such cases, it becomes unrealistic to try to identify each path and its duration accurately. The PERT/CPM methodology offers a much more efficient way of identifying the critical path and the slack of each activity on the network. It also produces an activity schedule by indicating when an activity should start and end.

Path
A sequence of activities that runs from the starting node to the ending node of the network diagram.

Critical Path
The longest path in a network diagram, which determines the duration of the project.

Critical Activities
Activities that are along the critical path.

Slack
Refers to the amount of time by which an activity can be delayed without delaying the entire project.

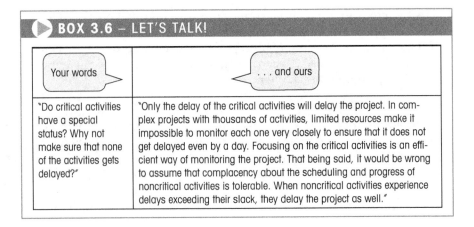

> **▶ BOX 3.6 – LET'S TALK!**
>
> | Your words | . . . and ours |
> |---|---|
> | "Do critical activities have a special status? Why not make sure that none of the activities gets delayed?" | "Only the delay of the critical activities will delay the project. In complex projects with thousands of activities, limited resources make it impossible to monitor each one very closely to ensure that it does not get delayed even by a day. Focusing on the critical activities is an efficient way of monitoring the project. That being said, it would be wrong to assume that complacency about the scheduling and progress of noncritical activities is tolerable. When noncritical activities experience delays exceeding their slack, they delay the project as well." |

Activity Schedule

Remember that some activities could be delayed without delaying the entire project. This means that they could start as soon as possible or later. The notion of earliest and latest start time—and by extension, finish time—of an activity is the basic premise of the algorithm used to schedule activities. This algorithm includes two passes through the network: the forward pass and the backward pass.

Forward Pass

The scheduling of activities from the Start node to the Finish node. It involves the computation of ES and EF times.

The **forward pass** involves the scheduling of activities from the Start node to the Finish node. It requires the computation of the earliest start (ES) and earliest finish (EF) times of each activity on the network.

ES = earliest time an activity can start if all preceding activities have begun at their earliest possible time.

- If an activity has no immediate predecessor, its ES is 0.
- If an activity has one immediate predecessor, its ES is equal to the EF of its predecessor.
- If an activity has multiple immediate predecessors, its ES is equal to the longest of the EF times of its predecessors:

ES = maximum (EF times of all immediate predecessors)   [3.1]

EF = earliest time an activity can finish = ES + activity time [3.2]

In our example, A and C are not preceded by any activity:

$ES_A = 0$
$EF_A = 0 + 1 = 1$ week

$ES_C = 0$
$EF_C = 0 + 2 = 2$ weeks

As soon as Activity A has been completed, Activities B and E can start. In other words, their ES time is equal to the EF of their predecessor, Activity A.

$ES_B = EF_A = 1$ week
$EF_B = 1 + 2 = 3$ weeks

$ES_E = EF_A = 1$ week
$EF_F = 1 + 4 = 5$ weeks

Similarly, Activity D can start as soon as Activity C is completed.

$ES_D = EF_C = 2$ weeks
$EF_D = 2 + 2 = 4$ weeks

Activity F is dependent on the completion of *both* Activities E and D. In other words, it cannot start until both activities are finished. Activity D will be finished in Week 4, but Activity E will only be finished in Week 5. Therefore, Activity F cannot start until Week 5.

$ES_F = $ maximum $(EF_E, EF_D) = 5$ weeks
$EF_F = 5 + 3 = 8$ weeks

It is common to display the ES and EF times of an activity on its node (Figure 3.6).

After the forward pass (Figure 3.7), the EF times of the two activities converging in the Finish node are 3 weeks for Activity B and 10 weeks for Activity I. Activity I would have to be completed before the project can be completed. Consequently, the project of remodeling the ACE unit is expected to last 10 weeks. The primary output of the forward pass is the expected project completion time. However, the critical path is still unknown. To determine the activities that are critical, a backward pass through the network is necessary.

The **backward pass** through the network involves scheduling activities from the Finish node to the Start node. While performing this pass, the latest finish (LF) and latest start (LS) times of each activity are computed. Because we go "backwards," the LF time of an activity is computed before its LS time.

Backward Pass
The scheduling of activities from the Finish node to the Start node. It involves the computations of LS and LF times.

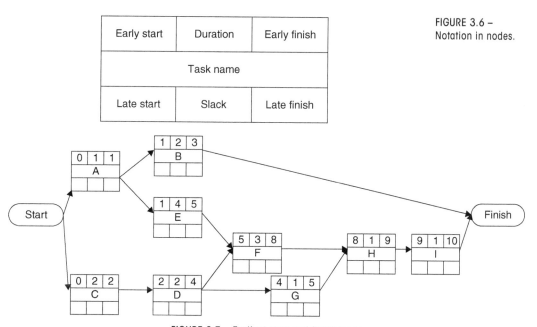

FIGURE 3.6 – Notation in nodes.

FIGURE 3.7 – Earliest start and finish times.

LF = latest time at which an activity can finish without delaying the project.

- If an activity has no immediate follower on the network, its LF is equal to the expected project completion time.
- If an activity has one immediate follower, its LF is equal to the LS of its follower.
- If an activity has multiple immediate followers, its LF is equal to the lowest of the LS times of all its followers:

$$LF = \text{minimum (LS of all immediate followers)} \qquad [3.3]$$

$$
\begin{aligned}
LS &= \text{latest time at which an activity can start without}\\
&\quad \text{delaying the project}\\
&= LF - \text{activity time} \qquad\qquad\qquad\qquad\qquad\quad [3.4]
\end{aligned}
$$

In our example, Activities B and I have no followers. Their LF times are therefore set equal to the expected project completion time. The explanation is simple, Activity B could end as early as in Week 3, but if it ends in Week 10, it will not delay the project because the project is expected to take 10 weeks to complete anyway.

$LF_B = 10$ weeks
$LS_B = 10 - 2 = 8$ weeks

$LF_I = 10$ weeks
$LS_I = 10 - 1 = 9$ weeks

Based on the precedence rules, we know that Activity H has to be completed before Activity I can start. If Activity I had an LS at 9 weeks, it means that Activity H could have ended at that time.

$LF_H = LS_I = 9$ weeks
$LS_H = 9 - 1 = 8$ weeks

Applying the same rules to the predecessors of Activity H, we find:

$LF_F = LS_H = 8$ weeks
$LS_F = 8 - 3 = 5$ weeks

$LF_G = LS_H = 8$ weeks
$LS_G = 8 - 1 = 7$ weeks

Note that Activity D precedes both F and G, which means that Activity D had to be completed before F or G could start. Because F had a late start in Week 5, which is earlier than the LS_G, the LF of Activity D is 5 weeks as well.

$LF_D = \text{minimum } (LS_F, LS_G) = 5$ weeks
$LS_D = 5 - 2 = 3$ weeks

After performing the backward pass, you will get a more detailed picture of how to schedule activities and monitor their progress (Figure 3.8). You will know, for example, that Activity C can start as early as Week 0, but it could start as late as Week 1 and not delay the project, assuming it does not take longer than 2 weeks to complete. In other words, Activity C has 1 week of slack time.

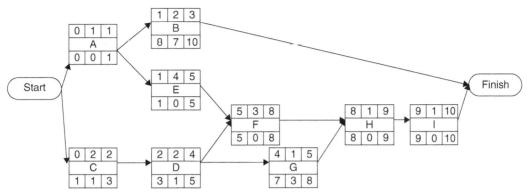

FIGURE 3.8 – Latest start and finish times.

TABLE 3.2 – Summary of Forward and Backward Passes

Activity	ES	t	EF	LS	LF	S
A	0	1	1	0	1	0*
B	1	2	3	8	10	7
C	0	2	2	1	3	1
D	2	2	4	3	5	1
E	1	4	5	1	5	0*
F	5	3	8	5	8	0*
G	4	1	5	7	8	3
H	8	1	9	8	9	0*
I	9	1	10	9	10	0*

Forward Pass	Backward Pass
For each activity beginning from the Start node, ES = 0 For all other activities, ES = EF of immediate predecessor EF = ES + t If an activity has multiple predecessors, ES = maximum (EF times of immediate predecessors) Expected project completion time = longest EF time of activities ending at the Finish node.	For each activity ending at the Finish node, LF = expected project completion time For all other activities, LF = LS of immediate follower LS = LF – t If an activity has multiple followers, LF = minimum (LS times of immediate followers)

$$\text{Stock} \text{ or } = \begin{cases} LF - EF \\ LS - ES \end{cases}$$

*Critical activities.

Computing Slack

What about the critical path? Remember that critical activities have zero slack. To compute slack, you need the numbers computed in the forward pass and in the backward pass:

$$S = LF - EF \qquad [3.5]$$

or

$$S = LS - ES \qquad [3.6]$$

Based on these computations, the Activities A-E-F-H-I make up the critical path, which is expected to take 10 weeks to complete. Table 3.2

displays the ES, EF, LS, LF, and S for each activity, as well as a summary of the computations.

PROBABILISTIC TIME ESTIMATES

The time for each activity in BPH's ACE unit remodeling project could be estimated rather accurately because the hospital staff, the architect, and the building contractor had likely worked on similar projects before. As a result, there was a single time estimate for each activity. When the project is a new endeavor, there is often some uncertainty in determining the duration of an activity. As an analogy, if you ask a plumber to give you the time estimate to fix a water leak in your bathroom, he may say: "If everything goes well, I should be done within an hour. If the pipe going to the shower head burst, I will need to remove some of the tiles and replace the pipe, which may take between 2 and 4 hours, depending on the severity of the problem."

This uncertainty or variability in activity times is captured by a probability distribution. For all practical purposes, it is assumed that activity times can be described by the beta distribution. Only three time estimates are necessary to approximate the mean and variance of the beta distribution. The beta distribution does not have a definite shape; it can be symmetrical or skewed.

Three Time Estimates

The three time estimates for an activity are:

Optimistic Time
The shortest estimated duration of an activity.

- The **optimistic time** (*a*): This is the time required to perform the activity under ideal conditions. Therefore, it is also the shortest estimated duration for the activity.

Pessimistic Time
The longest estimated duration of an activity.

- The **pessimistic time** (*b*): This is the time required to perform the activity under the worst possible conditions. It is thus the longest estimated duration for the activity.

Most Likely Time
The most probable time required to execute an activity.

- The **most likely time** (*m*): This is the most probable time required to execute the activity. It lies somewhere between the optimistic and pessimistic time estimates.

Although a project manager may wish to establish schedules based on optimistic, pessimistic, or likely conditions, the traditional approach involves averaging the three times using the following formula:

$$t_e = (a + 4m + b)/6 \qquad [3.7]$$

This is a weighted average in which both optimistic and pessimistic times are assigned a weight of 1, whereas the most likely time is emphasized more heavily with a weight of 4. The sum of the weights is 6, which is the denominator. As shown in Figure 3.9, when the beta distribution is symmetric, t_e is equal to the most likely time. When it is skewed, t_e is "pulled" by the more extreme value: *a* (skewed to the left) or *b* (skewed to the right).

The variation between *a* and *b* spans 6 standard deviations. Therefore, the standard deviation for an activity's time is:

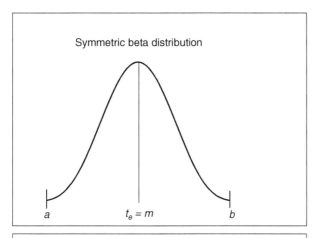

FIGURE 3.9 – Beta distribution.

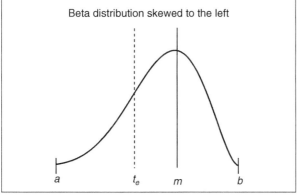

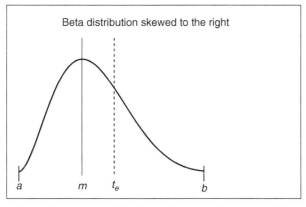

$$\sigma = \left(\frac{b-a}{6} \right)$$

[3.8]

For analysis purposes, the variance of the activity's time will be more useful. Based on Equation 3.8, the formula for the variance is:

$$\sigma^2 = \left(\frac{b-a}{6} \right)^2$$

[3.9]

BRADLEY PARK HOSPITAL 3.3

Jennifer began the ACE unit project kickoff meeting, "When I first started at Bradley Park Hospital, I was a nurse on the pulmonary floor. I took care of an elderly patient, Mary Griffin. She was a lovely person, and her three children and husband adored her. She was in the hospital for simple pneumonia. Mary would get confused at night and try to get out of bed. One day, when I came to work, she was no longer there. I was shocked because I knew that she was not scheduled to go home. My nurse supervisor pulled me aside and told me that she had died after falling in the night. She hit her head and never woke up. I was devastated.

"I have learned that ACE units are specifically designed to meet the unique needs of older patients and help prevent complications, such as falls. I believe we owe it to our patients and their families to deliver the best possible care. And that includes designing an ACE unit that will improve the quality of care given while reining in costs.

"But before we build the ACE unit, we need to understand our patients' needs. Who will volunteer to help Juan Blanco, director of patient services, get the needed information from our patients?"

A few hands went up and Jennifer recorded their names. "We will meet back here next week and outline our next steps."

Juan was very adept at gathering and analyzing data. He stood at the board while Shirley Sullivan, Cary Todd, and Fred Chan were gathered around a table. "We have an important task at hand. The Bradley Park board is meeting in 55 days, and we must have our survey results by then so that Jennifer can write and present her report. That seems like a long time, but there is a lot of uncertainty in the time it takes to develop and administer surveys! First, we need to identify all the patients who were admitted to Bradley Park in the last 2 years who were over the age of 65. That will give us a good pool from which to select a random sample of 2,500." Fred looked puzzled, "Why do we need so many?" Juan replied, "We need to have a comprehensive view of our patient needs so that we can build an ACE unit with adequate services for all our elderly patients."

Ⓠ Is it always a good idea to assess patients' needs before starting a capital project?

Figure 3.10 displays the network diagram for the survey project. The three time estimates are displayed for each activity. The time estimates and variances are shown in Table 3.3. The time estimates can be used

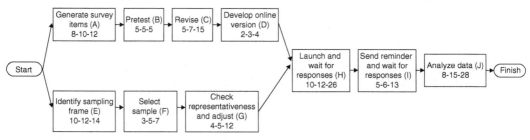

FIGURE 3.10 – Network diagram for survey project.

TABLE 3.3 – Time Estimates and Variances

Activity	Optimistic a	Most Likely m	Pessimistic b	Expected Time t_e	Variance σ^2
A	8	10	12	10	16/36 = 0.44
B	5	5	5	5	0
C	5	7	15	8	100/36 = 2.78
D	2	3	4	3	4/36 = 0.11
E	10	12	14	12	16/36 = 0.44
F	3	5	7	5	16/36 = 0.44
G	4	5	12	6	64/36 = 1.78
H	10	12	26	14	256/36 = 7.11
I	5	6	13	7	64/36 = 1.78
J	8	15	28	16	400/36 = 11.11

TABLE 3.4 – Forward and Backward Passes for Survey Project

Activity	ES	Expected Time t_e	EF	LS	LF	S
A	0	10	10	0	10	0
B	10	5	15	10	15	0
C	15	8	23	15	23	0
D	23	3	26	23	26	0
E	0	12	12	3	15	3
F	12	5	17	15	20	3
G	17	6	23	20	26	3
H	26	14	40	26	40	0
I	40	7	47	40	47	0
J	47	16	**63**	47	63	0

to determine the critical path, which is A-B-C-D-H-I-J (Table 3.4). The expected time to complete this project is 63 days, which is longer than the 55-day deadline.

Probability of Completing a Project

Are we sure that this project can be completed in 63 days? Not really, because the variability in the activity times also creates variability in the duration of each path. The variation in the critical path makes it susceptible to potential delays and casts some doubt on the project's completion in 63 days.

To measure the project's variability, PERT utilizes the standard deviation of the critical path:

$$\sigma_{cp} = \sqrt{\sum (\text{variances of activities on critical path})} \qquad [3.10]$$

In our example,

$$\sigma_{cp} = \sqrt{\left(\sigma_A^2 + \sigma_B^2 + \sigma_C^2 + \sigma_D^2 + \sigma_H^2 + \sigma_I^2 + \sigma_J^2\right)}$$

$$= \sqrt{\left(\frac{16}{36} + 0 + \frac{100}{36} + \frac{4}{36} + \frac{256}{36} + \frac{64}{36} + \frac{400}{36}\right)}$$

$$= \sqrt{\frac{840}{36}}$$

$$= 4.83 \text{ days}$$

Given this variability, how much confidence do we have in completing the survey project in 63 days? Another way of asking this question is, "What is the probability of completing the project in 63 days?" The answer lies in the probability distribution of the critical path. As shown in Figure 3.11, the critical path is described by the normal distribution with a mean of 63 days and a standard deviation of 4.83 days. There is a 50% chance (half the curve) of completing the project in 63 days or less and a 50% chance of completing it in 63 days or more (Box 3.7).

We can use this information to answer other questions as well:

- What is the probability that the project will be completed within 60 days?

- What is the probability that the project will take longer than 70 days?

Look at the standard normal distribution in Appendix A. It has a mean of 0 and a standard deviation of 1. The z-values indicate the number of standard deviations away from the mean. The numbers in the body of the table are the cumulative probabilities from 0 to a given

FIGURE 3.11 – Probability distribution of completion times for survey project.

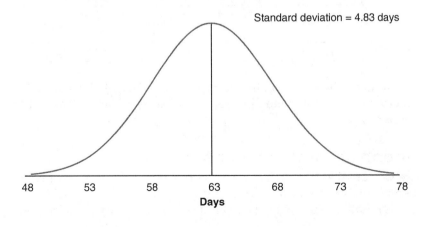

Standard deviation = 4.83 days

Days

48   53   58   63   68   73   78

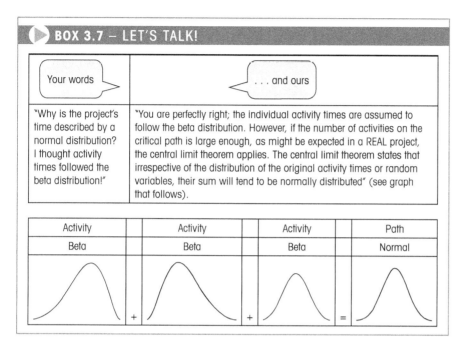

BOX 3.7 – LET'S TALK!

Your words	. . . and ours
"Why is the project's time described by a normal distribution? I thought activity times followed the beta distribution!"	"You are perfectly right; the individual activity times are assumed to follow the beta distribution. However, if the number of activities on the critical path is large enough, as might be expected in a REAL project, the central limit theorem applies. The central limit theorem states that irrespective of the distribution of the original activity times or random variables, their sum will tend to be normally distributed" (see graph that follows).

Activity		Activity		Activity		Path
Beta		Beta		Beta		Normal

positive z-value. What we need to do to answer our two questions is standardize our normal distribution with a mean of 63 days and a standard deviation of 4.83 days. It is easy to see that the mean of 63 is standardized to 0 (Figure 3.12). What about the numbers specified in the questions? We need to standardize them or convert them to z-values using the formula:

$$z = \frac{(\text{specified time} - \text{expected time})}{\sigma_{cp}} \qquad [3.11]$$

The specified time is the time specified in the question (e.g., 60); the expected time is the project's expected duration, or 63 days; and the standard deviation of the critical path is 4.83 days. Therefore:

$$z = \frac{(60 - 63)}{4.83} = -0.62$$

As shown in Figure 3.12, the probability of completing the project within 60 days is equivalent to finding $P(z \leq -0.62)$:

P (project completed within 60 days) $= P(z \leq 0.62) = 0.2676$ or 26.76% chance.

Similarly, to find the probability that the project will take longer than 70 days, we compute:

$$z = \frac{(70 - 63)}{4.83} = 1.45$$

P (project takes longer than 70 days) $= P(z \geq 1.45) = 1 - P(z \leq 1.45)$
$$= 1 - 0.9265 = 0.0735 \text{ or}$$
$$7.35\% \text{ chance.}$$

FIGURE 3.12 –
Standardizing the
normal distribution.

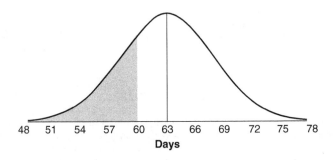

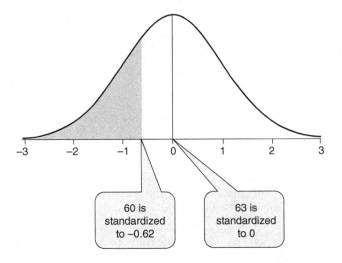

BRADLEY PARK HOSPITAL 3.4

Juan computed that the probability of completing the project in 55 days was about 5%! He got the team back together and said, "To speed up this project, we must devote more time and resources. I could ask all of you to work overtime and get as many helpers as possible in your departments, but there is a smarter way of doing this. It is called 'crashing.'"

As Juan mentioned in the BPH story, there is a procedure that enables project managers to reduce a project's duration efficiently. This procedure involves assessing trade-offs between time and cost. It is explained in the next section.

 ## TIME/COST TRADE-OFFS

Since the critical path is the longest path and governs the project's duration, time/cost trade-offs focus on reducing the critical path at the lowest possible cost. Therefore, activities along the critical path are "crashed" to shorten their durations. Doing so requires the use of more personnel, subcontractors, equipment, and so on, which adds to the cost of the project. Because two of a project's constraints are time and cost, you can appreciate the dilemmas project managers face when they have to sacrifice one for the other.

In order to crash activity times efficiently, the manager needs estimates of the potential time reductions for each activity and of the extra costs involved. These estimates are based on:

- t_n: the normal time to complete an activity. This is the time it takes to perform an activity with a normal amount of resources.

- t_c: the crash time to complete an activity. This is the shortest amount of time it takes to perform an activity when maximum resources are expended.

- c_n: the normal cost to complete an activity. This is the cost associated with the completion of the activity within its normal time.

- c_c: the crash cost to complete the activity. This is the cost associated with performing the activity within its crash time.

With this information, the manager will compute:

1. t_{RED} = maximum time reduction

$$= t_n - t_c \qquad\qquad [3.12]$$

2. S = crash cost per unit of time (assuming a linear relationship between crash cost and crash time)

$$= \frac{c_c - c_n}{t_{RED}} \qquad\qquad [3.13]$$

The **crash cost per unit of time** is the change in cost for a one-unit reduction in time. As depicted in Figure 3.13, the downward slope reflects the negative relationship—or trade-off—between time and cost.

There are two procedures to crash activity times: marginal cost analysis and linear programming.

Crash Cost per Unit of Time

The change in cost for a one-unit reduction in time.

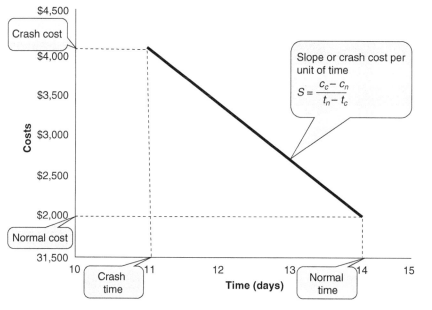

FIGURE 3.13 – The relationship between cost and time.

Marginal Cost Analysis

As its name indicates, the **marginal cost analysis approach** involves crashing activities along the critical path in such a way that incremental costs are minimized. As a critical path is shortened, other paths will become critical if their duration is equal to the duration of the original critical path. In that case, all critical paths will be reduced simultaneously until the desired project completion time is attained.

This crashing procedure comprises five steps:

STEP 1: Compute t_{RED} and S for each activity.
STEP 2: Identify all the paths and their respective durations.
STEP 3: Find the cheapest critical activity to crash and reduce its duration by the maximum time allowable without overlooking another critical path (i.e., a path that was originally shorter might become as long as the crashed critical path).
STEP 4: If one or more other critical paths emerge, proceed in a similar fashion by finding the cheapest activities to crash along those paths and sum their crashing costs. If these paths share a common activity, compare the cost of crashing the common activity with the sum of the crashing costs of the least expensive activities to crash on the separate critical paths.
STEP 5: Repeat this process until you have reached the desired project completion time.

Following these steps, we will crash the project to 55 days. The normal time, crash time, normal cost, and crash cost are shown in Table 3.5. Now, let us go through the crashing procedure step by step.

1. Compute t_{RED} and S for each activity (see Table 3.5).

2. Identify all the paths and their respective durations:

   • A-B-C-D-H-I-J: 63 days (critical path)

   • E-F-G-H-I-J: 60 days

TABLE 3.5 – Cost and Time Information for Survey Project

Activity	t_n	t_c	C_n	C_c	t_{RED}	S
A	10	7	$500	$950	3	$150
B	5	5	$300	$300	0	$0
C	8	6	$400	$600	2	$100
D	3	2	$1,500	$2,000	1	$500
E	12	10	$1,000	$1,700	2	$350
F	5	4	$200	$400	1	$200
G	6	4	$500	$800	2	$150
H	14	11	$2,000	$4,100	3	$700
I	7	6	$400	$650	1	$250
J	16	12	$3,000	$5,200	4	$550
Total Cost			$9,800			

3. Find the cheapest critical activity to crash and reduce its duration by the maximum time allowable without overlooking another critical path (i.e., a path that was originally shorter might become as long as the crashed critical path).

   On the critical path, Activity C is the cheapest to crash. We will crash it by its maximum duration, which is 2 days. The cost of doing so is 100×2 or $200. The cost of completing the project has thus increased from $9,800 to $10,000.

   - A-B-C-D-H-I-J: 61 days (critical path)

   - E-F-G-H-I-J: 60 days

   A-B-C-D-H-I-J is still the critical path. Because Activity C is fully crashed, the next cheapest activity to crash on that path is Activity A. If we crash it by the maximum possible time reduction, 3 days, this path's duration would be 58 days, but path E-F-G-H-I-J would still take 60 days to complete and would be the new critical path. We would have spent money to crash the project by 3 days, but it would have been reduced by only 1 day, from 61 to 60 days. Therefore, we will only crash Activity A by 1 day. The cost incurred will be $150, making the total cost of the project equal to $10,150.

   - A-B-C-D-H-I-J: 60 days (critical path)

   - E-F-G-H-I-J: 60 days (critical path)

4. Both paths are now critical. On path A-B-C-D-H-I-J, we could still crash Activity A for $150/day. On path E-F-G-H-I-J, the cheapest activity to crash is Activity G for $150/day as well. The total cost would amount to $300. However, the two paths share activities H, I, and J. Reducing any of these activities would reduce both paths at the same time. Activity I would only cost $250 to crash, which is lower than the cost of crashing both A and G simultaneously. We will therefore crash I by its maximum time reduction, which is 1 day. The cost of the project is now $10,400.

   - A-B-C-D-H-I-J: 59 days (critical path)

   - E-F-G-H-I-J: 59 days (critical path)

5. The cost of crashing the other two common activities, H and J, are $700 and $550, respectively. Either cost is higher than that of crashing both A and G simultaneously. Activity A can still be crashed by 2 days and so can G. We will therefore crash both by 2 days. The cost of the project will increase by $600 to reach $11,000.

   - A-B-C-D-H-I-J: 57 days (critical path)

   - E-F-G-H-I-J: 57 days (critical path)

   The next cheapest activities to crash on paths A-B-C-D-H-I-J and E-F-G-H-I-J are activities D and F, respectively. Their combined crashing cost for 1 day is $700. This amount is higher than the cost of crashing J, a common activity, for $550. We will

TABLE 3.6 – Summary of Crashing Project to 55 Days

Activities crashed	C (2)	A (1)	I (1)	A (2); G (2)	J (2)
Paths					
A-B-C-D-H-I-J 63 days*	61*	60*	59	57	55
E-F-G-H-I-J 60 days	60	60	59	57	55
Cost of crashing	$200	$150	$250	$600	$1,100
Total cost	$10,000	$10,150	$10,400	$11,000	$12,100
*Critical path.					

therefore crash J by 2 days and reach the target of 55 days. The total cost of the project is now $12,100.

- A-B-C-D-H-I-J: 55 days (critical path)
- E-F-G-H-I-J: 55 days (critical path)

The summary of the procedure is displayed in Table 3.6.

With large, complex projects, the marginal cost analysis quickly becomes cumbersome and error prone. In such instances, the linear programming method is both more effective and efficient.

Linear Programming

Linear Programming (LP)
A decision-making technique that provides an optimal solution given a specific objective and a set of constraints.

Linear programming is a decision-making technique that provides an optimal solution given a specific objective and a set of constraints. In the case of crashing,

- the **decision** to be made involves which activities to crash and by how much
- the **objective** is to minimize the cost of reducing the project's duration
- the **constraints** or limitations include (a) the amount of time by which each activity can be crashed, and (b) the amount of time by which each path must be reduced to reach a desired project completion time.

To formulate a linear programming model for crashing, you will still need to compute t_{RED} and S. In addition, you will follow three steps:

STEP 1: Formulate the **decision variables**. The decision variables are the key elements of the decision; their values make up the solution. They need to be defined very precisely. In the case of the survey project, the decision variables can be specified as:

X_i = number of days by which activity I must be crashed
    (i = A – J)

STEP 2: Formulate the **objective function**. The objective function expresses the objective of the model, which here is to minimize the cost of crashing. The cost of crashing each activity by 1 day is S. Accordingly, the objective function can be expressed as:

$$\text{Minimize cost} = 150 \, X_A + 0 \, X_B + 100 \, X_C + 500 \, X_D + 350 \, X_E$$
$$+ \, 200 \, X_F + 150 \, X_G + 700 \, X_H + 250 \, X_I + 550 \, X_J$$

Look at the additive effects in this function. If, for example, we decided to crash A by 1 day and C by 2 days, the cost would be ($150 × 1) + ($100 × 2) = $350.

STEP 3: Formulate the **constraints**. As mentioned earlier, there are two major sets of constraints: those limiting the amount of time by which an activity can be crashed and those ensuring that each path is crashed by a sufficient amount of time to achieve the desired project completion time. Additionally, at the end, we need to specify that the decision variables—time reductions—can only take on positive values.

First set:

$$X_A \qquad\qquad\qquad\qquad\qquad\qquad\qquad\qquad\qquad \leq 3$$
$$X_B \qquad\qquad\qquad\qquad\qquad\qquad\qquad\qquad\quad \leq 0$$
$$X_C \qquad\qquad\qquad\qquad\qquad\qquad\qquad\quad \leq 2$$
$$X_D \qquad\qquad\qquad\qquad\qquad\qquad\quad \leq 1$$
$$X_E \qquad\qquad\qquad\qquad\qquad\quad \leq 2$$
$$X_F \qquad\qquad\qquad\qquad\quad \leq 1$$
$$X_G \qquad\qquad\qquad \leq 2$$
$$X_H \qquad\qquad \leq 3$$
$$X_I \qquad \leq 1$$
$$X_J \quad \leq 4$$

The first constraint indicates that the number of days by which Activity A must be crashed (or X_A) has to be less than or equal to the activity's maximum time reduction, which is 3 days. The last constraint specifies that activity J cannot be crashed by more than 4 days.

Second set:
$$X_A + X_B + X_C + X_D + \qquad\qquad X_H + X_I + X_J \qquad \geq 8$$
$$X_E + X_F + X_G + X_H + X_I + X_J \qquad \geq 5$$

The length of path A-B-C-D-H-I-J is 63 days. To complete the project in 55 days, the total amount of time crashed on this path would have to be at least 8 days. Similarly, path E-F-G-H-I-J takes 60 days to complete and would have to be reduced by at least 5 days.

Logical constraint:
$$X_i \geq 0 \ (i = A - J)$$

All time reductions must be nonnegative. Because B cannot be crashed, the combination of $X_B \leq 0$ in the first set of constraints and $X_B \geq 0$ at the end enforces that it not be crashed.

The solution to this model was obtained with Microsoft Excel and is presented in Figure 3.14. It is identical to the one found using the marginal cost analysis method: A must be crashed by 3 days, C by 2, G by 2, I by 1, and J by 2. The total cost of crashing is $2,300. When adding this cost to the normal cost of the project, we obtain a total project cost of $12,100.

▲	A	B	C	D	E	F	G	H	I	J	K	L	M	N	O
1		Xa	Xb	Xc	Xd	Xe	Xf	Xg	Xh	Xi	Xj				
2	Cost	150	0	100	500	350	200	150	700	250	550				
3															
4															
5	Constraints											LHS	Sign	RHS	
6	A	1										0	≤	3	
7	B		1									0	≤	0	
8	C			1								0	≤	2	
9	D				1							0	≤	1	
10	E					1						0	≤	2	
11	F						1					0	≤	1	
12	G							1				0	≤	2	
13	H								1			0	≤	3	
14	I									1		0	≤	1	
15	J										1	0	≤	4	
16	A-B-C-D-H-I-J	1	1	1	1				1	1	1	0	≥	8	
17	E-F-G-H-I-J					1	1	1	1	1	1	0	≥	5	
18															TC
19	Solution														0
20															

Cell	Formulas	Corresponding LP model formulation
L6	=SUMPRODUCT(B6:K6,$B$19:$K$19)	$1X_A$
L7	=SUMPRODUCT(B7:K7,$B$19:$K$19)	$1X_B$
L8	=SUMPRODUCT(B8:K8,$B$19:$K$19)	$1X_C$
L9	=SUMP RODUCT(B9:K9,$B$19:$K$19)	$1X_D$
L10	=SUMPRODUCT(B10:K10,$B$19:$K$19)	$1X_E$
L11	=SUMPRODUCT(B11:K11,$B$19:$K$19)	$1X_F$
L12	=SUMPRODUCT(B12:K12,$B$19:$K$19)	$1X_G$
L13	=SUMPRODUCT(B13:K13,$B$19:$K$19)	$1X_H$
L14	=SUMPRODUCT(B14:K14,$B$19:$K$19)	$1X_I$
L15	=SUMPRODUCT(B15:K15,$B$19:$K$19)	$1X_J$
L16	=SUMPRODUCT(B16:K16,$B$19:$K$19)	$1X_A + 1X_B + 1X_C + 1X_D + 1X_H + 1X_I + 1X_J$
L17	=SUMPRODUCT(B17:K17,$B$19:$K$19)	$1X_E + 1X_F + 1X_G + 1X_H + 1X_I + 1X_J$
O19	=SUMPRODUCT(B2:K2,$B$19:$K$19)	$150\,X_A + 0\,X_B + 100\,X_C + 500\,X_D + 350\,X_E + 200\,X_F + 150\,X_G + 700\,X_H + 250\,X_I + 550\,X_J$

(a) Model

FIGURE 3.14 – Microsoft Excel model and solution of crashing problem. (*continued*)

Note: Microsoft Excel application interface is used with permission of Microsoft.

(*continued*)

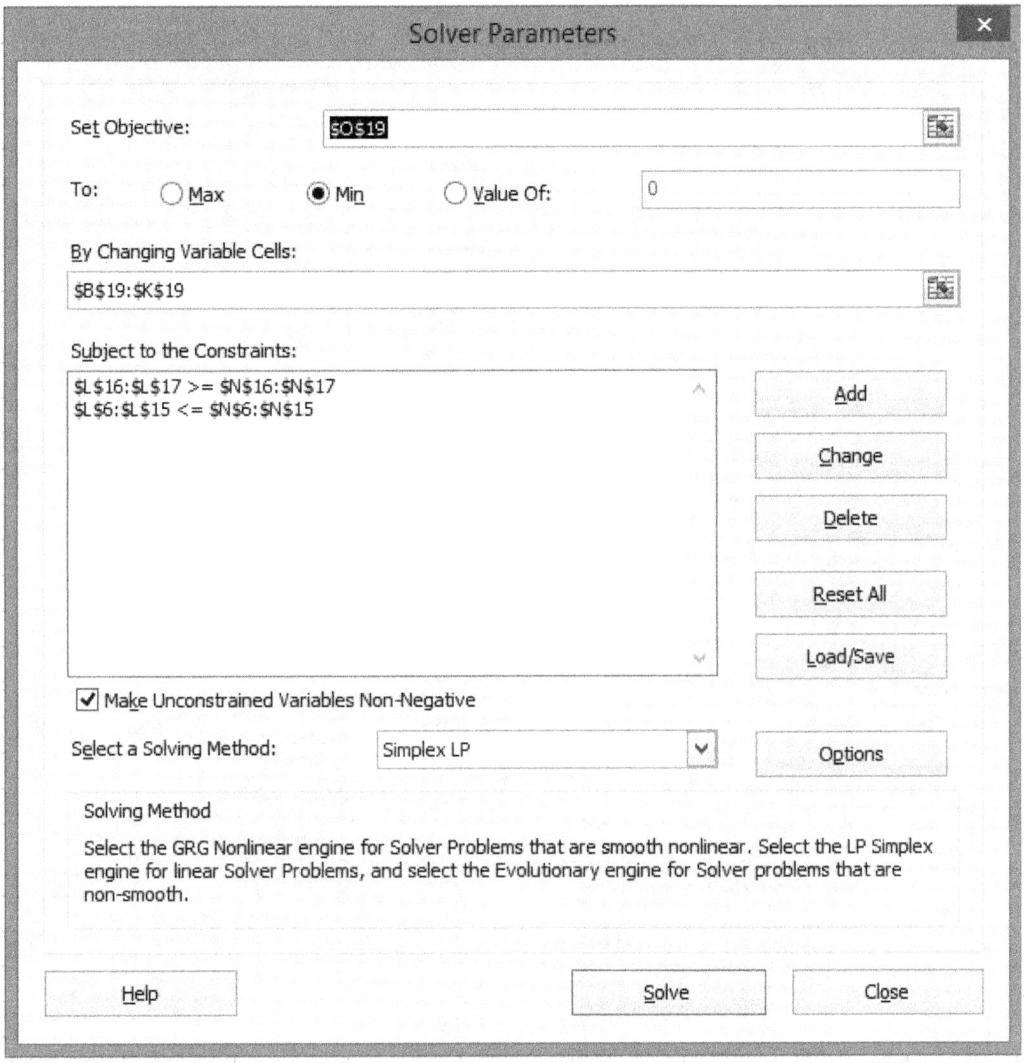

(b) Solver dialog box

FIGURE 3.14 – Microsoft Excel model and solution of crashing problem. (*continued*)

Note: Excel Solver interface reproduced by permission of Frontline Solvers (www.solver.com).

(*continued*)

Objective cell (Min)

Cell	Name	Original value	Final value
$N$19	Solution TC	0	2300

Variable cells

Cell	Name	Original value	Final value	Integer
$B$19	Solution XA	0	3	Contin
$C$19	Solution XB	0	0	Contin
$D$19	Solution XC	0	2	Contin
$E$19	Solution XD	0	0	Contin
$F$19	Solution XE	0	0	Contin
$G$19	Solution XF	0	0	Contin
$H$19	Solution XG	0	2	Contin
$I$19	Solution XH	0	0	Contin
$J$19	Solution XI	0	1	Contin
$K$19	Solution XJ	0	2	Contin

Constraints

Cell	Name	Cell Value	Formula	Status	Slack
$L$15	Min. time reduction for Path 1 LHS	8	$L$15>=$N$15	Binding	0
$L$16	Min. time reduction for Path 2 LHS	5	$L$16>=$N$16	Binding	0
$L$5	Max. time reduction for A LHS	3	$L$5<=$N$5	Binding	0
$L$6	Max. time reduction for B LHS	0	$L$6<=$N$6	Binding	0
$L$7	Max. time reduction for C LHS	2	$L$7<=$N$7	Binding	0
$L$8	Max. time reduction for D LHS	0	$L$8<=$N$8	Not binding	1
$L$9	Max. time reduction for E LHS	0	$L$9<=$N$9	Not binding	2
$L$10	Max. time reduction for F LHS	0	$L$10<=$N$10	Not binding	1
$L$11	Max. time reduction for G LHS	2	$L$11<=$N$11	Binding	0
$L$12	Max. time reduction for H LHS	0	$L$12<=$N$12	Not binding	3
$L$13	Max. time reduction for I LHS	1	$L$13<=$N$13	Binding	0
$L$14	Max. time reduction for J LHS	2	$L$14<=$N$14	Not binding	2

(c) Answer report (Solution)

FIGURE 3.14 – Microsoft Excel model and solution of crashing problem.

BRADLEY PARK HOSPITAL 3.5

Jennifer stood up in front of the BPH board. "Before I present the findings supporting the need for remodeling the old geriatrics unit into a modern and efficient ACE unit, I want to tell you what an exceptional job my teammates have done collecting information on patient needs. When they started, there was only a 5% chance of them completing the survey of our patients by today, but through teamwork, tenacity, and expert use of project management tools they provided me with the data that I will show you now."

EVALUATING PERT/CPM

Before using PERT/CPM, project managers must be aware of both their pros and cons.

Advantages

1. The technique forces project managers to organize the project information in a logical fashion and quantify it.

2. The network diagram provides a graphic display of the project and its activities. It is a common point of reference for all the parties involved in the project.

3. The technique is not overly complex and can be learned easily.

4. Knowledge of the critical activities enables the project manager to (a) monitor closely the activities whose delay would postpone the completion of the entire project, and (b) potentially allow delays for those activities that have slack. Resources can be allocated and managed accordingly.

Disadvantages

1. It is sometimes impossible to identify all activities, especially for complex projects. Omissions will emerge and may require a substantial modification of the schedule.

2. Time estimates are just that: estimates. They tend to be subjective and could be quite inaccurate—fudge factor—for first-time endeavors.

3. There is a tendency to focus too much on the critical path and overlook other paths that are near critical or become critical as a result of delays.

WHY PROJECTS FAIL

Planning is never perfect, execution is difficult, and sometimes projects fail. Failure can occur at any of the steps in the process. Major reasons for failure are as follows (Kerzner, 2013, p. 263; Box 3.8):

- **Goals are not understood throughout the organization.** If others within the organization do not know or understand the objectives of the project, it may be difficult to obtain the resources (people, time, money) needed to complete the project. Also, others may inadvertently interfere with the project team and may make decisions that prevent the goals from being achieved.

- **There is a misalignment of the organization's strategy and the goals of the project.** If the organization is going one way,

---

⊕ BOX 3.8 – DID YOU KNOW?

Project Disaster in Maine: Medicaid Claims System Upgrade
To comply with the Health Insurance Portability and Accountability Act of 1996 (HIPAA), Maine's Department of Human Services proceeded with a web-based Medicaid claims system for processing $1.5 billion in annual Medicaid claims and payments. The $25 million project was implemented in a manner that ignored sound project management principles and methods resulting in massive failures in claims processing for the states' Medicaid patients. The repercussions included:

- Hundreds of thousands of Medicaid patients were denied care.
- Physicians had to take loans to stay in business.
- Maine's credit rating was threatened.
- The new system had over $30 million in cost overruns.
- The new system was not HIPAA compliant.
- Jobs for project leads were lost.
- Trust between the providers and Medicaid was eroded.

The project failed because of poor planning, unrealistic timelines, inadequate and inexperienced resources, unproven technology, competing priorities, lack of piloting, poor contingency planning, and lack of an engaged subject matter expert (Holmes, 2006).

---

and the project team is going another way, the project will fail. There needs to be a common purpose within the organization for projects to be successful.

- **Timelines are unrealistic.** If a project timeline does not take into account the realization that team members have other responsibilities, project milestones will be missed. It is discouraging for team members to be asked to do things that are impossible to do. Lack of commitment and disengagement will occur and the project will fail.

- **Resources are not available.** If team members do not have the tools (time, people, funds, expertise, etc.) to do the work, the project will fail. It is important to define what is really needed to do the work and communicate the need to the executive sponsors of the project. If resources are not available, it is better not to even start the project.

- **Planning is poor.** If the project plan is not realistic and does not have the necessary resources allocated, it will not succeed. Realistic planning is the most important step in project management.

- **Rigorous project management methodology is not followed.** If appropriate tools are not applied, it becomes more difficult to monitor tasks and predict time and cost overruns. Visual displays make it easier for team members to see how completion of their tasks impacts completion of the overall project. If appropriate tools are not available, project managers lose sight of what needs to be done, and deadlines are missed.

- **Inadequate communication, progress tracking, and reporting.** If the project manager is not monitoring progress, communicating with his or her team and executive sponsors when milestones are met or unmet, and harnessing the necessary resources to be successful, the project will fail.

Team Dynamics and Communication

Another major reason for failure is team dynamics. Understanding what is happening within a team and being able to identify what is not working is important. In his book, *Five Dysfunctions of a Team*, Lencioni (2011) describes how the following issues can destroy successful project management:

- Absence of trust
- Fear of conflict
- Lack of commitment
- Avoidance of accountability
- Inattention to results

Effective communication is very difficult to achieve. Different people can view the same message in different ways. People tend to remember details of discussions when they are interested in the topic, but quickly forget them if they don't care about the issue. People come into discussions with preconceived notions about what will be said and don't actually listen to what the speaker is trying to communicate. Ambiguity makes us hear what we want to hear. Therefore, don't assume that the message that you are communicating always gets through to a group, or that decisions made within a group will be remembered several weeks later. Taking accurate minutes of the meetings and sending them to the group within a week can help people refresh their memories and ask for clarifications. Also, meeting transcripts documenting what was actually said (word for word) are very helpful in ensuring open, honest discussions. Communication goes many ways. A project manager must communicate upward to the executives who are interested in the project; laterally to peers, groups in functional areas, and stakeholders; and downward to others in the project office or at the operational level.

In any situation in which people with different perspectives work together, conflict should be expected. Conflict is a normal and necessary part of a healthy interaction and, if handled properly, can engender energy and excitement and lead to a better outcome. Unfortunately, conflict can also be destructive and lead to hard feelings and a dysfunctional process (Box 3.9). When conflict is mismanaged, it can harm relationships and sidetrack a project. But when handled in a respectful and positive way, conflict provides an opportunity to build trust and gain a deeper understanding of the issue as well as the person involved in the conflict. Learning to manage your emotions and to be willing to confront conflicts is addressed in *Crucial Conversations: Tools for Talking When the Stakes Are High* (Patterson, Grenny, McMillan, & Switzler, 2011). What is a crucial conversation? According to the authors, it is a discussion between two or more people in which (a) the stakes are high, (b) opinions vary, and (c) emotions are strong. In this book, there are several concepts that are important to keep in mind when dealing with highly charged situations:

- Conflicts escalate when ignored.
- We respond to conflicts based on our perceptions of the situation, not necessarily to an objective review of the facts.
- Conflicts trigger strong emotions.
- Conflicts are an opportunity for growth.

Although good project management is difficult, it is one of the most important skills one can develop in healthcare operations. Systems constantly need upgrading, regulations are frequently changed, and processes need continuous streamlining. Learning to be a constructive team member and developing the skills necessary to lead teams will help define you as a successful healthcare operations manager. Leaders of the future will be those who can harness the skills of groups and solve tough problems. Good luck in your journey!

⊕ BOX 3.9 – DID YOU KNOW?

Would You Buy a "Purple Suit"?

On the heels of two reports of deplorable care and conditions at Walter Reed Army Medical Center, Congress took action to create a superior healthcare delivery system for our military. However, the strategy for integrating the historic Walter Reed Army Medical Center with the National Naval Medical Center floundered because of a clash of cultures.

The project was daunting; it had an accelerated timeline, uncoordinated funding process, lack of defined goals, and a vision with no definition of "world class." However, the most significant hurdle to overcome was a clash of cultures. In 2009, The National Capital Region Base Realignment and Closure Health Systems Advisory Subcommittee of Defense Health Board reported that the differing cultures of the army, navy, and air force conflict with the needs of an integrated delivery system. Despite those shortcomings, the project moved forward and, as reported by National Public Radio in 2011, the new facility failed to meet its objectives. All the while, the legislators continued to debate the merits of combining the military medical operations. This "purple suit" debate—a reference to mixing army green with navy and air force blues—highlights the difficulties of combining cultures to implement a project. The debate continues on theoretic arguments around costs and efficiencies, but ignores Peter Drucker's pragmatic warning: "Culture eats strategy for breakfast" (Shapiro, 2011).

SUMMARY

In this chapter, we discussed the phases of project management and the roles that people must play in order to have a successful project outcome. Tools, such as the work breakdown structure (WBS), Gantt charts, and PERT/CPM, that are used to help plan, schedule, and control projects were discussed in detail. You also learned why projects fail and how project managers and team members can take steps to minimize the risks of failure.

KEY TERMS

Project	Variance	Forward pass
Project management	Work breakdown structure (WBS)	Backward pass
Project charter	Gantt chart	Optimistic time
Scope creep	Network diagram	Pessimistic time
Project manager	Path	Most likely time
Project management office (PMO)	Critical path	Crash cost per unit of time
Project team	Critical activities	Marginal cost analysis
Project champion	Slack	Linear programming

TOOLS USED IN THIS CHAPTER

TOOL	PURPOSE
Project charter	Provides a road map for the project
Traffic light flagging system	Communication tool that clearly depicts what projects (or tasks within the project) are on track (green), which ones are at risk of falling behind (yellow), and which ones are behind (red)
Work breakdown structure	Hierarchical depiction of a project's components at various levels of detail that helps the planner identify all the work requirements of a project and organize them in a logical fashion
Gantt chart	A chart that shows the scheduling of activities and/or resources

Network diagram	Diagram that represents tasks required for completing the project and the minimum time to complete the task
PERT	Planning and scheduling technique that takes into account uncertain times and helps determine the probability of completing a project by a certain date
CPM	An algorithm used to schedule a set of project activities. It is frequently used in conjunction with PERT
Crashing	Method used to shorten the project's duration by reducing the time of one (or more) critical activities by adding more resources

FORMULAS USED IN THIS CHAPTER

Technique	Metric	Formula	Number
CPM	ES	maximum (EF times of all immediate predecessors)	[3.1]
	EF	ES + activity time	[3.2]
	LF	minimum (LS times of all immediate followers)	[3.3]
	LS	LF – activity time	[3.4]
	S	LF – EF or LS – ES	[3.5] and [3.6]
PERT	t_e	$(a + 4m + b)/6$	[3.7]
	σ	$\left(\dfrac{b-a}{6}\right)$	[3.8]
	σ^2	$\left(\dfrac{b-a}{6}\right)^2$	[3.9]
	σ_{cp}	$\sqrt{\Sigma\left(\begin{array}{l}\text{variances of activities}\\ \text{on critical path}\end{array}\right)}$	[3.10]
	z	$\dfrac{(\text{specified time} - \text{expected time})}{\sigma_{cp}}$	[3.11]

Crashing t_{RED} $t_n - t_c$ [3.12]

$$S \quad \frac{c_c - c_n}{t_{RED}} \qquad [3.13]$$

WHAT DO YOU REMEMBER?

1. What is a project? What are the five phases of a project and what happens if you do not complete them all?
2. What is the triple constraint and what does it mean?
3. What is a project charter? What does it include?
4. What are the characteristics of good team members?
5. Why is communication so important when managing projects?
6. What is a Gantt chart? Where is it used?
7. List five reasons that projects fail.
8. What are the advantages and disadvantages of PERT and CPM?
9. The Denver VA project was over cost and over budget. What do you think should have been done to keep this project on track?

SOLVE BPH'S PROBLEMS

1. A group of physicians wants to establish a new protocol. They have identified a list of 13 activities and their precedence relationships to design the protocol, train staff, and implement the new protocol. Draw the appropriate network diagram using (a) the AOA convention, and (b) the AON convention.

Activity	Immediate Predecessors
A	—
B	A
C	B
D	B
E	C
F	C, D
G	F
H	E, G
I	H
J	H
K	J
L	J
M	K, L

2. The pathology department at BPH has planned a new project involving 20 activities. The activities and their immediate

predecessors are listed in the following table. Draw the appropriate network diagram using (a) the AOA convention, and (b) the AON convention.

Activity	Immediate Predecessors
A	—
B	—
C	—
D	A, B
E	B
F	C
G	D
H	E, F
I	G
J	G
K	I, J
L	H
M	H
N	M
O	M
P	N, O
Q	L
R	K
S	Q, R
T	P, S

3. For problem 1, assume the following activity times:

Activity	Time (days)
A	3
B	2
C	5
D	4
E	12
F	8
G	9
H	1
I	3
J	4
K	6
L	2
M	1

Based on this information,

a. Develop a Gantt chart assuming the project starts on Monday, March 3rd.

b. Determine the earliest start and finish times, the latest start and finish times, and slack for each activity.

c. Indicate the critical path and project duration.

4. For problem 2, assume the following activity times:

Activity	Time (weeks)
A	3
B	1
C	5
D	2
E	6
F	1
G	4
H	8
I	6
J	2
K	3
L	5
M	1
N	1
O	4
P	3
Q	5
R	2
S	3
T	2

Based on this,

a. Develop a Gantt chart assuming the project starts on Monday, April 28th.

b. Determine the earliest start and finish times, the latest start and finish times, and slack for each activity.

c. Indicate the critical path and project duration.

5. The layout redesign of the pediatric ward is expected to take 47 weeks. The standard deviation of the critical path is 2.17 weeks. Find the z-values and determine the probabilities that:

a. The project will be completed within 50 weeks.

b. The project will take 49 weeks or longer.

c. The project will be completed within 40 weeks.

d. The project will be completed within 47 weeks.

e. The project will take 46 weeks or longer.

6. A team of trauma surgeons is concerned about the time it takes to receive blood for transfusions. They have identified all the

activities involved in the process, their precedence relationships, and their durations.

Activities	Immediate Predecessors	Optimistic Time (min)	Most Likely Time	Pessimistic Time
A. Blood transfusion is ordered.	—	0.5	1	1.5
B. Phlebotomist draws blood sample.	A	30	38	46
C. Sample is sent to lab.	B	12	15	20
D. Nurse places blood band on patient.	B	1	2	5
E. Blood bank identifies blood type and checks for antibodies.	C	12	15	18
F. Blood bank cross-checks patient's plasma against red blood cells in blood bank.	E	25	30	40
G. Blood bank notifies nursing floor when blood is ready and sends to floor.	F	2	5	9
H. Blood is checked by two nurses to confirm patient date of birth.	D,G	17	21	24
I. Blood transfusion is performed.	H	50	60	80

a.　Draw the AON network.

b.　Determine the time estimate for each activity.

c.　Find the ES, EF, LS, LF, and S for each activity and determine the critical path. How long is this process expected to last?

d.　What is the probability of completing this process in 180 minutes and in 240 minutes?

e.　What is the probability that the process will take longer than 200 minutes?

7.　Bradley Park Hospital's environmental services team wants to reduce patient room turnover times without sacrificing safety and room cleanliness. Their first task involves identifying all the activities necessary to clean and disinfect a room after patient discharge and their respective durations (in minutes). Their efforts led to the following network diagram.

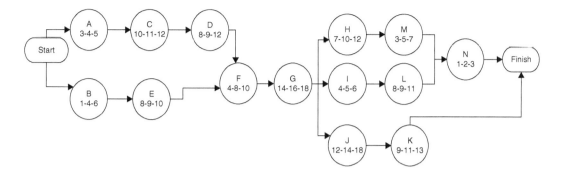

a. What is the time estimate for each activity?
b. Find the ES, EF, LS, LF, and S for each activity and determine the critical path. How long does it take to clean and disinfect a room?
c. What is the probability of completing the room cleaning and disinfection process in 65 minutes and in 75 minutes?
d. What is the probability that the process will take longer than 77 minutes?

8. Based on the following network and data, use the marginal cost analysis method to show how the project's duration can be reduced to 35 weeks. What is the extra cost incurred?

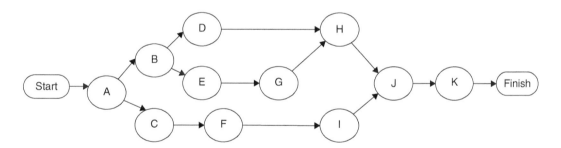

Activity	t_n (weeks)	c_n ($000)	t_c (weeks)	c_c ($000)
A	5	20	2	32
B	10	26	8	36
C	9	16	8	22
D	4	14	3	22
E	4	24	3	30
F	7	18	5	38
G	8	20	8	20
H	6	14	4	18
I	8	12	5	24
J	5	50	4	60
K	6	60	5	67

9. A team at Bradley Park Hospital is involved in a process improvement project involving six major activities. Because the improvement is viewed as essential to obtain reaccreditation by The Joint Commission, it must be completed before the audit, that is, in 19 weeks. Data on costs and times have been gathered by the team. Crash the project using (a) the marginal cost analysis method, and (b) the LP method. What is the extra cost incurred?

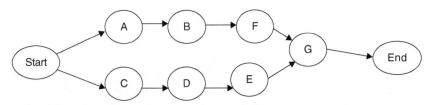

Activity	t_n (weeks)	$c_{n(\$)}$	t_c (weeks)	$c_{c(\$)}$
A	7	800	4	1,550
B	8	400	6	700
C	5	700	5	700
D	3	1,000	1	2,500
E	9	1,800	6	3,000
F	6	400	5	500
G	5	600	3	850

10. The environmental services team in problem 7 wants to complete the process in 65 minutes. Based on the following data, which activities should be crashed, and what is the resulting cost? Find the solution using (a) the marginal cost analysis method, and (b) the LP method. What is the extra cost incurred?

Activity	t_n (min)	$c_{n(\$)}$	t_c (min)	$c_{c(\$)}$
A	4	10	3	13
B	4	5	4	5
C	11	20	8	26
D	9	13	7	18
E	9	20	6	29
F	8	8	6	12
G	16	20	14	40
H	10	6	7	18
I	5	2	5	2
J	14	15	10	36
K	11	10	9	13
L	9	6	7	11
M	5	8	4	9
N	2	9	2	9

THINK OUTSIDE THE BOOK!

1. What attributes should a project manager have?

2. Do you think functional managers would make good project managers?

3. Identify a failed project that is in the news. Why do you think the project failed? Point to specific factors that may have contributed to the failure.

4. If conflicts develop into a situation where mistrust prevails, would you expect documentation of activities to increase or decrease? Why?

REFERENCES

Benjamin Franklin. (n.d.). *BrainyQuote.com*. Retrieved from http://www.brainyquote.com/quotes/quotes/b/benjaminfr138217.html

Bobera, D. (2008). Project management organization. *Management Information Systems, 3*(1), 3–9.

Elliott, D. (2015). VA employee says he was fired after warning of hospital cost. Retrieved from https://www.yahoo.com/news/lawmakers-va-fired-whistleblower-not-executives-191250764.html?ref=gs

Haughey, D. (2011). Understanding the project management triple constraint. Retrieved from http://www.projectsmart.co.uk/pdf/understanding-the-project-management-triple-constraint.pdf

Heizer, J., & Render, B. (2011). *Operations management*. Upper Saddle River, NJ: Prentice-Hall.

Holmes, A. (2006, April 15). Maine's medicaid mistakes. *CIO*. Retrieved from http://www.cio.com/article/2447010/project-management/maine-s-medicaid-mistakes.html

Kelley, J. E., Jr., & Walker, M. R. (1959, December 1–3). *Critical-path planning and scheduling* (pp. 160–173). Paper presented at the IRE-AIEE-ACM Conference, New York, NY.

Kerzner, H. R. (2013). *Project management: A systems approach to planning, scheduling, and controlling* (11th ed.). Hoboken, NJ: John Wiley & Sons.

Lencioni, P. M. (2011). *The five dysfunctions of a team: A leadership fable*. San Francisco, CA: Jossey-Bass.

Patterson, K., Grenny, J., McMillan, R., & Switzler, A. (2011). *Crucial conversations: Tools for talking when stakes are high* (2nd ed.). New York, NY: McGraw-Hill.

Peter, L. J., & Hull, R. (1969). *The Peter principle: Why things always go wrong*. New York, NY: William Morrow.

Russell, R. S., & Taylor, B. W. (2009). *Operations management: Creating value along the supply chain* (6th ed.). Hoboken, NJ: John Wiley & Sons.

Shapiro, J. (2011, September 2). Change is hard: Army, navy hospitals merge. *South Carolina Public Radio*. Retrieved from http://www.npr .org/2011/09/02/139641918/change-is-hard-army-navy-hospitals-merge

Stevenson, W. J. (2012). *Operations management* (11th ed.). New York, NY: McGraw-Hill.

Tate, C. (2015). Differing work styles can help team performance. *Harvard Business Review*. Retrieved from https://hbr.org/2015/04/differing-work-styles-can-help-team-performance

Thomas Edison. (n.d.). 50 Awesome quotes on vision. Retrieved from http://www.ideachampions.com/weblogs/archives/2010/11/50_awesome_quot_1.shtml

Weiss, J. W., & Wsocki, R. K. (1992). *5-phase project management: A practical planning and implementation guide*. Cambridge, MA: Perseus Books.

PART

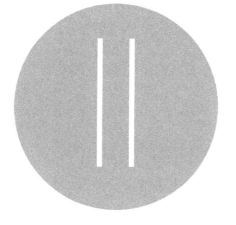

Competing on Quality

CHAPTER 4

QUALITY MANAGEMENT

BRADLEY PARK HOSPITAL 4.1

Don and Jennifer were sitting in the hospital cafeteria discussing the success of the acute care for the elderly (ACE) unit over a cup of coffee. "Just look at these patient satisfaction numbers. They are higher than I ever imagined! You know, it all goes back to understanding what the patients' needs are. I am so glad we worked so hard on our patient survey before planning the layout and the services. That made all the difference."

A few sips of coffee later, "I am so glad I ran into you two," Mike Chambers was walking through the cafeteria on his way back to his office. "Great job on the ACE unit. What a wonderful place for our older patients. No falls in a month!" "We now need to do something similar for our outpatient clinics. If we do not improve our patient satisfaction, I am afraid we will lose some of our physicians and many of our patients to Madison Hospital. They have beautiful facilities. Will you two look into that right away?" Mike's cell phone rang, and he answered it as he walked off toward his office.

Jennifer turned to Don, "Well, I learned a lot about ACE units during this project. I guess I now need to learn more about our clinics!" Don smiled, "I believe this project may be a bit more complicated, but I am up for it if you are."

Don and Jennifer were sitting in the windowless conference in the administration area of the clinic. Penny James, the director of ambulatory services walked into the room. "Thank you for coming. We need your help. The patient satisfaction numbers in the clinic have been dropping since Madison Hospital opened 3 years ago, but lately, patient wait times have increased significantly. Our no-show rate is getting worse and our physician productivity is decreasing."

"In addition to patient satisfaction scores, we have conducted several focus groups to find out what our patients want when they come to see us. The findings are not surprising, but they can focus our efforts."

Jennifer responded, "What specific things did the focus groups comment on?" "Wait times primarily," Penny continued, "They complained that the time to the appointment date is way too long. Sometimes, it takes months to find an opening. But once they get to the clinic, they have to wait too long to get into the room and then see the doctor. The staff have not kept patients informed of delays and sometimes patients leave the clinic without a clear understanding of what they should do. They say they then call the clinic for clarification, but it takes so long to hold the phone while someone finds the doctor."

"I am not sure where to start." Penny looked concerned. Don smiled, "Well, I am glad that Jennifer and I can help. Let us think about how we need to approach this and we can get back together the first of next week." Jennifer joined in, "I am looking forward to working with you and learning the complexities of ambulatory services. Have a great weekend."

 Have you had reasons to be dissatisfied when going to see a doctor? What were those reasons?

INTRODUCTION AND LEARNING OBJECTIVES

As a follow-up to its 1999 report on patient safety (see Chapter 1), the Institute of Medicine (IOM; 2001) published a set of recommendations to improve the quality of healthcare delivery in the United States. It notably advocated the redesign of a system that would make it difficult for errors to occur in the first place. More recent, under the Affordable Care Act (ACA), the U.S. Department of Health and Human Services (Agency for Healthcare Research and Quality [AHRQ], 2015) developed the first National Quality Strategy to guide local, state, and national efforts to improve the quality of care. The strategy presented three aims for the health care system, often referred to as the "triple aim":

1. **Better care:** improve the overall quality by making healthcare more patient centered, reliable, accessible, and safe

2. **Healthier people and communities:** improve the health of the U.S. population by supporting proven interventions to address behavioral, social, and environmental determinants of health in addition to delivering higher quality care

3. **Lower costs:** reduce the cost of quality health care for individuals, families, employers, and government

Consistent with the National Quality Strategy, and as we discussed in Chapter 2, we are making quality the cornerstone of all competitive priorities (Figure 4.1). Let us start with an important question: What does healthcare quality mean to you as a patient? You may think of safety, good outcomes, outstanding providers, state-of-the art facilities, and so on. Healthcare quality has indeed many facets, which make it difficult to pin it down precisely. Further complicating the issue, *quality* means different things to different people. Healthcare providers tend to view quality exclusively in terms of processes and clinical outcomes, whereas patients focus on the quality of their experience *in addition* to the outcomes. The payers (i.e., insurance companies health plan sponsors such as employers and unions and government agencies) insist not only on excellent health outcomes but also on efficiency. Besides the multidimensionality of the concept itself, this plurality of perspectives regarding its meaning magnifies the difficulty of building a coherent healthcare quality system. Yet, this challenge was one of the ACA's imperatives (White House, 2010). By requiring public reporting of providers' performance on key quality indicators and penalizing providers for poor performance, the ACA put quality on the forefront of the national healthcare policy. In this chapter, you learn how to develop a quality system in a healthcare organization. More specifically, you will:

1. **Define *quality* from the perspectives of providers, patients, and third-party payers**

2. **Capture the voice of the customer with subjective quality measures**

3. **Translate the voice of the customer into the voice of the process by developing internal, objective quality indicators**

4. **Gauge quality performance through benchmarking**

5. **Use a variety of quality tools**

6. **View quality improvement as a never-ending process**

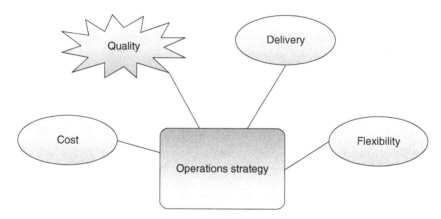

FIGURE 4.1 – Mind map with a focus on quality.

WHAT IS QUALITY?

Who defines quality? The customer! If the customer is responsible for defining the quality he or she wants, the provider of the product/ service is responsible for delivering that quality. As a result, a broad, common definition of *quality* involves *exceeding customers' expectations*. There are two elements in this definition: (a) the customers and (b) their expectations. Let us focus on customers first. For many businesses, it is easy to identify the customer: patrons in a restaurant, shoppers in a clothing store, readers in a library, and so on, but who is the "customer" in healthcare? Although the patient is the ultimate customer, there are many processes required to care for patients that involve multiple customers. So, from an operations management (OM) standpoint, all the entities mentioned in Table 4.1 are major customers of the healthcare system. If you consider treatment, the customer is the patient. If you examine the delivery of supplies to the operating room, the customers are the doctors and nurses. In the case of billing, the customer is an insurance company, an individual, or a third-party administrator. In fact, we could consider accrediting agencies as customers of the providers'

**Next Process
Concept**

View the customer
as the beneficiary of
the next step in the
process.

quality reports. One simple way to identify the customer is to adopt the **"next process"** concept: View the customer as the beneficiary of the next step in the process of healthcare delivery.

Now, let us consider these customers' different expectations. In the following paragraphs, we elaborate on each one's perspective.

TABLE 4.1 – Customers in Healthcare	
Customers	**Examples**
Patients	Young patients wanting convenient access to clinic Older patients with diabetes having difficulties with transportation
Providers and administrative staff	Community physicians or clinics referring patients to your hospital Physicians sending specimens to your laboratory Nurses in the intensive care unit (ICU) receiving patients admitted through the emergency department (ED) Bed control needing information when a patient is discharged
Third-party payers	Managed care organizations contracting with physician groups Self-insured employers contracting with third-party administrator Centers for Medicare & Medicaid Services

Patients' Perspectives

As healthcare *consumers*, individuals may focus on the future costs of their care, especially when choosing a plan. However, as *patients*, quality is their primary concern. They form perceptions about their healthcare experiences during care delivery and outcomes after care delivery. They are sensitive to their provider's expertise, courtesy, attentiveness to their needs, and respect for their time. They also appreciate the appearance, atmosphere, and ease of access of the facilities. With regard to health outcomes, patients often evaluate their results in terms of well-being (e.g., less pain or increased mobility). These perceptions are subjective; they are shaped by personal feelings, opinions, or outlook on life. For example, Patient A may feel that a 10-minute wait is acceptable, whereas Patient B finds it intolerable. Patient C may be delighted to walk unassisted for 20 minutes 1 month after knee surgery, whereas Patient D wishes he could already run a half marathon.

Providers' and Administrative Staff's Perspectives

🐾 BOX 4.1 – WORDS OF WISDOM

"Simply put, health care quality is getting the right care to the right patient at the right time—every time" (Clancy, 2009; http://www.hhs.gov/asl/testify/2009/03/t20090318b.html).

Providers are most interested in the process of providing care and its clinical outcomes (Box 4.1). The patient's health is their top priority. As a result, they may distrust cost-reduction programs, which, in their views, may be threats to both patient safety and their incomes. They often clash with hospital administrators who have a more business-oriented perspective of healthcare delivery and want to balance costs and quality. Providers may also be skeptical of the importance of the patient's experience, the subjective elements of which seem less relevant than sound, objective clinical indicators. They prefer to evaluate patients' care and health against "hard" measures with well-established standards: blood pressure, mortality rate, number of readmissions, number of patient falls, percentage of time a prophylactic antibiotic was received within 1 hour prior to surgical incision, and so on.

The Value-Based Purchasing (VBP) program under the ACA rewards providers for efficiency and quality of care in the domains of clinical practice, patient experience, and outcomes for Medicare beneficiaries (U.S. Department of Health and Human Services, 2013b; VanLare & Conway, 2012). By tying compensation to patient experience and efficiency (incentive payments for performance achievements or performance improvements, penalties for poor performance), VBP attempts to unify the patients', providers', administrators', and payers' (see next section) perspectives. As shown in Table 4.2, the importance of patient experience measures in evaluating a hospital's total performance is substantial. You will notice that the relative weight of process measures decreased by 25% from fiscal year (FY) 2014 to FY 2015. This loss was recaptured by a reallocation of 5 additional percentage points to outcomes and 20 points to efficiency (Medicare spending per patient). Efficiency is actually a measure of cost rather than quality, but as discussed in Chapter 2, quality improvements pave the ground for efficiency gains. As the government agency that pays for healthcare services for all Medicare or Medicaid recipients, the Centers for Medicare & Medicaid Services (CMS) has huge power over the U.S. healthcare enterprise, and it is using this power to transform care. This transformative role of payers is highlighted in the next section.

TABLE 4.2 – Value-Based Purchasing: Quality Domain Weights FY 2014 to FY 2015

Domain	FY 2014 Weight (%)	FY 2015 Weight (%)
Clinical process of care	45	20
Patient experience of care	30	30
Outcome	25	30
Efficiency	—	20

Third-Party Payers' Perspectives

Third-party payers are interested in both quality and efficiency. They do value positive clinical outcomes, but they are wary of costly, new treatments and procedures, the effectiveness of which may not be superior to older alternatives. As a result, they are often at odds with both patients and providers as they may deny coverage of treatments preferred by these two parties (Young, Olsen, & McGinnis, 2010). In fact, even though insurers and self-insured employers have been at times vocal against the ACA, many subscribe to the ACA's emphasis on evidence-based practice and cost-effectiveness of multiple treatment options. Under the ACA, the National Quality Strategy established six priorities to help focus public and private partners' efforts. These priorities are (U.S. Department of Health and Human Services, 2013a):

1. **Improve safety**. Patients should not be harmed (injuries, infections, etc.) by the care they receive.

2. **Increase patients' and families' engagement as partners in their care**. Providers should make patients and family members important participants in their care and take into account their preferences, value systems, and beliefs.

3. **Promote effective communication and coordination of care** among providers. All providers involved in a patient's care should have accurate and timely information regarding the patient's condition and treatment to eliminate errors, delays, and other costly inefficiencies.

4. **Adopt the most effective prevention and treatment practices** for the leading causes of mortality.

5. **Ensure wide use of best practices across communities** to enable healthy living. The care delivered should be based on scientific evidence of its successful outcomes. Both overuse and underuse should be eliminated, and all patients should receive quality care irrespective of their gender, ethnicity, socioeconomic status, or geographic location.

6. **Improve the affordability of quality care** for individuals, families, employers, and governments by developing new delivery models.

Some payers may welcome innovative options that they consider cost-effective in the long run. They may cover alternative treatments such as homeopathy, acupuncture, and restorative yoga. They may also offer incentives to participate in nutrition counseling and smoking-cessation programs. They may even encourage treatment away from home (another city or country) if the value proposition is favorable.

In summary, patients, payers, and providers have somewhat different perspectives and expectations. As healthcare managers, our challenge is to develop and improve the processes that will exceed those expectations. The house of quality (HOQ) provides a useful framework to meet this challenge and build quality throughout the system.

THE HOUSE OF QUALITY

Quality Function Deployment (QFD)

A systematic approach used to incorporate customers' needs into each step of a process.

In our quest to develop and manage a quality system, we must ensure that all processes are developed and managed to satisfy customers' needs. **Quality function deployment** is a systematic approach to incorporate these needs into each step of a process, that is, deploy quality into the design of a process. The tool used in QFD to merge the **voice of the customer (VOC)** with the **voice of the process (VOP)** is the

house of quality. The HOQ is a matrix that depicts clear relationships between customer and process requirements (Figure 4.2). Building the house comprises several steps. The first step involves asking customers what they want.

House of Quality (HOQ)
A matrix that depicts clear relationships between customer and process requirements.

FIGURE 4.2 – Overview of the house of quality.

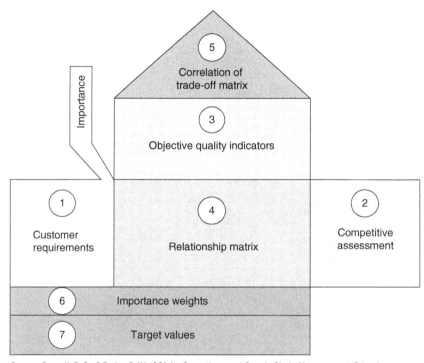

Source: Russell, R. S., & Taylor, B. W. (2014). *Operations and Supply Chain Management* (8th ed., pp. 178–182). Copyright © 2014, 2011, 2008, 2005 John Wiley & Sons, Inc.

1. **Capture the customers' requirements (VOC).** This can be done informally through discussions and/or formally through other methods of data collection, such as surveys or structured interviews. Customers are also asked to rate the importance of each requirement on a scale of 1 (low) to 5 (high). These customers' requirements and their relative importance are the inputs into the HOQ. For our example, patients want to get an appointment at the Bradley Park Hospital (BPH) clinic easily, be seen by the physician promptly after arrival, be diagnosed and treated correctly, and so forth. However, even though they value good communication skills on the part of their provider, they view a correct diagnosis as the most important requirement (Figure 4.3).

VOC (Voice of the Customer)
The customers' requirements.

2. **Conduct a competitive assessment by comparing your performance to your competitors' on the various customer requirements.** Access to the national norms of a patient satisfaction database, or the CMS databases on

hospitalcompare.gov and physiciancompare.gov, will facilitate this task. In our example, we see that Bradley Park physicians perform well in terms of courtesy and diagnosis skills. For those attributes in which BPH surpasses the competition, a design change may not be necessary. For those in which it trails the competition, change is imperative. If considered important to customers, these attributes are at least order

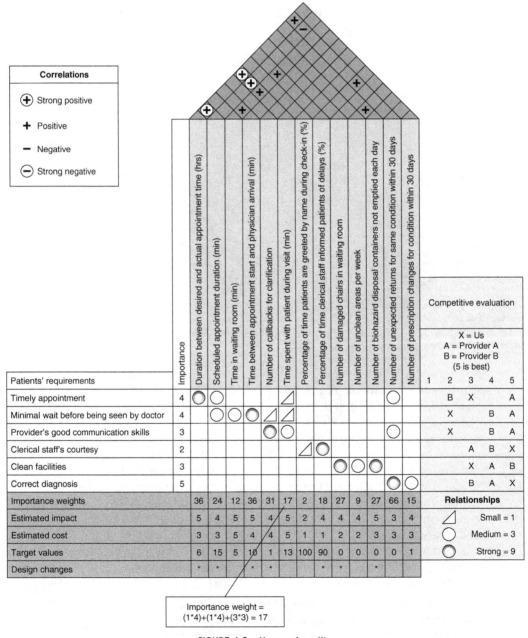

FIGURE 4.3 – House of quality.

qualifiers, and not being on par with the competition may result in revenue losses.

3. **Translate the customer's requirements (VOC) into observable process requirements (VOP).** At this point, the perceptual measures obtained from the customer are converted into objective quality indicators. **Indicators** are operationalized definitions of quality; they can be observed, measured, and tracked consistently by the service provider. For example, the ability to see the physician promptly could be measured by the following two indicators: (a) the number of minutes between appointment and exam times, or (b) the number of minutes spent in the waiting room. It is a good idea to generate a large number of indicators because some of them might be discarded later if deemed less adequate than others in capturing the VOC.

4. **Indicate the strength of the relationship between a given customer requirement and an observable quality indicator in the relationship matrix.** This can be done with a number or a symbol (see Figure 4.3). In our example, the elapsed time between when a patient arrives for an appointment and the physician enters the exam room is a stronger indicator of the patient's wish to be seen promptly than the number of minutes in the waiting room because the patient will likely wait in both the waiting room and the exam room before being seen by the physician. Although the time in the waiting room is a "weaker" indicator, it should not be discarded at this point as it may reveal the source of delay before the physician sees the patient.

5. **Determine the correlations or trade-offs between pairs of indicators.** Achieving excellence in one indicator may reinforce or hinder performance on another because they are interrelated. For example, increasing the average time of doctor–patient interaction would decrease the number of patients seen in a day, which would contribute to a larger gap between desired and actual appointment dates. Longer visits may also result in backlogs with the undesirable effect of other patients waiting well past their appointment time before the physician can see them. Similarly, return visits for the same condition may require schedulers to "work patients in" and, therefore, decrease the length of scheduling intervals. Considering all this information is necessary to build the most effective and efficient processes.

6. **Compute the indicators' importance weights.** This is done by multiplying the importance rating of a customer requirement by the strength of the relationship between the requirement and an indicator and summing through all customer requirements. See example on Figure 4.3.

VOP (Voice of the Process)
The process requirements or indicators.

Indicators
Operationalized definitions of quality that can be observed, measured, and tracked consistently by the service provider.

7. **Determine the target value for each indicator, and the cost and impact of achieving that target value.** As a general rule, process design improvements will be called for if:

   a. The provider is trailing the competition in areas customers consider important (e.g., being seen promptly by physician)

   b. The impact of a change exceeds its cost. In our example, Bradley Park Hospital may already be a leader in terms of staff courtesy, but they fall short in informing patients of delays (see Figure 4.3). The cost for improving that service is small compared to its impact. As a result, Bradley Park Hospital may want to train its staff to be even more vigilant about this issue.

To ensure a consistency of purpose at all levels of quality deployment, QFD relies on a series of matrices that look like interconnected houses (Figure 4.4). The first house is the *house of quality* shown in Figure 4.3. The other houses provide the structure to carry out the design changes proposed in the HOQ at increasingly greater levels of detail. Based on Figure 4.3, if Bradley Park Hospital decides to meet the customer requirement of minimal wait at the doctor's office, it will need to decrease the time patients spend waiting in the waiting room and/or the exam room. The second house, *resource requirements*, analyzes which resources would be affected by such changes. We might have to hire new clinical staff or "free up" some of the existing resources by automating some activities. In turn, these resource changes become inputs to the next house, *process planning*. With new inputs, a more responsive process with fewer steps can be designed, and human resources can be allocated to patients more efficiently. However, the adoption of more streamlined, automated processes requires a fourth house, *quality plan*, where specific instructions for training, software updates, equipment maintenance, and process control can be developed. The succession of houses maximizes the chances for a seamless deployment of customer-driven changes in the organization.

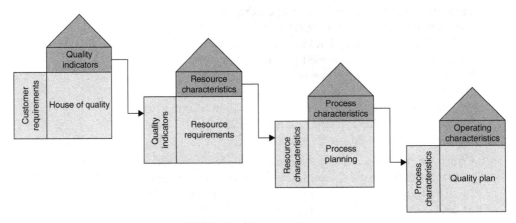

FIGURE 4.4 – Connected houses.
Source: Russell, R. S., & Taylor, B. W. (2014). *Operations and Supply Chain Management* (8th ed., pp. 178–182). Copyright © 2014, 2011, 2008, 2005 John Wiley & Sons, Inc.

QFD is an excellent communication system. It helps multidisciplinary groups to interact, focus on the same issues, and agree on measurement systems and performance targets. It can serve as a reference point during process improvement efforts and can be upgraded regularly (Russell & Taylor, 2014). Several healthcare organizations, such as De Grift (Box 4.2), have used the methodology to build and maintain a coherent quality system.

✦ BOX 4.2 – OM IN PRACTICE!

QFD at De Grift (Dijkstra & van der Bij, 2002)

De Grift is a clinic for alcohol and drug addicts in The Netherlands that decided to redesign its processes according to customer requirements. Five groups of stakeholders were selected: (a) patients; (b) reference group (e.g., family doctors, mental hospitals); (c) local, provincial, and national authorities; (d) insurance companies; and (e) management and staff. The groups expressed their requirements and were then asked to prioritize them using the method of paired comparisons. Under this method, each requirement is compared to every other requirement, and participants select the more important requirement in a pair. The number of times a requirement is preferred over another is recorded. In the De Grift case, it turned out that most of the requirements were perceived as equally important (Dijkstra & van der Bij, 2002).

The requirements were then translated into process parameters or indicators, and the strength of the relationships between a requirement and an indicator was indicated by the numbers 0, 1, 3, or 9 (0: no relationship, 9: strong relationship). The relationship matrix is represented here:

Requirements	Process Indicators								
	A	B	C	D	E	F	G	H	I
Correct diagnosis	9	0	1	3	0	1	0	1	0
Customer can express needs and wishes	0	9	3	3	3	1	1	9	3
Objective of treatment is clear	3	1	9	3	0	3	1	1	3
Treatment is tuned to following treatments	3	3	3	3	9	3	9	9	9
Match between clinical and outpatient help	0	1	1	3	3	1	9	9	9
Excellent information flow in healthcare process	1	1	1	3	3	3	9	3	3

A = standardization of diagnosis, B = protocol to uncover patient's requirements, C = protocol to set goals for process, D = monitoring and feedback, E = protocol to prepare for next treatment, F = protocol for internal information flow, G = protocol for external information flow, H = process management route guidance, I = protocol tuned to external healthcare.

This information was used to redesign the admissions department in which detoxification and diagnosis occur and treatment is discussed. Standardization and protocols were implemented, important failure modes were eliminated, and staff received additional training.

THE VOICE OF THE CUSTOMER

The HOQ starts with the VOC. Let us expand on this important driver of quality deployment. For the following discussion, we continue to focus on the patient as the customer. Because patient experience is intangible, measuring it is a complex task. Standardized survey instruments available to help you accomplish this task include the Consumer Assessment of Healthcare Providers and Systems (CAHPS) and SERVQUAL for healthcare. Some vendors also offer their proprietary instruments along with a gamut of survey administration and data analysis services (e.g., Press-Ganey and Professional Research Consultants).

CAHPS Survey Instrument

In response to a lack of information regarding the quality of health plans from a consumer perspective, the Agency for Healthcare Research and Quality introduced the CAHPS program in 1995. Several research organizations—known as the CAHPS Consortium—collaborated to develop and test standard instruments for enrollees to rate the quality of their plans. The purpose was to collect massive amounts of data and produce reports that health consumers could use in comparing and selecting plans against a predetermined set of criteria. Over the years, the program's scope was expanded to other health services provided in physicians' offices, hospitals, nursing homes, dialysis centers, and patients' homes (AHRQ, 2014).

The perceived quality of care is a multidimensional construct. In other words, several conceptual elements make up its domain. Therefore, a survey instrument should measure all these elements to render a valid account of a patient's experience of care. The core quality elements measured in various CAHPS instruments are presented in Table 4.3. Supplemental measures, such as the Patient-Centered Medical Home (PCMH) Item Set, are available as well. PCMH complements the list of topics covered in the Clinician & Group Survey with questions pertaining to access, coordination, self-management support, comprehensiveness of care, and shared decision making.

As a member of the CAHPS Consortium, CMS collects Hospital Consumer Assessment of Healthcare Providers and Systems (HCAHPS) data from all hospitals serving Medicare recipients. After eliminating incomplete surveys and surveys from ineligible patients, it calculates the provider's "top-box" score for each of the nine measures of the instrument. The **"top-box" score** is the percentage of a provider's patients who selected the most positive response to the HCAHPS survey items. CMS adjusts the nine scores for patient mix and calculates a Patient Experience of Care Domain Score used as one of the criteria for full reimbursement under the VBP program (see Table 4.2).

Top-Box Score
The percentage of a provider's patients who selected the most positive response to the HCAHPS survey items.

TABLE 4.3 – Selected CAHPS Surveys and Quality Measures	
Survey Instrument	**Measures**
Clinician and Group https://cahps.ahrq.gov/ surveys-guidance/cg/about/ index.html	• Getting timely appointments, care, and information • Providers' communication with patients • Helpful, courteous, and respectful staff • Overall rating of provider
Hospitals (HCAHPS) https://cahps.ahrq.gov/ surveys-guidance/hospital/ about/index.html	• Communication with doctors • Communication with nurses • Responsiveness of hospital staff • Pain management • Communication about medicine • Discharge information • Cleanliness of hospital environment • Quietness of hospital environment • Transition of care • Overall rating
Surgical Care https://cahps.ahrq.gov/ surveys-guidance/surgical/ about/index.html	• Information to help prepare for surgery • Surgeon's communication before surgery • Surgeon's attentiveness on day of surgery • Information to help recover from surgery • Surgeon's communication after surgery • Helpful, courteous, and respectful staff • Overall rating of surgeon
Nursing Home (Discharged Resident) https://cahps.ahrq.gov/ surveys-guidance/nh/resident/ index.html	• Environment (comfort, cleanliness, safety, etc.) • Care • Communication and respect • Autonomy • Activities
Home Health Care https://cahps.ahrq.gov/ surveys-guidance/home/index .html	• Care (gentleness, courtesy, problems with care) • Communication with healthcare providers and agency staff • Pain and medication • Overall rating

Because of their significant role in public reporting (e.g., hospitalcompare.gov) in general and in the Medicare program in particular, CAHPS surveys are the standard adopted by most providers. However, patient experience is not limited to the measures provided in these regulatory surveys. This is why other instruments may be used to complement CAHPS surveys.

SERVQUAL Survey Instrument

Originally developed in 1988, SERVQUAL is an instrument measuring the major facets of service quality (Parasuraman, Berry, & Zeithaml, 1991):

1. **Tangibles**: physical facilities, professional appearance of personnel, equipment
2. **Reliability**: ability to perform the promised service dependably and accurately

Tangibles
The physical facilities, professional appearance of personnel, and equipment.

Reliability
The ability to perform a service dependably and accurately.

Responsiveness
The willingness to help customers promptly.

Assurance
The knowledge and courtesy of employees; their ability to inspire trust.

Empathy
Refers to the caring, individualized attention given to customers.

3. **Responsiveness**: willingness to help customers and provide prompt service

4. **Assurance**: knowledge and courtesy of employees and their ability to inspire trust and confidence

5. **Empathy**: caring, individualized attention given to customers

As you can see, there are overlaps between CAHPS and SERVQUAL. Nevertheless, items in SERVQUAL can be used to collect supplemental data on patients' opinions regarding professionalism of employees, billing accuracy, knowledge of staff, and degree of personal attention. Just like CAHPS instruments, SERVQUAL uses multiple items/ questions to tap one measure, and the ratings on the items are later aggregated for each measure. A specific adaptation of SERVQUAL for healthcare services is publicly available (Babakus & Mangold, 1992).

SERVQUAL was tested in multiple consumer samples before its publication, and has been used extensively in academic research. Although the psychometric properties of the scale are not perfect, there is a general consensus that SERVQUAL provides a comprehensive measurement of consumers' perceptions of service quality.

In summary, patients may not be able to assess the clinical quality of the care they receive, but they can voice their opinion about their experience of care. These opinions or perceptions constitute the VOC, which is often captured in standardized questionnaires. We have discussed two examples, CAHPS and SERVQUAL, but there may be others that are more useful for a particular purpose. Figure 4.5 displays the mind map for quality and the VOC.

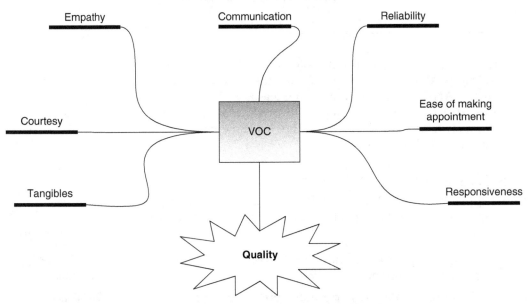

FIGURE 4.5 – Mind map for quality and VOC.

BRADLEY PARK HOSPITAL 4.2

Don, Jennifer, and Penny were sitting at the conference table looking over a drawing. "This is called the house of quality," *Don began. "In your focus groups, you outlined what the customer wants and the importance of each requirement. That is where we start. That is the voice of the customer. From patient satisfaction data, we know what we are doing well and how we compare to other clinics. You can see that our physicians are very competent in diagnosis and the clerical staff is courteous. That is a plus. But the wait times and clear communication of what the patients should do when they go home is what we need to focus on." Penny added, "And I did not know that so many chairs in the waiting room were broken."*

"Now we need to translate what the patients want using process indicators so we can use that to monitor improvements," Don continued. "Some changes may be too expensive—for example, we cannot hire twice as many doctors to see patients—we must balance our constraints with the desires of the patients. The house of quality is a good way to look at trade-offs, taking into account costs, to determine what steps should be taken to achieve our goals."

THE VOICE OF THE PROCESS (VOP)

> **◈ BOX 4.3 – WORDS OF WISDOM**
>
> "If you cannot measure it, you cannot improve it" (Lord Kelvin, n.d.).

As per the HOQ, once customers' needs have been identified, they need to be translated into objective quality measures known as *indicators* (Box 4.3). Indicators are purely quantitative; they yield actual numbers: number of patient falls, temperature, percentage of times discharge instructions were not given, and so on. In his seminal article, "Evaluating the Quality of Medical Care," Donabedian (1966), a physician and the father of quality assurance in healthcare, argued that quality indicators should measure performance along the three stages of the healthcare delivery system: input, process, and output. Accordingly, his measurement model—often called Donabedian's triad (Figure 4.6)—features three types of quality indicators: structure, process, and outcomes. This is also the way our mind map captures the VOP (Figure 4.7).

Structure

Structural indicators measure the quality of what went into the care process (input). They include facilities, equipment, human resources, managerial talent, organizational culture, and so on. For example, are the physicians trained well? Is the facility well maintained? Is the technology up-to-date and appropriate for the care of the patients served?

Structural Indicators
Refers to input measures such as facilities, equipment, and personnel.

FIGURE 4.6 – Donabedian's triad.

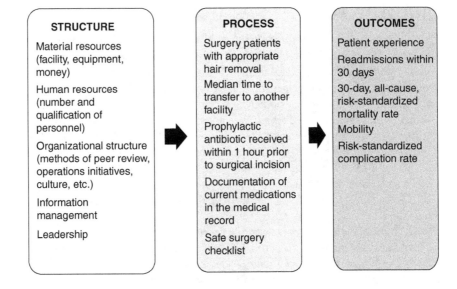

FIGURE 4.7 – Mind map for quality and VOP.

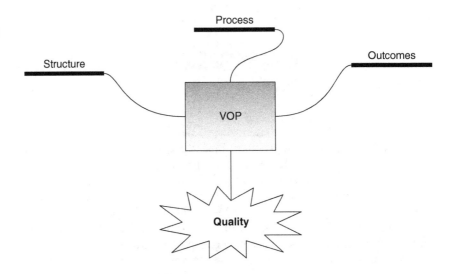

Process

Process Indicators
These are the measures of how the process is being performed.

Process indicators measure the quality of how the process is being performed. Many of the process indicators reflect whether evidence-based procedures have been followed. Are patients with diabetes getting tested to see whether their glucose level is high? Are patients with heart disease being treated with the proper medication? Has a "safe surgery" checklist been used?

Ideally, high compliance with process measures should lead to better outcomes, but it is not always the case. Indeed, the value of the indicators themselves needs to be scrutinized and the following criteria met (Chassin, Loeb, Schmaltz, & Wachter, 2010):

1. There is a strong evidence base (more than one study; mostly randomized trials) showing that the care process leads to improved outcomes.

2. The measure accurately captures whether the evidence-based care process has, in fact, been provided. This is where there is great variation in the value of measures to capture the quality of the care process. Whether aspirin was administered after an acute myocardial infarction or not ("yes/no") accurately reflects the action taken by the nurse to comply with evidence-based guidelines. However, whether a patient was given discharge instructions or not (also "yes/no") says nothing about the way this was done, that is, handing out an instruction sheet versus explaining all the steps of the discharge process and making sure the patient understands them.

3. The measure addresses a process that influences the desired outcome with only a few intervening steps. For example, properly administered medication that achieves the desired effect meets this goal. However, providing nutritional information to a patient believing that the effect will be weight loss does not.

4. Implementing the measure has little or no chance of inducing unintended, adverse consequences. For example, the practice of treating all upper respiratory infections with an antibiotic could lead to antibiotic-resistant organisms and is not good care. A quality indicator that captures the prescribing of antibiotics for a cough may therefore be inappropriate.

If process indicators meet these four criteria, they are more likely to lead to better clinical outcomes.

Outcomes

In principle, **outcome indicators** measure the end result of the care process (output). Did the patient improve? Did the patient's glucose level remain under control? Was the patient satisfied with the care experience? Although outcomes are assumed to be unambiguous and easy to determine objectively, they may not always be a reflection of the quality of care provided at the process stage. For example, a patient may die (bad outcome) while given the best possible care. Unfortunately, the patient was terminally ill, and her condition had no chance for improvement given the current state of science. Many providers have voiced their opposition to several outcomes, such as mortality rate, because they question the method for risk adjustment (Box 4.4). It is important to remember that if poor quality measures are chosen, resources are wasted. However, when good quality measures are chosen, healthcare organizations can make significant advances in the quality of patient care.

Outcome Indicators
Refers to output measures such as hospital-acquired infections, mortality, and patient satisfaction.

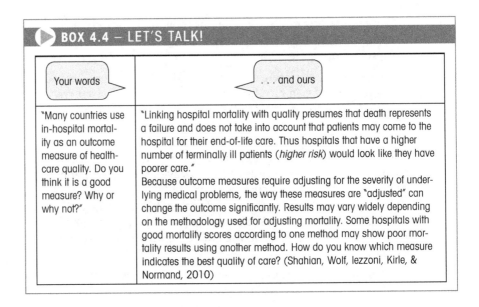

BRADLEY PARK HOSPITAL 4.3

Penny was standing at the screen explaining the house of quality to her leadership team. Sarah, the nurse manager in the surgery clinic spoke first. "This is so helpful. I had no idea that when we did not communicate clearly what the patient needed to do postoperatively that the patient would call his or her primary care physician and cause inefficiency in their clinic. I now understand how interconnected we all are and need to focus on the issues outlined. I am going back to be sure that we have clear, printed instructions with answers to the common patient questions to give to patients and their families before the surgery is done." LaQuinta, nurse manager in primary care commented, "Thanks, Sarah. And we will work on training our staff to communicate delays with patients in the waiting rooms and keeping the patients on schedule." "We all have a role in making our clinic work," Penny continued. "We can now develop specific indicators for each area and improve our processes so that patients will want to come here. Let's get back together next week and track our progress."

 Why do organizations need indicators? Why not use the exact, same measures as those used in patient surveys?

INDICATOR SELECTION AND BENCHMARKING

Besides the indicators required for reporting, there are other indicators that a provider selects to target improvement areas. A logical tool to aid in this selection process is the HOQ discussed earlier (Figure 4.3). The indicators most strongly related to customer requirements certainly demand the provider's full attention. In the BPH example, this would include duration between desired and actual appointment times, time between appointment time and physician arrival, number of call backs to clarify instructions, number of damaged chairs in waiting rooms, number of biohazard material containers not emptied each day, and number of unexpected returns for the same condition.

Benchmarking

Although it is tempting to select indicators that showcase the areas in which you excel—the *feel good* factor—it is much more productive to track indicators that highlight your weaknesses so that you can focus on improvements in areas critical to your competitiveness. **Benchmarking** is a useful tool to help you identify opportunities for improvement. Benchmarking involves comparing your organization's performance to the best organization's performance in a particular industry or a particular process in order to identify and follow best practices. The key word is "best." You are not simply gauging your performance against your competitors; rather you are evaluating yourself against the top performer in a given field. Similarly, a benchmark is not an aggregate performance target derived from averaging indicator values for multiple organizations. On the contrary, a **benchmark** is the score achieved by one organization: the leader. Indicators for which the difference between the score set by the leader and your own tends to be large are natural candidates for selection, as long as they are aligned with your strategic goals.

Benchmarking
Refers to the comparison of an organization's performance to the best in a particular industry or a particular process in order to identify and follow best practices.

Benchmark
Refers to a score achieved by the leading organization.

The Vital Few

The National Quality Forum's (2014) Measure Applications Partnership (MAP) recently created families or groups of "high impact" measures that can be used to identify areas for improvement. These families promote the use of the same measures for multiple purposes and across different external entities, thereby alleviating the measurement burden for the provider. There are 10 families of measures, and each family contains (a) a set of cross-cutting measures used in more than one family, and (b) a set of unique measures.

Chapter 2 introduced you to the concept of scorecards and dashboards. In this chapter, we focus on the quality scorecard and cascade it down to the tactical level. The quality dashboard in Table 4.4 displays the "vital few" (between 5 and 20) quality indicators, the criticality of which warrants monitoring in BPH's coronary care unit. As you can see, their performance is quite dismal, and drastic improvements are needed urgently.

The idea behind tracking quality performance with scorecards/dashboards is to identify weaknesses and performance shifts quickly and take remedial action before the situation becomes a crisis. Once a dashboard signals a problem area, several quality tools can be used to examine the problem, identify its roots, prioritize them, and therefore set the stage for improvement.

TABLE 4.4 – Quality Dashboard in the Coronary Care Unit

Measures	FYTD Actual	FY Target	Jan	Feb	Mar	Apr	May	Jun	Jul
MORTALITY	7.80%	2.93%	7.41%	10.44%	6.39%	8.43%	7.98%	7.28%	6.68%
# of deaths	71	N/A	10	11	12	10	7	12	9
# of CLABSI	20	2	2	3	3	3	3	4	2
# of CAUTIs	21	2	5	3	2	4	3	1	3
# of VAPs	11	2	2	1	2	3	0	1	2
Medication lists match	67%	100%	60%	70%	65%	62%	75%	70%	69%
PATIENT SATISFACTION (1–5)	3.0	4.5	2.9	3.2	3	2.6	3.2	3.2	3.1
Response time (min) after call button is pressed	29	5	40	34	20	35	24	31	18
Percentage of meals returned	2%	2%	3%	1%	5%	2%	1%	2%	1%

CAUTI, catheter-associated urinary tract infection; CLABSI, central line-associated bloodstream infection; FYTD, fiscal year to date; VAP, ventilator-associated pneumonia.

Note: It is common (and more accurate) to report CLABSI, CAUTI, and VAP as rates (e.g., CLABSI per 1,000 central line-days; CAUTI per 1,000 catheter-days), usually on a quarterly basis. Nevertheless, the raw frequencies per month still provide a timely snapshot of infections as they occur.

▭ RED FLAG! Needs improvement.

TOOLS

There are eight basic quality tools that an organization can use for problem solving. The following text provides a quick overview of these tools and their purposes.

Flowcharts

Flowchart
A tool that graphically represents the sequential steps of a process.

Flowcharts are graphic representations of the sequential steps of a process. At their most basic level, they include the boundaries (starting and ending points) of the process (ovals in Figure 4.8), the procedures involved in the process (rectangles), the decisions to be made (diamonds), and the flow of the process (arrows). Flowcharts are used to

- Develop process understanding
- Identify where problems occur in the process
- Document the process

In Figure 4.8, a flowchart of an ST segment evaluation myocardial infarction (STEMI) patient's transfer to the ED high-lights the inefficiency of a potentially unnecessary transfer to the ED.

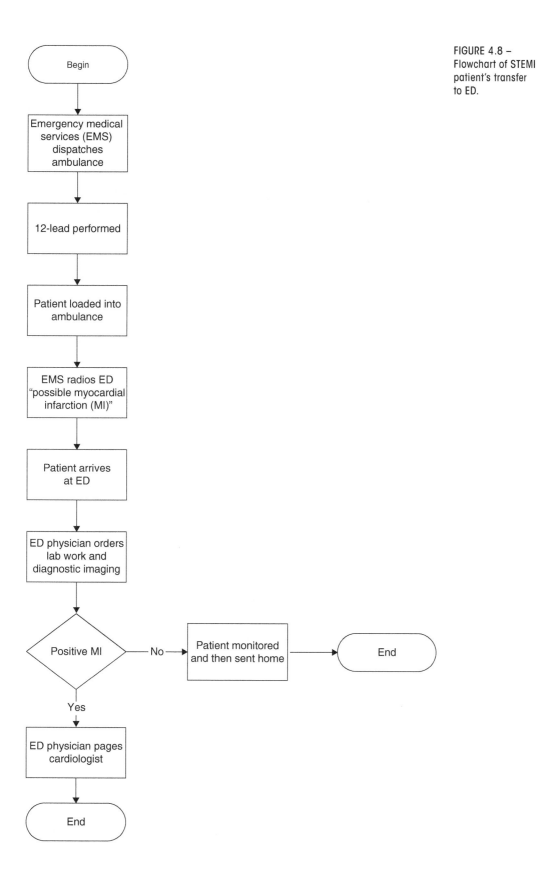

FIGURE 4.8 – Flowchart of STEMI patient's transfer to ED.

Failure Modes and Effects Analysis (FMEA)
A methodology designed to identify potential failure points in the process and to assess the relative impact of these failures.

Failure Modes and Effects Analysis

Failure modes and effects analysis is a proactive methodology designed to identify potential failure points in the process and assess the relative impact of these failures. The ultimate goal is to prioritize the steps in the process that need fixing in order to prevent serious failures (e.g., adverse events) from occurring in the first place. To maximize the chances of success, it is recommended that a subprocess rather than a very comprehensive process is chosen. For example, if one wants to review the administration of a blood thinner (Coumadin) to clinic patients who have blood clots, it might be a good idea to divide the whole process into manageable parts, such as (a) physician writes prescription, (b) pharmacist fills prescription, (c) patient takes daily dose, and so forth. Tackling one subprocess at a time would guarantee a more accurate description of the process steps and simplify the task of identifying failure points. Conducting an FMEA requires the formation of a multidisciplinary team with all the process participants. This collaborative approach discourages the "blame game" and increases the likelihood that the proposed solutions will receive broad support. The team should accomplish the following (U.S. Department of Health and Human Services, 2011):

1. Identify all steps of the process in a sequential manner. This is actually easier said than done. Even when a process is well defined and documented, there is a tendency for process participants to deviate from norms and perform steps that are unique to their way of working. For example, a nurse may call a colleague to help her with a computer problem, whereas another may call the Help Desk immediately.

2. Identify ALL (big and small; likely and unlikely) potential failures at each step of the process as well as their causes: What could go wrong and why?

3. For each failure, rate the following on a scale of 1 to 10:
   a. Likelihood of occurrence
   b. Likelihood of detection
   c. Severity

   Compute the risk priority number (RPN) by multiplying all three ratings. For example, if the likelihood of occurrence for a failure point was rated at 5, its likelihood of detection at 6, and its severity at 4, the RPN for the failure mode would be $5 \times 6 \times 4 = 120$.

4. Select the best candidates for improvement. These are usually the ones with the highest RPNs.

Ultimately, the purpose is to improve the process so that the incidence of important failures is minimized, or even eliminated. Table 4.5 provides a simplified example of an FMEA. Only one cause for failure at each step is listed, whereas there may be many potential failure points and causes at each step. In this example, you can see that educating the patient and the family on the importance and risks of Coumadin helps minimize the most critical points of failure in this analysis. A real-life use of an FMEA in an organization is featured in Box 4.5.

TABLE 4.5 – FMEA Example: Administering Coumadin (Blood Thinner) to Patients With a Blood Clot in the Leg

Process Steps	Failure Mode	Failure Causes	Failure Effects Likelihood of Occurrence (1–10)	Likelihood of Detection (1–10)	Severity (1–10)	RPN	Actions to Reduce Occurrence of Failure
MD writes order for Coumadin	Order not written	Not entered into computer	2	5	5	50	Create checking system to be sure patients with blood clot have Coumadin order
Coumadin prescription filled by pharmacist	Patient does not have prescription filled	Lack of understanding of the importance of the medication	4	8	5	160	Patient education
Patient takes daily dose	Patient misses doses	Family is not aware of need for medication	3	4	5	60	Family awareness and education
Initial response to Coumadin monitored	Patient does not come into clinic for lab test	Patient forgot appointment	3	10	5	150	Appointment reminders
Coumadin continued and dose adjusted according to lab test	Patient does not continue monitoring	Lack of understanding of the importance of medication	4	8	7	224	Patient and family education

RPN, risk priority number.

✚ BOX 4.5 – OM IN PRACTICE!

FMEA Analysis at SUNY Downstate Medical Center

From May 2012 through March 2013, SUNY Downstate Medical Center used an FMEA analysis to help identify potential causes of patient falls within their organization. Although the medical center compared favorably to national benchmarks, the nursing department assembled an interdisciplinary team and used this tool to identify areas where the quality of care was not optimal. As with many clinical challenges, there was no single easy answer to the challenges posed by patient falls.

The team analyzed the data, searched for the best evidence-based practices, learned from colleagues' successes, eliminated ineffective practices, and disseminated enhanced outcomes across the organization to reduce patient falls.

Their FMEA program and analysis can be accessed online: www.downstate.edu/patientsafety/FMEA_2012_Fall_Prevention.pdf

Spaghetti Diagrams

Spaghetti Diagram
A graph that depicts traffic intensity and patterns within an area or across areas. It helps visualize where movements are wasted.

Spaghetti diagrams are used mostly to redesign layouts. They depict traffic intensity and patterns within an area or across areas and help visualize where movements are wasted. In Figure 4.9, you can see that there is substantial traffic between the labs and the computer area, and between the labs and the reception area, where specimens are delivered. It would be logical to place computers inside each lab to avoid delays, fatigue, and overall inefficiency. If building constraints allow it, it would also make sense to have the reception area recede from the exterior wall and closer to both labs.

In order to develop a spaghetti diagram, you need to perform the following tasks:

1. Determine what you want to observe: patients, supplies, staff, paperwork, and so on. If you want to observe several units at the same time, simply use different colors.

2. Draw the layout of the area under study.

3. Follow the unit(s) you are observing and draw the flow of their movements through the area.

4. Identify locations between which there is repeated traffic and make sure that they are located close to one another.

Checksheets

Checksheet
A fact-finding table used to record problem occurrences and organize them by category.

Checksheets provide an easy way to record problem occurrences and organize them by category. They are fact-finding tools that enable identification of critical problem issues. As an example, there may be many problems occurring in the ED, and if you ask the staff, they will

FIGURE 4.9 –
Spaghetti diagram
in pathology lab.

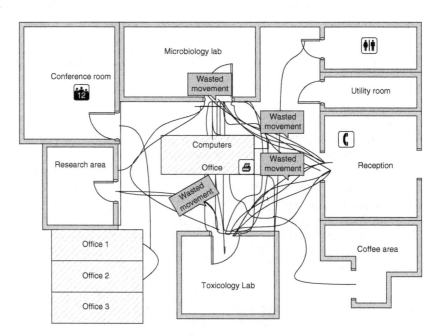

say that the problems affecting their own work are the most urgent ones that need immediate corrective action. These might be *guesses* rather than *facts*. Based on the checksheet presented in Figure 4.10, it can be established as a fact that of all the problems plaguing the ED, *patients leaving without being seen*, with 11 occurrences during the data-collection period, is the most prevalent one. To gather more data about this problem, the staff may want to develop a checksheet that organizes the occurrences per shift (day, evening, night) or even per hour (8:00–9:00 a.m., 9:01–10:00 a.m., 10:01–11:00 a.m., etc.). This might enable them to identify a specific pattern for these events and identify viable solutions more quickly.

Problem	Number of Occurrences	Total
Missing supplies in exam room	✓✓✓✓	4
Patients leaving without being seen	✓✓✓✓✓✓✓✓✓✓✓	11
Soiled linen	✓✓✓	3
Late lab results	✓✓✓✓✓	5
Malfunctioning blood pressure monitors	✓✓	2

FIGURE 4.10 – Checksheet.

Cause-and-Effect Diagrams

Cause-and-effect diagrams, also called fishbone (see shape) or Ishikawa diagrams, are commonly used in root cause analyses and display the potential sources of quality problems. The quality problems are the "effects" of the causes and are depicted by the "head of the fish" in the diagram. The causes are represented by the "bones" and typically fall into six major categories:

Cause-and-Effect Diagram
A tool used in root cause analyses to display the potential sources of quality problems.

1. **People:** the people involved in the process
2. **Materials:** the raw materials, parts, and supplies needed to produce the good or provide the service
3. **Methods:** the methods, approaches, practices, systems, and procedures used to perform the process
4. **Measurement:** the data collected to assess process quality
5. **Environment:** the nature of the surroundings (e.g., temperature, humidity, noise levels, lighting) in which the process is performed
6. **Equipment:** the machines, computers, tools, devices, and instruments used to perform the process

When developing a cause-and-effect diagram, all the individuals involved in various stages of the process should voice their opinions about the potential causes of a given problem. This plurality of opinions is instrumental in effective problem solving. The development of the diagram involves multiple phases:

- Identify the problem clearly.
- List the causes that have the most influence on the problem.
- Brainstorm to identify the "causes of the causes," that is, the secondary branches on the diagram. A useful supplemental tool that can be used at this stage is the "5 Whys," a Six Sigma technique (see Chapter 6) that drills down to the root causes. Why was the staff unfriendly? Because they are too busy? Why are they too busy? Because there is not enough capacity? Why is there insufficient capacity? Because of recent budget cuts . . .

Not all categories of causes are always relevant to a particular process. In the example provided in Figure 4.11, the problem-solving team seems to have determined that materials, equipment, and measurement factors did not contribute to patients leaving the ED. Nevertheless, many other causes in the process/methods, people, and environment categories have emerged as potential drivers of patients leaving without being seen. Because of limited time and resources, it is important to uncover the one or two factors that have the strongest influence on the problem. This is accomplished with the development of a Pareto chart.

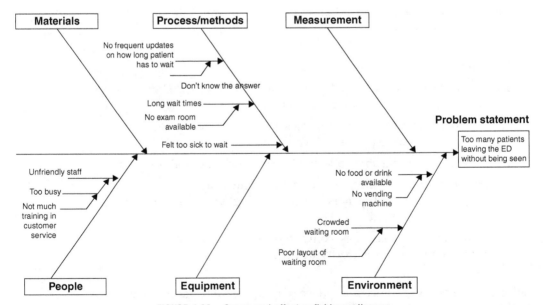

FIGURE 4.11 – Cause-and-effect or fishbone diagram.

Pareto Charts

Pareto charts get their name from Vilfredo Pareto, the Italian engineer and economist who observed that 20% of the population owned 80% of the wealth in Italy at the end of the 19th century. This 80/20 rule was later extended to quality management. It means that 80% of the effects come from 20% of the causes. In other words, there are very few ($\approx 20\%$) causes that account for the majority ($\approx 80\%$) of a problem's occurrences. The Pareto chart is used to identify these "vital few" causes and, therefore, facilitate prioritization. In order to construct a Pareto chart, the following steps need to be followed:

Pareto Chart
A chart that identifies the few causes responsible for the majority of the problems in a situation.

1. Determine the problem's frequency of occurrence (Table 4.6) resulting from the most influential causes. This is similar to the checksheet discussed earlier.

2. If necessary, relist the causes so that their contributions to the problem's frequency of occurrence are in descending order.

3. Compute the relative importance (percentages) of each cause as a contributing factor to the problem.

4. Compute the cumulative percentages.

5. Develop the Pareto chart. It is a bar graph that displays the relative frequencies of occurrence (percentages) and a line graph that represents the cumulative percentage. The line/curve usually has a steep incline reflecting that there are usually only a few strong influences on the problem, followed by a plateau, suggesting the diminished importance of the other factors. Figure 4.12 underscores the importance of "no frequent updates" and "long wait times" as the primary causes for patients leaving the ED without being seen.

Control Charts

Control charts depict the behavior of a process through continuous tracking of performance indicators, such as wait time, postoperative mortality rate, and percentage of noncompliance with a given protocol.

Control Chart
A chart that depicts the behavior of a process through continuous tracking of indicators.

TABLE 4.6 – Occurrences of the Various Causes			
Cause	Number of Occurrences	Percentage	Cumulative Percentage
No frequent updates	150	43.0	43.0
Long wait times	120	34.4	77.4
Crowded waiting room	36	10.3	87.7
Felt too sick to wait	25	7.1	94.8
Unfriendly staff	10	2.9	97.7
No food or drink available	8	2.3	100
Total	349	100	

FIGURE 4.12 – Pareto chart.

Patients who left without being seen (LWBS).

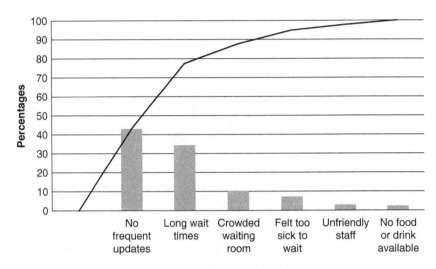

Indicators are random variables, but their variation follows a pattern called a *distribution*. On a control chart, the limits of the distribution are represented by a top line, the upper control limit (UCL), and a bottom line, the lower control limit (LCL). The centerline is simply the average or mean of the distribution (Figure 4.13). Systematic and continuous measurements of the indicators are plotted on the control chart to ascertain that the process is still behaving as expected, that is, the indicator values fall within the distribution limits and there is no detectable pattern suggesting nonrandomness. In case of nonrandomness, the assignable cause of variation is removed so that the process can "go back to normal."

FIGURE 4.13 – Control chart.

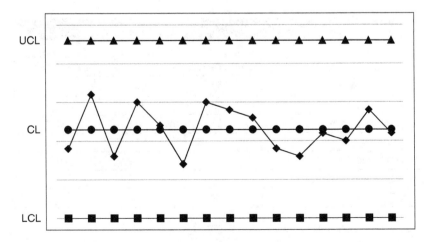

Run Charts

Run charts simply track the values of an indicator over time, again to see whether any patterns emerge. They are a powerful visual tool that also have the advantage of being easy to construct and understand. In Figure 4.14, you can see that over a period of a year, the number of patient falls has followed a steadily decreasing trend.

Run Chart
A chart that tracks the value of an indicator over time to see whether patterns emerge.

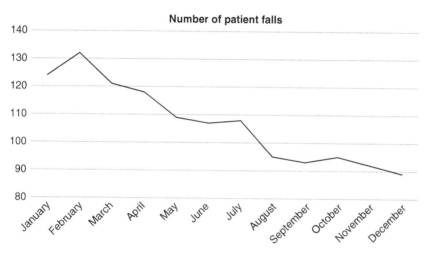

FIGURE 4.14 – Run chart.

TOTAL QUALITY MANAGEMENT

Quality must permeate all areas of the healthcare value chain. This managerial philosophy is commonly known as *total quality management* (TQM). The three major principles of TQM underscore what is meant by "total." The first principle is a commitment to provide customers with total satisfaction by exceeding their expectations. The second principle requires that all members of the value chain share this commitment. In other words, quality is the responsibility of suppliers, schedulers, physicians, vice presidents, chief executive officers, nurses, cooks, janitors, and so on. The third principle advocates a never-ending journey focused on continuous improvement. The relentless pursuit of perfect quality becomes an integral part of the organizational culture.

Deming's Wheel

TQM's orientation is definitely long term as incremental improvements are sought continuously. This approach is best illustrated by the plan–do–check–act (PDCA) cycle, also known as *Deming's wheel*. As shown in Figure 4.15, four stages make up the PDCA cycle:

1. **Plan.** Carefully select the process that needs improvement. Then develop a deeper understanding of the process by collecting data. Based on the data analysis, formulate a plan for improvement that includes performance measures.

2.   **Do.** Implement the improvement on a limited scale. During this phase, do not forget to collect data on the performance of the improved process.

3.   **Check.** Analyze the data collected during the Do phase and check whether the improvement has yielded the results anticipated in the Plan phase. If the results are negative, go back to the Plan phase and modify the improvement. If they are positive, proceed to the next phase.

4.   **Act.** Make the improved process the new standard and deploy it on a larger scale. During this phase, make sure that everyone involved in the process understands its new dynamics, and provide training on the new methods if necessary.

Is the process perfect? Certainly not! It is therefore time to plan the next improvement and repeat the cycle.

FIGURE 4.15 –
Deming's wheel.

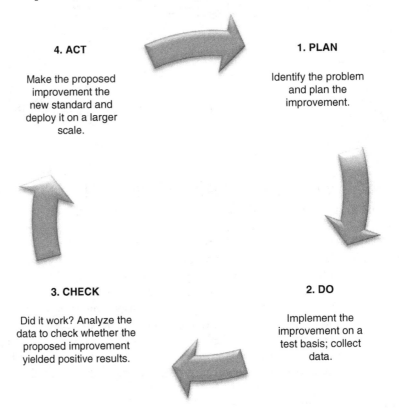

4. ACT

Make the proposed improvement the new standard and deploy it on a larger scale.

1. PLAN

Identify the problem and plan the improvement.

3. CHECK

Did it work? Analyze the data to check whether the proposed improvement yielded positive results.

2. DO

Implement the improvement on a test basis; collect data.

Deming's 14 Points

In 1984, the navy was one of the first adopters of TQM principles in the United States. It had asked researchers to evaluate some of its operations and make recommendations for improved performance. The researchers proposed TQM and Deming's works (Box 4.6). Deming's (1982) 14 points embody his ideas about quality. They emphasize the three principles of TQM as well as the importance of human capital development to its success.

⊕ **BOX 4.6 – DID YOU KNOW?**

W. Edwards Deming: Use of Statistical Methods to Help Rebuild Japan

After being raised in Cody, Wyoming, Deming (October 14, 1900–December 20, 1993) graduated with a bachelor's degree in engineering from the University of Wyoming, a master's degree in physics and mathematics from the University of Colorado, and a doctoral degree in mathematical physics from Yale. He applied statistical methods to search for knowledge. He is widely credited with initiating the TQM movement and resurrecting Japan's industrial complex after World War II (WWII).

In 1947, Deming was called by the supreme commander for the Allied Powers to help Japan study the nutritional and housing issues in the devastation after the war. His work over the ensuing years led to improved production in Japan. He was widely appreciated and recognized there for using statistical theory in the areas of consumer research, product design, and production to foster continuous improvement. His work provided the Japanese industry with the perspectives and methods to ascend as an economic power after WWII.

Despite his impressive career and recognition in Japan, it was not until the 1980s that Deming's work was appreciated by the people and companies in the United States. In June of 1980, NBC's documentary highlighted his work in "If Japan Can, Why Can't We?" After 30 years of practice in Japan, his methods came to the United States, and the TQM movement began. The core to TQM is outlined in Deming's 14 points on quality management, as presented in his classic book, *Out of Crisis* (1982). These management practices to improve quality and productivity remain at the epicenter of OM.

Deming was certainly a visionary whose teachings tend to be viewed as universal as their relevance transcends industry and geographic boundaries. Here is a list of the recognition he received for his substantial and various contributions.

- 1951: The Union of Japanese Scientists and Engineers (JUSE) established the Deming Prize.
- 1955: Was awarded the Shewhart Medal by the American Society for Quality Control (ASQC)
- 1960: Awarded the Second Order Medal of the Sacred Treasure by Emperor Hirohito
- 1983: Received the Taylor Key award from the American Management Association and the Samuel S. Wilks Award from the American Statistical Association
- 1986: Inducted into the Science and Technology Hall of Fame; received the Distinguished Career in Science award from the National Academy of Sciences
- 1987: Awarded the National Medal of Technology
- 1991: Inducted into the Automotive Hall of Fame
- 1992: Nominated for the Nobel Prize

Point #1: Create Constancy of Purpose Toward Improvement

This point underscores the importance of instituting a culture of continuous improvement to become or remain competitive.

Point #2: Adopt the New Philosophy

Leadership must rise to the challenge of letting go of the old ways and embrace change for improvement.

Point #3: Cease Dependence on Inspection to Achieve Quality

This point highlights the need for productive systems that focus on prevention rather than correction of defects or errors (see IOM's recommendation in the introductory section of this chapter). Inspections are basically needed because errors are made. If one could develop a system that makes it difficult for the most serious errors to occur, patient safety would improve greatly, and the scarce resources now consumed with error detection and correction would be utilized more efficiently (Box 4.7).

⊕ BOX 4.7 – DID YOU KNOW?

The Costs of Quality

There are four categories of costs associated with quality: (a) prevention costs, (b) appraisal costs, (c) internal failure costs, and (d) external failure costs.

Prevention costs are associated with decreasing the likelihood of making errors in the first place. They include training programs, process improvement efforts (e.g., collecting patient information, process analysis, process redesign), and maintenance of records and quality data.

Appraisal costs refer to evaluating the quality of products or services. They include the costs of conducting inspections or audits. Appraisal does not prevent errors from occurring, but it is to be hoped that, it will help identify them and correct them before the customer of the process is affected.

Internal failure costs are the costs of fixing the errors before the customer is affected. They include the costs of rework to correct the errors, of outdated supplies that must be discarded, and of downtime caused by failures in the process (e.g., malfunctioning equipment).

External failure costs are the costs of errors that affect the customer. They include customer complaints, readmissions, litigation, and loss of customers.

Point #4: End the Practice of Awarding Business on the Basis of Price Tag Alone

This point emphasizes abandoning the practice of switching from one vendor to another while pursuing the lowest possible price. Instead,

Deming advocated the selection of few suppliers based on their ability to deliver quality products and supplies consistently.

Point #5: Improve Constantly and Forever the System of Production and Service

As perfection does not exist, the pursuit of perfect quality is a never-ending journey. Seeking this perfection throughout the organization results in an overall decrease in costs associated with poor quality (e.g., rework, scrap, lost productivity; see Box 4.7).

Point #6: Institute Training

All employees must be trained to use the methods, tools, and techniques that help them achieve a higher quality output in their jobs.

Point #7: Institute Leadership

Because lives are at stake, good leadership is especially critical to a healthcare organization's success. The Joint Commission, a major healthcare accreditor, likens a healthcare organization to a watch (The Governance Institute, 2009). A watchmaker could gather the best components in the world and put them together, but the resulting watch would be unlikely to run. The individual components, although necessary, are not enough. It is how the components work together that creates a quality watch. In other words, healthcare organizations must be appreciated as a system, the components of which work together to provide high-quality care. Thus, when we talk of leadership in healthcare, it implies that the many leaders within the organization (the governing body, the chief executive and other senior leaders, and the leaders of the licensed independent practitioners) work well together to formulate and implement their shared vision of success.

Point #8: Drive Out Fear

Perfecting quality requires some experimentation with new concepts and processes. As a result, mistakes will be made. Penalizing workers for these mistakes is essentially guaranteeing that they will never try again. They will avoid improvement rather than seek it.

Point #9: Break Down Barriers Between Departments

As discussed in Chapter 1, a major problem of the U.S. healthcare system is fragmentation. This fragmentation is the result of an organizational structure that emphasizes silos rather than team collaboration. Collaboration across departments and units reduces the errors and inefficiencies resulting from a lack of communication and overall system perspective.

Point #10: Eliminate Slogans Asking for Zero Defects and Unattainable Productivity

Setting lofty goals that seem out of reach for the employees will only contribute to poor morale and adversarial relationships. Rather, it is important to set reasonable goals that will allow employees to feel pride once they attain them. Over time, these goals or targets will be revised to set higher standards, but again, meeting the new expectations must be perceived as achievable.

Point #11: Eliminate the Emphasis on Numerical Quotas

The piece-rate system of yesteryear often sacrificed quality for quantity. Point #11 does not call for the elimination of reasonable quotas. Rather, it urges supervisors and leaders to stop relying heavily on those for performance evaluations. Physicians could see a very large number of patients if they spent very little time with them. This might lead the physicians to overlook important symptoms and misdiagnose. The poor quality of care and deficient physician–patient interaction would threaten not only patient safety but also patient satisfaction. At the other extreme, a physician could extend the exam time beyond what is necessary, which would then hurt the bottom line because of low volume and make it difficult for patients to schedule timely appointments. Therefore, point #11 implies balance. A certain numerical target may be set, but it should never jeopardize quality.

Point #12: Remove Barriers That Rob People of Pride of Workmanship

This point is related to the previous one. Numerical goals that prevent employees from doing their jobs well and enjoying the pride of fully exercising their skills must be eradicated. These goals should be replaced with a system that emphasizes problem solving and the delivery of a superior product or service.

Point #13: Institute a Vigorous Program of Education and Self-Improvement

Deming recognized the importance of training and professional development. He viewed self-improvement as a driver of quality improvements throughout the organization.

Point #14: Put Everybody in the Company to Work to Accomplish the Transformation

Culture
Refers to the basic set of values, assumptions, and beliefs in an organization.

Point #14 stresses that quality becomes everyone's purpose and part of everyone's job. In other words, quality is engrained in the organizational culture. **Culture**, or the basic set of values, assumptions, and beliefs in an organization, is what guides people when no one is looking. A healthcare organization's culture reflects the beliefs, attitudes, and priorities of the staff, including physicians and leadership. When quality is approached as a set of values, as a general orientation, and an organizational ideology, there evolves a new style of working and thinking (Cameron & Sine, 1999).

Deming's 14 points have passed the test of time across industries. As shown in Box 4.8, constancy of purpose, a shared commitment to quality, strong leadership, and measurement have contributed to increased quality of care and patient safety. Regarding the importance of measurement, let us not forget that Deming was a statistician who urged the use of statistical process control (SPC) in improvement efforts. SPC is therefore the topic of the next chapter.

⊕ BOX 4.8 – DID YOU KNOW?

In a study of 79 academic medical centers, Keroack et al. (2007) found five themes associated with measurable differences in quality and safety:

1. A shared sense of purpose: Leaders articulated that "patients first" was the primary goal.
2. Leadership style: Leaders were passionate about quality and had an "authentic, hands-on" style.
3. Accountability system for quality, safety, and service: Strategic priorities and measures of success were developed and leaders were accountable for their achievement.
4. A focus on results: Leaders were relentless in their efforts to improve and measure their results.
5. Collaboration: Leaders recognized that contributions at every level within the organization were important.

SUMMARY

In this chapter, you learned that the customers of a process define the meaning of quality. This is the voice of the customer. The VOC reflects opinions and perceptions regarding the service provided. The house of quality helps ensure that the VOC remains heard by providing a framework that "translates" customer requirements into process characteristics or quality indicators, that is, the voice of the process. As opposed to the VOC, which reflects opinions and perceptions, the VOP is a set of objective measures capturing the quality of the inputs (structure), processes, and outputs (outcomes) of healthcare delivery.

Numerous tools are available to aid healthcare professionals in quality problem solving. These tools help identify problems, find their causes, and prioritize improvement efforts. They are widely used in organizations that have adopted total quality management in their endless search for perfect quality. With his pragmatic approach to problem solving, Deming greatly advanced our knowledge of TQM and disseminated its adoption across industries. In the next three chapters, you learn how to track quality performance with statistical process control (Chapter 5) and how to apply various methodologies to improve that performance (Chapters 6 and 7; Figure 4.16).

FIGURE 4.16 –
Mind map linking
indicators to other
quality concepts and
delivery.

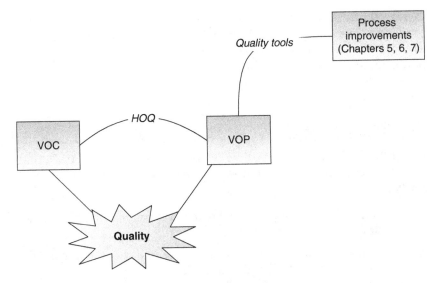

Although the quality competitive priority was showcased in this chapter, it overlaps with other competitive priorities. Deming's points #3 and #5 clearly link quality to appraisal and failure costs. Preventing errors from happening in the first place speeds up delivery as no time is wasted on excessive appraisals and corrections. Point #9 emphasizes the reduction or even elimination of fragmentation known to create errors, excess costs, and delays in healthcare. The connections among the competitive priorities are depicted in Figure 4.17.

FIGURE 4.17 – Mind
map linking TQM to
the other competitive
priorities.

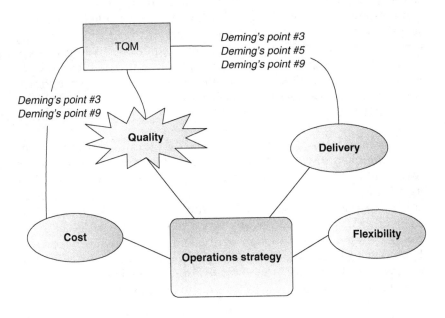

KEY TERMS

"Next process" concept	Responsiveness	Failure modes and effects analysis
Quality function deployment	Assurance	Spaghetti diagram
House of quality	Empathy	Checksheet
Voice of customer	Structural indicators	Cause-and-effect diagram
Voice of process	Process indicators	Pareto chart
Indicators	Outcome indicators	Control chart
Top-box score	Benchmarking	Run chart
Tangibles	Benchmark	Culture
Reliability	Flowchart	

TOOLS USED IN THIS CHAPTER

TOOL	PURPOSE
House of quality (HOQ)	Matrix that clearly depicts the relationship between the VOC and the VOP
Flowchart	Graphic representation of the sequential steps of a process
Checksheet	Fact-finding tool that tracks occurrences and organizes the issues by category to identify critical problem areas
Failure modes and effects analysis (FMEA)	Technique designed to identify potential failure points in a process and to assess the relative impact of these failures
Spaghetti diagram	Diagram that depicts traffic intensity and patterns within an area to help redesign layouts
Cause-and-effect diagram (fishbone diagram)	Diagram that displays potential sources of quality problems

TOOL	PURPOSE
Pareto chart	Visual display of prioritized causes (or problems) based on the 80/20 rule
Control chart	Chart that depicts the behavior of a process through continuous tracking of performance with upper and lower control limits displayed
Run chart	Chart that tracks values of an indicator over time to detect emerging patterns
Plan–do–check–act (PDCA) cycle	Continuous-improvement cycle

WHAT DO YOU REMEMBER?

1. The U.S. Department of Health and Human Services' first National Quality Strategy specifies three aims for quality improvement. What are they?

2. Differentiate among the quality expectations of patients, providers, and third-party payers?

3. What is value-based purchasing?

4. What is quality function deployment? What is the house of quality?

5. What are the seven steps involved in building the HOQ?

6. What is the VOC?

7. What is the VOP?

8. What is a quality indicator?

9. In Box 4.2, you learned about quality function deployment at De Grift. Review their process indicators. Which indicators appear to be the strongest in capturing customers' requirements? Which ones appear to be the weakest?

10. Describe Donabedian's triad.

11. What is the difference between a benchmark and benchmarking?

12. What are the definition and purpose of each one of the following tools?

    a. Flowchart

    b. Checksheet

    c. FMEA

    d. Spaghetti diagram

    e. Cause-and-effect diagram

    f.   Pareto chart

    g.   Control chart

    h.   Run chart

13. What are the three principles of TQM?

14. Describe Deming's wheel. How is it associated with continuous improvement?

15. Select three of Deming's 14 points and describe them.

SOLVE BPH'S PROBLEMS

1. One of the surgeons at BPH would like to complement the CAHPS survey with some additional measures pertaining to responsiveness. Generate a few questions that would tap this dimension of patient experience.

2. Assume there are two quality indicators: (a) percentage of cases when aspirin was administered after a myocardial infarction, and (b) percentage of patients who received discharge instructions. Which one is a better indicator of quality? Why?

3. Several of the pharmacists are brainstorming to develop process indicators to measure responsiveness. They have solicited your help for this task. Help them develop such indicators.

4. Following a survey of the clinical staff, the director of supply chain management is trying to translate customer requirements into process characteristics. Help him accomplish this task based on the following data:

Clinical Staff's Requirement	Importance Rating (1–5)
Supplies are available when needed	5
Different package sizes are available for latex gloves	2
Placing orders is quick and easy	4
Charging for identical supplies is equitable across departments	4

5. Based on the following relationship matrix, compute the importance weights.

Customer requirement	Importance	Indicators						
		1	2	3	4	5	6	7
A	4	●	○		●			
B	5		●			◁	●	
C	5	●		◁				○
D	3				●			

(continued)

(continued)

Customer requirement	Importance	Indicators						
E	2		○			△		●
F	3	△		△				●
Importance weights		?	?	?	?	?	?	?

6. Identify causes of a steady increase of supply shortages in the exam room. Classify these causes into the categories of people, methods, measurement, environment, equipment, and materials categories, and develop a cause-and-effect diagram.

7. Looking at a cause-and-effect diagram, the head of the radiology department identified reasons for long wait times (see table that follows). She wants to prioritize the factors that contribute to the problem. Her staff collected data on the frequency with which these causes contribute to long wait times over a period of a month. Based on these data, develop a Pareto chart and identify the cause(s) that require(s) immediate intervention.

Cause	Frequency of Occurrence
Patients scheduled too close together	536
Procedures that take too long	165
Patients not released on time from floor	314
Retakes on x-rays too frequent	130
Equipment inadequate for complex cases	97

8. At the hospital cafeteria, typical complaints about the food are: too salty, too mushy, too bland, too greasy, and too starchy. The manager of the cafeteria has compiled the following complaint data during the past month. Develop a Pareto chart and help him decide which problem(s) deserve(s) his immediate attention.

Complaint Type	Frequency
Too salty	60
Too mushy	210
Too bland	308
Too greasy	162
Too starchy	52

9. Develop a checksheet and Pareto diagram for the following complaints regarding patients' bills:

No.	Problem	No.	Problem	No.	Problem
1	Patient never received it	12	Patient charged for services not provided	23	Total amount is inaccurate
2	Patient charged for services not provided	13	Filed late with insurer	24	Patient never received it
3	Total amount is inaccurate	14	Filed late with insurer	25	Patient charged for services not provided
4	Patient charged for services not provided	15	Total amount is inaccurate	26	Received late
5	Patient never received it	16	Patient charged for services not provided	27	Patient charged for services not provided
6	Received late	17	Filed late with insurer	28	Total amount is inaccurate
7	Filed late with insurer	18	Total amount is inaccurate	29	Patient charged for services not provided
8	Filed late with insurer	19	Patient charged for services not provided	30	Filed late with insurer
9	Patient charged for services not provided	20	Filed late with insurer	31	Received late
10	Filed late with insurer	21	Received late	32	Patient charged for services not provided
11	Received late	22	Filed late with insurer	33	Filed late with insurer

10. This is the layout of a nurses' station. Based on this information regarding traffic, draw a spaghetti diagram and make recommendations for improvement.

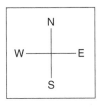

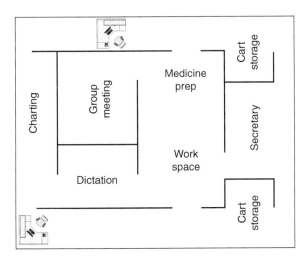

Number of trips per day

From \ To	Workstations on North wall	Workstations on South wall	Group meeting	Dictation	Charting	Medicine prep	Cart storage (North side)	Cart storage (South side)	Work space	Secretary
Workstations on North wall		30	4	10	150	100	80	10	90	30
Workstations on South wall			4	15	180	120	20	90	10	60
Group meeting				2	—	—	—	—	—	10
Dictation					—	—	—	—	10	60
Charting						60	20	10	30	25
Medicine prep							50	60	20	—
Cart storage (North side)								50	30	—
Cart storage (South side)									25	—
Work space										25
Secretary										—

11. The table here presents failure modes, causes, and effects for each process step involved in scheduling appointments at BPH's pediatrics clinic. Estimate the likelihood of occurrence of each failure mode, its likelihood of detection, and its severity. Compute the RPN for each step and for the entire process.

Steps	Failure Mode	Failure Causes	Failure Effects	Likelihood of Occurrence (1–10)	Likelihood of Detection (1–10)	Severity (1–10)	RPN
Patient calls pediatrics clinic	Talks to someone in pharmacy who transfers patient to pediatrics	Almost identical phone numbers	Staff at pharmacy gets annoyed				
Patient listens to automatic recording and chooses appropriate option	Patient often selects wrong option or hangs up	There are nine options to select from; patient stops paying attention or gets impatient	Poor satisfaction scores and/or possible loss of revenue				
Patient is transferred to central scheduling and is put on hold	Patient hangs up	Long wait times	Poor satisfaction scores and/or possible loss of revenue				
Scheduler finds patient's name and insurance information in system	Wrong patient is found	Some names are misspelled; there are sometimes duplicate Social Security numbers	Long time to "sort things out," find the right patient, and correct the patient info				
Scheduler asks for physician's name and reason for appointment and then selects visit type	Wrong visit type is selected	Discrepancy between patient's description of reason and scheduler's interpretation	Patient's condition may require a longer visit than the one scheduled; physician has to play "catch up" with other patients				
Scheduler reviews scheduling instructions for selected visit type and physician	Scheduler skips that step	The descriptions of visit types differ from one physician to the next, which makes the review a lengthy process	Wrong type of visit is scheduled; physician is dissatisfied; billing issues				
Appointment is scheduled	Patient does not show up	No reminder is sent	Loss of revenue				

12. Regarding question 11, identify actions to improve each step and reduce the occurrence of failure.

THINK OUTSIDE THE BOOK!

1. In this book, we used the term "third-party" payer. Who are the first and second parties?

2. Translate the VOC into VOP! Download the HCAHPS survey from the CMS website (www.hcahpsonline.org/surveyinstrument.aspx) and develop an indicator for each questionnaire item.

3. Select three scholarly articles discussing the reliability and/or validity of HCAHPS. What are the instrument's strengths and weaknesses?

4. Go to the Institute for Healthcare Improvement website (www.ihi.org/resources/Pages/Tools/FailureModesEffects AnalysisComparisonFiveMedicationDispensingScenarios .aspx) and download the sample FMEA tool comparing five medication dispensing scenarios. Choose one of the scenarios and develop a fishbone diagram. Hint: The problem is "medication error"; look at some of the failure causes and categorize them in terms of people, materials, methods, measurement, environment, and equipment.

5. Go to data.medicare.gov/data/hospital-compare and compare providers in your market. Which one would you choose and why? Do you think the data are relevant to all patients? Why or why not?

6. Look at the quality dashboard (see Table 4.4). Can you identify other quality indicators that would be appropriate?

REFERENCES

Agency for Healthcare Research and Quality. (2014). The CAHPS program. Retrieved from https://cahps.ahrq.gov/about-cahps/cahps-program/index.html

Agency for Healthcare Research and Quality. (2015). The national quality strategy. Retrieved from http://www.ahrq.gov/workingforquality

Babakus, E., & Mangold, W. G. (1992). Adapting the SERVQUAL scale to hospital services: An empirical investigation. *Health Services Research, 26*(6), 767–786.

Cameron, K., & Sine, W. (1999). A framework for organizational quality culture. *Quality Management Journal, 6*(4), 7–25.

Chassin, M. R., Loeb, J. M., Schmaltz, S. P., & Wachter, R. M. (2010). Accountability measures—Using measurement to promote quality improvement. *New England Journal of Medicine, 363*(7), 683–688.

Clancy, C. M. (2009). *What is health care quality and who decides?* Washington, DC: Committee on Finance, Subcommittee on Health Care, United States Senate. Retrieved from http://www.hhs.gov/asl/testify/2009/03/t20090318b.html

Deming, W. E. (1982). *Out of the crisis.* Cambridge, MA: The MIT Press.

Dijkstra, L., & van der Bij, H. (2002). Quality function deployment in healthcare: Methods for meeting customer requirements in redesign and renewal. *International Journal of Quality & Reliability Management, 19*(1), 67–89.

Donabedian, A. (1966). Evaluating the quality of medical care. *Milbank Memorial Fund Quarterly, 44*(3), 166–206.

Institute of Medicine. (1999). *To err is human*. Washington, DC: National Academies Press.

Institute of Medicine. (2001). *Crossing the quality chasm: A new health system for the 21st century*. Washington, DC: Author.

Keroack, M. A., Youngberg, B. J., Cerese, J. L., Krsek, C., Prellwitz, L. W., & Trevelyan, E. W. (2007). Organizational factors associated with high performance in quality and safety in academic medical centers. *Academic Medicine, 82*(12), 1178–1186.

Lord Kelvin. (n.d.). Lord Kelvin quotations. Retrieved from http://zapatopi.net/kelvin/quotes

National Quality Forum. (2014). *Finding common ground for healthcare priorities: Families of measures for assessing affordability, population health, and person-and family-centered care*. Washington, DC: Author.

Parasuraman, A., Berry, L. L., & Zeithaml, V. A. (1991). Refinement and reassessment of the SERVQUAL scale. *Journal of Retailing, 67*(4), 420–450.

Russell, R. S., & Taylor, B. W. (2014). *Operations and supply chain management* (8th ed.). Hoboken, NJ: John Wiley & Sons.

Shahian, D. M., Wolf, R. E., Iezzoni, L. I., Kirle, L., & Normand, S.-L. T. (2010). Variability in the measurement of hospital-wide mortality rates. *New England Journal of Medicine, 363*(26), 2530–2539.

The Governance Institute. (2009). *Leadership in healthcare organizations: A guide to joint commission leadership standards*. San Diego, CA: Author.

U.S. Department of Health and Human Services. (2011). *Report to congress: National strategy for quality improvement in health care*. Rockville, MD: Author.

U.S. Department of Health and Human Services. (2013a). *2013 annual progress report to congress: National strategy for quality improvement in health care*. Rockville, MD: Agency for Healthcare Research and Quality.

U.S. Department of Health and Human Services. (2013b). Hospital value-based purchasing program. *Medical Learning Network*. Retrieved from http://www.cms.gov/Outreach-and-Education/Medicare-Learning-Network-MLN/MLNProducts/downloads/Hospital_VBPurchasing_Fact_Sheet_ICN907664.pdf

VanLare, J. M., & Conway, P. H. (2012). Value-based purchasing—National programs to move from volume to value. *New England Journal of Medicine, 367*(4), 292–295.

White House. (2010). Health care that works for Americans. Retrieved from http://www.whitehouse.gov/healthreform/healthcare-overview #healthcare-menu

Young, P. L., Olsen, L., & McGinnis, J. (2010). *Value in health care: Accounting for cost, quality, safety, outcomes, and innovation.* Washington, DC: Institute of Medicine.

CHAPTER 5

STATISTICAL PROCESS CONTROL

BRADLEY PARK HOSPITAL 5.1

The quality office that Jennifer directed was receiving requests for improvement projects almost daily. Now that Jennifer had a better understanding of some of the issues that Bradley Park Hospital (BPH) was facing, she needed to find appropriate management tools to measure and monitor their efforts. She knew that everyone in the organization was watching her, and she needed to show everyone at BPH that she could help make meaningful change.

As she was contemplating this early one morning, she received a text message. The message indicated that the emergency department (ED) was on diversion. This familiar message perplexed her, as did the volumes of complaints she had received regarding the BPH ED. Many patients complained about long wait times and general dissatisfaction with the ED. It was so bad that she had heard that a number of patients would leave the waiting room without seeing a physician. In addition, the physicians in the clinic and community were reluctant to send patients to the BPH ED. They felt that the quality of care was good, but patients had to wait too long for service.

Just as she had done in the clinic, if she could improve on this area, the patients and physicians would be more satisfied. Additionally, she knew that the issues resulted in lost revenue.

She called Eric Wong, the ED manager.

"Eric, this is Jennifer. Looks like we have another crisis today. What's the problem?"

"Jennifer, I'm sick and tired of repeating the same thing. There are not enough exam rooms to place our patients. Some of the patients have been waiting for hours and are furious. I don't blame them. Everyone here is on a short fuse! Somebody's going to have to take our problems seriously."

"I understand your frustration, Eric. You're right. It's time to fix this problem. Can we meet Monday morning to discuss it?"

"We needed to meet 6 months ago, . . . but I guess Monday will do. Eight o'clock?"

"Eight is perfect. It would be helpful if you could bring some data on how the department has been running lately."

"I'll see if I can put some numbers together. I can't promise. The way things are going here, we're busy handling one crisis after another. There's no time for anything else, it seems."

Eric hung up. Jennifer looked at the receiver and thought, "This promises to be a lovely Monday morning."

INTRODUCTION AND LEARNING OBJECTIVES

In the previous chapter, you learned about the importance of using quality indicators to measure process performance. In this follow-up chapter, you apply basic statistical techniques to determine whether the processes are stable and generating output in a reliable fashion. There are many tools available to accomplish this task, but all depend on the type of data collected. Moreover, you will see that even if a process is behaving the way you expected, it may still not be good enough to meet specific targets.

Do you like numbers? If the answer is "yes," great! If the answer is "no," no problem! You are like millions of other highly educated individuals who may not like numbers because they are a little "intimidated" by math. As a result, we try to introduce you to this material in a step-by-step, nonthreatening way. After reading the chapter, you will:

1. **Understand the concept of variation, which affects all processes**

2. **Determine whether quality indicators are attributes or variables**

3. **Develop process control charts to track attributes (p-chart, c-chart, and u-chart) over time**

4. **Develop process control charts to track variables ($\overline{X}$ and R; $\overline{X}$ and s) over time**

5. **Evaluate a process control chart and determine whether the process being monitored is behaving as expected or becoming unstable**

6. **Decide whether a process is capable of meeting predetermined quality requirements**

7. **Know the basics of probabilistic sampling (see Appendix 5.3)**

VARIATION

As suggested in Box 5.1, it is impossible to determine exactly how long it takes to drive from your house to your best friend's. It depends on the time of day, the traffic, whether you hit every red light, whether a cop is right behind you, and so on. Even if you drove at the exact same

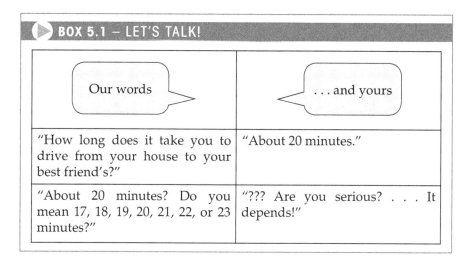

Our words	. . . and yours
"How long does it take you to drive from your house to your best friend's?"	"About 20 minutes."
"About 20 minutes? Do you mean 17, 18, 19, 20, 21, 22, or 23 minutes?"	"??? Are you serious? . . . It depends!"

time of day, got green lights all the way, and tried to drive consistently at the same speed, it might take you a little less time on some days and a little more time on others. This is the phenomenon of variation, and it exists in everything we do.

Process variation reflects the deviations of process output values from the mean or expected value for that process. When process output values deviate significantly from the mean, they create uncertainty about the ability of the process to produce quality output. For example, at a university health center, patients may usually wait 5 to 15 minutes before going to the exam room. However, it is possible that some will have to wait much longer than 15 minutes, in which case they will likely get irritated and dissatisfied with the responsiveness of the service. Why do some patients wait for 5 minutes, whereas others wait for 10, or even 30 minutes? There are many possible reasons, but they fall into two major categories.

Process Variation
Variation reflects the deviations of process output values from the mean or expected value for that process.

Assignable Causes of Variation

Assignable or **special causes of variation** occur for reasons that are external to the process. They reflect unusual faults arising from temporary situations. In the earlier example, the x-ray machine may have malfunctioned intermittently, resulting in the increased utilization of exam rooms by patients waiting for their x-ray results. Another possibility is that the clinical information system became uncharacteristically slow when various scheduled reports were printed. These sources of variation do not indicate a "bad" process per se; they signal atypical disturbances that can be identified and eliminated because they cause the process to be "out of control" and therefore unstable or unpredictable. In the previous examples, repairing the x-ray machine and scheduling the printing of reports at nonpeak times in the clinic will resolve a majority of the delays.

Assignable/Special Causes of Variation
Causes that occur for reasons that are external to the process. They reflect unusual faults arising from temporary situations.

Common or Random Causes of Variation

Common/Random Causes of Variation
Causes that are inherent to the process. They reflect the faults of the system and result from the combined influences of many regular, ordinary causes that occur randomly.

Common or **random causes of variation** are inherent to the process. They reflect the faults of the system and result from the combined influences of many regular, ordinary causes that occur randomly. Each one of these causes is insignificant by itself. Even if we could isolate and eliminate one, the impact on process variability would be negligible (Stevenson, 2008). As mentioned before, you may have to wait between 5 and 15 minutes before seeing a physician at the university health center. This would be expected given the number of doctors and nurses usually on duty, the number of exam rooms, and so on, to accommodate the existing student population. Why do patients sometimes wait 6 minutes and at other times 14 minutes? Because some patients arrive early for their appointments, whereas others arrive late; because some exams last longer than expected, whereas others are finished promptly. All these little variations add up, creating variation in wait times. Minimizing wait times and keeping them low for all patients would require changing elements of the process itself (e.g., building new facilities with additional exam rooms and increasing staff). In other words, an investment in process redesign would be necessary.

The type of variation that is intrinsic to the process is also referred to as the *natural* variation of the process because it determines the *natural* statistical variation, or width, in the distribution of the process output. The standard deviation is a measure of this type of variation. Most of the process values (99.7%) fall within ± 3 standard deviations from the mean or expected process value. Because this variation is expected, it does not impair the stability and predictability of the process. In fact, it provides the "control settings" (± 3 standard deviations from the mean) for the statistical process control charts, which were briefly introduced in Chapter 4 and are covered in depth in this chapter. This does not mean that random variation is desirable (Figure 5.1). For example, infection rates in a hospital could remain predictably high over time. This would of course be a stable but unacceptable situation. Continued surveillance and institution of sound infection control procedures would need to be implemented in order to change the process and, therefore, shift the average infection rate downward as well as reduce its variability.

FUNDAMENTALS OF SPC

Statistical Process Control (SPC)
Involves the use of statistical methods to determine whether a process is performing as expected.

Control Charts
SPC tools depicting whether sample output is within the statistical control limits established by the random variation of the process.

SPC involves the use of statistical methods to determine whether a process is performing as expected. **Control charts** are SPC tools depicting whether sample output is within the statistical control limits established by the random variation of the process. They help you detect process changes visually and take prompt, corrective action before a process becomes "out of control" and starts generating defective output consistently. A process is considered "in control" if (Russell & Taylor, 2009; Figure 5.2)

1. There are no points outside the control limits.

2. The majority of the points are close to the central line, that is, the process average, and only a few points approach the control limits.

At BPH, data were collected on waiting times in the ED for the past year. The frequencies of those times were plotted to obtain the process distribution. If you were Eric Wong, which one of the following normal distributions of the process would you prefer to see?

FIGURE 5.1 – Let's explore variability.

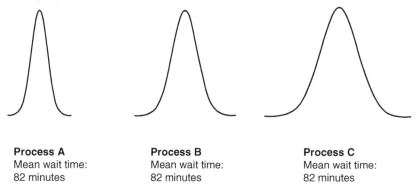

Process A
Mean wait time:
82 minutes

Process B
Mean wait time:
82 minutes

Process C
Mean wait time:
82 minutes

A? B? C? Not sure? Here is a little hint. As you recall, the standard deviation is a measure of random variation. Let's assume that the standard deviations in processes A, B, and C are 5, 10, and 15, respectively. Now, which one of the process distributions do you find more desirable?

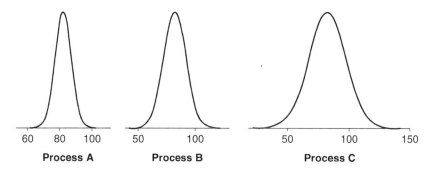

A! The more compact distribution (82 min ± 3 × 5 min) has less variation, giving the decision maker more certainty about the process output. On the other hand, process output values that are all over the place (82 min ± 3 × 15 min), make it very difficult to determine adequate staffing levels.

3. The points are approximately equally distributed above and below the centerline.

4. The points are randomly distributed around the centerline with no visible pattern.

To build control charts, we have to draw samples. A sample is a subset of observations taken from a population that it is supposed to represent. If you select a sample that is not representative, it will produce results that will be either better or worse than those obtained by using the entire population of observations. At BPH, the average wait time for *all* patients seen in the ED for the past year was 82 minutes. One day of data is shown in Appendix 5.3 (see Table A5.3.1). If we took a sample of 100 patients that is perfectly representative of the population, the sample

FIGURE 5.2 – Process control chart.

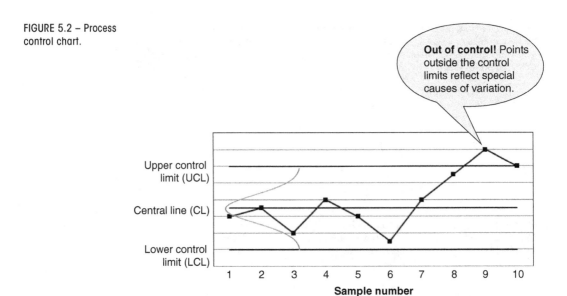

average wait time would also be 82 minutes. Realistically, close to 80 minutes will be good enough! The choice of the sampling technique has significant impact on the representativeness of the sample.

PROCESS CONTROL CHARTS

Samples are necessary to construct process control charts. There are several types of these charts, and one challenge is knowing which chart to use. This decision partly hinges upon whether the quality indicators (Chapter 4) you are monitoring are attributes or variables.

Attribute or Variable

Attributes

Discrete (i.e., identifiable, separate) units that are counted and can be classified as defective units in a sample.

Variables

Continuous measures obtained using some type of instrument such as a balance, ruler, or clock.

Attributes refer to discrete (i.e., identifiable, separate) units that are *counted* and can be classified as defective units in a sample (e.g., number of postoperative deaths in a sample of surgeries), or as number of defects per unit (e.g., number of medical errors per 1,000 patient-days). Attributes are counted with minimal effort. Was the outcome good or bad? Was an error made or not? On the other hand, **variables** are *measured* on a continuous scale using some type of instrument, such as a balance (e.g., weight), ruler (e.g., length), or clock (e.g., wait time). They therefore yield a more informative and precise assessment of the quality indicator. The control charts used to monitor attributes are p-charts, c-charts, or u-charts. The charts used to monitor variables are $\overline{X}$ and R charts, or $\overline{X}$ and s-charts.

Control Charts for Attributes

p-Charts

When the attribute data consist of two categories (defective versus nondefective; nonconforming versus conforming), it is appropriate to use the *p*-chart to assess process stability. *p*-**Charts** display the proportion of defective items in a sample. Although the theoretical basis for a *p*-chart is the binomial distribution, large samples ($n > 30$) enable a good approximation of the normal distribution (Stevenson, 2008). The ease of using the normal distribution justifies the extra effort required in drawing larger samples.

p-**Chart**
A process control chart that displays the proportion of defective items in a sample over time.

BRADLEY PARK HOSPITAL 5.2

At BPH, Eric Wong has been getting ready for his meeting with Jennifer. The problems involving wait times are plentiful. One of them is the number of patients who leave before being seen by a health practitioner. Because a picture is worth a thousand words, he has been building a control chart of patients leaving without being seen (LWBS) in September. He obtained the data shown in Table 5.1.

These are the numbers that will be plotted.

[1] Day	[2] Number of Visits (*n*)	[3] LWBS ("Defective Visits")	[4] Proportion (*p*) (LWBS/*n*)
1	161	17	0.1056
2	159	14	0.0881
3	165	16	0.0970
4	180	4	0.0222
5	167	7	0.0419
6	182	14	0.0769
7	168	28	0.1667
8	190	17	0.0895
9	109	0	0.0000
10	175	18	0.1029
11	172	19	0.1105
12	151	8	0.0530
13	153	9	0.0588
14	177	24	0.1356
15	153	7	0.0458
16	146	12	0.0822
17	171	17	0.0994
18	176	7	0.0398
19	171	7	0.0409
20	177	3	0.0169
21	146	1	0.0068
22	164	6	0.0366
23	155	15	0.0968

TABLE 5.1 – Proportion of LWBS Patients in September

(continued)

[1] Day	[2] Number of Visits (*n*)	[3] LWBS ("Defective Visits")	[4] Proportion (*p*) (LWBS/*n*)
24	193	18	0.0933
25	188	7	0.0372
26	164	9	0.0549
27	177	1	0.0056
28	187	29	0.1551
29	164	8	0.0488
30	177	12	0.0678
Total	5018	354	

TABLE 5.1 – Proportion of LWBS Patients in September (*continued*)

To construct the *p*-chart, Eric followed the steps that follow (see Appendix 5.2 to perform these steps in Excel).

STEP 1: Compute the mean proportion of LWBS patients, $\bar{p}$.

$$\bar{p} = \frac{\text{total number of nonconforming items}}{\text{total number of items inspected}}$$

This is the centerline of the control chart.

$$= \frac{\text{total number of patients who LWBS}}{\text{total number of patients who visited the ED}} \qquad [5.1]$$

$$= \frac{354}{5018} = 0.0705$$

This reflects the variation or spread in the data.

STEP 2: Compute the standard deviation of the proportion, S_p.

$$S_p = \sqrt{\frac{\bar{p}\,(1-\bar{p}\,)}{\text{number of items inspected in each sample (i.e., sample size)}}} \qquad [5.2]$$

Note: As the sample size changes every day, S_p will also change daily.

$$\text{On September 1 } (\text{day 1}), S_p = \sqrt{\frac{(0.0705)(1-0.0705)}{161}} = 0.0202$$

STEP 3: Determine the control limits or lower and upper bands of the chart (± 3 standard deviations from the centerline), UCL_p and LCL_p.

$$\text{Upper control limit } \left(UCL_p\right) = \bar{p} + 3\,S_p \qquad [5.3]$$

$$\text{Lower control limit } \left(LCL_p\right) = \bar{p} - 3\,S_p \qquad [5.4]$$

On September 1 (day 1),

$$UCL_p = 0.0705 + (3 \times 0.0202) = 0.1311$$

$$LCL_p = 0.0705 - (3 \times 0.0202) = 0.0099 \text{ (Box 5.2)}$$

▶ BOX 5.2 – LET'S TALK!

Your words	. . . and ours
"Is it possible to get a negative value when computing the LCL?"	"Yes! In fact, it happens on Day 9. The LCL is –0.0055."
"It doesn't make sense! How could a proportion of patients who left without being seen be negative?"	"You're right. It's impossible. That's why we have to round it up to 0. Anything else?"
"Yes. Why add and subtract 3 standard deviations to and from the average proportion?"	"Because the control chart essentially depicts the distribution of the process. Three standard deviations below and above the mean represent most of its natural width, that is, its random variation."

STEP 4: Draw the control limits (Figure 5.3).
Note that the control limits change for every sample point. This is because the number of observations or patient visits to the ED (the denominator in the standard deviation formula used to determine control limits) changes each day. If Eric Wong had decided to sample 50 visits each day and determine the number of LWBS patients in each sample, the control limits would have been straight lines.

STEP 5: Plot the proportion defective (proportion of LWBS patients) for each day (column 4 in Table 5.1), p.

$$p = \frac{\text{number of nonconforming items in a sample}}{\text{number of items in the sample (sample size)}} \qquad [5.5]$$

$$= \frac{\text{number of LWBS patients each day}}{\text{number of patients who visited the ED on that day}}$$

On day 1, $p = \dfrac{17}{161} = 0.1056$ (Figure 5.4)

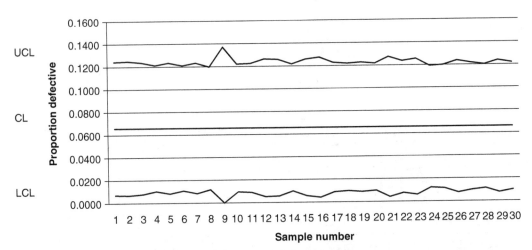

FIGURE 5.3 – Control limits of p-chart.

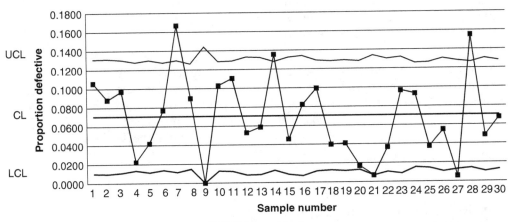

FIGURE 5.4 – p-Chart.

STEP 6: Determine whether the process is in control.

The process is out of control. The proportion of LWBS patients was outside the control limits on days 7, 14, 27, and 28. On days 7, 14, and 28, the special causes of variation that led to larger-than-expected proportions of LWBS patients should be investigated and eliminated. As for day 27 (same for day 9), the percentage of LWBS patients was lower than expected, which is a good thing! Again, the cause(s) should be investigated so that the favorable conditions which led to these outcomes can be reproduced.

c-Chart
A process control chart that displays the number of defects per unit over time.

c-Charts

c-Charts are used to plot the number of defects per unit over time. The **area of opportunity**, or number of units inspected, for the defect to occur must be constant (e.g., number of falls per patient per year in a long-term care facility, number of occurrences of system downtime per week, number of needle-stick injuries in a 10-bed ward). One important distinction between these attributes and those in *p*-charts is that *multiple* defects can be found in each unit or area of opportunity, whereas an item in a *p*-chart is determined to be defective or nondefective only once. In other words, a patient may fall multiple times, and the system could be down several times in a month. In contrast, LWBS patients leave or they don't (*p*-chart); they don't leave multiple times.

Area of Opportunity
The number of units inspected.

BRADLEY PARK HOSPITAL 5.3

Eric Wong was also disturbed by the number of shortages of essential supplies (gloves, gauze, etc.) in the exam rooms. Inadequate stocking of these rooms caused the staff to take the necessary supplies from other rooms (creating stock problems in those rooms as well), which delayed patient care. He prepared a c-chart that graphs the number of defects per unit. In this case, the defects were the shortages, and the unit was the exam room floor. To prepare the chart, Eric used the data gathered in September (see Table 5.2).

TABLE 5.2 – Number of Shortages in Exam Rooms	
Day	**Number of Shortages**
1	7
2	7
3	6
4	8
5	9
6	7
7	9
8	8
9	10
10	12
11	8
12	12
13	11
14	13
15	15
16	11
17	10
18	9
19	14
20	15
21	12

These are the numbers that will be plotted.

(continued)

TABLE 5.2 – Number of Shortages in Exam Rooms (continued)	
Day	Number of Shortages
22	17
23	10
24	11
25	18
26	17
27	19
28	20
29	19
30	21
Total	365

To construct the c-chart, Eric Wong used the following steps.

STEP 1: Compute the average number of defects per unit, $\bar{c}$.

$$\bar{c} = \frac{\text{total number of defects}}{\text{total number of inspection units}} \qquad [5.6]$$

$$= \frac{\text{total number of shortages}}{\text{total number of exam room floors inspected over 30 days}}$$

$$= \frac{365}{30} = 12.17 \text{ shortages}$$

STEP 2: Compute the standard deviation of the number of defects, S_c.

$$S_c = \sqrt{\bar{c}} \qquad [5.7]$$

$$= \sqrt{12.17} = 3.49 \text{ shortages}$$

STEP 3: Determine the control limits, UCL_c and LCL_c.

$$UCL_c = \bar{c} + 3S_c \qquad [5.8]$$

$$= 12.17 + (3 \times 3.49) = 22.64 \text{ shortages}$$

$$LCL_c = \bar{c} - 3S_c \qquad [5.9]$$

$$= 12.17 - (3 \times 3.49) = 1.70 \text{ shortages}$$

STEP 4: Draw the centerline and control limits.

STEP 5: Plot the number of defects, that is, shortages, c (Figure 5.5).

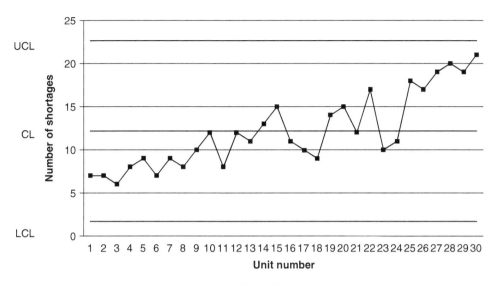

FIGURE 5.5 – *c*-Chart.

STEP 6:   Determine whether the process is in control.

No data points were outside the control limits, but Eric Wong was far from satisfied. There was clearly a pattern with the number of shortages increasing over time. The process was unstable and therefore out of control. He could see that if no action was taken, the upward trend would continue and the number of shortages would soon go over the upper control limit. Things were getting worse and worse!

His frustration was increasing. How could this happen? He pretty much dedicated himself to the ED and its patients, and so did the medical staff. Arriving early and staying late was just a way of life. He decided to take a break and went to the lounge to get a cup of coffee. Tina McBride, one of the registration clerks, was sitting on one of the couches.

"Hi, Tina. How's it going?"

"Hello, Mr. Wong. I'm just taking a short break. What a day! It seems like everyone is either sick or injured today. Patients just keep on coming, and we have no place to put them. Some have been in the waiting room for more than 3 hours, and I hear that boarding time is especially long today. Patients are frustrated and take it out on us. People can be so rude, you know!"

"Sorry to hear that. I've been asking for more resources, but every other administrator in the hospital is doing the same. They tell us that money's tight, that we need to find ways to be more efficient . . . as if we were not already squeezing everything out of the resources we've got. Anyway, patients complain all the time. That's the way it's always been . . ."

"This is the worst I've seen during my 12 years at the hospital. Another year like this and . . . well, some of us may be asking for a transfer to another department. Don't get me wrong, you're a great boss. It's just that it's easy to get burned out in the ED."

"Yeah, it sure is. . . . Let me see what I can do."

"Thanks. Well, time to get back to work. Thank you for letting me vent my frustration. Bye, Mr. Wong."

"Bye, Tina."

"Not exactly the coffee break I needed," Eric thought. "Patients are mad, the staff is mad, the boss is mad."

He poured himself a cup of coffee and went back to his office. He sat in his chair and reflected. Was the increase in complaints real or was it just a perception from people who were stressed out and fed up. He decided to get the facts and look at the incidence of complaints in the ED.

u-Charts

u-Chart

A process control chart that displays the number of defects per unit over time when the area of opportunity fluctuates.

u-**Charts** are similar to c-charts. They are used to plot defects per unit (or set of inspected units) when the area of opportunity fluctuates. Each day the number of patients visiting the ED varies. When there are more patients, one would expect more complaints and vice versa. Therefore, the set of inspected units, that is, the number of patients seen on a given day, is not constant; there is not an equal area of opportunity for defects to occur. Other examples include the number of needle-stick injuries in a hospital per month (the number of occupied beds fluctuates), or the number of discrepancies in surgery patient charts per week (the number of weekly surgeries fluctuates). In the absence of an equal area of opportunity for the defects to occur, we need to unitize, that is, make the set of inspected units constant, so that comparable values can be plotted on the *u*-chart.

Eric Wong used the data shown in Table 5.3.

> These are the numbers that will be plotted.

TABLE 5.3 – Number of Complaints in the ED

[1] Day	[2] Visits	[3] Complaints (c)	[4] n	[5] u
1	161	12	1.61	7.45
2	159	15	1.59	9.43
3	165	18	1.65	10.91
4	180	25	1.80	13.89
5	167	20	1.67	11.98
6	182	14	1.82	7.69
7	168	18	1.68	10.71
8	190	27	1.90	14.21
9	109	15	1.09	13.76
10	175	17	1.75	9.71
11	172	19	1.72	11.05
12	151	19	1.51	12.58
13	153	16	1.53	10.46
14	177	23	1.77	12.99
15	153	20	1.53	13.07
16	146	18	1.46	12.33
17	171	27	1.71	15.79

(continued)

TABLE 5.3 – Number of Complaints in the ED (*continued*)

[1] Day	[2] Visits	[3] Complaints (c)	[4] n	[5] u
18	176	20	1.76	11.36
19	171	21	1.71	12.28
20	177	24	1.77	13.56
21	146	18	1.46	12.33
22	164	19	1.64	11.59
23	155	25	1.55	16.13
24	193	34	1.93	17.62
25	188	37	1.88	19.68
26	164	29	1.64	17.68
27	177	28	1.77	15.82
28	187	30	1.87	16.04
29	164	26	1.64	15.85
30	177	29	1.77	16.38
Total		663	50.18	

To construct the *u*-chart, Eric followed the following steps.

STEP 1: Compute the number of sets of inspected units in each area of opportunity, *n* (column 4 in Table 5.3). For the data in Table 5.3, Eric Wong had decided to use a set of 100 visits to unitize.

$$n = \frac{\text{number of observations in the original area of opportunity}}{\text{number of observations in the agreed} - \text{upon set of inspected units}}$$

[5.10]

$$= \frac{\text{number of daily visits to the ED}}{100}$$

For day 1, $n = \dfrac{161}{100} = 1.61$

STEP 2: Convert *c* (column 3 in Table 5.3), the number of defects, to *u* (column 5 in Table 5.3), the unitized number of defects.

$$u = \frac{c}{n} = \frac{\text{number of defects in the original area of opportunity}}{\text{number of sets of inspected units}}$$

[5.11]

$$= \frac{\text{number of complaints}}{\text{number of sets of 100 visits}}$$

For day 1, $u = \dfrac{12}{1.61} = 7.45$ complaints

Step 3: Compute the average unitized number of defects, $\bar{u}$.

$$\bar{u} = \frac{\text{total number of defects}}{\text{total number of sets of inspected units}} \qquad [5.12]$$

This is the centerline of the control chart.

$$= \frac{\text{total number of complaints in September}}{\text{total number of sets of 100 visits in September}}$$

$$= \frac{663}{50.18}$$

$$= 13.21 \text{ complaints}$$

Step 4: Compute the standard deviation of the unitized number of defects, S_u.

$$S_u = \sqrt{\frac{\bar{\bar{u}}}{n}} \qquad [5.13]$$

$$\text{For day 1, } S_u = \sqrt{\frac{13.21}{1.61}} = 2.86$$

Step 5: Determine the control limits, UCL_u and LCL_u.

$$UCL_u = \bar{u} + S_u \qquad [5.14]$$

$$= 13.21 + (3 \times 2.86) = 21.79 \text{ complaints}$$

$$LCL_u = \bar{u} - 3S_u \qquad [5.15]$$

$$= 13.21 - (3 \times 2.86) = 4.63 \text{ complaints}$$

Step 6: Draw the centerline and control limits.

Step 7: Plot the unitized number of defects, u (Figure 5.6).

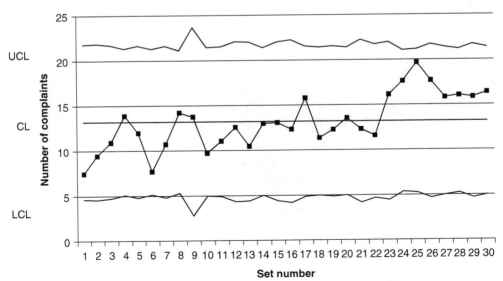

FIGURE 5.6 – u-Chart.

STEP 8: Determine whether the process is in control.

Although no data point is outside the control limits, two phenomena are worth discussing. It seems that at the beginning of the month, a large number of values were below average, whereas the opposite is true for the end of the month. It seems that the average is shifting to a higher value. Further supporting this observation is the presence of 8 consecutive data points above the average for the last days of September. The points, therefore, do not appear to be randomly distributed around the mean. The process is out of control.

BRADLEY PARK HOSPITAL 5.4

Eric Wong pondered these results. Why were patients complaining? According to the staff, they complained about long waits. But where? Did they wait too long in the waiting room or do they spend too much time in the ED from start to finish? He decided to examine the waiting room times first.

Control Charts for Variables

Unlike the number of LWBS patients or the number of complaints, time is a continuous variable. Other examples of variables include weight, height, and blood pressure. Variables are not counted; they are measured precisely using an instrument. The control charts for variables are (a) $\overline{X}$ and R charts or (b) $\overline{X}$ and s charts. The principles for constructing control charts for variables are the same as for attributes: draw a centerline and establish the control limits 3 standard deviations from the mean. However, there are always two charts for variables: one to track the process central tendency $(\overline{X})$ and the other (R or s) to track its variability or dispersion.

$\overline{X}$ and R Charts

Mean $(\overline{X})$ and range (R) charts are used when the sample size is small $(2 \leq n \leq 9)$. The $\overline{X}$ **chart** displays the sample means; the R **chart** displays the sample ranges. The range helps track the amount of variability or dispersion in the process. The range is the simplest measure of variability and is therefore easy and practical to use.

$\overline{X}$ Chart
A process control chart that displays sample means over time.

R Chart
A process control chart that displays sample ranges over time.

BRADLEY PARK HOSPITAL 5.5

Eric Wong retrieved the waiting room times for each patient seen in September. Thousands of patients had been seen in September! He decided to take random samples of five patients each day and their associated waiting time. He came up with the data presented in Table 5.4.

These numbers will be plotted on the $\overline{X}$ chart.

These numbers will be plotted on the R chart.

TABLE 5.4 – Waiting Room Times in September

Day	Patient 1	Patient 2	Patient 3	Patient 4	Patient 5	$\overline{X}$	R
1	53	281	14	57	21	85.2	267
2	117	3	7	136	190	90.6	187
3	9	30	55	106	100	60	97
4	2	20	63	53	164	60.4	162
5	28	31	66	163	125	82.6	135
6	20	81	87	202	236	125.2	216
7	6	227	194	161	30	123.6	221
8	83	13	245	4	202	109.4	241
9	38	131	13	165	140	97.4	152
10	113	74	89	57	133	93.2	76
11	106	183	21	169	29	101.6	162
12	7	128	64	205	170	114.8	198
13	24	137	86	16	76	67.8	121
14	130	16	8	203	31	77.6	195
15	32	253	18	149	115	113.4	235
16	69	125	28	75	119	83.2	97
17	68	112	72	132	149	106.6	81
18	109	23	195	109	6	88.4	189
19	15	54	160	13	188	86	175
20	98	196	191	167	192	168.8	98
21	165	17	157	263	221	164.6	246
22	32	120	273	307	33	153	275
23	99	56	42	287	183	133.4	245
24	28	109	191	8	178	102.8	183
25	59	20	99	195	117	98	175
26	138	86	33	40	10	61.4	128
27	103	78	256	279	152	173.6	201
28	25	286	59	37	146	110.6	261
29	30	49	177	44	34	66.8	147
30	116	1	14	81	115	65.4	115
Total						3065.4	5281

The following steps were used to construct the R chart.

STEP 1: Compute the range for each sample, R.

R = largest value in the sample − lowest value in the sample   [5.16]

= longest wait time in sample − shortest wait time in sample

For day 1, $R = 281$ min $- 14$ min $= 267$ min

This value shows the spread in the sample data.

STEP 2: Compute the mean range, $\bar{R}$.

$$\bar{R} = \frac{\sum R}{k} = \frac{\text{sum of the ranges across all samples}}{\text{number of samples taken}} \qquad [5.17]$$

$$= \frac{\text{sum of the waiting time ranges}}{\text{number of samples of five patients taken}}$$

$$= \frac{5281}{30} = 176.03 \text{ min}$$

STEP 3: Determine the control limits, UCL_R and LCL_R.
Table values (see Appendix 5.1) have been developed to determine the lower (D_3) and upper (D_4) control limits for the range charts based on different sample sizes. These values enable you to produce control limits that are similar to 3 standard deviations away from the mean.

$$UCL_R = D_4 \, \bar{R} \qquad [5.18]$$

$$= (2.11)(176.03)$$

$$= 371.43 \text{ min}$$

> 0 and 2.11 are the D_3 and D_4 values for a sample size of 5. (Box 5.3)

$$LCL_R = D_3 \, \bar{R} \qquad [5.19]$$

$$= (0)(176.03)$$

$$= 0 \text{ min}$$

STEP 4: Draw the control limits.

STEP 5: Plot all sample ranges, R (Figure 5.7).

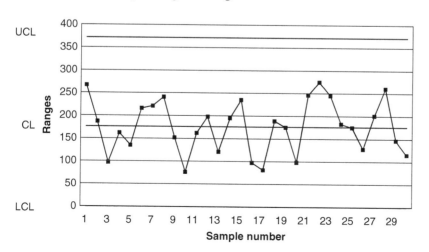

FIGURE 5.7 – *R* chart.

STEP 6:   Determine whether the process is in control.
The process dispersion appears to be in control.

The following steps are needed to construct an $\overline{X}$ chart.

STEP 1:   Compute the mean for each sample, $\overline{X}$.

$$\overline{X} = \frac{\sum X}{n} = \frac{\text{sum of sample values}}{\text{number of units in sample (sample size)}} \quad [5.20]$$

$$= \frac{\text{sum of wait times}}{\text{number of patients in sample}}$$

For day 1, $\overline{X} = \dfrac{53+281+14+57+21}{5} = 85.2$ minutes

STEP 2:   Compute the average of the sample means or grand mean, $\overline{\overline{X}}$.

$$\overline{\overline{X}} = \frac{\sum \overline{X}}{k} = \frac{\text{sum of the sample means}}{\text{number of samples taken}} \quad [5.21]$$

$$= \frac{\text{sum of the average wait times for each sample of five patients}}{\text{number of samples of five patients taken}}$$

$$= \frac{3065.40}{30} = 102.18 \text{ minutes}$$

STEP 3:   Compute the control limits, $UCL_{\overline{X}}$ and $LCL_{\overline{X}}$.
Just like for the R chart, table values (A_2) have been developed to determine the LCL and UCL for the $\overline{X}$ charts based on different sample sizes. These values enable you to produce control limits that are similar to 3 standard deviations away from the mean.

> The A_2 value for a sample size of 5 is 0.58.

$$UCL_{\overline{X}} = \overline{\overline{X}} + A_2\overline{R} \quad [5.22]$$

$$= 102.18 + (0.58)(176.03)$$

$$= 204.28 \text{ minutes}$$

$$LCL_{\overline{X}} = \overline{\overline{X}} - A_2\overline{R} \quad [5.23]$$

$$= 102.18 - (0.58)(176.03)$$

$$= 0.08 \text{ minutes}$$

STEP 4:   Draw the control limits.

STEP 5: Plot the sample means, $\overline{X}$ (Figure 5.8).

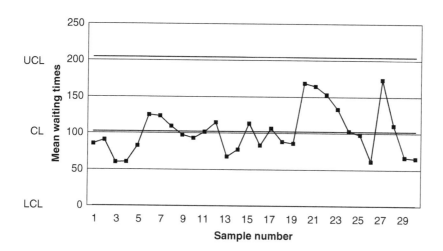

FIGURE 5.8 – $\overline{X}$ chart.

STEP 6: Determine whether the process is in control.

Although a few larger sample averages emerged in the last days of September, the process appears to be in control. Because both central tendency and dispersion are in control, the process is in control.

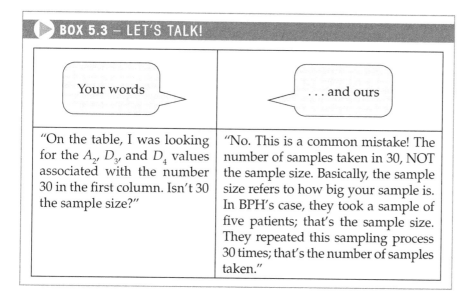

▶ **BOX 5.3 – LET'S TALK!**

Your words	. . . and ours
"On the table, I was looking for the A_2, D_3, and D_4 values associated with the number 30 in the first column. Isn't 30 the sample size?"	"No. This is a common mistake! The number of samples taken in 30, NOT the sample size. Basically, the sample size refers to how big your sample is. In BPH's case, they took a sample of five patients; that's the sample size. They repeated this sampling process 30 times; that's the number of samples taken."

$\overline{X}$ and R charts are used together. Because variables are evaluated both in terms of central tendency and dispersion, both the process average and its variability must be in control for the process to be in control. This makes sense. After all, the ranges could be consistently small, suggesting little variability, but the averages could be out of control. For example, if the control limits of the $\bar{X}$ chart were 5 and 10 minutes, and those of the R chart were 3 and 4 minutes, sample values of 9, 10, and 12.5 minutes would yield a range of 3.5 (within limits), but the sample mean of 10.5 minutes would be outside the limits. On the other hand, sample values of 1, 5, and 10 minutes would yield a mean of 5.33 minutes (within limits), but the sample range would be 9, a value clearly outside of the UCL.

BRADLEY PARK HOSPITAL 5.6

Despite finding out that the process was in control, Eric Wong had a bitter taste in his mouth. Somehow, it still did not feel good. There was something about the wait times that did not seem positive . . . he was just too tired to put his finger on it. He decided to put this issue aside for the time being and examine some other data. One other problem in the ED was the turnaround time for tests conducted on admitted patients. Both doctors and nurses complained that once they had ordered tests, it took way too long to get the results. This caused unnecessary delays. The patients were occupying exam rooms, thereby preventing staff from calling the patients in the waiting room. Everyone was waiting, and the system was at a standstill. Eric looked at the data compiled by his staff.

The staff had accessed the data on lab turnaround times in the health information system. They had taken daily samples of 10 patients and recorded the turnaround times for a complete blood count (CBC), one of the most common lab tests (Table 5.5).

$\bar{X}$ and s-Charts

Mean ($\bar{X}$) and standard deviation (s) charts are used when the sample size is larger than 9. These are the most powerful control charts, but compared to the R chart, constructing the **s-chart**, which displays the sample standard deviations, is more computationally demanding.

To develop the s-chart, Eric used the following steps.

s-Chart
A process control chart that displays sample standard deviations over time.

STEP 1: Compute the standard deviation for each sample, s

$$s = \sqrt{\frac{\sum_{i=1}^{n}(X_i - \bar{X})^2}{n-1}} \qquad [5.24]$$

$$= \sqrt{\frac{\text{sum of }(\text{each sample value} - \text{the sample mean})^2}{\text{sample size} - 1}}$$

$$\text{On day 1, } s = \sqrt{\frac{(16.47 - 14.71)^2 + (13.52 - 14.71)^2 + \ldots + (12.68 - 14.71)^2}{10 - 1}}$$

$$= 4.96 \text{ minutes}$$

These numbers will be plotted on the s-chart.

These numbers will be plotted on the X̄ chart.

TABLE 5.5 – CBC Turnaround Times in September

Day	Patient 1	Patient 2	Patient 3	Patient 4	Patient 5	Patient 6	Patient 7	Patient 8	Patient 9	Patient 10	X̄	s
1	16.47	13.52	2.75	20.28	16	13.8	19.03	18.77	13.8	12.68	14.71	4.96
2	10	13.05	15.85	12.88	17.67	12.98	12.58	9.53	10.62	9.77	12.49	2.68
3	6.9	38.5	24.15	147.5	11.47	38.5	15.28	13.95	74.72	8.95	37.99	43.64
4	7.58	12.67	32.9	27.13	19.2	45.07	32.9	119.53	59.98	23.93	38.09	32.44
5	14.73	19.15	15.8	47.5	13.88	26.97	19.15	26.97	13.88	9.77	20.78	10.92
6	19.47	24.88	11.5	25.95	18.47	16.92	11.5	18.47	24.88	10.12	18.22	5.85
7	9.78	11.32	19.05	12.68	16.07	7.58	32.32	46.85	12.33	11.8	17.98	12.30
8	67.65	11.38	30.52	10.75	17	14.17	10.75	7.73	12.12	13.17	19.52	18.03
9	13.28	12.65	10.08	16.85	20.03	12.65	35.42	11.3	10.93	30.9	17.41	8.88
10	10.85	8.27	27.35	10.97	10.38	16.02	7.6	10.85	20.48	10	13.28	6.24
11	26.15	9.58	13.22	35.87	33.53	35.87	13.22	35.87	38.88	13.05	25.52	11.91
12	99.97	21.28	20.88	16.33	15.5	10.88	17.23	16.33	21.05	15.85	25.53	26.35
13	12.68	9.77	8.95	23.93	9.77	10.12	11.8	13.17	30.9	12.88	14.40	7.21
14	12.57	12.57	4.82	37.05	95.9	10.25	11.33	14.03	15.23	17.67	23.14	26.93
15	7.42	14.77	51.08	39.35	19.22	30.62	9.3	8.95	36.65	12.98	23.03	15.31
16	8.08	16.1	65.4	8.08	7.77	19.72	12.32	13.07	12.43	12.58	17.56	17.22
17	14.38	67.45	23.52	13.9	19.9	7.52	13.9	20.43	14.3	9.53	20.48	17.21
18	15.2	46.25	30.87	25.87	3.5	22.42	27.72	3.5	13.88	10.62	19.98	13.33
19	37.73	18.32	6.48	49.52	19.12	6.4	19.38	17.53	19.53	12.23	20.62	13.42

(continued)

TABLE 5.5 – CBC Turnaround Times in September (continued)

Day	Patient 1	Patient 2	Patient 3	Patient 4	Patient 5	Patient 6	Patient 7	Patient 8	Patient 9	Patient 10	x̄	s
20	9.9	10.15	13.12	28.57	16.63	19.67	9.73	142.12	11.68	12.63	27.42	40.72
21	5.97	11.03	3.9	12.22	9.53	11.6	76.87	14.12	5.23	4.55	15.50	21.86
22	14.62	5.47	15.77	24.52	5.47	15.77	16.2	9.38	89.27	7.02	20.35	24.94
23	9.38	9.32	11.57	13.03	113.75	31.02	11.57	21.18	15.43	20.23	25.65	31.68
24	27.52	55.93	12.17	6.53	17	13.57	10.13	13.4	13.93	10.52	18.07	14.42
25	28.37	10.07	10.92	55.47	21.6	12.32	28.37	9.48	13.42	12.88	20.29	14.32
26	12.05	40.4	17.65	50.87	16.32	12.7	146.9	50.87	16.32	13.07	37.72	41.48
27	21	14.43	31.32	18.43	66.42	14.43	44.65	12.05	17.57	23.03	26.33	17.11
28	12.23	12.63	4.55	7.02	20.23	10.52	12.88	13.07	23.03	13.8	13.00	5.45
29	15.95	6.18	13.77	15.95	11.73	13.77	13.77	13.82	14.95	19.03	13.89	3.34
30	12.56	10.15	37.04	49.56	21.5	19.48	20.54	18.57	3.84	18.77	21.20	13.21
Total											640.16	523.35

STEP 2: Compute the average sample standard deviation, $\bar{s}$.

$$\bar{s} = \frac{\sum s}{k}$$ [5.25]

$$= \frac{\text{sum of standard deviations}}{\text{number of samples taken}}$$

$$= \frac{523.35}{30} = 17.45 \text{ min}$$

The B_3 and B_4 values for a sample size of 10 are 0.284 and 1.716 (see Appendix 5.1).

STEP 3: Determine the control limits, UCL_s and LCL_s.

$$UCL_s = B_4\bar{s}$$ [5.26]

$$= (1.716)(17.45) = 29.94 \text{ minutes}$$

$$LCL_s = B_3\bar{s}$$ [5.27]

$$= (0.284)(17.45) = 4.95 \text{ minutes}$$

STEP 4: Graph the control limits.
STEP 5: Plot the standard deviations for each sample, s (Figure 5.9).

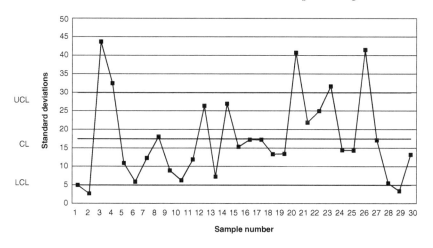

FIGURE 5.9 – s-chart.

STEP 6: Determine whether the process is in control.
Several standard deviations (samples #2, 3, 4, 20, 23, 26, and 29) are outside the control limits, indicating unstable variability. The process is out of control.

To build the $\overline{X}$ chart, the following steps were followed.

STEP 1: Compute the mean for each sample, $\overline{X}$.

$$\overline{X} = \frac{\sum X}{n} = \frac{\text{sum of sample values}}{\text{number of units in sample (sample size)}}$$ [5.28]

$$= \frac{\text{sum of turnaround times in a sample}}{\text{number of patients in sample}}$$

$$\text{For day 1, } \bar{X} = \frac{\begin{array}{c}16.47+13.52+2.75+20.28+16+13.8\\+19.03+18.77+13.8+12.68\end{array}}{10} = 14.71 \text{ minutes}$$

STEP 2: Compute the average of the sample means or grand mean, $\bar{\bar{X}}$.

$$\bar{\bar{X}} = \frac{\sum \bar{X}}{k} = \frac{\text{sum of the sample means}}{\text{number of samples taken}}$$

$$= \frac{\text{sum of the average turnaround times for each sample of 10 patients}}{\text{number of samples of 10 patients taken}}$$

$$= \frac{640.16}{30} = 21.34 \text{ minutes}$$

STEP 3: Compute the control limits, $UCL_{\bar{X}}$ and $LCL_{\bar{X}}$

$$UCL_{\bar{x}} = \bar{\bar{X}} + A_3\bar{s} \qquad\qquad [5.29]$$

$$= 21.34 + (0.975)(17.45)$$

$$= 38.35 \text{ minutes}$$

The A_3 value for a sample size of 10 is 0.975 (see Appendix 5.1).

$$LCL_{\bar{x}} = \bar{\bar{X}} - A_3\bar{s} \qquad\qquad [5.30]$$

$$= 21.34 - (0.975)(17.45)$$

$$= 4.33 \text{ minutes}$$

STEP 4: Graph the control limits.

STEP 5: Plot the $\bar{X}$ values for each sample (Figure 5.10).

FIGURE 5.10 – $\bar{X}$ chart.

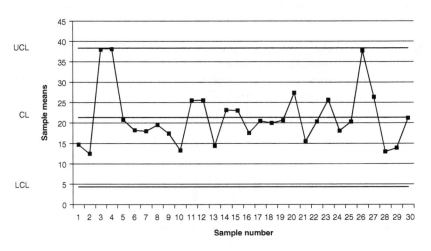

STEP 6: Determine whether the process is in control.
All sample values are within the control limits. Although the central tendency ($\overline{X}$ chart) of the process is in control, its dispersion (s-chart) is out of control, making the process unstable overall and out of control.

When using both charts together, you can see that for samples #2 and #29, the standard deviations are very low, indicating low variability. The average turnaround times for these two samples are also relatively low. This is a desirable situation that we would want to reproduce in the future! Identifying the conditions that led to these situations would be time well spent. On the other hand, the standard deviations for samples #3, 4, 20, 23, and 26 are high because of the unusually high turnaround times for some patients.

So many charts to remember! Figure 5.11 helps you determine which SPC chart is to be used based on the characteristics of the data.

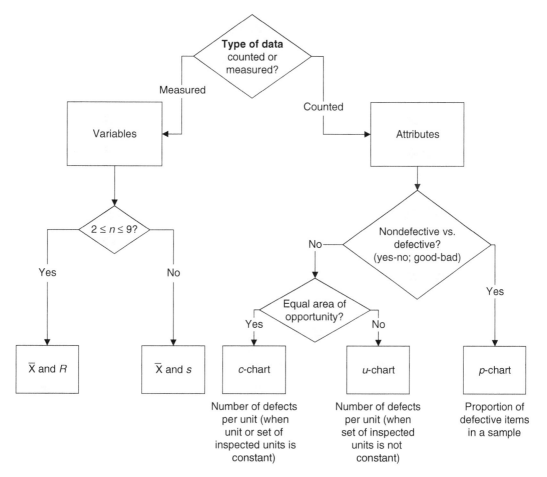

FIGURE 5.11 – Control chart decision tree.

CONTROL CHART PATTERNS

As previously mentioned, a sample value could be inside the control limits and yet the process could be deemed unstable or out of control. A consistent pattern, even inside the limits, would suggest the presence of assignable causes of variation, not the random variation that we normally expect in a process. In most cases, patterns—that are nonrandom—would warrant efforts to identify the causes of variation and eliminate them to get the process back in control. Three examples of patterns are shown in Figure 5.12. Note that if Figure 5.12(b) represented a p-chart, the proportion of defective items would decrease consistently, which is desirable! In this situation, just like for any out-of-control process, you would want to identify the causes of assignable variation. However, instead of eliminating the causes that led to a better outcome, you would ensure that they become permanent elements of the new, improved process.

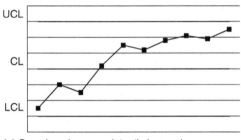

(a) Sample values consistently increasing

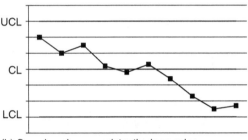

(b) Sample values consistently decreasing

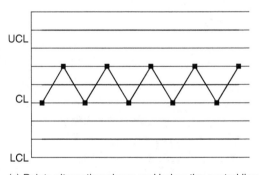

(c) Points alternating above and below the central line

FIGURE 5.12 – Examples of patterns.

Run Test
A test that detects patterns in a control chart divided into zones A, B, and C.

Sometimes, the patterns are not as obvious as those shown in Figure 5.12, and we need to do a **run test** to detect their presence (Lighter & Fair, 2004). To conduct a run test, we divide the control chart into three zones above and below the centerline. Zone A includes values between 2 and 3 standard deviations from the mean. Zone B contains values between 1 and 2 standard deviations from the mean. Zone C contains values that are less than 1 standard deviation from the mean. Remember that to reflect a process that is in control, sample value points should be *randomly* distributed around the mean, with most of the values close to the mean and a few values close to the control limits (Box 5.4). Figure 5.13 shows several deviations from this rule.

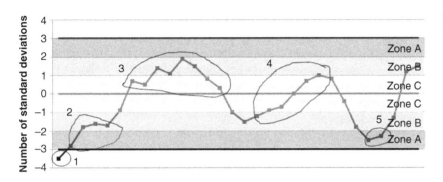

FIGURE 5.13 – Zones and patterns.

Pattern	Characteristics
1	Point outside the band determined by the control limits
2	4 of 5 consecutive points in zones A or B
3	More than 7 consecutive points either above or below the centerline
4	More than 5 points with consistently increasing or decreasing values
5	2 of 3 consecutive points in zone A

⚕ BOX 5.4 – OM IN PRACTICE!

Use of Quality Control to Guide Therapy for Asthma

At John Hunter Hospital in New South Wales, Australia, researchers collected data from an asthma management and education program over a 3-month period. The 150 patients enrolled in the study used a mini-Wright peak expiratory flow meter and recorded the best of three values after inhaled bronchodilator therapy twice a day. For each patient, $\overline{X}$ charts and pattern tests were developed to examine variations in peak expiratory flow. Out-of-control situations were investigated, and special causes were identified. This analysis enabled early detection of asthma problems and prompted immediate intervention such as increased aerosol bronchodilator therapy. Quality-control techniques proved superior to published "action points" in monitoring patients' conditions, thereby resulting in better care (Gibson et al., 1995).

At this point, you may think that once a process is in control, everything is fine, right? Not really! A process in control is not necessarily a "good" process in that it may not be capable of meeting established requirements.

BRADLEY PARK HOSPITAL 5.7

It was Thursday, and the meeting with Jennifer was on Monday. The list of problems was long enough, and Eric knew she would seriously question his management of the ED unless . . . he could come up with some of the solutions. He called Susan Clark, the ED nurse manager.

"Hi Susan, this is Eric. Can you come to the office for a minute?"

"Sure," Susan replied. "I'll be there in 5 minutes."

Eric knew that he could not tackle all the problems by Monday. However, he thought he'd have to explain why there was a major issue with patients leaving the ED before being seen even though the waiting room times were in control. This continued to puzzle him. The phone rang, and his secretary announced that Susan was there.

"Tell her to come in," Eric said.

Susan came in. She looked perplexed.

"Hello, Eric. Any problem?"

"Yes. I have a meeting with Jennifer Lawson on Monday morning. Management is concerned with the problems the ED faces. I put some charts together, and I am starting a dashboard. Nothing looks good. It's too late to do much about it before Monday, but I'd like to find out why we have so many LWBS patients.

Measures	FYTD Actual	FY Target	Sep-1	Sep-2	Sep-3	Sep-4	Sep-5	Sep-6	Sep-7
LWBS	14.2	0	17	14	16	4	7	14	28
Left without being treated (LWBT)	2.9	0	4	3	4	1	1	2	5
Average wait times	90	45	85	90	60	60	83	125	124
Average triage times	21	15	20	25	18	20	18	22	25
Arrival to treatment time	100	60	105	100	103	110	130	95	124
Data ready time	36	35	25	30	45	50	35	30	35

"Well, that's because they get tired of waiting for so long before a physician is available to see them."

"That may not be the entire story. My analysis shows that the waiting room times are in control. Susan, I'm desperate here. Management is not impressed with our performance. My job here may be on the line. Please. . . . Any chance you can do some digging and find out why these patients leave?"

"You're doing the best you can. We all are. We just don't have enough resources," Susan exclaimed.

"Well, that's the problem. Even though it is not enough to cover all our needs, our part of the hospital budget is far from shabby. Susan, I must offer some solution to our problems on Monday."

"Let's see. I'll talk to a few nurses and reception clerks and pick their brains. It won't be a thorough analysis of the situation, but perhaps there will be something useful you can report to Jennifer."

"That'd be great, Susan. I'll owe you!"

"Yes, you will, and I won't forget," Susan replied with a smile.

Friday afternoon, Susan called Eric in the office.

"Hi, Boss. How are you?"

"I don't know yet. It depends on what you're about to tell me."

"Let's put it this way. There were a lot of shrugs, eyes rolling to the back of the head, and always somebody else to blame. It was an interesting assignment, I'll tell you that. I'm summarizing the results of this discussion in writing. Unless things get crazy in the ED, I'll have the report on your desk by 5:00 this evening."

"Thanks, Susan. I'll be waiting."

At 5:30 p.m., the report was ready. It contained two charts: a cause-and-effect diagram and a Pareto chart. Eric looked at both charts for several minutes.

Eric Wong looked at Susan. "It appears that most LWBS patients leave the ED because they wait for too long and have no idea how much longer they will have to wait as we do not provide them with updates. Makes sense . . . we're just adding insult to injury; no pun intended.

"Yes, I'd be irritated too if I was a patient," Susan said. "Almost 80% of the patients who leave did so for these two reasons. I can't think of a quick solution to reducing wait times—although it is clearly a priority—but we could do a better job about informing patients about wait times. We could install monitors in the waiting room. These monitors would display estimates of wait times and would be refreshed every 10 minutes or so."

"This is about the best news I've heard all week! I'll be sure to tell Jennifer about the great job you've done in such a short period of time."

After a long day at work, Eric Wong was whistling on the way to his car. And then it hit him. Susan and her team had reemphasized the long wait times. It is not because a process is in control that it meets the patients' expectations!

 Although average wait times were within the control limits and did not follow a particular pattern, they do not meet the patients' expectations. Why not?

PROCESS CAPABILITY

Process capability indicates the ability of a process to produce outputs within specification limits. For example, the LCL and UCL for waiting times in the ED were 0.08 minutes and 204.28 minutes, respectively (see $\overline{X}$ chart in section on $\overline{X}$ and R charts). The spread represented the natural or random variation of the process. The process was found to be in control (see Figures 5.7 and 5.8), with no signs of assignable variation. However, what if surveys of low-acuity patients indicated that they would leave the ED if they had to stay longer than 2.5 hours (150 minutes) in the waiting room? In that case, the process, which is in control, would not be capable of meeting patient requirements. Of course, if the process was out of control, it would be too unpredictable to ever be capable of meeting preestablished requirements. In other words, being in control is a *necessary* but not *sufficient* condition for a process to be capable.

Process Capability
The ability of a process to produce outputs within specification limits.

Preestablished requirements are often called specification or tolerance limits. Unlike the LCL and UCL, they do not reflect the random variation of the process. Rather, the lower specification limit (LSL) and upper specification limit (USL) are determined independently from the process and reflect tolerable variation from the target value for a particular indicator. These limits may be imposed by the customer of the process, evidence-based guidelines, regulations, and so on. There are two reasons why a process that is in control may not be capable of meeting the specifications: (a) its natural distribution is too wide, and/or (b) its distribution is not properly centered.

Is the Process Distribution Too Wide?

Look at Figure 5.14. You can see that the natural or random variation in the process is too "spread out" to fit between the LSL and USL. You do not have to plot the distribution to determine whether a process distribution will fit within the band established by the LSL and USL. All you have to do is compute C_p, **the process capability ratio**, which compares the width of the process distribution (denominator in the following formula) with the width or range of the specifications (numerator in the following formula)

Process Capability Ratio

A metric that compares the width of the process distribution with the width of the specifications.

$$C_p = \frac{USL - LSL}{6\,\sigma} \qquad [5.31]$$

FIGURE 5.14 –
Process distribution is too wide.

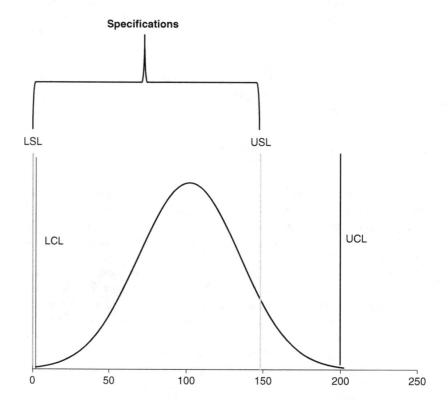

In our example, assume that the process standard deviation of waiting times is 33 minutes. The process capability ratio is therefore:

$$C_p = \frac{150 - 0}{6 \times 33} = 0.76$$

This value indicates that the denominator, or process variation, is larger than the tolerable range of specifications. The process, or random variation, is too large for the process to be capable. At a minimum, C_p should be equal to 1, which means that the width of the process and the range of the specifications are exactly the same. The larger the C_p, the tighter the process distribution compared to the spread of the specification limits, and therefore the greater is the ability of the process to meet specifications. Table 5.6 displays some guidelines regarding the interpretation of C_p values.

TABLE 5.6 – Interpretation of C_p and C_{pk} Values

C_p, C_{pk} Values	Interpretation
< 1	Process is not capable
= 1	Process is barely capable
≥ 1.33	Process is capable (good)
≥ 2.0	Process is capable (excellent)

Is the Process Well Centered?

In our example, because the process distribution is too wide, it is obvious that the process is generating unacceptable output. However, sometimes, even if the process distribution is narrower than the range of the specification limits, the process may not be capable of meeting the specifications because it is poorly centered. Ideally, the center of the process distribution should be equidistant from the LSL and the USL. In reality, it is likely to be somewhat off. The key is for the center of the process distribution to be as close as possible to the midpoint between the LSL and USL. In order to determine whether it is the case, you should compute C_{pk}, the **process capability index**:

Process Capability Index
A metric that determines whether the process output is properly centered.

$$C_{pk} = minimum\left(\frac{USL - \overline{\overline{X}}}{3\sigma}, \frac{\overline{\overline{X}} - LSL}{3\sigma}\right) \qquad [5.32]$$

$$= min\left(\frac{150 - 102.18}{(3 \times 33)}, \frac{102.18 - 0}{(3 \times 33)}\right)$$

$$= min\ (0.48, 1.03) = 0.48$$

The larger the C_{pk} value, the better it is; our concern is about the ability of the lower of the two computed values to meet process capability criteria. Based on Table 5.6, the C_{pk} value of 0.48 is unacceptable. This value is associated with the first term, that is, $\dfrac{USL - \overline{\overline{X}}}{3\sigma}$. It shows that the process mean is less than 3 standard deviations away from the USL and is therefore too close to it. Not only is our process distribution too wide, but it is also poorly centered.

A useful analogy to C_p and C_{pk} is driving your car into a garage (Figure 5.15). The garage door provides the specifications limits. The car's width is the distribution of the process output. If the car is wider than the garage, it does not matter whether you have it centered or not; it will not fit at all [Figure 5.15(a)]. If the car is only a little bit narrower than the garage, you must park it right in the middle of the garage, or it will not fit [Figure 5.15(b)]. If the car is significantly smaller than the garage, there is plenty of room on either side, and it will fit whether or not you center it [Figure 5.15(c)]. C_p and C_{pk} give you the relationship between the size of the car and the size of the garage. They also tell you how far away from the middle of the garage you parked the car.

FIGURE 5.15 –
Process capability
analogy.

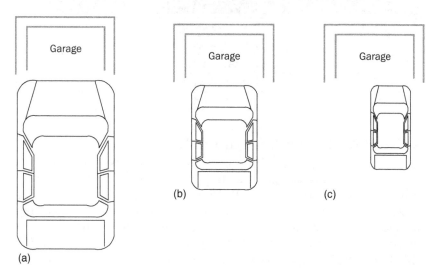

So, if the process is in control but incapable of meeting the specifications, what should be done? We are no longer talking about assignable causes of variation, here. Instead, we are looking at the natural variation of the process and realize that it must change. This means that the process must be changed or redesigned, which is the topic of Chapters 6 and 7.

SUMMARY

In this chapter, you were introduced to the concept of variation: assignable or random. Processes must be stable and predictable. In order to monitor their behavior, we use a multitude of statistical process control charts. For attributes, common charts are p-, c-, and u-charts. For variables, we use $\overline{X}$ and R or $\overline{X}$ and s-charts, depending on the sample size. If some of the process output values fall outside of the three limits of the distribution or follow a pattern, the process is deemed out of control. This means that assignable causes of variation are present and, in most cases, need to be eliminated. However, even if a process is in control, it may be incapable of meeting target specifications. The process capability ratio and the process capability index help you determine whether the process is capable. If it is not capable, it needs to be redesigned (Chapters 6 and 7). In Figure 5.16, we have expanded our mind map to show the links between the VOP and process performance through SPC and process capability. SPC monitors the process and tracks the consistency of its performance; process capability highlights gaps between performance and expected targets. Both provide sound metrics for improved redesign.

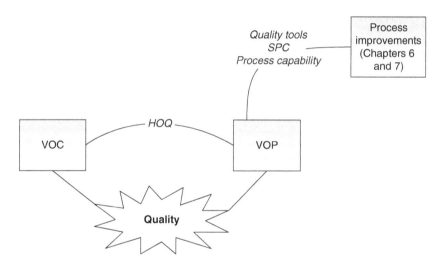

FIGURE 5.16 – Revised mind map linking indicators to other quality concepts and delivery.

KEY TERMS

Process variation	Variables	*R* chart
Assignable/special causes of variation	*p*-chart	*s*-chart
Common/random causes of variation	*c*-chart	Run test
Statistical process control	Area of opportunity	Process capability
Control charts	*u*-chart	Process capability ratio
Attributes	$\overline{X}$ chart	Process capability index

TOOLS USED IN THIS CHAPTER

TOOL	TYPE OF DATA	PURPOSE
p-chart	Attributes	SPC chart used to track the proportion defective in a sample
c-chart	Attributes	SPC chart used to track the number of defects per unit
u-chart	Attributes	SPC chart used to track the number of defects per unit over time when the area of opportunity fluctuates
$\bar{X}$ chart	Variables	SPC chart used to track sample means over time
R chart	Variables	SPC chart used to track sample ranges over time
s-chart	Variables	SPC chart used to track sample standard deviations over time
Run test	Attributes and variables	Test used to detect patterns in a control chart divided into zones A, B, and C
Process capability ratio	Variables (an equivalent measure is available for attributes)	Metric to determine whether a process in control has a distribution narrow enough to fit within specification limits
Process capability index	Variables (an equivalent measure is available for attributes)	Metric to determine whether a process in control is properly centered with respect to a specified target value

FORMULAS USED IN THIS CHAPTER

Technique	Definition	Formula	Number
p-chart	Mean $(\bar{p})$	$\dfrac{\text{total number of nonconforming items}}{\text{total number of items inspected}}$	[5.1]

Technique	Definition	Formula	Number
	Standard deviation (S_p)	$\sqrt{\dfrac{\bar{p}\,(1-\bar{p})}{\text{number of items inspected in each sample (i.e., sample size)}}}$	[5.2]
	UCL_p	$\bar{p}+3\,S_p$	[5.3]
	LCL_p	$\bar{p}-3S_p$	[5.4]
	Proportion defective (p)	$\dfrac{\text{number of nonconforming items in a sample}}{\text{number of items in the sample (sample size)}}$	[5.5]
c-chart	Mean $(\bar{c})$	$\dfrac{\text{total number of defects}}{\text{total number of inspection units}}$	[5.6]
	Standard deviation (S_c)	$\sqrt{\bar{c}}$	[5.7]
	UCL_c	$\bar{c}+S_c$	[5.8]
	LCL_c	$\bar{c}-3S_c$	[5.9]
u-chart	Number of sets of inspected units (n)	$\dfrac{\text{number of observations in the original area of opportunity}}{\text{number of observations in the agreed upon set of inspected units}}$	[5.10]
	Number of defects per set (u)	$\dfrac{c}{n}=\dfrac{\text{number of defects in the original area of opportunity}}{\text{number of sets of inspected units}}$	[5.11]

Technique	Definition	Formula	Number
	Mean $(\bar{u})$	$\dfrac{\text{total number of defects}}{\text{total number of sets of inspected units}}$	[5.12]
	Standard deviation (S_u)	$\sqrt{\dfrac{\bar{u}}{n}}$	[5.13]
	UCL_u	$\bar{u} + 3S_u$	[5.14]
	LCL_u	$\bar{u} - 3S_u$	[5.15]
R chart	Range (R)	largest value in the sample – lowest value in the sample	[5.16]
	Mean $(\bar{R})$	$\dfrac{\sum R}{k} = \dfrac{\text{sum of the ranges across all samples}}{\text{number of samples taken}}$	[5.17]
	UCL_R	$D_4\bar{R}$	[5.18]
	LCL_R	$D_3\bar{R}$	[5.19]
$\bar{X}$ chart $(2 \le n \le 9)$	Sample mean $(\bar{X})$	$\dfrac{\sum X}{n} = \dfrac{\text{sum of sample values}}{\text{number of units in sample (sample size)}}$	[5.20]
	Mean $(\bar{\bar{X}})$	$\dfrac{\sum \bar{X}}{k} = \dfrac{\text{sum of the sample means}}{\text{number of samples taken}}$	[5.21; 5.28]
	$UCL_{\bar{x}}$	$\bar{\bar{X}} + A_2\bar{R}$	[5.22]
	$LCL_{\bar{x}}$	$\bar{\bar{X}} - A_2\bar{R}$	[5.23]

Technique	Definition	Formula	Number
s-chart	Standard deviation (s)	$\sqrt{\dfrac{\sum_{i=1}^{n}(X_i - \bar{X})^2}{n-1}}$	[5.24]
	Average standard deviation ($\bar{s}$)	$\dfrac{\sum s}{k} = \dfrac{\text{sum of standard deviations}}{\text{number of samples taken}}$	[5.25]
	UCL_s	$B_4\bar{s}$	[5.26]
	LCL_s	$B_3\bar{s}$	[5.27]
$\bar{X}$ chart ($n \geq 10$)	$UCL_{\bar{x}}$	$\bar{\bar{X}} + A_3\bar{s}$	[5.29]
	$LCL_{\bar{x}}$	$\bar{\bar{X}} - A_3\bar{s}$	[5.30]
Process capability	Process capability ratio (C_p)	$\dfrac{USL - LSL}{6\sigma}$	[5.31]
	Process capability index (C_{pk})	$\min\left(\dfrac{USL - \bar{X}}{3\sigma}, \dfrac{\bar{X} - LSL}{3\sigma}\right)$	[5.32]

WHAT DO YOU REMEMBER?

1. What are the two major causes of variation? Explain each one.
2. What is statistical process control? What is the purpose of control charts?
3. How do you determine whether a process is in control?
4. Differentiate between attributes and variables.
5. How do you know when to use a p-chart versus a c-chart? A c-chart versus a u-chart?
6. When do you use $\bar{X}$ and R charts versus $\bar{X}$ and s-charts?
7. Distinguish between "sample size" and "number of samples taken." Use examples to illustrate your answer.
8. What are zones A, B, and C in a control chart?
9. What is process capability? What is the purpose of C_p? What is the purpose of C_{pk}?

SOLVE BPH'S PROBLEMS

1. Based on all the control charts produced by Eric Wong and his staff, anticipate Jennifer Lawson's reaction and concerns.

2. At BPH, wait times seemed to be in control (Figures 5.7 and 5.8). Does it mean that the situation is satisfactory? Explain why or why not?

3. Samples of 30 medication orders placed in the ED are checked each day against five potential types of errors. The following table shows the number of orders that were found to include errors during the last 15 days. Develop the appropriate control chart(s). Is the process in control? Why or why not?

Day	Number of Orders Containing Errors
1	2
2	5
3	3
4	1
5	0
6	4
7	10
8	3
9	5
10	0
11	1
12	7
13	4
14	3
15	1

4. For each sample of 30 medication orders described in problem 3, the number of medication errors is also recorded (see following table). Develop the appropriate control chart(s). Is the process in control? Why or why not?

Day	Number of Errors
1	3
2	8
3	4
4	3
5	0
6	5

(continued)

(continued)

Day	Number of Errors
7	15
8	6
9	12
10	0
11	2
12	12
13	6
14	3
15	1

5. Following are the average times spent in the ED and standard deviations for samples of 25 patients seen in the ED in February. Develop the appropriate $\overline{X}$ and s-charts. Is the process in control? Why or why not?

Day	Mean (hours)	SD (hours)
1	5.22	2.64
2	4.67	2.72
3	4.63	2.90
4	5.40	2.59
5	5.70	2.71
6	5.02	2.27
7	5.50	3.39
8	6.04	3.37
9	5.00	2.92
10	4.70	2.64
11	4.71	2.65
12	5.41	2.67
13	5.06	2.60
14	5.84	3.91
15	5.53	3.18
16	5.08	3.01
17	5.74	4.08
18	6.71	3.45
19	5.46	2.93
20	5.64	2.78
21	5.29	3.04
22	6.08	2.86
23	4.74	2.84
24	4.78	2.87
25	4.92	2.82

(continued)

(continued)

Day	Mean (hours)	SD (hours)
26	6.20	4.28
27	6.17	3.22
28	5.30	3.04

6. The dietitian at BPH has warned that the meals served at the cafeteria contain too much sodium. For the past 10 days, she has sampled four batches of the "entrée du jour" and recorded the sodium content per serving. Based on the data that follows, construct the $\overline{X}$ and R charts.

   a. Is the process in control? Why or why not?

   b. Given the fact that the sodium content should be between 450 and 520 mg per serving for meal-type products, does the dietitian have a valid concern? Assume that the standard deviation is 25 mg.

Day	Sodium Content (mg/serving)			
	Batch 1	Batch 2	Batch 3	Batch 4
1	502	485	516	550
2	495	519	514	480
3	482	516	530	495
4	543	496	402	516
5	475	489	526	502
6	513	489	497	526
7	532	462	523	495
8	495	485	521	505
9	512	523	452	476
10	500	502	513	487

7. Nosocomial infections result from treatment in a hospital. At BPH, the following incidences of nosocomial infection that appeared within 30 days after discharge were recorded for the first half of June. The number of patients discharged did not fluctuate much from day to day and can be assumed to be constant. Develop the appropriate chart(s). Is the process in control? Why or why not?

Day	Nosocomial Infections
1	4
2	3
3	5
4	4

(continued)

(*continued*)

Day	Nosocomial Infections
5	2
6	6
7	5
8	13
9	12
10	10
11	15
12	16
13	13
14	15
15	14

8. The head of the surgery department is concerned about the incidence of patient readmissions after being discharged from the hospital. In several cases, a patient had to be readmitted multiple times. The following data are available for the past 11 months. Develop the appropriate control chart and help the head of surgery determine whether the process involving readmissions per 500 discharges is stable. Based on your findings, does he have a reason to be concerned?

Month	Number of Discharges	Number of Readmissions
January	720	108
February	680	95
March	500	85
April	559	78
May	672	114
June	742	122
July	700	126
August	650	110
September	708	134
October	687	123
November	729	145

9. One of BPH's clinics is concerned about the number of patient records that get misplaced. They decide to record the number of misplaced patient records over a period of 15 weeks. The number of patients seen for whom the records were needed is indicated. Develop the appropriate control chart(s) and determine whether the process is in control.

Week	Number of Misplaced Records	Number of Records Needed
1	10	210
2	9	190
3	12	220
4	10	225
5	15	185
6	6	200
7	26	210
8	12	205
9	8	218
10	6	228
11	9	175
12	11	200
13	10	210
14	13	220
15	9	185

10. Dr. Barari wants to reduce the waiting times in her office. Six random observations of times spent between arrival and exam were made over a period of 17 days.

   a. Develop the appropriate chart(s) and determine whether the process is in control

   b. If patient surveys indicate that they are willing to wait between 10 and 30 minutes before seeing Dr. Barari, is the process capable? Assume a process standard deviation of 2.5 minutes.

Observations

Day	1	2	3	4	5	6
1	29	29	22	31	29	31
2	24	29	40	26	36	30
3	28	33	25	26	28	33
4	26	31	38	30	23	28
5	36	29	24	29	26	32
6	26	27	32	25	30	29
7	22	33	30	31	37	34
8	40	29	26	29	32	30
9	32	32	21	34	28	29
10	34	26	35	27	31	26
11	35	30	29	30	31	27
12	38	35	37	35	30	32
13	35	29	30	25	28	30

(continued)

(*continued*)

Day	1	2	3	4	5	6
14	22	29	26	30	36	28
15	26	26	34	34	25	36
16	29	26	20	31	32	33
17	28	30	34	28	31	30

11. You have been asked to determine whether the sound level at night is acceptable in cancer patient rooms. Using a digital sound-pressure-level meter, you collect data in 12 patient rooms, every day, for 20 days. Recommended sound levels are 35 dB ± 10 dB. Is the process in control? Why or why not? If the process mean and standard deviation are 40 dB and 3 dB, respectively, is the process capable of meeting recommended sound levels? Why or why not?

Day	1	2	3	4	5	6	7	8	9	10	11	12
1	31.2	39.8	41.0	39.1	40.0	37.9	41.7	45.8	37.7	35.6	33.8	40.3
2	43.1	37.0	43.9	41.7	38.2	41.7	39.0	43.2	39.1	40.4	38.7	40.6
3	41.2	41.6	44.0	37.7	39.8	33.7	39.9	44.2	41.2	40.1	40.1	41.4
4	36.8	36.7	41.8	38.2	40.2	42.0	39.7	40.4	37.5	35.1	41.2	40.3
5	41.9	39.7	38.3	39.9	37.6	43.3	35.9	43.4	38.5	43.5	41.9	41.7
6	41.4	42.1	38.2	40.3	41.6	39.9	39.1	41.1	43.4	40.0	46.2	42.5
7	38.4	34.4	38.9	40.8	42.7	42.8	43.1	40.8	40.6	42.0	38.2	39.6
8	31.3	40.8	35.9	40.0	41.2	38.8	39.4	45.1	31.1	37.0	35.3	38.2
9	43.4	41.2	37.1	42.2	42.1	35.6	39.3	39.0	41.0	38.5	41.8	40.0
10	43.5	42.9	36.0	34.7	41.4	40.5	44.2	41.1	41.4	38.8	47.3	42.1
11	36.5	35.7	37.9	44.2	39.4	40.8	41.0	43.6	37.6	34.2	38.5	40.8
12	43.5	36.3	38.4	45.4	38.9	45.8	39.9	41.6	40.3	40.1	43.5	41.9
13	39.7	41.6	37.6	44.1	39.0	45.1	40.0	36.8	35.4	40.0	37.2	37.8
14	40.5	37.4	43.6	36.9	38.1	41.8	38.8	33.1	40.7	42.1	37.3	40.7
15	35.6	39.7	38.2	40.2	44.6	35.4	39.1	39.2	40.6	38.5	38.4	42.8
16	38.4	37.4	42.2	38.3	45.8	37.8	37.7	44.0	43.1	37.7	35.5	37.6
17	38.2	39.3	37.0	37.4	37.6	34.5	38.2	36.8	37.7	40.9	38.5	39.8
18	46.9	46.2	35.6	35.8	40.3	37.8	41.6	39.5	38.4	41.4	42.0	42.0
19	41.7	44.3	40.2	39.0	38.2	41.9	40.0	35.0	40.4	40.2	33.6	36.3
20	38.8	35.1	39.1	41.6	41.1	41.8	46.7	41.3	39.8	39.6	34.2	37.2

12. Based on the following scenarios, determine the type of data (attribute versus variable) involved and identify the appropriate control chart.

Type of Measure	Scenario	Chart(s)
	Each day, an inspector checks the 4th floor of a clinic. He has a list of 30 items to check for cleanliness, and he places a check mark next to the items that did not meet cleaning standards.	
	At the hospital cafeteria, staff complaints about the food served are recorded for lunch and dinner each day.	
	At a clinic, the number of no-shows (patients who had an appointment but failed to show up for it) is recorded each day.	
	Each day, the registration clerk of a clinic records the time at which a patient checks in and the time when he or she is called by the nurse to see the doctor. The difference between these two times is the wait time. The registration clerk reports the number of patients who had to wait more than 20 minutes.	
	Hospital staff records the number of Medicare patients' rehospitalizations within 30 days following surgery.	
	Each week, the director of financial services determines the number of bills that contained errors.	
	Each week, the director of financial services reports the number of billing errors identified by her staff.	
	When billing Medicare outpatients, claims must be filed within 72 hours of service. Each week, a hospital administrator selects a sample of 20 late claims and records for each claim the number of hours by which the 72-hour deadline was exceeded.	
	A new hospital information system has just been implemented. This implementation required extensive training of the nursing staff. To assess the quality of the training program, the education specialist requests to see the daily log of calls (seeking assistance with the new system) to the information technology help desk.	

13. Use the supplemental BPH ED data set (LWBS & LWBT) for April. The proportion of LWBS + LWBT patients relative to the total number of visits is provided for each day (Column Q). Construct the appropriate p-chart. Is the process in control? Why or why not? Hint: convert percentages (LWBS + LWBT rate) to decimals.

14. Use the BPH ED data set (LWBS & LWBT) for May. The proportion of admissions relative to the total number of visits is provided for each day (Column BF). Construct the appropriate p-chart. Is the process in control? Why or why not?

15. Use the BPH data set (CBC-Stats) for October. Filter the data to extract the tests for CBC-d (Column A). From October 1st to

October 20th, randomly select samples of 5 total lab turnaround times (Column J) each day. Using the 20 samples (one for each day), construct an $\overline{X}$ chart and conduct a run test. Is there any reason for concern? Hint: use $\frac{1}{3}A_2\overline{R}$ for 1 standard deviation.

THINK OUTSIDE THE BOOK!

1. Find an article describing the reorganization of an emergency department. Explain the scope of their efforts to redesign processes and how these efforts contributed to higher efficiency and higher patient satisfaction.

2. Do a literature search and explain the "crowding" phenomenon in the ED.

3. SPC knowledge by itself is insufficient to bring about quality. Inability to apply this knowledge is a major obstacle to quality achievement and is the result of numerical illiteracy. "Numerical illiteracy is not a failure with arithmetic, but it is instead a failure to know how to use the basic tools of arithmetic to understand data. Numerical illiteracy is not addressed by traditional courses in elementary or secondary schools, nor is it addressed in advanced courses in mathematics. This is why even highly educated individuals can be numerically illiterate" (Wheeler, 1993, p. vi).

    Explain why and how numerical illiteracy can be a serious problem in healthcare management. What can be done to overcome this obstacle?

4. In healthcare, it is not uncommon to see Individual *X-MR* control charts. Research what these charts display and identify some healthcare indicators for which they are appropriate.

REFERENCES

Gibson, P. G., Wlodarczyk, J., Hensley, M. J., Murree-Allen, K., Olson, L. G., & Saltos, N. (1995). Using quality-control analysis of peak expiratory flow recordings to guide therapy for asthma. *Annals of Internal Medicine, 123*(7), 488–492.

Lighter, D. E., & Fair, D. C. (2004). *Quality management in health care.* Boston, MA: Jones & Bartlett.

Russell, R. S., & Taylor, B. W. (2009). *Operations management: Creating value along the supply chain* (6th ed.). Hoboken, NJ: John Wiley & Sons.

Stevenson, W. J. (2008). *Operations management* (10th ed.). Boston, MA: McGraw-Hill/Irwin.

Wheeler, D. (1993). *Understanding variation: The key to managing chaos.* Knoxville, TN: SPC Press.

APPENDIX 5.1 FACTORS FOR LIMITS OF CONTROL CHARTS

Sample Size (n)	Chart for Averages		Chart for Standard Deviations		Chart for Ranges	
	A_2	A_3	B_3	B_4	D_3	D_4
1	2.660	—			0	3.267
2	1.880	2.659	0.000	3.267	0.000	3.267
3	1.023	1.954	0.000	2.568	0.000	2.575
4	0.729	1.628	0.000	2.266	0.000	2.282
5	0.577	1.427	0.000	2.089	0.000	2.114
6	0.483	1.287	0.030	1.970	0.000	2.004
7	0.419	1.182	0.118	1.882	0.076	1.924
8	0.373	1.099	0.185	1.815	0.136	1.864
9	0.337	1.032	0.239	1.761	0.184	1.816
10	0.308	0.975	0.284	1.716	0.223	1.777
11	0.285	0.927	0.321	1.679	0.256	1.744
12	0.266	0.886	0.354	1.646	0.283	1.717
13	0.249	0.850	0.382	1.618	0.307	1.693
14	0.235	0.817	0.406	1.594	0.328	1.672
15	0.223	0.789	0.428	1.572	0.347	1.653
16	0.212	0.763	0.448	1.552	0.363	1.637
17	0.203	0.739	0.466	1.534	0.378	1.622
18	0.194	0.718	0.482	1.518	0.391	1.609
19	0.187	0.698	0.497	1.503	0.404	1.596
20	0.180	0.680	0.510	1.490	0.415	1.585
21	0.173	0.663	0.523	1.477	0.425	1.575
22	0.167	0.647	0.534	1.466	0.435	1.565
23	0.162	0.633	0.545	1.455	0.443	1.557
24	0.157	0.619	0.555	1.445	0.452	1.548
25	0.153	0.606	0.565	1.435	0.459	1.541
Over 25	$\dfrac{3}{\sqrt{n}}$	—	$1 - \dfrac{3}{\sqrt{2n}}$	$1 + \dfrac{3}{\sqrt{2n}}$		

APPENDIX 5.2 DEVELOPING A CONTROL CHART IN EXCEL

The p-chart shown in Figure 5.4 is based on the data in Figure A5.2.1 (the formulas for $\bar{p}$, UCL, and LCL were provided in the chapter material). Note that a column labeled "actual LCL" has been added. The LCL value for day 9 was negative. It is impossible to have a negative

proportion. As a result, it must be rounded up to 0. The formula in cell
H2 is = IF(G2 > 0, G2, 0).

	A	B	C	D	E	F	G	H
1	Day	Visits	LWBS	Proportio	p-bar	UCL	LCL	actual LCL
2	1	161	17	0.1056	0.0705	0.1311	0.0100	0.0100
3	2	159	14	0.0881	0.0705	0.1315	0.0096	0.0096
4	3	165	16	0.0970	0.0705	0.1303	0.0107	0.0107
5	4	180	4	0.0222	0.0705	0.1278	0.0133	0.0133
6	5	167	7	0.0419	0.0705	0.1300	0.0111	0.0111
7	6	182	14	0.0769	0.0705	0.1275	0.0136	0.0136
8	7	168	28	0.1667	0.0705	0.1298	0.0113	0.0113
9	8	190	17	0.0895	0.0705	0.1263	0.0148	0.0148
10	9	109	0	0.0000	0.0705	0.1441	-0.0030	0.0000
11	10	175	18	0.1029	0.0705	0.1286	0.0125	0.0125
12	11	172	19	0.1105	0.0705	0.1291	0.0120	0.0120
13	12	151	8	0.0530	0.0705	0.1331	0.0080	0.0080
14	13	153	9	0.0588	0.0705	0.1327	0.0084	0.0084
15	14	177	24	0.1356	0.0705	0.1283	0.0128	0.0128
16	15	153	7	0.0458	0.0705	0.1327	0.0084	0.0084
17	16	146	12	0.0822	0.0705	0.1341	0.0070	0.0070
18	17	171	17	0.0994	0.0705	0.1293	0.0118	0.0118
19	18	176	7	0.0398	0.0705	0.1285	0.0126	0.0126
20	19	171	7	0.0409	0.0705	0.1293	0.0118	0.0118
21	20	177	3	0.0169	0.0705	0.1283	0.0128	0.0128
22	21	146	1	0.0068	0.0705	0.1341	0.0070	0.0070
23	22	164	6	0.0366	0.0705	0.1305	0.0106	0.0106
24	23	155	15	0.0968	0.0705	0.1322	0.0088	0.0088
25	24	193	18	0.0933	0.0705	0.1258	0.0153	0.0153
26	25	188	7	0.0372	0.0705	0.1266	0.0145	0.0145
27	26	164	9	0.0549	0.0705	0.1305	0.0106	0.0106
28	27	177	1	0.0056	0.0705	0.1283	0.0128	0.0128
29	28	187	29	0.1551	0.0705	0.1267	0.0144	0.0144
30	29	164	8	0.0488	0.0705	0.1305	0.0106	0.0106
31	30	177	12	0.0678	0.0705	0.1283	0.0128	0.0128

FIGURE A5.2.1 – Data for p-chart shown in Figure 5.4.

Note: Microsoft Excel application interface is used with permission of Microsoft.

The values that you want to see plotted on your p-chart are: $\bar{p}$, UCL,
LCL (actual), and the sample proportion values. With your mouse,
select the cells $D$1:$F$31,$H$1:$H$31 (Press the Ctrl key to keep the
D–F columns marked while skipping Column G), click on Insert, then
click on the Line chart.

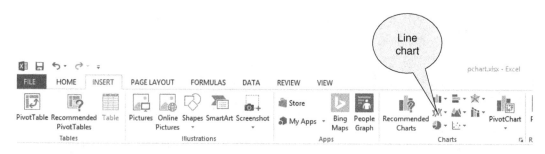

FIGURE A5.2.2

Note: Microsoft Excel application interface is used with permission of Microsoft.

Select the line chart format of your choice, and the corresponding control chart will appear on your monitor. Scroll through the *Chart Style* options to select your preferred layout.

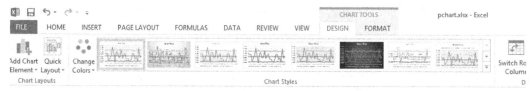

FIGURE A5.2.3 – Selecting the line chart format.

Note: Microsoft Excel application interface is used with permission of Microsoft.

Here is the result:

FIGURE A5.2.4

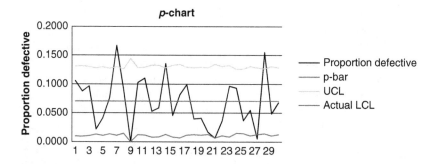

APPENDIX 5.3 SAMPLING

To select sample units for SPC, it is common to use a **probability sampling** method. This means that each unit in the population is assigned an objective probability or chance of being selected, irrespective of the personal preferences or biases of the person collecting the data. For example, a nurse keeping track of wait times could not arbitrarily (and conveniently!) select patients who show up during the first hour of her shift in order to be "done with it" early! This would be what we call *convenience sampling*, which is not a statistically sound sampling method.

There are several types of sound, probability-based sampling plans. The most common are simple random sampling, stratified sampling, and cluster sampling.

SIMPLE RANDOM SAMPLING

Simple random sampling is simple! It means that every sample of a certain size within a population has a known and equal probability of being selected in the sample.

Let us demonstrate this principle. A total of 100 patients visited the ED on September 1 (Table A5.3.1). The average wait time was 75.64 minutes. If you were going to pick a sample of 10 patients, there would be 17,310,309,456,440 possible samples of size 10! You could write them all out on 17,310,309,456,440 pieces of paper, put them in a hat, and pick one of them. Each sample of 10 patients would have a 1/17,310,309,456,440 chance of being selected.

Fortunately, this was just a demonstration of the concept. Nobody would actually do it this way. Instead, we could just put our finger on the list of patients and their associated wait times, close our eyes, pick one patient, write down the wait time for that patient, and repeat the process 10 times. Or we could use the sampling tool in Excel to select 10 patients and their wait times. When using this procedure, we obtain the sample shown in Table A5.3.2. For this sample, the average wait time is 84.9 minutes. Why is it so much higher than the average of 75.64 minutes found for the population of patients seen in the ED on September 1? Note that the sample included three patients from the day shift, six from the evening shift, and one from the night shift. However, the percentages of patients in the population seen during the day, evening, and night shifts were 48, 37, and 15, respectively. In other words, patients who arrived during the evening shift are overrepresented, whereas patients who arrived during the other two shifts are underrepresented in our sample. As wait times tend to be longer during the evening shift, it is therefore no surprise that the average waiting time for our sample of patients is substantially longer than that of the population. To overcome this problem, we can use a sampling procedure called "proportionate stratified random sampling."

TABLE A5.3.1 – Wait Times Data—September 1		
Patient	**Arrival Time**	**Wait Time (min)**
1	09-01 00:04:34	124
2	09-01 00:21:00	194
3	09-01 00:52:00	17
4	09-01 01:01:00	170
5	09-01 02:05:00	36

(continued)

TABLE A5.3.1 – Wait Times Data—September 1 (continued)

Patient	Arrival Time		Wait Time (min)	
6	09-01	02:24:24	4	
7	09-01	02:50:00	15	
8	09-01	05:02:10	3	Night Shift: Midnight to 8:00 a.m.
9	09-01	05:14:00	16	
10	09-01	05:43:00	9	15 patients
11	09-01	06:05:00	14	
12	09-01	07:09:00	12	Average wait time: 44 min
13	09-01	07:28:00	17	
14	09-01	07:44:41	20	
15	09-01	07:50:00	3	
16	09-01	08:14:00	34	
17	09-01	08:23:00	8	
18	09-01	08:24:02	0	
19	09-01	08:36:00	10	
20	09-01	08:37:00	2	
21	09-01	08:42:00	13	
22	09-01	08:47:50	5	
23	09-01	09:16:15	14	
24	09-01	09:36:00	18	
25	09-01	09:38:00	21	
26	09-01	09:41:00	29	
27	09-01	09:42:00	10	
28	09-01	09:42:00	10	
29	09-01	09:48:00	33	
30	09-01	09:52:00	20	Day Shift: 8:00 a.m. to 4:00 p.m.
31	09-01	10:04:00	23	
32	09-01	10:11:00	0	48 patients
33	09-01	10:12:00	88	
34	09-01	10:14:00	102	Average wait time: 64.31 min
35	09-01	10:31:26	62	
36	09-01	10:32:00	76	
37	09-01	10:38:36	112	
38	09-01	10:51:00	20	
39	09-01	10:52:00	119	
40	09-01	11:27:00	215	
41	09-01	11:33:00	142	
42	09-01	11:40:47	252	
43	09-01	11:49:00	16	

(continued)

TABLE A5.3.1 – Wait Times Data—September 1 (*continued*)

Patient	Arrival Time	Wait Time (min)	
44	09-01 11:55:00	59	
45	09-01 12:14:00	119	
46	09-01 12:46:00	92	
47	09-01 12:53:00	9	
48	09-01 12:57:10	62	
49	09-01 13:04:00	32	
50	09-01 13:05:00	5	
51	09-01 13:22:00	148	
52	09-01 13:47:00	152	
53	09-01 13:58:00	197	
54	09-01 14:10:58	213	
55	09-01 14:24:37	102	
56	09-01 14:31:00	4	
57	09-01 14:37:08	13	
58	09-01 14:49:00	18	
59	09-01 14:56:00	131	
60	09-01 15:20:00	19	
61	09-01 15:29:00	245	
62	09-01 15:42:00	2	
63	09-01 15:46:00	11	
64	09-01 16:00:25	134	
65	09-01 16:07:21	162	
66	09-01 16:14:00	225	
67	09-01 16:44:00	281	Evening Shift: 4:00 p.m. to midnight
68	09-01 16:54:00	248	
69	09-01 16:57:00	7	37 patients
70	09-01 16:59:45	5	
71	09-01 17:06:00	11	Average wait time: 103.32 min
72	09-01 17:06:16	217	
73	09-01 17:24:00	220	
74	09-01 17:35:59	1	
75	09-01 17:36:53	22	
76	09-01 17:46:00	11	
77	09-01 17:56:00	0	
78	09-01 18:37:00	168	
79	09-01 18:40:00	171	
80	09-01 18:51:00	166	
81	09-01 18:54:00	112	

(*continued*)

TABLE A5.3.1 – Wait Times Data—September 1 (continued)

Patient	Arrival Time	Wait Time (min)
82	09-01 18:59:00	6
83	09-01 19:07:00	13
84	09-01 19:33:00	221
85	09-01 20:09:00	93
86	09-01 20:10:29	139
87	09-01 20:29:00	72
88	09-01 20:36:00	183
89	09-01 20:39:00	82
90	09-01 21:11:10	70
91	09-01 21:26:00	168
92	09-01 21:39:00	129
93	09-01 21:49:00	57
94	09-01 21:54:00	37
95	09-01 21:58:00	77
96	09-01 22:31:00	78
97	09-01 22:36:00	108
98	09-01 22:54:00	35
99	09-01 23:24:00	12
100	09-01 23:27:00	82
	Average	75.64

TABLE A5.3.2 – Simple Random Sample of 10 Patients

Patient	Arrival Time	Shift	Wait Time (min)
93	09-01 21:49:00	Evening	57
69	09-01 16:57:00	Evening	7
5	09-01 02:05:00	Night	36
78	09-01 18:37:00	Evening	168
57	09-01 14:37:08	Day	13
24	09-01 09:36:00	Day	18
64	09-01 16:00:25	Evening	134
40	09-01 11:27:00	Day	215
97	09-01 22:36:00	Evening	108
85	09-01 20:09:00	Evening	93
Average			84.90

Simple Random Sampling Using Excel

It is quite simple to use Excel to generate samples. Below is the series of steps you need to follow to draw simple random samples (see Figures A5.3.1–A.5.3.5).

	A	B	C	D	E	F	G
1	Waiting Times Data - September 1st						
2							
3	Patient	Arrival Time		Wait time			
4	1	00:04:34		124			
5	2	00:21:00		194			
6	3	00:52:00		17		Night Shift	
7	4	01:01:00		170		12:00 a.m. - 8:00 a.m.	
8	5	02:05:00		36			
9	6	02:24:24		4			
10	.		.	.			
11	.		.	.			
12	42	11:40:47		252			
13	43	11:49:00		16			
14	44	11:55:00		59		Day Shift	
15	45	12:14:00		119		8:00 a.m. - 4:00 p.m.	
16	46	12:46:00		92			
17	47	12:53:00		9			
18	48	12:57:10		62			
19	.		.	.			
20	.		.	.			
21	95	21:58:00		77			
22	96	22:31:00		78			
23	97	22:36:00		108		Evening Shift	
24	98	22:54:00		35		4:00 p.m. to 12:00 a.m.	
25	99	23:24:00		12			
26	100	23:27:00		82			
27							

FIGURE A5.3.1 – Selection of waiting times data in Excel spreadsheet.

Note: Microsoft Excel application interface is used with permission of Microsoft.

Step 1: Click on the *Data* Tab, and select *Data Analysis*.

FIGURE A5.3.2 – Tool bar.

Note: Microsoft Excel application interface is used with permission of Microsoft.

STEP 2: Select *Sampling* and press *OK*.

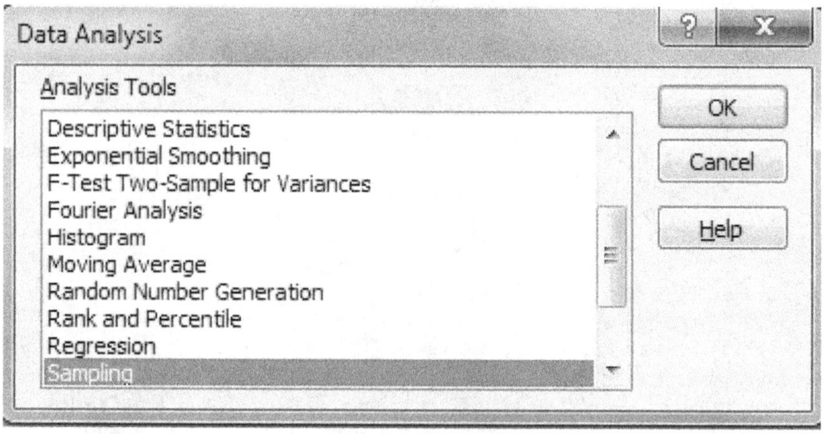

FIGURE A5.3.3 – Data analysis menu.

Note: Microsoft Excel application interface is used with permission of Microsoft.

STEP 3: In the *Input Range* box, specify the numbers from which the sample is going to be drawn. Here, it is patients 1 through 100. Click on *Labels* to indicate that the first cell corresponds to a column title. Select the number of units to be sampled (*Number of Samples*), and indicate where in the spreadsheet you want the sample to be displayed (e.g., K4).

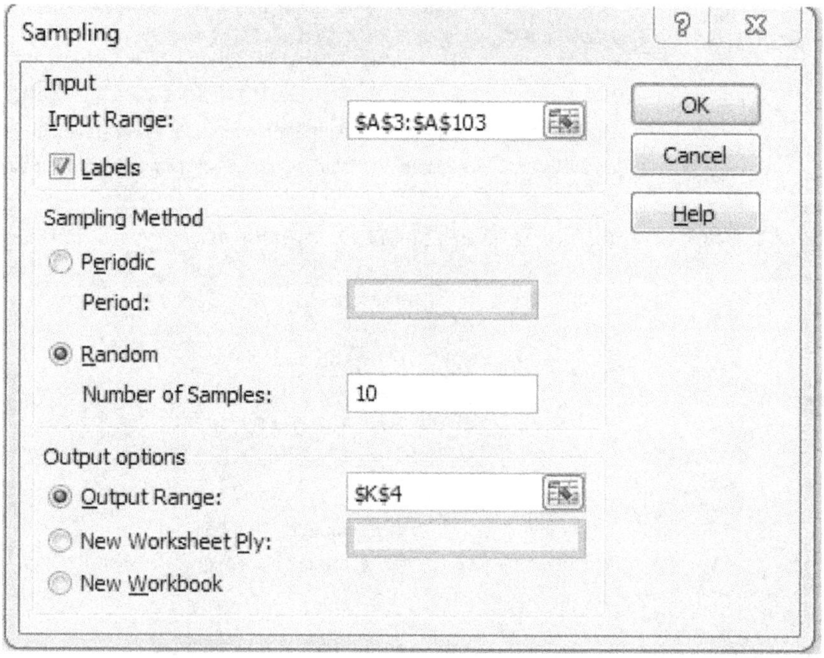

FIGURE A5.3.4 – Sampling dialog box.

Note: Microsoft Excel application interface is used with permission of Microsoft.

Ten patients were selected using this tool. Note that the procedure involves sampling with replacement. If you see that a patient was selected more than once, you will need to select another patient. Use the VLOOKUP function to extract the patients' wait times. For example, the formula in cell M4 is VLOOKUP(K4, $A$4:$C$103,3).

	K	L	M
1			
2	**Sampling Unit**	**Arrival Time**	**Wait time**
3			
4	11	06:05:00	14
5	80	18:51:00	166
6	50	13:05:00	5
7	34	10:14:00	102
8	79	18:40:00	171
9	14	07:44:41	20
10	19	08:36:00	10
11	97	22:36:00	108
12	39	10:52:00	119
13	4	01:01:00	170
14			

FIGURE A5.3.5 – Simple random sample generated in Excel.

Note: Microsoft Excel application interface is used with permission of Microsoft.

PROPORTIONATE STRATIFIED RANDOM SAMPLING

Proportionate stratified random sampling is a special case of simple random sampling. It requires the population to be divided into meaningful strata or categories (e.g., shift), such as in Table A5.3.1. The next two steps are then followed:

STEP 1: Ensure that the number of sample units from each stratum is proportionate to the size of the stratum in the population. In order to do so, use the following formula:

Number of sample units from a stratum = (number of population units in the stratum/total number of units in the population) × total sample size

For BPH's sample of 10 patients,

Number of patients from the day shift = (48/100) × 10 = 4.8 ≈ 5 patients.

Number of patients from the evening shift = (37/100) × 10 = 3.7 ≈ 4 patients.

Number of patients from the night shift = (15/100) × 10 = 1.5 ≈ 2 patients.

Due to rounding, we came up with a sample of 11 patients. To adjust, we will make a judgment call and select one rather than two patients from the night shift.

STEP 2: Select units from each stratum using the simple random sampling procedure (see above)

The results are presented in Table A5.3.3.

TABLE A5.3.3 – Proportionate Stratified Random Sample of 10 Patients

Patient	Arrival Time		Shift	Wait Time (10 min)
13	09-01	7:28:00	Night	17
21	09-01	8:42:00	Day	13
58	09-01	4:49:00	Day	18
26	09-01	9:41:00	Day	29
39	09-01	0:52:00	Day	119
56	09-01	4:31:00	Day	4
80	09-01	8:51:00	Evening	166
68	09-01	6:54:00	Evening	248
81	09-01	8:54:00	Evening	112
93	09-01	21:49:00	Evening	57
Average				78.3

The average wait time for the sample is now 78.3 minutes, which is quite close to the population average. Another popular sampling technique is systematic (or periodic) sampling.

SYSTEMATIC SAMPLING

This is a rather simple procedure, which involves selecting units from the population according to a fixed interval. The requirement is that the population units be assigned the numbers 1 to N (population size). For BPH, that would be patients 1 to 100. The following steps are then followed.

STEP 1: To sample n units, compute the sampling interval $k = N/n$. If you obtain a fractional amount, round k to the closest integer.

For BPH, $k = 100/10 = 10$.

STEP 2: Randomly select a number from 1 to k. This will be the first unit sampled from the population.

For BPH, let's assume that that number is 6. Patient #6 will be the first unit sampled.

STEP 3: The selected unit and every kth unit thereafter will be included in the sample until the desired sample size is obtained.

In BPH's case, the sampled patients would therefore be:

[1]   6
[2]   6 + 10 = 16
[3]   16 + 10 = 26
       .
       .
       .
[10]   86 + 10 = 96

The resulting sample and wait times are shown in Table A5.3.4.

TABLE A5.3.4 – Systematic Random Sample of 10 Patients

Patient	Arrival Time		Shift	Wait Time
6	09-01	02:24:24	Night	4
16	09-01	08:14:00	Day	34
26	09-01	09:41:00	Day	29
36	09-01	10:32:00	Day	76
46	09-01	12:46:00	Day	92
56	09-01	14:31:00	Day	4
66	09-01	16:14:00	Evening	225
76	09-01	17:46:00	Evening	11
86	09-01	20:10:29	Evening	139
96	09-01	22:31:00	Evening	78
Average				69.2

Although practical, systematic sampling can be problematic when the periodicity coincides with another phenomenon. For example, if the room temperature in the ED was recorded every hour over a period of 10 days, selecting a sample of 10 room temperatures would result in $k = 240/10 = 24$. This means that the sample data would all correspond to room temperatures recorded at the same time each day, let's say 5:00 a.m. Because room temperature is likely to fluctuate during the day because of sun exposure and volume of patients, it is likely that the average room temperature in our sample would be quite lower than the population's.

PROBLEMS

A.5.3.1. Differentiate among simple random sampling, proportionate stratified random sampling, and systematic sampling.

A.5.3.2. Your objective is to draw a sample of 500 patients. Use proportionate stratified random sampling in the following case.

Marital Status	N (population)	n (sample)?
Single (never married)	3,000	
Married	6,000	
Widowed	2,250	
Divorced	3,750	
Total	15,000	

A.5.3.3. Use the BPH ED data set (CBC stats); filter to obtain the data on the urine pregnancy tests (Column A) for the month of October. Select a simple random sample of five total lab turnaround times (Column J).

A.5.3.4. Use the BPH ED data set (CBC stats); filter to obtain the data on acetaminophen level tests (Column A) for October. Form a sample of 10 total lab turnaround times (Column J) using systematic sampling.

A.5.3.5. Use the BPH ED data set (LWBS & LWBT) for the month of November 2015:
   a.   Create a sample of 10 average lengths of stay (Column AO) using simple random sampling.
   b.   Create a sample of 10 average lengths of stay (Column AO) using systematic sampling.

CHAPTER 6

SIX SIGMA AND LEAN

BRADLEY PARK HOSPITAL 6.1

Brent Gregg caught up with Don and Jennifer as they were leaving the town hall meeting where Mike Chambers had outlined his quality strategy to the employees of Bradley Park Hospital (BPH).

"I thought Mike did a great job laying out his plan and setting expectations," Brent commented. "What did you two think?"

"It was powerful," Jennifer commented. "I could feel everyone's excitement. Particularly when Mike highlighted the successes to date. Eric was beaming!"

Don shook his head, "Mike does a great job engaging the staff and getting them to see how they are the key to BPH's success."

"And I am so glad that he linked our quality agenda to our financial success," Brent continued. "Everyone is worried about our finances, but now we all can see how our daily actions align with our overall success."

Don paused, "I will catch you later. Jennifer, I will see you tomorrow morning. Have a great evening."

 The new chief executive officer (CEO), Mike Chambers, seems to be respected by some of BPH's staff. Yet, he is not a clinician. Do you think that some clinicians will doubt his capabilities and criticize his ideas? Why?

INTRODUCTION AND LEARNING OBJECTIVES

In Chapters 4 and 5, we explored how to apply the concepts and tools for quality improvement. In this chapter, we describe how the complementary methodologies of Six Sigma and Lean can drive operational improvement. Many of the tools discussed in the previous chapters are used with Six Sigma and Lean. Both methodologies were derived from manufacturing, but each is being used more frequently in healthcare. Each brings to the improvement process something the other does not.

Lean is often used first, when the process needing improvement has not previously been refined. Think of Lean as a house painter, using broad strokes and a wide brush. It looks at steps in the activity fairly quickly, identifies areas for improvement, and allows you to check whether the change improves the process. After using Lean methods, if specific steps need refinement and a high level of reliability, the more technical Six Sigma tools may help decrease variation and improve process outcomes. Think of Six Sigma as an artist, using precise strokes to refine the picture.

We describe the methodologies of Lean and Six Sigma, illustrate how each methodology can be used, and show how tools from each methodology can be combined to drive improvement in healthcare. Specifically, you should be able to:

1. **Describe the types of waste found in healthcare processes**
2. **List the five Lean principles and explain briefly how each is used to examine a process**
3. **Learn how to map the value stream**
4. **Investigate the root cause of a problem**
5. **Understand the importance of flow in Lean**
6. **Explain the basis for Six Sigma**
7. **Describe the steps in DMAIC (define, measure, analyze, improve, control)**
8. **Elucidate how culture is important for organizations that adopt Lean or Six Sigma methodologies**

BRADLEY PARK HOSPITAL 6.2

Jennifer, with a cup of coffee in her hand, knocked on Don's office door.

"Come in. Ready to get down to work?"

"Yes," Jennifer replied. "But I must tell you that I feel overwhelmed. I went home last night and thought about Mike's vision for BPH and I realized that I have learned to lead some projects, but I do not know how to do everything that he says he wants to do. There is so much to be done. How are we going to change all that needs to be changed here?"

Don paused before he answered. "Jennifer, WE are not going to change everything, the people on the front lines are the ones who have the answers. Our job is to unleash their knowledge and creativity."

"How do we do that?" Jennifer looked puzzled.

Don continued, "Our job is to help create a culture of continuous improvement. It is not just about executing a handful of process improvement projects. The projects that we have completed are a good place to start, but more is required to drive sustainable results over time and embed continuous improvement into the fabric of this organization. That is where the real transformational changes take place.

"Mike started this transformation last night when he communicated his expectations and explained that it was everyone's job to improve how we care for patients. Our job will be to deliver training in how to improve the processes and give staff the tools to help them."

"What kind of tools?" Jennifer questioned. "Tools like Gantt charts and Pareto analyses?"

"Yes. Those are helpful. But there are other tools that help make problems in the process visible and help people think about processes differently. I am going to introduce you to the methodologies of Lean and Six Sigma."

 Have you ever been involved in Lean or Six Sigma projects? Were they successful? What were the primary roadblocks?

LEAN

Although some trace the rigorous process analysis back to the 1450s ship-building industry in Venice, most attribute Henry Ford with seizing the idea of streamlining the process of building automobiles (Ford & Crowther, 2014). He set up the moving assembly line and lined up fabrication processes in sequence to produce cheaper automobiles. However, a limitation of the assembly line was that it did not allow for variety. Henry Ford's famous quote, "Any customer can have a car painted any color that he wants so long as it is black" (Ford & Crowther, 1922, p. 72) sums up this problem!

In the 1930s, Kiichiro Toyoda and colleagues at Toyota built on the basic assembly-line concept and invented what is called the Toyota Production System. Toyoda was influenced greatly by the American scholar and visionary, W. Edwards Deming (The W. Edwards Deming Institute, 2015). Toyoda shifted the focus of the automobile assembly process to the flow of the automobile throughout the total process. The Toyota Production System began to right-size machines for the volume needed, introduce self-monitoring machines that insured quality, line up the machines in process sequence, and develop quick setups so each machine could make small volumes of many part numbers. The Toyota Production System was much more than an improved assembly line. It focused on the customer, and the push was to give the customer value. A major component of the Toyota Production System was treating employees with respect and allowing employees to think and improve processes when they saw the need.

Lean became a way of working, not just a set of tools. You can define **Lean** as "a set of concepts, principles, and tools used to create and deliver the most value from the customers' perspective while consuming the fewest resources and fully utilizing the knowledge and skill of the people performing the work" (Graban, 2012, p. 17). The core idea of Lean involves distinguishing what adds value to a process from what does not. The non–value-added steps are called "**waste**" (or *muda* in Japanese). In fact, the term "Lean" is derived from the meaning of the word, "containing little or no fat" (*Webster's New World Dictionary of the American Language*, 1968, p. 833). The goal is to ensure each process is as streamlined as possible, and designed to provide the customer with the most value. In its comprehensive form, Lean is a complete management system in which the values that permeate the organization are aligned with the guiding principles of Lean.

Lean
A set of concepts, principles, and tools used to create and deliver the most value from the customers' perspective while consuming the fewest resources and fully utilizing the knowledge and skill of the people performing the work.

Waste (or *muda* in Japanese)
Refers to the non–value-added steps in a process.

Healthcare organizations have shown that when Lean practices are rigorously applied throughout the organization, productivity, cost, and quality are dramatically improved (Toussaint & Gerard, 2010). The reason that Lean is so useful in healthcare is that care processes in large organizations have generally evolved over time and have rarely been the result of thoughtful analysis. The focus tends to be on optimal time utilization for doctors and nurses, and not on patients. Care is usually segmented into departments, and often the only people who experience the entire patient care process are the patients themselves. In these systems, a patient can spend hours going from area to area, waiting at each step, for only a few minutes of value-added effort. Lean has the potential to break down the silos between departments and provide care that will add value from the patient's viewpoint (Bozena, 2010; Box 6.1).

✚ BOX 6.1 – OM IN PRACTICE!

Virginia Mason Medical Center in Seattle, Washington

Virginia Mason Medical Center began using Lean management principles in 2002. By working to eliminate waste, Virginia Mason created more capacity in existing programs and practices so that planned expansions were scrapped, saving $6 million for a new surgery suite that was no longer necessary (Plsek, 2014).

Lean Culture

A Lean culture is the backdrop for the use of Lean principles. If you are a leader who wants to develop a culture in which Lean practices are pervasive, you cannot do it by edict. Your employees must learn the actions expected of them, and they will have to build these actions into their daily work. Not only do the frontline people need to learn what actions are expected, but leaders must also model the desired behaviors. Because respect is a necessary component of a Lean culture, everyone within the organization needs to be trained in the Lean methodology. Cultural change can take years to take root, so the leadership team must be committed to the practices as the new way of doing business.

To be a leader in a Lean organization, you must work differently. You need to understand that when making decisions, you need to know the reality of what is happening on the field. You need to go where the problem is occurring, personally observe how the product or service is delivered, and gather facts for yourself. You ask the frontline employees questions and understand that they are the experts when it comes to the activity under investigation. Because respect is a fundamental value in a Lean organization, leaders and frontline staff work together and listen to each other as problems are solved.

Waste Elimination

To initiate Lean, you need to understand which activities in a process create value. Everything else is considered "waste" (Table 6.1). There are eight types of waste:

1. **Overproduction**: doing more than necessary

2. **Inventory**: excess raw materials, end products that are stored, work-in-progress that has not been completed

3. **Defects, errors**: waste in the form of time wasted for rework, extra capacity to redo the work, litigation, and so on

4. **Motion**: unnecessary movements because supplies and tools are not easily accessible or visible

5. **Extra processing**: doing more than the customer actually values

6. **Waiting**: inactivity in a process because one or more activities have not been delivered in time

7. **Transport**: unnecessary movement of materials during the process

8. **Underutilization**: not distributing work smoothly to the people who can do the job

Healthcare is loaded with these wastes. Most healthcare workers will grossly underestimate the amount of inefficiency that can be taken out of their workday. The key is to get everyone in the organization to systematically find waste, make it visible, and eradicate it.

TABLE 6.1 – Types of Waste in Healthcare

Types of Waste	Examples	Causes
Overproduction	• Generating reports that are no longer used • Running more copies than needed • Batch processing that results in excess output	• Not evaluating benefit of reports • Not paying attention to detail • Avoiding running low on an item (lack of precise planning)
Inventory	• Having a higher par level than needed for supplies • Medications having to be thrown out because of expiration date	• Lack of streamlined ordering procedure • Clutter in cabinets making it difficult to see what is in the back
Defects	• Mislabeled specimen • Wrong diet given to a patient	• Batch processing • Process failure
Motion	• Looking for blood pressure cuff to take patient vital signs • Items not set up for easy use	• Cluttered work environment • Workstation design
Extra processing	• Asking the same question multiple times at registration desks • Regular meetings with no purpose	• Customer voice not heard • Lack of respect for people's time
Waiting	• Waiting to see the physician • Waiting to get test results	• Work imbalance • Batch processing

(continued)

TABLE 6.1 – Types of Waste in Healthcare (*continued*)		
Types of Waste	**Examples**	**Causes**
Transport	• Transporting supplies from central area to patient care rooms • Transporting patients long distances to see different providers	• Lack of local storage for commonly used supplies • Lack of coordination among care providers
Underutilization	• Manager performing tasks that can be done by nurses aide • Physician doing work that nurse can do	• Lack of clarification of roles • Poor workflow design

To continually identify and eliminate waste, organizations must learn to care about the little things. This means helping people see the waste around them and recognizing that eliminating waste will free them up to do more valuable and rewarding activities.

Lean Principles

Womak and Jones (1996) identified five Lean principles used to examine any process (Figure 6.1). Because no one can improve everything at once, the organization must decide what to prioritize. As we discussed in Chapter 4, methods, such as FMEA (failure modes and effects analysis), HOQ (house of quality), or Pareto, may help you set priorities. When adopting Lean for the first time, leaders may wish to begin with a relatively simple process so employees can be trained on Lean methods. Prior to moving forward, they need to be sure that everyone touching the process is on board and will contribute to the analysis and change, and that the parameters to gauge success are clearly articulated.

**FIGURE 6.1 –
Principles of Lean.**

Source: Lean Enterprise Institute (2015). Reproduced with permission.

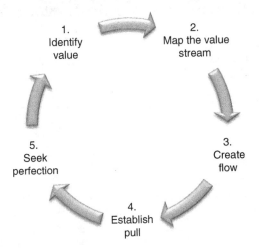

Identify Value

The customer of the process determines value (Box 6.2). The product or service being delivered must be what is wanted, at the right time, and at the right price. The customer expects the same product or service to be delivered the same way, every time. Listening to the voice of the customer (VOC; Chapter 4) will help you understand what the customer values.

When a process is being reviewed through the Lean lens, you need to ask the question, "Are we providing what the customer wants in the way he or she wants it?" If not, ask "What needs to be changed?" Only a small fraction of the total time and effort in any activity actually adds value for the customer. By clearly defining value for a specific product or service from the customer's perspective, all the non–value-added activities (waste) can be targeted for removal.

 BOX 6.2 – WORDS OF WISDOM

"Value is what a customer is willing to pay for" (Naisbitt, 1982, p. 36).

Map the Value Stream

Once you understand what your customer wants, the next step is to identify how you need to deliver it to them. The analysis and design of a process often starts with its depiction. A **flowchart** is a diagram that depicts each step of a process. A **value stream map (VSM)** is a flowchart depicting a process flow from a Lean perspective. Therefore, a process should create optimal value to the customer with no, or minimal, waste. The VSM incorporates the activities that are valuable to the customer as well as those that are considered wasteful. The visualization of waste on the process map facilitates its subsequent elimination and thus aids in planning process redesign. All the possible points in the process, such as delays, errors, and unnecessary movements that might dissatisfy the customer, should be identified in the process map. In the VSM shown in Figure 6.2, a physician has ordered a medication for a patient. The process has many steps, and the medication must pass through many hands. Although the patient does not see each of the steps, the value to the patient is to obtain the correct medication at the proper dose quickly.

For each step in the current state VSM (Table 6.2), you must designate whether this process step (a) creates value, (b) does not create value (waste) but cannot be eliminated at this time, or (c) is waste and can be eliminated. The process steps that are considered waste but cannot be eliminated should be targeted for improvement. In the example shown in Figure 6.2, the opportunities for improvement include minimizing wait times between when the pharmacist receives the order and the order is verified, decreasing the time waiting for a drug to come from inventory, and minimizing the time it takes for the nurse to administer the drug after it has arrived in the patient care area.

As each step is being scrutinized, an intense questioning exercise can help elucidate the steps that create the true value of the process (The 5 Whys). As steps are being categorized, a new VSM (future state) should be created to illustrate the new process with eliminated waste.

Value Stream Map
A flowchart that depicts a process flow from the Lean perspective.

Flowchart
A diagram that depicts each step in a process.

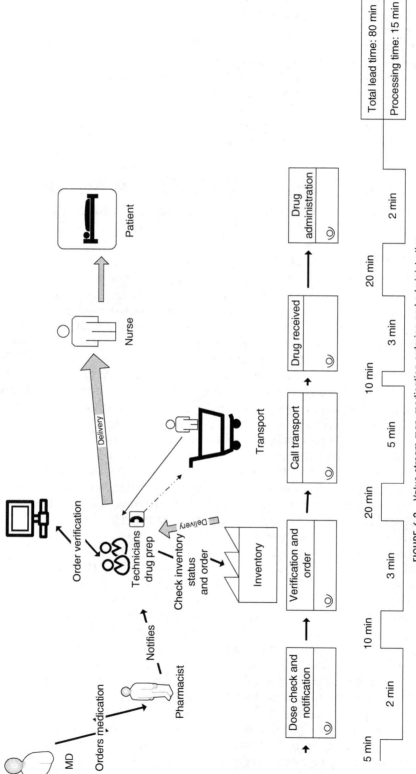

FIGURE 6.2 – Value stream map: medication ordering and administration.

TABLE 6.2 – Steps in Value Stream Mapping

Step	Description
1	Determine what service to map
2	Draw the current process flow with all the steps, delays, and information flows required to deliver the targeted service
3	Assess the current state process in terms of flow and waste
4	Identify and list all areas of waste and develop a list of opportunities for improvement based on this list
5	Validate the map

The 5 Whys

Once waste is identified, it is easy to see. However, it is often difficult to find it initially. This is because most waste is embedded in processes that have been performed the same way for long periods of time. The way to find waste is to look at each process differently. Instead of assuming that things are done properly, assume that things are being done incorrectly. Ask the "5 Whys." Continuing to ask the question "why?" gets to the root cause of the problem.

For example, patients are complaining because they need to wait for over an hour to see their physician.

Why are patients being asked to wait? Because the physician is seeing patients who are scheduled earlier.

Why is the physician seeing patients scheduled earlier? Because the clinic started late.

Why did the clinic start late? Because the doctor was seeing patients in the hospital prior to the clinic.

Why was the doctor seeing patients in the hospital on a clinic day? Because the physician had patients in the hospital that he needed to care for and the clinic scheduler did not get the message that she was going to be late.

Why did the clinic scheduler not get the message? Because there is no standard way to communicate changing physician schedules.

As you can see, this example unearthed the problem of communication. If the clinic scheduler knew that the physician was going to be late, the timing of patients could be changed and the patients would not need to wait.

The 5 Whys
The practice of asking the question "why?" at least five times until you get to the root cause of a problem.

Create Flow

Once the value to the customer is identified and the waste has been removed from the value stream, it is time to make the value-added steps flow. To create flow, we need to divorce ourselves from traditional thinking. We need to deconstruct the typical "departments" where activities are grouped by type and where batches of products, orders, documents, or people wait until resources are ready to process them. Instead, rearrange resources according to the process sequence so that processing can take place in a continuous flow.

Teams involved in Lean process improvements actually walk through the steps of the process and work to identify waste. Distances between the steps in a process are meticulously documented. Physical layouts of the space may change as the non–value-added distances are eliminated. The environment where the activity is ongoing is scrutinized to identify ways to make the use of the space more efficient. A tool used for this purpose is called the 5S (Table 6.3; Figure 6.3).

TABLE 6.3 – 5S

S	Description
Sort Out (*seiri*)	Organize and eliminate what is unnecessary
Systematize (*seiton*)	Arrange items in their correct places so that they can be accessed when needed
Scrub (*seisou*)	Keep the environment clean
Standardize (*seiketsu*)	Do the same thing every time
Sustain (*shisuke*)	Stick to the rules, build the previous 4Ss into the culture, and constantly improve when possible

FIGURE 6.3 – OR supplies before and after using the 5S methodology.

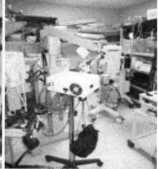

BEFORE
Operating room (OR) supplies need organization. Abundance of OR supplies leads to increased risk of expired inventory and duplication.

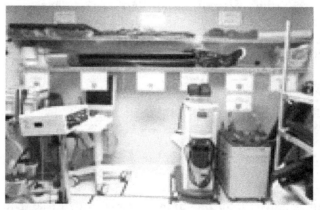

AFTER
Organized equipment room increases visibility of what is missing and what needs to be repaired or replaced.

Establish Pull

Before we discuss the concept of "pull" in Lean, let us talk about how traditional manufacturing processes work using "push." In a **"push"** environment, goods are produced without waiting for customer demand. For example, a hospital pharmacy may routinely make 100 saline intravenous (IV) bags per day. Why 100? Because it is the highest number of saline bags needed for patients in a day, and the pharmacy does not want to run out of bags. Because the hospital policy says that any IV bags not used in 24 hours must be discarded, many bags per day may be wasted. In a "push" system, process steps are executed independently, with little regard to the actual needs of the beneficiaries of their output. As a result, inventory accumulates, and materials may have to be discarded.

Push

Goods or services are produced without waiting for customer demand.

The **"pull"** principle is probably the most important logistical innovation of the Toyota Production System (Womack & Jones, 1996). "Pull" is the concept of producing a good or service in response to actual customer demand. The goal of "establishing pull" is to remove unnecessary waste and to be highly responsive to customers' needs. The next process is considered the "customer." Any demand (pull) from the downstream or "customer" process triggers activity at the upstream or "supplier" process. Anything that is not used immediately or is waiting at any point in time to be processed at the next step is considered waste. A pull system allows materials, patients, documents, and so on to flow smoothly from one step to the next; restocking takes place, but there is no overstocking. The steps in the process flow are balanced (Chapter 7) so that there is no buildup of partially processed unit, or idle resources sitting around waiting.

Pull

Goods or services are produced in response to actual patient demand.

A pull system works best when there is a relatively stable demand and the process is repetitive and standardized. This is more common for administrative support services than for clinical services. However, there are some medical procedures for which a pull system works very well. For example, cataract surgeries are high-volume, relatively standardized procedures. The sequential steps are (a) patients go from the waiting room to a prep/recovery area; (b) they are then taken to the OR for their surgery; (c) next, they are taken back to recovery area; (d) when patients have recovered and received discharge instructions, they leave. With a pull system, as soon as a bed in the recovery area becomes vacant after a patient leaves, a patient is pulled from the waiting room to be prepped. As soon as the OR is vacated by a patient and set up for the next one, a prepped patient from the prep/recovery area is pulled and placed in the OR (Figure 6.4). Because all surgery times are fairly consistent, the appointment times are set so that patients will not have to wait too long in the waiting room. The interdependence between processes requires frequent communication among the labor resources involved.

FIGURE 6.4 – Pull system for cataract surgery.

Just-in-Time

Just-in-Time (JIT)
An inventory strategy designed to receive materials at the time they are needed to eliminate excess inventory.

There is an inventory strategy in Lean called **just-in-time**. JIT is designed so that materials arrive only when they are needed, not early and not late. Toyota designed a process in which they ordered automobile parts in small quantities based on their short-term needs. The process was designed to ensure that a part would arrive just in time to be used, eliminating the need to keep it in inventory. Toyota found that the JIT system reduced lead time on orders by one third and reduced production costs by 50% (Thompson, 2015). Many healthcare organizations use a JIT system to eliminate the need to store excess supplies.

No system is completely based on "pull." "Push" and "pull" must be used in tandem to produce a flow with minimal waiting between steps. In manufacturing, when a downstream process step initiates demand, a little bit of inventory must be available to meet that demand immediately. The same applies to our cataract surgery example. Patients must be in the waiting room when availability in the prep/recovery area triggers the pull. That little "slack" is consistent with a push system, but it is kept to a minimum. Whether we have a push or pull process, the real goal in Lean is "flow"—with downstream demand being promptly met by upstream supply (Box 6.3). When you decrease the waste in the system, flow can happen.

✚ BOX 6.3 – OM IN PRACTICE!

Smoothing Patient Flow at Cincinnati Children's Hospital

A series of operations management interventions was implemented to smooth patient flow through the intensive care unit (ICU) and make bed occupancy more predictable. Staff analyzed which types of patients needed a particular type of service and evaluated surgeons' needs for intensive care services. The average length of stay of patients was calculated. When a procedure was scheduled, the surgeons helped the staff understand the complexity of the procedure and specific patient characteristics. Together, they estimated how long the patient would need intensive care. The scheduling system was designed to take reservations for space according to these estimates. Reserved beds were continuously monitored and elective cases were postponed if patient stay exceeded the estimates. Staff communicated daily on ICU bed availability and became expert at anticipating the needs for the next day. Demand for beds and bed capacity were coordinated so that patient flow increased and resources were utilized more effectively (Institute of Medicine, 2012).

Seek Perfection

As we discussed in Chapter 4, Deming's wheel (PDCA cycle) is the basis for continuous improvement. A Lean organization is always trying to achieve the perfect system, knowing that perfection is never attainable.

Even after a process has been redesigned using Lean methodology, people should begin to look at the process to see whether it can be refined further. The word for this continuous improvement in Japanese is *Kaizen*. The term **Kaizen** is derived from two Japanese characters: *kai*, meaning "change," and *zen*, meaning "continuous improvement." Continuously eliminating waste and improving flow in the value stream are the goals of Kaizen.

Poka-yoke, or "mistake-proofing," is a device or system that produces a signal before an error occurs so that corrective action can be taken (Box 6.4). An example is the use of barcoding to identify patients. A barcode is placed on a patient's wristband. When an order for a medication is written, the order is connected with the patient's barcode. Before the nurse administers the drug, he or she checks the barcode that was printed on the medication dose and the barcode on the patient's wristband. If the barcodes do not match, the system alerts the nurse that the medication was not ordered for that patient. A medication administration error was prevented.

Kaizen

The Japanese word for continuous improvement that uses Deming's wheel or the PDCA cycle.

Poka-yoke (or "mistake-proofing")

A Japanese term for a device or system that can help to prevent errors from occurring.

⚙ BOX 6.4 – OM IN PRACTICE!

Using Poka-yoke to Prevent Infant Abduction

There have been several instances in which infants have been abducted from a hospital. One organization decided to "mistake-proof" their prevention efforts by attaching an electronic device, or "tag," to the infant's umbilical cord. If the infant was removed without authorization, the tag triggered an alarm. Specific doors were locked, all elevators automatically returned to the secured maternity floor, and elevator doors remained open. The tag is an electronic means of preventing an undesirable event from occurring (Agency for Healthcare Research and Quality, 2015).

Poka-yoking a process does not necessarily require technology. You can set up a system that prevents you from forgetting to take an assignment to school by placing the assignment under your shoes the night before. When you awake and get dressed, you are alerted to the need to turn in your assignment.

BRADLEY PARK HOSPITAL 6.3

"There is a lot to learn with Lean, but I can see how powerful it can be. But how are we going to change our culture to be one of continuous improvement?" Jennifer asked Don as he was putting away an example of a value stream map.

"You build a culture of continuous improvement when everyone in the organization wants to continue to learn and believes that he or she is contributing to the overall goal."

"How do you do that?" Jennifer interrupted.

"Remember Deming's 14 points? Let's start there." Don's phone rang. "Hello. Oh, I will be there in just a minute. I was finishing up." "Jennifer, I must go to another meeting, but let's get back together next week and we can start making our plan. In the meantime, read about Six Sigma. We will want to incorporate some of its principles in our plan."

Jennifer picked up Don's book on Six Sigma. "May I borrow this?" "Of course," Don replied. "See you later."

 Why would people resist improvements?

SIX SIGMA

Six Sigma
Refers to six standard deviations from a target and the trademark name of a methodology for process improvement using the principles of DMAIC.

Six Sigma is a process improvement methodology that has the same general purpose as Lean—providing the customer with the best possible quality, cost, timeliness, and flexibility. As Lean is focused on driving out waste (non–value-added steps) and improving flow, Six Sigma focuses on eliminating defects and decreasing variation. Six Sigma uses a rigorous approach to identify the root causes of problems and reduce variation (Chapter 5). Both methodologies are focused on customer's needs.

History of Six Sigma

In the early and mid-1980s, Motorola engineers were not satisfied with the quality of their products. Bill Smith, Motorola's vice president and quality manager of the Land Mobile Product Sector, devised his theory of latent defect (Akpose, 2010). The core principle behind the latent defect theory is that variation in manufacturing processes is the main culprit for defects, and eliminating variation will help eliminate the defects, decrease overall costs, and increase customer satisfaction. Mr. Smith and colleagues at Motorola developed a methodology to reduce the variability of their products. This data-driven, defect-reduction process called **DMAIC**, was refined by companies, such as General Electric, and was trademarked as "Six Sigma."

The term **Six Sigma** refers to six standard deviations from a target value. In terms of process capability (Chapter 5), it would mean that the mean of the process distribution is 6 standard deviations away from the lower specification limit (LSL) and 6 standard deviations away from the upper specification limit (USL). In other words, the C_p value is at least 2. This implies that you meet your target 99.99966% of the time (Table 6.4). The core tenet of Six Sigma is that by removing variation from a process, you decrease the chances of introducing errors in a statistically measurable and controllable way. When variation is reduced, a process is more predictable and reliable.

TABLE 6.4 – Sigma Levels for Items Without Defects (Yield)		
Percentage of Items Without Defect (Yield)	DPMO	Sigma Level
30.9	690,000	1.0
62.9	308,000	2.0

(continued)

TABLE 6.4 – Sigma Levels for Items Without Defects (Yield) (*continued*)

Percentage of Items Without Defect (Yield)	DPMO	Sigma Level
93.3	66,800	3.0
99.4	6,210	4.0
99.98	320	5.0
99.99966	3.4	6.0

DPMO, Defects per Million Opportunities.

Principles of Six Sigma

Executing a process that brings a Six Sigma level of performance requires employees to use a well-defined set of data-driven tools to identify any small deviations in the process almost immediately. The methodology intrinsic to Six Sigma is called **DMAIC** (Morror, 2009; Figure 6.5). At each of these steps, qualitative and quantitative techniques and tools can help guide the process. Many of these tools are not unique to Six Sigma and are used in other methodologies, such as Lean.

DMAIC (Define, Measure, Analyze, Improve, Control)
A data-driven, error-reduction process that forms the basis of Six Sigma.

Six Sigma depends on employees to use standardized methods to identify problems and eliminate them. Six Sigma, a methodology originally based in statistics, has evolved from a metric used to measure product quality to a management philosophy that promotes collaborative problem solving. Trained employees must examine statistical graphs, understand when there is a deviation from the standard, determine the root cause of failure, and change what other employees do (Box 6.5). We examine each of these steps in more detail and describe the tools and statistical methods that can be used at each step. Many of these tools have already been presented in previous chapters.

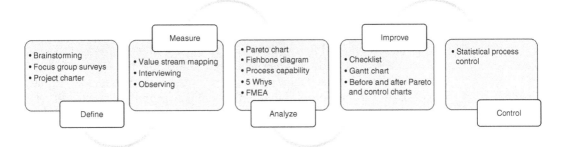

FIGURE 6.5 – Steps in DMAIC and tools used at each step.

Define

Just as we saw in the Lean methodology, the first step is to define what the customer wants. Six Sigma leaders use multiple techniques, such as brainstorming and focus group interviews, to begin to define what the customer requirements are. Once the customer's desires are clarified and the process indicators are defined, the organization's required

---

⊕ BOX 6.5 – DID YOU KNOW?

Standardizing With Checklists

In 2001, Peter Pronovost, a critical care specialist at Johns Hopkins Hospital in Baltimore, Maryland, decided to see whether checklists, like those used in aviation, could improve the reliability of care in the ICU. He chose to focus on one process, the insertion of central venous catheters (CVCs) in patients. Taking care of patients in an ICU setting is very complicated. In fact, previous research showed that to take care of a critically ill patient, 178 individual actions were required per day, many of which needed to be performed in a specific sequence. The same research also found that although only 1% of the individual actions were incorrectly performed, they added up to one to two errors per patient per day! Pronovost decided to see whether a five-step checklist could decrease the error rate when inserting CVCs. The five steps were simple:

1. Wash hands with soap.
2. Clean the patient's skin with chlorhexidine antiseptic.
3. Use sterile drapes that cover the entire patient.
4. Wear a sterile mask, hat, gown, and gloves.
5. Put a sterile dressing over the catheter insertion site once the line is placed.

When the checklist was first tried, a review of CVC placements for one month showed that physicians skipped at least one step in more than a third of patients. The next step was to give nurses the authority to stop the procedure if they saw them skip a step on the checklist. After one year, the infection rate of CVCs in place for over 10 days went from 11% to zero.

Pronovost observed that the checklists provided two main benefits. One, they helped with memory recall, especially when mundane tasks are being done and many chaotic events are going on all around you. Two, checklists provided explicit instructions on the expected steps to be taken in the process. This prompted physicians and nurses to talk about the clinical evidence that supported each step in the complex process. Checklists established a higher standard of baseline performance (Gawande, 2007).

---

capabilities can be specified. The project team must clearly delineate the focus, scope, and direction of the improvement effort. When projects are launched, a project charter is drafted to articulate why the project is being done, what the expected benefits are, who the team members are and what their roles will be, and the timeline for completion. This document is used as a communication tool by all members of the team (Chapter 3).

Measure

Just as in Lean, Six Sigma uses value stream process mapping as a valuable tool to outline all of the steps in the current process that will undergo improvement. The process must be mapped as it actually works, not how you think it should work. This is often difficult, particularly when there is significant variation in how different operators perform the work. Measuring the work of different people, at different times of the day, or on different days of the week is vital to understanding the variability within the process and in quality indicators. Data collection in Six Sigma is multipronged. It includes interviewing people, making first-hand observations, and asking questions.

Analyze

Once data are collected, they are analyzed to determine the root causes of the variability, increased costs, bottlenecks in the process, or barriers to providing a quality service. The root causes are the fundamental breakdowns or failures in a process that, when corrected, prevent the recurrence of the problem. Each problem can be viewed as an opportunity to learn about the system. Discovering the root cause(s) of a problem can tell you a lot about why and how the problem occurred. The reason you need to get at the root cause(s) is that the true problem must be understood before action is taken. If we do not identify them, we will waste time and resources trying to correct symptoms, rather than fundamental issues. Examples of symptoms versus root causes are provided in Table 6.5.

TABLE 6.5 – Symptoms Versus Root Causes

Symptom	Root Cause
Employees do not know what they are doing	The process is ambiguous and poorly defined
The upstream processes give us junk to work with	There is no feedback mechanism to communicate downstream processes' needs and expectations
Nurses take days off when we need them most	The scheduling system is based on providers' preferences rather than patient demand
Patients never arrive on time	The parking lot is too small to accommodate the patient volume

A simple root cause tool is the "5 Whys" described earlier in the Lean methods. Other methods introduced in Chapter 4 include the fishbone diagram and the FMEA.

When you go to the doctor's office, care providers try to find the root cause of your problem. For example, if you go in complaining of a painful hand, the doctor will ask many questions and look at your hand carefully. Likely, the doctor will order an x-ray to be sure that there are no broken bones. The doctor is actually looking for the root cause of your problem, which is pain. The doctor could easily give you pain medications, but if a bone is broken, the pain medicine will only mask the symptoms, and the problem will not be fixed.

Improve

Once you have identified the root cause of a problem, you begin to make changes that will prevent the problem from occurring again. You have to think through the effects, including the unintentional consequences of making a change. Once a modification is decided upon, you pilot the change to uncover other problems that may arise as a result of the change. If the pilot shows that the change improves the process so that fewer variations or defects are produced, you expand the implementation of the change.

Gantt charts can help keep track of activities and timelines for improvement. Following the process improvement with other tools, such as Pareto charts and control charts, can demonstrate that the changes made have actually resulted in improved performance. By the end of the improve step, you should be able to document that the process was actually enhanced by your actions.

Control

All of your work that has gone into identifying the root cause of a problem and improving the process will be lost if you do not monitor results. Statistical process control (SPC) is one method of monitoring results and identifying variation patterns before they result in defects (Chapter 5). Metrics help you monitor and document successes and failures. By following metrics, you can determine whether your interventions work. You start responding to other problems in a constructive way, and through this continuous group problem solving, you learn what works in your organization and help to build a culture of teamwork (Box 6.6).

BOX 6.6 – OM IN PRACTICE!

Successfully Applying Six Sigma in a Healthcare Organization

Heritage Valley Health System in Brighton Township, Pennsylvania, used Six Sigma to improve the processes surrounding the care of patients undergoing cataract extraction. Patient satisfaction was low and the profit margin was not healthy. Through teams of physicians and staff, the processes surrounding these patients were evaluated using the DMAIC methodology. The following changes were made:

- Preadmission testing for patients needing only topical anesthesia was eliminated.
- All supplies were standardized.
- Medications were prescripted.

Results were impressive. Customer satisfaction improved from 44% to over 90% and the profit margin increased from −16% to +7% (Beaver, 2015).

The Learning Culture in Six Sigma and Key Players

The power of Six Sigma to create a culture of continuous improvement lies in the combination of changing the way work gets done and teaching people to collaboratively solve problems. Implementing the methods of Six Sigma throughout an organization requires a serious business commitment. There needs to be a dedicated staff overseeing the steps of Six Sigma daily, and everyone in the organization must support the processes. The top professionals who drive the changes in a Six Sigma organization are (Figure 6.6) listed.

Executive sponsor or champion. This is often a clinical leader or senior manager who assigns the project, ensures that resources are available, sets a timeline for completion, and assures accountability for implementation. He or she will remove any roadblocks for the teams to guarantee successful project implementation.

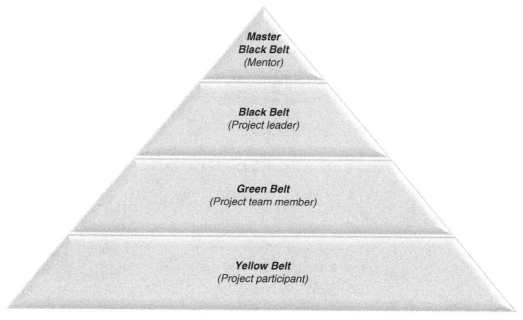

FIGURE 6.6 – Six Sigma pyramid.

Master Black Belts. They have extensive quantitative skills and Six Sigma experience, which enables them to monitor, review, and mentor Black Belts across projects. They develop key metrics and formulate the strategic direction of the projects.

Black Belts. They devote all of their time to Six Sigma projects. They have extensive training in statistics, quality tools, and project management. They may lead 8 to 12 projects in different areas (Box 6.7).

Green Belts. They are project team members who generally have an overview of the process and will be responsible for completing project benchmarks. Green Belts often are in charge of data collection and project monitoring. They assume Six Sigma responsibilities in addition to their regular roles in the organization.

Yellow Belts. They have very basic Six Sigma training and participate in the project, but they are not full members of the project team.

In addition to understanding the methods of Six Sigma, key players need to have the communication and leadership skills to involve and communicate with everyone on the team. They must be able to pull together multifunctional teams to focus on the problem. Having a team with diverse skills and experiences increases the likelihood of identifying variations and developing creative solutions.

⊕ BOX 6.7 – DID YOU KNOW?

Black Belts

"Black belt" has its roots in martial arts and was coined to indicate practitioners who were self-assured and knowledgeable, the result of intensive training and real-world experience. This term was adopted by Motorola and became part of their corporate culture. When other companies began using the Six Sigma methodology, the Black Belt designation was widely accepted.

BRADLEY PARK HOSPITAL 6.4

Jennifer and Don were finishing up their discussion on Six Sigma. "Mmm," Jennifer mused, "I need to think about the similarities and differences between Lean and Six Sigma. Many things seem similar, but there are differences."

"Yes," Don replied. "But the tools for Lean and Six Sigma can be used together, so it is important to understand the purpose of the tools and when one tool works best. Some people are even combining the names into 'Lean Six Sigma.'"

"That is interesting," Jennifer responded. "Dr. Levine in ear, nose, and throat is meeting me in the morning to discuss some issues he is having with patient delays for surgery. It will be helpful to have the principles of Lean and Six Sigma in mind when I am talking with him."

Don reminded her, "Don't forget to get the front-line staff involved when looking for a solution. Remember, our job is to help make the problems visible so that the people who actually perform the tasks can identify solutions. That is how we build a culture of continuous improvement."

"Thanks. Wish me luck!"

 Do you find the concepts of Six Sigma or Lean to be more intuitive? Why?

BENEFITS OF LEAN AND SIX SIGMA

Organizations that adopt a Lean or Six Sigma methodology and culture achieve significant benefits. Different organizations may choose one methodology over the other, but neither is considered "best." In fact, many organizations use all of these tools and methodologies, depending on the problem to be solved at the time (Table 6.6).

TABLE 6.6 – Use of Different Approaches to Solve Different Types of Problems

PROBLEM TYPE		
• Waste, rework, redundancy • Poor flow, multiple process steps • Non–value-added activities ⬇	• Poor quality and variation • Complex and multiple system interactions ⬇	• Poor process • Lack of standardization • Clinical issues ⬇
PROCESS IMPROVEMENT APPROACH		
Lean • Eliminate waste • Improve flow • Simplify and mistake-proof	Six Sigma • Minimize variation • Eliminate defects • Establish robust controls to sustain	Continuous Improvement • Testing based on theory • Iterative learning • Emphasis on teamwork
Identify value	Define	Establish aim
Understand the value stream	Measure	Plan
Eliminate waste	Analyze	Do
Establish flow	Improve	Check
Seek perfection	Control	Act

Adapted from M. R. Waldrum, CEO, Vident Health, personal communication (July 25, 2015).

In healthcare, the quality of services rendered depends a lot on human skills. These are sometimes difficult to measure and control, so the process improvement tools of Lean and Six Sigma may be shared depending on the circumstances. But if Lean and Six Sigma methodologies are followed and cultures are built around process improvement, there will be improved quality of the product/service as perceived by the customer, reduction in the process cycle times, improved communication throughout the organization, cost savings, and improved skill training for employees.

Both Lean and Six Sigma help to streamline operations and identify waste or variation that can lead to increased costs. In the next chapter, we explore additional tools and principles used for process redesign.

SUMMARY

The continuous improvement methodologies of Lean and Six Sigma developed separately in the manufacturing sector. However, both are now used extensively in healthcare. The Lean principles of (a) identify value, (b) map the value stream, (c) create flow, (d) establish pull, and (e) seek perfection are designed to drive "waste" out of the system and improve process efficiency. Six Sigma's principles of DMAIC are focused on decreasing variation and enhancing process effectiveness. Many of the tools used in each of these steps are shared between Lean and Six Sigma. In fact, if you look at the steps of Lean and Six Sigma side by side, you will see many similarities. Both methodologies, when used properly, create a culture of continuous improvement and focus efforts on creating value for the customer (Figure 6.7).

Through reductions in waste and variation, both Lean and Six Sigma not only improve quality, but they also lower costs and facilitate delivery. The expanded skill repertoire of the individuals involved in these projects fosters greater flexibility. In improving processes on multiple fronts, Lean and Six Sigma boost performance not only in quality, but also in the other competitive priorities. The process improvements achieved through Lean and Six Sigma are further explored and mind mapped with the other competitive priorities in Chapter 7.

FIGURE 6.7 – Revised mind map linking indicators to delivery (Chapter 7).

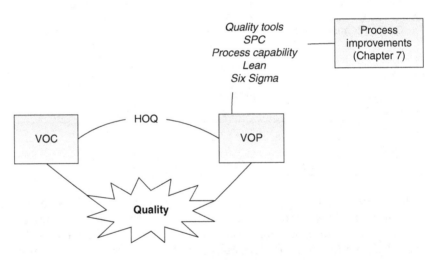

KEY TERMS

Lean	Pull
Waste	Just-in-time
Value stream map	Kaizen
Flowchart	Poka-yoke (mistake-proofing)
The 5 Whys	Six Sigma
Push	DMAIC

TOOLS USED IN THIS CHAPTER

TOOL	PURPOSE
Value stream mapping	Depicts all the activities in a process so that waste can be easily seen
The 5 Whys	Identifies the root cause(s) of a problem
5S	Organizes the work space for effectiveness and efficiency
Poka-yoke	Mistake-proofs a process so that errors are identified before they happen

WHAT DO YOU REMEMBER?

1. Name the eight types of waste (Lean methodology) and give an example of each in healthcare.
2. List the Lean principles and explain how each one is used to examine/improve a process.
3. Why is flow important in Lean?
4. What are the differences between push and pull systems?
5. Explain why culture is an important consideration when both Lean and Six Sigma are used in an organization.
6. What is a root cause and how do you identify it? Give an example.
7. What is poka-yoke? Name three examples of its use in healthcare.
8. What are the steps in Six Sigma?
9. What are the various roles of people involved in Six Sigma projects?
10. Give an example of a just-in-time system. Explain why it is beneficial.

THINK OUTSIDE THE BOOK!

1. Draw the actual value stream for one of the following processes:
   a. Making a cup of coffee using a regular coffeemaker
   b. Brushing your teeth and flossing
   c. Washing your car

   Time the various steps and identify and label the types of waste that can be eliminated.
2. Go to http://archive.ahrq.gov/professionals/quality-patient-safety/patient-safety-resources/resources/mistakeproof/mistake8.html. Explain why barcoding of specimens or drugs can be considered a method of poka-yoke. Name one mistake that can come with barcoding.

3. Describe a way to poka-yoke your morning routine so that you wake up on time and remember to take your cell phone to work.

REFERENCES

Agency for Healthcare Research and Quality. (2015). More examples of mistake-proofing in health care. In *Mistake-proofing the design of health care processes* (07-0020; pp. 134–147). Retrieved from http://archive .ahrq.gov/professionals/quality-patient-safety/patient-safety-resources/resources/mistakeproof/mistake8.html

Akpose, W. (2010). A history of Six Sigma. Retrieved from http://www .morganmckinley.co.uk/article/six-sigma-briefhistory

Akron Children's Hospital. (2015). Examples of Lean Six Sigma successes. Retrieved from www.akronchildrens.org/cms/lean-six-sigma-successes

Beaver, R. (2015). Successfully applying Six Sigma in a healthcare organization. Retrieved from www.slideshare.net/Vijay_Bijaj/ successfully-applying-six-sigma-in-a-healthcare-organization

Bozena, P. (2010). The current state of Lean implementation in health care: Literature review. *Quality Management in Health Care, 19*(4), 319–329.

Ford, H., & Crowther, S. (1922). *My life and work* (p. 72). New York, NY: Doubleday.

Ford, H., & Crowther, S. (2014). *My life and work*. San Diego, CA: Didactic Press.

Gawande, A. (2007, December 10). The checklist (Annals of medicine). *The New Yorker*. Retrieved from http://www.newyorker.com/ magazine/2007/12/10/the-checklist

Graban, M. (2012). *Lean hospitals: Improving quality, patient safety, and employee engagement* (2nd ed.). Boca Raton, FL: CRC Press.

Institute of Medicine. (2012). *Best care at lower cost: The path to continuously learning health care in America*. Washington, DC: National Academies Press.

Lean Enterprise Institute. (2015). Principles of Lean. Retrieved from http://www.lean.org/WhatsLean/Principles.cfm

Morror, C. M. (2009). *The certified quality engineer handbook* (3rd ed.). Milwaukee, WI: ASQ Quality Press.

Naisbitt, J. (1982). *Megatrends: Ten new directions transforming our lives*. New York, NY: Warner Books.

Plsek, P. E. (2014). *Accelerating health care transformation with Lean and innovation: The Virginia Mason experience*. Boca Raton, FL: CRC Press.

Pyzdek, T., & Keller, P. (2010). *The Six Sigma handbook: A complete guide for green belts, black belts, and managers at all levels* (3rd ed.). New York, NY: McGraw Hill.

Thompson, S. (2015). Differences between JIT & Lean manufacturing. Retrieved from http://smallbusiness.chron.com/differences-between-jit-lean-manufacturing-75614.html

Toussaint, J., & Gerard, R. A. (2010). *On the mend: Revolutionizing healthcare to save lives and transform the industry.* Cambridge, MA: Lean Enterprise Institute.

The W. Edwards Deming Institute. (2015). The man. Retrieved from www.deming.org

Webster's New World Dictionary of the American Language (College ed.). (1968). New York, NY: World Publishing Company.

Womack, J. P., & Jones D. T. (1996). *Lean thinking: Banish waste and create wealth in your corporation.* London, UK: Simon & Schuster.

PART

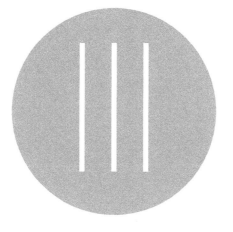

Competing on Delivery

CHAPTER 7

PROCESS ANALYSIS AND DESIGN

BRADLEY PARK HOSPITAL 7.1

"Good morning, Jennifer," Dr. Levine smiled. "I hope this is not too early. I have surgery this morning and I wanted to get going on fixing these patient delays."

Jennifer opened her notebook. Six-thirty in the morning was a bit early for her, but she wanted to do a good job for Dr. Levine. He was the head of the physician group, and she felt that if she could win him over, he could be a real champion for improving processes.

Jennifer started, "So what is the problem, Dr. Levine?"

"I do not know why this is happening, but I often receive patients' test results very late, which sometimes delays their surgery. Some patients drive long distances, only to be turned away when the test results are either not available or indicate that the patient is not healthy enough for surgery. I have told the staff to do better, but errors keep occurring. I was in the emergency department (ED) the other day admitting a patient and I mentioned my frustration to Eric Wong. He told me that you may be able to help me."

"Will you give me a list of patients who have experienced this problem? I will do a little investigating and get back with you."

INTRODUCTION AND LEARNING OBJECTIVES

Variations in process quality and flow times hinder a process's ability to deliver services in a timely manner. The only remedy is process change or redesign. With Six Sigma and Lean concepts, Chapter 6 introduced you to general methodologies to improve processes. In this chapter, we specifically target flow improvement and take a hands-on, tool-based approach to analyzing a process and redesigning it for prompt service delivery (Figure 7.1). Redesign does not occur in a vacuum. It is part of a cycle with multiple stages: (a) modeling, (b) analysis, (c) redesign, (d) implementation, (e) control, and (f) refinement of the design. It is always a good idea to represent the process graphically in order to develop an easily understandable view of its structure, intricacies, and boundaries. The depiction of the process thus facilitates

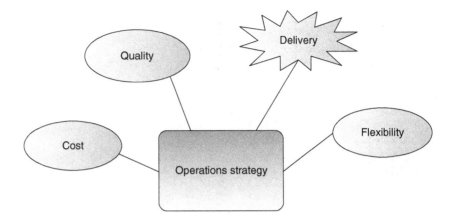

its analysis, which is primarily concerned with process understanding and performance assessment. Once you identify and properly define performance gaps, it is time to decide whether the process needs to be redesigned, or completely overhauled or reengineered. Following implementation, the process needs to be monitored on a regular basis, leading to further refinements.

A well-designed process should support the organizational strategy. At a time when the strategic emphasis is on producing value in healthcare, processes should be designed to minimize errors and maximize efficiency. In this chapter, you learn about various design tools and techniques that help you meet these challenges. More specifically, you will:

1. **Model a process using well-known visual tools: basic flowcharts, swimlane diagrams, and value stream maps**

2. **Develop a 5w2h (who, what, when, where, why, how, and how much) framework to develop a basic understanding of a process**

3. **Develop a process activity chart to identify value-added and non–value-added steps in a process**

4. **Propose approaches to reduce hand offs and to simplify processes**

5. **Design product, functional, or hybrid layouts based on process characteristics**

6. **Develop general process charts to evaluate the extent of improvement accomplished through redesign**

BRADLEY PARK HOSPITAL 7.2

Jennifer walks up to the ear, nose, and throat (ENT) clinic after going to the cafeteria for some coffee. "My head is a little clearer now that I have some caffeine in my system," she thought. Laverne, the nurse manager of the clinic, was in her office waiting.

"Thanks for agreeing to meet me on such short notice," Jennifer said.

"My pleasure," Laverne responded. "We cannot figure out the problem with Dr. Levine's patient delays. We are thankful for your help."

Jennifer started, "Here is the list of patients who have experienced delays. Can you and your staff show me what steps you take to get these patients ready for surgery?"

Laverne began, "After Dr. Levine and the patient agree to have surgery, we get a consent form."

"Wait," Jennifer stopped her. "Will you walk me through the process and let me talk to the staff who perform each step?"

"Sure," Laverne replied. "Let's go down the hall and I will introduce you to everyone."

 Does Jennifer need to go through all the process steps? Why can't she just trust Laverne?

PROCESS MODELING

A **process model** is essentially a simplified, graphic representation of a process. Modeling can be accomplished at various levels of detail. The model can be a simple diagram depicting the basic workflow of the activities comprising the process. The diagram can be refined to include the players as well as the various points of "waste" in the process. At its most advanced state, the process model is a sophisticated simulation model that mimics the existing, or planned process, and generates performance measures based on its configuration.

Process Model
A simplified, graphic representation of a process.

Flowchart

The analysis and design of a process often starts with its depiction. There are many established, as well as original, diagramming conventions available for the purpose. A popular one is a **flowchart** (Box 7.1; Chapter 6). A flowchart shows the movement of a **flow unit** through the process. A flow unit refers to any entity that enters the process, goes through a sequence of activities, and exits the process (Laguna & Marklund, 2005). Depending on the context, the flow unit could be a patient, a lab order, a medical record, or a purchase requisition. The flowchart displays the progress of the flow unit through the process as a left to right (or top to bottom) arrangement of symbols (Figure 7.2). It can show loops when rework needs to be done, decision points, alternative paths or routings, and activities that can be performed in parallel, independently from one another. For example, let us consider the surgery scheduling process at Bradley Park Hospital's (BPH's) ENT department. The flow unit is the patient, and the process consists of 13 steps (Figure 7.3). Once the patient has decided to undergo surgery, he or she must go through a multistep process: signing a consent form, getting several tests done, waiting for the results, and finalizing the scheduling procedure. Note that the two decision points in the process influence the logical sequence of steps.

Flowchart
A diagram that shows the movement of a flow unit through a sequence of activities.

Flow Unit
Any entity that enters the process, goes through a sequence of activities, and exits the process.

> ### ✚ BOX 7.1 – OM IN PRACTICE!
>
> **Preventing Suicides in the Psychiatry Unit at Johns Hopkins**
>
> After wrong-site surgery, inpatient suicide in psychiatry units is the second most common hospital error. Rather than focusing on the individual providers who might be "at fault" in such instances, Johns Hopkins decided to examine the *system* that allows for such errors to occur and improve it. Most critical was the monitoring process of patients at risk, and the communication flow among the various providers involved in their care. They developed flowcharts to depict the process, identified its weak points, and redesigned the process with a standardized path for observation and exchange of notes (Johns Hopkins Medicine, 2009).

FIGURE 7.2 – Basic flowchart symbols.

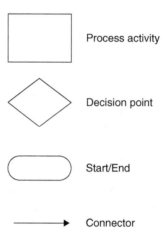

Process activity

Decision point

Start/End

Connector

Swimlane Diagram

Swimlane Diagram

A type of flowchart that identifies all the players in the process. It is composed of several bands or lanes, each one corresponding to a participant in the process.

A **swimlane diagram** is a type of flowchart that identifies all the players in the process. It is composed of several bands or lanes, each one corresponding to a participant or player in the process. This information is useful when determining the various resources involved in performing the process; it also hints at the subprocesses performed by the players. In our example, ordering lab tests would trigger a series of subactivities, such as retrieving a patient record, assigning a phlebotomist, labeling samples, analyzing, and logging the results. Figure 7.4 extends the basic flowchart for surgery scheduling (see Figure 7.3) by indicating the roles played by specific individuals/departments in the process. The surgeon recommends surgery, orders tests, contacts the insurance company if the request for PET scan is denied, reviews test results, and makes the appropriate final decision regarding the surgery. The medical assistant prepares the required forms and sends them to the scheduler. The scheduler consults with the patient to set a date for the surgery and faxes the surgical request form to the hospital's operating room (OR) scheduling department. Staff at the lab and imaging department perform the appropriate tests and forward the results for review.

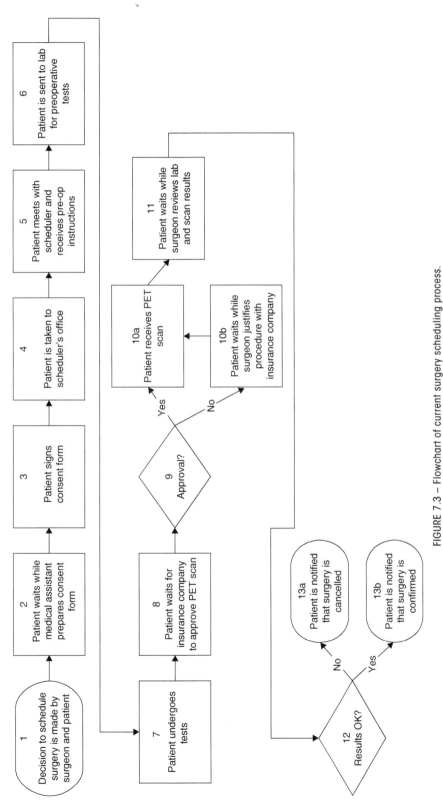

FIGURE 7.3 – Flowchart of current surgery scheduling process.

Based on Dr. D. Pinheiro's practice at the Mercy Clinic Ear, Nose, and Throat, Springfield, Missouri.

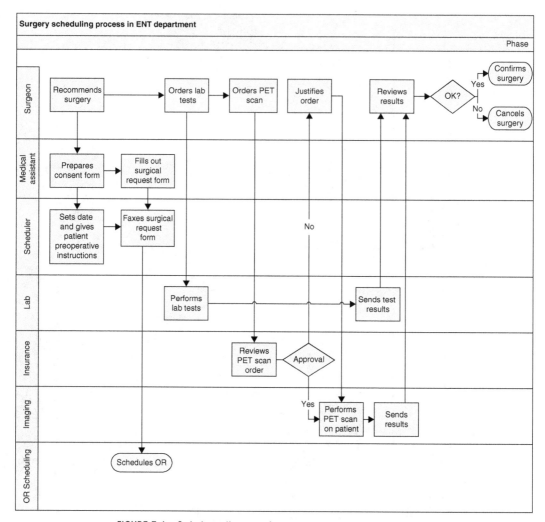

FIGURE 7.4 – Swimlane diagram of current surgery scheduling process.

Value Stream Map

Value Stream Map

A flowchart that depicts a process flow from a Lean perspective. As such, the process should create optimal value to the customer with no or minimal waste.

A **value stream map** is a flowchart depicting a process flow from a Lean perspective (Chapter 6). As such, the process should create optimal value to the customer with minimal or no waste. The value stream map therefore incorporates the activities that are valuable to the customer as well as those that are considered wasteful. The visualization of waste on the process map facilitates its subsequent elimination and thus aids in process redesign. Remember from Chapter 2 that value is defined from the perspective of the customer. Therefore, all the possible points in the process, such as delays, errors, and unnecessary movements that might dissatisfy the customer, should be identified in the process map. In the value stream map shown in Figure 7.5, it is clear that the major delays might occur between the visit with the scheduler at the surgeon's office and the lab test, and between the lab test and the PET scan. The criticality of these matters is highlighted in the map by the "burst Kaizen" icons urging for the redesign of a leaner, improved process. As indicated in the bottom, right-hand corner of the map, the total time for the process fluctuates between 6 days and 33 days approximately, but only 90 minutes of that time is of value to the patient.

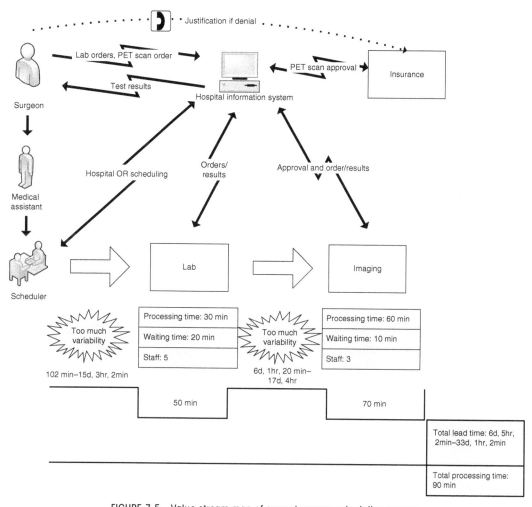

FIGURE 7.5 – Value stream map of current surgery scheduling process.

Simulation

The highest level of process modeling is simulation. As its name indicates, **simulation** involves the imitation or replication of a process. It is an abstraction of a real-world process. Although several types of simulation exist (e.g., physical prototype of a car), only computer simulation is addressed in this chapter. A simulation model of the process depicted in Figure 7.3 was developed using the software ExtendSim 9.1 (Figure 7.6). The patient flow from BPH's ENT department is represented by a series of activity blocks (e.g., sign

Simulation
Imitation or replication of a process. It is an abstraction of a real-world process. It produces performance metrics to guide redesign.

consent forms) and queues in front of these blocks. Blocks combining a queue and an activity—"workstations" in ExtendSim terminology— are also shown for illustrative purposes (see Chapter 8 for more detailed coverage of simulation with ExtendSim). The model is overly simplified because it does not take into account the flow of patients from other health facilities who also undergo lab tests and PET scans. If additional information on patient volumes at the lab and imaging department were collected, the model could be modified to reflect the extra load placed by other patients on the system.

Simulation is data intensive and requires the collection of historical data on any random variable. At a minimum, data will be collected on two variables: the arrival of flow units into the process and the processing time for each activity. Once simulation models are "run," they yield important performance statistics such as minimum, maximum, and average wait time before each activity; number of flow units held in the queue; utilization of resources, and so on. This is part of process analysis. One of the main advantages of simulation is that the process configurations can be changed easily, and the performance statistics are regenerated automatically, thereby allowing you to test different potential solutions before selecting and implementing one.

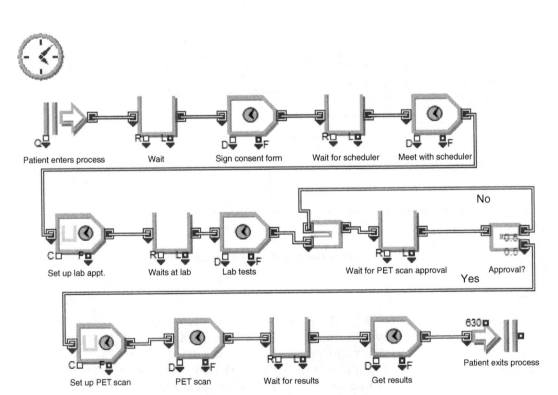

FIGURE 7.6 – Simulation model of surgery scheduling process.

BRADLEY PARK HOSPITAL 7.3

Jennifer and Laverne sat at the head of the conference room table with a projection screen behind them. The rest of the clinic staff sat around the table chatting.

Jennifer started. "As you all know, we are trying to figure out how to decrease the time it takes for Dr. Levine to get patients' lab test results and a PET scan prior to surgery. When you stepped me through the process to get patients ready for surgery, I took notes and developed this flowchart (see Figure 7.3) to show the current steps in the scheduling process. Will you all look at this and make sure that I got every step right?"

Mary, a clinic nurse, piped up, "When you look at the process this way, it looks so complicated. You also see how many times the patient is left waiting for an answer or for the next step to occur."

"Yes," Jennifer responded. "The flowchart helps you see where there may be unnecessary steps or delays. Another way of looking at the process is with the swimlane diagram (see Figure 7.4). This shows all the people who are involved in the process."

"Wow," Laverne uttered. "I had no idea that so many people were involved in getting these tests. But it makes sense. With approvals and billings, these processes are complicated."

Jennifer continued, "And finally, we get to the value stream map, which shows the complexity of the processes and includes the processing times. We also can begin to look at the steps that have too much variability and lead to inconsistent results. What we see is that there are delays of up to 15 days in scheduling lab tests and up to 17 days in scheduling PET scans."

"I don't think we can work any faster," Jamie, another staff nurse said. "I feel like I am working as hard as I can."

"I am not saying that you all need to work harder," Jennifer countered. "We all just need to work 'smarter'! I will be digging into these delays, and we can get back together when I have more information. I just wanted to confirm that the flowcharts looked right to you as you are the ones with firsthand knowledge of the process."

"I have a question," Tim, a clinic nurse, began. "I think you have done a great job in clarifying the process from the clinic perspective. However, I know patients who live an hour or so away from the clinic. If they must come back for a test, is this travel accounted for?"

"Great question, Tim. You are right that this travel time is not depicted in these maps. But we will need to take that into account if we are really going to make this a patient-friendly process. Thank you for your willingness to work with me to get to the bottom of these delays. We will be setting up a project focused on these delays and will be working with you on an ongoing basis to see how we can redesign your processes to eliminate as many delays as feasible. I look forward to working with you all." Jennifer stood up to leave.

Laverne thanked her for her help. "We are working to become the model clinic for BPH! Now, let's move on to the rest of the agenda," Laverne continued as the group turned to look at patient satisfaction scores for their clinic.

 Why is it a good idea to represent a process graphically?

PROCESS ANALYSIS

Process Analysis
An analysis that creates an understanding of the activities of the process and measures the success of those activities in meeting the goals set for this process.

The process model is the input to **process analysis,** which "creates an understanding of the activities of the process and measures the success of those activities in meeting the goals" (Association of Business Process Management Professionals, 2009, p. 58). Processes should be designed to support the organizational strategy. Their ability to do so is thus reflected by less time, higher flexibility, better quality, and/or lower cost. Both value stream maps and simulation models help signal problem areas and quantify their magnitude. For example, Figure 7.5 documented delays of up to 15 days in scheduling lab tests and up to 17 days in scheduling PET scans. Similarly, once run, the simulation model in Figure 7.6 generated queue statistics confirming extensive delays to set up the lab appointments, get PET scan approval, and set up the PET scan appointment after approval. Accounting for such long delays would compel the physician's staff to schedule surgeries further in the future, thereby putting patients at risk. Furthermore, the surgeon could get test results at such a late date that the procedure might need to be cancelled at the last minute if warranted. Clearly, these analyses call for process redesign. Other useful tools in process analysis are the 5w2h framework and process activity charts.

The 5w2h Framework

5w2h Framework
A framework that asks pertinent questions (*who, what, when, where, why, how,* and *how much?*) to paint an accurate and comprehensive picture of the process and signal improvement opportunities.

Originally used for benchmarking (Robinson, 1991), the **5w2h framework** also contributes to the understanding of the process by asking pertinent questions. Typically, the process analyst will consult multiple sources of information to answer these questions. Besides graphic models, interviews of process participants, internal documents, and video recording of the process in action may prove useful in painting an accurate and comprehensive picture of the process and signal improvement opportunities. Table 7.1 indicates how the activity of setting up a lab appointment in the surgery scheduling process should be questioned and evaluated for redesign.

Process Activity Chart
A tool that examines the flow of activities and assesses whether or not they create value. It categorizes activities as operations, inspections, transportation, delay, and storage.

Process Activity Charts

Process activity charts are popular process analysis tools that complement 5w2h frameworks. Process activity charts examine the flow of activities and assess whether or not they create value. As you may recall (Chapter 2), value establishes a relationship between quality and cost; it is essentially what the customer of the process is willing to pay. The process activities meeting or exceeding customers' expectations are therefore considered to add value. They deliver exactly what the customers want, and they do so without wasting time and resources. In our surgery scheduling process, a PET scan is certainly something the patient would be willing to pay for.

TABLE 7.1 – 5w2h Framework for Setting up Lab Appointment

Classification	5w2h Questions	Description
People	Who?	**Who is performing the activity?** The physician, the patient, and the scheduler at the lab **Why are these people doing it?** The physician must give the order, the patient must set a time that is convenient, and the scheduler must check whether the patient's request can be satisfied given the times available. **Could/should someone else perform the activity?** The patient could be less involved in the process if it is redesigned.
Subject matter	What?	**What is being done in this activity?** Orders are placed; patient decides whether to have lab test after visit or at a later time; scheduler checks times available and sets up appointment in system; patient may call lab to set up appointment before surgery if he or she does not meet with scheduler. **Can the activity in question be eliminated?** The doctor would still have to place order, but patient could walk in without appointment if he or she does not mind waiting.
Sequence	When?	**When is this activity performed?** After visit or at a later time **When is the best time to perform this activity?** Lab test should be right after visit. **Does it have to be done at a certain time?** At least 1 week before the surgery
Location	Where?	**Where is this activity carried out?** The appointment is set up either in the doctor's office immediately after the visit, or at the patient's whereabouts later on. **Does it have to be done at this location?** It does not have to be done at the patient's whereabouts if lab test is done right after visit.
Purpose	Why?	**Why is this activity needed?** The appointment is set up in order to accommodate the patient's schedule, to plan and schedule lab resources, and to ensure that surgeon receives results before surgery. **Clarify its purpose** Preopeartive tests are necessary to determine the general state of health and uncover possible conditions that may influence the outcome of the surgery.
Method	How?	**How is the activity carried out?** If the patient is available after the visit, a lab appointment is made, and the patient may get the tests done right away. If not, the patient goes home and schedules a lab appointment at his or her convenience. Given the time required to travel back to the health facility and get the tests done, the patient may procrastinate, resulting in late test results. The surgery then needs to be rescheduled at a later date or canceled at the last minute. **Is this the best way or are there alternatives?** This is not the best way because the patient wastes time coming back to the facility, and late lab results contribute to both the surgeon's and the patient's frustration and dissatisfaction. A better way would be to perform the lab tests immediately after visit.
Cost	How much?	**How much does it currently cost?** Lost revenue if dissatisfied patient decides to get surgery elsewhere (about eight occurrences per year). **What would the tentative cost be after improvement?** Lost revenue would decrease. Although it may not be possible to completely eliminate the number of surgeries lost because of patient's dissatisfaction, the number of yearly occurrences could be reduced to two or three.

**Value-Added
Activities**

Activities that benefit
the customer directly
and for which he or
she is "willing to pay."

**Non–Value-Added
Activities**

Activities that are
considered waste
from the customer's
perspective.

**Business–Value-
Added Activities**

Activities involving
inspection, verification,
and policy compliance
that benefit the
customer indirectly.

However, the PET scan is **value added** (V) only if it is performed correctly and does not require the patient to come back and also if the wait between appointment time and procedure is on par with or below the patient's expectations. Clearly, the customer or patient would not be willing to pay for delays, rework, and unnecessary transportation. These are therefore **non–value-added activities** (N). Control and policy compliance activities lie somewhere in between. They do not benefit the customer directly, but they do so indirectly. For example, having each member of the surgery team (surgeon, nurses, and anesthesiologist) verify the patient's identity may not be something the patient would associate with a successful surgery. Nevertheless, verification of the patient's identity by all members of the surgical team is a policy designed to ensure patient safety. This type of activity is categorized as **business–value-added** (B; Laguna & Marklund, 2005).

Process activity charts combine the value classification scheme with a descriptive system using symbols denoting operations; transportations, movements, or information transfers; storage; delays; and inspections (Figure 7.7). In our surgery scheduling process, undergoing a test is an operation; going to the lab is transportation; time spent in the waiting room is a delay; and checking the test results is an inspection. Storage often implies storing physical objects—such as paper medical records in a warehouse, equipment in a stock room, or documents in a filing cabinet—and is not explicitly captured in this example. Be aware that the classification of an activity can change depending on the process being examined. For example, when scheduling surgery, meeting with the scheduler and having lab tests are considered value-added. However, when looking at the entire surgery delivery process, meeting with the

FIGURE 7.7 –
Symbols in process
activity chart.

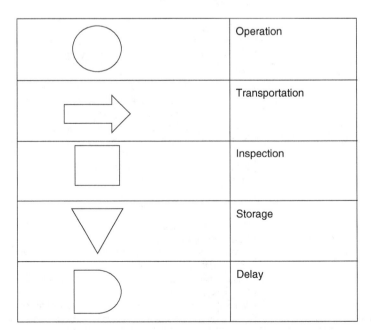

⬤	Operation
⬥	Transportation
▢	Inspection
▽	Storage
D	Delay

scheduler and tests might be downgraded to business–value-added. Moreover, the classification will vary based on the customer of the process (i.e., the recipient of its output). For example, PET scan approval may be a business–value-added step from the patient's perspective, but definitely a value-added one from the insurer's standpoint.

The process activity chart for the surgery scheduling process is depicted in Figure 7.8. The symbols corresponding to the steps listed in the same row are connected to show the nature of the patient flow. The time and/or distance for each step are also recorded. As can be seen from this chart, many activities do not pass the litmus test of meeting the patient's value expectations. The patient spends long periods waiting for appointments and traveling distances. The situation is especially alarming for patients who return home after their visit with the surgeon rather than go directly to the lab. In some cases, the patients live 60 miles from the health facility, which results in lengthy travel, inconvenience, and excess cost. In addition, the PET scan approval may take up to 10 days, causing anxiety for the patient and potentially harming the patient by delaying the scheduled surgery.

The current process comprises 21 steps: nine operations, six delays, one inspection, and five transports. The total value-added time is 133 minutes, whereas the total time fluctuates between 6 days, 7 hours, and 4 minutes (3,304 minutes based on 8-hour days) and 33 days, 4 hours, and 24 minutes (16,104 minutes). Much of this total time is non–value-added, signaling a need for corrective action. Computing the efficiency of a process helps us quantify the extent of improvement needed. The efficiency of a process expresses the proportion of time spent on value-added time in the entire process. It is computed as:

$$\text{Efficiency} = \frac{\text{Sum of the times of value-added steps in the process}}{\text{Sum of times of all steps in the process}} \quad [7.1]$$

$$= \frac{133}{3304} = 4.03\%$$

or $$= \frac{133}{16104} = 0.83\%$$

For the process depicted in Figure 7.8, efficiency varies between 0.83% and 4.03%, an indication that the process is cluttered with non–value-added time.

The main drawback of a process activity chart is that it does not allow for alternate paths following a decision point. When such situations arise, you may create a flow chart that also uses the symbols of the process activity chart (Figure 7.9)

Case for Action

The redesign of a process is a project (Chapter 3). Like many projects, process redesign faces many obstacles, the most daunting being people's natural resistance to change. Individuals performing the process will feel that it works just fine the way they do it, or they will

				Code (V/N/B)	
1	Decision for surgery made with patient	10 min		V	
2	Surgeon tells medical assistant to schedule procedure	1 min		V	
3	Surgeon enters orders in computer	4 min		B	
4	Patient waits while medical assistant fills out surgical case request form	5 min		N	
5	Patient signs consent forms	2 min		B	
6	Patient waits to meet with surgical scheduler	10 min		N	
7	Patient meets with scheduler and is given pre-op instructions and date of procedure	30 min		V	
8	Patient waits for or makes appointment for lab tests	20 min –15d, 20 min		N	
9	Patient goes to lab for preop testing at main hospital	40–120 min	1–60 miles	N	
10	Patient gets labs and preop testing done	30 min		V	
11	Patient goes home	40–120 min	1–60 miles	N	
12	Patient waits for PET scan approval from insurance	3–10 days		N	
13	PET scan scheduled	3–7 days		N	
14	Patient goes to imaging department	40–120 min	1–60 miles	N	
15	Patient waits	10 min		N	
16	Patient gets PET scan completed	60 min		V	
17	Patient goes home	40–120 min	1–60 miles	N	
18	Tests are processed and analyzed	60 min		B	
19	Test results are sent to surgeon	10 min		N	
20	Tests results are examined	10 min		B	
21	Patient is notified if surgery is confirmed	2 min		V	

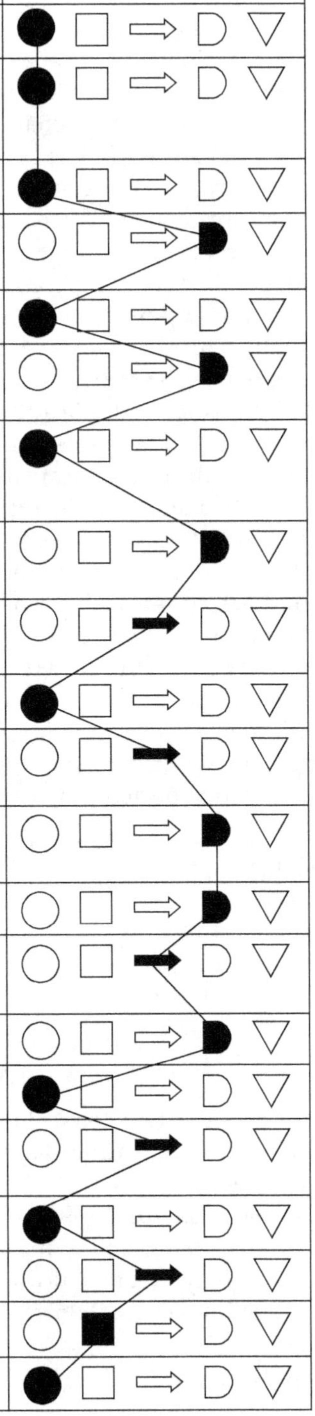

FIGURE 7.8 – Process activity chart for surgery scheduling process.
B, business–value-added; N, non–value-added activities; V, value added.

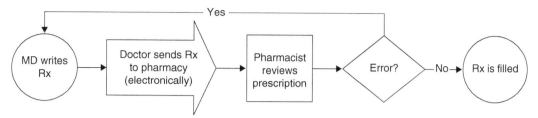

FIGURE 7.9 – Flowchart with activity chart symbols.

fear that efficiency gains will come at the expense of their job, power, or autonomy; people working upstream and downstream of the process will resent the adjustments they may have to make in their routines; and upper management will require evidence of substantial improvement in the bottom line. It is, therefore, very important to develop a **case for action**, a document or presentation that makes a compelling, clear, and concise argument for change and the resources to implement it. For process improvements, a case for action should comprise five short sections (Cassidy & Guggenberger, 2002):

Case for Action
A document or presentation that makes a compelling, clear, and concise argument for change and the resources to implement it.

1. **Business environment**. As processes are supposed to support the organizational strategy, the case for action should identify the environmental pressures that justify change. For example, wait times at a competing hospital's ED are 10 minutes shorter, on average.

2. **Problem**. The problem(s) stemming from the current process should be clearly articulated. For example, wait times are very long during certain times of the day when patient volume is higher.

3. **Diagnosis**. The reasons for the process's dysfunction should be listed and briefly explained. In the case of long wait times, a diagnosis could refer to (a) poor triage hindering a rapid and smooth flow of patients through the ED, (b) lack of provider capacity at peak times, and (c) inappropriate layout.

4. **Cost of inaction**. This section warns the various stakeholders of the consequences of maintaining the status quo in terms of lost business, loss of reputation, missed opportunities, and/or excess cost. Left alone, the processes in the ED would result in an increase in left-without-being-seen (LWBS) cases (lost revenue), poor patient satisfaction scores (lower reimbursements by Medicare, unfavorable contracts with payers), tarnished reputation (lost opportunities for future revenue), and even worse medical outcomes because of delayed treatment (litigation costs).

5. **Objectives**. The objectives section should list the tangible and intangible benefits to be derived from the improvement. In the ED example, redesigned processes might reduce wait times by 12 minutes on average, decrease LWBS cases by 30%, improve providers' morale and productivity, and increase competitiveness for future business.

The case for action is of utmost importance because it "sells" the need for the improvement. If it is well received, it should lead to process redesign.

PROCESS DESIGN

Process Design
The creation of a process that lowers the chances for error (quality), minimizes waste (cost), eases the flow (delivery), and allows for rapid modifications (flexibility).

Handoff
The act of passing the responsibility for an activity onto another person, unit, department, and so on.

Process design or redesign aims at creating a process that lowers the chances for error (quality), minimizes waste (cost), eases the flow (delivery), and allows for rapid modifications (flexibility; Box 7.2). How do we create such processes? As a general rule, simpler processes are more robust. Think of a process as a sequence of steps. The reliability of each step is the probability that it will function effectively, that is, without errors, for a given period of time. As each step presents an opportunity—even a small one—to make errors, the more steps in the process, the greater the chances that the system/process will fail at one time or another. Furthermore, each time the responsibility for an activity is passed on to another person (a **handoff**), there is opportunity for miscommunication and error. Sound process design principles should therefore focus on simplicity and parsimony of tasks and movements (Laguna & Marklund, 2005). You may recognize some of the principles in Figure 7.10 as they are aligned with the Lean philosophy presented in Chapter 6.

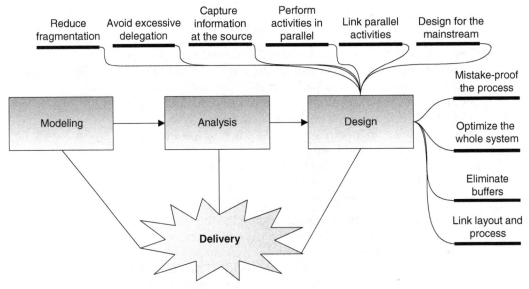

FIGURE 7.10 – Mind map of process design.

Design Principles

Principle #1: Reduce Fragmentation

For decades now, work with a narrow scope has been described as antiquated. Nevertheless, the concept remains popular thanks to well-entrenched ideas linking specialization to speed and efficiency. In an increasingly complex healthcare world, it is also tempting to divide up the work into narrowly defined areas of expertise as a justification to prevent errors. After all, one can only know so much. The problem with this approach is that it increases the fragmentation of the process, with handoffs and control/inspection points along the process. The result is more delays and errors. As much as possible, horizontal and/or vertical loading of activities should be pursued. Horizontal loading, also known as **job enlargement**, aims at increasing the variety of a job by having employees perform more activities that are immediately upstream or downstream. For example, a nurse may perform triage, provide discharge instructions, and schedule a patient for follow-up. Vertical loading, or **job enrichment**, extends the employee's regular activities to planning and control functions (Campion & McClelland, 1993). For example, the vertical loading of a nurse's tasks may entail the development of staffing schedules as well as checking proper medication reconciliation protocols. This "combination" of steps produces a simplified and continuous flow of activities.

Job Enlargement
A job design approach that increases the variety of a job by having employees perform more immediately upstream or downstream activities.

Job Enrichment
A job design approach that extends the employee's regular activities to planning and control functions.

Principle #2: Avoid Excessive Delegation

In line with principle #1, principle #2 attempts to prevent the proliferation of handoffs subsequent to delegating responsibilities and relying on others to "fix" problems. Lack of coordination and accountability ensue, affecting the effectiveness and efficiency of the process. In essence, principle #2 means, "Why have somebody else do it if you can do it yourself?" Physician order entry (POE) is an example of this principle in action. Computerized POE reduces delays and errors associated with transcription.

Principle #3: Capture the Information Once, at the Source

It is commonplace to have written data entered into a computer, or even digital information reentered in multiple computer systems. In addition to the time wasted on performing these redundant functions, human errors are also made during reentry. Point-of-care (POC) technologies enable healthcare providers to collect electronic test data directly at the patient's bedside. As a result, they eliminate the need for reentering information from a paper chart to an electronic health record. Nevertheless, when unresolved, incompatibility issues among different technological platforms may hamper seamless integration of POC data and electronic health records, thereby defeating their purpose. Therefore, a careful consideration of these challenges should precede a successful application of principle #3.

Principle #4: Perform Activities in Parallel Whenever Possible

Processes can often be depicted by perfectly linear sequences of activities. In the surgery scheduling example, the patient waits for the medical assistant to prepare the consent form, signs it, and then goes to the scheduler's office. The patient could go to the scheduler's office *while* the medical assistant prepares the form and then sign it in the scheduler's office. Performing these activities in parallel would decrease the amount of non–value-added time for the patient and speed up the entire process.

Principle #5: Link Parallel Activities Instead of Merely Integrating Their Output

A poor implementation of principle #4 would feature several activities being performed simultaneously and independently without much coordination. For instance, when working on a team project, you and your teammates might divide up the tasks. Assuming each individual knows exactly what his or her responsibilities entail, you may all work independently. When it is time to "assemble" all the parts of the project, you realize that some of the topics may have been covered by two or more of your teammates (redundancies), that some key parts of the project are missing (omissions/errors), and that the final output is essentially a very disjointed project report. If all of you had coordinated your activities frequently and had used a collaboration tool like SharePoint for document control, chances are that the finished report might require only few, minor revisions, if any.

Principle #6: Design for the Mainstream, Not the Exceptions

Inefficiencies are not part of the initial process design. Often, they emerge as new services are added, the patient mix changes, modern equipment is installed, new regulations are implemented, and so on. With these changes come ad hoc process "fixes" or add-ons. Over time, they become a web of paths with complicated and jumbled flows that make it hard to track the movements of flow units. When going to your dentist for your regular check-up, you may be asked to produce your insurance card so that the staff can make a photocopy even though the information is in their electronic dental record system. A simple check on their system would indicate whether the insurance information needs to be updated, but they continue to keep paper records because "they have always done it that way." Similarly, if supplies purchased from new vendors need to be inspected, it is not necessary to create a process with inspections for all purchases, including those from well-established, certified vendors. A design for the mainstream minimizes the number of paths and thus provides a simplified platform with lower variability and increased visibility and predictability.

Principle #7: Mistake-Proof the Process

In Chapter 6, one of the Lean tools mentioned was the *poka-yoke* system. This system is consistent with Deming's point #3—"Eliminate the need for inspection by building quality into the [process] in the first place" (see Chapter 4). A pharmacy system that signals drug interactions for a patient is an example of a poka-yoke system preventing medication error. A smart pump programmed to prevent infusion of an unsafe dose of a particular drug is another example.

Principle #8: Optimize the Whole System and Stop Focusing on Local Optimization

Very often, ingenious and motivated employees will work on ways to improve "their" system or process. Although their effort may improve their own operations, it may create a myriad of problems for upstream and/or downstream activities. For example, if a hospital has an integrated health information system and the surgery department decides to have a surgery module sold by another vendor, the surgery staff may be happy with the results. However, in the best case scenario, it may generate excess costs to interface the surgery system with other system modules, such as lab and billing. In the worst case scenario, information may have to be reentered, with potential for errors and additional clerical costs.

Principle #9: Eliminate Buffers

What is a buffer? A **buffer** is a group of flow units that has been temporarily held until capacity is freed to let them move through the process. A buffer can be an inventory of goods/supplies waiting to be used or a line of patients waiting to be seen by a provider. Buffers are often seen as an insurance policy against uncertainty in vendor lead times and demand (see safety stocks in Chapter 11). They also arise from variable arrivals of these flow units or variable activity times at any of the process steps the flow units go through. They are produced as well by batch processing systems that delay the movement of a flow unit from one activity to the next until a batch has been completed (see principle #10). In any case, buffers are visual process encumbrances that halt a smooth and rapid flow. Eliminating buffers exposes weaknesses and forces redesign. The example provided in Box 7.3 shows how a reorganization of surgical carts freed up capacity and improved OR times.

Buffer
A group of flow units that has been temporarily held until capacity is freed to let them move through the process.

⊕ BOX 7.3 – OM IN PRACTICE!

Supply Storage for Orthopedic Surgery at Mercy Hospital in Springfield, Missouri

When a surgery is scheduled, the supplies needed for the case are assembled onto a case cart, which is then wheeled into the operating room. In many cases, the supply requirements are very consistent. However, in orthopedic trauma cases, the injuries vary from person to person, and thus the supply needs also vary. Dr. David Merriman, one of the orthopedic surgeons, noticed that seemingly high-usage

---

(continued)

> **🔶 BOX 7.3 – OM IN PRACTICE! (continued)**
>
> supplies were unavailable on the cart and needed to be retrieved from the central storage area during surgery, thereby extending the time for surgery. Longer surgery time has been associated with increased risk of infection and blood loss. It also results in delays for later surgeries, increasing waiting times for those patients. Finally, OR time is a precious commodity that cannot be wasted. Dr. Merriman tracked the item types and their usage and found that 12 items comprised 88% of the additional supplies needed during surgery. The process was redesigned to allow for storage of these items in the operating room rather than in the central storage area. This change was estimated to save approximately 3 minutes per item, or about 125 hours per year (D. Merriman, personal communication, December 2014).

Principle #10: Link Layout and Process

Many of the non–value-added steps in a process consist of avoidable movements and travel. Ideally, the layout of the work environment should be designed to optimize the work flow and prevent wasteful traffic. Nursing staff spend a lot of time walking. This time would be better spent on patient care activities as well as interactions with family members. Recent nursing unit designs feature decentralized nurses' stations that permit the distribution of staff members closer to the point of care. The placement of storage and supply areas near the nurses' stations also decreases time spent walking, thereby boosting productivity (Zborowsky, Bunker-Hellmich, & Morel, 2010).

General Process Charts

The surgery scheduling process depicted in Figure 7.8 violates principles #1, 4, 7, and 10. The process is highly fragmented with numerous handoffs; several activities that could be performed in parallel are performed sequentially; the failure to properly justify the PET scan results in call backs and delays; and the patient must travel long distances. Based on these observations, the process was redesigned (Figure 7.11) with the following changes:

- The patient starts meeting with the scheduler while the medical assistant is preparing the consent form (principle #4).

- A lab has been set up in the surgery building to facilitate access. Patients no longer have to go to the main hospital to get tests done or go home and come back for tests at a later date (principle #10).

- After tests are completed, the patient goes home. As the test has already been done, there is no need for the patient to schedule an appointment and come back at a later date (principle #1).

- After reviewing records of PET scan approvals, it became clear that denials originated from one insurer whose requirements for approval included additional information. As soon as a request has to be placed with that insurer, the computer system now flags a warning to provide more detailed information. The change has resulted in virtually no denials (principle #7).

No.	Description	Time	Distance	Value Code (V/N/B)	Symbol
1	Decision for surgery made with patient	10 min		V	
2	Surgeon tells medical assistant to schedule procedure	1 min		V	
3	Surgeon enters orders in computer	4 min		B	
4	Patient waits to meet with scheduler while medical assistant prepares consent form	10 min		N	
5	Patient meets with scheduler, is given preop instructions and date of procedure, and signs consent form while appointment is being made at lab	32 min		V	
6	Patient goes to lab (same building) for preop testing	5 min	0.2 min	N	
7	Patient waits in lab	10 min		N	
8	Patient gets lab and preop testing done	30 min		V	
9	Patient goes home	40–120 min	1–60 min	N	
10	Patient waits for PET scan approval from insurance	3 days		N	
11	PET scan scheduled	3–7 days		N	
12	Patient goes to Imaging department	40–120 min	1–60 min	N	
13	Patient waits	10 min		N	
14	Patient gets PET scan completed	60 min		V	
15	Patient goes home	40–120 min	1-60 min	N	
16	Tests are processed and analyzed	60 min		B	
17	Tests results are sent to surgeon	10 min		N	
18	Tests results are examined	10 min		B	
19	Patient is notified if surgery is confirmed	2 min		V	

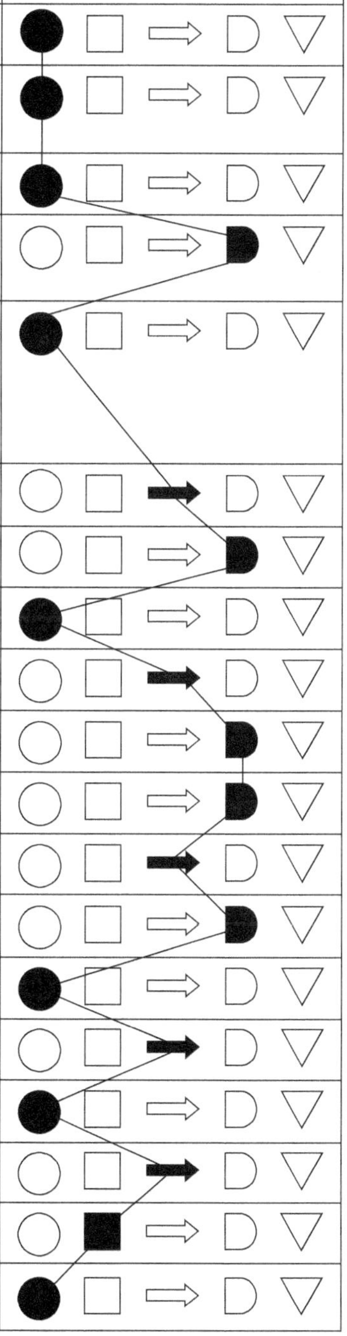

FIGURE 7.11 – Redesigned surgery scheduling process.

General Process Chart

Compares old and improved designs and displays the extent of improvement.

The performance of the proposed process can be compared to that of the original in a **general process chart**, which summarizes the improvements expected from redesign. Although the number of steps has only been reduced by two, the total time of the process has been reduced by 5,370 minutes or 11 days, 1 hour, and 30 minutes (Table 7.2)! This is mainly the result of a decrease of variability in scheduling the lab work and getting approval for the PET scan. The patient was able to get the lab tests done right away by placing a lab in the surgery building. The lower volume of patients at the lab also resulted in shorter wait times. Note that if this option was deemed to be cost prohibitive, a mini-phlebotomy lab could be set up at a lower expense. The blood samples would then be taken to the main hospital's lab without inconveniencing the patient.

TABLE 7.2 – General Process Chart

Activities	Current Process			Redesigned Process			Difference	
	No.	Time (min)	%*	No.	Time	%**	No.	Time
Operations	9	199	2.1	8	199	4.6	−1	0
Inspections	1	10	0.1	1	10	0.2	0	0
Transportation	5	170–490	3.4	5	135–375	5.9	0	−75
Storage	0	0	0	0	0	0	0	0
Delays	6	2,925–15,405	94.4	5	2,910–4,830	89.3	−1	−5,295
Total	21	3,304–16,104	100	19	3,254–5,414	100	−2	−5,370

*Shown for midpoint only (e.g., midpoint for transportation is 330; midpoint for total time = 9,704).
**Shown for midpoint only (e.g., midpoint for transportation is 255; midpoint for total time = 4,334).

BRADLEY PARK HOSPITAL 7.4

The ENT clinic staff and physicians congregated in the clinic conference room. Jennifer, Laverne, and Dr. Levine were standing at the front of the room while everyone was enjoying the cheese and crackers that Jennifer provided.

"May I have your attention," Dr. Levine started. "We are here to celebrate some success. We still have a long way to go, but when Jennifer showed me this dashboard (Figure 7.12), I wanted to share the good news. As you see, our lab results lead time is down, our productivity is up, and our PET scan denials are greatly reduced. This all translates into better patient care and better financial performance. Thank you all for your part in this project."

"But what about the wait time for the schedulers? It looks like that number is getting worse," Mary asked.

Jennifer jumped in, "It is normal that when you improve a process, you may bring out inefficiencies in another step. In this case, the schedulers are spending more time with the patients doing several steps at the same sitting. This means that patients are backing up because of the increased time required. The schedulers are doing a great job in getting consent, explaining the process, and collecting billing information. We now need to look at this step more closely and see what we can do to eliminate the backlog. That will be our next project!"

Is it premature for them to celebrate some successes? Shouldn't they wait until all problems have been resolved?

The metrics provided in the general process chart attest to the success of the redesign. Improvement will also be reflected in the performance metrics of a dashboard. Figure 7.12 displays a tactical dashboard for the delivery priority at the ENT department. After the process redesign in April, most performance metrics improved significantly, except for wait time to see the scheduler. This is the result of the longer meeting time with the scheduler, which is now creating a backlog due to insufficient capacity. This is the target for the next improvement.

Measures	FYTD Actual	FY Target	Jan.	Feb.	Mar.	Apr.	May	Jun.	Jul.
TIME									
Rescheduled appointments (%)	4.9	0	6	5	8	7	3	3	2
Rescheduled surgeries (%)	3	0	4	5	4	4	1	2	1
Visit—lab results lead time (days)	7.9	2	14	13	12	10	2	2	2
Wait time to see scheduler (min)	12.9	5	10	12	10	11	15	16	16
UTILIZATION									
Surgeons total hours	893	900	920	950	875	832	900	875	900
Surgeons productive hours	773	770	732	720	725	762	820	815	840
PET scan denials	2.3	0	5	6	2	3	0	0	0

FIGURE 7.12 – Dashboard for delivery at ENT department.

☐ RED FLAG! Needs improvement.
FY, fiscal year; FYTD, fiscal year to date.

THE RELATIONSHIP BETWEEN PROCESS AND LAYOUT

Ideally, the layout of the physical environment should facilitate the effective and efficient movement of flow units (patients, employees, materials, information, etc.) through the system. Common objectives include (Stevenson, 2012):

1. Reducing errors
2. Utilizing resources and space efficiently
3. Avoiding delays and bottlenecks
4. Minimizing handoffs
5. Minimizing movements and transfers

There are two basic layouts: a product layout and a functional layout. The main characteristics of each one are listed in Table 7.3. A product layout would be suitable for a lab: high and stable volume; a functional layout is the norm in hospitals where the various specialties (surgery, radiology, ophthalmology, etc.) are organized in separate departments, with each one experiencing variable demand.

TABLE 7.3 – Differentiating Between Product and Functional Layouts

	Product Layout	Functional Layout
1. Description	Sequential arrangement of activities dedicated to a specific service	Functional arrangement of activities accommodating a variety of services/patients
2. Process type	Standard and repetitive (with a few options)	Customized and variable
3. Demand	Stable	Fluctuating
4. Volume	High	Low
5. Resources	Specialized	Flexible
6. Flow	Fixed	Variable
7. Objective of design	Balance the workload at each step of process	Minimize wasted movements/transfers
8. Layout design techniques	Line balancing	Block diagramming; relationship diagramming
9. Advantages	Faster processing, fewer delays, less transportation, fewer handoffs, clear and streamlined flow	Flexibility, opportunity for high performance quality
10. Disadvantages	Low flexibility	High cost and time Jumbled flow

Adapted from Russell and Taylor (2014).

Designing Product Layouts for Repetitive Processes

Product Layout
Sequential arrangement of activities dedicated to a standard and repetitive process.

Traditionally, highly repetitive processes have been considered more common in support services (e.g., registration, scheduling, billing, and claims processing) than in clinical areas. However, keep in mind that blood sample processing and certain clinical procedures, such as cataract surgery, are high volume, repetitive operations, similar to an assembly line in manufacturing. The high volume requires a rapid flow through the process with as few hurdles and handoffs as possible. The best way to meet this requirement is to organize the resources (equipment and people) around the service and standardize procedures for consistent quality, that is, to adopt a **product layout** (Box 7.5).

Let us take the example of medical billing. Each day healthcare providers generate and send out a large number of bills to their payers. Table 7.4 provides a list of the tasks involved as well as their precedence relationships. If each task was performed sequentially by a different employee, people performing short tasks would often be idle, whereas people completing long tasks would see their backlog—or work-in-process—increase. The stop-and-go process would be extremely inefficient and frustrating. It is thus imperative to group tasks into process steps with approximately equal workloads, that is, balance the line.

 BOX 7.5 – OM IN PRACTICE!

From "Job Shop" to "Focused Factory" at Mayo Clinic

Because surgeons and hospital administrators often view cardiac surgical care as complex and unstructured, it has been organized and managed like a craftsmen's job shop with heavy reliance on customization. The customization is not only based on patients' needs, but also on providers' specific training and expertise. The problem with this model is that it generates great variability in terms of care and treatment for the same condition. The leaders of a clinical practice at Mayo Clinic, Rochester, Minnesota, decided to classify patients as focused factory vs. job shop candidates based on surgical complexity, medical comorbidities, and risk. Focused-factory care involved (a) clinical pathway of linked protocols for the operating room, intensive care unit, and progressive care unit; (b) empowerment of nonphysician care providers; and (c) placement of patients with similar conditions and medical complexity close together in order to create a "plant within plant" environment. Overall, the focused-factory model produced superior value: lower resource use, better clinical outcomes, and lower and stable costs of care per patient (Cook et al., 2014).

TABLE 7.4 – Tasks in Medical Billing Department

Task	Precedence	Time (min)
A Open coded report for existing patient	—	0.5
B Verify demographic and insurance information in billing software	A	6
C Update old or missing information	A	3
D Post charge	B, C	10
E Print and file copy of claim	D	4
F Submit electronic claim	D	1
	Total	24.5

Line Balancing

Line balancing is a trial-and-error technique that equalizes workload requirements subject to cycle time and precedence relationship constraints. Its objective is to develop an efficient layout with the lowest possible number of process steps. A balanced line is one of the requirements for a pull system (see Chapter 6).

Line Balancing
A layout design technique used for repetitive processes. It equalizes workload requirements subject to cycle time and precedence relationship constraints.

Cycle Time

The maximum amount of time allowed in a process step. It is also viewed as the time elapsed between two consecutive flow units exiting the process.

Cycle time is the maximum amount of time allowed in a process step. It is also viewed as the time elapsed between two consecutive flow units exiting the process. The desired cycle time is based on the total work time available and the number of jobs that need to be completed:

$$C_d = \frac{\text{Time available}}{\text{Desired output}} \qquad [7.2]$$

In the medical billing process example shown in Table 7.4, if we assume that 250 bills must be sent out daily and that six employees work 8 hours a day, the desired cycle time (Box 7.4) is:

$$C_d = \frac{6\,\text{employees} \times 8\,\text{hours} \times 60\,\text{minutes}}{250} = 11.52\,\text{minutes}$$

▶ BOX 7.4 – LET'S TALK!

Your words	. . . and ours
"Why is the cycle time in minutes?"	"Because the task times are given in minutes."

Flow Time

The total time needed to complete all process tasks.

Although the total time to process a bill—also known as **flow time**—is 24.5 minutes (see Table 7.4) the resources at process step #1 will not wait until a claim is sent to start working on the next bill. In fact, if everything goes as planned, there should be three bills in the system at any one time.

The other constraint is precedence relationships, which identify the tasks that must be performed before others can take place. Groupings must follow the logical sequence of the various tasks. In other words, task A cannot be grouped with task D unless B and C have been performed.

Line balancing is a step-by-step procedure:

STEP 1: Draw the precedence diagram.

STEP 2: Compute the desired cycle time, C_d.

STEP 3: Determine the theoretical minimum number of steps in the process.

> To minimize handoffs!

STEP 4: Group tasks to form process steps, using a heuristic or rule of thumb. Popular heuristics for line balancing are longest processing times, largest number of following tasks, lowest number of following tasks, and so forth (Table 7.5). Make sure that the longest time for a process step does not exceed C_d.

Efficiency

The ratio of time needed to complete all activities to the amount of time allocated by the newly designed process.

STEP 5: Compute the efficiency of the process created in step #4. The **efficiency** is the ratio of time needed to complete all activities to the amount of time allocated by the newly designed process.

STEP 6: Determine whether better efficiency or balance can be obtained.

Let us go back to our medical billing example.

1. The precedence diagram for the data shown in Table 7.4 is shown in Figure 7.13.

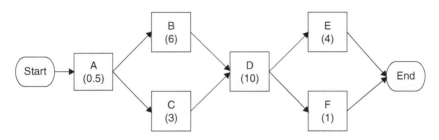

FIGURE 7.13 –
Precedence diagram
with task times.

2. $C_d = 11.52$ minutes (see Eqn. 7.2)

3. The theoretical minimum number of steps is the total amount of time required to complete all tasks divided by the longest time allowed at a process step, C_d.

$$TM = \frac{\text{Total task time}}{C_d} \qquad [7.3]$$

$$= \frac{24.5}{11.52} = 2.13 \approx 3\,\text{steps}$$

If the minimum number of steps is not an integer, always round UP. Rounding down would make it impossible to meet the daily demand.

4. Balance the line using a heuristic. Let us use the longest task time as a heuristic (Table 7.5).

TABLE 7.5 – Line Balancing Procedure

Process Step	Candidate Tasks	Assigned Tasks	Cumulative Time (C$_d$ = 11.52 min)	Idle Time
	A	A	0.5	11.02
1	B,C	B	6.5	5.02
	C	C	9.5	2.02
2	D	D	10	1.52
	F	F	11	0.52
3	E	E	4	7.52

- Task A must be completed before any other. At the start of the line balancing procedure, it is therefore the only candidate. It is assigned to process step #1 and takes 0.5 minute to complete. As the longest time allowed at a process step is 11.52 minutes, 11.02 minutes of time remain available at process step #1 after assigning task A.

- After assigning A, B and C are candidates as they meet the precedence relationship requirements (completed after A) *and* their respective durations are below the remaining time available at process step #1, that is 11.02 minutes. As B has the longer time (heuristic: Time$_B$ is greater than Time$_C$), it is assigned to process step #1.

- Now that A and B have been assigned, only 5.02 minutes of time remain available at that step. This is enough to fit in task C, which only takes 1 minute. Note: D is NOT a candidate because (a) it cannot start before both B and C are completed, and (b) its time of 10 minutes is longer than the remaining time available at process step #1. Keep in mind that only one reason is sufficient to exclude a task as a candidate. With 2.02 minutes of time remaining at process step #1, another process step must be created.

- The only candidate for process step #2 is task D, which must be completed before E or F. Once assigned, only 1.52 minutes of time remain at process step #2, which is sufficient to accommodate F, but not E.

- E is the only candidate left for process step #3. It is therefore assigned, and the idle time at that process step is 7.52 minutes.

The resulting process is shown in Figure 7.14:

FIGURE 7.14 –
Balanced process.

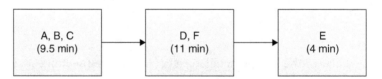

It includes the minimum number of three steps. Process step #2 is the longest with 11 minutes. Therefore, the actual cycle time of this process is 11 minutes, which is slightly lower than C_d. Assuming no delays, the implication is that a bill will come off this process every 11 minutes.

5. Compute the efficiency of the process, E.

$$E = \frac{\text{Total task time}}{\text{Number of steps created} \times \text{actual cycle time}} \times 100\% \quad [7.4]$$

$$= \frac{24.5\,\text{min}}{3 \times 11} \times 100\% = 74.24\%$$

Although the efficiency cannot improve dramatically as the number of steps created was equal to the theoretical number of steps, a little better balancing can be achieved by moving activity F to the third step. The resulting process would be as shown in Figure 7.15. Its efficiency would increase to $(24.5/(3 \times 10)) \times 100\%$ or 81.67% as bills exit the system every 10 rather than 11 minutes. Sometimes, other heuristics are used to determine whether higher efficiency or better balance can be achieved (Table 7.6).

FIGURE 7.15 –
Rebalanced process.

| A, B, C (9.5 min) | → | D (10 min) | → | E, F (5 min) |

TABLE 7.6 – Examples of Heuristics Used in Line Balancing

Heuristic	Rule to Select Candidate
Longest task time	Based on longest task time
Highest number of following tasks	Based on largest number of following tasks in process
Ranked positional weight	Based on the sum of the times for the candidate and all of its following tasks
Shortest task time	Based on the lowest task time
Lowest number of following tasks	Based on the smallest number of following tasks in process

Designing Functional Layouts for Nonrepetitive Processes

Functional layouts are suitable for customized, high-variety processes (job shops in manufacturing), which require flexible resources to perform diverse activities on diverse flow units. Dedicating resources assigned to fixed tasks, such as in the product layout, would result in low capacity utilization and excess cost. Instead, a **functional layout** organizes resources into departments or areas of expertise and supports variable paths among these areas. Although less efficient than product layouts, functional layouts should also be designed with the objective of reducing waste by eliminating excess movements and transfers along the paths. Two popular methods used to create functional layouts are block diagramming and relationship diagramming.

Functional Layout
Organizes resources into departments or areas of expertise for customized, high-variety processes.

Block Diagramming

Block diagramming is often used in material handling situations when the objective is to minimize the distances over which loads of material are carried. The technique prioritizes the transport of the heaviest loads over the shortest distances while relaxing this requirement for lighter loads. Although it seems more suitable for warehouse and manufacturing operations, the premise of the technique can easily be extended to service operations in which the amount of traffic between departments, as might be revealed in a spaghetti diagram, would influence their proximity.

Block Diagramming
A design technique used for functional layouts. It aims at minimizing the load–distance between departments, workstations, or offices.

For example, nurses in BPH's OB/GYN department have often complained about being tired and unable to handle the workload. Administrators have denied their requests multiple times for additional capacity because new expenses were incurred for remodeling. Sensing an opportunity for improved efficiency, Nurse Manager Janice Branson decided to use the block diagramming technique to suggest a better layout. She used the following steps.

STEP 1: Examine the floor plan, establish a list of all departments or rooms, and record the average amount of traffic as well as distances between the various rooms (Tables 7.7 and 7.8).

A Waiting room (1)	B Exam rooms (2)
C Nurses' station (3)	D Doctors' offices (4)

TABLE 7.7 – Distances Between Locations (in yards)

	Location			
To From	A	B	C	D
A	—	20	10	40
B			50	15
C				20

TABLE 7.8 – Daily Traffic Between Rooms

	Room			
To From	1	2	3	4
Waiting room (1)	—	62	50	3
Exam rooms (2)	22	—	101	25
Nurses' station (3)	43	65	—	15
Doctors' offices (4)	—	35	57	—

STEP 2: Determine the composite (two-way movements) load or traffic between pairs of departments or rooms.

Rooms	Composite Load
1 ⟷ 2	62 + 22 = 84
1 ⟷ 3	50 + 43 = 93
1 ⟷ 4	3 = 3
2 ⟷ 3	101 + 65 = 166
2 ⟷ 4	25 + 35 = 60
3 ⟷ 4	15 + 57 = 72

STEP 3: Compute the load–distance between pairs of departments or rooms.

Pair	Composite Load	Distance	Load × Distance
1–2	84	20	1,680
1–3	93	10	930
1–4	3	40	120
2–3	166	50	8,300
2–4	60	15	900
3–4	72	20	1,440
		Total	13,370

STEP 4: Examine the pairs with the highest composite loads and design a trial layout that would minimize the distances between them. Recalculate the load–distance.

A Exam rooms (2)		B Doctors' offices (4)
C Nurses' station (3)		D Waiting room (1)

Pair	Composite Load	Distance	Load × Distance
1–2	84	40	3,360
1–3	93	20	1,860
1–4	3	15	45
2–3	166	10	1,660
2–4	60	20	1,200
3–4	72	50	3,600
		Total	11,725

As you can see, locating the nurses' station closer to the exam rooms resulted in a reduction of 13,370 − 11,725 = 1,645 yards in total daily traffic. Please note that the current design ignored building constraints. For example, we could have assumed that the waiting room could not be displaced because of building entrance requirements. In that case, the waiting room would have been fixed in location A, and we would have only considered displacing the other rooms. Irrespective of physical constraints, the availability of quantitative data enables us to assess the merits of various design improvements in block diagramming. When quantitative data are unavailable, relationship diagramming is a more suitable layout design technique.

Relationship Diagramming

Relationship diagramming utilizes qualitative information provided by analysts, managers, and workers to establish relationship

Relationship Diagramming

A design technique used for functional layouts. It utilizes qualitative information provided by analysts, managers, and workers to establish relationship preferences between pairs of departments, workstations, or offices.

preferences between pairs of departments, workstations, or offices. It is common to use Muther's (1961) grid to reflect preferences coded as A, E, I, O, U, or X. Although X denotes an undesirable proximity between two rooms or departments, the vowels refer to various degrees of preferred proximity between such pairs. Figure 7.16 is an illustration of Muther's grid for a clinic. Although the waiting room should not (X) be next to the storage and supply room to prevent theft, it is absolutely necessary (A) to locate the nurses' station close to the exam rooms for easy access; it is especially important (E) to have the restrooms located close to the waiting room; it is important (I) to have the storage and supply room near the exam rooms to access medical supplies; it is okay (O) to have the nurses' station close to the offices; but it is unimportant (U) to have those offices located near the exam rooms.

FIGURE 7.16 – Muther's grid.

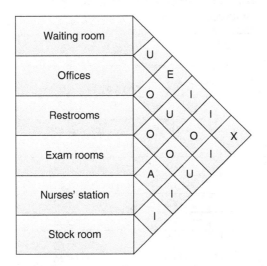

Key

A Absolutelynecessary
E Especially important
I   Important
O Okay
U Unimportant
X Undesirable

Muther's grid is then used to develop a relationship diagram to evaluate the appropriateness of current or proposed layouts. The thickness of the lines indicates the extent to which close proximity is desirable. Ideally, thick lines (I, E, and A) should be short and have few, if any, angles or zigzags, whereas thin or dashed lines (U and O) can be of any length and can even be omitted from the diagram to enhance clarity. As shown in Figure 7.17(a), the storage and supply room is in very close proximity to the waiting room when it should not be, the nurses' station is too far from the exam rooms, resulting in a lot of extra traffic every day, the restrooms are not conveniently located for patients in the waiting room, and the exam rooms are too far from the stock room to facilitate restocking. The layout in Figure 7.17(b) is much improved in that it fulfills most of the requirements expressed in Muther's grid. Perhaps, the building could also be remodeled to create a straight path between the nurses' station and the exam rooms.

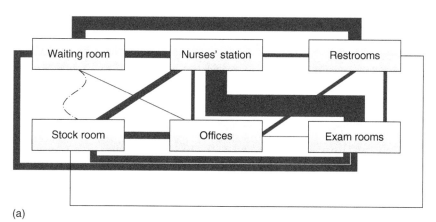

(a)

FIGURE 7.17 –
(a) Relationship
diagram for
existing layout,
(b) relationship
diagram for revised
layout.

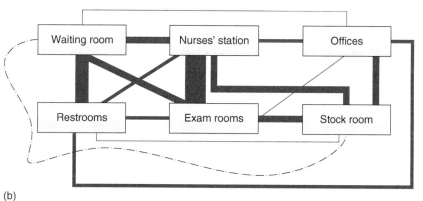

(b)

Software

Although useful for simple problems and to generate initial ideas about layout, the block diagramming and relationship diagramming methods are not sophisticated enough to handle complex layout decisions with building constraints. In those cases, professional software is used to generate facility layouts. CORELAP (computerized relationship layout planning) generates layouts based on closeness ratings and the number of departments and their respective square footage. CORELAP's algorithm attempts to place department pairs with A rating in close proximity first, then proceeds with the placement of department pairs with E rating, and so on, until a feasible layout is obtained. In other words, Muther's grid guides the order in which departments are placed in the layout plan. Another popular software package for facility layout is CRAFT (computerized relative allocation of facilities technique). CRAFT is based on the block diagramming method. Its required inputs are an initial layout, as well as interdepartmental traffic and travel costs/distances. It then determines which departments can be exchanged and estimates the cost savings of these exchanges. Once costs or load distances can no longer be reduced, the layout is finalized. CRAFT is sensitive to the initial layout. As a result, it works best when multiple initial layouts are examined for improvement. Finally, simulation software, such as Arena, PROMODEL, or ExtendSim, can be used to evaluate layout designs in terms of total distance traveled and total time spent on interdepartmental movements.

Cellular Layouts

By now, you must have grasped that the main benefits of the product layout are its simplicity and efficiency, whereas the main benefit of the functional layout is its versatility in accommodating a variety of flow units. A long-held view in healthcare is that all patients are different. Manufacturers faced the same issues decades ago when the relatively low volumes of some products made it too costly for them to dedicate resources to the production of these items. The solution involved the formation of "families" of products or services with similar processing requirements (e.g., motorcycles and jet skis). These natural groupings created a volume substantial enough to dedicate resources to their production. As the products within a family shared common process characteristics, the benefits of standardization could be reaped, and the cost penalties of switching from one product to the other were minimal.

Cellular Layout
A layout that is a hybrid between a product and a functional layout. It groups "families" of products or services with similar processing requirements.

The hybrid system that enables the coexistence of efficiency and diversity is the **cellular layout.** It does so by combining certain attributes of the product layout and certain attributes of the functional layout. It is essentially a mini plant within a plant. In healthcare, this concept is becoming increasingly popular. Let us take the example of a patient with prostate cancer. In a traditional system organized by functions, one patient may visit a urologist in one facility, then go to two separate locations for an ultrasound and lab tests. After another visit to the urology clinic, the patient may undergo surgery at the main hospital, followed by chemotherapy in yet another facility. One argument in favor of this functional layout is that it can accommodate an extremely diverse patient population with different ailments and treatment needs. The drawbacks are obvious: waste of time, waste of movements, handoffs, opportunities for communication breakdowns, patient's frustration, and fluctuations in providers' utilization. The solution is to create a urology center or wing that will diagnose and treat all urology patients. These patients are diverse, but they do share similar medical conditions. Grouping them as a "patient family" may generate the volume necessary to operate a facility dedicated to providing a comprehensive range of treatment services for these patients. The benefits are reduced movement, fewer care delays, easier tracking of patient's progress, more consistent utilization of resources, and increased standardization of care based on best practices (Figure 7.18).

SUMMARY

This chapter gives you the tools to examine a process, analyze it, and improve it. To examine the process, its graphic description or model is often preferred because it is an easy and universal communication

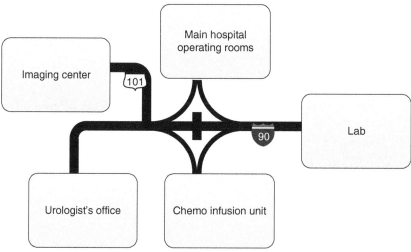

(a) Functional layout

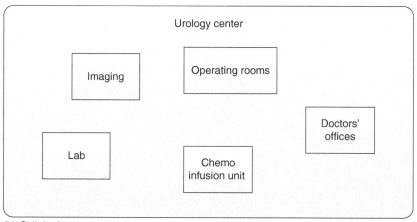

(b) Cellular layout

FIGURE 7.18 –
Functional layout vs.
cellular layout for
urology.

medium among all parties involved in the process. Flowcharts, swimlane diagrams, value stream maps, and simulation models are all popular process depictions that help visualize its flow, intricacies, and points of failure and stoppages. Further analysis is carried out by determining whether a process step adds value or not. A useful tool to uncover and document this analysis is the process activity chart, which categorizes activities as operations, inspections, transports, delays, or storage, and classifies them as value-added, business–value-added, or non–value-added. As we want the process to contribute as much value as possible, we design it or redesign it so that handoffs and other wasteful steps are eliminated. Ten principles guide us in this endeavor.

The flow of units (patients, documents, goods, etc.) through the system is also facilitated by the physical layout. Although the simplicity and efficiency of the product layout make it especially attractive in contributing value, the functional layout has the merits of supporting variety. Line balancing helps us design product layouts, and block diagramming and relationship diagramming help us design functional layouts. In healthcare, there has been a tendency to ignore efficiency to accommodate variety. Cellular layouts offer the opportunity to achieve both.

In our quest to add value in process flows, we have tied the competitive priority of on-time/fast delivery to cost, quality, and flexibility. Not only do we want to create a process that minimizes the chances of making errors and jeopardizing health outcomes and patient satisfaction, but we also want one that utilizes resources sensibly and economically. The tools presented in Chapters 4, 5, and 6 promote quality and chase waste away; they are most useful in creating value-added flows (Figure 7.19).

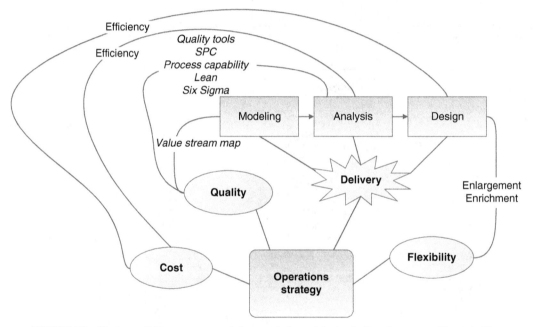

FIGURE 7.19 – Mind map linking process modeling, analysis, and design to the other competitive priorities.

KEY TERMS

Process model	Value-added activities	Product layout
Flowchart	Non–value-added activities	Line balancing
Flow unit	Business–value-added activities	Cycle time
Swimlane diagram	Case for action	Flow time
Value stream map	Process design	Efficiency

Simulation	Handoff	Functional layout
Process analysis	Job enlargement	Block diagramming
5w2h framework	Job enrichment	Relationship diagramming
Process activity chart	Buffer	Cellular layout
General process chart		

TOOLS USED IN THIS CHAPTER

TOOL	PURPOSE
Flowchart	Diagram used in process modeling to visualize the movement of flow units in a process. It displays the sequence of activities.
Swimlane diagram	Diagram used in process modeling to show the various participants in the sequence of process activities.
Value stream map	Diagram used in process modeling and analysis. It depicts a process flow from a Lean perspective, indicating areas that need improvement (Kaizen).
Simulation	Data analytical technique used in process modeling, analysis, and redesign. It generates important process performance metrics that help assess current and alternative designs.
5w2h framework	Framework used in process analysis to (a) understand the process by answering seven important questions, and (b) to identify improvement opportunities.
Process activity chart	Chart that displays all steps, categorizes them, and indicates whether they add value or not.
General process chart	Chart that shows gains between the old and improved process designs.

Line balancing	Technique used to produce equal task groupings when designing product layouts (repetitive processes).
Block diagramming	Technique used to minimize the amount of load–distance when designing functional layouts.
Relationship diagramming	Technique used to satisfy qualitative requirements when designing functional layouts.

FORMULAS USED IN THIS CHAPTER

Technique	Definition	Formula	Number
Process analysis	Efficiency	$\dfrac{\text{Sum of the times of value-added steps in the process}}{\text{Sum of times of all steps in the process}}$	[7.1]
Line balancing	Cycle time (C_d)	$\dfrac{\text{Time available}}{\text{Desired output}}$	[7.2]
	Minimum number of steps (TM)	$\dfrac{\text{Total task time}}{C_d}$	[7.3]
	Efficiency (E)	$\dfrac{\text{Total task time}}{\text{Number of steps created} \times \text{actual cycle time}}$	[7.4]

WHAT DO YOU REMEMBER?

1. Describe the modeling, analysis, and design phases briefly.
2. What are the modeling tools explained in this chapter? Explain each one.
3. What is the purpose of a 5w2h framework? Describe each of the 5 Ws and the 2 Hs.
4. What is a process activity chart? What are the symbols used in the chart to categorize process steps?
5. What are business–value-added activities? Give some examples.
6. From a value standpoint, what is the efficiency of a process?
7. What are the five sections of a business case for process improvement?
8. List five design principles and explain them.
9. What is the purpose of a general process chart?

10. What are common objectives of layouts?

11. Differentiate between functional and product layouts in terms of process type, demand, volume, and organization of resources.

12. What is the purpose of line balancing?

13. What is the purpose of block diagramming?

14. What is the meaning of the X and of each of the five vowels in Muther's grid?

15. What is a cellular layout? What is its primary advantage?

SOLVE BPH'S PROBLEMS

1. These are the steps for patients' paper records requests and recovery at one of BPH's clinics:
   - Staff member pulls list of patients with appointments to pick up their records (1 minute).
   - Staff member requests paper medical records from file clerk through e-mail, call, instant messaging, or paper note (10 minutes)
   - File clerk checks all communication methods (10 minutes).
   - File clerk finds the location of each requested file (5 minutes).
   - File clerk goes to record storage location (5 minutes).
   - File clerk places a request to have records pulled (2 minutes).
   - Storage clerk reviews the request (2 minutes).
   - File clerk collects the records (3 minutes).
   - Staff member makes copies of records and gives them to patient (20 minutes).
   - File clerk returns records to storage location (5 minutes).
     a. Develop a basic flowchart.
     b. Develop a swimlane diagram.

2. These are the steps for a patient to receive an echocardiogram:
   - Patient checks in (1 minute).
   - Patient sits in waiting area (1 minute).
   - Patient goes to registration booth and is registered (3 minutes).
   - Patient is sent to third floor for exam (3 minutes).
   - Patient sits in waiting area (11 minutes).
   - Echo staff checks paperwork and enters order (3 minutes).
   - Echo staff goes to procedure room and enters demographic patient data into machine (3 minutes).
   - Echo staff takes patient to procedure room (1 minute).
   - Echo staff gets a blanket and brings it to the room (1 minute).
   - Patient changes (2 minutes).

- Echo staff performs exam (23 minutes).
- Patient changes and is dismissed (2 minutes).
- Echo staff writes down exam information (3 minutes).
- Echo staff moves to control area (1 minute).
- Echo staff charges for exam (2 minutes).
  a. Develop a basic flowchart.
  b. Develop a value stream map.
  c. What improvements would you recommend? Why?
3. Develop a process activity chart for problem 1.
   a. Categorize activities as value-added, non–value-added, and business–value-added.
   b. Compute the efficiency of this process.
4. Develop a process activity chart for problem 2.
   a. Categorize activities as value-added, non–value-added, and business–value-added.
   b. Compute the efficiency of this process.
5. The billing department at BPH is redesigning the layout of its office to manage bottlenecks better. You are responsible for assigning each employee involved in this process to a set of tasks. One major goal is to achieve equal work groupings, that is, balance the line. The work elements to be performed are listed, along with their times and immediate predecessors.

Task	Time (sec)	Immediate Predecessors
A	60	—
B	40	A
C	30	B
D	20	B
E	40	B
F	60	C
G	70	D
H	50	F, G
I	20	E
J	60	H, I

If the desired output rate is 240 bills per day, and the facility operates 8 hours a day:

a. Construct a precedence diagram.
b. What is the desired cycle time?
c. What is the theoretical minimum number of steps (or task sets, in this context)?
d. Balance the line using the longest activity time as a heuristic and depict the process.
e. Compute the efficiency of the process.

6. These are the tasks necessary for the final assembly of a hospital bed, the time needed to perform each task, and the operations that must be completed prior to subsequent operations. The time available is 300 minutes per day, and the required output rate is 25 beds per day.

Task	Time (min)	Immediate Predecessors
A	4	None
B	5	None
C	8	None
D	4	A
E	3	A,B
F	3	B
G	5	D,E
H	7	F
I	1	G,H
J	7	I
K	4	C,J

a. Construct a precedence diagram.

b. Compute the desired cycle time.

c. Compute the theoretical number of process steps.

d. Balance the process using the longest activity time as a heuristic. If there is a tie, break it using the longest remaining time after the activity, that is, sum of the times of all its followers.

e. Compute the efficiency of the process.

7. Employees at BPH's Health Plans division process 200 claims during a 400-minute day. Based on the following precedence relationships, do the following:

Task	Time (min)	Immediate Predecessors
A	0.5	—
B	1.4	A
C	1.2	A
D	0.7	A
E	0.5	B,C
F	1.0	D
G	0.4	E
H	0.3	G
I	0.5	F
J	0.8	E,I
K	0.9	H,J
M	0.3	K

    a.   Draw the precedence diagram.

    b.   Compute the desired cycle time.

    c.   Compute the theoretical minimum number of process steps.

    d.   Balance the process using the longest activity time as a heuristic. If there is a tie, break it using the longest remaining time after the activity, that is, sum of the times of all its followers.

    e.   Compute the efficiency of the process

8.   The following is the current layout of a large storage area with items placed in rooms 1, 2, or 3 depending on their types. Based on the data regarding traffic and distance:

    a.   Fnd the load–distance for the current layout.

    b.   Redesign the layout to minimize load–distance. What is the total load–distance for your recommended layout?

A Room 1	B Room 2
C Room 3	

Distances between locations (in feet):

	Location		
From \ To	A	B	C
A	—	50	30
B			80

Daily traffic (number of trips) between rooms:

	Room		
From \ To	1	2	3
Room 1	—	27	5
Room 2	2	—	72
Room 3	—	29	—

9.   The following diagram is the existing layout of the nursing management office. Based on the data regarding traffic and distance, propose a new layout that will minimize the load–distance. What is the total load–distance of your layout?

A Room 1	B Room 2
C Room 3	D Room 4

Distances between locations (in yards):

To From	Location			
	A	B	C	D
A	—	20	10	30
B		—	25	15
C			—	10

Daily traffic (number of trips) between rooms:

To From	Room			
	1	2	3	4
Room 1	—	30	10	100
Room 2	40	—	110	25
Room 3	43	65	—	15
Room 4	70	35	42	—

10. A very satisfied patient has made a sizeable donation to the plastic surgery clinic at BPH. The funds will be used to remodel the outdated facility so that the new layout will support the work flow. After talking with the staff and making observations on her own, the office manager developed Muther's grid and then came up with the following relationship diagram. Redesign the layout according to the relationship diagram's requirements. The only constraint is that room E cannot be located anywhere else.

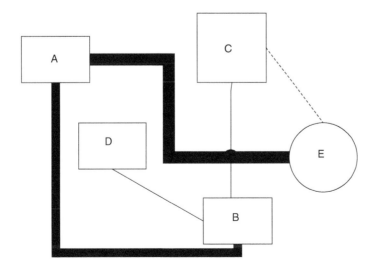

THINK OUTSIDE THE BOOK!

1. Search online for a process improvement in nursing homes and answer the following questions:
    a. What were the problems before the process redesign?
    b. Who took the initiative to recommend the redesign?
    c. What tools were used?
    d. What were the results of the redesign?

2. Box 7.1 describes a process change aimed at decreasing the suicide rate in the psychiatry unit at Johns Hopkins. Was Johns Hopkins right in focusing on the system rather than the individuals? Why or why not?

3. In Box 7.3, what would you consider to be "buffers"?

4. Box 7.5 describes the switch from a "job shop" to a "focused factory" model. Can you recommend this process transformation for another situation in healthcare? If so, which one and why?

5. In your work environment, select a process that is dysfunctional. Depict it using a swimlane diagram, analyze it using a process activity chart, and propose an improvement. Develop a general process chart to show the magnitude of the improvement.

6. In your work environment, select a process that is dysfunctional, develop a 5w2h framework, and make a case for action.

7. Look at the dashboard (Figure 7.12). Can you think of other indicators for the competitive priority of delivery?

REFERENCES

Association of Business Process Management Professionals. (2009). *Guide to the business process management common body of knowledge* (V. 2.0 ed.). Chicago, IL: Author.

Campion, M. A., & McClelland, C. L. (1993). Follow-up and extension of the interdisciplinary costs and benefits of enlarged jobs. *Journal of Applied Psychology, 78*(3), 339–351.

Cassidy, A., & Guggenberger, K. (2002). *A practical guide to information systems process improvement*. London, UK: CRC Press.

Cook, D., Thompson, J. E., Habermann, E. B., Visscher, S. L., Dearani, J. A., Roger, V. L., & Borah, B. J. (2014). From "solution shop" model to "focused factory" in hospital surgery: Increasing care value and predictability. *Health Affairs, 33*(5), 746–755.

Johns Hopkins Medicine. (2009). Preventing suicide may stem from how we watch. Retrieved from http://www.hopkinsmedicine.org/psychiatry/about/publications/newsletter/archive/09_spring/preventing%20suicide.html

Laguna, M., & Marklund, J. (2005). *Business process, modeling, simulation, and design*. Upper Saddle River, NJ: Pearson.

Muther, R. (1961). *Systematic layout planning*. Boston, MA: Industrial Education Institute.

Robinson, A. (1991). *Continuous improvement in operations: A systematic approach to waste reduction*. Cambridge, MA: Productivity Press.

Russell, R. S., & Taylor, B. W. (2014). *Operations and supply chain management* (8th ed.). Hoboken, NJ: John Wiley & Sons.

Steve Jobs. (n.d.). 20 Most memorable quotes from Steve Jobs. Retrieved from http://www.cheatsheet.com/technology/20-most-memorable-quotes-from-steve-jobs.html/?a=viewall

Stevenson, W. J. (2012). *Operations management* (11th ed.). New York, NY: McGraw-Hill.

Zborowsky, T., Bunker-Hellmich, L., & Morel, A. (2010, November). Centralized vs. decentralized nursing stations. *Healthcare Design, 10*, 50–78.

CHAPTER 8

CAPACITY AND DEMAND

BRADLEY PARK HOSPITAL 8.1

Mike Chambers was sitting drinking his morning coffee when he saw the paper's headline, "Early Flu Season Kills Three in New York City." "Wow," he thought. "We need to be sure that we vaccinate our patients soon. I need to check on how we are doing at the hospital and clinic. I will set up a meeting this morning to find out."

Francine and Todd Beringer, the chief pharmacist at Bradley Park Hospital (BPH), were waiting in Mike's office when he arrived. "Good morning, Mike," Francine said. "I hear you saw the news. Influenza is hitting hard this year. We have not yet seen a case in our state, but it is only a matter of time. The flu vaccine takes about 2 weeks to increase the body's antibodies so that it can fight infection. So we do not have any time to waste."

"Why are we starting so late to give vaccinations?" Mike asked.

Todd replied, "We are not late, the flu season is early! Each year, the drug companies make a vaccine that is directed against the most likely strains of influenza that are circulating and which viruses are likely to cause disease. In January, the WHO and the Food and Drug Administration decide what three to four flu strains the vaccine should be directed against and drug companies begin to grow them in large quantities to make the vaccine. It takes over 8 months to make the vaccine, process it, and ship it. We just got our first batch of vaccine yesterday. We will receive two more allotments over the next 4 weeks."

"We are setting up our vaccination stations," Francine continued, "but with this news of deaths from the flu, I wonder whether we have the capacity we need to serve the patient demand. I think I will get Jennifer involved to be sure that we design our stations to handle the volume of patients that we will likely see."

"Keep me posted," Mike said. "This is an important time for BPH and I do not want patient satisfaction to drop because we cannot deliver flu vaccinations. We are just beginning to earn the community's confidence."

"We will give you weekly reports," Todd said as he and Francine got up to leave. "Just don't forget to get your flu shot. We will be vaccinating all hospital employees ASAP."

 The last time you got your flu shot, was there a long line of people waiting to get the shot? Why?

INTRODUCTION AND LEARNING OBJECTIVES

Have you ever waited in line? Of course you have and you know that it can be an unpleasant experience. Now compound that with discomfort; let us say that you have burned your hand while barbecuing outside, and you have been waiting at the emergency department (ED) for more than 1 hour with no immediate relief in sight. Frustrated? As you know, these types of stories plague healthcare facilities, sometimes with tragic consequences (Box 8.1). So, what can be done about it?

The design principles presented in Chapter 7 provide a solid conceptual foundation on which to build smooth processes, but they should be strengthened with techniques grounded in flow theory (Figure 8.1). As discussed previously, waste, fragmentation, and redundancies can certainly hamper the flow of units through a process. Equally harmful is the inability to provide the capacity necessary to handle the demand placed on the process or system. You must have heard that businesses should match capacity with demand . . . well, this is WRONG. Actually, capacity should always exceed demand. Inefficient? Not if it is done properly. To this end, Chapter 8 introduces you to the scientific principles that govern waiting-line management. The contents will help you:

1. **Identify queuing characteristics and classify queuing models accordingly**

2. **Evaluate the performance of basic queuing systems and compute their costs**

3. **Extend the concepts of queuing theory to queuing simulation**

4. **Develop and run simulation models**

5. **Use simulation to analyze different process configurations and formulate design improvements**

6. **Identify bottleneck issues and understand the Theory of Constraints (TOC)**

✚ BOX 8.1 – OM IN PRACTICE!

Dead After 8-Hour Wait in Emergency Room for Rash

John Verrier went to the Saint Barnabas Hospital ER complaining of a rash. More than 8 hours later, he was found dead, still in the waiting room. An employee at the hospital blamed understaffing for Verrier's death. After his vitals were checked, he was told to wait. There was no system in place to ensure that patients' conditions remained stable while unattended for long periods of time (Shapiro, 2014).

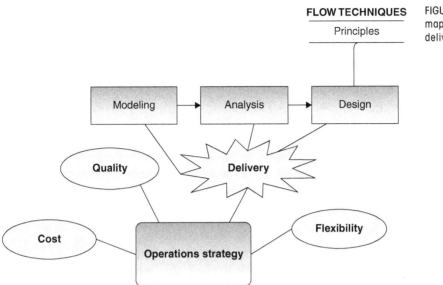

FIGURE 8.1 – Mind map focus on delivery.

CHARACTERISTICS OF QUEUING SYSTEMS

We first need to make the analogy between a process and a queuing system. As you know, a process is made up of a sequence of activities with various points of delay and stoppages. Flow units enter the process (arrivals), wait to be processed (queue), are processed (service), and then move to the next step in the process or exit it (Figure 8.2). The time spent in a line or queue is a function of the configuration and discipline rate at which the flow units enter the system, the rate at which they are processed or served, the queue, and the population of flow units.

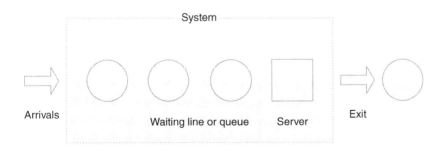

FIGURE 8.2 – General queuing system.

Arrivals

Claims will "arrive" on a third-party administrator's computer system; prescription orders will "arrive" at the pharmacy; calls will "arrive" at the central scheduling office. These arrivals coincide with the flow units' entrances into the process or system. Arrivals can be planned (e.g., patients arrive at the doctor's office at their preestablished appointment time), or they can be random (e.g., patients arrive at the ER or at a walk-in clinic). When arrivals are planned or known with relative certainty, it is easier for an organization to ensure that the system will be staffed adequately. Unfortunately, there is hardly anything certain in healthcare. Even with an appointment system, patients will arrive early or late, thereby injecting some randomness into the system. In most instances, arrivals are therefore random, that is, they occur at variable times.

The arrival rate is the number of flow unit arrivals per unit of time. It denotes the pace at which the flow units enter and place *demand* on the system. The rate varies. If you observe the customers who enter a fast-food restaurant, you may notice that one person arrives at 9:00 a.m., the next one at 9:03, then three people arrive at 9:10, and so on. Fortunately, the number of arrivals in a given period of time can be described by a probability distribution. Knowledge of the shape and parameters of this distribution reduces the uncertainty surrounding variability in arrivals and provides the basis for making decisions. Often, arrival rates follow a Poisson distribution (Figure 8.3). The variability occurs not only for a given time frame (e.g., peak vs. off-peak times) but also from day to day (e.g., Monday lunch vs. Sunday lunch times). In those cases, different distributions would be appropriate.

Average Arrival Rate, λ

The average number of arrivals per unit of time (minute, hour, day, week, etc.).

The **average arrival rate**, λ, is the average number of arrivals per unit of time (minute, hour, day, week, etc.). Related to the average arrival rate, is the average interarrival time or time between two consecutive arrivals: $1/\lambda$. For example, if λ is five patients per hour, the corresponding interarrival time is $1/5$ hour or 12 minutes. In other words, the average arrival rate and average interarrival time are each other's reciprocals. If arrival rates are Poisson distributed, their corresponding interarrival times will follow the negative exponential distribution (Figure 8.4). Note that the Poisson distribution captures *discrete* random variables that are *counted* (e.g., arrivals). On the other hand, the negative exponential distribution describes *continuous* random variables that are *measured* (e.g., time).

FIGURE 8.3 –
Poisson distribution
for arrival rates.

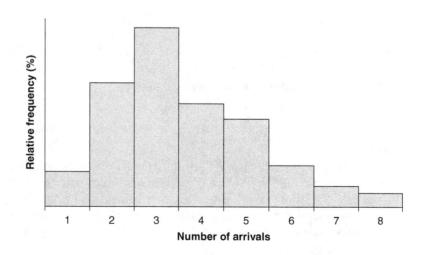

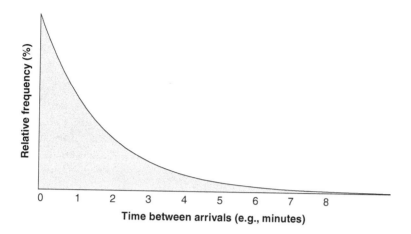

FIGURE 8.4 –
Negative exponential
distribution for
interarrival times.

Service

Flow units are "served" or processed. The rate at which the *capacity* (e.g., nurses, doctors, receptionists, or x-ray machines) can serve them is called the service rate. As you know, sometimes dentists can see four to five patients per hour; at other times, they may see only one or two. The Poisson distribution may also describe service rates, although this occurrence is less common than for arrival rates. The **average service rate**, μ, represents the average number of flow units served or processed per unit of time. Associated with a service rate is a service time or the time it takes to serve or process a flow unit. If service rates are Poisson distributed, service times can be described by the negative exponential distribution (Figure 8.5), and vice versa. If the average service time, $1/\mu$, is 3 minutes, then the corresponding service rate, μ, is 1/3 flow unit per minute or 20 flow units per hour.

**Average Service
Rate, μ**
The average
number of flow units
served or processed
per unit of time.

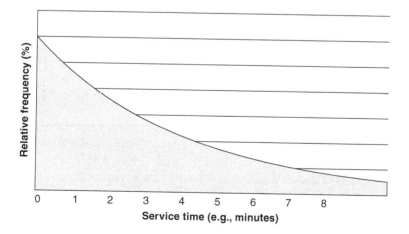

FIGURE 8.5 –
Negative exponential
distribution for
service times.

Queues

Flow units waiting to be processed constitute the queues. These queues can be lines of visitors at Disney World waiting to get on a ride, work-in-process inventory on a factory floor, prescription orders waiting to be filled, patients on a transplant waiting list, and so on. Queues are also referred to as "buffers" (Chapter 7).

Queue Configurations

One queue or multiple queues. If there is only one server, there is usually one queue. However, if there are multiple servers, one type of configuration may feature a line in front of each server (Figure 8.6a), whereas the other will involve a single, serpentine-like queue in which the first flow unit in line will go to the next available server (Figure 8.6b).

FIGURE 8.6 –
(a) Multiple queues, multiple servers;
(b) One queue, multiple servers.

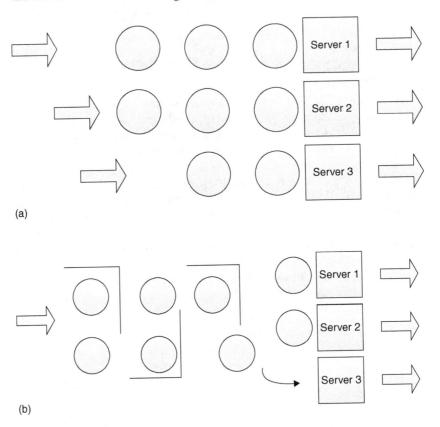

Which one of these two systems would you choose? As you know, the one depicted in Figure 8.6a is often more appealing because you have the opportunity to choose the shortest queue. However, you also know that the server for that line of customers may encounter a problem, slowing down the flow, whereas the flow at another line seems to reach a quick pace, and people who joined that line after you did are served before you! Customers often perceive this system as unfair because it is not first-come, first-served (FCFS) or first-in, first-out (FIFO). On the other hand, the system illustrated in Figure 8.6b ensures that customers are served in the order in which they arrived. Its disadvantage is that it often turns people off when they see a "long" line. The systems studied in this chapter will be FCFS systems.

One stage versus multiple stages. The systems in Figures 8.6a and 8.6b are single-stage systems involving one point of service. They are essentially "mini-processes." However, actual processes include multiple steps or stages, with a variety of queue and server configurations (Figure 8.7). Going through the security checkpoint at an airport, getting a house loan, getting a mammogram, and so on are examples of multistep processes or multistage queuing systems. These systems are more complex to study and require the use of queuing simulation.

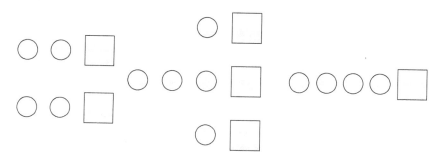

FIGURE 8.7 –
Multistage system.

Queue Discipline

Another factor in the order in which flow units are served is the **queue discipline**, or the order in which flow units are processed. Because of the fairness issue mentioned earlier, FCFS systems are very popular when the flow units are people. However, with parts, materials, and documents, last-in, first-out (LIFO) systems are not uncommon. For example, parts processed at a workstation may be placed on a pallet after completion. When the pallet is moved to the next workstation, the part at the top (last-in) will be processed first (first-out). The same is true with documents. Paper charts may be checked for errors and placed in two piles: those with errors and those without. In each case, the chart at the top (last checked) will be the first one to be either corrected or placed back into its storage location. In some cases, a **priority system** overrides the order in which the flow units arrived. The classic example is the emergency room. If a shooting victim is rushed to the ER, he or she will be treated ahead of anyone with a severe cough, irrespective of the time the person with the cough may have already been waiting.

Queue Discipline
Refers to the order in which flow units are processed.

Priority System
A system that overrides the order of arrivals for processing.

Population of Flow Units

Most systems are assumed to have an *infinite* population of flow units, also known as a **calling population**. "Infinite" is not an absolute term here; it simply indicates that the number of potential arrivals is neither restricted nor influenced significantly by the number of people waiting in line. Potentially, a large number of patients could enter a walk-in clinic offering free dental care, even though they know they will have to wait. Similarly, patients will ask physicians to send their prescription orders to a pharmacy of their choice even if they know that other prescriptions will get filled before theirs. Conversely, some systems will

Calling Population
Refers to the population of flow units.

have *finite* populations with a set number of potential arrivals into the system. For example, a nurse may be responsible for a 10-bed ward. In that case, the maximum number of patients who might be waiting for her to respond to their call at any given time is 10. There could not be an 11th arrival.

KENDALL NOTATION

Channel

A capacity unit such as one server or one team of servers.

The characteristics mentioned in the previous section are the basis for classifying queuing systems. The Kendall notation is a well-established classification scheme. Its most basic form includes three main symbols designating arrivals, service, and channels. **Channels** represent capacity units such as individual servers or teams of servers. The format of the Kendall notation is as follows:

Distribution of arrivals/distribution of service/number of channels.

To designate the probability distributions of arrivals or service, three letters are used: M, G, and D.

M = Poisson distribution for rates or exponential distribution for times

G = General—any—distribution with a known mean and variance

D = Deterministic or constant

Therefore, a queuing model with Poisson-distributed arrival rates, negative exponential service times, and one channel is called an M/M/1 model.

BRADLEY PARK HOSPITAL 8.2

Jennifer sat at the conference table with Francine, Todd, and a staff pharmacist, Frederick, and handed out the influenza vaccine administration report for week 1. "I have here the number of patients who came to our vaccine station, their time of arrival, and the times it took to administer each vaccine. You can see that we have a lot of variability when the patients arrive—both by time of the day and day of the week. What is also troubling is that our capacity to serve the patients is relatively limited. Frederick is working with a staff nurse to give the vaccine, but she can only give an average of one vaccine every 6 minutes."

"Why is it taking so long?" Francine asked.

"Well," Frederick responded, "We check the patients in and pull up their medical records. We then print out a consent form for the patients that they must read and sign. We talk to the patients so that they know what we are doing and why we are doing it, we prepare the syringe, and then the shot is given."

"I see. But when there are more patients coming to get the vaccine, there is a backup. Should we try scheduling the patients so that they do not come all at once?" Francine asked.

"I think a schedule may discourage people from coming to get the vaccine, and we do not want that. Also, it will take a lot more administrative time

and effort to schedule patients for a simple shot. I think our best option is to use queuing theory to help us figure out how best to serve our patients," Jennifer replied.

 What do you think of Jennifer's assumption that a schedule may discourage people from getting vaccinated? Wouldn't a long wait be even worse?

PERFORMANCE MEASURES FOR M/M/1 SYSTEMS

M/M/1 systems rely on the following assumptions:

- One channel (either one server or one team of servers)
- Poisson arrival rate
- Negative exponential service time
- FCFS queue discipline
- Infinite calling population

Moreover, a necessary condition for the system to be viable is that the arrival rate be strictly less than the number of channels, s, multiplied by the service rate (Box 8.2):

$$\lambda < s \times \mu.$$

Since $s = 1$ in an M/M/1 system, the requirement can be simplified to $\lambda < \mu$.

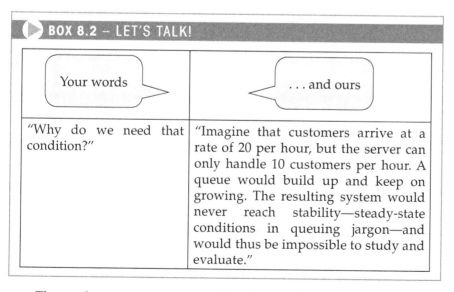

BOX 8.2 – LET'S TALK!

Your words	. . . and ours
"Why do we need that condition?"	"Imagine that customers arrive at a rate of 20 per hour, but the server can only handle 10 customers per hour. A queue would build up and keep on growing. The resulting system would never reach stability—steady-state conditions in queuing jargon—and would thus be impossible to study and evaluate."

The performance measures and their meanings are presented in Table 8.1. Many of these performance measures are useful in the healthcare field (Box 8.3).

TABLE 8.1 – Performance Measures and Formulas for the M/M/1 System

Performance Measure	Formula	Eqn. No.
System utilization • Probability that the system is in use • Percentage of time that the server is busy	$$\rho = \frac{\lambda}{\mu}$$	[8.1]
Probability of no customers in system • Percentage of time that the server is idle	$$P_0 = 1 - \frac{\lambda}{\mu}$$	[8.2]
Average number of customers waiting in line before service • Average number of flow units in the queue • Length of the queue	$$L_q = \frac{\lambda^2}{\mu\,(\mu - \lambda)}$$	[8.3]
Average number of customers in the system • Average number of flow units in the system (those waiting for service and those being served)	$$L = \frac{\lambda}{\mu - \lambda}$$ $$= L_q + \frac{\lambda}{\mu}$$	[8.4]
Average time spent waiting for service Average time spent waiting in the queue	$$W_q = \frac{\lambda}{\mu(\mu - \lambda)}$$	[8.5]
Average time spent in the system Average time spent waiting for service and being served	$$W = \frac{1}{\mu - \lambda}$$ $$= W_q + \frac{1}{\mu}$$	[8.6]
Probability of exactly *n* customers in the system	$$P_n = P_0 \left(\frac{\lambda}{\mu} \right)^n$$	[8.7]
Probability that the number of customers in the system does not exceed a certain number, *k*	$$P_{n \leq k} = 1 - \left(\frac{\lambda}{\mu} \right)^{k+1}$$	[8.8]
Probability that an arriving customer would have to wait for service	$$P_w = \frac{\lambda}{\mu}$$	[8.9]

⊕ BOX 8.3 – DID YOU KNOW?

Queuing Theory Applications in Healthcare

A survey of queuing theory applications in healthcare summarized research in the areas of waiting time and utilization analysis, system design, and appointment systems. Some of the findings are summarized in the following table.

Area	Queuing Concepts	Examples and Solutions
Waiting Time and Utilization Analysis	Reneging (patients forgo care because the wait is too long)	Use of triage
	Priority queue discipline	Assign different categories of patients to different queues with different priorities, which can be preemptive or nonpreemptive.

(continued)

BOX 8.3 – DID YOU KNOW? (*continued*)

Area	Queuing Concepts	Examples and Solutions
	Blocking (when capacity is full, patients are turned away)	Turn away walk-in patients when waiting room is full in outpatient clinics. Hold patients longer than necessary or send them to other facilities if the size of the queue at the downstream care step cannot exceed 0 (e.g., intensive care unit).
System Design	Capacity	Design for a capacity that exceeds demand.
		Redesign process to decrease service times.
		Vary staffing levels according to patient traffic or call-volume intensity.
		Design bed capacity to achieve a turn-away rate no larger than a set percentage (1%–5%). Patients turned away are sent to other facilities.
		Increase the number of beds until the cost of additional beds is equal to the benefits.
		Determine bed capacity based on the holding cost of an empty bed, a penalty when a patient is turned away, and a profit assigned to an occupied bed.
Appointment Systems	Reduction of patient waiting time and physician idle time	Set scheduling intervals equal to average patient processing time; make physician arrive at the same time as the second patient.
	Decrease rescheduling scheduled requests in case of emergency	Include a certain number of empty slots in the schedule to avoid rescheduling.
	Eliminate bottlenecks	Identify points in the system with long waits and find common-sense solutions for each one.

Source: Fomundam and Herrmann (2007).

Let us use the BPH example to determine the performance measures. During the flu season, patients wanting a flu shot arrive at the hospital's vaccine station at a rate of five per hour. Arrivals can be described by a Poisson distribution. Patients are seen by the care provider on an FCFS basis. The time to obtain consent, prepare the supplies, and administer the shot follows a negative exponential distribution with a mean of 6 minutes. Let us evaluate the performance of this system. Assume that the pharmacist wants no more than three patients in the system at least 95% of the time.

Because all performance measures require knowledge of λ and μ, it is always good practice to state them first.

$\lambda = 5$ patients per hour, as mentioned explicitly in the problem.

μ is not given, but the average service time, $1/\mu$, is known to be 6 minutes.

$$\mu = \frac{1}{\dfrac{1}{\mu}} = 1/6 \text{ patient per minute} = 10 \text{ patients per hour}$$

$$\rho = \frac{5}{10} = 0.50$$

$$P_0 = 1 - \frac{5}{10} = 0.50$$

$$L_q = \frac{5^2}{10(10-5)} = 0.50 \text{ patient}$$

$$L = \frac{5}{10-5} = 0.50 + \frac{5}{10} = 1 \text{ patient}$$

> How do we know that the time unit is in hours and not minutes? Because λ and μ in the formula are rates per *hour*.

$$W_q = \frac{5}{10(10-5)} = 0.10 \text{ hour} = 6 \text{ minutes}$$

$$W = \frac{1}{10-5} = 0.1 + \frac{1}{10} = 0.2 \text{ hour} = 12 \text{ minutes}$$

$$P_1 = (0.50)\left(\frac{5}{10}\right)^1 = 0.25$$

$$P_2 = (0.50)\left(\frac{5}{10}\right)^2 = 0.125$$

$$P_3 = (0.50)\left(\frac{5}{10}\right)^3 = 0.0625$$

$$P_{n \leq 3} = P_0 + P_1 + P_2 + P_3 = 1 - \left(\frac{5}{10}\right)^{3+1} = 0.9375$$

$$P_W = \frac{5}{10} = 0.50$$

Overall, this system's performance is acceptable. Some patients may mind waiting for 6 minutes before being served. On average, there is only one patient in the system, but there will be more than three patients 6.25% of the time, thus falling short of the pharmacist's expectations for customer service. Rather than hiring another provider and having a low server utilization, it might be a good idea to reduce the service time by preparing consent forms and/or doing part of the supply preparation ahead of time.

LITTLE'S FLOW EQUATIONS

There are some interesting and useful relationships among some of the performance measures (Little, 1961). To illustrate them, assume that you enter a bank on a Tuesday morning to deposit your paycheck. The arrival rate is 20 customers per hour, and you spend 15 minutes or 0.25 hour waiting in line. When it is your time to be served, how many people are behind you? The answer is five people because in 0.25 hour, you would expect 20 people × 0.25 to arrive and join the line. In other words, $L_q = \lambda \times W_q$. The same rationale applies to L and W. In summary:

$$L = \lambda W \qquad\qquad\qquad [8.10]$$

and therefore, $W = \dfrac{L}{\lambda}$ [8.11]

> These relationships hold true irrespective of the probability distributions of the arrivals and service time.

$$L_q = \lambda W_q \qquad\qquad\qquad [8.12]$$

and therefore, $W_q = \dfrac{L_q}{\lambda}$ [8.13]

Little's flow equations enable you to find W_q if you have already found L_q and vice versa. The same is true for W and L.

PERFORMANCE MEASURES FOR M/M/s SYSTEMS

Let us reformulate the aforementioned M/M/1 example with patients arriving at a rate of 10 per hour, and service time averaging 6 minutes. In this case, $\lambda = 10$ patients per hour and $\mu = 10$ patients per hour. This looks like a perfect match between capacity and demand, right? Wrong! If this system was allowed to run indefinitely, the length of the queue would grow to infinity, as shown in the following.

$L_q = \dfrac{10^2}{10(10-10)} = ???$ Clearly, a division by 0 is impossible, but even if the denominator approached 0, the resulting ratio would be a very large number.

This is a reminder that the condition $\lambda < s\mu$ must be satisfied. Therefore, the minimum number of channels required when $\lambda = 10$ and $\mu = 10$ is 2, making it an M/M/2 system. If the number of channels is more than 1, the formulas presented in Table 8.1 are no longer valid and those in Table 8.2 must be used.

$$\rho = \frac{10}{2 \times 10} = 0.50$$

$$P_0 = \frac{1}{\left(\frac{\left(\frac{10}{10}\right)^0}{0!} \right) + \left(\frac{\left(\frac{10}{10}\right)^1}{1!} \right) + \left(\frac{\left(\frac{10}{10}\right)^2}{2!} \left(\frac{2 \times 10}{2 \times 10 - 10} \right) \right)} = \frac{1}{1+1+1} = 0.333$$

$$L_q = \frac{\left(\frac{10}{10}\right)^2 (10 \times 10)}{(2 \quad 1)!(2 \quad 10 \quad 10)^2}(0.333) = 0.333 \text{ patient}$$

$$L = 0.333 + \frac{10}{10} = 1.333 \text{ patients}$$

$$W_q = \frac{0.333}{10} = 0.0333 \text{ hour} = 2 \text{ minutes}$$

$$W = 0.0333 + \frac{1}{10} = 0.1333 \text{ hour} = 8 \text{ minutes}$$

$$P_1 = (0.333)\frac{\left(\frac{10}{10}\right)^1}{1!} = 0.333$$

$$P_2 = (0.333)\frac{\left(\frac{10}{10}\right)^2}{2!} = 0.167$$

$$P_3 = (0.333)\frac{\left(\frac{10}{10}\right)^3}{2!(2)^{3-2}} = 0.083$$

$$P_{n \leq 3} = 0.333 + 0.333 + 0.167 + 0.083 = 0.916$$

$$P_w = \frac{1}{2!}\left(\frac{10}{10}\right)^2 \left(\frac{2 \times 10}{2 \times 10 - 10} \right)(0.333) = 0.333$$

The aforementioned system performs relatively well with an average wait time of 2 minutes before being served. This is reasonable. However, the pharmacist's goal of having no more than three customers in the system 95% of the time is not met. As recommended for the M/M/1 system, process design changes could be helpful. Using a third provider would lower the utilization to 0.333. Unless the third provider can be assigned other duties, the addition of a channel is not advisable.

TABLE 8.2 – Performance Measures and Formulas for the M/M/s System

Performance Measure	Formula	Eqn. No.
System utilization • Average utilization rate of servers	$\rho = \dfrac{\lambda}{s\mu}$	[8.14]
Probability of no customers in system • Probability that the system is empty • Percentage of time that all servers are idle	$P_0 = \dfrac{1}{\sum_{n=0}^{s-1}\left[\dfrac{\left(\frac{\lambda}{\mu}\right)^n}{n!}\right] + \left[\dfrac{\left(\frac{\lambda}{\mu}\right)^s}{s!}\left(\dfrac{s\mu}{s\mu-\lambda}\right)\right]}$	[8.15]
Average number of customers waiting in line before service • Average number of flow units in the queue • Length of the queue	$L_q = \dfrac{\left(\frac{\lambda}{\mu}\right)^s \lambda\mu}{(s-1)!(s\mu-\lambda)^2} P_0$	[8.16]
Average number of customers in the system • Average number of flow units in the system (those waiting for service and those being served)	$L = L_q + \dfrac{\lambda}{\mu}$	[8.17]
Average time spent waiting for service • Average time spent waiting in the queue	$W_q = \dfrac{L_q}{\lambda}$	[8.18]
Average time spent in the system • Average time spent waiting for service and being served	$W = W_q + \dfrac{1}{\mu}$	[8.19]
Probability of exactly *n* customers in the system	$P_n = P_0 \dfrac{\left(\frac{\lambda}{\mu}\right)^n}{n!}$ for $n \le s$ $P_n = P_0 \dfrac{\left(\frac{\lambda}{\mu}\right)^n}{s!s^{n-s}}$ for $n > s$	[8.20]
Probability that the number of customers in the system does not exceed *k*	$P_{n\le k} = \sum_{n=0}^{k} P_n$	[8.21]
Probability that an arriving customer would have to wait for service (all servers are busy)	$P_w = \dfrac{1}{s!}\left(\dfrac{\lambda}{\mu}\right)^s\left(\dfrac{s\mu}{s\mu-\lambda}\right)P_0$	[8.22]

You can see how a little change in our system—the addition of a channel—created a dramatic increase in the complexity of our formulas. Fortunately, Excel-based queuing macros (e.g., QueueMacros.xls from California State University, Northridge) are freely available on the Internet to help you obtain these performance measures with a few mouse clicks.

ECONOMIC ANALYSIS

The **goal of queuing analysis** is to find the optimal amount of capacity to provide an adequate service level. Often, the decision will be based on an evaluation of the performance measures of the queuing system.

Goal of Queuing Analysis
Find the optimal amount of capacity to provide an adequate service level.

For the flu shot example, the pharmacist wanted the probability of having no more than three patients in the system to be at least 95%. Other managers may want W_q not to exceed a prespecified amount of time.

Sometimes, the cost of a queuing system will influence system design. This is a balancing act because two competing forces influence that goal. As a manager, you want to provide adequate capacity to prevent unacceptable wait times while simultaneously ensuring that you do not waste monetary resources on idle capacity. Each unit of capacity (employee, machine, or bed) acting as a server costs money. The total amount disbursed for the servers is referred to as capacity or service costs. The higher the number of servers, the higher the cost of providing the service, as shown in Figure 8.8.

You must have noticed that when checkout lines are getting long at the supermarket, they open new ones, thereby increasing the number of servers to decrease the length of the lines. Why? Because customers' wait times also cost money and need to be controlled. Although they can rarely be obtained directly from accounting records, waiting costs are essentially penalties incurred for letting flow units congest the system. Examples include work-in-process inventory costs, lost business resulting from customers leaving the waiting line and going to a competitor, fuel costs for airplanes circling the airport landing because no runway is available for landing, space to accommodate waiting patients, lost reimbursements for late claims, and so on. The more the number of servers, the lower the waiting costs (Figure 8.8).

$$\text{Total costs} = \text{waiting costs} + \text{service costs} \qquad [8.23]$$

$$(C_w \times L) + (C_s \times \text{number of servers}),$$

where:
C_w = estimated waiting cost per flow unit per unit of time
L = number of flow units in the system
C_s = cost of service per server per unit of time

Two elements of this formula may seem counterintuitive:

1. C_w is essentially a penalty for waiting, yet it is multiplied by L, the number of flow units in the system. If C_w was multiplied by W, it would be the penalty for only one flow unit waiting. However, during let us say an hour, multiple flow units (λ) will enter the system and will have to spend time (W) in it. From Little's flow equations, we know that $L = \lambda W$.

2. C_s is multiplied by the number of servers rather than the number of channels. In many cases, the number of channels is equal to the number of servers. However, if one channel comprises a team of multiple servers, all of them will need to be paid.

Going back to our BPH example, let us assume that the arrival rate is Poisson distributed and averages five patients per hour, and that service time follows a negative exponential distribution with a mean

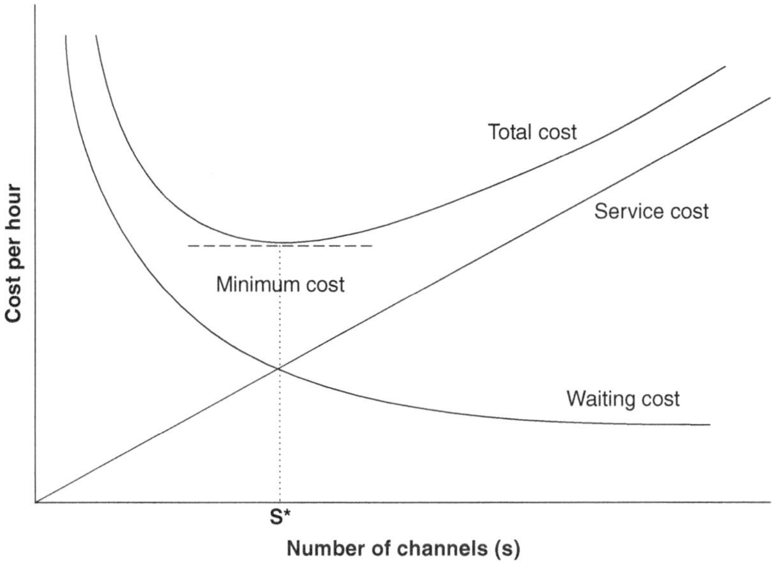

FIGURE 8.8 – Costs in queuing models.

of 8 minutes. C_w is \$30 per hour, whereas C_s is \$20 per hour. What is the optimal number of servers for this system?

The procedure to find the optimal number of servers based on cost involves three steps:

STEP 1: Determine the minimum number of servers needed, given λ and μ for that system. Compute the total cost.

STEP 2: Increase the number of servers by 1. Compute the total cost.

STEP 3: If the total cost obtained in Step 2 is higher than the cost computed previously, stop. It means that your total cost is now past the minimum point on the total cost curve (Figure 8.8). If the total cost is lower than the cost computed previously, repeat step 2 until the total cost starts increasing. The number of servers for which the total cost is lowest is optimal.

In the BPH example, let us assume that λ = 5 patients per hour and μ = 7.5 patients per hour. Because $\lambda < 1\mu$, the minimum number of servers is 1. The L value for this M/M/1 system is two patients. Let us follow the aforementioned three steps to find the optimal number of servers (TC denotes the total cost).

1. $TC_1 = (\$30 \times 2) + (\$20 \times 1)$

    $= \$60 + \$20 = \$80.$

2. Is it the lowest cost? To find out, we need to increment the number of servers by 1 and determine the new total costs. The L value for this M/M/2 system is 0.75 patients.

    $$TC_2 = (\$30 \times 0.75) + (\$20 \times 2)$$

    $$= \$22.50 + \$40 = \$62.50.$$

3. The expected decrease in waiting cost exceeded the increase in service cost, resulting in a lower overall cost. We increase the number of servers to three, and the L value for the M/M/3 system is 0.676 patients.

$$TC_3 = (\$30 \times 0.676) + (\$20 \times 3)$$

$$= \$20.28 + \$60 = \$80.28.$$

The total cost for three servers exceeds that for two servers, thereby indicating that after reaching the minimum on the curve, the total cost has started rising. The optimal number of servers for this system is therefore two.

PERFORMANCE MEASURES FOR M/G/1 AND M/D/1 SYSTEMS

So far we have examined queuing systems with Poisson-distributed arrivals and negative exponential service times. When the probability distribution of the service times is general with a mean and standard deviation, and when the number of channels is one, the model is designated as an M/G/1 model. The formulas for this system are presented in Table 8.3.

TABLE 8.3 – Performance Measures and Formulas for the M/G/1 System

Performance Measure	Formula	Eqn. No.
System utilization • Probability that the system is in use • Percentage of time that the server is busy	$\rho = \dfrac{\lambda}{\mu}$	[8.24]
Probability of no customers in system • Probability that the system is empty • Percentage of time that the server is idle	$P_0 = 1 - \dfrac{\lambda}{\mu}$	[8.25]
Average number of customers waiting in line before service • Average number of flow units in the queue • Length of the queue	$L_q = \dfrac{\lambda^2 \sigma^2 + \left(\dfrac{\lambda}{\mu}\right)^2}{2\left(1 - \dfrac{\lambda}{\mu}\right)}$	[8.26]
Average number of customers in the system • Average number of flow units in the system (those waiting for service and those being served)	$L = L_q + \dfrac{\lambda}{\mu}$	[8.27]
Average time spent waiting for service • Average time spent waiting in the queue	$W_q = \dfrac{L_q}{\lambda}$	[8.28]
Average time spent in the system • Average time spent waiting for service and being served	$W = W_q + \dfrac{1}{\mu}$	[8.29]
Probability that an arriving customer would have to wait for service	$P_w = \dfrac{\lambda}{\mu}$	[8.30]

Let us modify the initial example so that arrivals are Poisson distributed with an average rate of five patients per hour, and service time follows a general distribution with a mean of 10 minutes and a standard deviation of 1.2 minutes.

$$\lambda = 5 \text{ patients/hour}$$

$$\mu = 10 \text{ patients/hour}$$

$$\sigma = 0.02 \text{ hour}$$

> Notice that the unit of the standard deviation has been converted so that it is consistent with the time unit of the arrival and service rates.

$$\rho = \frac{5}{10} = 0.50$$

$$P_0 = 1 - \frac{5}{10} = 0.50$$

$$L_q = \frac{(5)^2 (0.02)^2 + \left(\frac{5}{10}\right)^2}{2\left(1 - \frac{5}{10}\right)} = 0.26 \text{ patient}$$

$$L = 0.26 + \frac{5}{10} = 0.76 \text{ patient}$$

$$W_q = \frac{0.26}{5} = 0.052 \text{ hour} = 3.12 \text{ minutes}$$

$$W = 0.052 + \frac{1}{10} = 0.152 \text{ hour} = 9.12 \text{ minutes}$$

$$P_W = \frac{5}{10} = 0.50$$

The M/D/1 model is applicable to situations in which service times are constant. This situation is relevant only in environments using automated equipment. The M/D/1 is a special case of the M/G/1 model because of the absence of variation in service time, $\sigma = 0$. All formulas shown in Table 8.3 can be used for the M/D/1 model, with the exception of L_q, whose computation no longer requires σ and simplifies to

$$L_q = \frac{\lambda^2}{2\mu(\mu - \lambda)} \qquad [8.31]$$

If arrivals are Poisson distributed with $\lambda = 5$ flow units/hour, and service times—and therefore rates—are constant with $\mu = 10$ flow units/hour, then

$$L_q = \frac{5^2}{(2)(10)(10 - 5)} = 0.25 \text{ flow unit.}$$

By extension,

$$L = 0.25 + 0.5 = 0.75 \text{ flow unit,}$$

$$W_q = 0.05 \text{ hour} = 3 \text{ minutes.}$$

Let us compare the M/M/1 and M/D/1 models. Even though both have identical arrival and service rates, the time and length of the queue in the M/D/1 model are exactly half of those computed for the M/M/1 model. As we mentioned before, it is the variation in arrival and/or service that creates uncertainty and therefore queues. With the removal of uncertainty associated with the service times in the M/D/1 model, the queues and waits are slashed by half.

So far in this book, we have used mathematical formulas to solve problems. With complex or very large real-world problems, these techniques often prove impractical. Finding an optimal solution is therefore not an option, but a very close approximation can be obtained with a good simulation.

QUEUING SIMULATION

As seen in Chapter 7, simulation involves developing a simplified representation of reality and experimenting with it to make better decisions. Simulation is appropriate in business situations that involve risk. **Risk** is uncertainty reduced through knowledge of probability distributions (Box 8.4). This knowledge enables the decision maker to formulate competing designs of a model or process and select the best performer.

Risk
The uncertainty reduced through knowledge of probability distributions.

▶ BOX 8.4 – LET'S TALK!

Your words	. . . and ours
"Is risk the same as uncertainty?"	"No, it is not. In a situation of uncertainty, you would have no idea how many customers would arrive at a facility within a given time frame. However, if you observed customer arrivals over several days during that same time frame, the data you collected would most likely follow a probability distribution with certain parameters (e.g., mean, standard deviation). You still would not know for sure how many customers would arrive, but you would not be completely in the dark either. Uncertainty would have been reduced to risk."

Simulation requires the completion of five steps (Stevenson & Ozgur, 2007):

1. **Define the problem and objectives**. For example, the problem might be congestion in a clinic's waiting room. The objective would be to decrease wait times to no more than 10 minutes so that patients move through the system faster.

2. **Collect data**. Simulation modeling is data intensive. It requires the collection of historical data on multiple variables, including the arrival of flow units into the process and the service/processing time for each activity. Representative samples of times between arrivals as well as service times for each activity in the process are vital to the accuracy of the simulation model (see concepts of random sampling in Chapter 5). These samples will yield probability distributions close to those of the real process, and their parameter values will be entered into the simulation model.

3. **Validate the model**. This phase involves running the simulation to see whether the performance of the simulated process reflects that of the actual one. If discrepancies between performance results are noted, the simulation model needs to be revised. In the case of a new process, there will not be a basis for comparison. In that case, subjective assessments of the adequacy of the results must be made.

4. **Generate different model/process configurations**. These experimental models are possible solutions to the problem(s) posed in step 1. Examples include deleting activities that may not be necessary, combining activities with people working in teams, adding capacity, changing the layout, and so on.

5. **Run the simulations and interpret the performance results**. Based on the simulation results, decide which potential configuration generates the lowest wait times, the lowest cost, the best labor utilization, and/or the least amount of rework. The best overall model provides the template for process redesign. Of course, the usefulness of the simulation results depends on the extent to which the model mimics the actual system. If the representation is a loose approximation of reality, the results will need to be interpreted with extreme caution. As with any system, if you put garbage in, you get garbage out.

The Monte Carlo Method

Probability distributions reflect the behavior of random variables. Randomness is most evident in the games of chance such as roulette. The roulette wheel has 36 numbers plus the number 0. Players place their bets on individual numbers and/or groups of numbers. The dealer spins the wheel, and a small, hard ball bounces around and eventually falls into one number slot. This game is especially popular at the famous casino in Monte Carlo. More important to us, it bears resemblance to many of the random events decision makers face: customer arrivals, service times, consumer demand, costs of supplies, delivery times, and so on. Monte Carlo simulation is similar to the game of roulette in that it involves drawing a number at random and recording it. Repeating this process over and over again should yield outcomes with the same probability of occurrence as those witnessed in the real-world system. Let us illustrate this concept with an example.

Collecting Data and Identifying Probability Distributions

Theoretical Probability Distribution

A probability distribution whose shape follows a well-established pattern (normal, Poisson, uniform, exponential, etc.).

At the BPH pharmacy, prescription orders are received at random times. Todd Beringer, the pharmacist, collected data on 200 orders and determined that interarrival times could be described by the *empirical* probability distribution shown in Table 8.4. Probability distributions can be **theoretical** or **empirical**. Both types are based on data collection, but the former implies that the shape of the distribution follows a well-established pattern (normal, Poisson, uniform, exponential, etc.), whereas the latter is unique to the problem data. We assume here that the interarrival times are discrete, which means that only the specific values shown in Table 8.4 are possible.

Empirical Probability Distribution

A probability distribution that is unique to the problem data.

TABLE 8.4 – Absolute Frequencies and Probability Distribution of Interarrival Times

Interarrival Time (min)	Frequency	Probability
3	10	0.05
4	20	0.10
5	60	0.30
6	50	0.25
7	30	0.15
8	20	0.10
9	10	0.05
Total	200	1.00

The expected value (denoted by EV) for the interarrival times is the sum of the products of the individual interarrival times and their respective probabilities:

$$\text{EV} = \sum_{i=1}^{\infty} x_i p_i \qquad [8.32]$$

EV = $(3 \times 0.05) + (4 \times 0.10) + (5 \times 0.30) + (6 \times 0.25) + \ldots + (9 \times 0.05)$

= 5.85 minutes.

Let us try to duplicate this expected value with simulation. Essentially, we have a "roulette wheel" with the interarrival times 3, 4, 5, 6, 7, 8, and 9 (Figure 8.9).

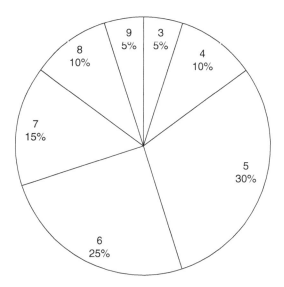

To simulate the randomness of the wheel, we need to draw random numbers and match them to a particular interarrival time. The random numbers can be drawn from Table 8.5, which displays 500 random numbers generated with Excel. These numbers will fall into one of the intervals shown in Table 8.6. To obtain the intervals, you must follow two steps:

STEP 1: Compute the cumulative probabilities for each interarrival time. (Note: Computing the cumulative probabilities is not critical to develop the intervals, but they provide a convenient reference to the upper boundary of the interval with which they are associated.)

STEP 2: Establish intervals so that the probability of a random number falling in that interval is equal to the probability of occurrence of the corresponding interarrival time. Make sure that the intervals are mutually exclusive so that no random number could fall into more than one interval.

TABLE 8.5 – Five Hundred Random Numbers Generated With Microsoft Excel

0.1059	0.9846	0.8058	0.5363	0.9005	0.4144	0.0679	0.9689	0.4556	0.5472
0.8505	0.6814	0.1945	0.2810	0.7061	0.5695	0.5121	0.2989	0.9714	0.7486
0.2194	0.1242	0.7061	0.3936	0.6767	0.7953	0.7361	0.8544	0.0552	0.7960
0.7146	0.5581	0.6310	0.8675	0.5828	0.6181	0.6080	0.0789	0.1100	0.5820
0.0816	0.5959	0.5732	0.7027	0.2743	0.4028	0.3224	0.2053	0.0421	0.9880
0.7191	0.7768	0.3435	0.4179	0.6536	0.5169	0.2530	0.8720	0.8069	0.6332
0.1164	0.6770	0.3321	0.8678	0.6513	0.6331	0.9076	0.0622	0.5565	0.5516
0.4068	0.8573	0.5394	0.3369	0.2180	0.8272	0.0723	0.3412	0.4337	0.0237
0.4473	0.0769	0.4627	0.0561	0.9625	0.4688	0.3730	0.6737	0.5206	0.9070

(continued)

TABLE 8.5 – Five Hundred Random Numbers Generated With Microsoft Excel (*continued*)

0.6453	0.8884	0.3438	0.8025	0.8043	0.8750	0.8114	0.2136	0.2966	0.2322
0.4359	0.1493	0.8015	0.4521	0.5130	0.6099	0.5214	0.6834	0.2874	0.9773
0.5279	0.0171	0.0916	0.1807	0.3703	0.5460	0.0234	0.4485	0.7832	0.6494
0.2751	0.4326	0.1995	0.3570	0.3860	0.8774	0.6317	0.8590	0.8269	0.7731
0.7914	0.7596	0.4441	0.6111	0.7357	0.8456	0.2007	0.3202	0.0776	0.3621
0.4467	0.4478	0.1254	0.6528	0.2794	0.0621	0.5859	0.4661	0.0656	0.8118
0.7778	0.9797	0.6456	0.2769	0.0137	0.5144	0.2127	0.0571	0.5982	0.0634
0.9732	0.2699	0.9511	0.2681	0.8399	0.7511	0.0796	0.9047	0.5520	0.9604
0.2330	0.6747	0.2237	0.0543	0.1924	0.5421	0.2164	0.5397	0.3914	0.4201
0.9187	0.3051	0.5054	0.0466	0.1317	0.9798	0.5254	0.9840	0.5495	0.2961
0.2938	0.1310	0.9733	0.3002	0.9325	0.3337	0.2945	0.5549	0.6271	0.3741
0.5434	0.4031	0.7382	0.2694	0.5920	0.7490	0.4843	0.8756	0.0168	0.7577
0.0924	0.6633	0.6156	0.4451	0.4818	0.3887	0.9206	0.6725	0.3470	0.0552
0.8981	0.5237	0.4123	0.5179	0.6049	0.0973	0.1510	0.3070	0.8806	0.4254
0.8449	0.2475	0.6585	0.5204	0.8422	0.4208	0.7036	0.9932	0.6154	0.4627
0.5190	0.7754	0.5915	0.2204	0.9320	0.0178	0.0000	0.4953	0.8288	0.7460
0.3256	0.7428	0.1478	0.0758	0.2370	0.0156	0.7457	0.7928	0.9764	0.4159
0.4444	0.3949	0.2742	0.4392	0.1505	0.3847	0.0411	0.6679	0.1880	0.4817
0.7828	0.5649	0.1860	0.6415	0.8317	0.3003	0.2968	0.0020	0.0869	0.8438
0.7405	0.5917	0.6800	0.0573	0.0740	0.8102	0.7460	0.0986	0.7190	0.7670
0.1310	0.0922	0.1334	0.2828	0.5391	0.5606	0.6935	0.4167	0.0479	0.0420
0.3117	0.8959	0.5731	0.5289	0.8546	0.5661	0.0981	0.7039	0.4355	0.3643
0.5191	0.4864	0.3348	0.9815	0.1958	0.3662	0.0541	0.3785	0.8295	0.6160
0.1003	0.5588	0.2008	0.2106	0.9159	0.5777	0.7509	0.6164	0.9570	0.4242
0.2231	0.2808	0.5627	0.4540	0.3874	0.1392	0.9903	0.2855	0.7189	0.8226
0.1649	0.7540	0.7977	0.7517	0.1018	0.2375	0.5264	0.5206	0.4264	0.0414
0.8154	0.9094	0.3489	0.2591	0.9850	0.4669	0.3494	0.9045	0.0124	0.8242
0.0530	0.1436	0.3741	0.5172	0.9621	0.6220	0.3920	0.5449	0.7057	0.3720
0.9725	0.9886	0.7309	0.1498	0.5059	0.6036	0.4523	0.8641	0.0928	0.3444
0.3830	0.4306	0.8873	0.9510	0.6260	0.4960	0.6027	0.6035	0.2115	0.8398
0.4160	0.0222	0.8978	0.7536	0.4737	0.0924	0.6244	0.3383	0.2676	0.1880
0.0520	0.2002	0.0005	0.1785	0.7976	0.9749	0.1436	0.8451	0.2214	0.0331
0.2129	0.1816	0.5229	0.7239	0.6780	0.8850	0.2195	0.1487	0.0844	0.0755
0.5884	0.4377	0.8697	0.8900	0.7393	0.4812	0.8810	0.6240	0.5423	0.3050
0.8698	0.8301	0.6769	0.6389	0.8423	0.7448	0.6341	0.8531	0.7960	0.1410
0.2536	0.7048	0.0712	0.7694	0.0238	0.0231	0.2177	0.1660	0.4283	0.0989
0.1655	0.8228	0.5138	0.5835	0.6703	0.7510	0.4473	0.6777	0.1489	0.7359
0.4406	0.6452	0.6153	0.0387	0.6413	0.3574	0.5523	0.5112	0.5398	0.4757
0.0105	0.4966	0.6256	0.3021	0.6574	0.2586	0.7775	0.9607	0.3014	0.7988
0.7043	0.9721	0.4876	0.9725	0.2186	0.2388	0.8280	0.1597	0.7437	0.0607
0.9333	0.9696	0.4357	0.9497	0.5692	0.3445	0.0745	0.0295	0.0684	0.6143

TABLE 8.6 – Cumulative Probability Distributions and Random Number Intervals

Interarrival Time (min)	Probability	Cumulative Probability	Random Number Interval
3	0.05	0.05	0.00–< 0.05
4	0.10	0.15	0.05–< 0.15
5	0.30	0.45	0.15–< 0.45
6	0.25	0.70	0.45–< 0.70
7	0.15	0.85	0.70–< 0.85
8	0.10	0.95	0.85–< 0.95
9	0.05	1.00	0.95–< 1.00

As shown in Table 8.6, if we select a random number that is less than 0.05, we will match it to the corresponding interarrival time of 3 minutes; a random number between 0.05 and a value less than 0.15 would be matched to an interarrival time of 4 minutes, and so on. We will repeat this process numerous times so that the simulated interarrival times occur with the same frequency as those obtained from historical records. These repetitions are called **trials**.

Trial
The repetition of an occurrence in simulation.

For our first trial, let us assume that we draw random number 0.3256. From Table 8.6, we see that it falls between 0.15 and less than 0.45, which is associated with an interarrival time of 5 minutes. Table 8.7 displays the interarrival times for 10 trials.

TABLE 8.7 Random Generation of 10 Interarrival Times

Trial	Random Number	Interarrival Time (min)
1	0.3256	5
2	0.2106	5
3	0.5214	6
4	0.7731	7
5	0.8102	7
6	0.2794	5
7	0.5179	6
8	0.0740	4
9	0.3920	5
10	0.0479	3
	Average	5.3

The average interarrival time for the 10 trials is 5.3 minutes, which is lower than the previously determined expected value of 5.85 minutes. Why? If you observe the interarrival times in Table 8.7, you will see that "3" was selected 10% of the time; "4," 10% of the time; "5," 40% of the time; "6," 20% of the time; and "7," 20% of the time. These percentages do not mirror the probabilities (see Table 8.4) used in computing the expected value of the interarrival times. The discrepancy is the result of the insufficient number of trials conducted in Table 8.7. The analogy with the game of chance sheds further light on this phenomenon. At a casino, the odds favor the house. However, you could play only once, win, take your gains and leave, and therefore defy the odds. If you continue playing, you know that you will eventually lose it all. The same concept is at play here. You continue drawing random numbers in order to meet the odds (Box 8.5). Due to space constraints, we will continue with 10 simulation trials for the remainder of the prescription order example.

⊕ BOX 8.5 – DID YOU KNOW?

How Many Simulation Trials Are Needed?

Practically speaking, the answer is "A LOT." The default in several simulation software packages is 1,000 trials, and it is not uncommon to see published simulation results based on 10,000 to 25,000 trials (Mooney, 1997).

Now, let us turn to the service times. Service times are commonly described by the exponential distribution, the normal distribution, or the uniform distribution. According to the data collected by the BPH pharmacist, the times required to fill prescription orders follow a normal distribution with a mean of 7 minutes and a standard deviation of 1 minute (Figure 8.10). The mathematical complexity of generating normal values would require an extensive explanation, which is beyond the scope of this book. Rather, we will use the following Excel function to generate the normally distributed service times:

$$=\text{NORM.INV}(\text{RAND}(), \text{Mean, Standard Deviation}). \qquad [8.33]$$

As the mean is 7 minutes and the standard deviation is 1 minute, the Excel formula will be

$$=\text{NORM.INV}(\text{RAND}(),7,1).$$

There are two options to select the random number. The first one is simply to enter RAND() in the formula and let Excel draw a random

FIGURE 8.10 – Normal probability distribution of service times.

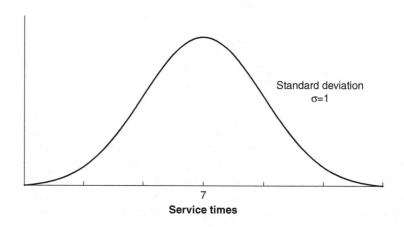

Standard deviation
σ=1

7

Service times

number automatically. The second one is to provide a list of random numbers from Table 8.5 and enter the corresponding Excel worksheet cells in the formula. Table 8.8 displays the first 10 random numbers of Table 8.5, Column 2, and their corresponding normally distributed service times.

TABLE 8.8 Random Generation of 10 Service Times

Trial	Random Number	Service Time (min)
1	0.9846	9.2
2	0.6814	7.5
3	0.1242	5.8
4	0.5581	7.1
5	0.5959	7.2
6	0.7768	7.8
7	0.6770	7.5
8	0.8573	8.1
9	0.0769	5.6
10	0.8884	8.2

Running the Simulation With One Pharmacist

We are first going to run the simulation for 10 prescription orders with one pharmacist/server filling the prescriptions (Table 8.9). A queuing simulation is dynamic because each trial affects the next one. For example, the server will not start work on the fifth order until the fourth is completed. We can use a timer or a clock to keep track of times. With a timer, we often initialize the simulation at time "0"; with a clock, we set a specific time such as 8:00 a.m. for the same purpose. To explain the logic of the simulation conducted in Table 8.9, we will discuss the simulation of the first three arrivals.

Order 1. The first interarrival time is 5 minutes, which means that the first order is received (arrival time) at $0 + 5 = 5$ minutes. Because this is the first order, the pharmacist is idle, and service can begin right away, at 5 minutes. Because the service time is 9.2 minutes, service ends at $5 + 9.2 = 14.2$ minutes. There is no difference between arrival time and time when service begins, indicating that the waiting time is 0. The order entered the system at 5 minutes and exited it at 14.2 minutes, making the time in the system $14.2 - 5 = 9.2$ minutes. As for the pharmacist, he or she was idle between the time of initialization, 0, and the time when the order was received, 5.

Order 2. The second interarrival time is 5 minutes, making the time of arrival 5 minutes later than the previous arrival: $5 + 5 = 10$ minutes. Service cannot start until the pharmacist has finished filling the first prescription order. Assuming that the time to switch from one order to the other is negligible, service will start at 14.2 minutes. As the service time is 7.5 minutes, service will end at 21.7 minutes. The order entered the system at 10 minutes and was not processed until 14.2 minutes, making the wait equal to 4.2 minutes. The time in the system is the time elapsed between the order's arrival in the system and its exit from the system, that is, 21.7 – 10 = 11.7 minutes. The pharmacist finished filling the first prescription order at 14.2 minutes and started working on the second one immediately, resulting in 0 idle time.

TABLE 8.9 Simulation of 10 and 1,000 Prescription Orders With One Server (See Excel Worksheet in Appendix 8.1)

	Cumulative IATs	Max(SE$_{i-1}$, AT$_i$)		SB + ST	SB – AT	SE – AT	SB$_i$ – SE$_{i-1}$
Order (*i*)	Interarrival Time (IAT)	Arrival Time (AT)	Service Begins (SB)	Service Time (ST)	Service Ends (SE)	Time in Queue (TQ)	Time in System (TS)	Server's Idle Time (I)
1	5	5	5	9.2	14.2	0	9.2	5
2	5	10	14.2	7.5	21.7	4.2	11.7	0
3	6	16	21.7	5.8	27.5	5.7	11.5	0
4	7	23	27.5	7.1	34.6	4.5	11.6	0
5	7	30	34.6	7.2	41.8	4.6	11.8	0
6	5	35	41.8	7.8	49.6	6.8	14.6	0
7	6	41	49.6	7.5	57.1	8.6	16.1	0
8	4	45	57.1	8.1	65.2	12.1	20.2	0
9	5	50	65.2	5.6	70.8	15.2	20.8	0
10	3	53	70.8	8.2	79	17.8	26	0
Average	**5.3**			**7.4**		**8.0**	**15.4**	**0.5**
⋮	⋮	⋮	⋮	⋮	⋮	⋮	⋮	⋮
⋮	⋮	⋮	⋮	⋮	⋮	⋮	⋮	⋮
991	6	5795	6890.2	6.2	6896.4	1095.2	1101.4	0
992	7	5802	6896.4	7.7	6904.1	1094.4	1102.1	0
993	7	5809	6904.1	7.1	6911.2	1095.1	1102.2	0
994	7	5816	6911.2	5.5	6916.7	1095.2	1100.7	0
995	8	5824	6916.7	8.2	6924.9	1092.7	1100.9	0
996	6	5830	6924.9	6.5	6931.4	1094.9	1101.4	0
997	5	5835	6931.4	6.3	6937.7	1096.4	1102.7	0
998	6	5841	6937.7	7.3	6945	1096.7	1104	0
999	6	5847	6945	7.3	6952.3	1098	1105.3	0
1000	4	5851	6952.3	7.7	6960	1101.3	1109	0
Average	**5.85**			**6.97**		**635.55**	**642.51**	**0.00**

First 10 Orders

Last 10 Orders

End of simulation

Order 3. The third interarrival time is 6 minutes, making the time of arrival 10 + 6 = 16 minutes. Service cannot begin until the pharmacist has completed the work on the second order, that is, 21.7 minutes. Service time is 5.8 minutes. Service ends at 21.7 + 5.8 = 27.5 minutes. The order enters the system at 16 minutes but is not processed until 21.7 minutes, making the wait equal to 21.7 − 16 = 5.7 minutes. The time elapsed between the order's arrival in the system and its exit from the system is 27.5 − 16 = 11.5 minutes. Upon completion of the second order, the pharmacist begins working on the third order immediately, making the idle time equal to 0.

After 10 simulation trials, the average interarrival time is 5.3 minutes (EV = 5.85 minutes), the average service time is 7.4 minutes (actual mean = 7 minutes), the average wait time before service is 8.0 minutes, the average time in the system is 15.4 minutes, and the average idle time for the server is 0.5 minutes.

When using Excel to run the simulation over 1,000 trials, the average interarrival and service times are equal to their expected averages. To compute the average values of the performance measures (Time in Queue, Time in System, and Idle Time for Server), we disregarded the first 100 trials in our computations. The first arrivals coincide with the start-up of the system, and therefore should be omitted (Box 8.6). The average time in queue is 635.55 minutes; the average time in the system is 642.51 minutes; and the pharmacist is never idle! The performance measures signal a dysfunctional system with poor customer service and an overloaded pharmacist. If the pharmacist is paid $60 per hour, and the cost of a prescription in the system is $100 per hour, the total hourly cost for this system is:

$$TC = \left(\$100 \times 1000 \text{ orders} \times \frac{642.51 \text{ min}}{60} \right) + \left(\$60 \times \frac{6960 \text{ min}}{60} \times 1 \text{ pharmacist} \right)$$

$$= \$1,070,850 + \$6,960$$

$$= \$1,077,810.$$

Notice the extremely high waiting costs. They are consistent with the ever increasing time in the queue and time in the system. The system is unstable, as could be expected because the demand placed on the system exceeds its capacity. We will therefore rerun this simulation with two rather than one server.

Running the Simulation With Two Pharmacists

For the sake of simplicity, let us assume that the second pharmacist has the same level of experience as the first one, and therefore the service times for both pharmacists follow the same normal distribution with a mean of 7 minutes and a standard deviation of 1 minute (Table 8.10). The arrivals are independent of service and are therefore not affected. For this simulation, we add two columns: time when pharmacist 1 is available and time when pharmacist 2 is available (Anderson, Sweeney, Williams, Camm, & Martin, 2012). For example, assuming

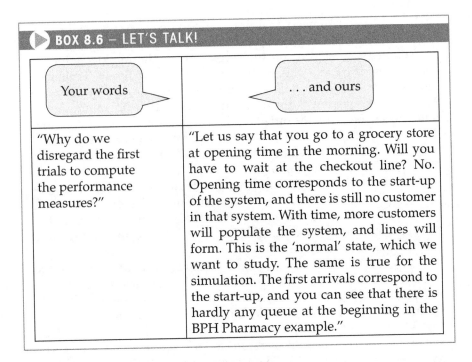

Your words	...and ours
"Why do we disregard the first trials to compute the performance measures?"	"Let us say that you go to a grocery store at opening time in the morning. Will you have to wait at the checkout line? No. Opening time corresponds to the start-up of the system, and there is still no customer in that system. With time, more customers will populate the system, and lines will form. This is the 'normal' state, which we want to study. The same is true for the simulation. The first arrivals correspond to the start-up, and you can see that there is hardly any queue at the beginning in the BPH Pharmacy example."

that pharmacist 1 was assigned to the first order, he or she would be available only after filling that prescription, that is, at 14.2 minutes, whereas pharmacist 2 would still be available. For the second order, we assign pharmacist 2, who was available at time 0.0, but will not be available again until the second order is completed, that is, at 17.5 minutes. We will assume that the pharmacist who has been idle longer will be assigned to the next order.

Only the 10th order experiences some delay in processing. We will therefore review orders 8, 9, and 10.

Order 8. The eighth order arrives 4 minutes after the seventh order. Its time of arrival is therefore 41 + 4 = 45 minutes. It was assigned to pharmacist 2, who was available at 42.8 minutes into the simulation. Service started at 45 minutes, processing lasted 8.1 minutes, and the prescription was ready at 45 + 8.1 = 53.1 minutes. Because service started right after the order was received, there was no wait. The time elapsed between the entry of the order in the system and its exit was 53.1 − 45 = 8.1 minutes.

Order 9. The ninth order was received 5 minutes later, at 45 + 5 = 50 minutes. Pharmacist 1 had been available since 48.5 minutes and was therefore free to process the order, which took 5.6 minutes. The prescription was ready at 50 + 5.6 = 55.6 minutes. Because the order had been processed right after its receipt, there was no wait. The time in the system is thus equal to the service time, which is 5.6 minutes.

Order 10. The 10th order is received at 50 + 3 = 53 minutes. Pharmacist 2 is available at 53.1 minutes, whereas pharmacist 1 is busy until 55.6 minutes. Pharmacist 2 is therefore assigned to the job, starts at

53.1 minutes, resulting in a 0.1 minute delay or wait. The time to fill the prescription is 8.2 minutes. The order is ready at 53.1 + 8.2 = 61.3 minutes, resulting in a total time in the system equal to 61.3 − 53 = 8.3 minutes.

TABLE 8.10 Simulation of 10 and 1,000 Prescription Orders With Two Servers

Cumulative IATs → AT column

Max(AT$_t$, Min (TimeP1$_{t1}$, TimeP2$_{t-1}$)) → SB column

SB + ST → SE column

SB − AT → TQ column

SE − AT → TS column

SB$_t$ − Min(TimeP1$_{t-1}$, TimeP2$_{t-1}$) → Idle Time column

	Order (t)	IAT	AT	SB	ST	SE	TQ	TS	Time P1 Is Free	Time P2 Is Free	Idle Time
First 10 Orders	1	5	5	5	9.2	14.2	0	9.2	14.2	0	5
	2	5	10	10	7.5	17.5	0	7.5	14.2	17.5	10
	3	6	16	16	5.8	21.8	0	5.8	21.8	17.5	1.8
	4	7	23	23	7.1	30.1	0	7.1	21.8	30.1	5.5
	5	7	30	30	7.2	37.2	0	7.2	37.2	30.1	8.2
	6	5	35	35	7.8	42.8	0	7.8	37.2	42.8	4.9
	7	6	41	41	7.5	48.5	0	7.5	48.5	42.8	3.8
	8	4	45	45	8.1	53.1	0	8.1	48.5	53.1	2.2
	9	5	50	50	5.6	55.6	0	5.6	55.6	53.1	1.5
	10	3	53	53.1	8.2	61.3	0.1	8.3	55.6	61.3	0
	Average	**5.30**			**7.40**		**0.01**	**7.41**			**4.29**
	⋮	⋮	⋮	⋮	⋮	⋮	⋮	⋮	⋮	⋮	
	⋮	⋮	⋮	⋮	⋮	⋮	⋮	⋮	⋮	⋮	
Last 10 Orders	991	6	5795	5795	6.2	5801.2	0	6.2	5801.2	5796.7	5.6
	992	7	5802	5802	7.7	5809.7	0	7.7	5801.2	5809.7	5.3
	993	7	5809	5809	7.1	5816.1	0	7.1	5816.1	5809.7	7.8
	994	7	5816	5816	5.5	5821.5	0	5.5	5816.1	5821.5	6.3
	995	8	5824	5824	8.2	5832.2	0	8.2	5832.2	5821.5	7.9
	996	6	5830	5830	6.5	5836.5	0	6.5	5832.2	5836.5	8.5
	997	5	5835	5835	6.3	5841.3	0	6.3	5841.3	5836.5	2.8
	998	6	5841	5841	7.3	5848.3	0	7.3	5841.3	5848.3	4.5
	999	6	5847	5847	7.3	5854.3	0	7.3	5854.3	5848.3	5.7
	1000	4	5851	5851	7.7	5858.7	0	7.7	5854.3	5858.7	2.7
	Average	**5.85**			**7.02**		**0.02**	**7.04**			**4.69**

AT, arrival time; IAT, interarrival time; SB, service begins; SE, service ends; ST, service ends; TQ, time in queue; TS, time in system.

After 10 simulation trials, the average wait before service is 0.01 minutes, the average time in the system is 7.41 minutes, and the average idle time for both servers combined is 4.29 minutes. When running the simulation over 1,000 trials, the average time in the queue remains negligible. A significant amount of non–value-added time has thus been eliminated (see Chapter 7), and the total cost of this system is now substantially lower:

$$TC = \left(\$100 \times 1000 \text{ orders} \times \frac{7.04\,\text{min}}{60} \right) + \left(\$60 \times \frac{5858.7\,\text{min}}{60} \times 2 \text{ pharmacists} \right)$$

$$= \$11{,}733.33 + \$11{,}717.40$$

$$= \textbf{\$23{,}450.73}.$$

The cost of service could have been split into the cost of compensating pharmacist 1 for 5,854.3 minutes and pharmacist 2 for 5,858.7 minutes. The overall cost difference would be minor.

The aforementioned examples illustrate one-stage processes. Although we can also model and run multistage processes in Excel, professional simulation software packages, such as ExtendSim, provide an easier platform to do so.

SIMULATING MULTISTAGE SYSTEMS WITH ExtendSim

After filling an order at the BPH pharmacy, Todd Beringer, the pharmacist, gives the prescription to an assistant who updates the patient's pharmacy record and files the insurance claim electronically. The time it takes the assistant to perform these tasks follows a uniform distribution with a minimum of 3 minutes and a maximum of 9 minutes. The process is depicted in ExtendSim in Figure 8.11.

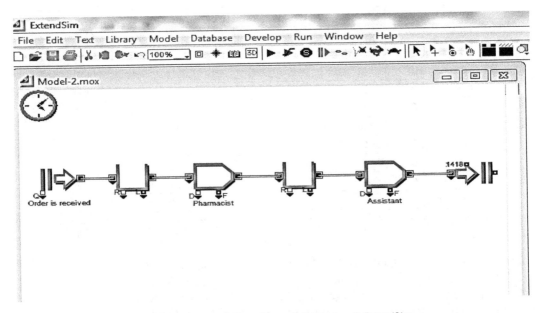

FIGURE 8.11 – Simulation of prescription orders in ExtendSim.

ExtendSim uses blocks to represent the various elements of the process or queuing system. The blocks used in Figure 8.11 are as follows:

Executive block
This block governs the system. It schedules the events and controls the simulation. It is always placed to the left of all other blocks.

Create block
This block generates arrivals according to a distribution specified by the user.

Queue block
This block holds flow units and releases them according to a queue discipline specified by the user.

Activity block
The activity block acts as the server in a queuing system. The distribution of the time to perform the activity, or service time, is specified by the user.

Exit block
This block removes the flow units from the system once their processing is completed.

Note: ExtendSim blocks Copyright © 1987–2016 Imagine That Inc. All rights reserved.

Simulation Input

Create Block

When double-clicking on the Create block, you will see the **Create**, **Options**, **Item Animation**, **Block Animation**, and **Comments** tabs. The Create dialog box requests the user to enter the most critical information for the simulation. As shown in Figure 8.12, items or flow units are created randomly. The time units for the arrivals are minutes (Note: the time unit can be specified for a particular block, or for the whole simulation in the Simulation Setup command). The distribution chosen from the menu is empirical discrete, and the probabilities of occurrence for the interarrival times listed in Table 8.4 are entered.

Queue Block

When double-clicking on the Queue block, the most important input will be in the Queue dialog box (Figure 8.13). Most noteworthy to our discussion is the sort method. In ExtendSim, the sort methods are equivalent to queue disciplines, and the available options are: Attribute Value; First in, First out; Last in, First out; and Priority. In our pharmacy example, we assumed that the orders were processed in their order of arrival. However, prescription orders could be given an attribute value

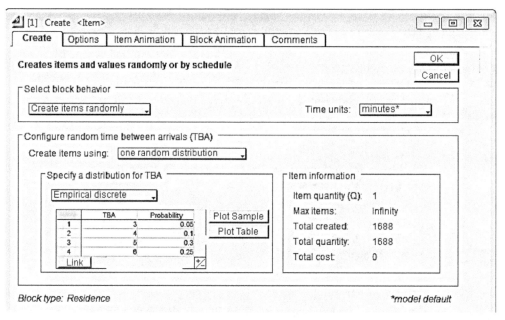

FIGURE 8.12 – Dialog box for Create block.

such that the order is categorized as (a) called in by the physician or (b) given by the patient who is on the premises. In the latter case, the pharmacist would likely process the prescriptions for the patients standing in the pharmacy before the call-ins.

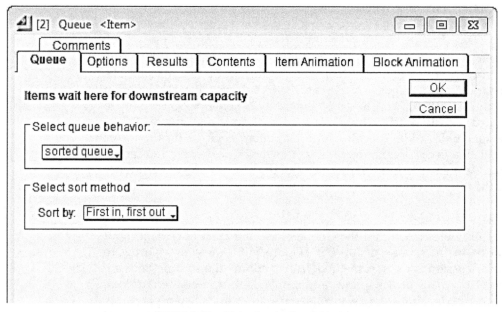

FIGURE 8.13 – Dialog box for Queue block.

Activity Blocks

In our simulation, we have two activity blocks corresponding to the two servers: the pharmacist and the assistant. As you will recall, the time to fill in the prescription followed a normal distribution with a mean of 7 minutes and a standard deviation of 1 minute (Figure 8.14). In the Process dialog box, the default for Maximum items in activity is 1, meaning that the pharmacist fills one prescription at a time, which is quite likely. You can specify the delay or service time distribution as well as its parameters, that is, the mean and the standard deviation.

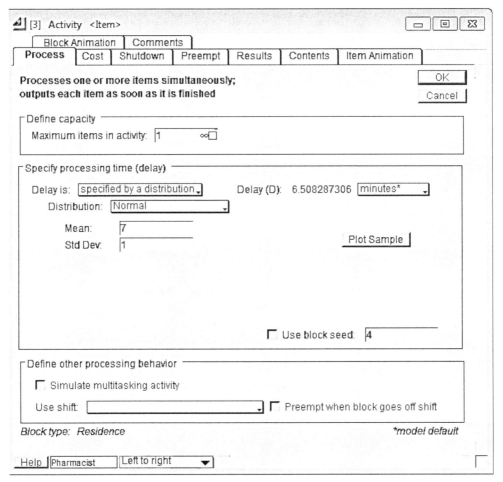

FIGURE 8.14 – Dialog box for Activity block (pharmacist).

The Assistant Activity block has similar entries, except that the selected distribution is uniform with a minimum of 3 minutes and a maximum of 9 minutes (Figure 8.15).

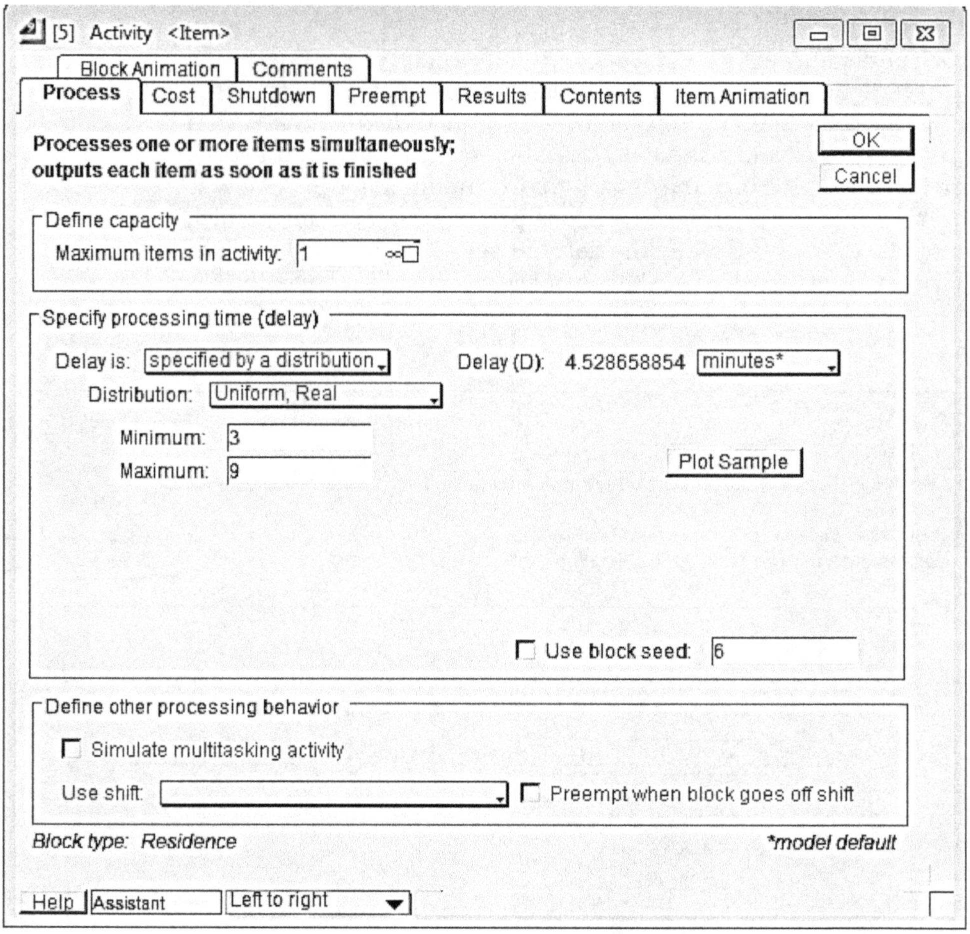

FIGURE 8.15 – Dialog box for Activity block (assistant).

Exit Block

No information needs to be entered in the Exit block. It simply lets flow units leave the system.

Simulation Setup

Before running the simulation, it is important to specify (a) the duration of the simulation, (b) the start time, (c) the time units for the duration of the simulation, and (d) the desired random number seed. Figure 8.16 (Setup tab) shows that we wanted the simulation to be run over a period of 10,000 minutes, starting at time 0. Figure 8.17 (Random Numbers tab) shows that we selected Random Number seed 1111 to generate random numbers (similar in concept to Column 1111 in Table 8.5 if there were that many columns listed).

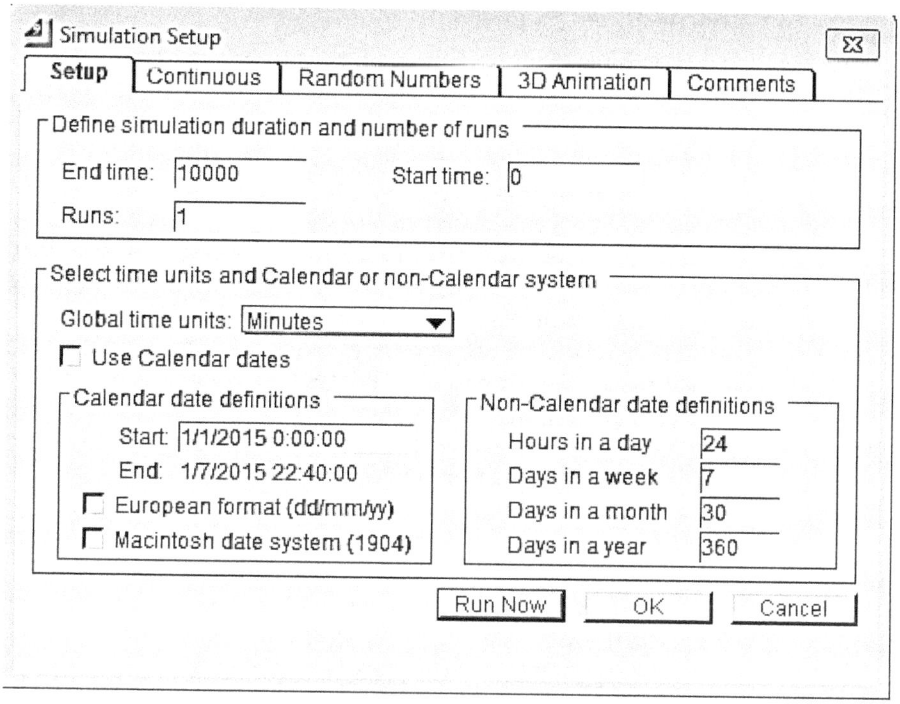

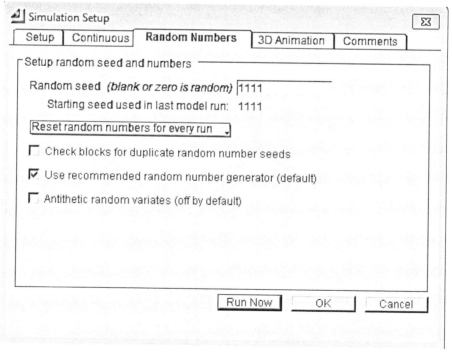

FIGURE 8.16 – Dialog box for Simulation Setup (Setup tab).

FIGURE 8.17 – Dialog box for Simulation Setup (Random Numbers tab).

Simulation Output

During the simulation with random number seed 1111, 1,688 orders were received and entered the queue in front of the pharmacist. The pharmacist finished processing 1,419 orders and was working on the 1,420th when the simulation ended. He was utilized 100% of the time. The assistant processed 1,418 of the 1,419 orders handed off by the pharmacist and was utilized 85% of the time (Figure 8.18).

The number of orders waiting to be processed by the pharmacist averaged 126.5 and reached up to 269 (Figure 8.19). The average wait time for these orders was 744.55 minutes, with a maximum of 1,558.2 minutes. Although 1,688 orders arrived into the system, only 1,420 reached the pharmacist to be processed, whereas the rest remained in the queue. The queue in front of the assistant had an average of 0.15467 orders and never exceeded 2. The average time in the queue was 1.09 minutes, and the maximum wait was 11.15 minutes.

Changing the random number seed will affect the results. Therefore, it is good practice to run the model with different random number seeds and base decisions on average results (Table 8.11).

As we already knew, the lack of capacity to fill the prescriptions is the main culprit for the delays in filling the prescriptions. The ExtendSim simulation with two pharmacists is depicted in Figure 8.20, and the

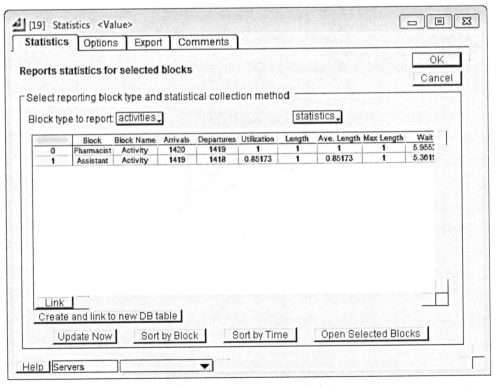

FIGURE 8.18 – Results (server utilization).

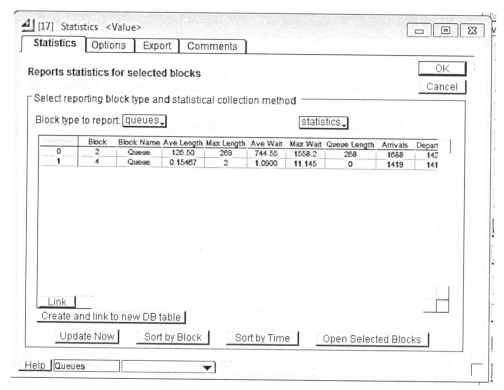

FIGURE 8.19 – Results (queue statistics).

Note: ExtendSim block Copyright © 1987–2016 Imagine That Inc. All rights reserved.

results with three random number seeds are shown in Table 8.12. In this model, two blocks have been added: one Activity block for pharmacist 2, and a Select Item In block, which pools the prescriptions filled by pharmacists 1 and 2, and places them in the queue in front of the assistant.

With random number seed 1111, 1,688 orders are generated. This is the same number of arrivals as with one pharmacist because arrivals are independent of service. The results indicate that 1,686 of these orders were processed by both pharmacists and were placed in the queue in

TABLE 8.11 Summary Results of Simulations With One Pharmacist and One Assistant for Three Random Number Seeds

Random Number Seed	Pharmacist			Assistant		
	Average Queue Length	Average Wait Time	Utilization (%)	Average Queue Length	Average Wait Time	Utilization (%)
1111	126.5	744.55	100	0.1547	1.09	85
2014	150.96	879.96	100	0.1303	0.92	84
678	141.23	823.65	100	0.1737	1.21	86
Average	**139.56**	**816.05**	**100**	**0.1529**	**1.21**	**86**

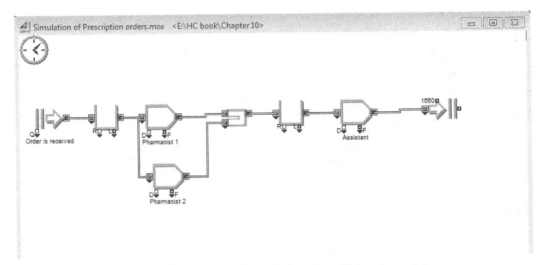

FIGURE 8.20 – Simulation of prescription orders with two pharmacists.

Note: ExtendSim block Copyright © 1987–2016 Imagine That Inc. All rights reserved.

front of the assistant; the assistant processed 1,660 of those. As capacity increases at the first service step, orders flow faster to the second step, thereby creating a situation in which demand exceeds the capacity provided by only one assistant. Whereas the queues and wait times essentially vanished at the pharmacist level, they started increasing at the assistant level, creating congestion at this process step (Table 8.12). This type of congestion is often referred to as a bottleneck.

TABLE 8.12 Summary Results of Simulations With Two Pharmacists and One Assistant for Three Random Number Seeds

Random Number Seed	Pharmacist				Assistant		
	Average Queue Length	Average Wait Time	Utilization Pharmacist 1 (%)	Utilization Pharmacist 2 (%)	Average Queue Length	Average Wait Time	Utilization (%)
1111	0.001	0.008	69	50	14.11	83.80	99
2014	0.001	0.008	68	53	11.60	67.03	100
678	0.002	0.011	68	51	37.85	223.13	100
Average	0.001	0.009	68.3	51.3	21.19	124.65	99.7

Bottleneck

A point in the system where capacity is less than or equal to demand.

As shown in Figure 8.21, a **bottleneck** involves a situation in which demand is greater than or equal to capacity. The bottleneck places a constraint on the system and restricts the flow. The TOC is a popular approach to managing bottlenecks.

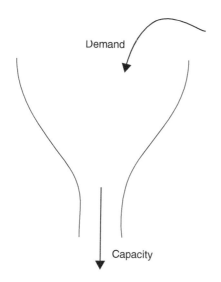

Demand

Capacity

FIGURE 8.21 –
Bottleneck = neck of
a bottle.

THEORY OF CONSTRAINTS

 BOX 8.7 – WORDS OF WISDOM

"The entire bottleneck concept is not geared to decrease operating expense, it's focused on increasing throughput" (Goldratt, 2004).

The **Theory of Constraints** is a scheduling method that focuses on the bottleneck or system constraint. It releases flow units into the system at the speed of the bottleneck server/resource. To demonstrate the viability of this concept to business organizations, Dr. Goldratt (2004) wrote a novel, *The Goal*, which covers the troubles and eventual success of a plant manager in a fictitious manufacturing organization (see Box 8.7). The plant is plagued by late deliveries to customers and huge amounts of work-in-process (or queues) inventory inside the plant. While on a trip with a troop of Boy Scouts, the plant manager notices the similarity between the flow of goods in his plant and the flow of Boy Scouts on the hiking trail. The Boy Scouts walk in file, with the guide at the end of the file to make sure that no one stays behind. Each Boy Scout walks at his own pace, unconcerned about what is happening behind him. Soon, gaps appear between the Boy Scouts (Figure 8.22a). One of them, Herbie, is not very athletic and carries a heavy backpack. As time passes, his slower pace pushes him further and further behind, and the gaps between the Boy Scouts keep widening (Figure 8.22b). These gaps worry the guide as he senses a loss of control over the hike. When the first Boy Scout arrives at the camp site, can the fun begin? No, the entire troop and the guide must be at the camp site to start the fire and set up the tents. As you can see from Figure 8.22c, this only happens when Herbie, the slowest Boy Scout, arrives. Moral of the story: *The pace of the bottleneck sets*

Theory of Constraints

A scheduling method that focuses on bottlenecks or system constraints.

FIGURE 8.22 (a) – Boy Scouts walking in file, (b) – Gaps widen; Herbie is behind, (c) – Entire troop's arrival at camp site.

the pace for the entire system. The plant manager realizes that the same happens at his plant. Every work center works at its own pace, and the volume of goods each one generates exceeds the capacity of the most constrained resource, that is, the bottleneck. The result is a growing amount of work-in-process inventory in front of the bottleneck. In the end, the product cannot be sold (The GOAL) until all processing steps, including the bottleneck step, have been completed.

TOC comprises five steps:

STEP 1: **Identify the constraint or bottleneck.** In process management, this would involve the identification of the slowest step in the process, that is, the one whose utilization $\left(\dfrac{\lambda}{\mu}\right)$ is highest and cannot fulfill the demand. Because the pace of upstream steps in the process is faster, you will see a lot of delays, queues, and work-in-process, at that step.

STEP 2: **Exploit the constraint.** It is important to keep the bottleneck resources utilized because every minute lost at the bottleneck is a minute lost for the entire system. Ways to accomplish this objective include:

- Make sure that the bottleneck resource always has work to do. A reasonable amount of work-in-process in front of the bottleneck is desirable because we do not want to "starve" that resource and further delay the work that it needs to perform.

- Make sure that resources are always available at the bottleneck, for example, by staggering lunch breaks.

- Always perform quality control before the bottleneck. The precious time at the bottleneck cannot be wasted on defective items that might be discarded anyway.

- If equipment is used, ensure that maintenance occurs during off hours. Again, we do not want to risk a loss of productive time because of a breakdown.

STEP 3: **Subordinate everything else to the constraint.** Make the speed of the bottleneck the speed at which work is released (i.e., arrivals) into the process and the speed at which all other process resources work. In other words, make Herbie lead the troop to the camp site.

STEP 4: **Elevate the constraint.** Find ways to increase the capacity of the bottleneck by pulling unutilized resources from some other area, or, if necessary, by subcontracting. Influence the demand placed on the bottleneck by making process changes that render the bottleneck step unnecessary for at least some flow units, and by eliminating as much non–value-added time at the bottleneck as possible. It is critical that the bottleneck resource work only on what is needed!

STEP 5: **If the constraint is broken, do not rest on your laurels.** Go back to step 1 and find a new constraint.

Let us illustrate the TOC with a data-entry process that includes the following three process steps (Figure 8.23):

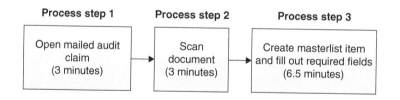

FIGURE 8.23 – Data entry process for audit claims.

1. The processing time for the first step follows a uniform distribution with (a) a minimum of 2 minutes and (b) a maximum of 4 minutes; the mean is $(2 + 4)/2 = 3$ minutes. To generate random numbers following a uniform distribution, use the following Excel function:

$$\text{Service time}_1 = a + (\text{RAND}() \times (b{-}a)) \qquad [8.34]$$

$$= 2 + (\text{RAND}() \times (4{-}2)).$$

2. The processing time for the second step follows a normal distribution with a mean of 3 minutes and a standard deviation of 0.5 minute. To generate random numbers following a normal distribution, use the following Excel function:

Service time$_2$ = NORM.INV(RAND(), mean, standard deviation) = NORM.INV(RAND(), 3, 0.5).

3. The processing time for the third step follows a uniform distribution with (a) a minimum of 5 minutes and (b) a maximum of 8 minutes; the mean is (5 + 8)/2 = 6.5 minutes. To generate random numbers following a uniform distribution, use the following Excel function:

Service time$_3$ = a + (RAND() × (b–a)) = 5 + (RAND() × (8–5)).

To keep this problem simple, we will assume that the interarrival time is 4 minutes and that this time is constant. The capacity at step 1 exceeds the demand (or arrivals); the capacity at step 2 exceeds the demand unless the service time is 2 or more standard deviations above the mean of 3 minutes; and the capacity at step 3 is insufficient to meet the demand. Therefore, step 3 is the bottleneck. As soon as they become available, the resources in step 1 start processing the arriving claims on an FCFS basis. In other words, in a traditional *push* system (see Chapter 6), the processing rate at step 1 governs the release of work into the system. The simulation of 10 and 1,000 claims is shown in Table 8.13.

As you can see, there are no delays until the claims reach step 3. Because of the slower processing time, the resources at step 3 are unable to keep up with the upstream stations' paces, and the number of unattended claims keeps growing. For 1,000 claims, the average time in the queue before the bottleneck is 1,240.4 minutes, after disregarding the first 100 arrivals.

To avoid this unnecessary queue, which is costly and frustrating for the resources at the third step, TOC advocates releasing work into the system at the speed of the bottleneck: "Subordinate everything else to the constraint." In principle, this synchronization is ideal, but it will result in idle time at the bottleneck once in a while, which is undesirable. Therefore, we will release the work at a pace slightly higher than that of the bottleneck, let us say every 6 minutes. This is consistent with the second step of TOC, which recommends that the bottleneck resource be utilized at all times. As shown in Table 8.14, the third queue is drastically reduced.

Has this change caused a decrease in process output? Not at all. The system is constrained by the bottleneck's speed of work, irrespective of the interarrival times. To show this phenomenon, we ran the simulations with three different sets of random numbers and obtained the results shown in Table 8.15. One thousand claims were processed in approximately 6,500 minutes, which is 1,000 claims × 6.5 minutes at the bottleneck. In order to accommodate the larger volume of claims that arrive every 4 minutes, the capacity of the bottleneck should be increased, that is, the constraint should be elevated (step 4 of TOC).

TABLE 8.13 Simulation With Work Released at Step 1's Speed (Push System)

Claim (t)	Time of Arrival	Process Step 1				Process Step 2				Process Step 3			
		Time in Queue	Service Begins	Service Time	Service Ends	Time in Queue	Service Begins	Service Time	Service Ends	Time in Queue	Service Begins	Service Time	Service Ends
1	0	0	0	2	2	0	2	2.6	4.6	0	4.6	5.1	9.7
2	4	0	4	3	7	0	7	2.4	9.4	0.3	9.7	6.9	16.6
3	8	0	8	3.1	11.1	0	11.1	3.6	14.7	1.9	16.6	5.6	22.2
4	12	0	12	3.1	15.1	0	15.1	3.1	18.2	4	22.2	5.1	27.3
5	16	0	16	3.6	19.6	0	19.6	2.4	22	5.3	27.3	7.5	34.8
6	20	0	20	3.3	23.3	0	23.3	3.5	26.8	8	34.8	5.3	40.1
7	24	0	24	3.4	27.4	0	27.4	2.6	30	10.1	40.1	7.7	47.8
8	28	0	28	2.9	30.9	0	30.9	2.3	33.2	14.6	47.8	5.6	53.4
9	32	0	32	3.2	35.2	0	35.2	2.8	38	15.4	53.4	7.1	60.5
10	36	0	36	4	40	0	40	3.5	43.5	17	60.5	6.7	67.2
Average		**0**				**0**				**7.66**			
..		..	..	..	..	..	..	..	..	..	..	..	..
..		..	..	..	..	..	..	..	..	..	..	..	..
991	3960	0	3960	3.7	3963.7	0	3963.7	2.5	3966.2	2456.6	6422.8	5.6	6428.4
992	3964	0	3964	2.5	3966.5	0	3966.5	3.4	3969.9	2458.5	6428.4	6.9	6435.3
993	3968	0	3968	3.2	3971.2	0	3971.2	2.5	3973.7	2461.6	6435.3	6.5	6441.8
994	3972	0	3972	3.7	3975.7	0	3975.7	3.1	3978.8	2463	6441.8	6.5	6448.3
995	3976	0	3976	2.8	3978.8	0	3978.8	3.5	3982.3	2466	6448.3	6.8	6455.1
996	3980	0	3980	2	3982	0.3	3982.3	2.9	3985.2	2469.9	6455.1	5.3	6460.4
997	3984	0	3984	2.8	3986.8	0	3986.8	3.3	3990.1	2470.3	6460.4	7.2	6467.6
998	3988	0	3988	2.7	3990.7	0	3990.7	2.1	3992.8	2474.8	6467.6	5.4	6473
999	3992	0	3992	3.4	3995.4	0	3995.4	2.5	3997.9	2475.1	6473	5.3	6478.3
1000	3996	0	3996	2.5	3998.5	0	3998.5	3.9	4002.4	2475.9	6478.3	6.2	6484.5
Average		**0**				**0.08**				**1240.4**			

First 10 Claims

Last 10 Claims

TABLE 8.14 Simulation With Work Released at Speed of Bottleneck (TOC)

Claim (t)	Time of Arrival	Process Step 1				Process Step 2				Process Step 3			
		Time in Queue	Service Begins	Service Time	Service Ends	Time in Queue	Service Begins	Service Time	Service Ends	Time in Queue	Service Begins	Service Time	Service Ends
1	0	0	0	2.4	2.4	0	2.4	2.4	4.8	0	4.8	6.8	11.6
2	6	0	6	2.1	8.1	0	8.1	2.5	10.6	1	11.6	6.2	17.8
3	12	0	12	3.1	15.1	0	15.1	2.6	17.7	0.1	17.8	7.8	25.6
4	18	0	18	2.4	20.4	0	20.4	2.9	23.3	2.3	25.6	6	31.6
5	24	0	24	2.4	26.4	0	26.4	2.6	29	2.6	31.6	6.8	38.4
6	30	0	30	3.8	33.8	0	33.8	2.1	35.9	2.5	38.4	6.1	44.5
7	36	0	36	2	38	0	38	3.5	41.5	3	44.5	6.4	50.9
8	42	0	42	2.3	44.3	0	44.3	3.2	47.5	3.4	50.9	7.7	58.6
9	48	0	48	2.5	50.5	0	50.5	2.8	53.3	5.3	58.6	7.3	65.9
10	54	0	54	2.2	56.2	0	56.2	3.3	59.5	6.4	65.9	5.6	71.5
Average		**0**				**0**				**2.66**			
..		..	..	..	..	..	..	..	..	..	..	..	..
..		..	..	..	..	..	..	..	..	..	..	..	..
991	5940	0	5940	3.1	5943.1	0	5943.1	2.9	5946	487.4	6433.4	6.8	6440.2
992	5946	0	5946	2.3	5948.3	0	5948.3	3.4	5951.7	488.5	6440.2	5.2	6445.4
993	5952	0	5952	3.3	5955.3	0	5955.3	3.6	5958.9	486.5	6445.4	5.2	6450.6
994	5958	0	5958	2.6	5960.6	0	5960.6	3.6	5964.2	486.4	6450.6	5.3	6455.9
995	5964	0	5964	2.3	5966.3	0	5966.3	2.8	5969.1	486.8	6455.9	6.2	6462.1
996	5970	0	5970	2	5972	0	5972	2.9	5974.9	487.2	6462.1	6.9	6469
997	5976	0	5976	3.9	5979.9	0	5979.9	2.2	5982.1	486.9	6469	6.2	6475.2
998	5982	0	5982	3.6	5985.6	0	5985.6	3.7	5989.3	485.9	6475.2	7.3	6482.5
999	5988	0	5988	3.9	5991.9	0	5991.9	3.8	5995.7	486.8	6482.5	6.5	6489
1000	5994	0	5994	2.6	5996.6	0	5996.6	2.3	5998.9	490.1	6489	7.6	6496.6
Average		**0**				**0**				**272.0**			

First 10 Claims

Last 10 Claims

TABLE 8.15 Summary Results for Simulations of Push and TOC Systems

Performance Measure	Release Work Every 4 Minutes				Release Work Every 6 Minutes			
	Run 1	Run 2	Run 3	Average	Run 1	Run 2	Run 3	Average
Average time in front of bottleneck	1240.4	1378.2	1417.2	**1345.3**	272.0	259.8	276.9	**269.6**
Ending time of simulation	6484.5	6518.3	6576.2	**6526.3**	6496.6	6482.7	6507.2	**6495.5**

BRADLEY PARK HOSPITAL 8.3

Mike Chambers welcomed Todd and Francine into his office, "Well, congratulations, you two. You certainly administered a record number of flu vaccines to our patients with great efficiency. I had several of our board members say that they had never seen such a well-run operation. You really showed that BPH is patient focused. Thanks for your hard work."

"We learned a lot from this process by using queuing models," Francine said. "In fact, Jennifer suggests that we begin to look at our clinics' flow in the same way. She just got simulation software so that we can begin to simulate flows within different areas and identify ways to improve our processes. This stuff is really helpful!"

 Should Jennifer advocate the use of the simulation software in the clinics or in the hospital? Why?

SUMMARY

In this chapter, you learned that the rate of arrivals into a process and the various processing times determine how congested the process will become. This was true for $M/M/1$, $M/M/s$, $M/G/1$, and $M/D/1$ systems. In fact, it is true for any queuing system! When you add the complexity of multistage queuing systems, there is an opportunity for a queue to form at each process step. The more steps in a process, the more potential delays, thereby buttressing the following process design principles from Chapter 7:

- Principle #1: Reduce fragmentation.
- Principle #2: Avoid excessive delegation.
- Principle #9: Eliminate buffers.

Additionally, the TOC taught you how to alleviate the congestion at the bottleneck by aligning the pace of the entire system with the pace of the bottleneck. This is consistent with another design principle in Chapter 7:

- Principle #8: Optimize the whole system and stop focusing on local optimization.

Powerful tools like computer simulation enable us to test various process configurations and assess their performance prior to implementation, which helps cement a successful redesign.

The topics covered in this chapter deal mostly with rapid and smooth flows, which is the essence of on-time or fast delivery. However, flow concepts also affect quality with regard to wait-time reduction. Being able to adjust levels of healthcare resources to minimize wait not only improves a patient's experience and health outcomes, but it also reflects the organization's flexibility. Both waiting and capacity have their associated costs. It takes expertise in queuing model analysis to balance these costs and achieve optimal or near optimal results (Figure 8.24).

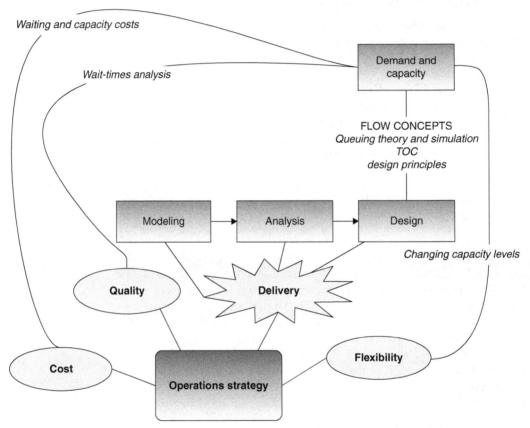

FIGURE 8.24 – Mind map showing links between demand/capacity and the competitive priorities.

KEY TERMS

Average arrival rate, λ	Goal of queuing analysis	Theory of Constraints
Average service rate, μ	Risk	

Queue discipline	Theoretical probability distribution
Priority system	Empirical probability distribution
Calling-customer population	Trial
Channel	Bottleneck

FORMULAS USED IN THIS CHAPTER

System	Performance Measure	Formula	No.
M/M/1	**System utilization** • Probability that the system is in use • Percentage of time that the server is busy	$\rho = \dfrac{\lambda}{\mu}$	[8.1]
	Probability of no customers in system • Percentage of time that the server is idle	$P_0 = 1 - \dfrac{\lambda}{\mu}$	[8.2]
	Average number of customers waiting in line before service • Average number of flow units in the queue • Length of the queue	$L_q = \dfrac{\lambda^2}{\mu(\mu - \lambda)}$	[8.3]

System	Performance Measure	Formula	No.
	Average number of customers in the system • Average number of flow units in the system (those waiting for service and those being served)	$L = \dfrac{\lambda}{\mu - \lambda}$ $= L_q + \dfrac{\lambda}{\mu}$	[8.4]
	Average time spent waiting for service Average time spent <u>wa</u>iting in the <u>q</u>ueue	$W_q = \dfrac{\lambda}{\mu(\mu - \lambda)}$	[8.5]
	Average time spent in the system Average time spent waiting for service and being served	$W = \dfrac{1}{\mu - \lambda}$ $= W_q + \dfrac{1}{\mu}$	[8.6]
	Probability of exactly n customers in the system	$P_n = P_0 \left(\dfrac{\lambda}{\mu} \right)^n$	[8.7]
	Probability that the number of customers in the system does not exceed k	$P_{n \leq k} = 1 - \left(\dfrac{\lambda}{\mu} \right)^{k+1}$	[8.8]
	Probability that an arriving customer would have to wait for service	$P_w = \dfrac{\lambda}{\mu}$	[8.9]

System	Performance Measure	Formula	No.
Little's flow equations	Average number of customers in the system	$L = \lambda W$	[8.10]
	Average time spent in the system	$W = \dfrac{L}{\lambda}$	[8.11]
	Average number of customers waiting in line before service	$L_q = \lambda W_q$	[8.12]
	Average time spent waiting for service	$W_q = \dfrac{L_q}{\lambda}$	[8.13]
M/M/s	System Utilization • Average utilization rate of servers	$\rho = \dfrac{\lambda}{s\mu}$	[8.14]
	Probability of no customers in system • Probability that the system is empty • Percentage of time that all servers are idle	$P_0 = \dfrac{1}{\displaystyle\sum_{n=0}^{s-1}\left[\dfrac{\left(\frac{\lambda}{\mu}\right)^n}{n!}\right] + \left[\dfrac{\left(\frac{\lambda}{\mu}\right)^s}{s!}\left(\dfrac{s\mu}{s\mu-\lambda}\right)\right]}$	[8.15]
	Average number of customers waiting in line before service • Average number of flow units in the queue • Length of the queue	$L_q = \dfrac{\left(\frac{\lambda}{\mu}\right)^s \lambda\mu}{(s-1)!(s\mu-\lambda)^2}P_0$	[8.16]

System	Performance Measure	Formula	No.
	Average number of customers in the system • Average number of flow units in the system (those waiting for service and those being served)	$L = L_q + \dfrac{\lambda}{\mu}$	[8.17]
	Average time spent waiting for service • Average time spent waiting in the queue	$W_q = \dfrac{L_q}{\lambda}$	[8.18]
	Average time spent in the system • Average time spent waiting for service and being served	$W = W_q + \dfrac{1}{\mu}$	[8.19]
	Probability of exactly n customers in the system	$P_n = P_0 \dfrac{\left(\dfrac{\lambda}{\mu}\right)^n}{n!}$ for $n \leq s$ $P_n = P_0 \dfrac{\left(\dfrac{\lambda}{\mu}\right)^n}{s! \, s^{n-s}}$ for $n > s$	[8.20]
	Probability that the number of customers in the system does not exceed k	$P_{n \leq k} = \displaystyle\sum_{n=0}^{k} P_n$	[8.21]
	Probability that an arriving customer would have to wait for service (all servers are busy)	$P_w = \dfrac{1}{s!}\left(\dfrac{\lambda}{\mu}\right)^s \left(\dfrac{s\mu}{s\mu - \lambda}\right) P_0$	[8.22]

System	Performance Measure	Formula	No.
Cost	Total costs	$TC = (C_w \times L) + (C_s \times$ number of servers$)$	[8.23]
M/G/1	System utilization • Probability that the system is in use • Percentage of time that the server is busy	$\rho = \dfrac{\lambda}{\mu}$	[8.24]
	Probability of no customers in system • Probability that the system is empty • Percentage of time that the server is idle	$P_0 = 1 - \dfrac{\lambda}{\mu}$	[8.25]
	Average number of customers waiting in line before service • Average number of flow units in the queue • Length of the queue	$L_q = \dfrac{\lambda^2 \sigma^2 + \left(\dfrac{\lambda}{\mu}\right)^2}{2\left(1 - \dfrac{\lambda}{\mu}\right)}$	[8.26]
	Average number of customers in the system • Average number of flow units in the system (those waiting for service and those being served)	$L = L_q + \dfrac{\lambda}{\mu}$	[8.27]

System	Performance Measure	Formula	No.
	Average time spent waiting for service • Average time spent waiting in the queue	$W_q = \dfrac{L_q}{\lambda}$	[8.28]
	Average time spent in the system • Average time spent waiting for service and being served	$W = W_q + \dfrac{1}{\mu}$	[8.29]
	Probability that an arriving customer would have to wait for service	$P_w = \dfrac{\lambda}{\mu}$	[8.30]
M/D/1	**Average number of customers waiting in line before service**	$L_q = \dfrac{\lambda^2}{2\mu(\mu - \lambda)}$	[8.31]
EV	**Expected value**	$EV = \sum_{i=1}^{\infty} x_i p_i$	[8.32]
Excel functions	**Normal distribution**	= NORM.INV(RAND(), Mean, Standard Deviation)	[8.33]
	Uniform distribution	$a + (RAND() \times (b\text{-}a))$	[8.34]

WHAT DO YOU REMEMBER?

1. What is the "average arrival rate?"
2. What is the "average service rate?"
3. What is the relationship between the arrival rate and the interarrival time?
4. What are the various queue configurations?

5. When using the Kendall notation, what do the letters M, D, and G represent?

6. What are the assumptions of the M/M/1 model?

7. What are Little's flow equations?

8. What is the primary goal of queuing analysis?

9. What are the two types of cost used in the cost formula? Describe their behavior.

10. What is risk?

11. What are the five steps in conducting a simulation?

12. What is the difference between an empirical and a theoretical probability distribution?

13. In ExtendSim, what are:
   a. The Executive block?
   b. The Create block?
   c. The Queue block?
   d. The Activity block?
   e. The Exit block?

14. What are the five steps of the TOC?

SOLVE BPH's PROBLEMS

1. Using the Kendall notation scheme (e.g., M/M/1), describe each of the following queuing systems:

   a. Clerks arrive according to a Poisson distribution to use a copy machine. Each clerk copies only one page.

   b. Syringes come off an assembly line at a constant rate to be inspected. The inspection time follows the normal distribution, and there are four inspectors.

   c. Patients call at a rate of 12 per hour (Poisson distribution) to preregister for a procedure. The preregistration time follows the exponential distribution with a mean of 5 minutes, and the minimum number of schedulers needed is available for preregistering.

   d. Patients and their families arrive randomly (Poisson distribution) at a rate of five per hour to use the automatic teller machine in the hospital lobby. Service time follows a uniform distribution.

   e. Patients arrive at one of BPH's clinics every 5 minutes (exponential), on average. The time it takes them to check in follows the normal distribution, and there are two receptionists.

2. Fill in the blanks (do not forget to indicate the units). Also give the definition of the item for which you provide an answer.

   $1/\mu = 3$ minutes $\mu = $ _____

   $1/\lambda = 28$ seconds $\lambda = $ _____

   $\mu = 12$ patients per day (8 hours) $1/\mu = $ _____

   $\lambda = 36$ test orders per minute $1/\lambda = $ _____

   $1/\mu = 0.5$ hour $\mu = $ _____

3. At a BPH walk-in clinic, patients arrive every 15 minutes on average (negative exponential distribution), and it takes about 10 minutes for the physician to diagnose the patient (negative exponential distribution).

   a. What are λ and μ?

   b. On average, how long do patients wait to see the physician?

   c. On average, how many patients are there at the clinic?

   d. In an 8-hour day, how many hours is the physician idle?

   e. What is the probability that there are more than five patients at the clinic?

4. One clerk is on duty at the information desk of a BPH clinic. The clerk can process information requests in an average time of 3 minutes, and this can be described by a negative exponential distribution that has a mean of 3. Requests are received at a rate of 15 per hour (Poisson distribution). Find:

   a. The expected number of requests waiting to be addressed.

   b. The average time people spend waiting in line for service.

   c. In an 8-hour shift, how many hours is the clerk idle?

   d. What is the probability that there are fewer than four people at the information desk (excluding the clerk)?

5. The deli counter in BPH's cafeteria has a ticket dispenser in order to maintain FCFS processing. The mean arrival rate during the morning hours is 84 per hour. Each server can handle an average of 30 customers per hour. Arrival and service rates can be reasonably well described by Poisson distributions, respectively. Assume that three servers are on duty.

   a. What is the average time between arrivals?

   b. What is the average time a customer spends at the checkout counter?

   c. What is the system utilization?

   d. What is the average number of customers waiting for service?

   e. How many clerks would be necessary to keep the average time customers spend waiting *in line* to no more than 2.5 minutes? How many clerks would be needed to keep the average time customers spend *in the system* to under 2.5 minutes?

6. Patients needing appointments call a central scheduling office. Calls arrive at an average rate of 20 per hour according to a Poisson distribution. The average time it takes an employee to schedule the appointment is 1/12 hr. Time in the system is valued at $30 per hour, and a scheduler is paid $18 per hour. Based on the following performance measures, what is the optimal number of schedulers for this system?

s	Wq	Lq	W	L	P$_0$
2	0.1894	3.7879	0.2727	5.4545	0.0909
3	0.0187	0.3747	0.1021	2.0414	0.1727
4	0.0037	0.0732	0.0870	1.7399	0.1859
5	0.0008	0.0151	0.0841	1.6818	0.1883

7. On New Year's Eve, during the night shift, emergency calls to paramedics arrive at a rate of three per hour. The director of operations can dispatch multiple vehicles during that time. The average time to make a trip and come back to base is 45 minutes. Arrival and service rates are both Poisson distributions.

   a. If the director wants the average time between when a call is made and when an emergency vehicle is dispatched not to exceed 20 minutes, how many vehicles should be scheduled for that night?

   b. If the number of vehicles scheduled is three, what proportion of the time are all emergency vehicles used? What is the probability that more than three calls will be in the system?

   c. If the number of vehicles scheduled is four, what proportion of the time are all emergency vehicles used? What is the probability that more than two calls will be in the system?

8. At the emergency department of BPH, nurses triage patients to determine the severity of their condition and establish the order in which they should be seen by the doctors. From 6:00 a.m. to 10:00 a.m., an average of 18 patients needing this service arrive per hour. Assume Poisson rates and exponential times. BPH is considering the following three alternatives:

- Three nurses do the triage, separately. Each nurse averages 7 minutes with a patient.

- Four medical assistants do the triage, separately. Each one has an average service time of 12 minutes.

- One nurse and two medical assistants work as a team with an average service time of 3 minutes.

The nurses are paid $50.00 per hour, the medical assistants are paid $35 an hour, and the patient time in the triage area is valued at $60.00 an hour.

Which system would you recommend?

9. At one of the clinics, an employee calls patients to remind them of their upcoming appointments and to verify their insurance. The number of patients to call follows a Poisson distribution with a mean of six per hour. The time it takes to complete a call follows a normal distribution with a mean of 4 minutes and a standard deviation of 1 minute.

   a. On average, how many calls wait to be processed?

   b. On average, how long does a call spend in the system (waiting and being processed)?

   c. What proportion of the time is the clerk free to do other tasks?

10. Calls requiring information technology (IT) support arrive at the help desk every 3 minutes (exponential distribution). The time it takes to troubleshoot the problem over the phone is exponentially distributed with a mean of 6 minutes. IT support staff is paid an average of $25 an hour. The lost time for the care provider making the call to have the issue resolved is valued at $70 an hour. Based on a cost analysis, what is the optimal number of servers?

11. Each month, the billing department of a nursing home where BPH sends some of its patients reviews each patient's bill for accuracy. This inspection process involves only two steps. The processing times in minutes at each step are described by the following probability distributions. Because it is a fairly standardized process, a pull system is utilized, that is, step 1 cannot start reviewing the next bill until "authorized" by step 2. Simulate the processing of five bills using the following template. Based on this simulation, what is the average output rate per hour and what is the average queue time in front of step 2?

Service Time at Step 1	RN Ranges
5	.00–< .20
6	.20–< .70
7	.70–< 1.00

RN, random number.

Service Time at Step 2	RN Ranges
5	.00–< .30
6	.30–< .80
7	.80–< 1.00

Bill	Start 1	RN	Service Time 1	End 1	Queue Time	Start 2	RN	Service Time 2	End 2
1	0	.25					.89		
2		.68					.45		
3		.92					.90		
4		.45					.88		
5		.18					.29		

12. Arrivals to an information desk have an interarrival time that follows the distribution shown in the next table. Service times follow another empirical distribution, also shown in the table. There is only one customer service representative who starts work at time 0.

Time Between Arrivals (min)	p
2	0.15
3	0.25
4	0.35
5	0.25

Minutes Spent on Service	p
2	0.10
3	0.20
4	0.40
5	0.20
6	0.10

Using the following table of random numbers, conduct the simulation for the next five arrivals. In setting up your simulation, some of the variables that you must keep track of are (a) the time of arrival of a customer (i.e., cumulative interarrival time), (b) the time at which service starts, (c) the time at which service ends, (d) the number of minutes the customer spent in the system, and (e) the number of minutes the service representative was idle. If time in the system is valued at $30.00 per hour and the service representative is paid $15.00 per hour, what is the total cost of this system?

Random Numbers for IAT	Random Numbers for Service Time
.08	.60
.16	.87
.29	.20
.93	.57
.54	.04
IAT, interarrival time.	

13. Charlotte Browning, the manager of BPH's hair salon (available to both patients and staff), has three chairs and two employees in her salon. She is contemplating hiring a third employee. Charlotte has observed that customers appear to arrive randomly; the data shown in the following table were collected on the time between arrivals. Charlotte also made some estimates of the time it takes to give a haircut; these are also shown in the table. She has noticed that, if two customers are in the salon waiting for service, a new customer will not join the queue and leaves. Moreover, she

estimates that she incurs a goodwill (waiting) cost of $15.00 per hour when customers wait before service. An employee makes $18.00 an hour. Presently the price of a haircut is $30.00.

Time Between Arrivals		Service Time	
Minutes	RN Ranges	Minutes	RN Ranges
5	.000–< .068	15	.00–< .10
6	.068–< .200	20	.10–< .45
7	.200–< .532	25	.45–< .75
8	.532–< .800	30	.75–< .90
9	.800–< 1.000	35	.90–< 1.00
RN, random number.			

Simulate 10 arrivals with **two** employees. Assume the salon opens at 8:00 a.m., and keep track of (a) the time of arrival, (b) the times at which service begins and ends, (c) the waiting time before a haircut for each customer, (d) the number of customers waiting for service, and (e) the idle time for each employee. Use the random numbers provided in the following table. What is the cost (lost business + waiting + servers) of this system?

Arrival	1	2	3	4	5	6	7	8	9	10
IAT	.304	.169	.005	.239	.788	.525	.050	.862	.679	.451
ST	.97	.55	.46	.84	.18	.26	.54	.61	.23	.04
IAT, interarrival time; ST, service time.										

14. Use ExtendSim to simulate the data entry process for audit claims presented in Figure 8.23. Release the work every 4 minutes, every 6 minutes, and every 6.5 minutes at a constant rate. Which system shows the best performance in terms of (a) average time in the queue at the bottleneck and (b) the average time in the system? Simulate for 10,000 minutes using random number seed 1289.

   To find the time in the system,

   • Insert the Information block from the Item library between the Step/Activity 3 block and the Exit block

   • Double click on the Create block. In the Options tab, check the window next to Timing attribute and click on the drop-down menu. Select New Value Attribute. You will be prompted to enter a New Value attribute. Type "Time System."

   • Double click on the Information block. In the Statistics tab, in the Cycle Time section, click on the timing attribute drop-down menu, and select "Time System."

15. Using StatFit in ExtendSim, find the probability distributions of the interarrival times and processing times at Steps A, B, C, D, E, and F in the supplemental BPH Queuing Simulation data set. In the process depicted below, Activities C and D, and E are performed in parallel. Simulate the process for 10,000 minutes using random number seeds 2123 and 1451. Where is the bottleneck? What is the average time in the system?

Notes:

- Click on the Help tab in ExtendSim to get the step-by-step instructions on how to use StatFit. You will need the Random Number block from the Value library to launch StatFit.

- To simulate a parallel sub-process, place the Unbatch block (to split jobs) from the Item library right after Activity B, and place the Batch block (to integrate the split outputs) right before Activity F.

- You may use workstation blocks (which include both a queue and an activity) rather than separate queue and activity blocks to unclutter the simulation model.

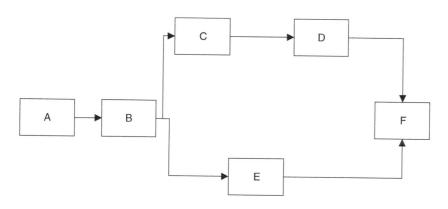

THINK OUTSIDE THE BOOK!

1. Give examples of process and flow units.

2. Read this following article:

    Jun, J. B., Jacobson, S. H., & Swisher, R. (1999). Application of discrete-event simulation in health care clinics: A survey. *Journal of the Operational Research Society 50*, 109–123.

    a. What are the primary areas where simulation has been used?

    b. What are the most fertile areas for future research?

3. Research the use of the TOC in healthcare. Is it really applicable in that industry? Why or why not?

REFERENCES

Anderson, D. R., Sweeney, D. J., Williams, T. A., Camm, J. D., & Martin, K. (2012). *An introduction to management science: Quantitative approaches to decision making.* Mason, OH: South-Western Cengage Learning.

Fomundam, S., & Herrmann, J. (2007). *A survey of queuing theory applications in healthcare.* College Park, MD: The Institute for Systems Research.

Goldratt, E. M. (2004). *The goal* (3rd rev. ed.). Great Barrington, MA: North River Press.

Little, J. D. C. (1961). A proof for the queuing formula: L = IW. *Operations Research, 9*(3), 383–387.

Mooney, C. Z. (1997). *Monte Carlo simulation.* Thousand Oaks, CA: Sage.

Shapiro, R. (2014, January 26). Man, 30, found dead after 8-hour wait in Bronx emergency room for rash. *New York Daily News.* Retrieved from http://www.nydailynews.com/new-york/bronx/man-30-dies-8-hour-wait-bronx-emergency-room-article-1.1591629

Stevenson, W. J., & Ozgur, C. (2007). *Introduction to management science with spreadsheets.* New York, NY: McGraw-Hill.

APPENDIX 8.1 – QUEUING SIMULATION WITH EXCEL

Excel Worksheet for Simulation With One Pharmacist (Web File)

	A	B	C	D	E	F	G	H	I
1		Interarrival	Arrival	Service	Service	Service	Time Waiting	Time in	Time Server
2	Order	Time	Time	Begins	Time	Ends	in Queue	the System	Is Idle
3	1	5	5	5	9.2	14.2	0	9.2	5
4	2	5	10	14.2	7.5	21.7	4.2	11.7	0
5	3	6	16	21.7	5.8	27.5	5.7	11.5	0
6	4	7	23	27.5	7.1	34.6	4.5	11.6	0
7	5	7	30	34.6	7.2	41.8	4.6	11.8	0
8	6	5	35	41.8	7.8	49.6	6.8	14.6	0
9	7	6	41	49.6	7.5	57.1	8.6	16.1	0
10	8	4	45	57.1	8.1	65.2	12.1	20.2	0
11	9	5	50	65.2	5.6	70.8	15.2	20.8	0
12	10	3	53	70.8	8.2	79	17.8	26	0
13									
14		5.3	30.8	38.75	7.4	46.15	7.95	15.35	0.5

Note: Microsoft Excel application interface is used with permission of Microsoft.

Formulas

	A	B	C	D	E	F	G	H	I
	Order	Interarrival Time	Arrival Time	Service Begins	Service Time	Service Ends	Time Waiting in Queue	Time in the System	Time Server Is Idle
3	1	5	5	5	=ROUND(NORM.INV(M3,7,1),1)	=SUM(D3:E3)	=D3-C3	=F3-C3	5
4	2	5	=C3+B4	=MAX(C4,F3)	=ROUND(NORM.INV(M4,7,1),1)	=SUM(D4:E4)	=D4-C4	=F4-C4	=D4-F3
5	3	6	=C4+B5	=MAX(C5,F4)	=ROUND(NORM.INV(M5,7,1),1)	=SUM(D5:E5)	=D5-C5	=F5-C5	=D5-F4
6	4	7	=C5+B6	=MAX(C6,F5)	=ROUND(NORM.INV(M6,7,1),1)	=SUM(D6:E6)	=D6-C6	=F6-C6	=D6-F5
7	5	7	=C6+B7	=MAX(C7,F6)	=ROUND(NORM.INV(M7,7,1),1)	=SUM(D7:E7)	=D7-C7	=F7-C7	=D7-F6
8	6	5	=C7+B8	=MAX(C8,F7)	=ROUND(NORM.INV(M8,7,1),1)	=SUM(D8:E8)	=D8-C8	=F8-C8	=D8-F7
9	7	6	=C8+B9	=MAX(C9,F8)	=ROUND(NORM.INV(M9,7,1),1)	=SUM(D9:E9)	=D9-C9	=F9-C9	=D9-F8
10	8	4	=C9+B10	=MAX(C10,F9)	=ROUND(NORM.INV(M10,7,1),1)	=SUM(D10:E10)	=D10-C10	=F10-C10	=D10-F9
11	9	5	=C10+B11	=MAX(C11,F10)	=ROUND(NORM.INV(M11,7,1),1)	=SUM(D11:E11)	=D11-C11	=F11-C11	=D11-F10
12	10	3	=C11+B12	=MAX(C12,F11)	=ROUND(NORM.INV(M12,7,1),1)	=SUM(D12:E12)	=D12-C12	=F12-C12	=D12-F11
13									
14		=AVERAGE(B3:B12)	=AVERAGE(C3:C12)	=AVERAGE(D3:D12)	=AVERAGE(E3:E12)	=AVERAGE(F3:F12)	=AVERAGE(G3:G12)	=AVERAGE(H3:H12)	=AVERAGE(I3:I12)

Note: Microsoft Excel application interface is used with permission of Microsoft.

Excel Worksheet for Simulation With Two Pharmacists (Web File)

Order	Interarrival Time	Arrival Time	Service Begins	Service Time	Service Ends	Time Waiting in Queue	Time in the System	P1 free	P2 free	Time Server Is Idle
1	5	5	5	9.2	14.2	0	9.2	14.2	0	5
2	5	10	10	7.5	17.5	0	7.5	14.2	17.5	10
3	6	16	16	5.8	21.8	0	5.8	21.8	17.5	1.8
4	7	23	23	7.1	30.1	0	7.1	21.8	30.1	5.5
5	7	30	30	7.2	37.2	0	7.2	37.2	30.1	8.2
6	5	35	35	7.8	42.8	0	7.8	37.2	42.8	4.9
7	6	41	41	7.5	48.5	0	7.5	48.5	42.8	3.8
8	4	45	45	8.1	53.1	0	8.1	48.5	53.1	2.2
9	5	50	50	5.6	55.6	0	5.6	55.6	53.1	1.5
10	3	53	53.1	8.2	61.3	0.1	8.3	55.6	61.3	0
	5.3			7.4		0.01	7.41			4.29

Formulas

	A	B	C	D	E	F	G	H	I	J	K
1	Order	Interarrival Time	Arrival Time	Service Begins	Service Time	Service Ends	Time Waiting in Queue	Time in the System	P1 free	P2 free	Time Server Is Idle
2											
3	1	5	5	5	=ROUND(NORM.INV(P3,7,1),1)	=SUM(D3:E3)	=D3-C3	=F3-C3	14.2	0	5
4	2	5	=C3+B4	=IF(C4<=MIN(I3:J3),MIN(I3:J3),C4)	=ROUND(NORM.INV(P4,7,1),1)	=SUM(D4:E4)	=D4-C4	=F4-C4	=IF(J3=MIN(I3:J3),F4,I3)	=IF(J3=MIN(I3:J3),F4,J3)	=D4-MIN(I3:J3)
5	3	6	=C4+B5	=IF(C5<=MIN(I4:J4),MIN(I4:J4),C5)	=ROUND(NORM.INV(P5,7,1),1)	=SUM(D5:E5)	=D5-C5	=F5-C5	=IF(J4=MIN(I4:J4),F5,I4)	=IF(J4=MIN(I4:J4),F5,J4)	=D5-MIN(I4:J4)
6	4	7	=C5+B6	=IF(C6<=MIN(I5:J5),MIN(I5:J5),C6)	=ROUND(NORM.INV(P6,7,1),1)	=SUM(D6:E6)	=D6-C6	=F6-C6	=IF(J5=MIN(I5:J5),F6,I5)	=IF(J5=MIN(I5:J5),F6,J5)	=D6-MIN(I5:J5)
7	5	7	=C6+B7	=IF(C7<=MIN(I6:J6),MIN(I6:J6),C7)	=ROUND(NORM.INV(P7,7,1),1)	=SUM(D7:E7)	=D7-C7	=F7-C7	=IF(J6=MIN(I6:J6),F7,I6)	=IF(J6=MIN(I6:J6),F7,J6)	=D7-MIN(I6:J6)
8	6	5	=C7+B8	=IF(C8<=MIN(I7:J7),MIN(I7:J7),C8)	=ROUND(NORM.INV(P8,7,1),1)	=SUM(D8:E8)	=D8-C8	=F8-C8	=IF(J7=MIN(I7:J7),F8,I7)	=IF(J7=MIN(I7:J7),F8,J7)	=D8-MIN(I7:J7)
9	7	6	=C8+B9	=IF(C9<=MIN(I8:J8),MIN(I8:J8),C9)	=ROUND(NORM.INV(P9,7,1),1)	=SUM(D9:E9)	=D9-C9	=F9-C9	=IF(J8=MIN(I8:J8),F9,I8)	=IF(J8=MIN(I8:J8),F9,J8)	=D9-MIN(I8:J8)
10	8	4	=C9+B10	=IF(C10<=MIN(I9:J9),MIN(I9:J9),C10)	=ROUND(NORM.INV(P10,7,1),1)	=SUM(D10:E10)	=D10-C10	=F10-C10	=IF(J9=MIN(I9:J9),F10,I9)	=IF(J9=MIN(I9:J9),F10,J9)	=D10-MIN(I9:J9)
11	9	5	=C10+B11	=IF(C11<=MIN(I10:J10),MIN(I10:J10),C11)	=ROUND(NORM.INV(P11,7,1),1)	=SUM(D11:E11)	=D11-C11	=F11-C11	=IF(J10=MIN(I10:J10),F11,I10)	=IF(J10=MIN(I10:J10),F11,J10)	=D11-MIN(I10:J10)
12	10	3	=C11+B12	=IF(C12<=MIN(I11:J11),MIN(I11:J11),C12)	=ROUND(NORM.INV(P12,7,1),1)	=SUM(D12:E12)	=D12-C12	=F12-C12	=IF(J11=MIN(I11:J11),F12,I11)	=IF(J11=MIN(I11:J11),F12,J11)	=D12-MIN(I11:J11)
13											
14		=AVERAGE(B3:			=AVERAGE(E3:E12)		=AVERAGE(G3:G12)	=AVERAGE(H3:+			=AVERAGE(K3:K12)
15											

Note: Microsoft Excel application interface is used with permission of Microsoft.

CHAPTER

SCHEDULING STAFF, PATIENTS, AND JOBS

BRADLEY PARK HOSPITAL 9.1

Jennifer was sitting at her desk looking over quality dashboards for the past 6 months and highlighting the numbers that she wanted to track closely when her phone rang.

"Jennifer?" the voice on the other end of the phone said. "I need your help. We are getting so many patient complaints about not being able to get into our clinic within a reasonable time frame. I don't know what has changed, but patients are getting a lot more demanding about being seen in a timely manner."

"I do know that Bradley Park Hospital's (BPH) reputation in the community for being patient-friendly is improving. Maybe people are expecting more of us!" Jennifer responded, "Who is this?"

"Oh, sorry. This is Dan Pinheiro in dermatology. As you know, dermatology is a high-volume clinic with many different procedures. I just saw this stack of complaints and know that if we want to continue to have patients come all the way across town to see us, we must address their concerns. Can you help?"

"Dr. Pinheiro! I will be happy to do what I can to help," Jennifer said. "When is a good time for us to meet?"

"Why don't you come by the clinic later this morning. You will see how busy we are and will meet Sally, our nurse manager."

"See you then," Jennifer responded as she began shuffling papers to find the dermatology dashboard.

INTRODUCTION AND LEARNING OBJECTIVES

Chapters 7 and 8 covered the challenges of balancing demand and capacity for a timely delivery of care. They highlighted the need to purge waste for smoother flows and demonstrated the relationships between patient arrivals and provider service times. Expanding on the latter concept, this chapter addresses the specific issues of workforce, job, and patient scheduling. It starts with the failure of the

Phoenix Veterans Administration (VA) Healthcare System (Box 9.1) to offer timely care to its patients, thus putting them at risk. This national scandal prompted the Department of Veterans Affairs to partner with the Institute of Medicine (IOM) to review the issues of scheduling, wait times, and timely access to care. The IOM (2015) report, *Transforming Health Care Scheduling and Access: Getting to Now*, brought to light promising strategies and best practices, which are thoroughly covered in this chapter. We also present new analytical tools appropriate for scheduling. Learning the materials in this chapter will help you to:

1. **Determine the major causes of care delays and waits**
2. **Identify the outcomes of excessive waits and delays**
3. **Establish staffing schedules using linear programming**
4. **Use job scheduling rules to speed up the flow of jobs through a process**
5. **Understand and evaluate various approaches to patient appointment scheduling**

✚ BOX 9.1 – OM IN PRACTICE!

Delays Continue at Phoenix VA

A 2014 investigation of the Phoenix VA Health Care System revealed that thousands of veterans had been waiting to see doctors, with 40 veterans dead while on the electronic waiting list. Scheduling records had been edited to hide the delays because there was not enough capacity to deal with the influx of patients. Much of the substandard care stemmed from the severe understaffing of the urology department. Despite legislation granting $16.3 billion for the VA to hire more doctors and nurses as well as patient referrals to private physicians, the backlog remained high with hundreds of cases behind. The office in the department was so shorthanded that clerks were unable to process the test results coming from private providers. As of 2015, efforts were under way to provide staffing relief (Zoroya, 2015).

BRADLEY PARK HOSPITAL 9.2

Sally met Jennifer at the registration desk. "Dr. Pinheiro is in with a patient, but he should be with us soon."

"Why don't you tell me what you think is going on, from your perspective," Jennifer asked.

Sally began, "This is a clinic with three, busy providers—Dr. Pinheiro, Dr. Baker, and Dr. Barari. All have very different styles of practicing. Dr. Pinheiro likes to have three patients come each hour on the hour so that he does not have to wait if someone is late. The problem is that one of those patients must wait at least 40 minutes to see him. And that is if he is on time!"

"Dr. Baker likes to see patients every 30 minutes, but there is a lot of time when she is just sitting waiting, and even then patients sometimes have to wait to see her. Dr. Barari uses a lot of the clinic staff because he wants patients put in an exam room as soon as they arrive, and he likes to have a nurse with him at all times as he moves from room to room."

"I believe that the patient complaints have made these physicians realize that they cannot continue to practice in their old, traditional way. But I am not sure what we need to do. I am so glad that Dr. Pinheiro called you!"

"Hello! Thanks for coming," Dr. Pinheiro bellowed as he approached Jennifer and Sally. "I told Sally that we need to approach the scheduling problem in a new way. I look forward to seeing what you suggest."

"This is a tough problem," Jennifer responded. "Let me gather some data on your patient schedules, staff schedules, and job duties. We can then get back together and talk."

"Why do you need information about the staff?" Dr. Pinheiro asked.

"The number of patients you can see in an hour, the clinic flow, and the bottlenecks all result from the interplay of demand and capacity. And one variable that you can control is the provider's willingness to change the way he or she is doing things!" Jennifer teased.

"We can talk about that!" Dr. Pinheiro smiled. "You will need to give me a good reason to change."

"I will get back with you soon," Jennifer ended. As she walked back to her office, she thought, "If we can get the dermatology clinic to flow better, we can begin to make BPH the provider of choice in our region!"

 What do you think of the dermatology clinic's current scheduling system? Is it patient centered?

WHAT ARE THE THREATS TO TIMELY CARE?

In Chapter 8, we learned that wait times originate from variability in arrivals (demand) and service (capacity). Although we then focused on wait times occurring during an appointment, the same dynamics regarding capacity and demand apply to the delays *before* getting an appointment (Box 9.3), which is the primary topic of this chapter (Box 9.2). As described in Box 9.1, the devastating consequences of care delays call for dependable scheduling solutions. **Scheduling** establishes the efficient timing of resources to provide services with minimal or no delay. Its effectiveness in ensuring timely delivery (Figure 9.1) rests not only on flow improvements and queue management (Chapters 7 and 8), but also on *accommodation,* the ease with which patients can make an appointment (Chapter 1).

Scheduling
Refers to the efficient timing of resources to provide services with minimal or no delay.

 BOX 9.2 – WORDS OF WISDOM

"There cannot be a crisis today; my schedule is already full" (Henry Kissinger quotes, n.d.).

FIGURE 9.1 – Mind map for delivery with scheduling.

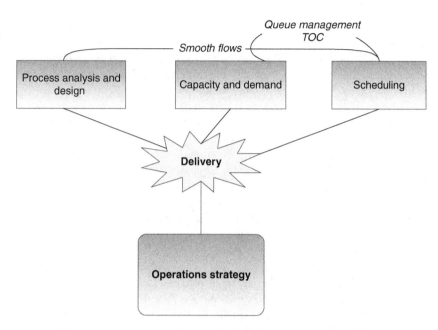

Demand
The number of calls for appointments received over a certain period of time, plus the number of walk-ins, emergencies, and follow-up appointments.

Capacity
The number of slots available plus additional resources such as alternative clinicians, backup arrangements with other clinics, and telemedicine.

There are several reasons why many scheduling systems fall short of meeting patients' needs and expectations.

1. **Superficial examination of variations in capacity and demand.** This is caused by poor operationalizations of capacity, demand and deficient record keeping. Most providers define *capacity* in terms of the number of slots available for a period of time, say a day, and by default view demand as the number of filled appointment slots. Both are inaccurate. **Demand** represents the number of calls for appointments received over a certain period of time, plus the number of walk-ins, emergencies, and follow-up appointments. In addition to the number of slots available, **capacity** should include additional resources

such as alternative clinicians, backup arrangements with other clinics, and telemedicine. **Telemedicine** involves the exchange of medical information (e.g., patient consultations, transmission of images, monitoring of vital signs) via telecommunication technologies (American Telemedicine Association, 2012). Providers fail to keep detailed records of the *actual* demand and capacity for their services as well as real-time data on call volume, waiting times, waiting lists, walk-ins, capacity utilization, and no-shows (Murray & Berwick, 2003).

Telemedicine
The exchange of medical information (patient consultations, transmission of images, monitoring of vital signs, etc.) via telecommunication technologies.

2. **Provider-centered systems misaligned with patients' needs**. The traditional scheduling systems accommodate providers' convenience rather than patients'. In primary care settings, demand is quite predictable, with a surge early in the morning and in the evening following work hours. Demand for services is also higher on Mondays and during the winter months. Capacity is also relatively stable. With such predictability, you would expect that scheduling decisions might accommodate patients' needs, but this is hardly the case. As mentioned previously, providers may not keep the records necessary to *plan for* rather than *react to* demand increases, and they try to avoid extending their office hours beyond 6:00 p.m. Patients' frustrations when trying to make timely appointments with their PCPs have spurred the growth of walk-in retail clinics.

3. **Shortage of clinical staff.** Box 9.1 stressed the role of understaffing in delaying access to care. Many claim that the Affordable Care Act intensified physician and nurse shortages by expanding access to care. Demand increases certainly squeeze an already tight capacity. However, the failure to construe demand and capacity properly exacerbates the situation. First, it is estimated that up to 25% of the calls do not require an on-site visit but could easily be addressed with telemedicine (Pearl, 2014). Second, failing to exploit resources other than physicians does little to improve the situation. The responsibilities of non-physician clinicians should be redefined to include services such as immunizations and previsit record screens. Nurse practitioners and physician assistants especially could facilitate care coordination among various providers, manage informatics, and even serve as primary care providers themselves in some situations.

4. **Inefficient process design with disrupted flows**. The non–value-added activities along with fragmented care replete with uncoordinated handoffs (Chapter 7) among providers are obvious sources of delays. Compounding the problem is that when multiple providers are involved in a patient's care, the variabilities in each one's capacity and demand accumulate and worsen the magnitude of delays. Even if one provider

has a clear perspective of demand and capacity in his or her own practice, the flow of the system is constrained by the performance of the weakest link in the system (see Theory of Constraints in Chapter 8).

The shortcomings have negative consequences for both providers and patients.

CONSEQUENCES OF CARE DELAYS

It is evident that care delays may have a negative impact on a patient's health. It is less obvious that they also result in lower revenue for providers.

1. **Lower quality of care** ensues from the inability to make a timely appointment as patients seek alternative, sometimes unorthodox, forms of treatment or decide to forgo healthcare altogether. Even if they manage to see their provider of choice at a later point in time, delayed diagnosis and treatment may affect their health adversely, leading to prolonged and/or more radical treatment. There is evidence to show that these unfortunate effects increase mortality and morbidity while decreasing the quality of life as a result of pain and illness (Coates, 1999; Desmeules, Dionne, Belzile, Bourbonnais, & Fremont, 2012; Sobolev, Levy, Kuramoto, Hayden, & Fitzgerald, 2006). Deterioration of one's health status is especially severe for elderly patients and those suffering from mental illnesses.

2. Patients incur **higher costs** resulting from no or lower reimbursement from their insurer when they seek noncovered forms of care or when they elect to see another provider who is out of network (IOM, 2015). If their condition worsens, preventable hospitalizations and more aggressive treatments will inflate their health-related expenses. Similarly, the inability to get a quick appointment with their PCP may lead to expensive visits to the emergency department (ED) or an urgent care facility. Finally, patients may miss work or experience declines in productivity, both of which affect their incomes. When patients who are insured through corporate contracts are involved in these situations, the provider runs the risk of losing a lucrative business contract.

3. Long delays in getting an appointment often lead to **patient dissatisfaction**. The unpleasant experience shapes the perception of the quality of care and of the medical facility's image (Llanwarne et al., 2013). Longer wait times even influence patients' opinions of the quality of treatment and instructions received (Bleustein et al., 2014).

4. **Increase in no-shows**. Long wait times increase patients' frustration and feelings of inconvenience, leading them to miss their first appointment or the return appointment for

follow-up care. In these cases, care is not delayed, but it is missed altogether, resulting in adverse health outcomes. Even if patients do not intend to miss their appointment, the long time span between the call and the appointment makes it more likely that they will simply forget the appointment. Assuming they decide to reschedule an appointment, which is uncertain, they will likely have to wait for their next appointment, delaying care even further.

5. **Loss of revenue for providers**. No-shows decrease the utilization of the resources involved in those patients' care: providers, space, and equipment. PCPs may recapture these losses if there are enough walk-ins to fill the now-open slots in their schedules. Other providers are very unlikely to have that opportunity. Basically, a no-show translates into a loss of income, especially if patients decide to switch providers. For patients postponing care with a provider because of care delays, poor health outcomes and patients' experiences affect reimbursement levels by payers (see value-based payment in Chapter 4) and therefore providers' bottom lines.

There have been many efforts aimed at improving scheduling systems. All require accurate estimates of capacity and demand. These estimates help formulate adequate staff schedules. They also assist in scheduling jobs associated with patient care (lab tests, minor health [information technology] IT system fixes, etc.). In providing adequate staff availability and alleviating job backlogs, both staff and job scheduling lay the foundations for reliable appointment scheduling systems.

STAFF SCHEDULING

Staff scheduling involves the assignment of personnel in various departments and time slots such as shifts. There are several commercial scheduling packages for medical groups with complex requirements. For simple cases with fairly stable demand and capacity, integer linear programming can be used to generate optimal schedules.

For example, assume that the nurse manager of the orthopedics department is preparing the nursing schedule for Friday, the busiest day. The staff consists of both part-time and full-time nurses. Part-time nurses work 4-hour shifts and are paid $100 per shift, whereas full-time nurses work the normal 8-hour shift for $330. The day is divided into six different time periods, each corresponding to a 4-hour period. Using queuing models, the following capacity needs have been determined (Table 9.1). For each time period, the number of full-time nurses should exceed or be on par with that of the part-time nurses. Moreover, there should be at least three full-time nurses in each time period. The objective of the schedule is to meet Friday's capacity needs at the lowest possible cost.

Staff Scheduling
The assignment of personnel in various departments and time slots such as shifts.

TABLE 9.1 – Staffing Requirements in Orthopedics Department

Time Period	Required Number of Nurses
1. 8:00 a.m.–12:00 p.m.	8
2. 12:00–4:00 p.m.	12
3. 4:00–8:00 p.m.	16
4. 8:00 p.m.–12:00 a.m.	10
5. 12:00– 4:00 a.m.	6
6. 4:00–8:00 a.m.	5

You may recall from Chapter 3 that the first step in simple linear programming is to specify the decision variables. In this problem, there are two sets of six decision variables:

FN_i = number of full-time nurses starting in period i ($i = 1$–6)

PN_i = number of part-time nurses starting in period i ($i = 1$–6).

The next step is to formulate the objective function, which is to minimize the total cost of staffing:

Minimize: Cost = $330\,FN_1 + 330\,FN_2 + 330\,FN_3 + 330\,FN_4 + 330\,FN_5 + 330\,FN_6 + 100\,PN_1 + 100\,PN_2 + 100\,PN_3 + 100\,PN_4 + 100\,PN_5 + 100\,PN_6$.

The constraints are then formulated. There are several sets of constraints in this problem: (a) the total number of part-time and full-time nurses working during a particular time period must be enough to meet the capacity needs for that period, (b) there must be at least three full-time nurses starting their shift in a given time period, (c) the number of full-time nurses may not be lower than that of the part-time nurses in a given time period, and (d) the logical constraints require that all decision variables take on positive, integer values.

First Set

$FN_1 + FN_6 + PN_1 \geq 8$ (the number of full-time nurses who started their shift at 8:00 a.m. + the number of full-time nurses who started their shift at 4:00 a.m. + the number of part-time nurses who started their shift at 8:00 a.m.)

They work 8 hours, so they will be working until noon.

$FN_1 + FN_2 + PN_2 \geq 12$ (capacity requirement for nurses working from 12:00 to 4:00 p.m.)

$FN_2 + FN_3 + PN_3 \geq 16$ (capacity requirement for nurses working from 4:00 to 8:00 p.m.)

$FN_3 + FN_4 + PN_4 \geq 10$ (capacity requirement for nurses working from 8:00 p.m. to 12:00 a.m.)

$FN_4 + FN_5 + PN_5 \geq 6$ (capacity requirement for nurses working from 12:00 to 4:00 a.m.)

$FN_5 + FN_6 + PN_6 \geq 5$ (capacity requirement for nurses working from 4:00 to 8:00 a.m.)

Second Set

$FN_1 \geq 3$ (the number of full-time nurses must be 3 or more in a given time period)

$FN_2 \geq 3$

$FN_3 \geq 3$

$FN_4 \geq 3$

$FN_5 \geq 3$

$FN_6 \geq 3$

Third Set

$FN_1 + FN_6 \geq PN_1$ (the number of full-time nurses must be greater than or equal to the number of part-time nurses)

$FN_1 + FN_2 \geq PN_2$

$FN_2 + FN_3 \geq PN_3$

$FN_3 + FN_4 \geq PN_4$

$FN_4 + FN_5 \geq PN_5$

$FN_5 + FN_6 \geq PN_6$

Logical Constraints

$FN_i, PN_i \geq 0$ and integer $(i = 1\text{–}6)$ (the decision variables must take on positive integer values because people cannot be split into fractional parts; this is a special case of linear programming called *integer linear programming*)

The Excel solution is presented in Figure 9.2 (formulas and solver dialog boxes are shown in Appendix 9.1). The schedule calls for:

	A	B	C	D	E	F	G	H	I	J	K	L	M	N	O	P
1				COST MATRIX									SOLUTION			
2																
3			Friday 1	Friday 2	Friday 3	Friday 4	Friday 5	Friday 6			Friday 1	Friday 2	Friday 3	Friday 4	Friday 5	Friday 6
4		PN1	100							PN1	2	0	0	0	0	0
5		PN2		100						PN2	0	4	0	0	0	0
6		PN3			100					PN3	0	0	8	0	0	0
7		PN4				100				PN4	0	0	0	4	0	0
8		PN5					100			PN5	0	0	0	0	0	0
9		PN6						100		PN6	0	0	0	0	0	0
10		FN1	330							FN1	3	0	0	0	0	0
11		FN2		330						FN2	0	5	0	0	0	0
12		FN3			330					FN3	0	0	3	0	0	0
13		FN4				330				FN4	0	0	0	3	0	0
14		FN5					330			FN5	0	0	0	0	3	0
15		FN6						330		FN6	0	0	0	0	0	3
16																
17									Nurses assigned		8	12	16	10	6	6
18									Sign		≥	≥	≥	≥	≥	≥
19									Nurses needed		8	12	16	10	6	5
20									FT nurses		6	8	8	6	6	6
21																
22										TC			8400			
23																

FIGURE 9.2 – Excel solution for nurse scheduling problem.
Note: Microsoft Excel application interface is used with permission of Microsoft.

- Six full-time nurses and two part-time nurses from 8:00 a.m. to 12:00 p.m.

- Eight full-time nurses and four part-time nurses from 12:00 to 4:00 p.m.

- Eight full-time nurses and eight part-time nurses from 4:00 to 8:00 p.m.

- Six full-time nurses and four part-time nurses from 8:00 p.m. to 12:00 a.m.

- Six full-time nurses and zero part-time nurses from 12:00 to 4:00 a.m.

- Six full-time nurses and zero part-time nurses from 4:00 to 8:00 a.m.

The total cost of the Friday schedule is \$8,400.[1] Please note that this was a very simple problem. Yet, the model included 12 decision variables and 18 constraints (excluding non-negativity). Imagine what the model would be if the schedule were generated for each day of the month and included nurses' personal scheduling preferences, days off, and so on. This is why many staff scheduling software packages with built-in algorithms are available in healthcare.

JOB SCHEDULING

Job Scheduling

A tactic used to sequence a series of jobs for processing in order to decrease tardiness, congestion, or some other criterion.

Job scheduling is a tactic used to sequence a series of jobs for processing. For example, a hospital lab receives multiple specimens with processing requirements. The selected processing sequence can have a significant impact on the turnaround times and average tardiness for the lab. Similarly, the IT staff in a large hospital typically receives numerous requests for small system changes every day. The time estimates to make some of those changes are fairly well established and the change orders can be first triaged and then queued in a sequence that will reduce the backlog quickly or lower the average turnaround times. Finally, if you have had surgery before, you must have realized that your time of arrival at the hospital did not necessarily determine the order in which surgeries were performed. Rather operating room (OR) schedulers may have used sequencing rules that boosted the utilization of the OR.

Sequencing Rules

First Come, First Served (FCFS) Sequencing Rule

A rule that states that jobs are processed in their order of arrival into the system.

The rules are essentially heuristics, that is, rules of thumb that help people solve problems quickly. They do not guarantee an optimal solution, but their simplicity makes them very attractive in practice. The most popular rules are as follows.

First Come, First Served

According to this rule, jobs are processed in their order of arrival into the system. Although not the most efficient rule, it is often used when customers are present and witness the process. Why? Because they perceive FCFS as being a fair system. However, you must also know from your own experience that when customers ahead of you require longer service times, queues build up, and service for the remaining customers slows down. For these reasons, FCFS typically does not promote a smooth and rapid flow through a system.

Shortest Processing Time

With this rule, the jobs are processed according to the time it takes to complete them, starting with the job that takes the least amount of time to perform, followed by the job that takes the next least amount of time, and so on. This is a very popular rule that is effective in reducing overall congestion or backlog in the system. An example of this rule in practice is ED patients with low-acuity illnesses being fast tracked. As jobs or patients move faster through the system, queues tend to be more manageable, and downstream idle time is reduced. However, longer jobs will be postponed, sometimes for very long periods of time if short jobs keep on entering the system. For this reason, the SPT rule may be modified to place a job ahead of the queue when the wait time exceeds a certain limit (Stevenson, 2012).

Earliest Due Date

As its name indicates, the EDD rule involves the processing of jobs according to their due date, with the job having the earliest due date being processed first, the job with the second earliest due date being processed second, and so on. This rule decreases the tardiness of jobs, which makes it attractive to many users. Despite its appeal, it does not take processing time into consideration. Short jobs may remain in the queue for quite some time and clog the process unnecessarily.

Slack Time Remaining

Slack time is the difference between the time remaining before a job's due date and the time needed to complete it. The STR rule will process the job with the least slack time—the one with the least laxity—first, followed by the job with the next least slack time, and so on:

$$STR = (Due\ date - Today's\ date) - Processing\ time \qquad [9.1]$$

Critical Ratio

The critical ratio is computed by dividing the time remaining until a job's due date and its processing time. Using this rule, priority is given to the job with the lowest critical ratio. This is a dynamic rule that reevaluates the situation after scheduling each job, one at a time. CR tends to perform better than other rules in terms of average lateness or tardiness:

$$CR = \frac{Due\ date - Today's\ date}{Processing\ time} \qquad [9.2]$$

Shortest Processing Time (SPT) Sequencing Rule

Jobs are processed according to the time it takes to complete them, starting with the job that takes the least amount of time to perform, followed by the job that takes the next least amount of time, and so on.

Earliest Due Date (EDD) Sequencing Rule

Jobs are processed according to their due date, with the job having the earliest due date being processed first, the job with the second earliest due date being processed second, and so on.

Slack Time Remaining (STR) Sequencing Rule

The job with the least slack time—the least laxity—is processed first, followed by the job with the next least slack time, and so on.

Critical Ratio (CR) Rule

Priority is given to the job with the lowest critical ratio. This is a dynamic rule that reevaluates the situation after scheduling each job, one at a time. After reevaluation, the job with the lowest critical ratio will be processed, and so on.

Here are the rules:

- If CR = 1, there is just enough time to complete the job.
- If CR > 1, there is more than enough time to complete the job.
- If CR < 1, there is not enough time to complete the job.

Rush
A job is given priority because it is an emergency or is for preferred customers.

Rush

A job is given priority because it is an emergency or is for preferred customers. This rule should only be applied when warranted because it disrupts schedules and creates backlogs for other jobs.

Performance Measures

A schedule must meet several objectives associated with the process: maximize output over a certain period of time, satisfy customers' needs, maximize resource utilization, and so on. Achievement of these objectives is determined by performance on certain measures. Some of the most common performance measures are as follows.

Makespan
The total time required to complete a set of jobs.

Makespan

Makespan is the total time required to complete a set of jobs; it should be *minimized*. Note that if only one resource is available, the makespan will be uniform across all sequencing rules.

Tardiness
The amount of time by which the completion time exceeds the due date.

Tardiness

Tardiness is the amount of time by which the completion time exceeds the due date; it should be *minimized*.

Weighted Tardiness
The product of a weight assigned to a job and its tardiness.

Weighted Tardiness

When some jobs are more important than others, they may be assigned a weight reflecting their importance (contribution to revenue, preferred customer, etc.). Weighted tardiness is the product of the weight assigned to a job and its tardiness; it should be *minimized*.

Tardy Job
A job that is completed after its due date.

Number of Tardy Jobs

A job is tardy if its completion date is past its due date. The number of tardy jobs in the whole set of jobs should be *minimized*.

Flow Time
The total time a job spends in the system (from arrival to completion).

Flow Time

Flow time is the total time (waiting + processing) a job spends in the system (from arrival to completion); it should be *minimized*.

At Bradley Park Hospital, one lab employee has just been assigned the five following jobs in the sequence shown in Table 9.2. She knows that late test results are unacceptable to both physicians and patients. Although she usually processes the specimens on an FCFS basis, she decides to evaluate multiple sequencing rules on their ability to minimize tardiness. Time 0 is now and the importance of these jobs is reflected by the weight they have been assigned (1–20). For the sake of simplicity, she assumes that the time to switch from one job to the other is negligible. In other words, if job A is completed after 20 minutes, the lab technician can start processing the next job immediately.

TABLE 9.2 – Assigned Jobs at BPH Lab

Job	Arrival Time	Processing Time (min)	Due Date/ Time (min)	Importance Weight (1–20)	Slack Time	Critical Ratio
A	0	20	20	5	0	1
B	0	10	15	14	5	1.5
C	0	30	50	8	20	1.67
D	0	15	30	12	15	2.0
E	0	12	40	6	28	3.33

Tables 9.3 to 9.10 show the schedules generated by each rule. Based on their arrival times, the jobs were received in the lab in the following order: A, B, C, D, and E. This is the order in which they will be processed according to the FCFS rule (Table 9.3).

TABLE 9.3 – Schedule With FCFS

Job Sequence	Start Time	Proc. Time	End Time/ Flow Time	Due Date	Tardiness	Weighted Tardiness	Tardy? (Yes/No)
A	0	20	20	20	0	0	No
B	20	10	30	15	15	210	Yes
C	30	30	60	50	10	80	Yes
D	60	15	75	30	45	540	Yes
E	75	12	87	40	47	282	Yes
Total			272 min		117 min	1,112 min	4 jobs

The SPT rule focuses on the shortest processing times. The processing times in ascending order are 10, 12, 15, 20, and 30 minutes for jobs B, E, D, A, and C, respectively (Table 9.4).

TABLE 9.4 – Schedule With SPT

Job Sequence	Start Time	Proc. Time	End Time/ Flow Time	Due Date	Tardiness	Weighted Tardiness	Tardy? (Yes/No)
B	0	10	10	15	0	0	No
E	10	12	22	40	0	0	No
D	22	15	37	30	7	84	Yes
A	37	20	57	20	37	185	Yes
C	57	30	87	50	37	296	Yes
Total			213 min		81 min	565 min	3 jobs

The EDD rule emphasizes the due dates. The due dates in ascending order are 15, 20, 30, 40, and 50 minutes for jobs B, A, D, E, and C, respectively (Table 9.5).

TABLE 9.5 – Schedule With EDD

Job Sequence	Start Time	Proc. Time	End Time/ Flow Time	Due Date	Tardiness	Weighted Tardiness	Tardy? (Yes/No)
B	0	10	10	15	0	0	No
A	10	20	30	20	10	50	Yes
D	30	15	45	30	15	180	Yes
E	45	12	57	40	17	102	Yes
C	57	30	87	50	37	296	Yes
Total			229 min		79 min	628 min	4 jobs

For the STR rule, the slack times remaining in ascending order are 0, 5, 15, 20, and 28 minutes for jobs A, B, D, C, and E, respectively (Table 9.6).

TABLE 9.6 – Schedule With STR

Job Sequence	Start Time	Proc. Time	End Time/ Flow Time	Due Date	Tardiness	Weighted Tardiness	Tardy? (Yes/No)
A	0	20	20	20	0	0	No
B	20	10	30	15	15	210	Yes
D	30	15	45	30	15	180	Yes
C	45	30	75	50	25	200	Yes
E	75	12	87	40	47	282	Yes
Total			257 min		102 min	872 min	4 jobs

In Table 9.2, the CRs were 1, 1.5, 1.67, 2, and 3.33, in ascending order. These CRs correspond to jobs A, B, C, D, and E. However, the CR rule is dynamic, which means that the CRs will be recomputed for each remaining job after a job has been scheduled (Table 9.7a–9.7d).

Because it has the lowest CR, job A is started first at time = 0. It takes 20 minutes to process. At minute 20 (job A completed), the CRs are recomputed (Table 9.7a).

TABLE 9.7(a) – Job A Was Assigned

Job Sequence	Proc. Time	Due Date	CR
A	—	—	—
B	10	15	$(15 - 20)/10 = -0.5$ *
C	30	50	$(50 - 20)/30 = 1$
D	15	30	$(30 - 20)/15 = 0.67$
E	12	40	$(40 - 20)/12 = 1.67$
* Lowest CR			

Because job B has the lowest CR, it will be scheduled next. It takes 10 minutes to process and will be completed at minute 20 + 10 = 30. When B is completed, the CRs are recomputed (Table 9.7b).

TABLE 9.7(b) – Job B Was Assigned

Job Sequence	Proc. Time	Due Date	CR
A	—	—	—
B	—	—	—
C	30	50	(50–30)/30 = 0.67
D	15	30	(30–30)/15 = 0*
E	12	40	(40–30)/12 = 0.83
* Lowest CR			

Job D has the lowest CR and will be scheduled next. D requires 15 minutes of processing time and will be completed at minute 30 + 15 = 45. When D is scheduled, the CRs are recomputed (Table 9.7c).

TABLE 9.7(c) – Job D Was Assigned

Job Sequence	Proc. Time	Due Date	CR
A	—	—	—
B	—	—	—
C	30	50	(50 – 45)/30 = 0.17
D	—	—	—
E	12	40	(40 – 45)/12 = – 0.42*
* Lowest CR			

Job E has the lowest CR and will be scheduled next. E requires 12 minutes of processing time and will be completed at minute 45 + 12 = 57. Only job C will remain to be processed and will therefore be scheduled last. The final schedule using the CR rule is presented in Table 9.7d.

TABLE 9.7(d) – Schedule With CR

Job Sequence	Start Time	Proc. Time	End Time/ Flow time	Due Date	Tardiness	Weighted Tardiness	Tardy? (Yes/No)
A	0	20	20	20	0	0	No
B	20	10	30	15	15	210	Yes
D	30	15	45	30	15	180	Yes
E	45	12	57	40	17	102	Yes
C	57	30	87	50	37	296	Yes
Total		239 min			84 min	788 min	4 jobs

Each sequencing rule produced different results (Table 9.8). The FCFS rule produced the worst results by far. The SPT rule performed very well with a total tardiness of 81 min, a weighted tardiness of 565 minutes, and a flow time of 213 minutes. Only three jobs were late when using this rule. The EDD rule yielded the lowest tardiness but did not fare as well as the SPT rule in terms of tardy jobs and flow time. The STR rule yielded poor results. As for CR, it yielded low tardiness as well. Overall, the SPT, EDD, and CR rules performed the best in terms of tardiness. As far as weighted tardiness is concerned, the SPT rule fared better, but the results are tied to the weights in this example. Another set of weights might have been more favorable to another rule. In fact, the performance of a rule depends on the circumstances and the environment. Organizations should be well informed about these circumstances before selecting a rule.

TABLE 9.8 – Comparison of Five Rules in BPH Lab Example				
Rule	Tardiness (min)	Weighted Tardiness (min)	Number of Tardy Jobs	Flow Time (min)
FCFS	117	1,112	4	272
SPT	81	565	3	213
EDD	79	628	4	229
STR	102	872	4	257
CR	84	788	4	239

Moore's Algorithm

Moore's Algorithm
An algorithm used to minimize the number of tardy jobs when the jobs are equally important.

Moore's algorithm can be used to minimize the number of tardy jobs if the jobs are of equal weight or importance (Laguna & Marklund, 2005). It involves the following steps.

STEP 1: Use the EDD rule to sequence the jobs (see Table 9.5).

STEP 2: If there are no tardy jobs, the optimal solution has been found, and there is no need to continue.

There are four tardy jobs in our example.

STEP 3: Find the first tardy job in the sequence. Let us call it the kth job, where k designates its place in the sequence.

In Table 9.5, job A is the first tardy job. It is the second job in the sequence.

STEP 4: Remove the job with the longest processing time from the top of the list down to, and including, the kth job. It will be placed at the end of the sequence obtained when the algorithm stops.

In the example, job A, the kth job, has the longest processing time, that is, 20 minutes. It is removed from the sequence (Table 9.9).

STEP 5: Revise the EDD schedule (Table 9.9) and go back to step 2.

Job C, the last job, is the only tardy job in the revised EDD schedule. It is removed. After removing jobs A and C, the remaining jobs are not tardy. The algorithm ends, and we add A and C at the bottom of the sequence (Table 9.10). There are now only two tardy jobs, and the total tardiness is only 74 minutes. In this example, not only did Moore's algorithm minimize the number of tardy jobs, as expected, but it also minimized tardiness. Its flow time is also very close to that achieved with the SPT rule.

TABLE 9.9 – Steps 4 and 5 of Moore's Algorithm

Job Sequence	Start Time	Proc. Time	End Time	Due Date	Tardiness	Tardy? (Yes/No)
B	0	10	10	15	0	No
D	10	15	25	30	0	No
E	25	12	37	40	0	No
C	37	30	67	50	17	Yes

Next job to be deleted

TABLE 9.10 – Schedule With Moore's Algorithm

Job Sequence	Start Time	Proc. Time	End Time/ Flow Time	Due Date	Tardiness	Tardy? (Yes/No)
B	0	10	10	15	0	No
D	10	15	25	30	0	No
E	25	12	37	40	0	No
A	37	20	57	20	37	Yes
C	57	30	87	50	37	Yes
Total		216 min			74 min	2 jobs

PATIENT APPOINTMENT SCHEDULING

Scheduling staff and jobs is a necessary but not sufficient condition to develop schedules that minimize patients' time to get an appointment and use provider resources efficiently. When established on the basis of accurate demand and capacity data, staff schedules mesh with patient appointment scheduling systems. There are three major types of appointment scheduling systems in healthcare: (a) block scheduling, (b) modified block scheduling, and (c) individual scheduling. **Block scheduling** is common for surgery cases. Surgeons are assigned blocks of time in the OR, and patients' surgeries are scheduled within those time frames. In the case of elective surgeries, the patients are often scheduled on an FCFS basis (Gupta & Denton, 2008). One of the problems with this technique is that it results in substantial unused OR time. **Modified block scheduling** assigns a small number of patients to short time blocks such as 2 hours. Based on a review of block use, a medical executive committee establishes a schedule to maximize OR utilization (McLane, 2005). **Individual scheduling** is the predominant type of scheduling in the United States; a single patient is scheduled at a particular time on a specific day according to the provider's availability (IOM, 2015). It is the system of choice for most primary care practices.

In its review of the current state of patient scheduling in the United States, the 2015 IOM report referenced at the beginning of the chapter deplored the lack of patient centeredness in most systems. Most appointment scheduling systems reflect a bias toward providers' convenience while ignoring patients' preferences. New technologies

Block Scheduling
Blocks of time are made available, and multiple patients are scheduled within those time frames.

Modified Block Scheduling
A small number of patients are assigned to short time blocks such as 2 hours. Based on a review of block use, a medical executive committee establishes a schedule to maximize capacity utilization.

Individual Scheduling
A single patient is scheduled at a particular time on a specific day according to the provider's availability.

and systems have been tested at multiple health centers across the country, enabling the IOM to issue a set of best practices for ambulatory and emergency/inpatient care. We review these practices in the remainder of the chapter.

Ambulatory Care

For ambulatory care, an immediate-response approach for new and returning patients should be emphasized. One of the early models for outpatient care scheduling was Welch and Bailey's (1952) model. This model is similar to an individual scheduling system, but it assigns two patients to the first appointment slot and none to the last one. It has shown robust performance over a wide range of situations (Sickinger & Kolisch, 2009). Many other models have emerged over the years, such as the Kaandorp and Koole (2007) optimal outpatient appointment scheduling model, which is available for public use at http://calculator.gerkoole.com/appointment-scheduler. The time that a facility is available for care is divided into time intervals of equal length. The objectives of the schedule are to minimize the weighted average of patients' wait times, providers' idle time, and tardiness. The weight (alpha) reflects the importance of the performance measure in the optimization function (here, minimization). The percentage of no-shows based on historical data can also be inputted.

BRADLEY PARK HOSPITAL 9.3

In an effort to improve patient flow in the dermatology clinic, Dr. Pinheiro and his partners, Drs. Baker and Barari, tested the Kaandorp and Koole tool recommended by Jennifer to improve their appointment schedule. Patient surveys had indicated that some patients complained of delays before getting an appointment and long wait times before seeing the doctor. Despite this apparent congestion, some of the physicians were idle at various times of the day. They first tested the model with Dr. Baker's patients. Dr. Baker usually sees patients from noon to 6:00 p.m. A careful analysis of the service times showed that they were exponentially distributed with an average of 25 minutes. She likes to schedule appointments every 30 minutes, which gives her time to schedule 12 patients per day. Because she was quite concerned about delays, she assigned weights of 2.0 to wait time, 0.5 to idle time, and 0.8 to tardiness in the model.

The results shown at the bottom of Figure 9.3 indicate that the individual schedule she had developed with one patient in each time slot (left column) produces an average wait time of about 20 minutes for the patient, an idle time of 91.05 minutes, and a tardiness of 31.75 minutes. The probability that the last patient finishes his or her treatment after the end of the day (fraction of excess) is about 0.60. The average total time to see all patients, the makespan, is 385.05 minutes. The Kaandorp and Koole model follows the Welch–Bailey rule. It assigns two patients to the first time slot, and leaves the last slot unfilled. The result (right column) shows an increased wait time of nearly 26 minutes, but much lower idle time and tardiness. Moreover, Dr. Baker sees that there is a lower probability that her last patient's visit will extend past the end of the day (fraction of excess is only 0.37) so that she can go home early. However, she realizes that 26 minutes of wait time is an average . . . some patients would have to wait longer than that. There should be a better way to accommodate patients.

Why did the tool generate a schedule with rather long wait times?

			Optimal outpatient appointment scheduling tool
Average service time	25	minutes	
Number of intervals	12		
Length of interval	30	minutes	Press the button to
Total number of arrivals	12		compute the solutions
Percentage no-shows	2	%	Finished searching.
alpha waiting	2.0		
alpha idle time	0.5		
alpha tardiness	0.8		

		☑ Number of patients of your choice (calc time: several seconds)	☑ ⦿ Small Neighborhood (Suboptimal, calc time: several minutes) ◯ Full Neighborhood (Optimal, calc time: several hours)
Interval	*Time*		
1	0:00	1	2
2	0:30	1	1
3	1:00	1	1
4	1:30	1	1
5	2:00	1	1
6	2:30	1	1
7	3:00	1	1
8	3:30	1	1
9	4:00	1	1
10	4:30	1	1
11	5:00	1	1
12	5:30	1	0
Waiting time		19.94 minutes	25.87 minutes
Idle time		91.05 minutes	63.76 minutes
Tardiness		31.75 minutes	19.74 minutes
Fraction of excess		59.94 %	36.99 %
Makespan		385.05 minutes	357.76 minutes
Lateness		25.05 minutes	-2.24 minutes
Object Value		110.79	99.41

FIGURE 9.3 – Appointment schedule for Dr. Baker's patients.
Note: Appointment scheduler Copyright © 2007 Guido Kaandorp and Ger Koole (http://calculator.gerkoole.com/appointment-scheduler). Interface reproduced with permission.

The schedule generated for Dr. Baker's patients rearranged the individual scheduling system, but did little to empower the patients themselves to make appointments suiting their own needs and schedules. For primary care especially, many patients would prefer same-day scheduling. The open/advanced access model of patient scheduling offers this opportunity.

Open Access Patient Scheduling

⊗ BOX 9.4 – WORDS OF WISDOM

"[Advanced access scheduling] has one very simple yet challenging rule: Do today's work today" (Murray & Tantau, 2000, p. 46).

Open-Access Scheduling

Also known as advanced access or same-day scheduling, makes it possible for patients to obtain an appointment on the day they call if they so desire, most likely with their own physician.

Open-access scheduling, also known as advanced access or same-day scheduling, makes it possible for patients to obtain an appointment on the day they call if they so desire, most likely with their own physician (Agency for Healthcare Research and Quality, 2015). The system was created by Dr. Murray and Ms. Tantau when they were managing a very large primary care clinic (see Box 9.4). The long waits and delays to get an appointment (about 55 days) had convinced them that they needed to hire more physicians and staff to absorb their huge backlog. After several attempts to refine the system with no measurable success, they decided to create a brand-new kind of patient-centered system. This system required physicians to let go of well-entrenched beliefs that there are two types of cases: urgent (patients need to be seen now!) and routine (patients can wait). With open access, all patients who can be seen today will be seen today because contrary to the traditional, individual scheduling system in which 100% of the capacity is booked for the day, the open-access system has most of its capacity available for the day. How does this happen? The principles of the open-access model are listed here (Murray & Tantau, 2000).

1. **Gain capacity by doing all of today's work today.** A priori, demand seems to be unlimited, but in reality, in most cases, it is pretty close to the capacity available. It is hard to even imagine this because the backlog creates the impression of unending work. With open-access systems, most of the appointment slots are open for patients who want same-day appointments.

2. **Trim the backlog or appointment debt.** This is by far the most demanding task, which will require quite a bit of overtime for several weeks or even months (Box 9.5). Setting a deadline for backlog elimination and agreeing not to make appointments past that date are helpful tactics to smooth implementation of the open-access model. To determine the deadline, it is important to assess the current backlog and then evaluate the impact of increasing capacity.

$$\text{Current backlog} = \text{All future appointments on the schedule} \qquad [9.3]$$

$$\text{Extra capacity provided} = \text{Number of extra patients} \atop \text{who will be seen every day} \quad [9.4]$$

$$\text{Days to reduce the backlog} = \frac{\text{Current backlog}}{\text{Extra capacity}} \quad [9.5]$$

For example, if the backlog is 300 appointments, and the provider decides to see five more patients every day, the time to reduce the backlog will be 60 days. Reevaluating the frequency with which follow-ups are needed is a good method to reduce the "bad backlog," that is, provider-recommended appointments that are not based on clinical necessity. When smart strategies are followed, the actual time needed to reduce the backlog is less than the computed number.

 BOX 9.5 – OM IN PRACTICE!

Advanced/Open-Access Scheduling at Southcentral Foundation's Alaska Native Medical Center

In response to long wait times for nonurgent appointments, Southcentral Foundation's Alaska Native Medical Center undertook a series of measures aimed at facilitating the implementation of an open access scheduling model. They matched patients with physicians, worked to decrease the appointment backlog, and increased capacity by expanding the roles and responsibilities of nonphysicians. Although the elimination of the backlog was a long and arduous process, once achieved, it freed up half of the appointment slots for same-day appointments. Initial kinks with the system, such as a large number of patients calling right before 4:00 p.m., had to be resolved, but overall the system was considered a major improvement over the old one (Murray, Bodenheimer, Rittenhouse, & Grumbach, 2003).

---

3. **Simplify the system with fewer appointment types**. According to Murray and Tantau (2000), the open-access system should include only three classifications:
   - P (personal) for patients seeing their regular provider
   - T (team) for patients seeing an alternate provider in the medical practice
   - U (unestablished) for patients who are not associated with any provider in particular

4. **Standardize appointment times**. Historical data should be utilized to determine average appointment lengths. Even though some appointments may take longer, the face-to-face time between the patient and the physician fluctuates between 15 and 20 minutes.

5. **Plan for unusually high demand**. Despite the best efforts to examine demand patterns, there will be times when the daily demand surges cannot be met with the existing capacity. Even increasing the number of appointment slots later in the day to absorb unmet demand earlier in the day may be insufficient. In those cases, it might be advisable, as long as the patient agrees, to break the patient–provider continuity of care and have patients see midlevel providers or available colleagues.

6. **Reduce demand for face-to-face appointments** by using telecommunication media. These appointments are especially recommended for patients with chronic diseases that require regular monitoring.

After several years of implementation in primary care across the country, what is the verdict on open-access scheduling? When the implementation is successful, proponents of open-access scheduling are emphatic about its benefits (O'Hare & Corlett, 2004):

- Better continuity of care because of increased efforts to match patients with their preferred physicians

- Decreased number of no-shows

- More productive visits as patients forge relationships with their preferred providers and feel more comfortable discussing a wider range of health concerns

- Increased utilization of physicians' time resulting in higher revenues

- Lower use of urgent care services because patients are able to make same-day appointments

- Lesser need for triage nurses due to the simplification of visit types

- Improved patient satisfaction because patients tend to regard their regular provider as more competent and knowledgeable about their health history

- Less frustration among schedulers, nurses, and physicians as they stop struggling with the backlog

Anecdotal evidence of the success of open-access scheduling abounds, but research reveals some caveats. A review of 28 studies describing 24 implementations in primary care settings showed mixed results (Rose, Ross, & Horwitz, 2011). Decreased wait time for an appointment was reported in all studies although very few facilities were able to achieve same-day access. No-show rates improved as well. Changes in visit volume, physician compensation, and productivity were either neutral or positive. Although the number of urgent care visits decreased following an open access model implementation, there was no clear effect on ED visits and hospitalizations. That being said, even though health outcomes may not have *improved* as a result of open-access scheduling, they did not worsen either. As for patient satisfaction, it did not consistently improve because of differences in implementation. Because none of the studies involved a randomized trial of open-access scheduling, the authors of the review concluded that limited success (e.g., little success with same-day appointments, inconclusive improvements in health outcomes and patient satisfaction) was not a condemnation of open-access scheduling per se but rather reflected the quality of the implementations themselves, which tended to focus on same-day appointments while ignoring the other equally (if not more) critical principles.

Same-day appointments need not be a stringent benchmark. In fact, patients with strict work schedules may prefer an appointment at a convenient time rather than an appointment on the same day. A next-day appointment is also a reasonable benchmark for primary care, and third next available appointment with a wait of 10 days or less is appropriate for specialty care unless it is an urgent matter. **TNA** is a common indicator of access. It captures the number of days between a patient's request for an appointment and the next third available appointment. It provides an accurate assessment of the scheduling system's performance because first and second available appointments often indicate availability as a result of last-minute cancellations (IOM, 2015).

Third Next Available (TNA)

The number of days before a patient can get the third next available appointment. It provides an accurate assessment of the scheduling system's performance because first and second available appointments are often due to cancelations or no-shows.

BRADLEY PARK HOSPITAL 9.4

Dr. Baker's satisfaction with her own schedule was not matched by her patients'. Survey results and her own discussions with patients and staff convinced her that the scheduling system was not exactly patient friendly. *Some of her colleagues at the hospital had talked about open-access scheduling, the front-end effort it required to decrease the backlog, and the difficulty in achieving same-day appointments. However, Jennifer had reminded her that in her practice, patients rarely needed to be seen on the same day they called. The priorities were to free up slots in the schedule and give patients options for timely appointments. Perhaps the clinic could invest in an online appointment scheduling system. Patients would see all the slots available and select the ones most convenient to them. She would talk to her colleagues about it. Maybe they could set a "go live" date 6 months from now. That would give her enough time to reduce her backlog if she worked a couple of hours in the morning as well. Self-discipline and constant monitoring were needed. Tracking the metrics in the following dashboard (Figure 9.4) would help her stay focused.*

 Can you think of people who might not want to use an online scheduling system when making an appointment to see their doctor? Explain their reasons.

Measures	FYTD Actual	FY Target	Jan.	Feb.	Mar.	Apr.	May	Jun.	Jul.
TIME									
Average TNA (days)	12.3	9	12	15	16	13	11	10	9
Fraction of excess (%)	37%	20%	42	40	40	37	35	34	30
Average lateness per patient (min)	12	5	20	15	22	13	5	7	5
UTILIZATION									
Hours busy/total hours worked (%)	71%	85%	65	67	67	60	78	80	79
No-shows (%)	2%	1%	3	2	1	2	2.5	3	1.5

FIGURE 9.4 – Dashboard for Dr. Baker's scheduling system.

FY, fiscal year; FYTD, fiscal year to date.

Smoothing Flow Scheduling

Improving access is also achieved by smoothing flows. The technique can be used in both primary and specialty care. Litvak and Fineberg (2013) pointed out that hospitals tend to schedule as many surgeries as requested by surgeons on a given day. If the number of surgeries scheduled is high, it produces artificial peaks in demand, which distort the true demand pattern and increase variability. Variability cannot be totally avoided but it can be somewhat managed. Smoothing flow scheduling involves three phases (IOM, 2015).

PHASE 1:   Use 3 months of historical data to analyze the case mix in terms of urgency and establish a schedule with a number of slots matching the demand both in terms of volume and mix. Adjust the capacity accordingly (Chapter 8).

PHASE 2:   Streamline the flow for scheduled patients and address bottlenecks as explained in Chapters 6, 7, and 8. A smooth flow for scheduled patients will free up capacity for unscheduled visits (e.g., same-day referrals). Monitor flow performance. Track cancellations and no-shows. Overbook appointments if the percentage is less than 10%. For example, if for a particular weekday, there are usually two no-shows, then two patients can be overbooked.

PHASE 3:   Examine the artificial variability resulting from provider and staff preferences that is injected into the scheduling system.

A thorough review and better understanding of variability patterns is certainly applicable to all settings and generates positive results. An example of how a reduction in the peaks and valleys caused by variability lead to improved access is presented in Box 9.6.

BOX 9.6 – OM IN PRACTICE!

Smoothing the Flow at Cincinnati Children's Hospital and Medical Center Outpatient Clinic

In response to increased demand, Cincinnati Children's Hospital reviewed the management of its capacity to create a better balance between capacity and demand. It simplified the flow of patients by reducing the number of appointment types to new and return visits and reduced the backlog by increasing the number of appointments in a given day. These measures were deployed and standardized across clinic operations, which reduced variability and thus enhanced predictability. A scheduling tool and decision tree algorithm based on capacity management was implemented to reach their goal of TNA wait times within 10 days (Cincinnati Children's Hospital, 2015).

Inpatient and Emergency Care

Smoothing flow scheduling also applies to inpatient and emergency care facilities. Again, the accurate assessment of demand and capacity is paramount to creating flows that facilitate the movement of patients through the hospital. Artificial variability in admissions, discharges, and transfers must be reduced through adherence to standard protocols. Because of the complexity of hospital environments, patient flows involve a large number of steps, each with its own processing capacity. In these multistage systems, throughput at one step determines arrivals to the next. In such cases, the use of simulation models is highly recommended to test different process configurations and determine adequate capacity levels (see Chapter 8).

Because so many variations accumulate along the path, it is also recommended to use **patient-tracking technologies** to know where patients are in the system. This information can be used to set timers triggering events at the downstream locations. Such a proactive approach helps diffuse some of the chaos associated with uncertain patient arrivals, uncertain timing of capacity deployment, and congestion buildup. It also eliminates the wasted time spent searching for patients. A few vendors provide real-time information about patient location. The solutions often involve the placement of tags on a patient. As the patient moves through the hospital, a network of sensors mounted throughout the hospital detect the patient's location in real time. These solutions are fairly new and not commonplace. Most tracking solutions today rely on caregivers' timely input into the integrated health information system at each step of the process (Drazen & Rhoads, 2011). Irrespective of the technology used, patient tracking improves flows through more effective care coordination among the hospital's units and subunits (Box 9.7). For example, intensive care unit (ICU) nurses may be placed on call and asked to come in to work when the electronic

Patient-Tracking Technologies

Refers to technologies that tracks patients' movements through the hospital. Some technologies provide real-time information about a patient's location.

health record (EHR) schedule notifies the ICU that cardiac surgery is being completed on a patient. The ICU nurse is not asked to come in until the patient leaving the OR is headed to recovery. By the time the patient is ready to leave recovery and be transported to the ICU, the ICU nurse has arrived and is ready to receive the patient just in time to provide skilled care. This communication system enables a greater continuity of care for the patient with skilled staff made available at the bedside on short notice.

⊕ BOX 9.7 – OM IN PRACTICE!

Use of Real-Time Location System at Christiana Hospital in Newark, Delaware

Christiana Hospital used to have a traditional tracking system, which depended on caregivers' input. In 2003, large increases in demand strained the system. Consumed with patient care activities, caregivers often delayed inputs into the hospital information system. Deducing patient location from the patient charts proved to be a challenge because the information on the patient's record lagged actual movement. Christiana Hospital adopted real-time location system using infrared technology. This system was integrated with the hospital's inpatient bed management system. As patients moved through the hospital, clinicians were able to view their up-to-date locations on a whiteboard with a map of the hospital. As a result of the improved patient flow, non–value-adding time was reduced, thereby improving throughput and capacity utilization (Drazen & Rhoads, 2011).

Staff scheduling, job scheduling, and patient scheduling are highly interrelated because they involve the alignment of patient demand with capacity resources. Staff schedules should accommodate patient demand. Patients should not be scheduled to create artificial peaks in demand, which stress capacity and disrupt the ability to build reliable schedules. Job scheduling depends on the staff available to do the job and the volume of jobs that needs to be done. Job scheduling also smooths the flow when multiple transfers are involved. For example, if providers in the ED are waiting for lab tests to proceed with patient discharge, admission, or further testing, it is vital for the lab to release test results promptly and avoid congestion in the lab and ED (Figure 9.5).

BRADLEY PARK HOSPITAL 9.5

Jennifer was sitting in Dr. Pinheiro's office, looking at the latest dashboard. "Things are slowly improving," Jennifer noted.

"Yes," Dr. Pinheiro continued. "It certainly has not been easy, but we are all much happier with the clinic flow. I have even gotten several compliments from patients! That certainly beats complaints."

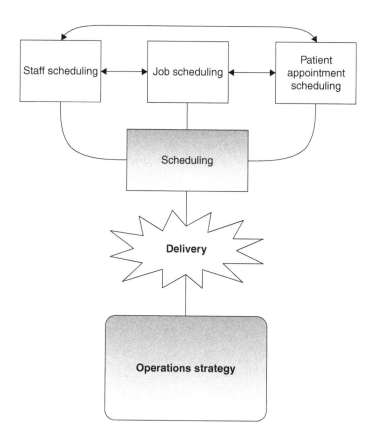

FIGURE 9.5 – Interrelationships among scheduling types.

"I think the major factor in the clinic's improvement is your and your colleagues' willingness to look at the clinic from your patients' perspective. Your commitment to change how things are done made it easier to get the staff to change, as well. Thanks for leading the charge!" Jennifer said.

"The data that you showed me were pretty compelling," Dr. Pinheiro stated. "Thanks for showing us what can be done when we put our minds to it."

SUMMARY

Scheduling is an operational activity that releases resources on a timely basis to meet demand needs. It is, therefore, intrinsically linked to the topics and tools learned in Chapter 8. In this chapter, we considered three types of scheduling: staff, job, and patient. Ideally, all three should be connected to ensure an easy and efficient movement of patients through the care paths. Staff scheduling involves balancing labor resources with patient demand. Job scheduling sequences the jobs to be performed in order to boost on-time or fast delivery. Patient or appointment scheduling sets the timing of care at a single point (e.g., PCP office) or through a network of points (e.g., hospital) in the system.

Because of its emphasis on timing, scheduling primarily enables the achievement of the delivery-competitive priority. Nevertheless, it affects cost, quality, and flexibility as well. When care is delayed, patients resort to alternative sources of care, which may not be reimbursed at the same rate by their insurer. Their conditions may also deteriorate, causing preventable hospitalizations and treatments, which increase costs. If appointments are set far in the future, patients may be upset at first and even forget about the appointments and miss them. Patient dissatisfaction coupled with lower utilization caused by no-shows impacts providers' revenues and efficiency. As we said in Chapter 8, capacity should always exceed demand. This enables the provider to respond to demand variabilities and work in emergencies (Figure 9.6).

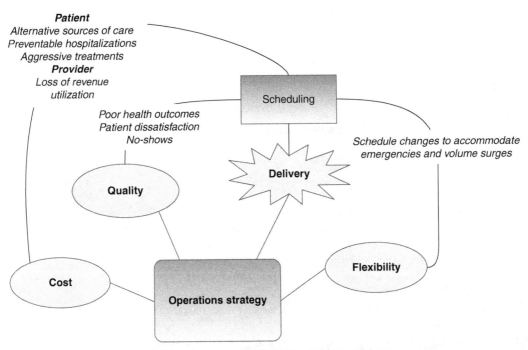

FIGURE 9.6 – Connecting scheduling to competitive priorities.

KEY TERMS

Scheduling	EDD sequencing rule	Flow time
Demand	STR sequencing rule	Moore's algorithm
Capacity	CR rule	Block scheduling
Telemedicine	Rush	Modified block scheduling
Staff scheduling	Makespan	Individual scheduling

Job scheduling	Tardiness	Open-access scheduling
FCFS sequencing rule	Weighted tardiness	Third next available appointment
SPT sequencing rule	Tardy job	Patient tracking technologies

NOTE

1. There is an alternate schedule yielding the same cost: six full-time nurses and two part-time nurses from 8:00 a.m. to 12:00 p.m., six full-time nurses and six part-time nurses from 12:00 to 4:00 p.m., eight full-time nurses and eight part-time nurses from 4:00 to 8:00 p.m., eight full-time nurses and two part-time nurses from 8:00 p.m. to 12:00 a.m., six full-time nurses and zero part-time nurses from 12:00 to 4:00 a.m., six full-time nurses and zero part-time nurses from 4:00 to 8:00 a.m.

TOOLS USED IN THIS CHAPTER

TOOL	PURPOSE
Linear Programming	Optimization model used to schedule labor resources according to a preset objective (e.g., minimize cost).
Sequencing rules	Rules used to sequence the jobs to be performed in order to appear fair (FCFS), minimize congestion (SPT), minimize tardiness (EDD), minimize the number of tardy jobs (Moore's algorithm), and so on.
The Kaandorp and Koole (2007) optimal outpatient appointment scheduling model	Individual appointment-scheduling algorithm used to optimize waiting, tardiness, and idle time.

FORMULAS USED IN THIS CHAPTER

Technique	Definition	Formula	Number
Job scheduling	STR	(Due date – Today's date) – Processing time	[9.1]
	CR	$\dfrac{\text{Due date – Today's date}}{\text{Processing time}}$	[9.2]

Appoint-ment scheduling	Current backlog	=	All future appointments on the schedule	[9.3]
	Extra capacity provided	=	Number of extra patients who will be seen every day	[9.4]
	Days to reduce the backlog	=	$\dfrac{\text{Current backlog}}{\text{Extra capacity}}$	[9.5]

WHAT DO YOU REMEMBER?

1. List and explain three threats to timely care.
2. List and explain the consequences of care delay.
3. What is the purpose of staff scheduling?
4. How is integer linear programming used to schedule staff?
5. What is job scheduling?
6. Discuss how each of the following rules works:
   a. FCFS
   b. SPT
   c. EDD
   d. STR
   e. CR
7. What is Moore's algorithm and what is its purpose?
8. List and briefly describe three performance measures for job scheduling.
9. What is block scheduling? What is its main disadvantage?
10. What is individual scheduling? What is its main disadvantage?
11. List and explain the six principles of open-access scheduling.
12. Why is TNA an accurate indicator of a scheduling system's performance?
13. Briefly explain how artificial variability hinders smooth flow scheduling.

SOLVE BPH'S PROBLEMS

1. The lab supervisor needs to establish a weekly schedule for the morning shift. Based on distributions of arrival times and service times, she has conducted a queuing analysis and found that the minimal number of lab technicians for each day is the following:

Day	Number of Technicians Needed	Pay per Technician/Day
Monday	6	$160
Tuesday	5	$160
Wednesday	4	$160
Thursday	4	$160
Friday	5	$160
Saturday	6	$240
Sunday	4	$240

Each technician is also allowed to take 2 days off every week. Technicians prefer to have 2 consecutive days off. There are therefore seven possible schedules (Monday and Tuesday off, Tuesday and Wednesday off, Wednesday and Thursday off, etc.). Formulate and solve an integer linear programming model that will determine the number of technicians for each one of the seven schedules while minimizing weekly cost and providing the necessary capacity and giving each lab technician 2 days off. Hint: Define the decision variables as the number of technicians in schedule 1, 2, 3, . . .

2. Besides technicians (see problem 9.1), the lab supervisor also needs to schedule part-time and full-time phlebotomists for Mondays. Some part-time phlebotomists work 2-hour shifts, whereas others work 4-hour shifts. Full-time phlebotomists work 8 hours. The supervisor has divided the day into 2-hour blocks and, based on historical interarrival and service times on Mondays, she has determined the minimum number of phlebotomists needed for each time slot. Below are all data pertaining to this problem. Please note that shift and time blocks do not coincide even though there are 12 of each.

Shift	Type	Daily Salary
1. 6 a.m.–8 a.m.	Part-time	$30
2. 6 a.m.–10 a.m.	Part-time	$60
3. 6 a.m.–2 p.m.	Full-time	$144
4. 10 a.m.–2 p.m.	Part-time	$60
5. 10 a.m.–6 p.m.	Full-time	$144
6. 2 p.m.–6 p.m.	Part-time	$60
7. 2 p.m.–10 p.m.	Full-time	$144
8. 6 p.m.–10 p.m.	Part-time	$60
9. 10 p.m.–6 a.m.	Full-time	$144
10. 10 p.m.–12 a.m.	Part-time	$30
11. 12 a.m.–4 a.m.	Part-time	$60
12. 4 a.m.–6 a.m.	Part-time	$30

Time Block	Number of Phlebotomists Needed
1. 6 a.m.–8 a.m.	8
2. 8 a.m.–10 a.m.	10
3. 10 a.m.–12 p.m.	22
4. 12 p.m.–2 p.m.	15
5. 2 p.m.–4 p.m.	12
6. 4 p.m.–6 p.m.	18
7. 6 p.m.–8 p.m.	12
8. 8 p.m.–10 p.m.	22
9. 10 p.m.–12 a.m.	15
10. 12 a.m.–2 a.m.	10
11. 2 a.m.–4 a.m.	8
12. 4 a.m.–6 a.m.	8

The lab supervisor wants at least 40% of the phlebotomists at the peak times of 10 a.m. to 12 p.m. and 8 p.m. to 10 p.m. to be full-time employees. Also, she wants at least two full-time phlebotomists at full-time shift changes: 6:00 a.m., 2:00 p.m., and 10 p.m. Formulate and solve an integer linear programming model to establish a schedule for phlebotomists that will meet all requirements while minimizing daily costs.

3. The weekly cafeteria cooking staff schedules need to be established. All cooks work 12-hour shifts, 4 days in a row. Then they take 3 consecutive days off. There are seven possible schedules (Monday, Tuesday, Wednesday off; Tuesday, Wednesday, Thursday off; etc.) The following table lists the number of cooks needed each day of the week as well as their pay.

Day	Number of Cooks Needed	Pay per Cook/Day
Monday	10	$180
Tuesday	12	$180
Wednesday	14	$180
Thursday	8	$180
Friday	8	$180
Saturday	12	$270
Sunday	14	$270

Formulate and solve an integer linear programming model that will determine the number of cooks in each schedule while minimizing weekly costs and ensuring that minimum capacity needs are met.

4. Requests for solutions to billing-related IT problems have been received. Six of those jobs were assigned to Joel Williams, one of the support specialists. Joel has latitude in deciding the order in

which these requests will be processed, but his performance is evaluated in terms of turnaround times or flow times. All jobs are equally important. Help Joel find the sequence that will minimize flow time based on the following data. Try the following rules: FCFS, SPT, EDD, and CR. Requests will start being processed after the last one's arrival, that is, 65 minutes.

Request	Arrival Time (min)	Processing Time (min)	Due Date
A	15	100	200
B	20	150	300
C	30	60	150
D	40	120	250
E	55	30	400
F	65	90	350

5. The next day, Joel was assigned six more jobs (see problem 4). However, for this set of jobs, Joel's supervisor told him to minimize tardiness and the number of tardy jobs. All jobs are equally important. Try the following rules: FCFS, SPT, EDD, CR, and Moore's algorithm. Requests will start being processed after the last one's arrival, that is, 200 minutes.

Request	Arrival Time (min)	Processing Time (min)	Due Date
U	20	60	310
V	80	120	380
W	100	90	400
X	120	45	500
Y	150	150	520
Z	200	100	560

6. Because physicians at a BPH clinic use an EHR system that is not fully interfaced with the system used by the hospital, some patient data have to be manually reinputted into the hospital's system. The clerk in charge of this task has just received a list of five patient charges. Their importance is evaluated in terms of their contribution to revenue. The clerk wants to minimize weighted tardiness. The data input will start now, at time 0. Help her find the best sequence to achieve that objective using the FCFS, SPT, EDD, and CR rules.

Patient Record	Arrival Time (min)	Processing Time (min)	Due Date	Weight
A	−5	10	65	9
B	−4	20	30	18
C	−3	15	20	15
D	−2	5	15	7
E	−1	12	40	10

7. In this chapter, we saw that Dr. Baker was booking patients every 30 minutes over a 6-hour time period, allowing her to see 12 patients a day. No-shows accounted for about 2% of her appointments. The exam time averaged 25 minutes. In her efforts to reduce the backlog, she is now seeing patients from 9:30 a.m. to 6:00 p.m. Even though she could schedule 17 patients (17 intervals) during that time period, she has decided to see only 16 (number of arrivals) and leave the last 30 minutes of the day to catch up on paperwork.

   a. Use the Kaandorp and Koole (2007) appointment scheduling tool to evaluate her new schedule (http://calculator .gerkoole.com/appointment-scheduler). Use weights of 1 for waiting, tardiness, and idle time. Compare the schedule with the small neighborhood schedule. Which one is better and why?

   b. Now assign a weight of 7 for waiting and compare the results of Dr. Baker's schedule and the small neighborhood schedule. Which one is better and why?

   c. Dr. Baker's office has been sending multiple appointment reminders, which decreased the no-show rate to 1.5%. Reassess the results (based on those you obtained in part b).

   d. A nurse now pulls the patient's record on the computer before Dr. Baker enters the exam room. Visit time has now gone from 25 to 22 minutes. Reassess the results (based on those you obtained in part c).

8. Dr. Heath is a very jovial PCP whose backlog has increased to 200 appointments. Because he is already working long hours, he figures that he can only work 1 more hour each day and can see four patients during that time. How many business days will it take him to eliminate the backlog?

9. Dr. Heath (see problem 8) wants to reduce his backlog in no more than 30 business days. How many extra patients will he have to see every day?

THINK OUTSIDE THE BOOK!

1. Some companies (Teladoc, MDLive, American Well, etc.) offer 24/7 access to doctors via webcam. Go to one of the websites and identify some of the benefits and drawbacks of the company's services.

2. Read Mitchel Zoler's article (available online), "Novel OR scheduling and staffing boosts efficiency," in *Clinical Psychiatry News*, January 17, 2013. Explain how some of the concepts covered in this chapter were used to schedule the OR at the Mayo Clinic in Jacksonville, Florida.

3. Do a search on online appointments and online check-in. Explain how they work.

4. Add a few other measures to Dr. Baker's scheduling dashboard (Figure 9.4).

REFERENCES

Agency for Healthcare Research and Quality. (2015). Open access scheduling for routine and urgent appointments. Retrieved from https://cahps.ahrq.gov/quality-improvement/improvement-guide/browse-interventions/Access/Open-Access.html

American Telemedicine Association. (2012). What is telemedicine? Retrieved from http://www.americantelemed.org/about-telemedicine/what-is-telemedicine#.VbK-ImbbK70

Bleustein, C., Rothschild, D. B., Valen, A., Valatis, E., Schweitzer, L., & Jones, R. (2014). Wait times, patient satisfaction scores, and the perception of care. *American Journal of Managed Care, 20*(5), 393–400.

Cincinnati Children's Hospital. (2015). 3rd next available appointment. Retrieved from http://www.cincinnatichildrens.org/about/quality-measures/system-level-measures/3rd-next-available-appointment

Coates, A. S. (1999). Breast cancer: Delays, dilemmas, and delusions. *Lancet, 353*(9159), 1112–1113.

Desmeules, F., Dionne, C. E., Belzile, E. L., Bourbonnais, R., & Fremont, P. (2012). The impacts of pre-surgery wait for total knee replacement on pain, function, and health-related quality of life six months after surgery. *Journal of Evaluation in Clinical Practice, 18*(1), 111–120.

Drazen, E., & Rhoads, J. (2011). *Using tracking tools to improve patient flow in hospitals*. Oakland, CA: California Healthcare Foundation.

Gupta, D., & Denton, B. (2008). Appointment scheduling in health care: Challenges and opportunities. *IIE Transactions, 40*, 800–819.

Institute of Medicine. (2015). *Transforming health care scheduling and access: Getting to now*. In G. Kapla, M. Hamilton Lopez, & J. M. McGinnis (Eds.). Washington, DC: National Academies Press.

Kaandorp, G. C., & Koole, G. (2007). Optimal outpatient appointment scheduling. *Health Care Management Science, 10*(3), 217–229.

Henry Kissinger. (n.d.). Scheduling quotes. Retrieved from http://thinkexist.com/quotes/with/keyword/scheduling

Laguna, M., & Marklund, J. (2005). *Business Process, Modeling, Simulation, and Design*. Upper Saddle River, NJ: Pearson.

Litvak, E., & Fineberg, H. V. (2013). Smoothing the way to high quality, safety, and economy. *New England Journal of Medicine, 369*, 1581–1583.

Llanwarne, N. R., Abel, G. A., Elliott, M. N., Paddison, C. A. M., Lyratzopoulos, G., Campbell, J. L., & Roland, M. (2013). Relationship between clinical quality and patient experience: Analysis of data from the english quality and outcomes framework and the National GP Patient Survey. *Annals of Family Medicine, 11*(5), 467–472.

McLane, K., D. Q. (2005). *Scheduling strategies for ambulatory surgery centers.* Danvers, MA: HCPro.

Merritt Hawkins. (2014). *Physician appointment wait times and Medicaid and Medicare acceptance rates.* Irving, TX: AMN Healthcare.

Murray, M., & Berwick, D. M. (2003). Advanced access: Reducing waiting and delays in primary care. *Journal of the American Medical Association, 289*(8), 1035–1040.

Murray, M., Bodenheimer, T., Rittenhouse, D., & Grumbach, K. (2003). Improving timely access to primary care: Case studies of the advanced access model. *Journal of the American Medical Association, 289*(8), 1042–1046.

Murray, M., & Tantau, C. (2000). Same-day appointments: Exploding the access paradigm. *Family Practice Management, 7*(8), 45–50.

O'Hare, D., & Corlett, J. (2004). The outcomes of open-access scheduling. *Family Practice Management, 11*(2), 35–38.

Pearl, R. (2014). Kaiser Permanente northern California: Current experiences with Internet, mobile, and video technologies. *Health Affairs, 33*(2), 251–257.

Rose, K. D., Ross, J. S., & Horwitz, L. I. (2011). Advanced access scheduling outcomes: A systematic review. *Archives of Internal Medicine, 171*(13), 1150–1159.

Sickinger, S., & Kolisch, R. (2009). The performance of a generalized Bailey–Welch rule for outpatient appointment scheduling under inpatient and emergency demand. *Health Care Management Science, 12*(4), 408–419.

Sobolev, B. L., Levy, A. R., Kuramoto, L., Hayden, R., & Fitzgerald, J. M. (2006). Do longer delays for coronary artery bypass surgery contribute to preoperative mortality in less urgent patients? *Medical Care, 44*(7), 680–686.

Stevenson, W. J. (2012). *Operations management* (11th ed.). New York, NY: McGraw-Hill.

Welch, J. D., & Bailey, N. T. (1952). Appointment systems in hospital outpatient departments. *Lancet, 1*(6718), 1105–1108.

Zoroya, G. (2015, January 29). At troubled Phoenix VA, delays continue in one department. *USA Today.* Retrieved from http://www.usatoday.com/story/news/nation/militaryintelligence/2015/01/29/va-scandal-wait-times-urology-phoenix/22527589

APPENDIX 9.1 EXCEL FORMULAS AND SOLVER DIALOG BOXES FOR STAFF SCHEDULING EXAMPLE

Figure A9.1 displays the formulas entered for this model. Please note that the row for the number of full-time nurses was added to the matrix. The sum is used to enter the set of constraints pertaining to the number of full-time nurses exceeding or being equal to the number of part-time nurses (see $K$20 ≥ $K$4; $L$20 ≥ $L$5; etc. in Figure A9.2).

	J	K	L	M	N	O	P
1				SOLUTION			
2							
3		Friday 1	Friday 2	Friday 3	Friday 4	Friday 5	Friday 6
4	PN1	2	0	0	0	0	0
5	PN2	0	4	0	0	0	0
6	PN3	0	0	8	0	0	0
7	PN4	0	0	0	4	0	0
8	PN5	0	0	0	0	0	0
9	PN6	0	0	0	0	0	0
10	FN1	3	0	0	0	0	0
11	FN2	0	5	0	0	0	0
12	FN3	0	0	3	0	0	0
13	FN4	0	0	0	3	0	0
14	FN5	0	0	0	0	3	0
15	FN6	0	0	0	0	0	3
16							
17	Nurses assigned	=K4+K10+P15	=L5+K10+L11	=M6+L11+M12	=N7+M12+N13	=O8+N13+O14	=P9+O14+P15
18	Sign	≥	≥	≥	≥	≥	≥
19	Nurses needed	8	12	16	10	6	5
20	FT nurses	=K10+P15	=K10+L11	=L11+M12	=M12+N13	=N13+O14	=O14+P15
21							
22			TC	=SUMPRODUCT(B4:G15,K4:P15)			
23							
24							

FIGURE A9.1 – Excel formulas.

Note: Microsoft Excel application interface is used with permission of Microsoft.

Figure A9.2 shows the following:

- Set Objective: cell with formula of objective function ($M$22 in Figure A9.1)
- Changing Variable Cells: matrix where values of the decision variables appear after solving ($K$4:$P$15 in Figure A9.1)
- Subject to the Constraints: list of constraints corresponding to the three sets presented in the model as well as the logical constraints ($K$4:$P$15 = integer)

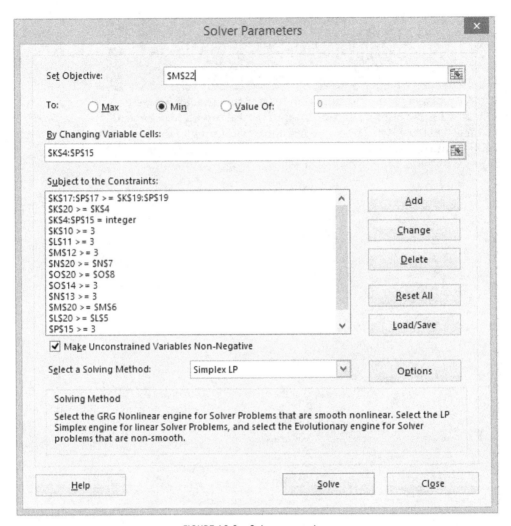

FIGURE A9.2 – Solver parameters.

Note: Excel Solver interface reproduced by permission of Frontline Solvers (www.solver.com).

PART

IV

Competing on Cost

CHAPTER 10

FORECASTING DEMAND

INTRODUCTION AND LEARNING OBJECTIVES

Chapters 8 and 9 focused on setting capacity levels and schedules to meet demand. Demand was predetermined, and the emphasis was on achieving on-time or fast delivery. Because demand is variable, it is difficult to predict. This chapter addresses this complexity and introduces you to popular techniques used to forecast demand. Correct demand estimates are important not only to set appropriate resource levels for timely delivery, but also to contain costs. Cost overruns occur when demand is overestimated (excessive capacity and supplies on hand) or underestimated (overtime and expedited deliveries to respond to shortages); see Figure 10.1 and Box 10.1.

This chapter introduces you to qualitative and quantitative forecasting techniques. Neither type of technique is superior to the other, and often, a mix of both seems to be most effective. In the end, solid quantitative skills combined with sound judgment and instincts produce the most accurate forecasts. Yes, forecasting is both an art and a science. We do not pretend to teach you the art of forecasting here. Only time and experience can accomplish that. However, we expose you to its scientific or technical aspects, which are necessary conditions for the pursuit of accuracy. More specifically, after reading this chapter, you will be able to:

1. **List the most popular qualitative approaches and mention their advantages and disadvantages**
2. **Identify the various components of a time series**
3. **Develop forecasts based on time series models: moving averages, weighted moving averages, exponential smoothing, and trend projections**
4. **Adjust forecasts for trend and seasonality**
5. **Modulate the stability and responsiveness of a forecast**
6. **Assess the accuracy of forecasts**
7. **Develop forecasts based on associative models**

FIGURE 10.1 –
Mind map with
focus on cost.

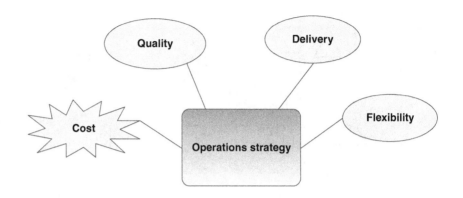

BRADLEY PARK HOSPITAL 10.1

*Sheila was the vascular surgery administrator. She knew that job backwards
and forwards and had the complete faith of the surgeons with whom she worked.
When Dr. Vaughn, the division chief, asked her why stents were not always
available before an endovascular stenting procedure, Sheila was perplexed.
Because stents cost over $10,000 each, she had kept a close eye on the inventory,
making sure that orders were placed at regular intervals. Yet, sometimes the
stents stayed in inventory for too long. At other times, there were not enough.
"I think I need to review the number of surgeries more closely," she said. "It
looks like I might be missing something."*

FORECASTING DEMAND

Demand Forecast
A prediction of future
demand.

A **demand forecast** is a prediction of future demand. These predictions are
never perfect! The actual demand is rarely equal to that indicated in the
forecast. In this chapter, you will learn how to select forecasting techniques
that decrease the chances and magnitudes of errors, but you will always
need to make allowances for these errors when using demand forecasts to

make decisions (e.g., setting capacity levels). Aggregate demand forecasts that focus on combined lines of products or services tend to be more accurate because the forecasting errors for single lines of services tend to cancel one another when the service lines are grouped together. For example, the prediction of the total demand for hospital beds is generally more accurate than the demand forecast for beds in the intensive care unit (ICU). Furthermore, short-term forecasts (a few months) tend to be more accurate than long-term forecasts because uncertainties increase and business conditions change over a long time span.

There are two main approaches to forecasting demand: qualitative and quantitative. **Qualitative approaches** rely on subjective human inputs and judgments. They are most appropriate when data on prior demand are unavailable, when political and economic conditions are changing, when available data are outdated or irrelevant, or when new products and services are introduced to the market. **Quantitative approaches** project historical demand into the future (time series models) or use multiple variables to predict demand (associative models). Some organizations favor one type of approach over another, but a combination of the two is usually most effective (Box 10.2).

Qualitative Approaches
Forecasting approaches that rely on subjective human inputs and judgments.

Quantitative Approaches
Forecasting approaches that project past demand into the future or use multiple variables to predict demand.

🔷 BOX 10.2 – WORDS OF WISDOM

"The key to making a good forecast is not in limiting yourself to quantitative information" (Silver, 2012).

QUALITATIVE APPROACHES

Qualitative techniques that are relevant to predict the demand for healthcare services include the jury of executive opinion, the Delphi method, and consumer market surveys.

Jury of Executive Opinion

This technique is mostly used when new products and services are considered or when existing forecasts need to be revised due to unusual circumstances. The opinions, judgments, and knowledge of high-level executives from various functions of the organization are summarized to formulate demand forecasts. The main advantages of this technique are that it incorporates experts' opinions and that it can yield fast results. One disadvantage is that some executives exert more power than others, a situation that may produce forecasts reflecting those executives' biases. Another is the potential waste of valuable executive time when reaching a consensus proves to be difficult and the situation gets out of control.

Delphi Method

The Delphi method is used for long-term forecasting (e.g., future demand for harvesting stem cells). The Delphi method pools experts' demand estimates in an iterative fashion. Experts, often in different locations, are asked to develop forecasts independently. Staff aggregate the results to produce a single forecast. These aggregated, anonymous forecasts are sent back to the experts who may then revise their original estimates. The revised estimates are again aggregated and sent to the experts until a consensus is reached. The main advantages of this method are the lack of bias resulting from the experts' anonymity and the strength of a forecast built on consensus. The disadvantage is that the process may be exceedingly time-consuming.

Consumer Market Surveys

Market research is a popular tool used to obtain existing and potential healthcare consumers' intentions to buy products and services. The surveys help estimate demand and design or redesign processes to accommodate customers' needs and wants. For example, cancer patients' opinions about their care experience may make a compelling argument for building a cancer center with lab, imaging, surgery, therapy, and counseling services under one roof. Although this method provides a useful input to forecasting demand, it may produce overly optimistic estimates of potential as opposed to actual demand.

QUANTITATIVE APPROACHES
Times Series Models

Time Series

A sequence of past data points that are spaced at even time intervals.

A **time series** is a sequence of past data (demand, in our case) points that are spaced at even time intervals (hour, day, week, month, quarter, year, etc.). The primary assumption of time series forecasting is that the behavior or pattern of this historical demand is likely to continue in the future (Box 10.3). Another assumption is that future demand can be predicted exclusively from past demand, thereby ignoring the potential influence of other variables, such as price.

◈ BOX 10.3 – WORDS OF WISDOM

"The best qualification of a prophet is, to have a good memory" (Marquis of Halifax, 1912).

Components of a Time Series

In order to reproduce the patterns of past data in our projections, we must break down the time series into its components. The four components of a time series are a trend, a cycle, seasonality, and an irregular movement (Figure 10.2).

Trend

A long-term, upward or downward movement of demand.

Cycle

A demand pattern that occurs every several years because of economic fluctuations.

1. **Trend.** A trend is a long-term, upward or downward movement of demand. Demand trends occur as a result of changes in demographics, competition, or societal changes. For example, the increasing population of aging baby boomers creates a higher demand for geriatric care services over time.

2. **Cycle.** A cycle (not represented in Figure 10.2) is a pattern that occurs every several years. It is often caused by changes in economic conditions, political elections, war, and so on. For

example, the economic recession starting in December 2007 resulted in fewer visits at private physician practices, but it fueled demand at community health centers (Robert Wood Johnson Foundation, 2009).

3. **Seasonality**. A seasonal pattern is a movement in the data that repeats itself every day, every week, every month, every quarter, every year, and so on. For example, the number of patients in the emergency department (ED) is lowest between midnight and 8:00 a.m. The number of hip fractures peaks during the winter months.

Seasonality
A demand pattern that repeats itself every day, week, month, quarter, or year.

4. **Irregular movement**. The irregular movement is a random variation. It occurs by chance and cannot be predicted. It pretty much guarantees that your forecast will never be perfect! Why did 120 patients show up at the emergency room (ER) today when only 97 showed up the day before? Nobody knows.

Irregular Movement
A random variation that occurs for no specific reason.

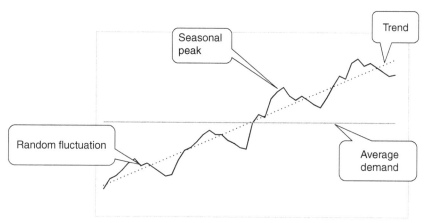

FIGURE 10.2 – Time series components.

BRADLEY PARK HOSPITAL 10.2

Sheila pulled the number of stent surgeries performed over the past 3 years. Because Bradley Park Hospital's (BPH's) cardiac unit had a strong reputation, it attracted patients from all over the state. Clearly, rescheduling surgeries because stents were not available would tarnish the hospital's image and threaten its status as a center of excellence. When looking at the spreadsheet, she did not see much variation. There was a slight increase from 1 year to the other due to BPH's growing reputation, but she had already accounted for that when ordering supplies. She then decided to plot the data (Table 10.1 and Figure 10.3). What she saw puzzled her: The number of stent surgeries was lower in April, November, and December. Although emergency surgeries were unpredictable, elective surgeries were often scheduled based on patients' and physicians' preferences. On a hunch, she checked the surgeons' schedules. "There it is," she thought. "Several of our surgeons attend the Annual Meeting of the American Association for Thoracic Surgery in April. And of course, with all the holidays, November and December tend to be slow months. Patients prefer to be at home rather than in the hospital during that time of year. The problem is that I only know the number of surgeries once they have been scheduled. That's a short time window. I can't really be proactive in placing orders . . ."

Sheila a walked to the finance department. Those people spent their lives working with spreadsheets and making all kinds of projections. They should be able to help her.

 What patterns do you see in the 3 years of data?

TABLE 10.1 – Monthly Volume of Stent Surgeries at BPH		
Year	**Month**	**Surgeries**
1	January	42
1	February	50
1	March	63
1	April	58
1	May	67
1	June	73
1	July	80
1	August	83
1	September	87
1	October	72
1	November	70
1	December	68
2	January	96
2	February	98
2	March	105
2	April	92
2	May	106
2	June	114
2	July	118
2	August	124
2	September	128
2	October	102
2	November	96
2	December	92
3	January	128
3	February	122
3	March	134
3	April	118
3	May	140
3	June	136
3	July	146
3	August	152
3	September	154

(continued)

TABLE 10.1 – Monthly Volume of Stent Surgeries at BPH (*continued*)		
Year	**Month**	**Surgeries**
3	October	128
3	November	124
3	December	122

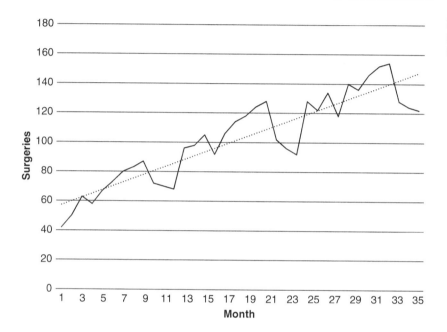

FIGURE 10.3 – Time series of stent surgeries.

Stability and Responsiveness

Random variations in demand can confuse and mislead the forecaster. If the number of patients visiting the ED is 120 on September 1, 97 on September 2, and 85 on September 3, it might be tempting to conclude that the demand for ED services is falling and adjust the capacity accordingly for September 4. However, because the changes reflect random fluctuations, the number of patient visits to the ED could well be 124 on September 4. Therefore, a forecast should not overreact to simple, random fluctuations. This property is called **stability**.

Stability
The ability of a forecast to play down the influence of simple, random fluctuations.

However, if demand changes for a reason, the forecast should reflect the change as soon as possible. For example, when a new statin enters the market, there is often a decline in the demand for older cholesterol-lowering drugs. When placing orders to their suppliers, pharmacists should account for these changes in demand. The ability of a forecast to react quickly to true changes in demand is called **responsiveness**.

Responsiveness
The ability of a forecast to respond quickly to true changes in demand.

Forecasts must be both stable and responsive. This is a balancing act because the actions required to make a forecast more responsive decrease its stability and vice versa. It all comes down to the forecaster's judgment and experience in deciding whether the change in demand is real or whether it is a simple "blip."

Naïve Approach

Naïve Approach

A simple forecasting technique that assumes that demand in the next time period will be equal to the demand in the current period.

As its name indicates, the **naïve approach** is simple. It merely assumes that demand in the next time period will be equal to the demand in the current period. In other words, if the demand for hospital beds averaged 220 last month, we forecast that it would be the same this month. Clearly, this approach produces extremely responsive forecasts. Its main advantages are its simplicity and low cost. It works best if the random fluctuations are very small. If they are large, the naïve forecast will produce erratic forecasts, which cannot be used for planning purposes.

Simple Moving Average

Simple Moving Average

A technique that averages demand over a certain number of time periods to forecast demand in the next period.

A **simple moving average** forecast averages demand over a certain number of past periods to forecast demand in the next period. A 3-month moving average would use the average of the 3 previous months to project demand next month; a 7-day moving average would average the demand over the past 7 days to predict tomorrow's demand, and so on. As time passes, each time a new data point is added to the historical data, the moving average includes the most recent period's data to compute the average and excludes the oldest demand point used in computing the previous average. This practice tends to smooth out the irregular component. The formula for a simple moving average in period t is

$$SMA_t = \frac{(A_t - n + ... + A_{t-2} + A_{t-1})}{n}$$ [10.1]

where SMA_t is the simple moving average forecast for period t,
n is the number of periods included in the average,
A_{t-1} is the actual demand in the previous period,
A_{t-2} and A_{t-n} are the actual demand two periods ago and n periods ago, respectively.

Table 10.2 displays 3-month and 5-month simple moving average forecasts for January of year 4. As you can see, the two simple moving average models produce different demand forecasts. The 3-month moving average forecast reflects the lower values of actual demand in the months of October, November, and December of year 3, whereas the 5-month moving average forecast includes the higher demand values in August and September (see the smoother—less jagged—5-month forecasts in Figure 10.4). Increasing the number of periods in a simple moving average increases its stability and decreases its responsiveness. The forecaster's ability to modulate responsiveness in a simple moving average model is nevertheless limited. Figure 10.4 (based on 3 years of data) shows that both the 3-month and 5-month moving average forecasts are always below the actual demand when it increases, and they are always above the actual demand when it decreases significantly. Simple moving averages are only appropriate when demand is fairly stable over time.

Weighted Moving Average

Weighted Moving Average

An averaging technique that includes weights to place more emphasis on recent demand.

Although a simple moving average forecast weighs each data point equally, the **weighted moving average** includes weights that place

TABLE 10.2 – Three-Month and Five-Month Simple Moving Averages

Year	Month	Actual Demand	Simple Moving Average, SMA, ($n = 3$)	Simple Moving Average, SMA, ($n = 5$)
3	Jan.	128		
3	Feb.	122		
3	Mar.	134		
3	Apr.	118	(128 + 122 + 134)/3 = 128.00	
3	May	140	(122 + 134 + 118)/3 = 124.67	
3	Jun.	136	(134 + 118 + 140) = 130.67	128.40
3	Jul.	146	(118 + 140 + 136)/3 = 131.33	130.00
3	Aug.	152	(140 + 136 + 146)/3 = 140.67	134.80
3	Sep.	154	(136 + 146 + 152)/3 = 144.67	138.40
3	Oct.	128	(146 + 152 + 154)/3 = 150.67	145.60
3	Nov.	124	(152 + 154 + 128)/3 = 144.67	143.20
3	Dec.	122	(154 + 128 + 124)/3 = 135.33	140.80
4	Jan.		(128 + 124 + 122)/3 = 124.67	136.00

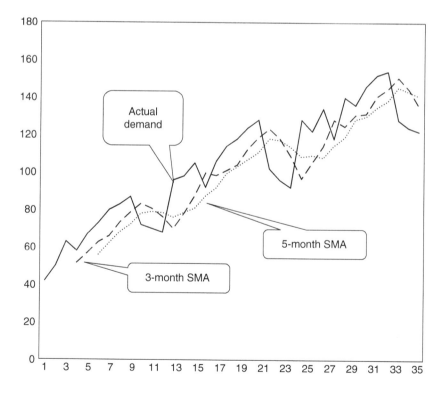

FIGURE 10.4 – Comparison of actual demand with 3-month and 5-month moving averages.

more emphasis on recent demand. The resulting forecast is more responsive because it will react to a true change in demand faster. The weights take on values between 0 and 1, and their sum must equal 1. There is no rule to determine the weights. Judgment and trial and error are the best ways to choose the weights. The formula for the weighted moving average for period t is

$$WMA_t = w_{t-1}(A_{t-1}) + w_{t-2}(A_{t-2}) + \ldots + w_{t-n}(A_{t-n})$$ [10.2]

where WMA_t is the weighted moving average forecast for period t,
A_{t-1} is the actual demand in the previous period,
W_{t-1} is the weight assigned to the actual demand in the previous period,
A_{t-2} and A_{t-n} are the actual demand two periods ago and n periods ago, respectively,
W_{t-2} and W_{t-n} are the weights assigned to the actual demand two periods ago and n periods ago, respectively.

In the Table 10.3 example, we selected the weights 0.5, 0.3, and 0.2. Note that the demand in December is assigned the heaviest weight of 0.5. The forecast for the January of next year is 123.8, which emphasizes the low demand in December. This is even more pronounced in another example with the weights 0.7 and 0.3. With a heavier emphasis placed on the most recent demand, the forecast reacts more quickly. Nevertheless, because it is an average of *past* values, it will always lag behind a seasonal pattern or a trend. This is demonstrated in Figure 10.5 for a 3-year time interval. Although the weighted moving average placing a heavier weight—0.7—on the most recent demand follows the actual demand more closely than does the weighted moving average with weights of 0.5, 0.3, and 0.2, it never catches up with the actual demand. The weighted moving average forecasting method is therefore appropriate for short-term forecasts only.

TABLE 10.3 – Weighted Moving Averages With Weights (0.5, 0.3, 0.2) and (0.7, 0.3)

Year	Month	Actual Demand	Weighted Moving Average, WMA_t (0.5, 0.3, 0.2)	Weighted Moving Average, WMA_t (0.7, 0.3)
3	Jan.	128		
3	Feb.	122		
3	Mar.	134		123.80
3	Apr.	118	$(0.5 \times 134) + (0.3 \times 122) + (0.2 \times 128) = 129.20$	130.40
3	May	140	$(0.5 \times 118) + (0.3 \times 134) + (0.2 \times 122) = 123.60$	122.80
3	Jun.	136	$(0.5 \times 140) + (0.3 \times 118) + (0.2 \times 134) = 132.20$	133.40
3	Jul.	146	$(0.5 \times 136) + (0.3 \times 140) + (0.2 \times 118) = 133.60$	137.20
3	Aug.	152	$(0.5 \times 146) + (0.3 \times 136) + (0.2 \times 140) = 141.80$	143.00
3	Sep.	154	$(0.5 \times 152) + (0.3 \times 146) + (0.2 \times 136) = 147.00$	150.20
3	Oct.	128	$(0.5 \times 154) + (0.3 \times 152) + (0.2 \times 146) = 151.80$	153.40
3	Nov.	124	$(0.5 \times 128) + (0.3 \times 154) + (0.2 \times 152) = 140.60$	135.80
3	Dec.	122	$(0.5 \times 124) + (0.3 \times 128) + (0.2 \times 154) = 131.20$	125.20
4	Jan.		$(0.5 \times 122) + (0.3 \times 124) + (0.2 \times 128) = 123.80$	122.60

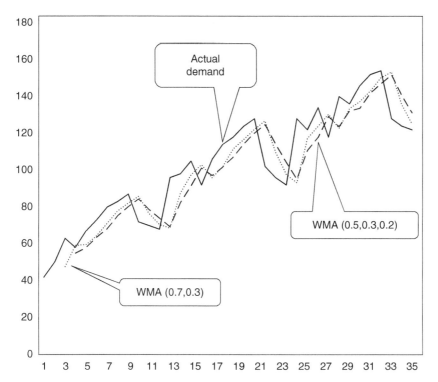

FIGURE 10.5 –
Comparison of
actual demand with
weighted moving
averages (Weights:
0.5, 0.3, 0.2 and
0.7, 0.3).

Exponential Smoothing

Exponential smoothing is one of the most popular forecasting techniques. It is similar to a weighted moving average technique in the sense that it assigns (a) a weight between 0 and 1 (called the smoothing constant), α, to the actual demand in the previous period and (b) a weight $(1 - \alpha)$ to the exponential smoothing forecast for the previous period (Box 10.4). The formula for the exponential forecast of demand in period t is

Exponential Smoothing

A weighted moving average technique that gives more weight to recent demand values than to earlier ones.

$$ES_t = \alpha\, A_{t-1} + (1 - \alpha)\, ES_{t-1}, \qquad [10.3]$$

where ES_t is the exponentially smoothed forecast for period t,
ES_{t-1} is the exponentially smoothed forecast for the previous period,
A_{t-1} is the actual demand in the previous period,
α is the smoothing constant ($0 \leq \alpha \leq 1$).

Note that the exponentially smoothed forecast is based on the actual demand and exponentially smoothing forecast for the previous period. In turn, the forecast for the previous period is based on the actual demand and the forecast two periods prior to the current period, and so on. The forecasts for previous periods are assigned a weight of $(1 - \alpha)$. Over time, the importance of past demand decreases exponentially, whereas greater emphasis is placed on more recent demand. Also note that we always need a forecast for the previous year. How far back can we go? In the BPH example, the first data point is for January. The exponential smoothing forecast for January cannot be computed if we have no prior

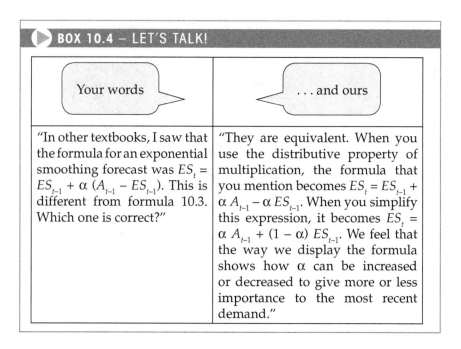

> **BOX 10.4 – LET'S TALK!**
>
> | Your words | . . . and ours |
> |---|---|
> | "In other textbooks, I saw that the formula for an exponential smoothing forecast was $ES_t = ES_{t-1} + \alpha (A_{t-1} - ES_{t-1})$. This is different from formula 10.3. Which one is correct?" | "They are equivalent. When you use the distributive property of multiplication, the formula that you mention becomes $ES_t = ES_{t-1} + \alpha A_{t-1} - \alpha ES_{t-1}$. When you simplify this expression, it becomes $ES_t = \alpha A_{t-1} + (1 - \alpha) ES_{t-1}$. We feel that the way we display the formula shows how α can be increased or decreased to give more or less importance to the most recent demand." |

data. Therefore, it is common procedure to choose an arbitrary forecast value that is realistic.

In our example (Table 10.4), we first chose an alpha value of 0.4. The forecast for January is 128.91. In another example, we selected an alpha value of 0.8. The forecast for January decreased to 122.76 because of the greater influence of the most recent demand value—122—in determining the forecast for January. As shown in Figure 10.6, the exponential smoothing forecast with $\alpha = 0.8$ is more responsive than the one with $\alpha = 0.4$, but it still lags behind the trend and the seasonal pattern. However, the benefit of the lower alpha is that it dampens the forecast's reaction to simple random fluctuations. Notice that in January, February, and March, the number of surgeries is fairly stable, except for the little dip in February. The exponential smoothing forecast with an alpha value of 0.4 overreacts to this random fluctuation (March forecast of 124.52), but to a lesser extent than does the exponential forecast with an alpha value of 0.8 (March forecast of 123.08). So, which alpha value should we select? The one that produces the most accurate forecast! As a general rule, when demand is fairly stable (e.g., demand for hospital gowns), we would prefer a lower value to minimize the effects of short-term or random changes. When demand changes for a reason (e.g., surge of flu-related visits at a community health center from December to February), we would favor a higher value to keep up with the pace of change. We could also adjust the exponential smoothing forecast for a trend if such a pattern exists (see section on techniques for trends).

The main advantage of the exponential smoothing technique over other averaging techniques is that it uses only two data points—the actual demand and forecast for the previous period—rather than demand values over multiple periods. This parsimony has contributed to its popularity in business.

TABLE 10.4 – Exponential Smoothing With α = 0.4 and α = 0.8

Year	Month	Actual Demand	Exponentially Smoothed Forecast, ES_t (α = 0.4)	Exponentially Smoothed Forecast, ES_t (α = 0.8)
3	Jan.	128	125.00	125.00
3	Feb.	122	$(0.4 \times 128) + (0.6 \times 125) = 126.20$	127.40
3	Mar.	134	$(0.4 \times 122) + (0.6 \times 126.2) = 124.52$	123.08
3	Apr.	118	$(0.4 \times 134) + (0.6 \times 124.52) = 128.31$	131.82
3	May	140	$(0.4 \times 118) + (0.6 \times 128.31) = 124.19$	120.76
3	Jun.	136	$(0.4 \times 140) + (0.6 \times 124.19) = 130.51$	136.15
3	Jul.	146	$(0.4 \times 136) + (0.6 \times 130.51) = 132.71$	136.03
3	Aug.	152	$(0.4 \times 146) + (0.6 \times 132.71) = 138.02$	144.01
3	Sep.	154	$(0.4 \times 152) + (0.6 \times 138.02) = 143.61$	150.40
3	Oct.	128	$(0.4 \times 154) + (0.6 \times 143.61) = 147.77$	153.28
3	Nov.	124	$(0.4 \times 128) + (0.6 \times 147.77) = 139.86$	133.06
3	Dec.	122	$(0.4 \times 124) + (0.6 \times 139.86) = 133.52$	125.81
4	Jan.		$(0.4 \times 122) + (0.6 \times 133.52) = 128.91$	122.76

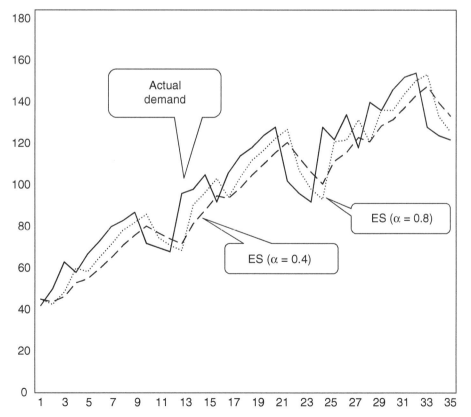

FIGURE 10.6 – Comparison of actual demand with exponentially smoothed forecasts (α = 0.4 and α = 0.8).

FORECAST ACCURACY

Forecast Error

The difference between actual demand in a given period and the forecasted value for that period.

The techniques covered so far have produced different forecasts for January of Year 4. Which forecast is likely to be more accurate? Forecast accuracy is determined by how closely the forecast matches the actual demand. Any deviation from the actual demand is a **forecast error**:

$$\text{Forecast error} = \text{Actual demand} - \text{Forecast.} \qquad [10.4]$$

Because a forecast *predicts* future demand, we cannot compare it to actual demand. However, because we have assumed that historical demand is representative of future demand, we can formulate "forecasts of the past" using a particular model and compare those forecasts to historical demand. In fact, this is precisely what we have done in Tables 10.2 to 10.5. Although we were then only interested in the forecast for January of year 4, we formulated "forecasts of the past" for several periods in year 3. There are three popular measures to assess forecast error: the mean absolute deviation, the mean squared error, and the mean absolute percentage error.

Mean Absolute Deviation

Mean Absolute Deviation (MAD)

A measure of forecast error that averages absolute values of forecast errors over n periods.

As its name indicates, the **mean absolute deviation** is the average of absolute forecast errors. Its formula is

$$\text{MAD} = \frac{\sum |\text{Actual demand} - \text{Forecast}|}{n} \qquad [10.5]$$

where n is the number of periods included in computing the sum of errors.

For example, the computation of the MAD for the simple moving average with $n = 5$ is

$$\text{MAD} = \frac{\begin{aligned} &|136 - 128.4| + |146 - 130.0| + |152 - 134.8| + |154 - 138.4| \\ &\quad + |128 - 145.6| + |124 - 143.2| + |122 - 140.8| \end{aligned}}{7}$$

$$= \frac{7.6 + 16.0 + 17.2 + 15.6 + 17.6 + 19.2 + 18.8}{7}$$

$$= 16.00.$$

An MAD of 16 means that on average, the forecasts generated by the SMA with $n = 5$ are "off" (above or below) the actual demand for surgeries by 16. Table 10.5 shows the MAD values for all the simple moving average, weighted moving average, and exponential smoothing models we formulated in earlier sections. Based on the MADs, both the weighted moving average model with weights of 0.7 and 0.3 and the exponential smoothing model with an alpha value of 0.8 produce the most accurate forecasts even though, on average, they underestimate or overestimate the actual demand by about 10

TABLE 10.5 – MAD Values for Simple Moving Average, Weighted Moving Average, and Exponential Smoothing Models

Month	Actual Demand	SMA_t (n = 3)	Abs. Error	SMA_t (n = 5)	Abs. Error	WMA_t (.5,.3,.2)	Abs. Error	WMA_t (.7,.3)	Abs. Error	ES_t (α = .4)	Abs. Error	ES_t (α = .8)	Abs. Error
Jan.	128									125.00		125.00	
Feb.	122									126.20	4.20	127.40	5.40
Mar.	134							123.80	10.20	124.52	9.48	123.08	10.92
Apr.	118	128.00	10.00			129.20	11.20	130.40	12.40	128.31	10.31	131.82	13.82
May	140	124.67	15.33			123.60	16.40	122.80	17.20	124.19	15.81	120.76	19.24
Jun.	136	130.67	5.33	128.40	7.60	132.20	3.80	133.40	2.60	130.51	5.49	136.15	0.15
Jul.	146	131.33	14.67	130.00	16.00	133.60	12.40	137.20	8.80	132.71	13.29	136.03	9.97
Aug.	152	140.67	11.33	134.80	17.20	141.80	10.20	143.00	9.00	138.02	13.98	144.01	7.99
Sep.	154	144.67	9.33	138.40	15.60	147.00	7.00	150.20	3.80	143.61	10.39	150.40	3.60
Oct.	128	150.67	22.67	145.60	17.60	151.80	23.80	153.40	25.40	147.77	19.77	153.28	25.28
Nov.	124	144.67	20.67	143.20	19.20	140.60	16.60	135.80	11.80	139.86	15.86	133.06	9.06
Dec.	122	135.33	13.33	140.80	18.80	131.20	9.20	125.20	3.20	133.52	11.52	125.81	3.81
MAD			**13.63**		**16.00**		**12.29**		**10.44**		**11.83**		**9.93**

units. Note that we did not include the first forecasts for exponential smoothing in computing their respective MADs. Because the first forecasts were determined arbitrarily, they do not reflect the accuracy of the selected forecasting technique and therefore their deviations from the actual demand are irrelevant. The MAD relies on absolute deviations. Therefore, the positive and negative errors do not cancel out when they are summed to obtain the average.

Mean Squared Error

Mean Squared Error (MSE)
A measure of forecast error that averages squared forecast errors over n periods.

Another measure of forecast error is the **mean squared error**. The MSE captures the average of the squared deviations between the forecast and the actual demand:

$$\text{MSE} = \frac{\sum (\text{Actual demand} - \text{Forecast})^2}{n} \qquad [10.6]$$

For example, the computation of the MSE for the weighted moving average with weights 0.5, 0.3, and 0.2 is as follows:

$$\text{MSE} = \frac{\begin{array}{c}(118-129.2)^2 + (140-123.6)^2 + (136-132.2)^2 + (146-133.6)^2 \\ + (152-141.8)^2 + (154-147)^2 + (128-151.8)^2 \\ + (124-140.6)^2 + (122-131.2)^2\end{array}}{9}$$

$$= \frac{\begin{array}{c}125.44 + 268.96 + 14.44 + 153.76 + 104.04 + 49.00 \\ + 566.44 + 275.56 + 84.64\end{array}}{9}$$

$$= 182.48$$

Table 10.6 shows the MSE values for all the simple moving average, weighted moving average, and exponential smoothing models we formulated in earlier sections. As expected, the weighted moving average model with weights of 0.7 and 0.3 as well as the exponential smoothing model with an alpha value of 0.8 yields the most accurate forecasts. Because of the squaring of the error term, the MSE accentuates large errors. Penalizing large errors to a greater extent is especially useful in environments where errors may have severe consequences, such as in healthcare. For example, underestimating the actual demand for plasma would place patients at risk if emergency stocks cannot be replenished fast enough.

Mean Absolute Percentage Error (MAPE)
A relative measure of forecast error that averages absolute values of forecast errors with respect to actual demand.

Mean Absolute Percentage Error

With both the MAD and MSE, the size of the deviations depends on the volume of the item being forecast. For example, if the demand is in thousands of units, the absolute and squared deviations could be quite

TABLE 10.6 – MSE Values for Simple Moving Average, Weighted Moving Average, and Exponential Smoothing Models

Month	Actual Demand	SMA, (n = 3)	(Error)²	SMA, (n = 5)	(Error)²	WMA, (.5,.3,.2)	(Error)²	WMA, (.7,.3)	(Error)²	ES, (α = .4)	(Error)²	ES, (α = .8)	(Error)²
Jan.	128									125.00		125.00	
Feb	122									126.20	17.64	127.40	29.16
Mar.	134							123.80	104.04	124.52	89.87	123.08	119.25
Apr.	118	128.00	100.00			129.20	125.44	130.40	153.76	128.31	106.34	131.82	190.88
May	140	124.67	235.11			123.60	268.96	122.80	295.84	124.19	250.04	120.76	370.05
Jun.	136	130.67	28.44	128.40	57.76	132.20	14.44	133.40	6.76	130.51	30.11	136.15	0.02
Jul.	146	131.33	215.11	130.00	256.00	133.60	153.76	137.20	77.44	132.71	176.69	136.03	99.39
Aug.	152	140.67	128.44	134.80	295.84	141.80	104.04	143.00	81.00	138.02	195.32	144.01	63.90
Sep.	154	144.67	87.11	138.40	243.36	147.00	49.00	150.20	14.44	143.61	107.86	150.40	12.95
Oct.	128	150.67	513.78	145.60	309.76	151.80	566.44	153.40	645.16	147.77	390.81	153.28	639.09
Nov.	124	144.67	427.11	143.20	368.64	140.60	275.56	135.80	139.24	139.86	251.58	133.06	82.01
Dec.	122	135.33	177.78	140.80	353.44	131.20	84.64	125.20	10.24	133.52	132.64	125.81	14.53
MSE			212.54		269.26		182.48		152.79		158.99		147.39

large. The **MAPE** remedies this problem by expressing the deviation as a percentage of the actual demand. Its formula is

$$MAPE = \frac{\sum \left(\dfrac{|\text{Actual demand} - \text{Forecast}|}{\text{Actual demand}} \times 100 \right)}{n} \qquad [10.7]$$

For example, the computation of the MAPE for the exponentially smoothed forecast with an alpha value of 0.4 is

$$MAPE = \frac{\begin{array}{l} 100\left(|22 - 126.2| / 122\right) + 100\left(|134 - 124.52| / 134\right) \\[4pt] \qquad + 100\left(|118 - 128.31| / 118\right) + \ldots\ldots \\[4pt] \qquad + 100\left(|122 - 133.52| / 122\right) \end{array}}{11}$$

$$= \frac{3.44 + 7.07 + 8.74 + \ldots\ldots + 9.44}{11}$$

$$= 8.85\%$$

The MAPE value of 8.85% means that on average, the forecasts generated by the exponential smoothing model with an alpha value of 0.4 are 8.85% off the actual demand. The MAPE values for the weighted moving average model with weights of 0.7 and 0.3 and for the exponential smoothing model with an alpha of 0.8 are 7.87% and 7.52%, respectively. The MAPE confirms that these two models produce the most accurate forecasts (Table 10.7).

TECHNIQUES FOR TRENDS

The models covered so far are appropriate when the demand fluctuates around an average. If there is a seasonal or trend pattern, they fail to anticipate the movement.

Trend-Adjusted Exponential Smoothing

Remember that an exponentially smoothed forecast will always lag behind an upward or downward trend in the data. To compensate for this deficiency, it is possible to adjust the exponentially smoothed average for the positive or negative trend. We simply introduce a second smoothing constant, a, to adjust for the trend. The revised formula is

$$TAES_t = F_t + T_t \qquad [10.8]$$

$$F_t = \alpha\, A_{t-1} + (1 - \alpha)\, TAES_{t-1} \qquad [10.9]$$

$$T_t = \beta\, (F_t - F_{t-1}) + (1 - \beta)\, (T_{t-1}), \qquad [10.10]$$

where $TAES_t$ is the trend-adjusted exponentially smoothed forecast for period t,

F_t is the exponentially smoothed forecast for period t,

TABLE 10.7 – MAPE Values for Simple Moving Average, Weighted Moving Average, and Exponential Smoothing Models

(|Actual − Forecast| / Actual) × 100

Month	Actual Demand	SMA_t (n = 3)	Abs.% error	SMA_t (n = 5)	Abs.% error	WMA_t (.5,.3,.2)	Abs.% error	WMA_t (.7,.3)	Abs.% error	ES_t (α = .4)	Abs.% error	ES_t (α = .8)	Abs.% error
Jan.	128									125.00		125.00	
Feb	122									126.20	3.44	127.40	4.43
Mar.	134							123.80		124.52	7.07	123.08	8.15
Apr.	118	128.00	8.47			129.20	9.49	130.40	10.51	128.31	8.74	131.82	11.71
May	140	124.67	10.95			123.60	11.71	122.80	12.29	124.19	11.29	120.76	13.74
Jun.	136	130.67	3.92	128.40	5.59	132.20	2.79	133.40	1.91	130.51	4.04	136.15	0.11
Jul.	146	131.33	10.05	130.00	10.96	133.60	8.49	137.20	6.03	132.71	9.10	136.03	6.83
Aug.	152	140.67	7.46	134.80	11.32	141.80	6.71	143.00	5.92	138.02	9.19	144.01	5.26
Sep.	154	144.67	6.06	138.40	10.13	147.00	4.55	150.20	2.47	143.61	6.74	150.40	2.34
Oct.	128	150.67	17.71	145.60	13.75	151.80	18.59	153.40	19.84	147.77	15.44	153.28	19.75
Nov.	124	144.67	16.67	143.20	15.48	140.60	13.39	135.80	9.52	139.86	12.79	133.06	7.30
Dec.	122	135.33	10.93	140.80	15.41	131.20	7.54	125.20	2.62	133.52	9.44	125.81	3.12
MAPE			10.25%		11.81%		9.25%		7.87%		8.85%		7.52%

T_t is the exponentially smoothed trend estimate for period t,
A_{t-1} is the actual demand in the previous period,
$TAES_{t-1}$ is the trend-adjusted exponentially smoothed forecast for the previous period,
F_{t-1} is the exponentially smoothed forecast for the previous period,
T_{t-1} is the exponentially smoothed trend estimate for the previous period,
α is the smoothing constant for the average ($0 \le \alpha \le 1$),
β is the smoothing constant for the trend ($0 \le \beta \le 1$).

There are therefore several steps needed to compute a trend-adjusted exponentially smoothed forecast. They are (Heizer & Render, 2011) as follows:

Step 1: Compute the exponentially smoothed forecast for period t, F_t (Equation 10.9).

Step 2: Compute the exponentially smoothed trend estimate, T_t (Equation 10.10).

Step 3: Compute the trend-adjusted exponentially smoothed forecast for period t, $TAES_t$, by adding the values calculated in steps 1 and 2 (Equation 10.8).

The rationale for choosing appropriate values is the same as that for α values: a lower β is less responsive to change, and vice versa. In our example, using $\alpha = 0.4$, $\beta = 0.3$, an initial forecast of 125, and an initial trend value of 1, we obtain a trend-adjusted forecast of 127 surgeries for January of year 4 (Table 10.8). Computations for period 2 are explained as follows.

Step 1: $F_2 = \alpha A_1 + (1 - \alpha)\, TAES_1$
$\qquad = (0.4)(128) + (0.6)(126)$
$\qquad = 126.80.$

Step 2: $T_2 = \beta\,(F_2 - F_1) + (1 - \beta)\,(T_1)$
$\qquad = (0.3)(126.80 - 125.00) + (0.7)(1)$
$\qquad = 1.24.$

Step 3: $TAES_2 = F_2 + T_2$
$\qquad = 126.80 + 1.24$
$\qquad = 128.04.$

Computations for period 3 are as follows:

Step 1: $F_3 = \alpha A_2 + (1 - \alpha)\, TAES_2$
$\qquad = (0.4)(122) + (0.6)(128.04)$
$\qquad = 125.62.$

Step 2: $T_3 = \beta\,(F_3 - F_2) + (1 - \beta)\,(T_2)$
$\qquad = (0.3)(125.62 - 126.80) + (0.7)(1.24)$
$\qquad = 0.52.$

Step 3: $TAES_3 = F_3 + T_3$
$\qquad = 125.62 + 0.52$
$\qquad = 126.14.$

Year	Month	Actual Demand	Exponentially Smoothed Forecast, F_t $(\alpha = 0.4)$	Exponentially Smoothed Trend Estimate, T_t $(\beta = 0.3)$	Trend-Adjusted Forecast, $TAES_t$
TABLE 10.8 – Trend-Adjusted Exponential Smoothing with $\alpha = 0.4$ and $\beta = 0.3$					
3	Jan.	128	125.00	1	126.00
3	Feb.	122	126.80	1.24	128.04
3	Mar.	134	125.62	0.52	126.14
3	Apr.	118	129.28	1.46	130.74
3	May	140	125.65	–0.07	125.57
3	Jun.	136	131.34	1.66	133.01
3	Jul.	146	134.20	2.02	136.22
3	Aug.	152	140.13	3.19	143.33
3	Sep.	154	146.80	4.23	151.03
3	Oct.	128	152.22	4.59	156.81
3	Nov.	124	145.28	1.13	146.42
3	Dec.	122	137.45	–1.56	135.89
4	Jan.		130.34	–3.22	127.11

Figure 10.7 shows that the trend-adjusted forecast follows the trend quite closely over a 3-year period. However, the forecast still lags behind the seasonal pattern. There are more sophisticated exponential smoothing models that adjust for seasonality as well, but they are beyond the scope of this chapter.

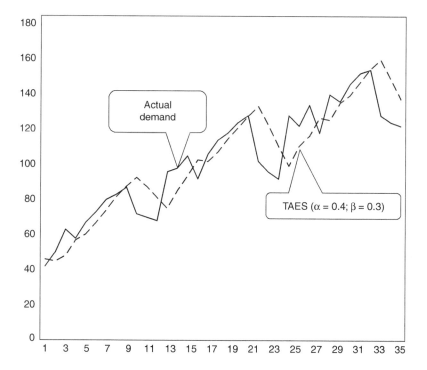

FIGURE 10.7 – Comparison of actual demand with trend-adjusted exponentially smoothed forecasts ($\alpha = 0.4$ and $\beta = 0.3$).

Linear Trend Projections

Another time series model that accounts for trends is a version of the **linear regression** technique, which is covered later in this chapter. It involves fitting a trend line to the historical demand data points and forecasting demand into the future. The ability to forecast for multiple periods in the future sets this technique apart from those presented so far in this chapter. The other forecasting methods required the inclusion of the actual demand in the previous period (A_{t-1}), making it impossible to forecast beyond the current period. Although this is suitable for short-term forecasting, there are many situations for which a medium or long-time horizon is desirable.

The *least-squares* method enables us to develop a trend line that minimizes the sum of the squared deviations between the line and the actual data points. That line illustrates the upward or downward relationship between an independent and a dependent variable. In time series models, we assume that demand changes as a function of time. Therefore, the independent variable is the time period, and the dependent variable is demand. The equation of the line—or regression equation—includes a y-intercept and a slope. The **y-intercept** is the value of y at the point where the trend line crosses the y-axis. In other words, it is the demand (y) value when $x = 0$. The **slope** indicates the change in the dependent variable for a one-unit increase in the independent variable. Therefore, it is the change in demand expected from one time period increment. The regression equation is expressed as follows:

$$\hat{y} = a + bx \qquad [10.11]$$

where $\hat{y}$ is the predicted value of the dependent variable, that is, demand,
a is the y-intercept,
b is the slope,
x is the value of the independent variable, that is, time period;

a and b can be computed using the following formulas:

$$a = \bar{y} - b\bar{x} \qquad [10.12]$$

$$b = \frac{\sum xy - n\bar{x}\bar{y}}{\sum x^2 - n\bar{x}^2} \qquad [10.13]$$

where $\bar{y}$ is the average of the y values,
$\bar{x}$ is the average of the x values,
n is the number of data points used to compute b.

Because trends typically occur over several years, we will use the surgery volume at BPH for the past 3 years. To simplify the illustration, we have aggregated the monthly data into quarterly data (Table 10.9).

Linear Regression
A statistical technique that fits a trend line to historical data points by minimizing the sum of the squared deviations between points on the line and the actual data points.

y-intercept
The value of y at the point where the trend line crosses the y-axis.

Slope
Indicates change in the value of y for a one-unit increase in x.

TABLE 10.9 – Computations for Trend-Line Equations

Year	Quarter	Actual Demand, y	xy	x²
1	1	155	155	1
1	2	198	396	4
1	3	250	750	9
1	4	210	840	16
2	5	299	1,495	25
2	6	312	1,872	36
2	7	370	2,590	49
2	8	290	2,320	64
3	9	384	3,456	81
3	10	394	3,940	100
3	11	452	4,972	121
3	12	374	4,488	144
Sum	78	3,688	27,274	650

$$\bar{x} = \frac{\sum x}{n} = \frac{78}{12} = 6.5$$

$$\bar{y} = \frac{\sum y}{n} = \frac{3,688}{12} = 307.33$$

$$b = \frac{\sum xy - n\bar{x}\bar{y}}{\sum x^2 - n\bar{x}^2} = \frac{27,274 - (12)(6.5)(307.33)}{650 - (12)(6.5^2)} = 23.09$$

$$a = \bar{y} - b\bar{x} = 307.33 - (23.09)(6.5) = 157.24$$

The regression equation is $y = 157.24 + 23.09x$. Using this equation, we can now forecast the demand for surgeries for the first three quarters of year 4 (Box 10.5):

Predicted demand for surgeries in year 4, quarter 1 (13th quarter):

$$\hat{y}_{13} = 157.24 = 23.09(13)$$

$$= 457.41.$$

Predicted demand for surgeries in year 4, quarter 2 (14th quarter):

$$\hat{y}_{14} = 157.24 + 23.09(14)$$
$$= 480.50.$$

Predicted demand for surgeries in year 4, quarter 3 (15th quarter):

$$\hat{y}_{15} = 157.24 + 23.09(14)$$

$$= 503.59.$$

Figure 10.8 indicates that the trend fits the data quite well. However, it does not account for seasonal fluctuations. Before we explain how to incorporate seasonality into our forecasts, it is important to keep in mind that the least-squares method is suitable when:

1. The trend movement is linear. If it is curvilinear, another model is required.

FIGURE 10.8 – Trend line fitted to actual demand and projections for quarters 13–15.

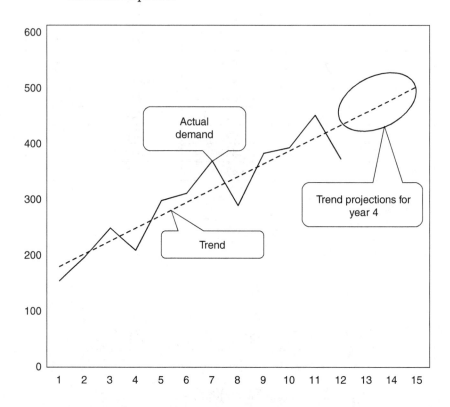

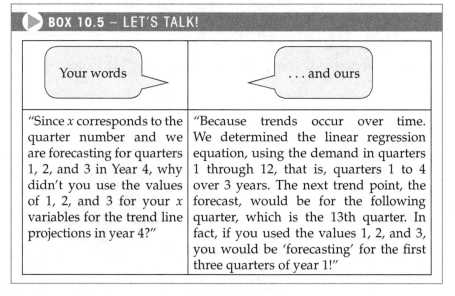

BOX 10.5 – LET'S TALK!

Your words

"Since x corresponds to the quarter number and we are forecasting for quarters 1, 2, and 3 in Year 4, why didn't you use the values of 1, 2, and 3 for your x variables for the trend line projections in year 4?"

...and ours

"Because trends occur over time. We determined the linear regression equation, using the demand in quarters 1 through 12, that is, quarters 1 to 4 over 3 years. The next trend point, the forecast, would be for the following quarter, which is the 13th quarter. In fact, if you used the values 1, 2, and 3, you would be 'forecasting' for the first three quarters of year 1!"

2. Future projections are not made too far into the future. For example, stock market projections are more likely to be accurate for the next few months than for the next 10 years. Over long periods of time, new patterns may emerge. In a similar vein, the number of periods for which demand is projected should never exceed the number of periods included in the database.

3. The deviations between actual demand and the computed trend line are assumed to be normally distributed with most of the demand points close to the line, and only a few points scattered further out.

TECHNIQUES FOR SEASONALITY

Remember that seasonality does not necessarily refer to a calendar season. It is any recurring variation that may happen daily, weekly, monthly, and so on. In a time series, seasonality is expressed as the amount of deviation between the actual demand values and the average value of the series. If demand is fairly constant, the average value is simply the mean of the data. When a trend is present, the average value is the trend value. There are two types of seasonal patterns: additive and multiplicative. With an additive model, a certain amount, let us say 20 units, is added to and subtracted from the trend value or average to reflect the upward and downward movements of the seasonal pattern. With a multiplicative model, seasonality is a percentage of the average value or trend. Because the multiplicative model is predominant in business, we will focus on it exclusively in this chapter. Seasonal percentages are known as **seasonal indices**. For example, a seasonal index of 0.7 during the month of November would indicate that the demand during that month is only 70% of the average. Knowledge of the seasonal indices can be very useful to *deseasonalize* or remove the seasonal pattern from the data and identify some other pattern (e.g., trend or cycle), or lack of it, which may not be apparent at first.

Seasonal Index
A demand expressed as a percentage of an average or trend.

Computing Seasonal Indices and Forecasting

Incorporating seasonality into our forecasts involves several steps (Stevenson, 2012). To illustrate, we will refer to the quarterly data previously shown in Table 10.9. All computations and steps are displayed in Table 10.10.

STEP 1: Calculate the average demand for each season. For example, the average demand for quarter 1 is $(155 + 299 + 384)/3 = 279.33$.

STEP 2: Calculate the overall average demand per season. This is done by averaging the average demand for each season (computed in step 1). In our case, the overall average quarterly demand is $(279.33 + 301.33 + 357.33 + 291.33)/4 = 307.33$.

STEP 3: Calculate the seasonal index. This is done by dividing the average demand per season (step 1) by the overall average demand per season (step 2).

STEP 4: Calculate the average demand in the next periods for which you want to obtain demand forecasts. The actual demand seems to increase by about 400 surgeries per year. With this upward trend in mind, we predict that the surgery volume in year 4 will be about 2,000, or 500 per quarter.

STEP 5: Multiply the average demand projections by the seasonal indices. The demand in quarters 1, 2, 3, and 4 in year 4 will be:

Seasonally adjusted demand for surgeries in quarter 1 = $500 \times 0.91 = 455$

Seasonally adjusted demand for surgeries in quarter 2 = $500 \times 0.98 = 490$

Seasonally adjusted demand for surgeries in quarter 3 = $500 \times 1.16 = 580$

Seasonally adjusted demand for surgeries in quarter 4 = $500 \times 0.95 = 475$.

TABLE 10.10 – Adjusting Forecast for Seasonality

Quarter	Year 1	Year 2	Year 3	Quarter Average	Seasonal Index	Forecast (Year 4)
1	155	299	384	279.33	0.91	$500 \times 0.91 = 455$
2	198	312	394	301.33	0.98	$500 \times 0.98 = 490$
3	250	370	452	357.33	1.16	$500 \times 1.16 = 580$
4	210	290	374	291.33	0.95	$500 \times 0.95 = 475$
Total	813	1,271	1,604			2,000
Overall average demand per quarter				307.33		

(Step 1 → Quarter Average; Step 3 → Seasonal Index; Step 5 → Forecast (Year 4); Step 2 → Overall average demand per quarter; Step 4 → 2,000)

Decomposing a Time Series Using Least-Squares Regression

When there is a trend, as is the case in our data set, it is common to first decompose the time series into its components and then forecast future values of each component (Chase, Aquilano, & Jacobs, 2006). Again, we follow a series of steps to quantify trend and seasonality and then develop forecasts (Table 10.11). We will use the same data as in the previous example.

STEP 1: Calculate the seasonal index as described in steps 1, 2, and 3 of the previous section. In other words, we compute the average demand for each quarter based on our 3 years of data. Then we compute the overall average demand per quarter. Finally, we divide the average demand for each quarter by the overall average.

STEP 2: Deseasonalize the actual demand by dividing each original data point by the appropriate seasonal index. For example, the demand in the first quarter of year 1 is 155. When we divide it by the seasonal index for quarter 1, we obtain 155/0.91 = 170.33.

STEP 3: Develop a regression equation for the deseasonalized data. The deseasonalized data are the dependent or y variable. The quarter numbers (1–12 over 3 years) are the independent or x variable. Using Excel, we obtain the following regression equation: $y = 162.14 + 22.33x$.

STEP 4: Use the regression equation to project demand in future periods. Because we want to forecast the volume of surgeries in quarters 13 to 16 (quarters 1–4 in year 4), the trend values are as follows:

Trend value for surgeries in quarter 13 = 162.14 + (22.33)(13) = 452.43
Trend value for surgeries in quarter 14 = 162.14 + (22.33)(14) = 474.76
Trend value for surgeries in quarter 15 = 162.14 + (22.33)(15) = 497.09
Trend value for surgeries in quarter 16 = 162.14 + (22.33)(16) = 519.42.

STEP 5: Adjust the trend forecasts for seasonality by multiplying the trend value by the appropriate seasonal index. The demand in quarters 1, 2, 3, and 4 in year 4 will be:

Seasonally adjusted demand for surgeries in quarter 13 = 452.43 × 0.91 = 411.71
Seasonally adjusted demand for surgeries in quarter 14 = 474.76 × 0.98 = 465.26
Seasonally adjusted demand for surgeries in quarter 15 = 497.09 × 1.16 = 576.62
Seasonally adjusted demand for surgeries in quarter 16 = 519.42 × 0.95 = 493.45.

The forecasts are different from those obtained using an approximation of the trend, but not by much. Figure 10.9 reveals a very good fit to the actual data.

BRADLEY PARK HOSPITAL 10.3

Sheila was headed toward the cafeteria when she ran into Sebastian Giles, one of the budget officers. "Hi Sheila, I haven't seen you for a while. How are you?" he said cheerfully. "Hi Sebastian. I feel much better than the last time I saw you. Thanks for all your help!" Sheila exclaimed. "I have run several models. The demand for stent surgeries has both an upward trend and a seasonal pattern. I computed the average seasonal index for each quarter and was able

TABLE 10.11 – Trend Projections Adjusted for Seasonality

			Step 1	Step 2	Step 4*	Step 5
Year	Quarter	Actual Demand, y	Seasonal Index	Deseasonalized Demand	Trend, $\hat{y}$	Forecasts
1	1	155	0.91	155/0.91 = 170.33	184.47	184.47 × 0.91 = 167.87
1	2	198	0.98	198/0.98 = 202.04	206.80	206.80 × 0.98 = 202.66
1	3	250	1.16	250/1.16 = 215.52	229.13	229.13 × 1.16 = 265.79
1	4	210	0.95	210/0.95 = 221.05	251.46	251.46 × 0.95 = 238.89
2	1	299	0.91	299/0.91 = 328.57	273.79	273.79 × 0.91 = 249.15
2	2	312	0.98	312/0.98 = 318.37	296.12	296.12 × 0.98 = 290.20
2	3	370	1.16	370/1.16 = 318.97	318.45	318.45 × 1.16 = 369.40
2	4	290	0.95	290/0.95 = 305.26	340.78	340.78 × 0.95 = 323.74
3	1	384	0.91	384/0.91 = 421.98	363.11	363.11 × 0.91 = 330.43
3	2	394	0.98	394/0.98 = 402.04	385.44	385.44 × 0.98 = 377.73
3	3	452	1.16	452/1.16 = 389.66	407.77	407.77 × 1.16 = 473.01
3	4	374	0.95	374/0.95 = 393.68	430.10	430.10 × 0.95 = 408.60
4	1 (13)		0.91		**452.43**	**452.43 × 0.91 = 411.71**
4	2 (14)		0.98		**474.76**	**474.76 × 0.98 = 465.26**
4	3 (15)		1.16		**497.09**	**497.09 × 1.16 = 576.62**
4	4 (16)		0.95		**519.42**	**519.42 × 0.95 = 493.45**

*Step 3: $y = 162.14 + 22.33x$.

FIGURE 10.9 – Comparison of actual demand with forecasts adjusted for trend and seasonality.

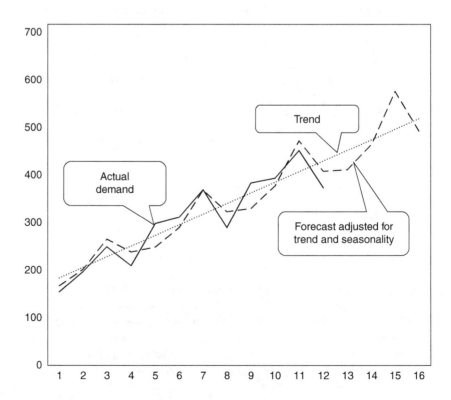

to forecast for several quarters into the future. Having a sense of what our future demand will be makes me feel more confident in my ability to manage supplies. Would you mind if I showed you the numbers? I just want to be sure that I am on the right track." Sebastian replied, "No problem. I am quite busy this afternoon, but stop by tomorrow, any time after 10:00. Just one thought: I recall that the volume of surgeries was lower during certain months of the year. I am wondering whether computing seasonal indices on a monthly basis might yield more accurate results. Let's check it out." "Good point!" said Sheila, " I'll see you tomorrow. Bye, Sebastian." "Bye, Sheila."

 Do you think it would be preferable to compute seasonal indices for each month rather than for each quarter? Use the 3 years of monthly data (Table 10.1) to justify your answer.

ASSOCIATIVE MODELS

So far, we have assumed that demand fluctuated as a function of time only. However, demand may be influenced by a myriad of other variables such as price, geographic distance from target market, age distribution of patient population, and so on. If the relationships between these variables and demand are linear, we can use the multiple linear regression technique to show the effect of predictor (or independent) variables on a dependent variable (demand); see Box 10.6. The model is expressed as follows:

$$\hat{y} = a + b_1x_1 + b_2x_2 + \ldots + b_nx_n \qquad [10.14]$$

where $\hat{y}$ is the predicted value of the dependent variable, that is, demand

a is the y-intercept, a constant

b_1, b_2, and b_n are the regression coefficients of x_1, x_2, and x_n, respectively

x_1, x_2, and x_n are the values of the first, second, and nth independent variables.

Let us assume that the demand for nursing home beds in a metropolitan area depends on the size and income level of the population 65 years and older. Table 10.12 shows the data collected in 25 metropolitan areas. The computations to obtain the regression coefficients are beyond the scope of this book. We used Excel (see Appendix 10.1 for steps) to obtain the model parameters (Figure 10.10). A very important regression statistic is R^2, also known as the **coefficient of multiple determination**. It indicates the proportion of variance in the dependent variable explained by the regression equation. We see here that population size and income level account for 81% of the variation in the demand for nursing home beds. The intercept is 2,905.081. The regression coefficient for population size (x_1) is 19.92. It means that the demand for beds increases by 19.92 for every one-unit (here 1,000) increment in population size. The p-value of .000000161 indicates that

Coefficient of Multiple Determination, R^2

A proportion of variance in the dependent variable explained by the regression equation.

the probability of concluding that population size affects the demand for beds when in fact it does not (Type 1 error) is almost zero. Similarly, the regression coefficient for the number of people living below the poverty level (x_2) is −63.15. It means that the demand for beds decreases by 63.15 for every one-unit (here 1,000) increment in the number of people living below the poverty level. The rationale is that people with low incomes usually cannot afford nursing homes. The p-value of .0079 indicates that that probability of making a Type 1 error is very low (below the typical 0.05 threshold). Therefore, we can say that both population size and income level are statistically significant predictors of the demand for nursing home beds. If we wanted to predict the demand for nursing home beds given a population of 100,000 people 65 years and older and 12,000 living below the poverty level, we would use the following equation:

$$\hat{y} = 2,905.081 + 19.92(100) - 63.15(12)$$

$$= 4,139.28 \text{ beds} \approx 4,139 \text{ beds.}$$

TABLE 10.12 – Data for Multiple Regression Example

Nursing Home Beds, y	Population 65 + (in thousands), x_1	Number of People 65 + Below Poverty Level (in thousands), x_2
4420	90.2	8.5
3159	80.2	11.2
4180	89.6	9.5
3855	86.1	8.7
3416	84.3	17.5
2955	48.6	15.1
2732	30.5	14.2
3542	80.0	11.2
2713	52.6	15.4
4336	91.7	8.5
3230	61.5	12.5
3148	59.8	9.7
3561	74.1	12.8
4668	98.3	6.5
3697	85.2	14.5
3620	87.1	15.2
2070	28.4	13.1
4310	87.3	9.6
3376	39.5	10.0
2945	32.1	15.1
3315	46.9	14.2
3228	44.8	13.2
2659	28.5	10.0
2863	35.6	12.5
3309	61.2	16.5

SUMMARY OUTPUT									
Regression Statistics									
Multiple R	0.900239								
R Square	0.81043								
Adjusted R Square	0.793196								
Standard Error	285.7224								
Observations	25								
	Coefficients	*Standard Error*	*t Stat*	*P-value*	*Lower 95%*	*Upper 95%*	*Lower 95.0%*	*Upper 95.0%*	
Intercept	2905.081	366.9271	7.91732555	7.01E-08	2144.121	3666.041	2144.121	3666.041	
Population size	19.91911	2.647974	7.522397	1.61E-07	14.42755	25.41067	14.42755	25.41067	
Below poverty	−63.151	21.59984	−2.92367799	0.007866	−107.946	−18.3557	−107.946	−18.3557	

FIGURE 10.10 – Partial Excel output for nursing home beds.

BOX 10.6 – OM IN PRACTICE!

Forecasting Patient Volume in the Emergency Department

Demand forecasting is important for the allocation of resources in the ED. A study explored and evaluated several quantitative forecasting methods to predict daily ED patient volumes: seasonal autoregressive integrated moving average, exponential smoothing, time series regression with and without climatic variables, and artificial neural networks. The benchmark was a multiple linear regression model based on calendar variables and holidays. The analysis confirmed annual and weekly seasonal patterns in ED visits. Based on the MAPE, the various forecasting methods proved to be only marginally better than the simple benchmark model (Jones et al., 2008).

SUMMARY

Forecasting demand is important to be able to plan and allocate the resources necessary to provide uninterrupted, quality customer service and avoid the excess costs arising from mismatched demand and resource supply. Furthermore, because flexibility is the ability to respond effectively and efficiently to changes in demand, accurate demand forecasts are a prerequisite for adequate performance in that competitive priority. In other words, accurate demand forecasts help support quality, delivery, flexibility, and cost (Figure 10.11).

It is good practice to use both judgment-based qualitative approaches and data-driven quantitative approaches when forecasting demand. Popular qualitative techniques include the jury of executive opinion, the Delphi method, and consumer research. Quantitative techniques include time series and associative models. Time series models assume that past demand data are representative of future demand. Such models include simple moving average, weighted moving average, exponential smoothing, and trend projections. Associative models assume that several variables influence demand.

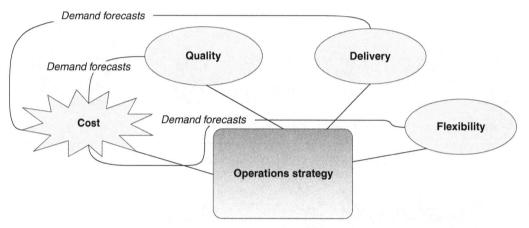

FIGURE 10.11 – Mind map with demand forecasts linking the competitive priorities.

KEY TERMS

Demand Forecast	Stability	Mean squared error (MSE)
Qualitative approaches	Responsiveness	Mean absolute percentage error (MAPE)
Quantitative approaches	Naïve approach	Linear regression
Time series	Simple moving average	y-intercept
Trend	Weighted moving average	Slope
Cycle	Exponential smoothing	Seasonal index
Seasonality	Forecast error	Coefficient of multiple determination, R^2
Irregular movement	Mean absolute deviation (MAD)	

FORMULAS USED IN THIS CHAPTER

Model	Definition	Formula	Number
Time series	Simple moving average	$SMA_t = \dfrac{(A_t - n + ... + A_{t-2} + A_{t-1})}{n}$	[10.1]
	Weighted moving average	$WMA_t = w_{t-1}(A_{t-1})$ $+ w_{t-2}(A_{t-2})$ $+ .... + w_{t-n}(A_{t-n})$	[10.2]
	Exponential forecast of demand	$ES_t = \alpha A_{t-1} + (1 - \alpha)\, ES_{t-1}$	[10.3]
	Trend-adjusted exponential smoothing	$TAES_t = F_t + T_t$	[10.8]
	Exponentially smoothed forecast	$F_t = \alpha A_{t-1} + (1 - \alpha)\, TAES_{t-1}$	[10.9]
	Exponentially smoothed trend estimate	$T_t = \beta\,(F_t - F_{t-1})$ $+ (1 - \beta)\,(T_{t-1})$	[10.10]
	Linear trend	$\hat{y} = a + bx$	[10.11]
	y-intercept	$a = \bar{y} - b\bar{x}$	[10.12]
	Slope	$b = \dfrac{\sum xy - n\bar{x}\bar{y}}{\sum x^2 - n\bar{x}^2}$	[10.13]
Associative	Multiple linear regression	$\hat{y} = a + b_1 x_1 + b_2 x_2$ $+ ... + b_n x_n$	[10.14]
Forecast accuracy	Forecast error	Error = Actual demand − Forecast	[10.4]
	Mean absolute deviation	$MAD = \dfrac{\sum \left| \text{Actual demand} - \text{Forecast} \right|}{n}$	[10.5]
	Mean squared error	$MSE = \dfrac{\sum \left(\text{Actual demand} - \text{Forecast} \right)^2}{n}$	[10.6]

Model	Definition	Formula	Number

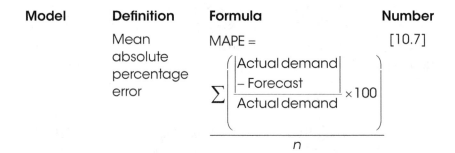

$$MAPE = \frac{\sum\left(\frac{|Actual\,demand - Forecast|}{Actual\,demand}\times 100\right)}{n} \qquad [10.7]$$

WHAT DO YOU REMEMBER?

1. List and explain the three qualitative approaches to forecasting.
2. What is a time series?
3. What are the components of a time series?
4. Differentiate between stability and responsiveness.
5. What is the naïve approach? When does it work best?
6. What is a simple moving average? How can you increase the stability of a simple moving average forecast?
7. How does a weighted moving average model differ from a simple moving average model?
8. What is the smoothing constant?
9. What are the various ways to determine a forecast's accuracy?
10. What are the two techniques that take trends into account?
11. In a regression equation, what is the slope and what is the intercept?
12. What is a seasonal index?
13. What are the steps to compute seasonal indices and formulate forecasts that incorporate them?
14. What are associative models?

SOLVE BPH'S PROBLEMS

1. The following shows the number of pints of Type O blood used at BPH for the past 7 weeks.

Week	Pints Used
January 31	460
February 7	490
February 14	500
February 21	485
February 28	479
March 7	464
March 14	482

a. Forecast the demand for the week of March 21 using a 2-week simple moving average.

b. Forecast the demand for the week of March 21 using a weighted moving average with weights of 0.4, 0.3, 0.2, and 0.1.

c. Forecast the demand for the week of March 21 using exponential smoothing with a forecast of 450 pints for the week of January 31 and $\alpha = 0.6$.

2. The actual demand for germicidal chemicals at one of BPH's clinics is as follows.

Quarter	Gallons of Germicidal Chemicals Used
1	550
2	490
3	510
4	590
5	595
6	550
7	565
8	610
9	635
10	565
11	572
12	655

a. Plot the data in the previous table on a graph. Do you detect any trend, seasonal pattern, or random variations?

b. Forecast demand from quarter 5 to quarter 13 using a 4-quarter simple moving average. Plot your forecast on the same graph as the actual demand.

c. Forecast demand from quarter 3 to quarter 13 using a weighted moving average with weights 0.6 and 0.4. Plot your forecast on the same graph as the actual demand and the simple moving average.

d. Looking at the graph in part c, which forecasting method seems to be more appropriate?

3. Use the data provided in problem 2.

a. Starting with a forecast of 550 for quarter 1, forecast the demand for quarter 13 using exponential smoothing with $\alpha = 0.6$. Plot the actual data and the exponentially smoothed forecasts on the same graph.

b. Forecast demand from quarter 2 to quarter 13 using the naïve approach. Plot your forecasts on the graph developed in part a.

    c. Looking at the graph in part b, which forecasting method seems to be more appropriate?

    d. Determine the MAD (disregard quarter 1 from computations) to confirm your answer in part c.

4. BPH is considering an expansion of its ED department. Currently, the maximum capacity is set for 83,000 visits per year. Develop a trend projection for the following data and determine if and when BPH would need the expanded facility.

Year	ED Visits
1	75,000
2	72,800
3	76,000
4	76,400
5	78,000
6	77,300
7	79,200
8	78,000
9	81,000
10	81,500

5. Use the data from problem 4.

    a. Develop a 3-year simple moving average forecast (starting in year 4).

    b. Develop a weighted moving average forecast using the weights 0.5 and 0.5.

    c. Develop an exponential smoothing forecast using a forecast of 74,000 visits for year 1 and $\alpha = 0.7$.

    d. Develop a trend-adjusted exponentially smoothed forecast using an initial forecast of 74,000 visits for year 1 and an initial trend adjustment of 0.5. The smoothing constants selected are $\alpha = 0.7$ and $\beta = 0.4$.

    e. Compute the MSE for each one of the aforementioned methods (disregard the first data point for the exponential smoothing and trend-adjusted exponential smoothing models). Based on your results, which forecasting method would yield the best results? Using that method, what is the forecast for next year?

6. Dr. Bumberry is a plastic surgeon at one of BPH's clinics. He and his partners have the data for the botulinum toxin injections given during each season from 2013 to 2016. He has forecasted that the annual demand for botulinum toxin injections at the clinic will remain rather stable with 3,940 in 2017. Use the multiplicative model to predict the demand in each season of 2017 (Hint: Use overall average demand to compute the seasonal indices).

Season	2013	2014	2015	2016
Winter	1080	1000	1010	1100
Spring	950	960	940	875
Summer	1200	1175	1175	1200
Fall	800	790	770	750

7. At the BPH pharmacy, the demand (number of tablets) for a particular drug has been declining over the years as new treatments have emerged. Demand is higher in winter and spring, as shown in the following table. The pharmacist wants to make sure that he does not order more tablets than needed.

Season	2013	2014	2015	2016
Winter	5200	4800	4500	4200
Spring	4900	4600	4400	3800
Summer	2100	1500	1200	1000
Fall	1800	1700	1500	1400

a. Deseasonalize the data.

b. Develop the regression equation for the deseasonalized data.

c. Formulate the trend forecasts for each season of 2017.

d. Adjust the trend forecasts for seasonality and round your estimates to the nearest hundred.

8. Because healthcare services provided through workmen's compensation generate relatively high profit margins, the director of the occupational therapy department wants to increase the number of patients with work-related injuries. He believes that the funds spent to promote BPH's services to employers in the community as well as the number of physicians assigned to those cases influence the volume of patient cases. He has compiled the following data.

Year	Patient Volume	Promotional Expenditures	Number of Physicians
1	420	$8,000	10
2	629	$10,200	12
3	390	$7,000	5
4	489	$7,800	7
5	540	$8,100	8
6	708	$10,800	10
7	650	$9,800	7
8	590	$8,200	8
9	700	$9,000	8
10	740	$10,000	7

a. Use Excel to obtain a regression equation. What is the regression equation?

b. Which one(s) of the two independent variables significantly influence(s) patient volume? Explain.

c. What is the R^2 value? What is its meaning?

9. The BPH board is considering a partnership with a hospital in Mexico for a limited line of surgical services. The hospital is accredited by The Joint Commission International. BPH has just conducted a survey to determine their patients' likelihood to get surgery at that hospital in Mexico based on patients' cosmopolitanism, perceptions of care quality in Mexico, and familiarity with the concept of medical travel. They ran a multiple regression model in IBM SPSS 20 and obtained the following results.

Model Summary

Model	R	R Square	Adjusted R Square	Std. Error of the Estimate
1	.541ª	.293	.292	1.64973

ªPredictors: (Constant), familiarity, perceptions of quality, cosmopolitanism

Coefficientsª

Model		Unstandardized Coefficients		Standardized Coefficients	t	Sig.
		Beta	Std. Error	Beta		
1	(Constant)	−1.213	.161		−7.541	.000
	Cosmopolitanism	.239	.239	.170	8.709	.000
	Perceptions of quality	.648	.031	.406	20.863	.000
	Familiarity	.176	.025	.133	7.072	.000

ªDependent Variable: Likelihood to get surgery in Mexico

a. What is the R^2 value? What does it mean?

b. Which independent variable(s) is (are) a significant predictor(s) of the likelihood to get surgery in Mexico?

c. What other variables could be included in the model?

10. Use all 36 months of data in Table 10.1.
a. Compute the MAD and MAPE for the 3-month simple moving average.

b. Compute the MAD and MAPE for the weighted moving average model with weights of 0.5, 0.3, and 0.2.

c. Compute the MAD and MAPE for exponential smoothing with $\alpha = 0.8$. Use 45 as the initial forecast in Month 1.

d. Based on your previous computations, which model would you recommend?

11. Use all 36 months of data in Table 10.1.
a. Deseasonalize the data. Use each month as a season.

b. Develop the regression equation for the deseasonalized data.

c. Formulate the trend forecasts for each month of next year.

d. Adjust the trend forecasts for seasonality.

e. Plot the surgery volume over the past 36 months along with the forecasts for the same periods. Does the forecasting model provide a good fit to the actual data?

THINK OUTSIDE THE BOOK!

1. If you use an alpha value equal to 1 in exponential smoothing, do you have a stable or responsive forecasting model? What if you use an alpha value equal to 0?

2. Read the following article:

    Boulkedid, R., Abdoul, H., Loustau, M., Sibony, O., & Alberti, C. (2011). Using and reporting the Delphi method for selecting healthcare quality indicators: A systematic review. *PLoS ONE*, 6(6), e20476. Retrieved from http://www.ncbi.nlm.nih.gov/pmc/articles/PMC3111406

    What are the authors' recommendations to improve the use and reporting of the Delphi method in quality indicator search?

3. Read the following article:

    Boyle, J., Wallis, M., Jessup, M., Crilly, J., Lind, J., Miller. P., & Fitzgerald, G. (2008). *Regression forecasting of patient admission data* (pp. 3819–3822). Thirtieth Annual International IEEE EMBS Conference, Vancouver, Canada, August 20–24.

    Describe the regression models. Which model(s) produced the most accurate forecasts?

REFERENCES

Chase, R. B., Aquilano, N. J., & Jacobs, F. R. (2006). *Operations management forcompetitive advantage* (11th ed.). Boston, MA: McGraw-Hill.

Heizer, J., & Render, B. (2011). *Operations management*. Upper Saddle River, NJ: Prentice-Hall.

Jones, S. S., Thomas, A., Evans, R. S., Welch, S. J., Haug, P. J., & Snow, G. L. (2008). Forecasting daily patient volumes in the emergency department. *Academic Emergency Medicine, 15*(2), 159–170.

Marquis of Halifax, G. S. (1912). *The complete works of George Savile, first Marquess of Halifax*. Ithaca, NY: Cornell University Library.

Robert Wood Johnson Foundation. (2009). *Impact of the economy on health care*. Princeton, NJ. Retrieved from http://www.rwjf.org/content/dam/farm/reports/issue_briefs/2009/rwjf44843

Silver, N. (2012). *The signal and the noise: Why most predictions fail but some don't*. New York, NY: Penguin Press.

Stevenson, W. J. (2012). *Operations management* (11th ed.). New York, NY: McGraw-Hill.

Whitehurst, B. (2015). Use continuous demand forecasting to improve your operating margins. Retrieved from http://www.mckesson .com/blog/continuous-demand-forecasting

APPENDIX 10.1 – MULTIPLE REGRESSION WITH EXCEL

To generate the multiple regression model shown in Figure 10.10, we entered the data from Table 10.12 in Excel as follows.

	A Beds	B Population size	C Below poverty
1			
2	4420	90.2	8.5
3	3159	80.2	11.2
4	4180	89.6	9.5
5	3855	86.1	8.7
6	3416	84.3	17.5
7	2955	48.6	15.1
8	2732	30.5	14.2
9	3542	80.0	11.2
10	2713	52.6	15.4
11	4336	91.7	8.5
12	3230	61.5	12.5
13	3148	59.8	9.7
14	3561	74.1	12.8
15	4668	98.3	6.5
16	3697	85.2	14.5
17	3620	87.1	15.2
18	2070	28.4	13.1
19	4310	87.3	9.6
20	3376	39.5	10.0
21	2945	32.1	15.1
22	3315	46.9	14.2
23	3228	44.8	13.2
24	2659	28.5	10.0
25	2863	35.6	12.5
26	3309	61.2	16.5
27			

Then, we clicked on the Data tab and selected "Data Analysis."

Note: Microsoft Excel application interface is used with permission of Microsoft.

In the Data Analysis menu, we selected "Regression."

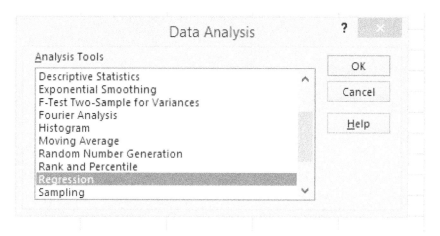

In the Regression dialog box, we selected the number of beds in Column A as the dependent variable (or as in Excel) and population size and number of people below the poverty level as the independent variables (or as in Excel dialog box). We clicked on "Labels" because we included the first row (text) with the column headings so that the Excel output would include the variable names. This is also a way of "telling" the Excel program that the first row does not include our numerical data. Finally, we indicated that we wanted the regression output on a separate worksheet.

	A	B	C
	Beds	Population size	Below poverty
1			
2	4420	90.2	8.5
3	3159	80.2	11.2
4	4180	89.6	9.5
5	3855	86.1	8.7
6	3416	84.3	17.5
7	2955	48.6	15.1
8	2732	30.5	14.2
9	3542	80.0	11.2
10	2713	52.6	15.4
11	4336	91.7	8.5
12	3230	61.5	12.5
13	3148	59.8	9.7
14	3561	74.1	12.8
15	4668	98.3	6.5
16	3697	85.2	14.5
17	3620	87.1	15.2
18	2070	28.4	13.1
19	4310	87.3	9.6
20	3376	39.5	10.0
21	2945	32.1	15.1
22	3315	46.9	14.2
23	3228	44.8	13.2
24	2659	28.5	10.0
25	2863	35.6	12.5
26	3309	61.2	16.5
27			

Note: Microsoft Excel application interface is used with permission of Microsoft.

The regression output displayed in Figure 10.10 is as follows.

	A	B	C	D	E	F	G	H	I	J
1	SUMMARY OUTPUT									
2										
3	*Regression Statistics*									
4	Multiple R	0.900239								
5	R Square	0.81043								
6	Adjusted R Square	0.793196								
7	Standard Error	285.7224								
8	Observations	25								
9										
10	ANOVA									
11		*df*	*SS*	*MS*	*F*	*Significance F*				
12	Regression	2	7678145	3839073	47.02595	1.14E-08				
13	Residual	22	1796021	81637.32						
14	Total	24	9474166							
15										
16		*Coefficients*	*Standard Error*	*t Stat*	*P-value*	*Lower 95%*	*Upper 95%*	*Lower 95.0%*	*Upper 95.0%*	
17	Intercept	2905.081	366.9271	7.917326	7.01E-08	2144.121	3666.041	2144.121	3666.041	
18	Population size	19.91911	2.647974	7.522397	1.61E-07	14.42755	25.41067	14.42755	25.41067	
19	Below poverty	-63.151	21.59984	-2.92368	0.007866	-107.946	-18.3557	-107.946	-18.3557	
20										
21										

Note: Microsoft Excel application interface is used with permission of Microsoft.

CHAPTER 11

SUPPLY CHAIN MANAGEMENT

BRADLEY PARK HOSPITAL 11.1

Now that she had a better understanding of the demand patterns for stent surgeries, Sheila had abandoned the placement of orders at regular intervals and had worked out a deal with the supplier to receive orders within 48 hours.

As Sheila was reading the latest e-mails she had received, Clara, a tech in the stockroom called, "The stents have come in. Where should we put them?" "I will be down shortly," Sheila responded. Sheila met Clara and they decided to place the stents on the shelf in order of size.

What do you think of Sheila's decision to request a lead time of 48 hours?

INTRODUCTION AND LEARNING OBJECTIVES

Have you ever worked on an important project with a tight deadline and discovered that you do not have a key item needed to finish the project? If so, you know the frustration that comes with attempting to rectify the issue as soon as possible. Now, imagine that the project is in healthcare, and someone's life and well-being depend on the immediate availability (supply) of that item for treatment. Ensuring that needed supplies are available to provide safe and efficient care is the domain of supply chain management (SCM). Supply chain management has a major impact on healthcare costs because supplies make up a significant proportion of the care process inputs. As is the case for several topics previously covered in the book (Chapters 7–9), SCM requires a good estimate of demand to plan for adequate inventories (Figure 11.1).

In this chapter, we introduce you to both conceptual and technical aspects of SCM. When you finish reading the chapter, you will be able to:

1. **Describe the domain of SCM**
2. **Explain the strategic importance of SCM**

3. Understand the nature and importance of inventories
4. Classify inventory systems
5. Determine how much to order
6. Determine when to order
7. Discuss the criteria used for supplier selection

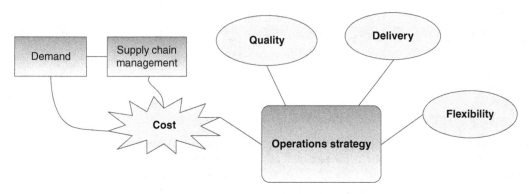

FIGURE 11.1 – Mind map with focus on cost.

WHAT IS A SUPPLY CHAIN?

Supply Chain
Multiple entities (organizations or individuals) that are directly involved in the upstream and downstream flows of products, services, capital, information, and so on, from a source to a customer.

Group Purchasing Organization (GPO)
An entity that negotiates contracts with manufacturers or distributors for multiple healthcare providers. The aggregate volume enables the GPO to negotiate discounts that the individual providers would be unable to obtain on their own.

A **supply chain** is "a set of three or more entities (organizations or individuals) directly involved in the upstream and downstream flows of products, services, finance, and other information from a source to a customer" (Mentzer et al., 2001, p. 4). In healthcare, the chain starts with the manufacturers of pharmaceuticals, medical/surgical supplies, medical devices, and equipment, and ends with their use in patient care (Burns & Wharton School Colleagues, 2002; see Figure 11.2). Health systems may acquire products directly from manufacturers if they have substantial purchasing power. Otherwise, they may elect to purchase from wholesalers and specialty distributors, or, as is often the case, use the services of a **group purchasing organization**. A GPO is an entity that negotiates contracts with manufacturers or distributors for multiple healthcare providers. The aggregate volume enables the GPO to negotiate discounts that the individual providers would be unable to obtain on their own. Hospitals and other providers remain free to make non-GPO contracted purchases if they so desire (Healthcare Supply Chain Association [HSCA], 2015).

The Council of Supply Chain Management Professionals (2015) defines **supply chain management** as "the planning and management of all activities involved in sourcing and procurement, conversion, and all logistics management activities (. . .). Supply chain management integrates supply and demand management within and across companies." It involves activities such as (Schneller & Smeltzer, 2006):

- Identifying and selecting supply sources
- Managing suppliers

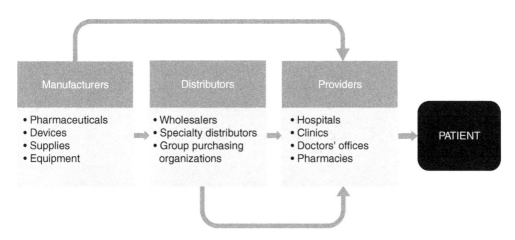

FIGURE 11.2 – Supply chain in healthcare.

- Forecasting demand
- Managing procurement
- Selecting and using distribution models
- Identifying and using adequate inventory systems

You will note that the entire supply chain encompasses not only relationships with entities outside the organization, but also internal processes delivering value to their customers. Some people distinguish between internal and external supply chains, but a seamless, well-integrated supply chain functions in a holistic fashion. In that respect, it is consistent with design principle #8 (Chapter 7), which advocates the optimization of the whole system rather than a focus on local optimization.

The goal of SCM is therefore to develop a chain of suppliers and providers that strive to deliver optimal value to the final customer. In healthcare, this final customer is the patient. To reach this ideal goal, SCM should involve (Storey, Emberson, Godsell, & Harrison, 2006):

- An information-technology (IT)-supported, seamless flow from initial supply sources to patient
- Customer-driven demand (pull system)
- Shared information and transparency across the value chain
- Collaboration rather than competition among the chain links
- Elimination of middlemen from supply source(s) to healthcare facility
- Inventory investments aligned with demand
- Responsiveness to customers' needs
- Elimination of waste
- Mass customization
- Market segmentation

Supply Chain Management

The planning and management of all activities involved in sourcing and procurement, conversion, and all logistics management activities: identifying and selecting supply sources, managing suppliers, forecasting demand, managing procurement, selecting and using distribution models, identifying and using adequate inventory systems, and so on.

In a number of industries, such as retail (e.g., Wal-Mart) and auto manufacturing (e.g., Toyota), SCM practices are mature, support the organizational strategy, and stretch from the executive suite to front-line operations. Unfortunately, in healthcare, these practices are still in their infancy and are not pervasive. Why is it a problem?

A McKinsey & Company report indicated that supply chain expenses represent approximately 25% of pharmaceutical costs and more than 40% of medical device costs. With an annual spending of about $400 billion on both pharmaceuticals and medical devices, even the smallest efficiency gains in the supply chain can have a dramatic impact on cost savings. Such gains are achieved through lower manufacturing lead times, lower inventory levels, and lower product obsolescence. Furthermore, better SCM can improve patient safety by reducing shortages, medication error rates, and recalls (Ebel, George, Larsen, Shah, & Ungerman, 2013). Therefore, improving SCM has many benefits in healthcare (Box 11.1).

 BOX 11.1 – OM IN PRACTICE!

Redesigning the Supply Chain for Blood Transfusions

Areas of concern in the blood supply chain include poor identification of usage patterns, suboptimal storage and transport, and inadequate donor recruitment. In order to improve the blood supply chain, the Finnish Red Cross established a program called *ketju*, which means "chain" in Finnish. The program sought to make the supply chain more cost-efficient and reliable with (a) compatible information systems between the Finnish Red Cross Blood Service and hospitals to track inventory levels throughout the supply chain, (b) deliveries matching demand, and (c) efficient internal management of blood products in the hospitals. They started with two pilot hospitals. In one, they focused on demand forecasting and the development of inventory models to ensure adequate stock levels. In the other, the focus was on inventory management and control. The initial success with these pilot projects (lower costs, higher customer satisfaction, less variation in stock levels, and simplification of the order process) fostered the expansion of the redesign program to other hospitals (Rautonen, 2007).

Effective SCM strategies (Croxton & Rogers, 2001) emphasize many of the topics we have discussed so far in the book:

1. **Customer relationship management** through market identification, customer research, and design of services matching customers' needs (Chapters 2 and 4)

2. **Customer service management** with the design of service processes fulfilling the customers' needs (Chapters 4–9)

3. **Demand management** through selection of demand forecasting techniques and synchronization procedures to match the forecasts to supplies and capacity levels (Chapters 8 and 10)

4. **Order fulfillment** through review of supply/distribution lead times and costs as well as customer service requirements

5. **System flexibility** to respond to environment and demand changes (Chapter 13)

6. **Supplier relationship management** with supplier selection and relationship terms between the healthcare organization and its suppliers

In this chapter, we will address order fulfillment and supply-relationship management. Ideally, orders are placed according to supply usage and corresponding inventory levels. Inventory management is therefore a key component of SCM.

WHAT IS INVENTORY?

✪ BOX 11.2 – WORDS OF WISDOM

"Nearly every business collects metrics on inventory, sales, and workplace process. Health care has been slow to measure these kinds of outcomes. Increasingly, general medicine, via either managed care or large practice settings, is improving by collecting data through electronic records and refining practice based on what works" (Insel, 2014).

An **inventory** is a stock of goods or supplies. There are different types of inventory:

Inventory
A stock of goods or supplies.

- **Raw materials and purchased parts.** These types of inventory are found in manufacturing (e.g., pharmaceutical companies or manufacturers of medical equipment).

- **Work-in-process.** These partially completed items would also be found in manufacturing.

- **Finished goods.** These are completed products, which can be sold by manufacturers (e.g., drug manufacturers) and retailers (e.g., pharmacies).

- **Supplies.** All hospitals store supplies such as surgical equipment, anesthetics, gauze, wheelchairs, and so forth.

- **Maintenance, repair, and operating supplies (MRO).** These are needed to keep the facilities clean (e.g., detergents and disinfectants) and to keep equipment running properly (e.g., tools, oil, lubricants).

Inventory Management

Balancing customer service and cost containment to provide the right goods, in sufficient quantities, in the right place, at the right time.

Because inventories represent a large portion of a firm's invested capital (Chapter 12), they need to be properly managed (see Box 11.2). **Inventory management** must balance customer service and cost containment. It is important to provide the right goods, in sufficient quantities, in the right place, at the right time. Therefore, adequate stock levels should be maintained to avoid service interruptions. At the same time, excessive stock levels represent excess costs and should be avoided. There are two important decisions in inventory management: how much to order (quantity) and when to order (timing). Both decisions will be determined by the type of items being stored.

ABC ANALYSIS

ABC Analysis

A technique that divides on-hand inventory items into three classes based on their annual dollar volume: A (very important), B (semi-important), and C (least important).

The **ABC approach** divides on-hand inventory items into three classes based on their annual dollar volume: A (very important), B (semi-important), and C (least important). This approach follows the Pareto principle (Chapter 4) in identifying the few critical items from the trivial many. It helps design inventory systems appropriate for each classification. When you manage inventories, you would not want to devote the same level of control to both stents and surgical gloves. The ABC analysis helps target the control efforts. In general, class A items account for 10% to 20% of the number of inventory items, but 70% to 80% of the annual dollar volume. Class B items represent about 30% of the number of inventory items and about 15% to 20% of the dollar volume. Class C items account for 50% to 60% of the number of inventory items, but only about 10% of the annual dollar volume. These percentages may vary from firm to firm. Furthermore, some organizations may choose to divide their inventories into more than three classes.

Because of their high dollar volume, A items are monitored very closely and their stock levels are reviewed continuously to ensure accuracy. C items are usually controlled loosely with visual inspections or two-bin systems and are ordered in bulk (Box 11.3). Control of B items lies somewhere between the two. The procedure to classify items into A, B, and C categories involves three steps:

STEP 1: Multiply the annual demand for each item by its unit price to obtain the annual dollar volume.

STEP 2: Rearrange the items in descending order based on their annual dollar volume.

STEP 3: Look for natural "breaks" or gaps between annual dollar volumes. They may not correspond exactly to the percentages mentioned earlier, but you will see a few items with a high dollar volume (A items), a larger group of items with a medium dollar volume (B items), and the majority of the items with a low dollar volume (C items).

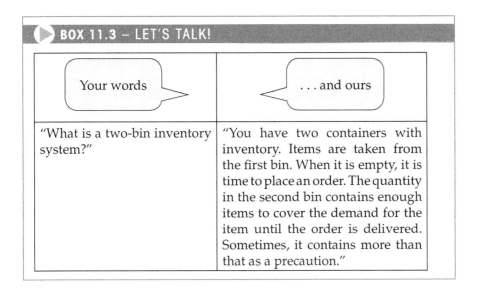

BRADLEY PARK HOSPITAL 11.2

Last week, Sheila had discussed some of the inventory problems with a friend from the accounting department. With all the things she already had to do, she realized that she had neither the time nor resources to dedicate to all the inventory items. However, stent grafts and vascular kits seemed to require a lot more attention than she had given them lately. The friend had told her that she should do an ABC analysis before setting up inventory policies for all the items used in vascular surgery. She vaguely remembered the ABC analysis from her cost accounting course in college many years ago. She checked a couple of books to refresh her memory and felt relieved. It looked quite simple!

Sheila was looking at a list of the items used for stent surgeries over the past year and their unit prices. There were great variations in usage and price. First, she had to compute the annual dollar volume.

Item	Usage (1)	Price per Unit (2)	Annual Dollar Volume (1) × (2)
Graft Sm	500	$6,000.00	$3,000,000
Graft M	700	$8,000.00	$5,600,000
Graft L	400	$10,000.00	$4,000,000
Guide-wire #1	1,000	$100.00	$100,000
Guide-wire #2	300	$200.00	$60,000
Guide-wire #3	200	$400.00	$80,000
Guide-wire #4	100	$1,000.00	$100,000
Cortis	1,600	$200.00	$320,000
Saline	4,000	$25.00	$100,000
Vascular Kit	1,600	$1,000.00	$1,600,000
Needle 18 g	900	$0.50	$450

(continued)

(continued)

Item	Usage (1)	Price per Unit (2)	Annual Dollar Volume (1) × (2)
Needle 20 g	2,000	$0.50	$1,000
Needle 22 g	2,000	$0.50	$1,000
Gloves (nonsterile) S (box)	400	$2.50	$1,000
Gloves (nonsterile) M (box)	800	$2.50	$2,000
Gloves (nonsterile) L (box)	400	$2.50	$1,000
Surgical Sterile Gloves S (box)	100	$10.00	$1,000
Surgical Sterile Gloves M (box)	350	$10.00	$3,500
Surgical Sterile Gloves L (box)	100	$10.00	$1,000

She then reorganized all the items in descending order based on their annual dollar volume. The various classes of items became obvious rather quickly.

Item	Annual Dollar Volume	Classification	
Graft M	$5,600,000	A	
Graft L	$4,000,000	A	21% of the items
Graft Sm	$3,000,000	A	94% of the annual $ volume
Vascular Kit	$1,600,000	A	
Cortis	$320,000	B	
Guide-wire #1	$100,000	B	
Guide-wire #4	$100,000	B	32% of the items
Saline	$100,000	B	5% of the annual $ volume
Guide-wire #3	$80,000	B	
Guide-wire #2	$60,000	B	
Surgical Sterile Gloves M	$3,500	C	
Gloves (nonsterile) M	$2,000	C	
Needle 20 g	$1,000	C	
Needle 22 g	$1,000	C	
Gloves (nonsterile) S	$1,000	C	47% of the items
Gloves (nonsterile) L	$1,000	C	<1% of the annual $ volume
Surgical Sterile Gloves S	$1,000	C	
Surgical Sterile Gloves L	$1,000	C	
Needle 18 g	$450	C	

"Well," she thought, "the percentages for annual dollar volume are some-what different from the general rule for the B and C items. That's because our A items are so outrageously expensive. Just the nature of our business, I guess. From now on, I will make sure that I have extremely accurate records on stock levels, open orders, and withdrawals."

What do you think of Sheila's earlier decision to place the stent grafts on a shelf with other items?

HOW MUCH TO ORDER?

Economic order quantity models help determine order sizes by minimizing the sum of annual costs that depend on order quantity and frequency. In this chapter, we will address the basic EOQ model and the EOQ model with quantity discounts.

Basic EOQ Model

The **basic EOQ model** is used to find a fixed order quantity that minimizes the sum of holding costs and ordering costs. **Holding costs** refer to the variable costs associated with carrying inventory and include interest or opportunity cost, storage and handling, insurance, taxes, and shrinkage. To purchase inventory, the organization may need to take a loan and pay interest on the debt. Conversely, it may use cash on hand and forgo an investment opportunity that would yield a return. Stored inventory takes up space, which costs money (building, light, heating, security, etc.). Moreover, it needs to be taken in and out of storage, which may require special handling equipment. On a balance sheet, inventory is an asset that is resold, often at a profit (e.g., medications). More taxes are paid if end-of-year inventories are high. Similarly, higher insurance premiums will be necessary to cover more expensive assets. Finally, shrinkage or loss of inventory may occur due to pilferage, damage, obsolescence, and so on. Holding costs are expressed either as a percentage of the item's cost or as a dollar amount per item. Annual holding costs typically range from 20% to 40% of the item's cost. If the cost of an item is $1,000, the cost of carrying that item for a year would be $200 to $400. Given their impact on profit margins, holding costs put pressure on healthcare organizations to keep their inventories at low levels. The annual holding cost increases linearly with Q, the order quantity:

$$\text{Annual holding cost} = \text{Average inventory} \times \text{Holding cost per unit per time period}$$

$$= \frac{Q}{2}H \qquad [11.1]$$

where Q is the order quantity,
$Q/2$ is the average inventory,
H is the cost of holding one particular item for one time period.

The average inventory is a function of the minimum and maximum inventory levels. Figure 11.3 shows that ideally, orders would be received when inventory levels reach zero. Therefore, the minimum inventory level is equal to zero, and the highest inventory level is equal to the order quantity. The average inventory is therefore:

$$\text{Average inventory} = \frac{\text{Minimum Inventory} + \text{Maximum Inventory}}{2}$$

$$= \frac{0+Q}{2} = \frac{Q}{2} \qquad [11.2]$$

Economic Order Quantity (EOQ) Models

Models that help determine order sizes by minimizing the sum of annual costs that depend on order quantity and frequency.

Holding Costs

Variable costs that are associated with carrying inventory and include interest or opportunity cost, storage and handling, insurance, taxes, and shrinkage.

FIGURE 11.3 –
Inventory cycles.

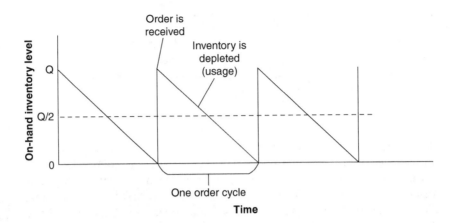

Ordering Costs

Costs of placing and receiving an order.

Ordering costs are the costs of placing and receiving an order. They include the costs associated with the preparation of requisitions and purchase orders, follow-up, inspection of goods upon arrival, movement to temporary storage, processing of suppliers' invoices, and so on. For a given item, order size does not influence the ordering cost, which is expressed as a fixed dollar amount. However, larger order sizes contribute to decreasing the frequency with which orders are placed. The costs of placing orders are incurred fewer times per year, resulting in overall lower ordering costs. Ordering costs place pressure on organizations to order in large quantities and therefore keep larger inventories on hand. The annual ordering cost is inversely and nonlinearly related to the number of orders placed per year:

Annual ordering cost = Number of orders placed per year
× Cost of placing one order

$$= \frac{D}{Q} S, \qquad [11.3]$$

where D is the annual demand for the item,
    Q is the order quantity,
    D/Q is the number of orders placed per year,
    S is the cost of placing one order.

The basic EOQ model attempts to balance holding costs and ordering costs. As the order size increases, holding costs increase and ordering costs decrease, and vice versa. The optimal order quantity minimizes the total cost, which is the sum of the holding cost and ordering cost (Figure 11.4):

Total cost = Annual holding cost + Annual ordering cost

$$TC = \frac{Q}{2} H + \frac{D}{Q} S \qquad [11.4]$$

The EOQ or optimal order size is found using the following formula:

$$EOQ = \sqrt{\frac{2DS}{H}}$$ [11.5]

You will notice that the ordering cost curve and the holding cost line intersect at the EOQ. In other words, they are equal. Let us demonstrate using an example.

At Bradley Park Hospital (BPH), the usage of medium-sized stent grafts is 700 annually, and their unit cost is $8,000 (see Bradley Park Hospital 11.2). BPH estimates that the cost of placing an order is about $200 and the holding cost per unit per year is 30% of the item's cost. The optimal order quantity is

$$EOQ = \sqrt{\frac{2 \times 700 \times \$200}{0.30 \times \$8,000}} = \sqrt{\frac{\$280,000}{\$2,400}} = 10.80123 \approx 11 \text{ grafts}$$

The total annual cost is

$$TC = \text{Holding cost} + \text{Ordering cost}$$

$$= \left(\frac{11}{2} \times \$2,400\right) + \left(\frac{700}{11} \times \$200\right)$$

$$= \$13,200 + \$12,727.27$$

$$= \$25,927.27$$

The ordering cost and holding cost are not perfectly equal because we rounded the order quantity to 11. If we had used exactly 10.80123, then both costs would have been $12,961.48 (Box 11.4).

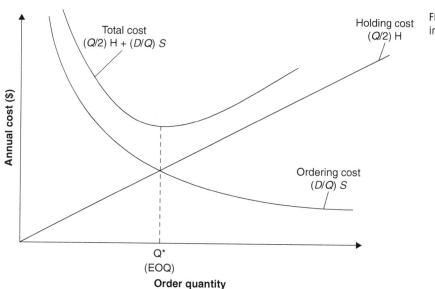

FIGURE 11.4 Total inventory costs.

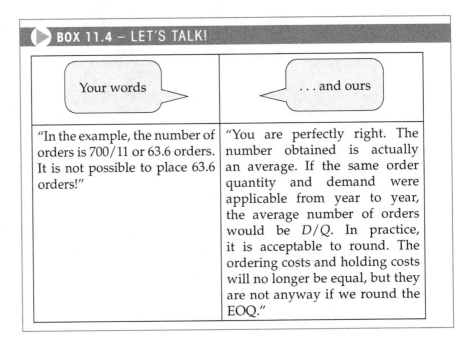

> **BOX 11.4 – LET'S TALK!**
>
> | Your words | ...and ours |
> |---|---|
> | "In the example, the number of orders is 700/11 or 63.6 orders. It is not possible to place 63.6 orders!" | "You are perfectly right. The number obtained is actually an average. If the same order quantity and demand were applicable from year to year, the average number of orders would be D/Q. In practice, it is acceptable to round. The ordering costs and holding costs will no longer be equal, but they are not anyway if we round the EOQ." |

You will notice that purchasing costs were not included in the total cost formula. This is because the basic EOQ model assumes that the purchasing cost of one item remains fixed, irrespective of the quantity ordered (no quantity discounts). As a result, purchasing costs are irrelevant in the determination of the optimal order quantity. The basic EOQ model is based on several assumptions:

- The demand rate is known and constant (e.g., 300 syringes per day).

Lead Time
Time elapsed between the placement of an order and its receipt.

- The order **lead time** (time elapsed between the placement of an order and the receipt of that order) is known and constant.

- The item's unit price is constant; there are no quantity discounts.

- Inventory replenishment is instantaneous; an order is received in a single delivery.

- The order size decision involves only one item; it is not advantageous to combine several orders with the same supplier.

These assumptions may seem overly restrictive. Nevertheless, the basic EOQ model has been shown to be quite robust. In other words, the order quantity derived from formula 11.5 results in minimal costs over a wide range of values (Figure 11.5). Because the holding cost per unit per year, the cost of placing an order, and even demand are estimated, it is reassuring to know that small deviations from the true EOQ have very little impact on costs. The order quantity derived from the model is therefore a good approximation of the optimal order quantity.

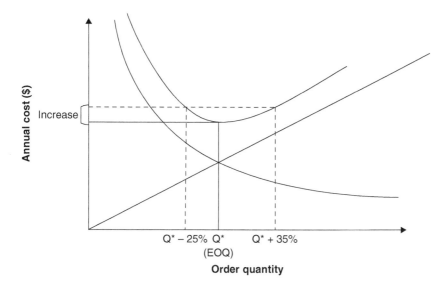

FIGURE 11.5
Robustness of the
EOQ model.

Quantity Discounts

When suppliers offer quantity discounts, it is possible to relax the assumption that the unit price of an item is constant. In that case, purchasing costs become relevant, and the total annual cost becomes a function of purchasing cost, holding cost, and ordering cost:

Quantity Discount Model
A model that helps determine the order size by minimizing total annual costs for a set of curves (one curve for each price).

$$TC = \text{Purchasing cost} + \text{Holding cost} + \text{Ordering cost}$$

$$= PD + \frac{Q}{2}H + \frac{D}{Q}S \qquad [11.6]$$

where P is the purchasing cost (price) of an item,
$\quad$ D is the annual demand for the item,
$\quad$ $(Q/2)\,H$ is the annual holding cost,
$\quad$ $(D/Q)\,S$ is the annual ordering cost.

In the **quantity discount model**, each price results in a separate total cost curve. The objective becomes finding the order quantity that will minimize the total cost for the entire set of curves. Each curve will have its own EOQ, but the EOQ is not feasible if its value does not fall within the range required to obtain a quantity discount. The relevant portion of the total cost curve for a given price range is displayed as a solid arc in Figures 11.6a and 11.6b. Let us assume that BPH's supplier of stent grafts offers the following pricing:

Order Quantity	Price per Unit
1 to 19	$8,000
20 to 30	$7,500
31 or more	$6,750

If the holding cost per unit per year is constant, then the cost curves have their minimum point at the same order quantity (Figure 11.6a). If the holding cost is expressed as a percentage of the unit price, then each curve has a different minimum point (Figure 11.6b). More often than not, the holding cost will be expressed as a percentage to reflect the value of the item kept on hand. In that case, the procedure to find the optimal order quantity is as follows:

FIGURE 11.6 –
(a) Cost curves with constant holding cost; (b) cost curves with holding cost expressed as a percentage of the item's cost.

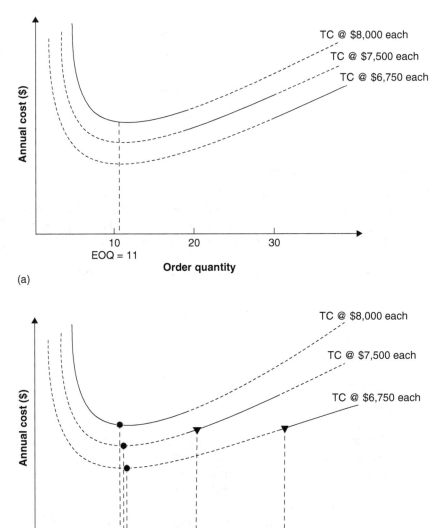

STEP 1:   Beginning with the lowest price, find the first feasible EOQ. If the first feasible EOQ is at the lowest unit price, stop. This is the optimal order quantity. If not, go to step 2.

STEP 2: Compute the total annual cost at the first feasible EOQ and at all the **price breaks**—minimum quantity needed to get a discount—for all the lower price ranges. The quantity that produces the lowest total cost is the optimal order quantity.

Price Break

The minimum quantity needed to get a discount.

In the previous example, the lowest price is $6,750 per graft. The EOQ at this price is as follows:

1. $\text{EOQ}_{\$6,750} = \sqrt{\dfrac{2 \times 700 \times \$200}{0.30 \times \$6,750}} = 11.76 \approx 12 \text{ grafts.}$ This quantity

is not feasible as an order of 31 or more is required for that price.

$\text{EOQ}_{\$7,500} = \sqrt{\dfrac{2 \times 700 \times \$200}{0.30 \times \$7,500}} = 11.16 \approx 11 \text{ grafts.}$ This quantity is

not feasible because an order of at least 20 grafts is necessary to obtain this price.

$\text{EOQ}_{\$8,000} = \sqrt{\dfrac{2 \times 700 \times \$200}{0.30 \times \$8,000}} = 10.80 \approx 11 \text{ grafts.}$ as mentioned in

the previous section.

2. $\text{TC}_{11} = (\$8,000 \times 700) + \left(\dfrac{11}{2} \times \$2,400\right) + \left(\dfrac{700}{11} \times \$200\right)$

$= \$5,600,000 + \$13,200 + \$12,727.27$

$= \$5,625,927.27.$

$\text{TC}_{20} = (\$7,500 \times 700) + \left(\dfrac{20}{2} \times \$2,250\right) + \left(\dfrac{700}{20} \times \$200\right)$

$= \$5,250,000 + \$22,500 + \$7,000$

$= \$5,279,500.00.$

$\text{TC}_{31} = (\$6,750 \times 700) + \left(\dfrac{31}{2} \times \$2,025\right) + \left(\dfrac{700}{31} \times \$200\right)$

$= \$4,725,000 + \$31,387.50 + \$4,516.1$

$= \$4,760,903.63.$

The last result is the lowest total cost. The optimal order quantity is 31 grafts.

WHEN TO PLACE AN ORDER?

Now that we know the optimal quantity to order, we need to explore the other important question: when to place the order. The **reorder point** is a predetermined inventory level that triggers the placement of an order. When demand and lead time are known and constant (basic

Reorder Point (ROP)

A predetermined inventory level that triggers the placement of an order.

EOQ model), the ROP is exactly the amount of inventory needed to cover demand during the lead time period (Figure 11.7). More specific, it is as follows:

$$ROP = \text{demand during lead time}$$

$$= d \times LT,\qquad\qquad [11.7]$$

where d is the demand per period (same time unit as lead time) and LT is the lead time or time required to replenish the inventory after placing the order.

In the BPH example, if the demand for medium-sized stent grafts is the same every day and surgeries are performed 350 days a year, the daily demand (or demand rate) is $700/350 = 2$ grafts. If the lead time is always 2 days, the reorder point is

$$ROP = 2 \text{ grafts per day} \times 2 \text{ days} = 4 \text{ grafts.}$$

This means that an order should be placed whenever the inventory level goes down to four grafts.

FIGURE 11.7 – Reorder point when demand and lead time are constant.

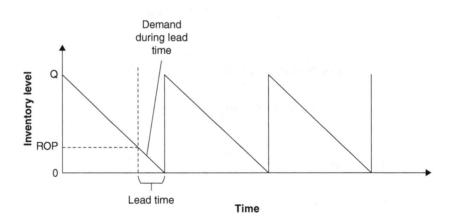

In reality, we know that this rarely happens. Demand could vary as is the case for BPH, and so could lead time. When there is variation, there is uncertainty. In such cases, an organization needs a "cushion" or safety stock to cover the demand during lead time. A **safety stock** is excess inventory that is held in addition to the expected demand during lead time (Figure 11.8). The reorder point becomes:

Safety Stock

Excess inventory that is held in addition to the expected demand during lead time.

$$ROP = \text{Expected demand during lead time} + \text{Safety stock} \quad [11.8]$$

You will note that this "just-in-case" inventory is in sharp contrast to "just-in-time" inventory (when inventory is replenished exactly when it is needed—Chapter 6). When there is variability, an inventory buffer reduces the risk of the service provider running out of stock, that is, experiencing a **stockout**. The risk of a stockout is only present during the lead time period. At any other point during the inventory cycle, an

Stockout

Running out of stock.

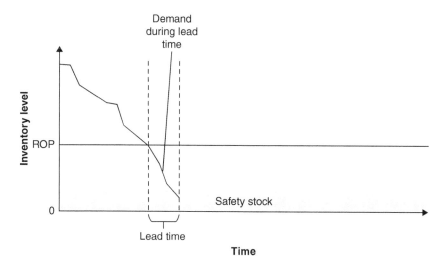

FIGURE 11.8 –
Reorder point
with probabilistic
demand.

emergency order could be placed if demand surged unexpectedly, and the likelihood of a stockout would be insignificant.

Safety stocks are expensive to maintain. Therefore, it is important to weigh the costs of holding excess inventory against the risk of a stockout. To do so, safety stock quantities are established according to service levels. The **service level** is the probability that inventory on hand will be sufficient to meet the needs during the lead time period:

Service Level
Probability that inventory on hand will be sufficient to meet the needs during the lead time period.

$$\text{Service level} = 1 - \text{Stockout risk}$$

If an organization wants to limit the chance of a stockout to 5%, it means that it adopts a service level of 95% in determining safety stock levels. Assuming that records on demand during lead time are available and that demand during lead time is normally distributed (Box 11.5), the formula for the reorder point is

$$\text{ROP} = \text{Expected demand during lead time} + z\sigma_{dLT} \qquad [11.9]$$

where z is the number of standard deviations associated with a given service level on the standard normal curve
σ_{dLT} is the standard deviation of lead time demand.

In the BPH example, if the expected demand for medium-sized stent grafts during the lead time period is four with a standard deviation of 1, and if BPH desires a service level of 97%, the reorder point is

$$\text{ROP} = 4 + 1.88\,(1)$$

$$= 5.88 \approx 6 \text{ grafts.}$$

A safety stock of two extra grafts would be carried as a protection against the risk of a stockout.

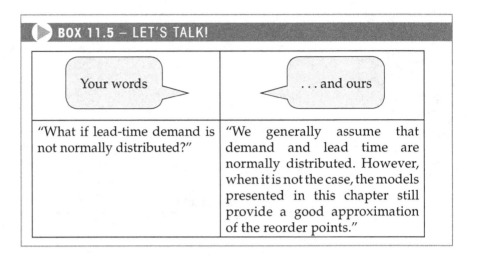

Sometimes, records on lead-time demand are not available. In those situations, other models are available. The model we need to use depends on whether:

1. Demand is constant, but lead time is variable.
2. Lead time is constant, but demand is variable.
3. Both demand and lead time are variable.

Constant Demand and Variable Lead Time

When the demand rate (e.g., demand per day) is known and constant but the lead time varies, the formula for the reorder point is

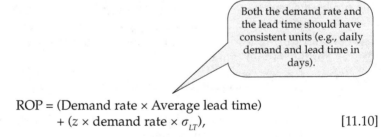

$$\text{ROP} = (\text{Demand rate} \times \text{Average lead time}) + (z \times \text{demand rate} \times \sigma_{LT}), \qquad [11.10]$$

where σ_{LT} is the standard deviation of lead time.

For BPH, let us assume that the daily demand for medium-sized stent grafts is almost always two and that lead time is normally distributed with a mean of 2 days and a standard deviation of 0.5 day. With a desired service level of 95%, the reorder point is

$$\text{ROP} = (2 \text{ grafts/day} \times 2 \text{ days}) + (1.645 \times 2 \text{ grafts} \times 0.5)$$

$$= 4 + 1.645$$

$$= 5.645 \approx 6 \text{ grafts.}$$

Constant Lead time and Variable Demand

When the lead time is known and constant but the demand fluctuates, the formula for the reorder point is

$$\text{ROP} = (\text{Average demand rate} \times \text{Lead time}) + z\sigma_d\sqrt{LT} \qquad [11.11]$$

where σ_d is the standard deviation of the demand per day, week, month, and so on.

In the BPH example, let us assume that the supplier guarantees a delivery of stent grafts exactly 2 days after an order has been placed and that daily demand is normally distributed with a mean of 2.2 grafts and a standard deviation of 0.3 grafts. If BPH establishes a service level of 98%, the reorder point is

$$\text{ROP} = \left(2.2 \text{ grafts / day} \times 2 \text{ days}\right) + \left(2.05 \times 0.3 \text{ grafts} \times \sqrt{2}\right)$$

$$= 4.4 + 0.87$$

$$= 5.27 \text{ grafts.}$$

Variable Lead Time and Variable Demand

When both demand and the lead time vary, the formula for the reorder point is more elaborate:

$$\text{ROP} = (\text{Average demand rate} \times \text{Average lead time}) \qquad [11.12]$$
$$+ z\sqrt{\left(\text{Average lead time} \times \sigma_d^2\right) + (\text{Average demand rate})^2\, \sigma_{LT}^2}$$

If daily demand for medium-sized stent grafts is normally distributed with a mean of 2.2 and a standard deviation of 0.3 and lead time is normally distributed with a mean of 2 days and a standard deviation of 0.5 days, the reorder point for a 98% service level is

$$\text{ROP} = \left(2.2 \text{ grafts / day} \times 2 \text{ days}\right) + (2.05)\sqrt{\left(2 \times 0.3^2\right) + (2.2)^2\,(0.5)^2}$$

$$= 4.4 + (2.05)\sqrt{0.18 + 1.21}$$

$$= 4.4 + (2.05)(1.18) = 6.819 \approx 7 \text{ grafts.}$$

The compounded variability in both demand and lead time results in a higher safety stock.

SELECTING SUPPLIERS

As healthcare organizations increasingly embrace lean systems (Chapter 6), they adopt supply management principles emphasizing close ties with suppliers. These suppliers are expected to deliver exactly what is needed when it is needed. This requires making frequent deliveries of small quantities of high-quality goods. In a traditional environment, buyers switch from one supplier to the other in the pursuit of low cost. The advantage of that approach is that buyers can secure low prices in the short term through cut-throat negotiations with a large number of vendors. The drawback is that buyers' lack of loyalty is matched by suppliers' lack of commitment. This adversarial relationship is contrary to a lean environment in which trust and high predictability ensure smooth operations with little or no waste. In a lean environment, healthcare organizations forge strong, long-term relationships with a few suppliers. This practice has multiple advantages. With few suppliers, the buyer commits to a substantial volume of business with each one. As a "major customer," the buyer will typically be entitled to sustained, discounted prices without the hassle of "renegotiating deals" constantly. Moreover, the buyer will be able to request special accommodations such as frequent and/or emergency deliveries of small quantities. Healthcare organizations can also certify established suppliers as vendors of high-quality supplies. This certification relieves the buyer from the burden of inspecting incoming shipments because they come from trusted sources. Relationships between the parties can evolve toward a collaboration in which the buyer shares consumption information with the vendor, and the vendor assumes the responsibility of replenishing the inventory when needed. This business model is known as a **vendor-managed inventory system** (Box 11.6).

Vendor-Managed Inventory (VMI) System

System based on a collaborative relationship between the buyer and the supplier. The buyer shares consumption information with the vendor, and the vendor assumes the responsibility of replenishing the inventory when needed.

🔆 BOX 11.6 – OM IN PRACTICE!

Vendor-Managed Inventory With Baxter

Baxter, a hospital supply company, implemented a VMI with large hospital customers. Hospitals specify stock requirements for each ward. A Baxter employee keeps track of inventory levels on a regular basis and transmits the information electronically to a Baxter warehouse, where a replenishment is activated when the reorder level is reached. The orders are placed in containers specific to each ward and delivered the next day; the invoices are generated and sent to the hospital. This system enables large hospitals to outsource a noncore function (Li, 2007).

Selecting long-term suppliers is the result of a rigorous process based on multiple criteria (Stevenson, 2012):

1. **Quality**. Does the supplier have sound procedures to ensure quality? What are the supplier's policies when quality problems occur?

2. **Flexibility**. Does the supplier allow changes in delivery schedules? Is the supplier willing to engage in a collaborative relationship?

3. **Location**. How far is the supplier located? How does that affect costs and timely deliveries?

4. **Price**. How much room is there for negotiation? How does the supplier's prices compare with other vendors? Are there quantity discounts?

5. **Lead time**. What lead times can the supplier guarantee? What is the policy if the supplier does not deliver on time?

6. **Reputation**. What is the supplier's reputation? How reliable is the supplier? What is the supplier's financial stability?

7. **Information system capability**. What are the supplier's e-procurement capabilities? What about vendor-managed inventory systems?

BRADLEY PARK HOSPITAL 11.3

Sheila felt she had made significant progress. Because the hospital experienced a high volume of surgeries, she could take advantage of quantity discounts and place orders for 31 medium-sized stent grafts at a time. She believed that the 48-hour lead time negotiated with the supplier would be constant. However demand was variable. Therefore, she would place orders of 31 grafts when five or six grafts were left in inventory. With so much money involved, there was no way she could leave the grafts on the shelf. The opportunity for theft was just too great. What would be a secure place to put them with limited access?

Also, Sheila wanted to keep track of the inventory management performance in her department. She was going to start a dashboard. The measures would be:

1. *Vendor's lead time*

2. *Holding costs*

3. *Stockouts*

4. *Shrinkage*

5. *Supply expense as a percentage of revenue*

6. *Supply expense per adjusted patient day*

 Can you help Sheila identify other performance indicators to place on the dashboard?

SUMMARY

In this chapter, you learned about SCM and its importance in controlling costs, meeting quality requirements, delivering services on time, and adapting to change. Careful selection of suppliers, prompt responses to customers' needs, elimination of middlemen, customer-driven demand (pull), collaboration, and information sharing drive SCM strategies and help boost performance on multiple competitive priorities (Figure 11.9).

Supply chain expenses are substantial. Not only do healthcare organizations incur the costs of purchasing, ordering, and holding supplies, but they have to be vigilant about obsolescence, shrinkage, and stockout problems, which jeopardize the timely delivery of quality care. Close ties with reliable vendors enable healthcare organizations to secure discounted prices and deliveries within agreed upon lead times. The relevance of order quantities and the reorder levels not only depend on good estimates of demand, but also on the quality of the inventory control systems, and the strength of the relationships with suppliers.

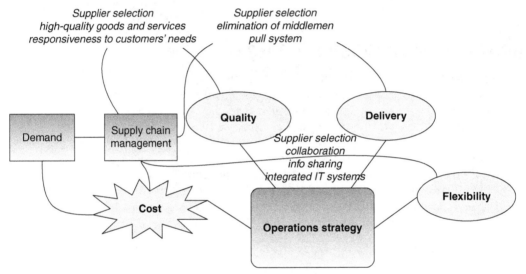

FIGURE 11.9 – Mind map linking SCM to the other competitive priorities.

KEY TERMS

Supply chain	Economic order quantity (EOQ) models	Reorder point
Group purchasing organization (GPO)	Holding costs	Safety stock
Supply chain management	Ordering costs	Stockout
Inventory	Lead time	Service level
Inventory management	Quantity discount model	Vendor-managed inventory system
ABC analysis	Price break	

TOOLS USED IN THIS CHAPTER

TOOL	PURPOSE
ABC analysis	Approach used to classify inventory items into three or more classes based on their annual dollar volume. It helps design inventory systems appropriate for each classification.
Basic EOQ model	Inventory model used to determine the order size that will minimize the sum of annual holding and ordering costs.
Quantity discount model	Inventory model used to determine the order size that will minimize the sum of annual holding, ordering, and purchasing costs for different prices.
Reorder point model	Inventory model used to help determine the timing of an order based on inventory levels.

FORMULAS USED IN THIS CHAPTER

Technique	Definition	Formula	Number
Basic EOQ	Annual holding cost	$\dfrac{Q}{2}H$	[11.1]
	Average inventory	$\dfrac{Q}{2}$	[11.2]
	Annual ordering cost	$\dfrac{D}{Q}S$	[11.3]
	Total cost (TC)	$\dfrac{Q}{2}H + \dfrac{D}{Q}S$	[11.4]
	EOQ	$\sqrt{\dfrac{2DS}{H}}$	[11.5]
Quantity discounts	TC	$PD + \dfrac{Q}{2}H + \dfrac{D}{Q}S$	[11.6]
Reorder point	ROP (demand and lead time are known and constant)	$d \times LT$	[11.7]
	ROP (variation is present)	Expected demand during lead time + Safety stock	[11.8]

ROP (records on demand during lead time are available)	Expected demand during lead time $+ z\sigma_{dLT}$	[11.9]
ROP (demand is constant; lead time is variable)	$\left(\begin{array}{l}\text{Demand rate} \\ \times \text{ Average lead time}\end{array}\right) +$ $(z \times \text{demand rate} \times \sigma_{LT})$	[11.10]
ROP (lead time is constant; demand is variable)	(Average demand rate $\times$ Lead time) $+ z\sigma_d\sqrt{LT}$	[11.11]
ROP (demand and lead time are variable)	(Average demand rate $\times$ Average lead time) $+ z$ $\sqrt{\begin{array}{l}\left(\text{Average lead time} \times \sigma_d^2\right) \\ + (\text{Average} \\ \text{demand rate})^2 \sigma_{LT}^2\end{array}}$	[11.12]

WHAT DO YOU REMEMBER?

1. What is a supply chain?
2. What is a GPO?
3. What is SCM? List some of the activities involved in SCM.
4. To deliver optimal value to the patient, what should SCM strategies emphasize?
5. What are the various types of inventory?
6. What are the two important decisions in inventory management?
7. What are the three steps of ABC analysis?
8. What is the purpose of the basic EOQ model?
9. Why is the average inventory equal to $Q/2$ in the basic EOQ model?
10. Describe holding costs and ordering costs.
11. What are the assumptions of the basic EOQ model?
12. Which assumption of the basic EOQ model is relaxed when quantity discounts are applied? What is the impact on the computation of total cost?
13. Is the EOQ the same as the optimal order quantity when quantity discounts are offered?
14. What is the reorder point?
15. What is the difference between just-in-time and just-in-case inventories?

16. What is meant by "service level?"

17. List five criteria used to select suppliers.

18. How does SCM support the quality, delivery, and flexibility competitive priorities?

SOLVE BPH'S PROBLEMS

1. One of BPH's pharmacists wants to establish different levels of inventory control for the following items. Help her classify those items into A, B, and C items.

Item Code	Annual Demand	Unit Price
J365	80	$600
K789	100	$12
H322	800	$2
J541	200	$55
J566	150	$10
K852	2,000	$5
H897	750	$3
H453	50	$1,000
J856	1,200	$4
K847	5,000	$3

2. The inventory manager wishes to use a two-bin inventory system for C items. Which ones of the following items are C items? Use the ABC approach to find out.

Item Code	Annual Demand	Unit Price
4556	10,000	$1
2564	52	$3,000
1289	128	$100
3265	300	$4
7896	90	$50
6842	600	$5
2589	35	$7,000
8496	420	$7
3564	560	$3
8547	136	$28
7826	30	$5,000
6514	85	$235
8951	450	$5
7265	76	$142
4235	100	$20
9898	2,000	$12

(continued)

(*continued*)

Item Code	Annual Demand	Unit Price
9542	400	$13
8474	300	$56
5454	600	$10
1236	700	$9

3. The annual demand for vascular kits is 1,600. The holding cost is $300 per kit per year, and the cost of placing an order is estimated at $50. The purchase price per unit is $1,000. Assume that demand is known and constant.

   a. Determine the optimal order quantity of vascular kits.

   b. Determine the total annual ordering and holding costs.

   c. Management would prefer to set the holding cost as a percentage of purchase price. Thirty-five percent of the item's price seems appropriate. Determine the new optimal order quantity and total costs.

   d. What is the relative difference between the EOQs found in parts a and c? What is the relative difference in total annual costs found in parts b and c? What is your conclusion?

4. The annual demand for a particular drug is 1,800 tablets. The purchase price of a tablet is $20. The holding cost per unit per year is 25% of the item's price, and the cost of placing an order is $30. The pharmacist orders the drug in quantities of 200. Demand is known and constant.

   a. Determine the optimal order quantity.

   b. Determine the total annual ordering and holding costs for the quantity determined in part a.

   c. Determine the total annual cost associated with the quantity ordered by the pharmacist. Which cost (holding or ordering) is higher and why?

   d. If the pharmacist used the EOQ, how many orders per year would be placed on average? What would the length of an order cycle (time between two consecutive orders) be, assuming 300 work days in a year?

5. BPH's supplier of surgical sterile gloves offers the following quantity discounts:

Quantity (20-pair boxes)	Price per Box
1–100	$18
101–200	$15
201–300	$12
301 and above	$10

BPH uses 11,000 pairs annually. The cost of placing an order is $30, and the holding cost per box per year is 20% of the item's cost. What is the optimal order quantity (round to the nearest integer if needed) and the total costs associated with that quantity?

6. BPH's consumption of a certain detergent is 1,000 gallons per year. Four-gallon cases can be purchased at the following prices:

Quantity (4-gallon cases)	Price per Case
1–99	$30
100–299	$25
300 and above	$22

Holding cost per case per year is 40% of the item's cost, and the cost of placing an order is $30. What is the optimal order quantity (round to the nearest integer if needed) and the total costs associated with that quantity?

7. At BPH, the mean lead time demand for Gauze AX-7 was 70 boxes (normally distributed). The standard deviation of demand during lead time was 5. The manager of hospital supplies wants to maintain a 90% service level.

   a. What safety stock level would you recommend?

   b. What should the reorder point be?

8. An inventory ordering system must be set up for Bandage T-150 based on the following data (assume the normal distribution):

Average weekly demand	80 packages
Standard deviation of weekly demand	4 packages
Lead time	2 weeks

   a. What safety stock would you recommend if a stockout risk of 5% is considered acceptable?

   b. What safety stock would you recommend if a stockout risk of 3% is considered acceptable?

   c. A reorder point of 172 packages has been set. What is the service level?

9. An inventory ordering system must be set up for Bandage BX-62 based on the following data (assume the normal distribution):

Daily demand	100 packages
Average lead time	4 days
Standard deviation of lead time	1 day

   a. What safety stock would you recommend if a stockout risk of 8% is considered acceptable?

b. What safety stock would you recommend if a stockout risk of 4% is considered acceptable?

c. A reorder point of 560 packages has been set. What is the service level?

10. An inventory ordering system must be set up for Ointment CX-30 based on the following data (assume the normal distribution):

Average daily demand	50 tubes
Standard deviation of demand	6 tubes
Average lead time	5 days
Standard deviation of lead time	1 day

a. What safety stock would you recommend if a stockout risk of 10% is considered acceptable?

b. What safety stock would you recommend if a stockout risk of 5% is considered acceptable?

c. What is the reorder point for a service level of 98%?

THINK OUTSIDE THE BOOK!

1. Based on the following article, what challenges does the hospital supply chain face? Explain.

Sutton, K. (2014, October 9). 5 challenges for the hospital supply chain. *Healthcare Finance*. Retrieved from http://www.healthcarefinancenews.com/blog/5-challenges-hospital-supply-chain

2. Identify three medical inventory software packages and their special features. Summarize any reviews that might be available on the software. Which software would you recommend and why?

3. There are too many drug shortages in the United States. What are the primary causes? You may want to do a literature review to answer that question. Reading the following article will be a good starting point.

DeBenedette, V. (2014, August 10). Drug shortages continue; hospitals cope. *Drug Topics: Voice of the Pharmacist*. Retrieved from http://drugtopics.modernmedicine.com/drug-topics/content/tags/ashp/drug-shortages-continue-hospitals-cope?page=full

REFERENCES

Burns, L. R., & Wharton School Colleagues. (2002). *The health care value chain: Producers, purchasers, and providers* (1st ed.). San Francisco, CA: Jossey-Bass.

Council of Supply Chain Management Professionals. (2015). CSCMP supply chain management. Retrieved from https://cscmp.org/about-us/supply-chain-management-definitions

Croxton, K. L., & Rogers, D. S. (2001). The supply chain management processes. *International Journal of Logistics Management, 12*(2), 13–36.

Ebel, T., George, K., Larsen, E., Shah, K., & Ungerman, D. (2013). *Building new strengths in the healthcare supply chain.* New York, NY: McKinsey & Company. Retrieved from http://www.mckinsey.com/search?q=building%20new%20strengths%20in%20the%20healthcare%20supply%20chain%20pharmaceuticals%20and%20medical%20products%20operations

Healthcare Supply Chain Association. (2015). *A primer on group purchasing organizations: Questions and answers.* Washington, DC: Author.

Insel, T. R. (2014, May 14). *May is for meetings and mental health.* Bethesda, MD: National Institute of Mental Health. Retrieved from http://www.nimh.nih.gov/about/director/2014/may-is-for-meetings-and-mental-health.shtml

Li, L. (2007). *Supply chain management: Concepts, techniques and practices—Enhancing value through collaboration.* Singapore: World Scientific.

Mentzer, J. T., DeWitt, W., Keebler, J. S., Min, S., Smith, C. D., & Zacharia, Z. G. (2001). Defining supply chain management. *Journal of Business Logistics, 22*(2), 1–21.

Rautonen, J. (2007, August). Redesigning supply chain management together with the hospitals. *Transfusion, 47*, 197S–200S.

Schneller, E. S., & Smeltzer, L. R. (2006). *Strategic management of the health care supply chain.* Hoboken, NJ: Jossey-Bass.

Stevenson, W. J. (2012). *Operations management* (11th ed.). New York, NY: McGraw-Hill.

Storey, J., Emberson, C., Godsell, J., & Harrison, A. (2006). Supply chain management: Theory, practice and future challenges. *International Journal of Operations & Production Management, 26*(7), 754–774.

CHAPTER 12

COST: BASIC CONCEPTS

BRADLEY PARK HOSPITAL 12.1

Mike Chambers was a bit confused and frustrated after the call from a new board member, Marcus Lynn, who wanted to understand the costs of care for Bradley Park Hospital (BPH). Mr. Lynn had just read a news article about the escalating costs of care in the United States and about new payment methods for healthcare services. Mike reminded him that the expenses for BPH were down over the past few years and that the hospital was profitable. He tried to reassure Mr. Lynn that they had appropriate cost controls. Mr. Lynn stated that he understood, but felt that there was something missing. He knew that the costs for insurance had been increasing for his large pipe manufacturing company, that the bills sent from the hospital were confusing; and that the press often talked about the high prices that health providers charged for simple things like aspirin. He felt he needed to understand these issues and he wanted the board to be educated on the costs of healthcare. Mike understood. However, he did not know how to approach educating his board on this confusing topic. He asked Mr. Lynn to send the article and he would get to work on the board's education.

INTRODUCTION AND LEARNING OBJECTIVES

The U.S. healthcare system is frequently described as being unsustainable because the costs of healthcare services continue to grow despite being the highest for all Organisation for Economic Co-operation and Development (OECD) countries (Chapter 1). In this chapter, we explore the concepts related to the costs of healthcare services (Figure 12.1). Several factors contribute to these high costs and are reviewed here. We also describe the payment system and its relationship to costs. Finally, we explain how to capture costs and improve financial performance. The measurement of cost is a complex endeavor and this chapter will be a high-level introduction to this evolving discipline. Remember that cost should not be considered in isolation from the quality, delivery, or flexibility of the services provided. As an operations management (OM) professional, you need to strive constantly to minimize costs while improving performance on the other competitive priorities. After reading this chapter, you will be able to:

1. **List the factors that increase healthcare costs in the United States**

2. **Describe the different payment models for healthcare services**

3. **Explain the various categories of costs**

4. **Describe how costs are measured**

5. **Evaluate services that promote financial success**

6. **Recognize actions that can be taken to improve costs**

FIGURE 12.1 –
Mind map with
focus on cost.

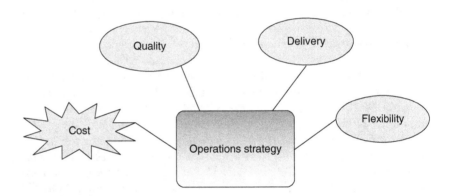

BRADLEY PARK HOSPITAL 12.2

After reading the article "Healthcare Costs Continue to Escalate and Will Sink the US Economy," Mike Chambers understood why Marcus Lynn was concerned and confused. He knew he had his work cut out for him to educate the board.

Mike called his administrative intern, Misty. "Hey, Misty, I need your help in preparing some board education on the costs of healthcare. I have an article I will send you as a reference."

Misty, who was eager to help, responded. "No problem, I loved finance and accounting in school. I should be able to have this to you next week."

Mike was not so certain that it would be that easy, but thanked her and left the office for the day. When Misty got the article she became concerned. Much of the article was not about the costs inside the walls of the hospital, but the costs of healthcare services to the federal government and what the United States is getting for spending this money. She knew she would have to answer a few questions: What is the relationship of costs to the United

States and expenses inside the hospital? How is cost related to payment for healthcare services? Do we have good methods to measure cost for healthcare services?

MACROECONOMICS ISSUES AND THE RELATIONSHIP TO OM

Much has been written about the cost of healthcare services and the relationship of costs to outcomes such as life expectancy. From a macroeconomics perspective, the United States has seen a growth in healthcare costs, which has consistently outpaced that of the gross domestic product (GDP), and per capita spending has been twice as high as the average for Europe (Davis, Stremikis, Squires, & Schoen, 2014). This growth has not been associated with significant improvement in life expectancy when compared to other developed countries. This suggests that we are not getting value for our healthcare dollar. This fact has been a major impetus for healthcare reform and was the driving factor for passage of the Affordable Care Act (ACA). If U.S. costs are higher, what are their drivers? The Institute of Medicine (IOM) identified that total excess costs approached $750 billion in 2009 (Young, Saunders, & Olsen, 2010). The sources of this excess are unnecessary services, inefficiently delivered services, excess administrative costs, excessive prices, missed prevention opportunities, and fraud (see Chapter 1). Several of the sources of excess costs are under the influence or direct control of OM professionals.

OM professionals are challenged with managing the costs of the processes for which they are responsible and maximizing the value of the services rendered. Measuring and minimizing cost are difficult to accomplish. Current costing systems do not provide accurate measurements at the patient condition level, which can lead to poor decision making and unintended consequences. We discuss this challenge more in detail later in this chapter. For now, remember that managing costs is embedded in the finance and operations strategies of the organization.

DEFINITION OF TERMS

In order to explore cost management, we first need to review some cost concepts.

Cost is an amount that has to be paid or given up in order to obtain something. In business, cost is usually a monetary valuation of (a) effort, (b) material, (c) resources, (d) time and utilities consumed, (e) risks incurred, and (f) opportunities forgone in producing a product and delivering a service.

Expenses represent the amount of money spent on something for providing services and are captured directly in accounting systems.

Cost
An amount that has to be paid or given up in order to get something.

Expense
Refers to the amount of money spent on something.

Price
The amount of money that is paid, requested, or expected for something that is bought, sold, or offered for sale.

Charges
The amount of money requested for an item or service.

Revenue
The amount of money received for a product or service.

Profit (Loss)
The positive or negative difference between revenue and costs.

Price is the amount of money paid (or requested or expected) for a product or service. **Charges** represent the amount of money requested (price) for an item or service. In healthcare, as you will see, payment for services is often not the amount requested with the charges. These terms are highly related but capture different concepts. An in-depth exploration is beyond the scope of this chapter. For our purposes, the price is what you pay for something (labor, supplies, insurance), is measured in monetary terms, and is captured in the accounting system as an expense. These expenses are used to measure the cost to provide a service. It is important to note that limiting the price paid for inputs is a fundamental way to reduce costs of services.

Revenue is the amount of money received for a product or service.

Profit (or loss) is the difference between the amount received for a product or service (revenue) and the cost to produce or deliver it. If the difference is positive, a profit is made. If the costs exceed the revenue, a loss is incurred.

Making a profit is important to the viability of the organization. OM professionals must promote the financial health of the organization by boosting profits where they can be made and minimizing losses where they might inevitably occur. In order to accomplish this goal, an understanding of payment methodologies and cost measurement is vital.

PAYMENT METHODOLOGIES

Payment methods for healthcare services are complex. Generally speaking, the methods for reimbursing hospitals and physicians for services rendered are determined by the federal government through the Centers for Medicare & Medicaid Services (CMS). Other non-governmental payers often follow similar methods as those set by CMS. Hospitals and physicians are paid separately, using different methodologies. Despite those differences, payments to both hospitals and physicians are dependent on the documentation of services rendered using standard code sets and on a prospectively defined price. We explore the respective payment methodologies for hospitals and physicians a little later. First, let us review some basic concepts.

Traditional Systems

Fee-for-Service
A payment system in which providers are paid separately for each service (office visit, test, or procedure) they perform.

Many healthcare services are paid using a *fee-for-service* method (Chapter 1). **Fee-for-service** just means that the provider (physician or hospital) is paid for each service rendered. Seems to make sense—right? This is what happens when you go to a restaurant. Each time you go and receive service, you pay the price for the service rendered. However, in healthcare this may lead to a perverse incentive, which destroys value. Suppose you are a patient and have a disease that requires follow-up. One physician may suggest that you be seen every 6 months, but another physician may feel that follow-up visits every 12 months are adequate. If there is no difference in outcome, the first physician creates excess cost, thereby decreasing value. The first physician gets paid twice as much as does the second physician and earns more money, but there is no benefit to the patient.

This simple example illustrates why fee-for-service payment methods can drive over utilization of healthcare services. In order to rectify these issues, other payment methodologies have been developed. These include different forms of *capitation payments*, according to which, service providers get paid a set amount for treating a condition or patient over time. In the previous example, the insurance company could contract with the physician and agree to pay him or her a set amount per year to care for the patient. The physician would get paid the same no matter how many times he or she saw the patient or how many tests were ordered. This was the model implemented under *managed care*, which became widespread in the 1980s and 1990s. Note that in this type of managed care, an important and needed service could be rationed because it would increase the costs of care without an increase in the capped payment. This created another perverse incentive to limit care for financial gain, thereby contributing to lower value. This rationing of value-added services led to the decreased use of traditional managed care methods in the 1990s.

Another type of capitated payment to hospitals that is becoming less common is the per diem (by day) payment method. In this method, hospitals are paid a certain amount for every day the patient is in the hospital regardless of the reason or resources needed to care for the patient. In this method, there is little incentive for hospitals to get patients out of the hospital. The hospital makes more money the longer the patient stays in the hospital. Again, this can lead to a perverse incentive to keep patients longer than necessary, resulting in lower value. Consequently, in 1983, CMS implemented a *case rate* method for paying hospitals using diagnosis related groups (DRGs); see Chapter 1, Box 12.1, and Table 12.1.

Capitation Payment

A payment system in which providers receive a set amount for treating a condition or patient over time.

⊕ BOX 12.1 – DID YOU KNOW?

What Is a DRG?

The Diagnosis-Related Group is a classification scheme that groups patients into approximately 500 categories by demographic, diagnostic, and therapeutic characteristics. Hospital cases within the same group have similar hospital resource use. Complications and comorbidities (CC) are used to adjust the severity of the diagnosis groups. Major CCs significantly increase the expected resource utilization beyond that of the base DRG. These DRGs have been used by the Centers for Medicare & Medicaid Services since 1983 for hospital payment for Medicare patients (CMS, 2015a).

In this method, the hospital is paid a set (capitated) amount to treat a condition (case) no matter how long the patient stays in the hospital or how many resources are utilized to provide the care. If you are

TABLE 12.1 – Examples of DRGs	
DRG	**Description of Diagnosis-Related Group**
207	Patients on the ventilator for over 96 hours
234	Heart bypass surgery without complications
282	Heart attack without complications and discharged alive
682	Kidney failure with complications
Source: CMS (2015a).	

Prospective Payment System (PPS)

A Medicare payment system in which a fixed payment rate is based on a predetermined calculation.

getting paid a set amount to treat a condition, you are motivated to decrease the resources (days in the hospital, supplies, etc.) utilized to treat that condition. This motivates hospitals to decrease costs for treating that condition. So, does this increase value? Overall, healthcare value may not be improved from the patient's perspective. How can this be? Suppose you run a hospital that does hip replacements and you get a set amount per patient. You are motivated to implant hips that cost the least amount. Suppose you implant hips that are cheap and appear to be of reasonable quality, but the implants fail after 5 years, requiring additional surgeries. By implanting the cheaper hip, you have decreased value to the patient while increasing the financial gain to your institution. This same dynamic applies when treating other diseases and conditions as discrete, isolated episodes of care.

As mentioned earlier, hospitals and physicians are paid by CMS using two different methods with similar characteristics. Both use a **prospective payment system** in which Medicare pays a fixed amount based on a predetermined calculation. The hospital system is covered by Medicare Part A insurance, and the fixed amount is determined by the inpatient prospective payment system (IPPS) using a classification system called the DRG. Physicians receive a separate payment in a predetermined amount based on a coding and classification system that is different from that used to pay the hospital. Generally, physicians are paid based on submission of a Current Procedural Terminology (CPT®) code, which categorizes the type of service provided. CPT is a proprietary system of the American Medical Association. The CPT code captures the type of service. For instance, a procedure in the hospital operating room, a procedure in the office, a hospital consult, and an office visit all have different codes and command different rates. Similar to the DRG system, there are mechanisms to modify the codes for specific situations such as providing the service while training a young physician. The physician must support the CPT code with documentation that describes the disease or symptom that leads to the service. The classification mechanism to capture this information is called the International Classification of Diseases (ICD). This classification system is managed by the WHO and has evolved to keep up with new knowledge and the need for more specificity. The current version most widely used in the world is the ICD-10, and this is the standard classification method adopted by CMS in 2015.

New Systems

The majority of traditional payment methods pay for discrete episodes of care and may lead to erosion of value. They need to be rectified to solve the cost crisis in healthcare (Kaplan & Porter, 2011). Fortunately, newer payment methods have emerged. These include **value-based payments** adjusted for quality metrics, **bundled payments** offering one payment amount for all services associated with treating a condition over a defined period of time, and **accountable care organization** models in which payment is tied to improving quality and reducing costs for a population of patients over time. These new payment models are the foundation of the ACA and have been developed with the hope of driving overall value improvement. Time will tell whether these new systems result in lower costs and higher quality over the long run.

It is important to note that providers are often paid according to different methods for similar services. For instance, for the same condition, the provider may be paid a fee-for-service by one insurance company and paid under a capitation method by another insurance carrier. This increased complexity can cause poor alignment of incentives. In addition, as more insurance companies move toward VBP methods, there have been no universal standards to measure quality. The providers may be held accountable for different quality metrics by different insurers. Confusion and increased administrative and reporting costs may ensue. Now that we have addressed providers' revenues, let us look at cost measurement.

Value-Based Payments (VBPs)
Payments that are adjusted for quality metrics.

Bundled Payments
Payments for all services associated with treating a condition over a defined period of time.

Accountable Care Organization (ACO)
A healthcare organization in which the payment and care delivery model is tied to improving quality and reducing costs for a population of patients over time.

BRADLEY PARK HOSPITAL 12.3

Misty was interested in understanding the costs from a process perspective. This was how patients received care, and this approach seemed to make the most sense to her. Maybe this would be the best way to explain it to the board. What is the total cost for taking care of a patient? Surely, if she could explain that, the board would understand.

TOTAL COSTS

The total cost of a process is the sum of input, process, and output costs (Figure 12.2).

Total cost = Cost of inputs + Cost of process + Cost of outputs   [12.1]

Input Costs

Input costs include the costs of resources, such as material, equipment, people, and facilities (Chapter 1), utilized to provide a given service. The input costs can be fixed or variable in nature. **Fixed costs** are expenses that are not dependent on the quantity of services provided. Fixed costs are usually managed by spreading these costs over a larger base of services, which decreases the cost per unit of service and creates economies of scale. For instance, the unit costs of serving 10 patients in an operating room would exceed those of serving 20 patients in the

Input Costs
Resources that are utilized to provide a given service.

Fixed Costs
Expenses that are not dependent on the level of goods or services produced.

FIGURE 12.2 –
Mind map of input,
process, and output
costs.

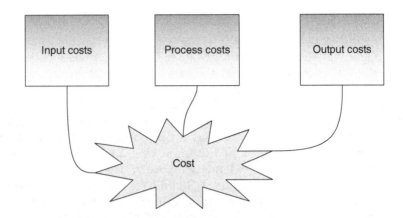

Variable Costs

Expenses that are
dependent on the level
of goods or services
produced by the
business.

Direct Costs

Costs of inputs that
are consumed during
the process of care.

Indirect Costs

Costs that are not
consumed during the
process of care but
are needed in order to
provide the service.

same operating room. **Variable costs** are expenses that are dependent on the volume of services provided. As more services are rendered, costs increase. These costs can be adjusted more rapidly than fixed costs. Examples of variable costs include the costs of supplies used in care processes and the costs of nurses needed to care for increasing volumes of patients.

In addition to being classified as fixed or variable, costs are also frequently classified as direct or indirect. **Direct costs** are the costs of inputs that are consumed during the process of care, which include items like pharmaceuticals, nursing care, and use of an operating room. **Indirect costs** are costs that are not consumed during the process of care but are needed in order to provide the service. They include the costs of items like administrative supervisors, information systems, or accounting staff. These costs are not traced back to specific patient service. These indirect costs are frequently described as overhead and are costs that must be covered by revenue-generating activities. When we evaluate the methods for measuring costs, you will see that how these overhead expenses are allocated can have a significant impact on the reporting of cost data. Table 12.2 provides a few examples of input cost classifications.

TABLE 12.2 – Types of Input Costs and Their Classifications

Input Cost	Fixed/Variable	Direct/Indirect
Pharmaceuticals	Variable	Direct
Nurses	Variable	Direct
MRI machine depreciation	Fixed	Direct
Information system	Fixed	Indirect
Administration	Fixed	Indirect

Reducing the amount paid for the input, eliminating the input, or substituting it with a less costly alternative are all ways to control input costs, whether they are fixed or variable. For instance, eliminating the admission lab tests on patients who had recent lab work would decrease both direct and variable costs. If it is safe to perform a surgery in a lower cost ambulatory surgery center rather than the larger more expensive hospital surgery suite, the direct and fixed input costs for the facility will be lower in the ambulatory setting. This last example highlights an important concept when categorizing costs. You should note that fixed costs and indirect costs capture different concepts and are not interchangeable. If a fixed cost can be traced to a specific patient activity, it is considered a direct cost of providing care.

Process Costs

Staff, supplies, and facilities are organized to affect service delivery and are brought together to provide value-added activities that serve the patient. **Process costs** are the costs inherent in the transformation process (Chapter 1) and are determined by its efficiency and the types of patients served. Process costs are related to the physical layout of the area, steps to accomplish tasks, process variability, rework, errors, and all forms of waste (Chapter 6). Using the tools for process redesign (Chapter 7), you can increase the efficiency of the process and lower its costs. For instance, by eliminating the number of duplicate tests ordered, the variable costs of the redundant tests vanish and the total cost of caring for the patient is decreased (Box 12.2). In order to calculate the process costs, you will need to be able to capture the cost of providing the needed capacities to provide the needed activities. With the newer methods for measuring costs, which attempt to capture the cost to provide the needed capacity to serve patients, you will have tools to measure the process costs.

Process Cost
The inherent cost of the process, which is determined by the efficiency of the process.

 BOX 12.2 – OM IN PRACTICE!

Reducing Process Waste

Cleveland Clinic initiated a project to reduce unnecessary, same-day, duplicative laboratory tests. A clinical decision support tool detected when same-day duplicate tests had been ordered and initiated an immediate notification alert that a duplicate test had been ordered. The system displayed the laboratory results if available, or informed the physician that the test result was pending. In a 2-year time frame, the tool blocked close to 12,000 unnecessary duplicate orders, which resulted in significant savings (Procop, Yerian, Wyllie, Harrison, & Kottke-Marchant, 2014).

When errors occur during the care process, costs increase. For a healthcare organization, these costs can be attributed to an error that does not affect the patient, for example, a prevented adverse drug event (Chapter 4, Box 4.7, internal failure costs). Alternatively, the error in the process can be a preventable event that does harm the patient and increases the cost of care as a result of additional treatments (Chapter 4, Box 4.7, external failure costs). Other costs are incurred when auditing the process or determining the causes of the errors (Chapter 4, Box 4.7, appraisal costs). For instance, if a patient gets a serious infection from a large intravenous catheter in the central vein (known as a central-line-associated bloodstream infection [CLABSI]) because the proper protocol was not followed, costs associated with treating the complications of this serious infection and with assessing why the event occurred in the first place will be incurred. Box 12.3 displays a list of preventable errors.

In healthcare, the term *attributable costs* is often used to describe costs associated with events that could be prevented. For

Attributable Costs
Additional costs associated with events that could be prevented.

⊕ BOX 12.3 – DID YOU KNOW?

Preventable Errors

Medication Errors

Mishaps that occur during prescribing, transcribing, dispensing, administering, adhering to a regimen, or monitoring a drug (CMS, 2015b, 2015c).

Hospital-Acquired Conditions

Events determined to be avoidable by CMS, which adjusts reimbursement to penalize hospitals for these complications.

Nosocomial Infection

Infection acquired during hospital stay.

Hospital-Acquired Pneumonia

Pneumonia acquired during hospital stay.

Ventilator-Associated Pneumonia

Lung infection occurring in patients who are on breathing machines in a hospital.

Central-Line-Associated Bloodstream Infection

Infection occurring as a result of having a catheter placed in the central circulation.

Failure to Diagnose

A patient condition that is not diagnosed appropriately. Harm may be inflicted if effective treatment is withheld or delayed, and/or if unnecessary treatments are provided.

Failure to Treat

Result of failure to diagnose or withheld treatment.

Failure to Rescue

Lack of response to a complication from an underlying illness or a complication of medical care during hospital stay.

CLABSI, that attributable cost is about $17,000 on average (The Joint Commission, 2012). Additionally, there is an ***attributable mortality.*** This is the mortality resulting from preventable events. A patient who gets a CLABSI has a 24% increased likelihood of dying while in the hospital (Rosenthal, Guzman, & Orellano, 2003). Obviously, because the health outcomes are worse for patients who endure these avoidable and costly situations, the value of their care is significantly reduced.

Attributable Mortality
Mortality associated with events that could have been prevented.

Cost avoidance, also known as prevention costs (Chapter 4, Box 4.7), is used to describe systems or technologies that are put in place to prevent future error-related costs. Cost avoidance engenders higher costs in the short run, but leads to lower costs and better quality in the long run. Examples of cost-avoidance items include "bundles" and checklists (Box 12.4).

Cost Avoidance
Activities, processes, or technologies that are put in place that prevent future costs.

⊕ BOX 12.4 – DID YOU KNOW?

Ventilator Bundle

Patients who require a ventilator to breathe are at risk for ventilator-associated pneumonia (VAP), or an airway infection that develops more than 48 hours after the patient was placed on the ventilator. Of all hospital-acquired infections, VAP has the highest mortality rate (Ibrahim, Tracy, Fraser, & Kollef, 2001). VAP is a major complication and leads to prolonged times on the ventilator, increased length of stay in the intensive care unit, and increased overall hospital stay, and VAP adds an average of $12,000 to a hospital admission (Warren et al., 2003).

The ventilator bundle is a series of interventions derived from best evidence-based practices. When implemented consistently, the ventilator bundle results in significantly improved patient morbidity and mortality (Institute for Healthcare Improvement, 2012).

The key components of the IHI Ventilator Bundle are as follows:

- **Elevate the head of the bed to 30 to 45 degrees**
  This prevents the aspiration of stomach contents.

- **Daily breaks in patient sedation and active assessment of the readiness to remove the patient from the ventilator**
  Patients are more awake and able to breathe better on their own. The time that the patient must stay on the ventilator is reduced.

- **Prevent stomach ulcers with medications**
  Patients on the ventilator are at increased risk for bleeding ulcers.

- **Prevent blood clots from forming in the legs**
  Patients who are on the ventilator are at increased risk for blood clots.

- **Daily mouth washing with chlorhexidine**
  This kills bacteria in the mouth, which can be aspirated into the lungs.

The process errors described earlier are important because they erode value and have been incorporated into VBP programs, where providers are penalized for having these types of errors. These process failures are evaluated and improved using quality tools learned about in Chapters 4 to 6.

Output Costs

Output Costs

Costs incurred once the service has been rendered and the process is no longer serving the customer.

Output costs are incurred once the service has been rendered, and the process is no longer serving the customer. For example, output costs are higher for angry or dissatisfied customers. They may log complaints, post negative comments on websites such as Healthgrades, discredit provider(s), or pursue legal actions (Chapter 4, Box 4.7, external failure costs). Besides the costs incurred when addressing complaints and lawsuits, providers also face lost revenue from potential patients who select other providers after seeing poor ratings on the Internet and from lower reimbursements according to the VBP program. High levels of patient complaints lead to higher litigation costs (Hickson et al., 1992). In turn, the malpractice costs (output costs) lead to higher malpractice insurance costs (input costs).

Now that we have explained input, transformation process, and output costs, we need to understand how the costs are measured.

BRADLEY PARK HOSPITAL 12.4

Misty felt she had a better understanding of the total costs of a process and what things influence the cost. She had seen reports from finance and was not sure how to relate what she has learned to those reports. So she called David in finance.

"David, this is Misty, the administrative intern working for Mike Chambers. I am working on a presentation for the board on the cost of healthcare. I was wondering whether you could help me?"

David was happy to help. "We implemented a cost-accounting system about 7 years ago. We have a firm understanding of our cost." He went on to explain, "Most institutions use their charges to measure costs, which means they use a ratio to estimate costs, but we invested in a more accurate way to measure cost. Come by tomorrow at 4 p.m. and we can talk."

Misty wondered why charges would not be good for estimating cost. She remembered that cost accounting was difficult and hoped that there was a simple solution. She knew that David was in the hospital finance department and wondered whether he had a way to capture costs that were outside the hospital accounting systems.

COST-ACCOUNTING METHODS

Cost accounting is the discipline of assigning costs to a product or service. It is a complex field, and an in-depth analysis of the subject is beyond the scope of this text. Nevertheless, an OM professional should have a general understanding of cost-accounting principles to determine the most appropriate costing method for the purpose at hand and make well-informed decisions. Cost accounting generally involves a five-step procedure to compute unit costs (Shepard, Hodgkin, & Anthony, 2000).

STEP 1: Identify the decision that is to be made and establish the objectives of the costing analysis (timeline, perspective).

STEP 2: Define the objects of the cost analysis (services, diagnosis, physician, etc.). Be explicit and specific.

STEP 3: Identify and categorize (direct/indirect) resources used to provide the service.

STEP 4: Measure resources utilized in natural units.

STEP 5: Place monetary value on these resources utilized and calculate unit costs of services.

There are many different cost-accounting methodologies for determining the cost of products or services, and the methods have evolved. There is no one right method, and the choice of a method depends on the perspective, the purpose of the analysis, and the availability of information or tools. The OM perspective is usually internal to the organization and concentrated on the business operations under the manager's responsibility. The purpose is to determine the costs per unit of service. With this knowledge, the OM professional can identify the different drivers of financial performance and work to improve it.

We explore the traditional methods for measuring costs, which are derived using the reimbursement system as the primary basis for identifying and allocating costs. These methods include the cost-to-charge ratio (CCR) and the relative value unit (RVU) methods. In these approaches, the assumption is that the costs of services are related to the charges, and that costs can be calculated and allocated based on the demand on resources as measured by charges. In addition, we explore the newer methods used to measure cost, which include activity-based costing and time-driven activity-based costing (TDABC). In these methods, there is an attempt to measure the actual consumption of resources rather than using charges as a surrogate for resource consumption.

Cost-to-Charge Ratio: Traditional Hospital Costing Methodology

A common way to measure costs in hospitals is the CCR method. So how does this work? As services are provided and resources consumed (medications, room, supplies, staff, etc.), the items consumed are entered into the information system. Each item has an associated charge, which is stored in the charge description master (CDM), often called the "charge master." These charges are used to generate bills so that revenue can be collected for services rendered. If we *assume* that there is a relationship between the charges generated and the costs of services rendered, a cost can be calculated. The first step in this process is to calculate a ratio, the CCR. Using the information from the accounting systems, a simplified CCR can be calculated by dividing the total expense incurred by the gross revenue:

$$CCR = \text{Total expense}/\text{Total gross patient revenue} \quad [12.2]$$

The total expense is what you paid to provide services as captured in the accounting system; this is your cost. It includes the amount paid for the inputs (supplies, people, and facilities). The total gross revenue captured is generated from charges and represents what you charged for the services provided. The CCR is typically calculated at the organizational level and is calculated annually. Next, in order to estimate the cost of a service you would take the charges generated by providing that service and multiply that number by the CCR. The formula for cost using the CCR method is as follows:

Cost = Gross charges for the service or product of interest × CCR [12.3]

Using this method, costs are often allocated to departments, services, or patients and are used to calculate profitability by these different units of analysis. An example will illustrate this concept. Let us assume that the CCR is 0.5 and the pharmacy charges for a patient are $500. For the pharmacy, the cost allocated to serve that patient would be calculated as $250 (0.5 × $500). Note that the actual cost to purchase and supply the pharmaceuticals is not used for this patient.

The CCR method remains popular because the data are readily available. However, the assumption that there is a relationship between costs and charges may not be accurate and this could lead to poor decision making. In general, the relationship of charges and costs may not hold at a service level or patient level because of how charges are managed. The charges generated are used to bill for services and are managed to maximize revenue. Services are rendered to patients with different types of insurance, and charges are used to generate bills for the many payer types. Some of these payers (i.e., Medicare and Medicaid) reimburse at levels that do not cover the costs to provide the service. In order to compensate for lower reimbursement levels from some payers, the charges may be increased for particular services or items, leading to increased reimbursement from payers with higher reimbursement. So, charges may be increased with no associated increase in cost to provide the service. In this case, the charges have been generated to bill for services rendered but are unrelated to the costs of these services. The practice of charging more for a service to patients with better insurance and therefore higher reimbursement in order to cover the costs of services not fully covered by the reimbursement of other insurers (Medicare and Medicaid) is called **cost shifting**.

Cost Shifting
Charging more for a service to the insured patients to cover the cost associated with serving patients who are under or uninsured.

Relative Value Unit Method for Determining Costs: A Common Physician Costing Methodology

The RVU method also uses charges and not actual resources to determine costs. It is another example of using a reimbursement-derived method to allocate costs. As we have discussed, when the physician provides a service and generates a bill, a CPT is generated. A Medicare panel reviews these codes and assigns an RVU. This unit captures the intensity, time, skill, practice expense, and malpractice expense for the service. This is used to calculate the reimbursement for the services rendered. It is not a measure of the costs incurred to provide services. However, it is common practice to use the RVU as a proxy for the amount of resources needed to provide services and is used to allocate expenses. In a physician practice, dividing the total expense by total RVUs generated will yield a reasonable measure of productivity and an understanding of the cost needed to accomplish that productivity. This is true because the RVU measures the amount of work produced (the output) and the expense measures the cost of the inputs. Still, just like the CCR method, when the RVU is used to allocate costs to particular services or patients it may not accurately capture the actual resources consumed to provide that service and therefore may not accurately measure the costs to provide that service. For example, if a physician consumes a large amount of human resources and incurs large malpractice expenses, and if these overhead cost centers and their associated expense are allocated based on RVU generated, the cost/RVU for this provider will be underestimated compared to a physician with less consumption of these overhead areas and the same amount of RVU production. This simple example highlights the deficiencies with using reimbursement-derived costing methodologies to allocate and measure costs. We need a method that better reflects true resource consumption and associated costs in order to make better decisions. Activity-based costing (ABC) methods can provide you with that information.

Activity-Based Costing

In this method, there is an attempt to measure the actual use of resources and their associated costs to determine the cost to provide services. When compared to the previous methods that we have reviewed, in this method more of the overhead costs are specifically measured and assigned as direct costs. By identifying the activities that are performed to serve the customer and the associated costs to provide those resources, a cost can be computed. In this method, you determine the activities that a given resource supports and the amount of time that the resource spends on each activity as the basis for measuring costs. It is important to note that resources often have many different tasks and activities and the perspective taken is from the resource that is available and the activities that resource performs. For instance, a physician may spend time in the operating room doing surgery, time seeing patients in the hospital, time doing clinic consults, and time returning patient calls. In this case, the surgeon will spend a certain percentage of time on each of these activities. By knowing how much a surgeon is paid, the cost to supply these different activities can be calculated. For instance, if it costs $500,000 to have a surgeon available, and the surgeon spends 50% of the time in surgery, then it costs $250,000 to have the surgeon doing surgery. This simple example illustrates the basics of ABC.

Now we will look at a more complicated example. Suppose you are the manager of the central clinic scheduling group for a large multidisciplinary practice. You are tasked with understanding how much it costs to provide services to some patients whose insurance started requiring preauthorization for services requested. The insurance company does not increase the reimbursement to you for this new requirement. You know that the costs of the space, phones, equipment, and personnel for scheduling are $640,000 per year. This number is usually obtained from historical accounting information. To set up the ABC model, the activities performed by the scheduling group need to be identified: processing requests for clinic visits, managing requests for medication refills, and obtaining insurance preauthorization for services. You need an estimate of the percentage of time spent on each of these activities. This can be achieved by surveying employees, which is subjective, or through work sampling. **Work sampling** is a work measurement technique that provides estimates of the percentage of time spent on various activities. Observations are made at random times, and the activity performed by the employee during the observation is recorded. Eventually, the tally marks or records of each activity are compiled to derive the percentage of time spent on each activity. Let us assume that the percentages are 60, 20, and 20 for processing requests for clinic visits, managing requests for medication refills, and obtaining preauthorization, respectively. Then you need to know the volume of each activity (e.g., the past year). Looking at these data, you find that 32,000 clinic visits were scheduled, 10,500 medications were refilled, and 5,000 insurance preauthorizations were obtained in the past year. With all this information, you calculate the unit cost for each of these activities, which is called the activity cost driver (Table 12.3). These calculations show that the new preauthorization requirement will cost you an additional $25.60 per patient without any new revenue.

Work Sampling

Measurement technique that provides estimates of the time spent on various activities.

TABLE 12.3 – Computation of Activity Cost Driver Rate Based on Total Costs of $640,000

Activity	%	Activity Cost (Total Cost x %)	Volume	Activity Cost Driver (Activity Cost/ Volume)
Process requests for clinic visits	60	$384,000	32,000	$12
Manage requests for medication refills	20	$128,000	10,500	$12.20
Obtain preauthorization	20	$128,000	5,000	$25.60
Total	100	$640,000		

ABC systems are costly to set up, and the percentage estimates are difficult to adjust when process changes or spending modifications occur. Additionally, the estimates of time spent on activities often add up to 100%, which overestimates capacity because there is always some idle time. Because of these shortcomings, TDABC is gaining traction in healthcare.

BRADLEY PARK HOSPITAL 12.5

Mike Chambers was at his desk going through mail when his eye caught a letter from the CMS. "I wonder what this is about," he thought to himself. His eye settled on the bolded sentences:

> **"The Centers for Medicare & Medicaid Services has chosen your metropolitan service area (MSA) to participate in the** *Comprehensive Care for Joint Replacement (CCJR) model* **for a demonstration project related to knee replacement surgery. Beginning July 1, 2016, CMS will pay a specified, bundled amount under the inpatient prospective payment system for the surgical procedure, all costs associated with hospital care and rehabilitation, and any follow-up for a period of 90 days postoperatively. The details of this project, including the reimbursement amount, will be forthcoming."**

Mike picked up the phone and dialed. "Misty, I know you are working on the board presentation on the cost of healthcare. I was wondering whether you have looked into ways to manage costs for bundled payments? I am concerned that we are going to be paid a set amount of money to care for these patients and we don't have a method to understand the costs for all the care needed. I mean there are things that we will be at risk for that are outside of our control, like the physician services and rehabilitation services, if needed."

Misty thought to herself, "This whole cost thing is really complicated and I am not sure anyone really understands it." She told Mike, "Yes, I have been doing some research and have learned of a new way to measure the costs. Maybe it would help with bundled payments."

Time-Driven Activity-Based Costing

TDABC has been promoted by Kaplan and Porter (2011) as a method to improve cost measurement and has been adopted in leading delivery systems (Beck, 2014). TDABC is similar to traditional ABC in that it provides an estimate of costs, requires identification of the groups of resources that perform activities, and produces unit costs. The difference is that the time required to perform an activity replaces the percentage of time that a resource spends on an activity. The perspective on the time distribution is no longer the provider's. Rather, the perspective on capacity utilization measurement is now based on the patient's consumption of resources. Knowing the cost of capacity available for work and how much of it is consumed by the patient in the process, an accurate picture of costs can be derived (Tablan, Anderson, Besser, Brides, & Hajjeh, 2004). This captures the process costs that we discussed earlier.

For example, consider a patient who calls the central scheduling service and needs to make an appointment to replace a medication with side effects with a new one. To provide this service, three resources are needed: a scheduler, an insurance specialist, and a nurse. The first step is to determine the extent (time) to which the patient consumes each of the resources. In evaluating the process, you find that the patient consumed 12 minutes (0.2 hours) with the scheduler, 28 minutes (0.47 hours) with the insurance specialist getting preauthorization completed, and 10 minutes (0.17 hours) with the nurse. Next, the **capacity cost rate** for each of the resources is calculated. This is the cost per unit of time (minute, hour, or day) that the resource is available to do patient-related work. This is calculated using the following formula:

Capacity Cost Rate
The cost per time that the resource is available for work.

Capacity cost rate = Expenses attributable to resource/Available
capacity of resource.   [12.4]

The numerator captures the costs needed to provide the capacity. This would include direct costs of salary, benefits, space, administrative oversight, equipment, and technology needed to enable the resource to provide the service. In our example, the cost of the scheduler would be as follows:

Annual salary/Benefits	$45,000
+ Administrative oversight	$5,000 (her supervisor is paid $100,000 a year and has 20 employees)
+ Space	$7,000
+ Technology and equipment	$15,000
= Total	$72,000/year or $ 6,000/month.

The denominator refers to the scheduler's availability for work. Subtracting weekends (104 days), vacation days (15), and sick days (5) from 365 days yields the number of days available per year, which in this example is 241 days a year or 20 days a month. An 8-hour workday minus breaks (1.0 hour) and education/administrative time (0.5 hours) leaves 6.5 hours a day available for work. Multiplying the hours available a day by the number of days the resource is available (6.5 × 20 = 130 hours/month) yields the monthly capacity. Dividing this monthly cost by the monthly capacity will produce the cost per hour for having this capacity available ($6,000 per month/130 hours per month = $46.15/hour). Using a similar process for the insurance specialist and nurse, the total hourly cost can be derived. If we assume that the insurance specialist capacity costs are $52.55/hour and the nurse $63.60/hour, the cost to serve this patient can be determined (Table 12.4).

As you can see, the TDABC method follows a process orientation. By understanding the full process of treating a patient over time, the OM professional can identify the costs for treating different types of patients and work to minimize the overall cost of treating a patient for a condition over a defined time period. As Kaplan and Porter (2011) noted, this costing method appeals to the clinical stakeholders. By

TABLE 12.4 – Calculation of the Cost to Serve a Patient			
	Time Spent on Activity	**Capacity Cost Rate**	**Cost**
Scheduler	0.2 hr	$46.15/hr	$9.23
Insurance specialist	0.47 hr	$52.55/hr	$24.70
Nurse	0.17 hr	$63.60/hr	$10.81
Total			**$44.74**

taking the patient perspective and representing the cost data for the process, it appeals to the clinicians because this is inherent in how they view the care process. This orientation is more logical to clinical staff than the traditional methods and leads to increased engagement, understanding, and trust. With this, the clinicians become more open to evaluating opportunities to evaluate process redesign that leads to reductions in waste, variation, and cost of care. TDABC is becoming more commonplace and, with time, will likely replace the traditional ABC methods. Next, we explore the typical output from the cost-accounting system.

BRADLEY PARK HOSPITAL 12.6

Mike Chambers was confident that Misty would be able to educate the board on the issues around measuring costs for healthcare. He was also glad that there may be a new method to measure cost that could help with bundled payments. However, he was concerned. He knew he had better get prepared for some tough questions from the board.

He knew that Marcus Lynn's request was important and the board would want to make sure he was managing appropriately. The board's responsibility is to oversee the success of their hospital. All this education was interesting, but where the rubber hits the road is how they are doing financially. That is their responsibility, and his bonus is dependent on making sure the hospital is doing well. He knew he would have to show how he is improving the organization and answer questions like: "What are you doing to improve revenue?" "How do you know what services make money for you?" "What actions are you taking to control costs?" "How do you know where to grow or where to cut?"

He called David in finance and asked for the past quarter's reports from the cost-accounting system.

COST-ACCOUNTING SYSTEMS

Cost-accounting systems are information systems within organizations that categorize expenses that are incurred and captured while providing services and use these categorized expenses to calculate costs. Currently, for the most part, these systems categorize expenses and model costs using traditional ABC methods. Expenses are traced to departments that are revenue-generating areas and to areas that provide services to the revenue-generating areas. These service centers include overhead areas (i.e., central administration and information services) and cost centers (i.e., the pharmacy supports the revenue generation in the hospital). Costs are then allocated to areas and categorized into direct or indirect, and reports can be generated for specific objects (services, physicians, diagnoses, etc.). The allocation process is complex and discussion of this topic is beyond the scope of this text. However, it is important to note that the more detailed and explicitly the expenses are captured, categorized, traced, and allocated, the better the cost measurement. This improved measurement comes with increased costs to implement and to maintain the system. Figure 12.3 illustrates a typical cost report, and in this example data for the entire hospital are shown.

Service Line: Show All   Refresh

DRG: Show All

Measure	Recent 3 Month History				Current Fiscal YTD	Prior Fiscal YTD	Achievement
	Jun	Jul	Aug	Sep			
				Financial			
Total Amounts							
Gross Revenue	239,470,315	216,106,237	239,947,349	217,298,669	2,667,140,091	2,397,642,175	11.24% ✓
Actual Payment	73,004,984	64,098,804	71,052,474	66,922,986	786,685,987	618,208,379	27.25% ✓
Actual Payment IP	47,022,480	42,871,798	47,594,648	44,638,938	520,226,509	443,149,959	117.39% ✓
Variable Cost	34,185,191	31,434,112	35,316,735	32,124,778	378,844,691	324,125,972	-16.88% ✗
Contribution Margin	38,819,793	32,664,692	35,735,739	34,798,207	407,841,297	294,082,408	38.68% ✓
Total Cost	62,966,886	57,809,898	65,427,338	59,339,805	700,150,950	595,691,884	-17.54% ✗
Net Income	10,038,098	6,288,907	5,625,136	7,583,180	86,535,037	22,516,495	284.32% ✓
Per Case Amounts							
Gross Revenue per Case	59,733	55,228	59,378	56,840	57,565	53,311	7.98% ✓
Actual Payment per Case	18,210	16,381	17,583	17,505	16,979	13,746	23.52% ✓
Contribution Margin per Case	9,683	8,348	8,843	9,102	8,802	6,539	34.61% ✓
Net Income per Case	2,504	1,607	1,392	1,984	1,868	501	272.85% ✓
Total Cost per Case	15,706	14,774	16,191	15,522	15,111	13,245	-14.09% ✗
Variable Cost per Case	8,527	8,033	8,740	8,403	8,177	7,207	-13.46% ✗
				Quality			
Mortalities	117	116	123	127	1,462	1,383	-5.71% ✗

FIGURE 12.3 – Cost dashboard for an endovascular lab.

For our purposes, we do not discuss all the items on the cost report shown in Figure 12.3. However, a few items should be emphasized. As you can see at the top, you can pick the object for consideration (i.e., what DRG and service to analyze), and the report displays the amount paid for the service (revenue) and the associated costs. The **contribution margin** is the difference between revenue and variable expenses. To calculate a per-unit metric, you can divide the revenue or expense of interest by the number of patients served. All the metrics can be compared with previous time periods. Not shown in this example are items, such as volume indicators, which measure the number of patients served for the time period under consideration. Additionally,

Contribution Margin

Revenue minus direct costs.

within the cost-accounting information system you are able to drill down to get a breakdown of the different items. For instance, you can drill down to see what the variable expense items are for the group that is being analyzed.

With this information at his or her disposal, let us look at some of the actions the OM professional can take to improve the organization's financial performance.

IMPROVING FINANCIAL PERFORMANCE: ENHANCING REVENUE AND DECREASING COSTS

Improving financial performance can be done by increasing revenues received or reducing the costs incurred in providing a service. So what methods and approaches can be used to accomplish these goals?

As we have discussed in the cost-accounting section, OM professionals need to familiarize themselves with the tools that can be used to understand where to target their efforts. By using the cost-accounting system and evaluating the revenue, costs, contribution margin, and **net income** (which equals the amount of money received minus all costs) for a service, OM can identify services that have the most potential for improvement and services that most or least support the overall financial health of the organization. Monitoring cost trends over time can help identify services or processes needing improvement.

Net Income
Revenue minus all costs.

Now we will review the typical scenarios you may encounter. If a service has a negative contribution margin, which means that the direct costs are higher than the revenue received, there are limited options. Seeing more patients would result in higher losses, and the overall financial performance of the institution would be harmed. Because much of the revenue is capped, the only way to improve the financial performance would be to limit the amount of service provided or cut the costs to provide the service. For example, if the hospital gets paid $10,000 for hip replacement service, but the implant cost is $12,000 (a direct and variable cost), the hospital would lose $2,000 every time this service was provided. In this simple example, your only option would be to decrease the input cost of the implant or limit the amount of services. From a strategic perspective, these would be services that you would look to divest or whose growth you would want to curb.

On the other end of the spectrum are services that have a high contribution margin and high net income. The revenue received by the organization for providing these services covers the direct variable expenses (has a positive contribution margin) and the costs allocated for indirect expenses (has a positive net income). From a strategic perspective, these are services the organization would want to expand by increasing the volume of services provided and, as with all scenarios, decrease the input costs to maximize the contribution margin.

In between these two extremes are services that produce a positive contribution margin but have a negative net margin. These services do support the financial health of the organization and may be targets for expansion. For example, if the hip surgery had a direct cost of $8,000 with a revenue of $12,000, this service would contribute $4,000 per case to cover fixed costs. For these services, you will want to calculate a **breakeven point** (BEP), which is the volume at which costs equal revenue.

$$BEP = \text{Fixed costs/Contribution margin per case} \qquad [12.5]$$

If each hip replacement produces $4,000 to cover fixed costs, and the total fixed costs for hip surgeries are $120,000, you would need to perform $120,000/$4,000 = 30$ cases to break even. More than 30 surgeries would produce a net income. For these services you will want to decrease the direct expenses, which will improve the contribution margin per case and decrease the breakeven number.

Table 12.5 summarizes the various actions that can be undertaken to improve financial performance. Regardless of the service's contribution margin and net margin, the OM professional should understand the underlying costs of the service and work to minimize the costs while working to maintain or enhance the quality of services. By doing so, the OM supports the overall strategic objectives of the organization while maximizing the value of the services rendered.

TABLE 12.5 – Actions to Improve Financial Performance

Cost Analysis Output	Options
Negative contribution margin	Decrease input costs Decrease volume of services
Positive contribution margin with negative net margin	Decrease input costs Increase volume of services
Positive contribution margin with positive net margin	Decrease input costs Increase volume of services

Reducing Input Costs

Caring for patients in the lowest cost facility for their needs (less fixed cost), staff efficiencies with flexible staffing (decreased variable cost), low supply costs (lower direct cost), supply-chain efficiencies, and energy conservation are all examples of reducing input costs. Additionally, high fixed overhead from investments in large, complex facilities can increase input costs and reduce flexibility.

Reducing Process Costs

Colocation of services, standardized processes, smoother flows, and elimination of waste/error are all ways to reduce process costs. As you have seen, many of the opportunities for improving process costs in healthcare are related to improving quality of care (fewer nosocomial infections etc.; see Chapters 4–6), and many are related to improved flow, increased throughput, and better capacity utilization (see Chapters 7–9).

Reducing Output Costs

Output costs are contained by proactively managing complaints, service recovery, preventable readmissions, regulatory fines, and so on. It is important to understand these costs and to manage issues related to the voice of the customer (Chapter 4).

BRADLEY PARK HOSPITAL 12.7

Misty's presentation to the board was excellent and cleared up many of the questions. Mike Chambers thanked her. "Misty, you did a great job. I think the board understands the global economic issues raised in the article. More important, they understand that we have tools to measure our costs." Misty thanked Mike, "Thanks, that was hard to put together. Cost has so much to do with one's perspective and I am glad we have new tools to measure the cost of care." Mike replied, "I agree but we must remember to always balance the cost with our quality and it is really hard to manage our costs when we are paid so many different ways."

Global or Enterprise Perspective

Much of the current reimbursement and costing systems are oriented toward parts of the care process and not oriented to measure or reimburse care across the continuum of the care. In this fragmented, misaligned healthcare environment, OM professionals are usually incentivized to manage the costs of care in their area of control and should understand that by doing so, they may actually increase the total costs of care. These historical issues are in a process of transformation, and this realization has driven national health policy. New payment models attempt to drive total cost down and to change the incentives/penalties for providers. Penalties for readmissions, bundling of payments, and formation of ACOs attempt to move the payment for services across care settings and time and decrease fragmentation. As the healthcare financing system changes, the systems that measure cost must evolve and capture the more global perspective. The OM professional will then have better tools and incentives to manage costs that are driving the overall value of healthcare services. At the time of writing, it is not clear that these efforts will lead to the desired effect of driving overall value in healthcare. However, as the system evolves, the perspective that the OM professional takes when managing costs must also evolve.

SUMMARY

In this chapter, we have reviewed the topic of cost for healthcare services. The macroeconomic drivers of the excess cost for healthcare in the United States were reviewed, and the ones that are under the influence of the OM professional were discussed. In order to understand the relationship of cost to financial performance, the major payment methodologies were reviewed. With an understanding of the cost of the process, we looked at different cost drivers. An overview of how costs are captured and measured was explored. With an understanding of how costs are measured, the OM professional can use cost information to target areas for improvement. With these targets for improvement the OM professional should recognize the relationship of the cost control initiatives and their relationship to the other competitive priorities (Figure 12.4).

FIGURE 12.4 – Mind map linking cost to the other competitive priorities.

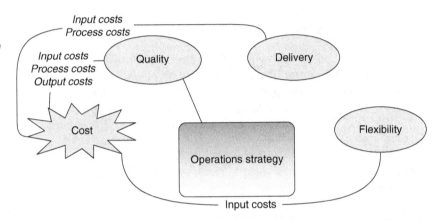

KEY TERMS

Cost	Capitation payments	Variable costs	Output costs
Expense	Prospective payment system	Direct cost	Cost shifting
Price	Value-based payment	Indirect cost	Work sampling
Charges	Bundled payments	Process cost	Capacity cost rate
Revenue	Accountable care organization	Attributable cost	Contribution margin
Profit	Input costs	Attributable mortality	Net income
Fee-for-service	Fixed costs	Cost avoidance	Breakeven point

TOOLS USED IN THIS CHAPTER

TOOL	PURPOSE
Cost-to-charge ratio (CCR) cost method	A method used to estimate the costs of service that uses charges as the basis to estimate and allocate costs

TOOL	PURPOSE
Relative value unit (RVU) cost method	A method used to estimate the costs of services that uses a standard estimate of the intensity and costs of work for services rendered
Activity-based costing (ABC)	A method used to calculate costs by assigning costs to activities needed to provide a service and knowing the amount of activity that is consumed to provide the service
Time-driven activity-based costing (TDABC)	A method used to measure cost that is calculated by multiplying the cost to have a capacity available for a period of time by the amount of time that capacity is consumed in the process of providing a service.

FORMULAS USED IN THIS CHAPTER

Definition	Formula	Number
Total cost	Total cost = Cost of inputs + Cost of process + Cost of outputs	[12.1]
Cost-to-charge ratio (CCR)	CCR = Total expense/Total gross patient revenue	[12.2]
Cost using CCR	Cost = Gross charges × CCR	[12.3]
Capacity cost rate	Capacity cost rate = Expenses attributable to resource/Available capacity of resource	[12.4]
Breakeven point (BEP)	BEP = Fixed cost/Contribution margin per case	[12.5]

WHAT DO YOU REMEMBER?

1. What is the difference among price, expense, and cost?
2. What is fee-for-service? How can it lead to increased costs?
3. List the different capitation payment methods.

4. What is the cost of a process?

5. Describe different types of input costs. Give examples for each.

6. What are process costs?

7. Describe output costs. When doing so, give examples for cost that would be captured as an expense and for costs that would not be captured.

8. What is a cost-to-charge ratio?

9. What are the common elements between ABC and TDABC?

10. How do they differ?

11. What is a contribution margin?

12. How do you calculate a breakeven point?

13. If a service has a negative contribution margin, what are the actions that you could take to improve the financial performance of the organization?

14. What is cost avoidance? Give examples of systems/processes that have been used for cost avoidance.

SOLVE BPH'S PROBLEMS

1. As the cardiology director, you have enjoyed the position you hold in the organization. Everyone knows that your area "always makes money." This perception was generated by the cost-accounting reports generated and distributed by finance. You knew that your area has had stable volumes and payer mix, so you were surprised when your finance liaison called to tell you that the past month's data are not looking all that good. She wanted to give you a heads up prior to the directors' meeting at the end of the week. She said that the reports were not ready to be distributed, but she shared the following information.

    • Volume of service and payer mix had not changed and this did not appear to be a revenue problem.

    • Procedures were at target and not significantly different, with 378 procedures done.

    • Net revenue was the same as the running average at $3,201,875.

    • Expenses seemed out of line with the recent past trends, with the direct labor expense at $1,280,500 and supplies expense at $1,205,867.

    • Indirect expenses, which are allocated on the basis of patient volume, were down slightly from historical trends and were $730,254.

She told you that the recent overhead reduction initiatives have been successful and this decreased these allocations.

What is the contribution margin for the past month? Has this improved or worsened compared to historical trends?

a. What is the ratio of labor expense and direct expense to net revenue?

b. What is the net margin?

2. You are concerned and want to get in front of this prior to the directors' meeting. You know that historically the labor expense runs at about 32% of net revenue and supplies run at 20%. Considering that the volumes of service are not significantly different you surmise that these inputs must be more expensive, so you call an urgent meeting with the manager. In the meeting with the manager, he is mystified that you are concerned. He told you he was working with a multidisciplinary team to improve the care of these patients. The goal was to decrease the total cost of care to the hospital and he had made changes to accomplish that goal. You tell him that is fine, but that you want to understand more. You learn that the labor expense increased because the staffing was changed and that this change has improved the process of care significantly. You learn that these process improvements have reduced complications that led to rework, increased need for staff on the floor, and a reduction of the length of stay in the hospital. You are impressed, but want to make sure this is quantified. You learn that the finance staff is working on a new method for costing the process of care called time-driven activity-based costing and you will have to wait a few months for that to be complete. You are fine with that but want to go to the directors' meeting knowing how much expense needs to be offset in other areas of the hospital.

a. How much has the labor expense increased when compared to the past?

Satisfied that you have a better idea about the labor expense you begin to explore the supply expenses. The manager explains the increase in supply expense may be related to a new cardiologist. This new physician is not using the standard supplies and has introduced a new, more expensive stent. You learn that these changes have not improved the quality of care and this has not contributed to improving quality, safety, or decreased expenses elsewhere.

b. How much has the supply expense increased when compared to the past? Has this increased supply expense enhanced value or eroded value?

With this information you are prepared to go to the directors' meeting and begin to plan on interventions that can be taken for improvement.

3. As the orthopedic manager, you are reviewing the past 2 years of data from the cost-accounting system. You know that you worked hard to improve the services but note that the volumes are lower in 2015, and this concerns you.

Cost-Accounting Report: Orthopedics	FY2014	FY2015
Cases	100	80
Gross revenue	$327,825	$320,825
Actual payments	$108,625	$104,280
Variable cost	$68,205	$52,980
Contribution margin	$40,420	$51,300
Indirect cost	$62,378	$50,290
Net margin	– $21,958	$1,010
FY, fiscal year.		

a. Explain what happened to reimbursements between 2014 and 2015. What could have changed to explain the differences in revenue and payments?

b. What is the variable cost per case for each year? What could explain the changes from one year to the other?

c. What is the breakeven point for each year?

d. Assuming that you have unused capacity, there is demand for the services, and you can get the volume back to 2014 levels for 2016, calculate your estimated 2016 contribution margin and net margin (assume the 2015 revenue per case and the allocation of indirect cost would be based at the same rate as 2015 and is allocated on the number of cases).

THINK OUTSIDE THE BOOK!

1. Search the Internet for time-driven activity-based costing and healthcare. What did you find? Describe an institution that used TDABC and process redesign to increase value.

2. Find the *Harvard Business Review* posting, "The Big Ideas: How to Solve the Cost Crisis in Healthcare." Read the article, but pay special attention to the section on myths in cost accounting. What are the myths and why are they important to dispel?

REFERENCES

Beck, M. (2014, February 23). Searching for the true cost of health care. *Wall Street Journal*. Retrieved from http://www.wsj.com/articles/SB10001424052702304888404579379122507671850

Centers for Medicare & Medicaid Services. (2015a). Prospective payment systems—General information. Retrieved from https://www.cms.gov/Medicare/Medicare-Fee-for-Service-Payment/ProspMedicareFeeSvcPmtGen/index.html

Centers for Medicare & Medicaid Services. (2015b). Prospective payment systems—General information. Retrieved from https://www.cms.gov/Medicare/Medicare-Fee-for-Service-Payment/HospitalAcqCond/Hospital-Acquired_Conditions.html

Centers for Medicare & Medicaid Services. (2015c). Prospective payment systems—General information. Retrieved from https://www.cms.gov/Research-Statistics-Data-and-Systems/Statistics-Trends-and-Reports/MedicareFeeforSvcPartsAB/downloads/DRGdesc08.pdf

Davis, K., Stremikis, D., Squires, D., & Schoen, C. (2014). *Mirror, mirror on the wall*. Washington, DC: The Commonwealth Fund. Retrieved from http://www.commonwealthfund.org/~/media/files/publications/fund-report/2014/jun/1755_davis_mirror_mirror_2014.pdf

Hickson, G., Federspiel, J., Pichert, J., Miller, C., Gauld-Jaeger, J., & Bost, P. (1992). Patient complaints and malpractice risk. *Journal of the American Medical Association*, *287*(22), 2951–2957.

Institute for Healthcare Improvement. (2012). *How-to guide: Prevent ventilator-associated pneumonia*. Cambridge, MA: Author. Retrieved from http://www.ihi.org/resources/Pages/Tools/HowtoGuidePreventVAP.aspx

Ibrahim, E., Tracy, L., Fraser, V., & Kollef, M. (2001). The occurrence of ventilator-associate pneumonia in a community hospital: Risk factors and clinical outcomes. *Chest*, *120*(2), 555–561.

Kaplan, R., & Porter, M. (2011). The big idea: How to solve the cost crisis in health care. *Harvard Business Review*, *89*, 46–52.

Procop, G., Yerian, L., Wyllie, R., Harrison, A., & Kottke-Marchant, K. (2014). Duplicate laboratory test reduction using a clinical decision support tool. *American Journal of Clinical Pathology*, *141*(5), 718–723.

Rosenthal, V., Guzman, S., & Orellano, P. (2003). Nosocomial infections in medical-surgical intensive care units in Argentina: Attributable mortality and length of stay. *American Journal of Infection Control*, *31*(5), 291–295.

Shepard, D., Hodgkin, D., & Anthony, Y. (2000). *Analysis of hospital costs: A manual for managers*. Geneva, Switzerland: World Health Organization. Retrieved from http://people.brandeis.edu/~shepard/w-manual.PDF

Tablan, O. C., Anderson, L. J., Besser, R., Brides, C., & Hajjeh, R. (2004). Guidelines for preventing health care-associated pneumonia, 2003: Recommendations of CDC and the healthcare infection control practices advisory committee. *Morbidity and Mortality Weekly Report*, *53*(RR-3), 1–36.

The Joint Commission. (2012). *Preventing central line-associated bloodstream infections: A global challenge, a global perspective*. Oakbrook, IL: Joint Commission Resources. Retrieved from http://www.jointcommission.org/preventing_clabsi

Warren, D., Shukla, S., Olsen, M., Kollef, M., Hollenbeak, D., Cox, M., . . . Fraser, V. (2003). Outcome and attributable cost of ventilator-associated pneumonia among intensive care unit patients in a suburban medical center. *Critical Care Medicine, 31*(5), 1312–1317.

Young, P., Saunders, R., & Olsen, L. (2010). *The healthcare imperative: Lowering costs and improving outcomes—Workshop series summary.* Washington, DC: National Academies Press.

PART

V

Competing on Flexibility

CHAPTER 13

ANTICIPATING AND ADAPTING TO CHANGE

BRADLEY PARK HOSPITAL 13.1

Francine Sutton and Brent Gregg stayed after a hospital operation meeting to talk about the cost of staffing the hospital units.

"Our nurse staffing is running way over budget in four of our units because the weekend census is low. There are times that the census is around 80% over the weekend, but it is rare. We are staffed for the number of beds in each unit so that we can handle maximum capacity, if it comes. I cannot help it if doctors and patients don't want to come into the hospital on the weekends," Francine complained.

Brent responded, "We may want to talk with the medical staff about working 7 days a week, but that is a long-term discussion. Let's look at what we can do short term or midterm to help with the problem."

"I will see what data I can pull together and I will set up a meeting with you early next week."

"Thanks, Francine. We will figure something out. I look forward to working with you on this."

 What could Bradley Park Hospital's (BPH's) rationale be for staffing at full capacity on weekends?

INTRODUCTION AND LEARNING OBJECTIVES

Of all the competitive priorities, flexibility is the most difficult to achieve because it requires the mastery of all other three: quality, cost, and timeliness. In business, flexibility remains a rather elusive, poorly defined concept. As a result, it is not measured and managed systematically like cost or quality. **Flexibility** is the ability to accelerate intentional changes, to continuously respond to unanticipated changes, and to adapt to the unexpected consequences of predictable

Flexibility
The ability to accelerate intentional changes, to continuously respond to unanticipated changes, and to adapt to the unexpected consequences of predictable changes with minimal penalties in terms of quality, time, and cost.

changes (Bahrami, 1992) with minimal penalties in terms of quality, time, and cost (Koste & Malhotra, 1999). Still struggling to produce value in care delivery, most healthcare organizations focus on quality and cost and may even see some of their flexibility attributes (e.g., varied patient mix) as deterrents to high quality and efficiency. Again, it is important to remember the lessons of the cumulative model (Chapter 2), which establishes quality as the foundation to rein in costs and enable timely delivery, ultimately positioning an organization to develop flexible capabilities. In a nutshell, only those with strong and consistent performance in quality, cost, and timeliness can vie for flexibility (Figure 13.1).

FIGURE 13.1 – Mind map focus on flexibility.

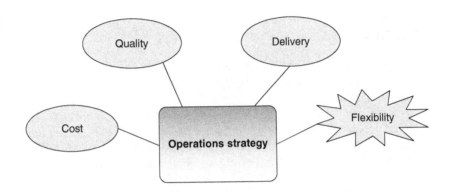

Flexibility is a complex, multidimensional concept. Each type or dimension of flexibility can be mapped along four elements reflecting levels of diversity achieved and penalties incurred. The impact of the dimensions of flexibility is cumulative, with resource flexibilities supporting process flexibility, which enables strategic flexibility.

After reading this chapter, you will be able to:

1. **List all the dimensions of flexibility and explain their interrelatedness**
2. **Map each dimension along four elements**
3. **Identify the interventions necessary to boost each type of flexibility**
4. **Explain the flexibility pyramid**
5. **Connect flexibility to all other competitive priorities**

STRATEGIC FLEXIBILITY

At the strategic level, competitive healthcare organizations pursue mix flexibility, volume flexibility, and innovation flexibility in order to expand their market share (Box 13.1).

> ### ✦ BOX 13.1 – WORDS OF WISDOM
> "The measure of intelligence is the ability to change" (Albert Einstein).

Mix Flexibility

Mix flexibility refers to the ability to serve a variety of patients, that is, a wide-ranging patient mix. The **patient mix** relates to diversity in terms of demographic characteristics (age, gender, education, primary language, etc.) as well as diagnostic characteristics (medical condition, severity of illness, comorbidity, etc.). As the population becomes increasingly diverse, we can take for granted that healthcare organizations must accommodate the needs of a broader patient mix. Furthermore, the higher reimbursements associated with certain diagnoses may make it attractive for providers to handle high-risk, complex cases. It is thus no wonder that multihospital systems and large provider networks are attempting to care for separate types of patients in different locations according to condition or disease severity. Although some of these integrative strategies are viable, others only deliver the *illusion* of mix flexibility. True flexibility implies no or minimal loss in terms of quality, cost, and timeliness. In other words, higher flexibility should not come at the expense of the other competitive priorities. This is why each dimension of flexibility is itself defined by four elements: range number, range heterogeneity, mobility, and uniformity.

Mix Flexibility
The ability to serve a variety of patients.

Patient Mix
A patient population that is diverse in terms of demographic characteristics (age, gender, education, primary language, etc.) as well as diagnostic characteristics (medical condition, severity of illness, comorbidity, etc.).

Elements of Flexibility

Range number. RN flexibility refers to the number of viable options for a given flexibility dimension (Slack, 1983; Upton, 1994). In the case of mix flexibility, the number of medical conditions or age groups treated by a healthcare organization would tap the RN element. So, a hospital handling 800 medical conditions has more RN flexibility than one handling 500. Similarly, a cancer center treating different types of cancer has more RN flexibility than a facility that limits its services to breast cancer patients.

Range Number (RN)
The number of viable options for a given flexibility dimension.

Range heterogeneity. RH flexibility captures the degree of differentiation between the viable options. RH would thus be higher for a healthcare organization treating cardiac and cancer patients than for a clinic focusing on cancer patients only. Although RN refers to the breadth of services in general, RH focuses on the distinct variations among the types of services.

Range Heterogeneity (RH)
The degree of differentiation between the viable options.

Mobility. Mobility denotes the ease with which an organization moves from one option to another (Gupta & Buzacott, 1989; Slack, 1987). It measures the transition penalties in terms of the time and cost that are incurred when switching from one option to the other. This is an important element because it highlights that expanding the patient mix does not imply greater mix flexibility if excessive costs and delays are generated as a result.

Mobility (M)
Mobility denotes the ease with which an organization moves from one option to the other.

Uniformity (U)
The similarity of quality outcomes for a range (RN and RH) of options.

Uniformity. Uniformity refers to the similarity of quality outcomes for a range (RN and RH) of options. This poses a serious challenge for healthcare organizations. Increasing the patient mix makes it harder to provide patient-centered care and obtain high patient satisfaction scores. In the same vein, a higher patient mix may lead to higher mortality rates. In both cases, the claims of higher mix flexibility would be futile if quality performance decrements had taken place.

Strategies for Mix Flexibility

Lately, there has been a great deal of interest in large, integrated multispecialty medical groups intended to increase market share, to lower costs through economies of scale and scope, and to reduce care fragmentation. Physician groups can be formed when physicians join one another in the same facility or across multiple facilities. They can also be formed via mergers with other physician groups or be assembled by hospital systems.

Although the evidence for higher quality, lower costs, and lower fragmentation is mixed, some large multispecialty groups, such as the Mayo Clinic and Cleveland Clinic, have achieved high levels of performance (Box 13.2). Some of the reasons for their success include the following (Burns, Goldsmith, & Sen, 2013):

1. **Unified clinical and administrative cultures**. Both clinicians and administrators have the same perceptions of corporate values and their significance. This shared perspective takes many years to develop and nurture, which is why many of the newly formed groups may not enjoy comparable success.

2. **Physicians remain the key decision makers in clinical issues**. Hospitals that sponsor the groups assume subordinate roles in supporting the physician enterprises and act as capital accumulation entities that hold funds for future investments.

3. **Strong interdependence among physician groups, hospitals, and health plans**. Physician groups supply hospital admissions, health plans supply patients, and hospitals supply capital and administrative support. Often, there are leadership overlaps among those groups to maintain a unified focus. Sharing risks and rewards facilitates strategic and cultural alignment.

 BOX 13.2 – OM IN PRACTICE!

Replicating Cleveland Clinic's Success

The Cleveland Clinic is one of the country's premier medical institutions that is famous worldwide. It is able to achieve high quality care at costs below the national average. Some say that one of the keys to its success is its level of integration. Its approach allows for the creation of teams of specialists that collaborate in treating patients, the deployment of evidence-based treatments across specialties, and the reduction of red tape for referrals.

(continued)

BOX 13.2 – OM IN PRACTICE! *(continued)*

Nevertheless, the model is difficult to replicate. Most physicians are very independent and want to practice medicine the way they see fit. Moreover, most hospitals cannot capitalize on international prestige to attract foreign patients who will pay two to three times more than Medicare recipients (Fuhrmans, 2009).

Volume Flexibility

Volume flexibility is the ability to respond quickly to sudden increases and decreases in midterm (12–18 months) demand. The concept of volume flexibility is rooted in the economics literature and is often discussed in terms of cost curves. Figure 13.2 displays U-shaped cost curves for two organizations. The bottom of the cost curve represents the lowest cost and is related to a certain output level. As volume flexibility increases, or as output levels shrink or grow, marginal costs increase. For organization X, the "flat" bottom indicates that costs remain low over a wider range of output levels, making it more flexible than organization Y (Carlsson, 1989).

Volume Flexibility
The ability to respond quickly to sudden increases and decreases in midterm (12–18 months) demand.

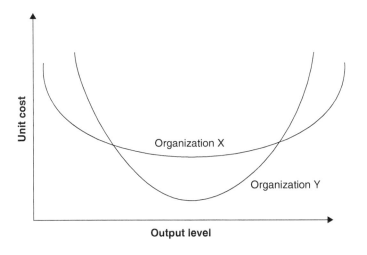

FIGURE 13.2 – Volume–cost relationships.

Several factors contribute to demand uncertainty in healthcare services: (a) the fluctuating size of the population from which healthcare organizations draw patients; (b) the economic swings affecting patients' ability to afford healthcare services; (c) the demographic and societal changes, such as increases in elderly and diabetic patients, triggering growth in some specialty services; and (d) the surge of healthcare and technological innovations making it possible to care for a larger number and variety of patients (Vissers, Van Der Bij, & Kusters, 2001). The challenges for healthcare organizations are substantial. They can have idle capacity ready to absorb increases in demand, which would threaten their efforts to control costs; or they can let demand exceed capacity, which means substandard timeliness and more erratic quality of care from an overloaded staff. Poor quality is not acceptable in healthcare services, and, therefore, it can be easily argued that demand uncertainty is most taxing when capacity constraints force managers to acquire additional resources when needed.

The RN element of volume flexibility involves the amount of aggregate output (e.g., number of beds) that can be achieved effectively and efficiently by the healthcare organization. The RH element reflects the number of departments or specialties for which changes in volume can be attained. The time and cost required to alter output levels capture the mobility element. Performance on quality indicators over different output levels would indicate uniformity.

Strategies for Volume Flexibility

Based on a review of the literature and field interviews of healthcare administrators, Jack and Powers (2004) proposed four strategies to cope with demand uncertainty. The first two strategies are coping schemes for organizations with limited adaptive capabilities, whereas the last two are progressive policies intended to build system and resource capabilities to face and even anticipate demand uncertainty (Figure 13.3).

1. **Shielding from uncertainty**. When demand uncertainty is high and volume flexibility is low, a healthcare organization will choose a shielding strategy. Healthcare organizations that do not have the means to deploy changing levels of capacity may opt to protect themselves from the negative effects of demand uncertainty. To do so, organizations often decide to manage demand rather than adjust capacity levels. Options would include closing the emergency department, limiting the range of services to highly specialized care with undetermined delivery times, or transferring patients to other facilities. Clearly, this approach would not be feasible for all hospitals, especially large trauma centers. Another approach used to stabilize demand and control increases is to limit patient population based on geographic distance, health maintenance organization (HMO) or preferred provider organization (PPO) membership, and the availability of services at close competitors' facilities.

2. **Absorbing uncertainty**. When both demand uncertainty and volume flexibility are low, the firm will likely select to absorb demand fluctuations through buffers. Although common in the service industry, appointment systems—or time buffers— are not uniformly effective at stabilizing the flow of patients through the system. Decentralized systems make it difficult for administrators to have a clear understanding of demand patterns and to control them. Even with centralized systems, individual doctors often prefer to set their own appointment classifications and intervals, leading to overall system inefficiencies (Chapter 9). Inventory or queue buffers also absorb uncertainty (Chapter 8). If time buffers are inadequate,

patients wait longer either to get an appointment scheduled or to see the provider once in the waiting room. Controlling service time variability through standardized protocols (refer back to Box 6.5 in Chapter 6) is one way to produce satisfactory time buffers. If demand is uncertain, safety stocks of supplies are kept "just in case" demand increases unexpectedly (Chapter 11). Finally, capacity buffers—slack capacity—can be maintained to handle walk-ins, emergencies, early or late arrivals of patients, and so on. Although buffers represent excess costs, they are likely small and manageable in environments characterized by low uncertainty.

3. **Containing uncertainty**. If demand uncertainty is low but flexibility is high, healthcare organizations will choose to contain uncertainty through the deployment of their flexible resources (workforce and technology). The quantitative flexibility of human resources can be manipulated through inventive shift schedules. Reducing error and therefore rework rates will also free up greater amounts of capacity. The qualitative flexibility is achieved through skill expansion involving job enlargement, job enrichment, and cross-training. Job enlargement (Chapter 7) involves a broader range of tasks requiring the same skill level. Job enrichment (Chapter 7) adds planning and control responsibilities to current job duties. **Cross-training** prepares employees to perform a variety of jobs within a reasonable scope. The greater skill repertoires permit the redeployment of human resources to better match demand patterns as they fluctuate across areas and disciplines.

Cross-training
Training for the mastery of multiple jobs.

Information technology (IT) may also provide opportunities to respond quickly to changes in demand by easing the processes with which patient records are accessed and reviewed, bills are generated, rescheduling is performed, and patient transfers are executed. In the same vein, telemedicine, the use of telecommunication and IT to deliver care at a distance (Chapter 9), enables a healthcare organization to increase patient access to its services. In addition, inpatient telemedicine involving the use of remote video and telemetry monitoring enables one person to observe the care of several patients at once. This is used more and more in intensive care units (ICUs) and emergency departments (EDs) to increase the number of patients physically assigned to a nurse as someone else is remotely monitoring the patients and communicating with the on-site nurse.

4. **Mitigating uncertainty**. When both demand uncertainty and flexibility are high, a healthcare organization may choose to mitigate uncertainty by developing tighter internal controls and closer relationships across the value chain. Such a strategy requires a heavier reliance on part-time staff, layoffs, reassignment of staff across facilities, and regionalization of services for larger systems. It may also entail the outsourcing of

patient care to other providers through strategic alliances, or the ownership of sourcing and distribution channels for medical supplies. Although a mitigating strategy seems more attractive to a large health system, small rural hospitals have also become affiliated or formed alliances with other providers to benefit from the volume flexibility that a multihospital system offers.

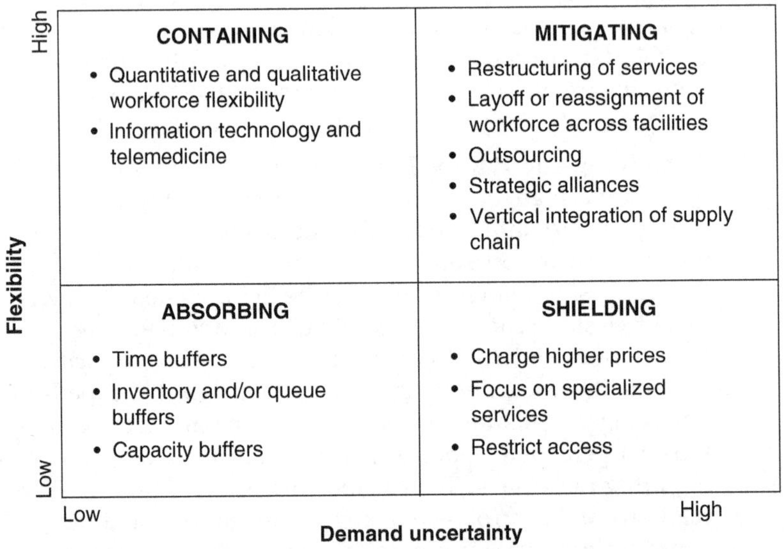

FIGURE 13.3 –
Volume flexibility
strategies.

Adapted from Jack and
Powers (2004).

Innovation Flexibility

Innovation flexibility refers to a healthcare organization's capability to pioneer clinical treatments and/or care delivery processes with ease. Innovating conveys the idea of anticipating or even influencing change. There can be no innovation without flexibility because innovation relies on the impulse and capability to change. The healthcare industry has been fertile ground for innovation. One example that comes to mind is Dr. Devi Shetty's Narayana Hrudayalaya Hospital complex in Bangalore, India, which provides very high-volume, top-quality yet low-cost cardiac surgery services through efficiency and innovative financing (Roy, 2012). Another is the perioperative surgical home (PSH; Box 13.3), which can serve as the integrator to achieve the triple aim in healthcare: (a) better experience of care, (b) improved population health, and (c) lower costs per capita (Berwick, Nolan, & Whittington, 2008; Vetter, Boudreaux, Jones, Huneter, & Pittet, 2014).

**Innovation
Flexibility**
Refers to the capability
to pioneer clinical
treatments and/or care
delivery processes
with ease.

🏥 BOX 13.3 – OM IN PRACTICE!

Perioperative Surgical Home at UC Irvine

Perioperative care amounts to about 60% of all hospital costs. The traditional model of perioperative care is replete with waste resulting from inconsistent, autonomous, and uncoordinated medical practice. The perioperative surgical home (PSH) model, on the contrary, is a

(continued)

⊕ BOX 13.3 – OM IN PRACTICE! (*continued*)

patient-centered, physician-led, team-based approach to coordinated and evidence-based care from the time a decision for surgery is made until discharge. At UC Irvine Health, staff from anesthesiology, perioperative care and services, and orthopedic surgeons initiated a PSH for total-joint replacement. Lean and Six Sigma principles and techniques were used to reduce variability and standardize the clinical processes for preoperative, intraoperative, postoperative, and postdischarge care. The total-joint replacement PSH was a success with all pathways agreed upon by the team before the patient entered the process. Plans to deploy this model through the entire orthopedic surgical line are under way (Cannesson, Schwarzkopf, Vakharia, & Kain, 2014).

The number of innovations that a healthcare organization creates is the RN element of innovation flexibility. The degree of variety of innovations is its RH element. For example, organizations with innovations solely in hip replacement and hip resurfacing surgery techniques would exhibit less RH innovation flexibility than their counterparts innovating in hip replacement surgeries and medical home systems. The mobility element refers to the development time and cost of these innovations. The uniformity element reflects the organization's ability to maintain consistent quality, timeliness, and financial performance while innovating.

Organizational Requirements for Innovation Flexibility

Innovations can be classified as technological or administrative. **Technological innovations** focus on the diagnosis and treatment of disease, whereas **administrative innovations** are related to the management of a healthcare organization. Several organizational characteristics that facilitate both types of innovation include functional differentiation, specialization, decentralization, managerial openness to change, technical knowledge resources, and slack financial resources (Damanpour, 1991; Kimberly & Evanisko, 1981).

Technological Innovations
Innovations that focus on the diagnosis and treatment of disease.

Administrative Innovations
Innovations that focus on the management of a healthcare organization.

1. **Functional differentiation** exists when coalitions of professionals form in different units and introduce and/or influence change. Invariably, many people in an organization will be extremely averse to change. In such cases, an individual with an innovative idea or concept would find it very frustrating to persuade all other individuals in his or her unit of the need for change. Rather, targeting other individuals in the unit who are open to innovations and forming a coalition will prove a more effective way to innovate. In functionally differentiated organizations, the multiple interest groups or coalitions will expand the scope and accelerate the pace of change.

2. **Specialization** refers to the variety of specialists within an organization. In healthcare, a large number of medical specialties create a substantial and diverse knowledge base, which spurs the development of new concepts and techniques in multiple domains. The more specialties, the more opportunities for innovation development. Moreover, the existence of multiple disciplines increases the opportunities for cross-fertilization of ideas and spillover of new managerial programs. If a PSH model (see Box 13.3) is successful in one department, it can be adapted and deployed in another department.

3. **Decentralization** involves the dispersion of power and decision making throughout the organization. For innovations to sprout in multiple areas, healthcare professionals must feel free to initiate, shape, and implement change. When initiatives are pushed from the top down through a rigid, centralized power structure, there is little incentive for employees to be creative and experiment with new ideas.

4. **Managers' openness to change** is a vital predictor of innovativeness because it creates a cultural climate that encourages the generation of new ideas and concepts and does not penalize for failed experimentation. Of particular value is managerial support at the implementation phase when conflict and coordination problems emerge. Managers and leaders most open to change tend to be receptive to new methods and procedures, better educated (not relevant in the case of physician leaders), and more involved in policy decisions and in professional development.

5. **Technical knowledge resources** both at the clinical and administrative levels provide the skill pool necessary not only to develop the innovations but also to understand their value and impact. For example, developing new vaccines and treatments will be more easily attained in an academic hospital where most physicians are actively involved in research and assisted by numerous technicians and medical or PhD students.

6. **Slack financial resources** enhance a healthcare organization's ability to finance innovations, absorb the potential losses resulting from failure, and push for change before it becomes a pressing need. Financial resources often correlate with size, which explains why large organizations are better able to sustain rapid and frequent innovation cycles.

Mix flexibility, volume flexibility, and innovation flexibility are crucial to capture markets and face competition. In order to build these strategic capabilities, the healthcare organization must develop flexible processes.

PROCESS FLEXIBILITY

After emphasizing the benefits of process standardization in previous chapters, it may come as a surprise that we now feature the need to boost process flexibility. Actually, they are not incompatible at all. Remember from Chapter 2 that processes support business strategies, which evolve as external and internal conditions change. As a result, processes are not static. Their planned and controlled—as opposed to ad hoc—transformations are vital to the survival of the organization.

Process flexibility is the ease with which a process can be modified to improve competitiveness. The number of processes that can be changed with minimal penalties measures the RN flexibility element. The number of process types (e.g., admission, discharge, billing, scheduling) that can be altered easily represents the RH element. The cost and time required—adjusted for scope—to change the process refer to its mobility, whereas the consistency of quality performance during change implementation captures the uniformity element.

Process Flexibility
The ease with which a process can be modified to improve competitiveness.

In Chapter 7, one of the design principles stressed the need to design for the main flow, not exceptions. Nevertheless, exceptions occur and must be handled with even effectiveness.

Exception Handling

Many types of exceptions often exist. They result from violations of the assumptions used to create a process model and may require changes in resources and procedures. The Process Handbook project at the Massachusetts Institute of Technology (MIT) Center for Coordination Science has been developing a system to resolve exceptions promptly with little or no impact on process performance. The project involves the creation of a massive repository of process knowledge and solutions to generate software that will automatically trigger a response to handle exceptions. The following step-by-step procedure summarizes the system's operation (Klein & Dellarocas, 1998).

STEP 1: The process designer determines where and how exceptions are most likely to occur. This can be done in conjunction with a failure modes and effects analysis (FMEA; Chapter 4). Failure points are identified along with their associated exception types.

STEP 2: Risk priority numbers (RPNs) are assigned to failure points. For robust processes and subprocesses (with low RPNs), the process designer may decide that it is not necessary to augment existing processes with additional exception handling capabilities.

STEP 3: In the case of failure-prone processes (with high RPNs), the process designer prioritizes exception types based on their likelihood to cause a failure, for example, by performing a Pareto analysis (Chapter 4). The characteristics of important exception types should be clearly defined.

STEP 4:   Based on these characteristics, the process designer should devise sentinel systems, such as poka-yokes (Chapter 6), that promptly recognize exceptions and their expected outcomes. Ideally, this diagnosis step is automated.

STEP 5:   Once an exception is identified and diagnosed, there should be a prescription in the knowledge repository to resolve it.

Besides handling exceptions, processes must also be flexible enough to adapt or even anticipate adaptation. Adaptation can be sudden or evolutionary, as described in the following.

Revolutionary Change

Process Reengineering

The total redesign of a process in order to achieve dramatic improvements.

If the organization is slow to react to changes in the external environment, such as different customers' needs, heightened competition, and new technologies, eventually it will be forced to reengineer its processes. **Reengineering** seeks drastic performance improvements through a complete process redesign. Not only does it involve dramatic changes in process design, but it also requires a revolutionary implementation. Reengineering adopts a clean-slate approach in that it wipes out existing process structures and procedures and replaces them with a process in which WHAT is being done and HOW it is being done conform to an ideal—or almost ideal—state. Often, IT systems designed for best practices are enablers of the transformation. If reengineering delivers what it promised and can be achieved rapidly and within budget, it is considered a success. However, because of unrealistic expectations, it is not uncommon for reengineering projects to fail (Box 13.4). The most pervasive reasons for these failures (Dorsey, 2005; Hammer & Champy, 1993; Petrozzo & Stepper, 1994) are listed in Table 13.1.

TABLE 13.1 – Reasons Why Engineering Projects Fail

Reengineering Phase	Reason
Planning	Inability to distinguish between reengineering and other improvement projects
	Poor understanding of the infrastructure needed for project redesign
	Inability to secure buy-in from all process stakeholders
	Lack of expertise to plan the project
	Focus on fixing problems rather than transforming the process
	Lack of strong leadership at the top
	Limit plans so that nobody will end up being unhappy
Implementation	Skip the testing phase because the project is behind schedule
	Customize the new IT system so that it supports most elements of the old process
	Lack of expertise to implement the project
	Lack of strong leadership at the project level
	Wavering commitment from top leaders
	Spread the resources over too many reengineering projects
	Back off when people start resisting change
	Quit early because results are not immediate

⊕ BOX 13.4 – DID YOU KNOW?

Does Reengineering Really Work? Outcomes of Hospital Reengineering Initiatives

A study of the effects of reengineering on the competitive cost position of hospitals revealed that reengineering by itself was not a panacea. When undertaken without integrative and coordinative efforts, reengineering projects may actually increase hospital costs relative to costs of competitors. However, reengineering *in conjunction with* project teams, steering committees, and codification of the innovative process to reduce ambiguity yielded improvements in the hospitals' competitive positions (Walston, Burns, & Kimberly, 2000).

Evolutionary Change

Despite their potential returns, reengineering projects do not necessarily reflect process flexibility. They may signal a desperate response to change rather than true adaptability and anticipation. A flexible process has a planned and controlled evolution as time passes. This change model assumes that the people who will be affected by the change must design and implement it. In other words, process change initiatives come from within. Because of the more limited scope, fewer resources will be allocated, meaning that deadlines will be more flexible. Process redesign will be executed on a pilot basis, for example, in one department, and if successful, will be expanded to other areas of the organization. The challenge is to ensure that deadline extensions do not become elusive and stifle people's enthusiasm and energy.

The evolutionary model is very much attuned to the total quality management (TQM) and Lean/Six Sigma principles of incremental improvement (see Chapters 4–6). Besides being less risky than the revolutionary method, the evolutionary approach nurtures a culture of continuous change, which is the essence of flexibility. Furthermore, it provides the foundations (attitude toward change, focus on learning and improvement, skills, use of tools and methodologies, performance measurement, etc.) to effect successful reengineering when external conditions shift dramatically and a more radical method is required. By reducing the cost, effort, and time to implement successful change—whether it is drastic or incremental—an evolutionary approach to process redesign embodies a dynamic emphasis on flexibility. Moreover, it is vital to sustain and further the improvements achieved through reengineering as business conditions continue to evolve (Laguna & Marklund, 2005). The synergy between the revolutionary and evolutionary approach to process change is illustrated in Figure 13.4.

As implied in the previous paragraphs, process flexibility depends on the inputs to the process. These inputs are the organization's resources.

FIGURE 13.4 –
Revolutionary
and evolutionary
changes.

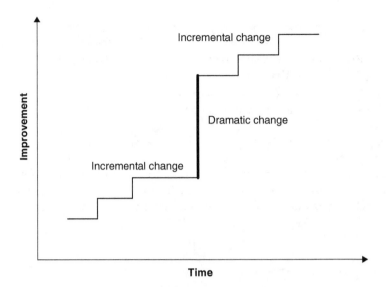

BRADLEY PARK HOSPITAL 13.2

Francine and Jennifer were ushered into Brent's office. "I hope you don't mind that I asked Jennifer to join us. She helped me gather information, and I thought that if we wanted to look into this issue further, she could assist us with data analysis and work with the medical staff to identify workable solutions," Francine began.

"Jennifer, welcome. I look forward to hearing your thoughts."

Jennifer smiled, "Here is what we have so far. The units with lowest census numbers on the weekends are shown in this table."

Unit	Percentage of Occupancy (Sat/Sun)	Severity of Illness	Staffing Ratios (Specialty Needs)
Ear, nose, and throat	5 to 8 pts/20 bed unit (25–40)	Medium	1 nurse: 4 patients respiratory
Hepatology	9 to 12 pts/20 bed unit (45–60)	High	1 nurse: 3 patients complex care
Thoracic surgery	10 to 12 pts/25 bed unit (40–48)	High	1 nurse: 4 patients respiratory
Obstetrics	10 to 12 pts/20 bed unit (50–60)	Low	1 nurse: 2 patients obstetrics

Francine continued, "You can see that of the four units, two have less than 50% occupancy and require respiratory expertise from the nursing staff. These units have been difficult to staff because the nurses must be comfortable with acute airway problems. We have had to contract with outside services to get us the nurses we need. Both of these services are surgery units with patients of similar, but not identical, acuity levels. And although there are some differences in the units' procedures, the nurses are familiar with working in the operating room. Interestingly, these units are located adjacent to each other. With standard protocols and cross-training, I think that we can possibly share staff between these units on the weekend and decrease the total number of staff needed to care for them. But I will have to get the physicians involved to be sure."

"What about the other units? The numbers suggest we can combine the staff on these units as well," Brent said.

"Obstetrics patients are generally healthy, but delivering a baby takes special expertise. And hepatology patients are generally very ill. Because these patient groups are so unlike each other, they require very different types of care. The staff in these units has skills that are not transferable. As we try to gain efficiencies, we cannot decrease the quality of care that we provide to our patients. We will need to find other ways to manage the low census in these units, Francine explained.

"We thought we would perform a pilot in the ear, nose, and throat (ENT) and thoracic surgery units to see whether we can decrease costs through flexing staff while not affecting care delivery or quality. We are planning to get the nurses and physicians together to explain why we are moving in this direction and get their thoughts on how best to proceed. We need our physicians to be the key decision makers on clinical issues, but the nurses should look at the training required to cover these two units. I am optimistic that if everyone works together, we can come up with a good model of care. Dr. Levine in ENT has been such a supporter of our quality efforts since we helped him with his clinic. I am going to see whether he will champion this project."

 If BPH had the financial resources and time to train OB/GYN nurses to work in the hepatology unit and vice versa, should it pursue this type of cross-training? Why or why not?

RESOURCE FLEXIBILITY

A flexible workforce, flexible technologies, and flexible facilities, collectively known as resource flexibility, are the underpinnings of process flexibility.

Workforce Flexibility

Workforce flexibility refers to employees' ability to perform a variety of tasks or jobs effectively and efficiently. There is a strong consensus in the literature that a multiskilled workforce is vital to creating and sustaining flexibility at the process and strategic levels. Furthermore, it supports improvements in the other competitive priorities: timeliness, cost, and quality (Karuppan & Ganster, 2004). When staff is able to move across areas and/or process steps where demand starts exceeding existing capacity, flow time is reduced (e.g., Bobrowski & Park, 1993), and costly inventory cushions and capacity buffers shrink (Malhotra & Ritzman, 1990; Box 13.5). Finally, the higher skill levels and continued learning necessary to support flexibility are also required for quality (Youndt, Snell, Dean, & Lepak, 1996).

Workforce Flexibility

Employees' ability to perform a variety of tasks or jobs effectively and efficiently.

> ### ⊕ BOX 13.5 – OM IN PRACTICE!
>
> **Nursing Resource Teams to Improve Quality of Care**
>
> Nursing resource teams—or flex pools—comprise RNs and licensed practical nurses who are used as needed to work in any unit, including intensive care units and emergency departments. They are cross-trained and may demand higher pay, but their versatility makes up for these costs as they are deployed to solve demand–capacity imbalances across the hospital. Empirical evidence supports their effectiveness in reducing overtime costs and adverse patient outcomes (Mendez de Leon & Klauzer Stroot, 2013).

The number of different *tasks* performed by an individual at his or her current job measures the RN element of workforce flexibility. It may involve job enlargement with an expansion of duties, typically requiring similar skill levels, and/or job enrichment with the addition of planning and control activities. For example, the addition of computerized physician-order entry responsibilities to exams and diagnoses is an example of enhanced RN flexibility. The number of different *jobs* an individual can perform captures the RH element. It always involves cross-training for the mastery of different jobs. For example, a hospitalist monitoring the care of cardiac and pediatric patients would demonstrate higher RH flexibility than a hospitalist caring for cardiac patients alone. The time and cost to switch from one task or job to the other reflects the mobility element. The quality performance across tasks or jobs denotes the uniformity element.

Strategies for Workforce Flexibility

Workforce flexibility revolves around the acquisition of skills to keep abreast of new procedures, technological systems, improvement methodologies, and so on. Training programs should promote the expansion of the skill repertoire in the long run. Several strategies that consider knowledge accuracy, retention, and adaptability to new situations are as follows.

1. **Do not deploy *total* flexibility**. Total flexibility involves intradepartmental and interdepartmental deployment of personnel, with maximal expansion of RN and RH flexibility. Taken to the extreme, total flexibility would imply that anyone can do any job in the organization, which is obviously a myth, especially in healthcare organizations where the nature of the work can be extremely complex. Complex knowledge is learned slowly and forgotten rapidly, especially in the absence of practice; for a review of this literature, see Karuppan (2011). In an increasingly complex medical field, it is no surprise that specialties are diving into narrow subspecialties and subsub-specialties; this is the era of superspecialization (Gawande, 2009). Although it has increased care fragmentation, this trend

has also yielded remarkable success, especially in the surgical area. Several studies have shown that surgeons with the best performance rates also had the highest volume of same surgeries (Osterweil, 2014; Stavrakis, Ituarte, Ko, & Yeh, 2007; Box 13.6).

The limits of flexibility are consistent with Champoux's (1978) suggestion that very high levels of "good" job characteristics—such as flexibility—might produce a dysfunctional, overstimulation effect. At low levels of flexibility, a lack of alertness or boredom causes understimulation, which hinders performance. Initially, increases in job variety are matched by performance increases. Then a leveling-off effect occurs as variety increases no longer yield the proportionate increases in job outcomes. Eventually, overstimulation occurs and further increases in variety become counterproductive (Singh, 1998) as a result of impaired information-processing capability (Humphreys & Revelle, 1984). Karuppan (2008) showed this curvilinear pattern for both RN and RH workforce flexibility. The curve for RN flexibility was smoother than that for RH, indicating that RN flexibility can be deployed to a larger extent than RH flexibility before performance suffers (Figure 13.5).

⚙ BOX 13.6 – WORDS OF WISDOM

"In surgery, you don't want a jack-of-all trades, master-of-none" (Youn, 2014).

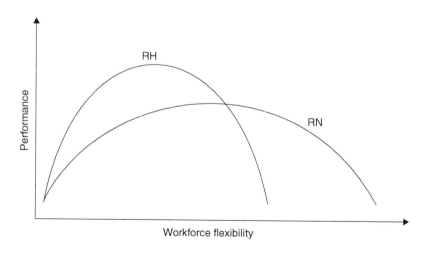

FIGURE 13.5 – Relationship between workforce flexibility (RN and RH) and performance.

Because complexity intensifies overstimulation effects, we advise you expand deployments of RN flexibility for simple tasks (e.g., paperwork) and curb deployments of RH flexibility as job complexity increases (e.g., ICU care).

2. **Adjust the skill mix to the situation**. The large number of studies on skill mix in healthcare environments has produced inconclusive, mixed results, which provide few normative guidelines (Buchan & Dal Poz, 2002):

    *   In general, a high ratio of skilled staff to occupied bed improves health outcomes.

    *   The growing practice of mixing qualified and unqualified nurses for cost containment can result in operational efficiency if care assistants are used to complement rather than replace qualified nurses. Nevertheless, the practice has its fallacies: higher absenteeism and turnover rates among less qualified staff, care assistants' inability to make decisions or solve problems independently, greater risk of harming patients, and higher workloads for RNs.

    *   The skill and role overlaps between doctors and nurses should be exploited. There is a growing body of evidence showing that expanding the roles and deployments of nurse specialists, nurse practitioners, and nurse midwives, in *specific and well-defined* situations, will control costs without compromising the quality of care.

3. **Train for conceptual rather than procedural learning**. Procedural training involves the instruction of step-by-step procedures or predetermined sequences and is often associated with rote memorization. There is no effort to establish logical relationships among the various materials learned or to link them to prior knowledge. The trainee makes assumptions regarding the linkages and corrects them as learning and practice progress. Think of a global positioning system (GPS). It provides step-by-step driving directions with no overall view of the road and street network. If the driver follows the same route repeatedly, he or she will eventually learn the correct route without the GPS. Contrast that with a map that shows the relative location of each street with respect to another as well as various points of reference with which the driver is familiar. This is an example of a conceptual model or external aid, which helps the trainee link the new knowledge to existing knowledge, through analogy (e.g., the GPS–map example) or through explicit relationships between concepts (e.g., Deming's wheel).

    When the new knowledge is simple, procedural learning may be effective. Otherwise, conceptual learning should be the preferred training method as trainees develop a more robust understanding of the new knowledge.

4. **Enforce overlearning**. Overlearning results from training beyond what is necessary for initial mastery (Farr, 1987). Some may consider it redundant effort and a source of excess cost, but it is strongly related to knowledge retention. Even for

individuals with high cognitive abilities, such as surgeons, frequent practice solidifies knowledge. It also increases automaticity of responses and promotes self-confidence, which reduce stress. Because stress compromises knowledge retrieval, overlearning acts as a shield against memory loss (Bremner & Narayan, 1998). Because of its extra cost, one question comes to mind: How much learning is enough? This is answered in the next paragraph.

5. **Test for ability to transfer knowledge to novel situations**. To determine the adequacy of learning and preparedness for actual performance, trainees are often required to demonstrate their knowledge acquisition via testing. For simple tasks, test material can be comparable to that learned during training sessions or in training manuals. For complex material, however, it is best to judge performance in creative (or far-transfer) tasks or testing scenarios, which require the completion of original task and decision sequences that are not presented during training (Mayer, 1981; Sein & Bostrom, 1989). High performance on these sequences attests to learners' comprehension of the new knowledge and their ability to apply it. Training and overlearning could thus be halted once preestablished performance standards for far-transfer tasks have been achieved.

Technology Flexibility

Technology flexibility refers to the ability of the equipment/ information system to handle a variety of patient cases and conditions as well as new regulations with little or no time/cost penalty or performance decrement. Many of the new developments in medical technologies reflect the flexibility trend: multipurpose technologies to both prevent pregnancy and protect against HIV, multipurpose valves to accommodate a wide variety of patient needs in hydrocephalus management, portable ultrasound system for multipurpose ultrasound imaging, oxygen therapy treatment units with adjustable therapy flow controls to be used for multiple patients simultaneously, and so on. This increased flexibility stems from technological innovation (see the Innovation Flexibility section of this chapter). The same is true for health information technologies (health ITs), which have evolved from electronic health record systems to integrated systems for all types of care and facilities at every stage of life (Chapter 13).

Integrated technologies are also starting to incorporate electronic health paths, which display short- and long-term healthcare plans for each patient (Glaser, 2015). Eventually, all the patient data collected from these records will be aggregated to help identify patterns for population health, that is, health outcomes of a group of individuals (disabled persons, African Americans, and so on). The evolving nature of health ITs attests to the constant changes and growing

Technology Flexibility
Refers to the ability of the equipment/ information system to handle a variety of patient cases and conditions as well as new regulations with little or no time/cost penalty or performance decrement.

expectations in the healthcare field. It also requires a high degree of information sharing between individuals and providers. Because providers often use different systems, which do not "talk" to each other, there is an urgent need to increase interoperability among health IT systems.

Interoperability

The ability of systems and devices to exchange and interpret electronic health data, irrespective of the system's vendor and the user's organizational boundaries.

Interoperability involves the exchange and interpretation of electronic health data among systems and devices for use by clinicians, lab, hospital, pharmacy, and patients, irrespective of the system's vendor and the user's organizational boundaries (Chapter 13; Health Information and Management Systems Society, 2013). Ironically, this increased flexibility in the exchange and use of health data requires the standardization of various health IT domains (HealthIT.gov, 2015). HealthIT.gov has published a list of best available standards and implementation specifications for the following domains:

1. **Semantics:** Vocabulary/code set/terminology (e.g., standard code set for immunizations, national drug codes, unified code of units of measure, unified medical language system)

2. **Syntax:** Content/structure (e.g., clinical document architecture, structured data capture, clinical decision support knowledge artifacts)

3. **Transport:** Method by which information is transferred (e.g., hypertext transfer protocol, simple object access protocol, transport layer security protocol)

4. **Services:** Infrastructure components needed to meet specific information exchange objectives (e.g., cross-enterprise document reliable interchange, messaging platform, patient demographic query, cross-community access, and patient discovery)

The RN dimension of technology flexibility is the number of applications/users the technology can support. The RH dimension refers to the dissimilarity of the applications/users of the technology. For example, the interoperability of a vendor's system across its network of adopters would reflect less RH than the ability of that vendor's system to "talk" to other vendors' systems. The mobility element captures the lack of time and cost penalties involved in switching from one application/user to the other. As far as health IT is concerned, clinicians often have to resort to faxing medical records to other clinicians, sometimes even within the same health information system network. Clearly, interoperability would greatly enhance the mobility of such technologies. The uniformity element relates to the evenness of outcomes across applications and users. For example, in the case of the multipatient oxygen therapy treatment units mentioned earlier, flow control should be as precise and accurate as it is for a single treatment unit. Moreover, data transferred from one system to another should be normalized to ensure that their integrity is preserved.

Strategies for Technology Flexibility

The inherent flexibility of technology rests with the designer of the technology, not the healthcare facility. Although there is little hospitals or other facilities can do to enhance the flexibility of technologies, they can intervene to facilitate their deployment and acceptance. With regard to medical technologies, there is usually little resistance from clinicians to adopt them. The same cannot be said about health IT. The following recommendations may be useful in securing a smooth diffusion of health IT among its most reluctant users: clinicians (Greenhalgh, Robert, MacFarlane, Bate, & Kyriakidou, 2004).

1. **Address concerns in preadoption, early use, and later use stages**. Before adoption, the intended adopters must be aware of the technology, of its capabilities and ease of use, and of what it can do for them specifically. At the early-use stage, adopters will need to be informed about implementation progress, training content and schedules, individualized training opportunities, and so on. Later, it is important for leaders to communicate the impact of the technology on the organization: benefits, problem areas, adequacy of support, and opportunities for improvement. Often, if adopters are involved in refining the technology to improve its functionality, they will be more willing to accept it in the long run.

2. **Identify and engage opinion leaders**. Some individuals in a healthcare organization exert a great deal of influence on other individuals within their social networks. It is very important to persuade these nurses, physicians, lab specialists, or pharmacists of the usefulness of the technology and of the benefits that can be derived from its use. If convinced, they should be asked to play an active role in disseminating positive information about the technology and facilitating its acceptance.

3. **Select champions**. Several clinicians will not be convinced of the merits of a particular technology and will resist its adoption. An effective strategy is to let a few innovators try the new technology, describe its benefits to less enthusiastic members of their department or social network, and harness their support (see functional differentiation in the section on innovation flexibility).

4. **Plan the dissemination**. If the dissemination of the technology is going to span the entire organization, proper communication planning is extremely important. The communication plan should (a) take into account all adopters' needs and concerns; (b) tailor communication strategies to different demographics, backgrounds, and mind-sets; (c) use multiple communication channels; and (d) include target versus current state comparisons as well as milestones.

5. **Ensure system expandability**. Implementing new technologies is a long and costly process. The human and capital investments that are required at the beginning can be daunting. The worst possible scenario is to make those investments and realize that the technology cannot grow to meet the expanding needs of a growing business. It is therefore critical to select technology solutions that will (a) support the ever increasing data collection and processing requirements for legal, administrative, and clinical decision-making purposes; (b) incorporate reporting and analytics capabilities; and (c) be seamlessly integrated with existing systems and databases (Thacker, 2011).

The last point alludes to flexible infrastructures, which is the primary focus of facility flexibility.

Facility Flexibility

Facility Flexibility
Refers to the ability of a facility to accommodate a variety of patients' needs and new regulations as well as volume changes with little or no time/cost penalty or performance decrement.

Facility flexibility is the ability of a facility to accommodate a variety of patients' needs and new regulations as well as volume changes with little or no time/cost penalty or performance decrement. The number of changes the facility can make to adapt to new patients' needs and demands is the RN element. The number of types of changes (building additions, repurposing rooms or wards, adding multipurpose rooms, etc.) captures the RH element. The ease with which facility changes (expansions, repurposing, etc.) are made is the mobility element. The ability to keep services functioning during construction or remodeling with no loss in effectiveness reflects uniformity.

Hospital infrastructures are usually designed to last for at least 40 years. During this time span, many changes in environmental constraints and patient demand will occur, making it imperative that the infrastructure be flexible enough to accommodate those changes. Although forecasting capacity requirements in terms of the number of beds is a typical input into hospital design, it is insufficient by itself. With decreasing average lengths of stay and shifts from inpatient to outpatient care, it is easy to see how such a forecast conducted decades earlier would have proved to be inaccurate today. Rather, *ranges* of capacity requirements should be projected and reprojected over time based on demographic patterns, technological advances, epidemiological patterns, regulations, payment/revenue/charge structures, and their interactions (de Neufville, Lee, & Scholtes, 2008). Planning for future expansion in the following decades would require the selection of a site with sufficient land around the initial premises. Flexible designs in hospital buildings include structural foundations that are strong enough to permit the construction of additional floors, free-ends features to accommodate lateral extensions, and modular design (Box 13.7). **Modular design** is an approach that subdivides a large and complex building into smaller parts, which can be prebuilt off-site and connected together. The main advantage of modular architecture is that you can replace a module or add another with

Modular Design
A design approach that subdivides a large and complex building into smaller parts, which can be prebuilt off-site and connected together.

BOX 13.7 – WORDS OF WISDOM

"Chance only favors the mind that is prepared" (Louis Pasteur).

relative ease, which is essentially *standardized flexibility*. Other examples of standardized flexibility include (The Joint Commission, 2008):

- **Indoor expansion flexibility** with shell spaces for future growth. The spaces are built but not medically equipped.

- **Adaptable flexibility** in which spaces can be designed for multiple uses (see Box 13.8 for an example).

- **Convertible flexibility** in which spaces can be converted rapidly for other uses (e.g., storage room with a knockout panel in the slab to allow for a future elevator).

 BOX 13.8 – OM IN PRACTICE!

Modular Design at Miami Valley Hospital Heart and Orthopedic Center

The Miami Valley Hospital Heart and Orthopedic Center in Dayton, Ohio, was the first U.S. hospital to use modular prefabrication extensively for patient rooms, exam rooms, single-toilet rooms, and patient-unit overhead utilities. The modular units were perfect for the hospital's focus on standardization with 178 identical rooms on five identical floors. The rooms are prebuilt to accommodate the widest range of patient types and clinical activities from low-acuity to maximum-acuity use. The identical layouts make it easy for staff to locate supplies and equipment (Horwitz-Bennett, 2014).

Strategies for Facility Flexibility

1. **Forecast ranges of capacity needs under different scenarios**. No single forecast by itself provides a reliable projection.

2. **Demonstrate the economic value of flexible designs**. Valuation can only be convincing if the economic value is demonstrated under different forecasting scenarios. Build for the most likely scenario and plan for ±10% variation in demand.

3. **Build for immediate and foreseen needs**, with room for possible developments. Let future leaders build to meet unknown future needs.

4. **Add the costs of relocating services** in order to minimize disruptions during construction when budgeting for expansion or redesign (de Neufville et al., 2008).

BRADLEY PARK HOSPITAL 13.3

Jennifer began to speak at the joint medical, nursing, and administrative meeting of ENT and thoracic surgery. "As you know, since cross-training staff between your services and developing standard protocols, we have been able to share nurses between the units. This has decreased not only staffing costs but also the number of contract nurses who are needed. I want to hear from you what you think. We want to be sure that we identify problems or educational needs early so our patients are well taken care of."

Dr. Levine jumped in, "I like the fact that our staffing has stabilized. It is wonderful to work with the same nurses day after day, even if we share them between the units. I believe that has actually increased the quality of care that my patients have received. If the hospital has saved money, that is great. But I am focusing on how well we are taking care of our patients. In that regard, I am very happy."

Dr. Long, a thoracic surgeon interjected, "From my standpoint, things are going well. Some of the former ENT nurses need to brush up on chest tube management, but I think that can be fixed easily. I agree that it is nice to have a dedicated staff to work with and get to know."

Marie, a staff nurse, spoke next, "I have been working in ENT for 5 years and have enjoyed working with thoracic surgery nurses and physicians. I have learned so much that is applicable to our ENT patients. I am more satisfied in my work because I get to learn new ways of doing things."

As the discussion continued, Jennifer and Francine looked at each other. Jennifer gave a "thumbs up," and Francine smiled.

Ⓠ Identify a way that Francine can address the overstaffing in the hepatology or obstetrics units that does not involve cross-training and sharing of staff.

FLEXIBILITY PYRAMID

There are many facets of flexibility across three layers: strategic, process, and resources. Strategic flexibility aims at conquering market share through mix, volume, and innovation flexibilities. Process flexibility is achieved through modifications that are either sudden and dramatic or continuous and incremental. Resource flexibility primarily involves the flexibility of inputs to the process: people, technology, and facilities (Figure 13.6).

The three layers form the flexibility pyramid (Figure 13.7), which encapsulates the incremental effects of flexibility. Resource flexibilities constitute the foundations. They represent the adaptability of inputs, which is necessary to promote the flexibility of processes. In turn, flexible processes pave the way for healthcare organizations to respond to market demands by expanding their mix, responding to volume surges and contractions, and establishing a supple structure for innovative ideas to germinate and flourish. Just like the stones at one level of the pyramid support the stones at the next, higher level, one layer of flexibility provides a strong, resting base for the next layer. The strength of the pyramid is reflected in the soundness of its measurements. The tactical dashboard presented in Figure 13.8 was developed for the ICU. It displays performance metrics for multiple dimensions of flexibility.

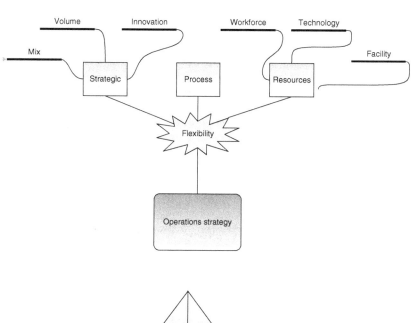

FIGURE 13.6 – Mind map with dimensions of flexibility.

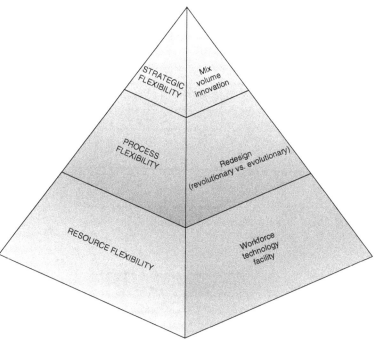

FIGURE 13.7 – Flexibility pyramid.

Measures	FYTD Actual	Target	Jan.	Feb.	Mar.	Apr.	May	Jun.	Jul.
MIX									
Number of different ICD codes as primary diagnosis	19	20	16	17	18	20	20	21	23
Total # of ICD codes in patient mix	57	60	55	55	54	56	58	59	60
VOLUME									
Backlog (number of times a patient was unable to get a bed immediately)	6	0	12	8	5	4	7	4	3
Low census (# of hours RNs sent home not needed)	26	0	36	12	65	52	20	0	0
Number of patients pulled from ED due to chest pain unit program expansion	54	60	40	45	52	55	60	62	63
PROCESS									
Number of new ideas on managing daily improvement board	10	10	5	6	8	9	10	15	14
Number of pending process improvement projects (PIPs)	6	0	6	4	5	7	8	7	6
Number of completed PIPs	6	10	6	8	3	7	5	4	6
WORKFORCE									
Use of nursing/float pool (hours)	9.7	20	0	0	0	0	24	32	12
Overtime percentage	2.9	3.0	3.5	3.2	3.0	3.0	2.8	2.1	2.7
Total number of experienced RNs accepting $5,000 bonus to transfer from day to night shift for 1 year	1	3	0	0	0	0	1	0	0
Number of RNs participating in guidance councils (job enrichment)	3	6	2	2	3	3	4	4	4
Number of RNs floated to other units (job enlargement)	2	6	1	1	2	1	3	1	2
Mandatory web-based-training completion rate	96%	100%	65%	68%	76%	85%	88%	93%	96%

FIGURE 13.8 – Flexibility dashboard for the ICU.
FYTD, fiscal year to date.

SUMMARY

There are three layers of flexibility: strategic, process, and resource. Mix, volume, and innovation are strategic flexibilities; workforce, technology, and facility are resource flexibilities. Ideally, process flexibility is ensured on a continuous basis with frequent, relatively small changes. However, sometimes, lethargy in the organization or major changes in the environment may require a dramatic process redesign, that is, reengineering.

The flexibilities have cumulative effects. Resource flexibilities provide the foundational support for other flexibilities to develop, culminating with capabilities vital for market share expansion. With its four elements (RN, RH, M, and U), flexibility is intrinsically linked to the other competitive priorities, as shown in Figure 13.9. RN and RH reflect the capacity to change, which is inherent to the concept of flexibility. However, to be labeled *flexibility*, the ability to change must involve little or no penalty in terms of time and cost. Similarly, while they occur, the changes cannot trigger performance decrements in existing services.

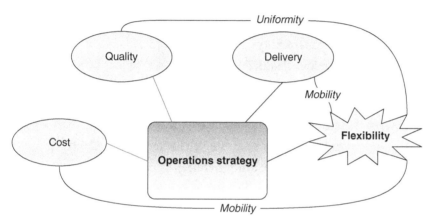

FIGURE 13.9 – Mind map connecting flexibility to the other competitive priorities.

KEY TERMS

Flexibility	Uniformity	Process flexibility
Mix flexibility	Volume flexibility	Process reengineering
Patient mix	Cross-training	Workforce flexibility
Range number (RN)	Innovation flexibility	Technology flexibility
Range heterogeneity (RH)	Technological innovations	Interoperability
Mobility	Administrative innovations	Facility flexibility
		Modular design

WHAT DO YOU REMEMBER?

1. What are the types of strategic flexibility?
2. What are the four elements of each flexibility dimension?
3. List and describe the three strategies for mix flexibility.

4. In Figure 13.2, why is organization X more volume flexible than organization Y?

5. List and describe the four strategies for volume flexibility.

6. What is the difference between technological and administrative innovations?

7. List and describe the organizational characteristics that foster innovation flexibility.

8. Describe the step-by-step procedure used to handle exceptions.

9. Distinguish between revolutionary and evolutionary changes.

10. Is reengineering or evolutionary change better aligned with process flexibility?

11. List and describe the five strategies for workforce flexibility.

12. What is interoperability? Why is it important?

13. What are the four health IT domains for which lists of best available standards have been compiled? Briefly describe each one.

14. List and describe the five strategies for technology flexibility.

15. Give three examples of standardized flexibility.

16. List and describe the four strategies for facility flexibility.

17. What is meant by "flexibility pyramid?"

18. Which elements connect flexibility to the other competitive priorities?

THINK OUTSIDE THE BOOK!

Find an article about reengineering the discharge process. Examine what steps need to be taken before the project starts and during implementation.

1. Are surgeons today required to be more or less flexible?

2. Sometimes, medical innovations are not necessarily better than the old devices/treatments they are intended to replace. Can you provide some examples?

3. Discuss the pros and cons of specialty versus multispecialty clinics.

4. Develop other flexibility measures that could be added to the dashboard (Figure 13.8).

REFERENCES

Bahrami, H. (1992). The emerging flexible organization: Perspectives from Silicon Valley. *California Management Review, 34*(4), 33–52.

Berwick, D. M., Nolan, T. W., & Whittington, J. (2008). The triple aim: Care, health, and cost. *Health Affairs, 27,* 759–769.

Bobrowski, P. M., & Park, P. S. (1993). An evaluation of labor assignment rules when workers are not perfectly interchangeable. *Journal of Operations Management, 11*, 257–268.

Bremner, J. D., & Narayan, M. (1998). The effects of stress on memory and the hippocampus throughout the life cycle: Implications for childhood development and aging. *Development and Psychopathology, 10*, 871–885.

Buchan, J., & Dal Poz, M. R. (2002). Skill mix in the health care workforce: Reviewing the evidence. *Bull World Health Organ, 80*(7), 575–580.

Burns, L. R., Goldsmith, J. C., & Sen, A. (2013). Horizontal and vertical integration of physicians: A tale of two tails. In J. Goes, G. T. Savage, & L. Friedman (Eds.), *Advances in health care management* (Vol. 15, pp. 39–147). Bingley, UK: Emerald Group Publishing.

Cannesson, M., Schwarzkopf, R., Vakharia, S. B., & Kain, Z. (2014). UC Irvine health experience with the PSH. *American Society of Anesthesiologists Newsletter, 78*(10), 30–33.

Carlsson, B. (1989). Flexibility and the theory of the firm. *International Journal of Industrial Organization, 7*(2), 179–203.

Champoux, J. E. (1978, August). *A preliminary examination of some complex job scope-growth need strength interactions.* Academy of Management Proceedings (pp. 59–63). San Francisco, CA.

Damanpour, F. (1991). Organizational innovation: A meta-analysis of effects of determinants and moderators. *Academy of Management Journal, 34*(3), 555–590.

de Neufville, R., Lee, Y. S., & Scholtes, S. (2008, November 10–12). *Using flexibility to improve value-for-money in hospital infrastructure investments.* Paper presented at the Infrastructure Systems and Services: Building Networks for a Brighter Future (INFRA), Rotterdam, The Netherlands.

Dorsey, P. (2005). Top 10 reasons why system projects fail. Retrieved from http://www.hks.harvard.edu/m-rcbg/ethiopia/Publications/ Top%2010%20Reasons%20Why%20Systems%20Projects%20Fail .pdf

Farr, M. J. (1987). *Long-term retention of knowledge and skills: A cognitive and instructional perspective.* New York, NY: Springer-Verlag.

Fuhrmans, V. (2009, July 23). Replicating cleveland clinic's success poses major challenges. *The Wall Street Journal.* Retrieved from http://www.wsj.com/articles/SB124831191487074451

Gawande, A. (2009). *The checklist manifesto: How to get things right.* New York, NY: Metropolitan Books.

Glaser, J. (2015, August 11). From the electronic health record to the elctronic health plan. *Hospitals & Health Networks Daily.* Retrieved from http://www.hhnmag.com/Daily/2015/August/electronic-health-record-plan-glaser-blog?utm_source=daily&utm_medium= email&utm_campaign=HHN&eid=257900606&bid=1148165

Greenhalgh, T., Robert, G., MacFarlane, F., Bate, P., & Kyriakidou, O. (2004). Diffusion of innovations in service organizations: Systematic review and recommendations. *The Milbank Quarterly, 82*(4), 581–629.

Gupta, D., & Buzacott, J. A. (1989). A framework for understanding flexibility of manufacturing systems. *Journal of Manufacturing Systems, 8*(2), 89–97.

Hammer, M., & Champy, J. (1993). *Reengineering the corporation: A manifesto for business revolution.* New York, NY: Harper Business.

Health Information and Management Systems Society. (2013). What is interoperability? Retrieved from http://www.himss.org/library/interoperability-standards/what-is-interoperability

HealthIT.gov. (2015, January 30). The 2015 interoperability standards advisory. Retrieved from http://www.healthit.gov/policy-researchers-implementers/2015-interoperability-standards-advisory

Horwitz-Bennett, B. (2014, December 19). Best of 2014: Modular construction delivers flexibility to healthcare. *Healthcare Design.*

Humphreys, M. S., & Revelle, W. (1984). Personality, motivation, and performance: A theory of the relationship between individual differencesand information processing. *Psychological Review, 91,* 153–184.

Jack, E. P., & Powers, T. L. (2004). Volume flexible strategies in health services: A research framework. *Production and Operations Management, 13*(3), 230-244.

The Joint Commission. (2008). *Health care at the crossroads: Guiding principles for the development of the hospital of the future.* Oakbrook Terrace, IL: Author.

Karuppan, C. M. (2008). Labor flexibility: Rethinking deployment. *International Journal of Business Strategy, 8*(2), 108–113.

Karuppan, C. M. (2011). Learning and forgetting: Implications for workforce flexibility in AMT environments. In M. Y. Jaber (Ed.), *Industrial learning curves: Theory, model, and applications* (pp. 173–190). London, UK: Taylor & Francis Group.

Karuppan, C. M., & Ganster, D. C. (2004). The labor-machine dyad and its influence on mix flexibility. *Journal of Operations Management, 22*(4), 533–556.

Kimberly, J. R., & Evanisko, M. J. (1981). Organizational innovation: The influence of individual, organizational, and contextual factors on hospital adoption of technological and administrative adoptions. *Academy of Management Journal, 24*(4), 689–713.

Klein, M., & Dellarocas, C. (1998). *A knowledge-based approach to handling exceptions in workflow systems.* Cambridge, MA: Center for Coordination Science, MIT Sloan School of Management. Retrieved from http://ccs.mit.edu/papers/CCSWP203

Koste, L. L., & Malhotra, M. K. (1999). A theoretical framework for analyzing the dimensions of manufacturing flexibility. *Journal of Operations Management, 18*(1), 75–93.

Laguna, M., & Marklund, J. (2005). *Business process, modeling, simulation, and design.* Upper Saddle River, NJ: Pearson.

Malhotra, M. K., & Ritzman, L. P. (1990). Resource flexibility issues in multistage manufacturing. *Decision Sciences, 21*, 673–690.

Mayer, R. E. (1981). The psychology of how novices learn computer programming. *Computing Surveys, 13*(1), 121–141.

Mendez de Leon, D. M., & Klauzer Stroot, J. A. (2013). *Using nursing resource teams to improve quality of care.* Westchester, IL: Healthcare Financial Management Association.

Osterweil, N. (2014, April 10). High-volume surgeons have best adrenalectomy outcomes. *ACS Surgery News.* Retrieved from http://www.acssurgerynews.com/specialty-focus/general-surgery/single-article-page/high-volume-surgeons-have-best-adrenalectomy-outcomes.html

Petrozzo, D. P., & Stepper, J. C. (1994). *Successful reengineering.* New York, NY: John Wiley & Sons.

Roy, P. (Writer). (2012). Indian hospital [Television series, episode 1]. *Indian hospital.* Doha, Qatar: Al Jazeera English.

Sein, M. K., & Bostrom, R. P. (1989). Individual differences and conceptual models in training novice users. *Human-Computer Interaction, 4*(3), 197–229.

Singh, J. (1998). Striking a balance in boundary-spanning positions: An investigation of some unconventional influences of role stressors and job characteristics on job outcomes of salespeople. *Journal of Marketing, 62*, 69–86.

Slack, N. (1983). Flexibility as a manufacturing objective. *International Journal of Operations and Production Management, 3*(3), 4–13.

Slack, N. (1987). The flexibility of manufacturing systems. *International Journal of Operations and Production Management, 7*(4), 34–45.

Stavrakis, A. I., Ituarte, P. H., Ko, C. Y., & Yeh, M. W. (2007). Surgeon volume as a predictor of outcomes in inpatient and outpatient endocrine surgery. *Surgery, 142*, 887–899.

Thacker, T. (2011). *Perspective on deploying hospital technology.* The Netherlands: Phillips Healthcare Consulting.

Upton, D. M. (1994). The management of manufacturing flexibility. *California Management Review, 36*(2), 72–89.

Vetter, T. R., Boudreaux, A. M., Jones, K. A., Huneter, J. M., Jr., & Pittet, J.-F. (2014). The perioperative surgical home: How anesthesiology can collaboratively achieve and leverage the triple aim in healthcare. *Open Mind, 118*(5), 1131–1136.

Vissers, J. M., Van Der Bij, J. L., & Kusters, R. J. (2001). Toward decision support for waiting lists: An operations management view. *Health Care Management Science, 4*(2), 133–143.

Walston, S. L., Burns, L. R., & Kimberly, J. R. (2000). Does reengineering really work? An examiniation of the context and outcomes of hospital reengineering initiatives. *Health Services Research, 34*(6), 1363–1388.

Youn, A. (2014). Opinion: You don't want a jack-of-all trades surgeon. Retrieved from http://www.cnn.com/2014/06/05/health/picking-surgeon-youn

Youndt, M. A., Snell, S. A., Dean, J. W., & Lepak, D. P. (1996). Human resource management, manufacturing strategy and firm performance. *Academy of Management Journal, 39*(4), 836–866.

CHAPTER 14

HEALTH IT: AN ENABLER OF FLEXIBILITY

BRADLEY PARK HOSPITAL 14.1

Jennifer watched the elevator doors open on the fifth floor. Surrounding the entrance to the information technology (IT) department, stacks of computer monitors and boxes allowed only enough room for her to pass through. She knocked on Don Nguyen's door.

"Come in."

"Wow, you must be cleaning house," Jennifer commented.

Don looked up from his computer and smiled, "Hello! Yes, we cleaned out the storeroom. We need more space up here since we are growing. How are you? To what do I owe this pleasure?"

Jennifer sat down at his table, "Don, our data show that Bradley Park Hospital's (BPH's) deaths from sepsis are higher than the national average. I wanted to pick your brain to see whether we can use our electronic health record (EHR) system to identify patients at risk of sepsis so that our clinicians can intervene earlier. I read that some hospitals were having great success using their computerized systems to identify those patients who needed intervention."

Don replied, "Sure. We will be happy to see what we can do. Now that we have the physicians and nurses using the EHR system more comfortably, I am interested in making the EHR work for them. Health information technology is a great way to standardize protocols and introduce evidence-based practice throughout the institution. Let's get a group together to brainstorm."

"Great. I can always count on you. I will set up the meeting, just let me know from your end who needs to be there." Jennifer got up to leave, "See you soon. And, good luck on your housecleaning!"

INTRODUCTION AND LEARNING OBJECTIVES

As we saw in Chapter 12, organizations need to be flexible to respond to the rapidly changing healthcare environment. Health IT has provided the platform for faster and more accurate communication, as well as for streamlined processes needed to drive flexibility as a competitive priority. EHRs, in particular, have enabled the expansion of reliable, rapid, and efficient access to more patient information (Figure 14.1).

545

Data permeate all aspects of healthcare delivery: collecting patient information, interpreting data to make diagnoses, communicating test results to health providers, sending data to insurers for payment, and managing data to provide long-term follow-up to patients. However, the healthcare industry has woefully lagged other data-intensive industries in collecting data electronically and making the data available to all who need it.

Office of the National Coordinator for Health Information Technology (ONC)
A federal office that has the authority to establish programs to improve healthcare quality, safety, and efficiency through the promotion of health IT, including EHRs.

In 2009, Congress passed the Health Information Technology for Economic and Clinical Health (HITECH) Act, which gave the **Office of the National Coordinator for Health Information Technology** the authority to establish programs improving healthcare quality, safety, and efficiency through the promotion of health IT, including EHRs (HealthIT.gov, 2015). As a result of Medicare and Medicaid's EHR Incentive Programs, hospitals have significantly increased their adoptions of EHRs with 59% of nonfederal acute care hospitals having adopted at least basic components of a system with clinicians' notes by 2013 (ONC, 2014b). As more providers rely on electronic data, the foundation of a health IT infrastructure is being realized.

The vision for electronic health information involves immediate availability to patients and their providers, use of data to help support decision making, and use of patient information to advance science (Accenture Solutions, 2013). As IT and EHRs become more prevalent in healthcare, it is important for everyone involved in healthcare operations to understand the principles and importance of governance of health IT.

In this chapter, you will learn:

1. **The importance of EHRs in promoting better patient care**
2. **The benefits and challenges of using an EHR**
3. **How telemedicine can help improve access to healthcare**
4. **Why governance is so important in health IT**
5. **How data are keys to promoting population health**
6. **How healthcare analytics can transform healthcare delivery**

FIGURE 14.1 – Mind map for flexibility with health IT.

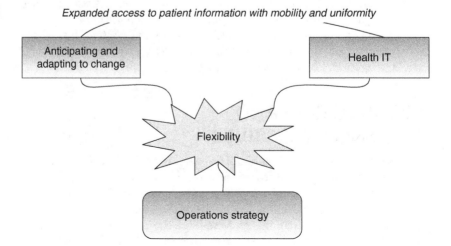

ELECTRONIC HEALTH RECORDS

So what exactly is an EHR? An **EHR** is a computerized documentation system that medical practices use instead of a paper chart. Paper charts have many drawbacks: they are accessible from only one location, papers can be misplaced or misfiled, and it is difficult to find needed and up-to-date information in thick charts. Identifying all patients with similar conditions or in need of a test is difficult when information on paper must be sorted through. EHRs have many benefits, including improved practice management, communication, and health monitoring (Table 14.1). But implementing an EHR requires significant institutional investment and buy-in by providers and staff.

Electronic Health Record
Refers to a digital version of a patient's medical record.

EHR projects are large-scale, organizational and cultural transformation projects. Before embarking on an EHR implementation, leaders must prepare the organization for the significant cultural and workflow process changes needed to achieve benefits. Some concerns include (Smaltz & Berner, 2007):

- Are the users of the systems engaged and committed to the change and implementation processes?

- Is there a respected physician leader who can champion the change process required?

- Which processes will be modified and which ones will be reengineered?

- How will the institution train users and continue to update the system to meet ongoing demands?

TABLE 14.1 Benefits of Adopting an Electronic Health Record

Benefit	Example
Improved efficiency	• Access to information • Better organization of data • Claims-processing efficiency
Improved monitoring	• Aggregate patient data • Provider performance
Improved clinical processes	• Quality improvement • Disease management

Source: Based on Smaltz and Berner (2007).

EHRs can improve efficiencies, but the efficiencies are not evenly distributed. An EHR may speed up the process of a patient receiving a medication, but some parts of the process may take longer with the use of an EHR than without. For example, time needed to document care by physicians and nurses may increase. However, reducing the search time for patient-related information may compensate for that increase. Physicians can view results and document remotely, thus improving physicians' quality of life.

There are also significant barriers to adopting an EHR. An EHR is not a technology that will solve the problem of inefficient care processes (Smaltz & Berner, 2007). Even with the cost of the software and hardware being significant, the bulk of the costs of implementing an EHR is consumed by workflow reengineering that is required to reap the benefits of the investment. Ongoing support, maintenance, and system upgrades must be part of the initial cost projections of adopting an EHR (Table 14.2). Physicians and staff must subscribe to and adopt the new EHR-enabled processes and workflows. In addition, the technical infrastructure required to implement and maintain the complex computer system, training requirements, resistance to change, and interoperability failures cannot be underestimated (Silow-Carroll, Edwards, & Rodin, 2012; Table 14.3). These factors need to be understood and addressed early.

TABLE 14.2 General Categories and Estimated EHR Costs Over a 10-Year Period

Categories of Cost	Estimated Cost
Capital costs	$67M
Operating expenses	$170M
Hardware maintenance	$15M
Software maintenance	$50M
Work redesign	$36M
Training	$16M
Implementation	$22M
Ongoing support	$22M
Total	**$398M**

Source: Silow-Carroll et al. (2012). Used with permission from The Commonwealth Fund.

TABLE 14.3 · Barriers to Adoption of Electronic Health Records

Category	Examples
Financial	• Start-up costs of hardware and software • System administration and maintenance
Technical	• Lack of computer skills or support staff • Lack of technical training • Lack of reliability or interoperability
Time	• Reduced productivity due to providers needing to document in real time • Training time to learn to use the system properly
Psychological	• Changes to work styles and processes • Loss of control
Social	• Fear that electronic health records interfere with face-to-face patient–provider communication
Privacy and security	• Concerns about data hackers • Frustration with security procedures that make using systems sometimes cumbersome
Organizational	• Larger organizations with more support for administration and training adopt EHRs at a higher rate; smaller organizations have limited resources

Source: Based on Agency for Healthcare Research and Quality (2012).

Components of an EHR

EHRs have multiple components: (a) physician/nurse documentation and test results, (b) computerized provider order entry, (c) clinical decision support systems (DSSs), (d) e-prescribing, (e) administrative support, and (f) telemedicine support.

Physician/Nurse Documentation and Test Results

Historically, physician/nurse notes were handwritten. These notes were not easy to abstract for coding or quality assurance, and they were often illegible. Physician dictation and transcription of the notes improved legibility but did not improve the ease of abstraction. Document scanning got the information in one place, but did not allow for abstraction or data aggregation. An EHR must have structured text that forms the basis of documentation but can be easily aggregated and abstracted. However, there is a trade-off between ease of abstraction and coding and clear communication. When a physician or nurse checks off a box instead of describing in words what he or she sees, information may be lost (Box 14.1).

⊕ BOX 14.1 – DID YOU KNOW?

Perceptions of the impact of physician documentation in the Electronic Health Record

A study was done in a Veterans Administration hospital to determine the perceived impact of electronic health record physician documentation on the care of patients. Ten faculty members and 10 residents were interviewed. The four major themes that were identified included:

1. Improved availability of documentation
2. Changes in work processes and communication
3. Alterations in document structure and content
4. Mistakes, concerns, and decreased confidence in the data.

Although the faculty and residents felt documentation was more available, with benefits for education and patient care, other impacts were largely seen as detrimental to aspects of clinical practice and education, including documentation quality, professional communication, and patient care (Embi et al., 2004).

Much work has been done to balance the effort needed for physicians to document their findings using free text and the ease of using checklists and template language. Most systems combine free text fields with structured inputs. Documentation templates can be customized for individual diseases and/or clinicians. Because the Medicare and Medicaid programs encourage use of EHRs through monetary incentives and penalties—also known as **Meaningful Use**—problem lists, medication lists, drug allergies, vital signs, and

Meaningful Use
A federal program that encourages use of EHRs through monetary incentives and penalties.

smoking status tend to be put into the system in a more structured way for easy abstraction (Box 14.2).

⊕ BOX 14.2 – DID YOU KNOW?

Meaningful Use

The Health Information Technology for Economic and Clinical Health Act, including the Medicare and Medicaid EHR Incentive Programs (Meaningful Use), improved EHR adoption. Meaningful Use means to use EHRs to achieve significant improvements in patient care. The legislation ties payments specifically to the achievement of advances in medical care processes and outcomes. It is a multiyear effort that occurs in stages.

Stage 1: Data Capture and Sharing

This stage began in 2011 and focused on capturing structured clinical data such as problem, medication, drug allergies, vital signs, and smoking status; providing health information to patients; and reporting clinical quality metrics.

Stage 2: Advance Clinical Processes

Stage 2 first went into effect in 2014 and had more complex requirements—electronic transmission of patient care summaries across settings, engagement of patients with personal health records, reporting of quality metrics.

Stage 3: Improve Outcomes

This stage, beginning in 2016, focuses on improving quality, safety, efficiency, and health outcomes; using decision support for high-priority conditions; engaging patients in a higher capacity; enhancing information exchange; and reporting population health metrics (The Advisory Board Company, 2014).

Test results from laboratory, radiology, or other procedures are a necessary part of a functional EHR. Most hospitals have ancillary laboratory, radiology, and pharmacy information systems that can feed into the EHR. Often, the actual image of the test results can be linked to the patient's EHR so that providers do not need to sign onto another system to view them. The integration of test results into the patient's record makes clinical decision making much faster and easier.

Computerized Provider Order Entry (CPOE)

A requirement that the provider treating the patient enter patient's orders directly into the electronic system.

Computerized Provider Order Entry

Although not absolutely necessary for an EHR, **CPOE**, which requires that the physician or another licensed provider treating the patient enter the patient's orders directly into the electronic system, is necessary to ensure effectiveness and efficiency. The reason is that decision-support features of EHRs rely on the interaction between the ordering provider and the computer. For example, if a nurse or clerk enters an order for penicillin into the computer, and the system produces an **alert** saying the patient is allergic, the nurse or clerk cannot take corrective action. He or she must halt the order placement, find the physician, and ask for a change to the order. This takes time and may create an error if communication is not good. If the physician places the order and receives the alert, he or she can respond to the alert immediately and change the order. CPOE realizes a true benefit of EHRs that allows integration of decision-support capabilities at the point where decisions are made.

CPOE is still a problem today because many practicing physicians object to spending the time to use the computer system directly. It seems that adoption rates vary with specialty type and practice size. It is interesting to note that although some believe that younger physicians adapt to the EHR more readily, Furukawa et al. (2014) found that physician age did not have a significant impact on adoption rates. However, as academic medical centers train the next generation of physicians to use EHRs and enter orders into the system, eventually all physicians will be trained on EHR systems and CPOE. CPOE may just become part of medical practice.

Clinical Decision Support Systems

Clinical DSSs are information systems designed to improve clinical decision making (Garg et al., 2005). Patient characteristics are matched to a computerized knowledge base, and software algorithms generate appropriate recommendations (Blumenthal, 2010). Most of the major EHR systems have the capability of generating clinical decision-making recommendations via alerts or reminders. Decisions as to what alerts to include are dependent on the organization and require physician direction. Too many alerts lead to "alert fatigue," and providers tend to ignore them (Blumenthal, 2010). Conversely, not enough alerts result in the system not providing optimal support to clinicians. Because these decisions are based on clinical practice, physicians should lead the discussion as to how alerts should be used.

E-Prescribing

Physicians can prescribe medications through the EHR, where the medications and dosages are recorded. **e-prescribing** helps eliminate problems with illegible penmanship, reduces pharmacy staff time, and avoids paper waste (Box 14.3). E-prescribing also eliminates the need for the patient to keep track of the prescription, because the physician transfers it electronically to the pharmacy. However, some patients like the flexibility of having a written prescription that they can use at any pharmacy. As both physicians and patients get used to this technology, it will become increasingly prevalent.

Alert
A computerized message that signals the provider that an order may be contraindicated in a specific patient due to allergies or abnormal results from laboratory studies.

Clinical Decision Support Systems (DSSs)
Information systems designed to improve clinical decision making.

e-Prescribing
Writing a prescription through an EHR that goes electronically to the pharmacy so that it can be filled.

 BOX 14.3 – OM IN PRACTICE!

Reducing Costs Through e-Prescribing

Geisinger Health System, a large, integrated health services organization that is widely recognized for innovative delivery of healthcare, uses their electronic health record to improve many administrative functions. To improve quality and enhance efficiency at 40 of their outpatient clinics, Geisinger implemented e-prescribing modules into their EHRs. They found that more than $500,000 were saved per year from reduced nursing and staff time through electronic management of prescriptions (Institute of Medicine, 2013).

Administrative Support

EHRs are useful from an administrative standpoint. Data, including patient demographics, diagnoses, insurance information, and employer information, are helpful when staff is registering a patient in a clinic, admitting or discharging a patient from the hospital, transferring a patient between facilities, or dropping a bill for services. For administrative data to be useful, patients must have a unique identifier, or a way to be sure that the "Mary Jones" who is being admitted is the same "Mary Jones" who was seen by another physician in the past month (NIH National Center for Research Resources, 2006). This unique identifier links all clinical data, diagnoses, laboratory tests, and doctor notes to a single individual. This is important so that a longitudinal picture of the patient's care can be seen. Because the unique identifier is specific to an organization (Box 14.4), it is sometimes difficult to match the individual with records at another institution.

 BOX 14.4 – DID YOU KNOW?

Why Social Security Numbers Are Not Used as Unique Identifiers

Some may wonder why a person's Social Security number (SSN) is not used as the unique identifier in his or her health record. The SSN is typically linked to an individual's financial resources. An SSN is tied to bank accounts, credit cards, and utility records. Thus, when it is stolen, it puts a person at great financial risk. In recent years, identity theft has become a real problem. With so many people in a hospital having access to a patient's health record, the risks of exposing a person's SSN are substantial. It is bad enough to have your financial information compromised by identity theft, but when thieves get access to your health records and perhaps fill your prescriptions, life gets really frustrating (Demster et al., 2011).

ICD-10 Codes

Codes from the _ICD_ that are used when physicians bill for their services.

In addition to linking administrative data for patient care, EHRs allow providers to bill insurers for their services. In order to communicate with all payers, the Centers for Medicare & Medicaid Services set up a series of codes to indicate the diagnosis of all patient encounters. The ***International Classification of Diseases and Related Health Problems, 10th Revision* (ICD-10) inpatient hospital codes** contain up to seven characters compared to a maximum of five for _ICD-9_ codes. This allows more detailed differentiation and description of symptoms, diagnosis, and procedures performed. Compared to _ICD-9_, _ICD-10_ provides greater ability to capture healthcare services, monitor population health, compile specific data, cut down on paperwork when submitting claims, and, one hopes, collect more revenue by getting paid for the correct services rendered (Medicaid.gov, 2015).

Telemedicine Support

Telemedicine or telehealth (Chapter 9) uses telecommunication and information technologies to connect providers and patients for the purpose of providing medical care, education, and/or clinical support. Telemedicine can provide clinical care to patients at a distance and is one way to increase access to medical care, particularly in rural areas. Faster Internet connections, better video software, and availability of EHRs make it possible for physicians to care for patients at a distance. Primary care physicians can follow up on patients' questions or symptoms without requiring the patient to come in for a visit. Specialty physicians can support providers when caring for complicated patients in the same hospital's intensive care unit or over a long distance. Telemedicine can leverage a physician's expertise so that patients can benefit, no matter where they live. As medicine becomes more sophisticated and expertise becomes more concentrated in urban areas, the use of telemedicine will likely grow.

There are many different types of telemedicine, and commercial companies are springing up all over the country to provide these services. Most of these commercial ventures are directed toward connecting with patients directly via telephone or video conferencing. Generally, minor problems are diagnosed and treated in these interactions. But there are more sophisticated uses of telemedicine in which monitors are placed in a patient's home. They transmit readings such as blood pressure, weight, blood sugar levels, and prescription compliance to providers who are caring for patients with chronic illnesses. When the transmitted readings are outside the range specified by the provider, the patient is contacted directly to intervene before the patient's condition worsens and he or she needs to go to the hospital. Radiology readings are also being increasingly performed through telehealth services. The radiological image is transmitted to a radiologist, either within the healthcare organization or across distances, for interpretation.

Telemedicine can also be used to support physicians in more remote locations. Telemedicine can provide education for primary care physicians in the care of complex medical problems and provide consultation between providers. Patients benefit because they are able to be treated closer to home (Box 14.5).

 BOX 14.5 – OM IN PRACTICE!

Primary Care Visits Through Telemedicine

Carolinas HealthCare System recently rolled out a virtual visit program that allows any of their one million eligible patients to access a provider at any time for a flat fee. The provider on the virtual consultation can see the patient's medical record and notes can be accessed by the primary care doctor and care team. As Dr. Greg Weidner, medical director of primary care innovation and proactive health at Carolinas, sees it, "We are able to provide convenience and simplicity, while compromising none of the benefits of carefully coordinated care" (Fleshman, 2015).

IT GOVERNANCE

How do we develop effective systems to support the creation and use of EHRs? Imagine that you are going to build a house that will serve as a home for you, your children, and your in-laws. All have their own ideas of what they want. Your children want a door that opens to the outside so that you will not know when they sneak out. Your in-laws want their own kitchen. You want peace and quiet with a bedroom on the far side of the house. Think about what the house would look like if you did not have an architect! Just as you need an architect and plan to build a house, you need an architect and a plan to build and connect IT systems. Without good governance, everyone starts stumbling over one another, going in different directions, and the end result is not optimal.

IT Governance
A system that establishes chains of responsibility, authority, and communication to empower people so that information can flow appropriately.

IT governance determines what goes where, which systems are connected, and what processes need to be followed. IT governance helps make the connections so that information can flow appropriately. But IT governance does not just determine the wiring of an EHR, it helps ensure the quality of data so that knowledge can be generated. So what are we talking about when we talk about data quality?

Data Accuracy

The first component of data quality is data accuracy. The good thing about computers is that they can handle large amounts of information. The bad thing about computers is that they cannot distinguish between good and bad information. How many of you have tried to search for a name in your inbox and found that you could not find it because you had misspelled the last name? In healthcare, it is even more complicated because the number of people's names that need to be searched may run into the millions. And what about searching for a diagnosis? Some people will write "asthma," and others will write "wheezing." Terminology, placement of periods, and spelling are important when you are dealing with data. Just remember that if you are sloppy on the input, the value of the data is questionable. IT governance helps drive data quality. Remember, the best IT people drive you crazy! They obsess over every period and space. Learn to love them.

Incomplete Data

The second component of data quality is completeness. We never have all of the data that we need, but if the important data are missing, providers cannot do their jobs. Statistics are meaningless, and trends cannot be detected if the data are incomplete.

Timeliness of Data

The third component of data quality is timeliness. If you receive the necessary data, but it arrives late, patients may suffer. Providers will have to track someone down to find the information. In the worst-case scenario, the wrong treatments will be prescribed. If we are to care for patients, we need to be sure that data are input in a timely way, are complete, and are accurate. Patients' lives are at stake.

HURDLES AND CHALLENGES

Just as with any large project, EHR implementations can fail. The reasons for failure may be related to poor project management in general (see Chapter 3). However, there are some specific reasons, both technical and user-related, for EHR implementation failure (Table 14.4).

EHR systems are complex and need significant functionality. Those who purchase a system must do a thorough analysis of its features and be sure that the system can perform adequately in their specific setting. Beware of IT vendors' flashy presentations of systems that do not perform outside the demonstration booth.

The organization must have a robust IT network infrastructure, including qualified IT professionals, hardware, and network capability. Without the proper bandwidth, response times will be slow and staff will be dissatisfied. The organization needs to have adequate personnel for maintenance of the system. When problems arise, there needs to be a rapid response for correction.

Providers expect that an EHR will have the ability to retrieve information quickly. Therefore, laboratory systems, radiology services, and other support areas within the healthcare organization must be integrated with the EHR to make it useful for patient care. Integrating these systems is not easy. Significant planning and resources need to be directed toward ensuring that all systems work together seamlessly.

TABLE 14.4 Causes of Electronic Health Record Implementation Failures	
Causes	**Examples**
Technical	• Buying an IT system without the necessary functionality • Inadequate IT network infrastructure • Not integrating "back-end" systems—laboratory, radiology, pharmacy, and so on to support the EHR
People	• Lack of physician leadership and participation • Inadequate IT training and support • Inadequate skills, such as typing • Lack of clear expectations
Source: Based on Smaltz and Berner (2007).	

EHRs absolutely require physician leadership and participation. You cannot substitute nonphysicians for this role. Significant workflow analyses and redesign must be sensitive to clinical demands. Providers must design the appropriate clinical decision support tools to support their work. Weak physician leadership or weak participation by a physician design team can lead to poor configuration designs. Organizations should select key influence leaders to serve on the oversight team for the EHR design/implementation and obtain participation from varied specialists.

All staff must be adequately trained on the new system. Clinical care is fast paced and complex. If interaction with the EHR is cumbersome or staff is not facile in its use, then frustration will build up. One common problem with older physicians and staff is the lack of typing skill. In circumstances in which individuals must document care and are unable to type quickly, templates or voice recognition dictation capability may be helpful.

INTEROPERABILITY

As more hospitals and physician practices adopt EHR systems, the next challenge is how to connect them so that information can flow between sites of care. Interoperability allows data to be exchanged and interpreted between systems (Chapter 12). Only when data are available across the continuum of care will patients be able to address their health issues beyond the confines of one healthcare system. Over the past decade, there has been much progress in building a national health IT infrastructure, but more needs to be done to allow for easy exchange of data between EHRs and to increase their ability to add different types of information such as genetic sequences, telephone conversations, photographs, and so on.

Health IT Ecosystem

All the sites where a patient's health information is collected and needed so that appropriate data are available to the right people across organizations so that it can be used to improve health.

The ONC has the critical responsibility to advance the connectivity of electronic health information and the interoperability of health IT throughout the United States (HealthIT.gov, 2015). It has defined the **health IT ecosystem** to include clinicians, hospitals, public health agencies, technology developers, payers, researchers, policy makers, patients, and many others. The vision is to build an interoperable health IT ecosystem that makes the appropriate data available to the right people across organizations in a way that enables the data to be used meaningfully to improve health. Health IT is expanding its boundaries beyond a single healthcare setting for two major reasons:

1. Healthcare is becoming more patient-focused and patients move from one setting to another.

2. Many of the determinants of health are influenced by actions and encounters outside the traditional healthcare settings. These settings may include school, the job site, and community organizations.

Health Insurance Portability and Accountability Act (HIPAA)

An Act passed by Congress that regulates health information and contains a privacy rule that sets boundaries on the use and release of health records.

With so many entities potentially connected to an individual's EHR, it becomes increasingly difficult to keep patient information confidential. Health information must be secure and providers must protect an individual's privacy. In 1996, Congress passed the **Health Insurance Portability and Accountability Act (HIPAA)**, which contains a provision designed to protect an individual's health information. The HIPAA Privacy Rule gives patients more control over their health information and sets boundaries on the use and release of health records (Box 14.6). It establishes safeguards that providers must follow when accessing information and holds violators accountable when they breach the Privacy Rule (Department of Health & Human Services, 2006).

⊕ BOX 14.6 – DID YOU KNOW?

HIPAA Privacy Rule

The Health Insurance Portability and Accountability Act of 1996 Privacy Rule provides federal protection for individually identifiable health information held in databases. It allows healthcare entities to use medical records for treatment, payment, and healthcare operations without specific patient consent. Other organizations (termed business associates) with whom information is shared must enter into a privacy agreement that gives patients specific rights associated with their shared information.

The HIPAA Security Rule specifies administrative, physical, and technical safeguards for healthcare entities and their business associates to ensure the confidentiality, integrity, and availability of electronic protected health information (Department of Health & Human Services, 2006).

The ONC has published a list of priorities that include and extend beyond privacy concerns for patient information. Its Health IT Strategic Plan goals for 2015–2020 (ONC, 2014a) are as follows:

- Expand the adoption of health IT.
- Advance secure and interoperable health information.
- Strengthen healthcare delivery.
- Advance the health and well-being of individuals and communities.
- Advance research, scientific knowledge, and innovation.

You can see from the fourth ONC goal that health IT spans a continuum from the individual to a population. At the individual level, the EHR keeps track of medical problems, tests performed, medications taken, and treatments administered, no matter where the service was delivered. At the group level, health information exchanges can aggregate and share data for those individuals who can be clustered geographically or by disease state. At the population level, the large numbers of data points can be pooled and used to identify specific patient characteristics or responses to treatment that cannot be identified when information from only small numbers of patients is analyzed (see Figure 14.2).

FIGURE 14.2 –
Evolution of
health information
technology.

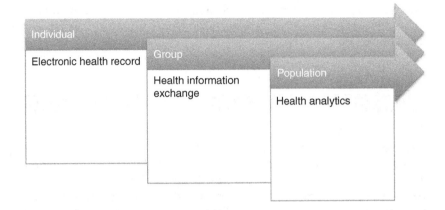

HEALTH INFORMATION EXCHANGE

**Health Information
Exchange (HIE)**
The transmission of
health information
electronically across
organizations within a
region, community, or
hospital system.

**Health Information
Organization (HIO)**
An organization that
oversees and governs
the exchange of health
information and
ensures that the data
adhere to recognized
standards.

How do we get from the data collected in an EHR to improved population health? HIEs are the bridge between these two ends. **Health information exchange** is the transmission of health information electronically across organizations within a region, community, or hospital system. There are multiple types of HIEs with different scopes (Table 14.5). The organizations that facilitate the development and use of HIEs are called **health information organizations**. An HIO oversees and governs the exchange of health information and ensures that the data adhere to recognized standards. HIEs enable reliable and secure transmission of data among these diverse systems and facilitate access and retrieval of data. An HIE may also be used by public health authorities to assist in the analysis of the health of populations.

TABLE 14.5 Types of Health Information Exchanges	
Types of HIE	**Functions**
State-wide HIEs	Operated by state governments or designee
Proprietary HIEs	Centered at an institution or directed toward a specific disease
Hybrid HIEs/HIOs	Collaboration between health information organizations that operate within a shared geographic area
Regional/community HIOs	Interorganizational HIOs that are focused on a community or region

Source: Based on Healthcare Information and Management Systems Society (2014).

BRADLEY PARK HOSPITAL 14.2

Jennifer and Don were standing by the whiteboard as groups of physicians, nurses, IT staff, and laboratory personnel were discussing the early signs of sepsis.

Jennifer summarized, "So we know that early on, when bacteria enter the bloodstream, there are signs of a systemic inflammatory response. These are usually increased fever, increased heart rate, increased respiratory rate, and an abnormal white blood cell count. These signs occur before full-blown sepsis appears. But these signs are subtle and often missed by clinicians. However, all of these data points are charted in the medical record on a regular basis."

Don continued, "By setting alerts within the system, we can identify changes in these values and alert the bedside nurse and the attending physician."

Dr. Levine interjected, "We can set up protocols to evaluate the patient, administer fluids and antibiotics, and, we hope, stop sepsis from becoming severe. This will be a huge benefit for our patients."

Francine Sutton interjected, "We will set up nurse protocols and, if you will help standardize the physician response, we can get started as soon as Don can set up the alerts."

Dr. Levine looked pleased. "This will be wonderful for our patients. The computer will detect changes much more consistently than we can by periodically reviewing the record. This is finally a good reason to use the EHR!"

Jennifer chuckled. "Thank you all. I will follow our sepsis response numbers and report them on a monthly basis. We can get back together to tweak our processes once this gets up and running."

HEALTHCARE ANALYTICS

As stated, the goal of HIE is to provide data from EHRs that can benefit individual and population health. Obviously, just transmitting the data is not enough. The vast array of information contained in EHRs must be carefully categorized and analyzed in order to impact population health. As more patient-specific data are collected and stored, information on groups of similar patients can be analyzed and tracked. Treatments and outcomes for specific diseases can be assessed to determine what factors lead to success. By tapping into large databases, providers will be able to access knowledge relevant to the individual patient and make better decisions for whole populations.

Healthcare analytics is a term used to connote the systematic use of data and related business insights to drive fact-based decision making for patient care and healthcare delivery (Cortada, Gordon, & Leniban, 2012). Analytics can be used at the individual level, group level, or population level (Figure 14.3). We will discuss how data can be used

Healthcare Analytics
The systematic use of data and related business insights to drive fact-based decision making for patient care and healthcare delivery.

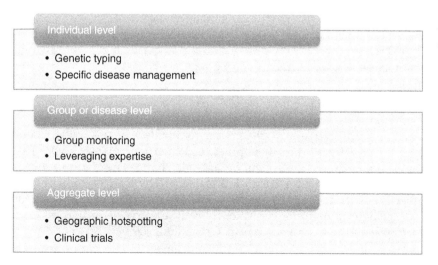

FIGURE 14.3 – Types of healthcare analytics.

at each of these levels to improve care and lower costs. Each year, healthcare analytics become more sophisticated and their use expands. The growth and expansion of EHRs in medical practice will fuel an explosion in the use of data.

Use of Healthcare Data at the Individual Level

 We like to think that we are all unique, but when we get ill, we want to know that the treatments that providers prescribe will work for us based on our similarities to other patients. Healthcare analytics can search through massive amounts of data and analyze it to predict outcomes for individual patients. Data from EHRs can be mined to predict responses to medication or predict who will be readmitted to the hospital. This leads to better care at lower costs.

Physicians can use analytics to help them make more accurate diagnoses. For example, a patient coming to the emergency room with chest pain can have his or her characteristics, laboratory tests, and family history compared to hundreds of similar patients. A predictive algorithm can inform the doctor as to the likelihood that the patient will need to be hospitalized. The physician's clinical judgment will be enhanced by the collective experience of hundreds of physicians. Patients are not needlessly admitted to the hospital and expensive testing can be minimized (Raghupathi & Raghupathi, 2014; Box 14.7).

🕂 BOX 14.7 – OM IN PRACTICE!

Targeting a Specific Type of Ovarian Cancer Based on Genetic Sequence

Ovarian cancer is the fourth leading cause of death in American women and most patients who develop this cancer have low survival rates. Investigators, using large databases of genome scans of cancers, are now able to separate cancers into similar clusters based on genetic variants. This will hopefully lead to targeted therapies based on these genetic sequences. In this study, a genetic analysis of 1,644 women with a specific type of ovarian cancer was compared to a genetic analysis of 21,000 women who did not have ovarian cancer. This type of research using large databases may revolutionize cancer treatment (Kelemen et al., 2015).

Comparative Effectiveness Research

A field of study that utilizes data to inform healthcare decisions by providing evidence on the effectiveness, benefits, and harms of different treatment options.

Algorithms can allow physicians to identify at-risk patients for specific diseases within their practice. When patients are identified, the provider can counsel them on lifestyle changes needed to prevent the development or progression of disease. The field of **comparative effectiveness research** depends on the analysis of large amounts of data to determine more clinically relevant and cost-effective ways to diagnose and treat patients (Sox & Greenfield, 2009).

Use of Healthcare Data at the Group or Disease Level

Critically ill patients are beginning to benefit from healthcare analytics as well. Sophisticated monitoring of patients is leading to large amounts of data flashed up on screens at the patient's bedside. Physicians and nurses looking at these monitors can be aided by healthcare analytics, which can "see" associations between readings that humans may easily miss. For example, a slowing of the pulse rate, a slight increase in temperature, and an elevated white blood cell count may not be noticed by a nurse working at the bedside. But this can be caught in the background with a computer algorithm that puts the disparate pieces of data together to flag a patient who may be developing an infection (Institute for Health Technology Transformation, 2013). The provider can then prescribe antibiotics earlier to prevent complications of infection.

This type of patient monitoring can be performed at the patient's bedside or across the world. Patient monitoring using telemedicine allows hospitals to leverage the expertise of specialties to help care for patients, even in provider shortage areas.

Use of Healthcare Data at the Population Level

Public health is finding new ways to use data analytics to analyze diseased patients and track disease outbreaks. When large amounts of data can be analyzed quickly, healthcare providers are able to respond in a more timely way (Box 14.8).

BOX 14.8 – OM IN PRACTICE!

Google Flu Trends May Be an Early Warning Sign for Emergency Departments

Investigators at Johns Hopkins University found that there was a strong association between Google searches for information about influenza and an increase in patients showing up in the emergency room for treatment with flu-like symptoms. Through monitoring of Internet searches, a surveillance system could be developed that would warn emergency rooms within a community about emerging illness. This "real-time" data would allow the hospitals to prepare for the influx of patients through staffing increases or diversion of elective procedures (Dugas et al., 2013).

Geographic "Hotspotting"
The process of combining health information with geographic location to identify clusters of patients who are in close proximity for targeted interventions.

By combining health data with geographic location, health departments and health systems can identify areas where disease is prevalent. **Geographic hotspotting** allows a provider to identify clusters of patients with the same condition and target interventions to the areas of most need. Because patients within a neighborhood may see multiple physicians, no one provider can see all the patients with a similar condition without aggregation of EHR information. This is the power of data analytics.

The potential of healthcare analytics lies in combining traditional data with new forms of data, both individually and at a population level. We are already seeing how data sets from a multitude of sources can help healthcare organizations be more responsive to patients' needs. The vast amounts of new data collected in increasingly large numbers of EHRs should significantly enhance the ability to impact individual, group, and population health in the years ahead.

BRADLEY PARK HOSPITAL 14.3

Jennifer stood in front of the BPH board of directors showing the graph of sepsis deaths at BPH. "And here is when we implemented the EHR sepsis alert system and protocol. You can see that the number of deaths dropped and has stayed down. Our physicians and nurses are very responsive to these alerts because they understand the tremendous benefit that they have to our patients."

Mike Chambers was the first to speak, "Jennifer, your report is impressive. It is exciting to see that technology is really changing the way we deliver healthcare. The drop in sepsis deaths was so rapid and showed that everyone in the hospital adopted the new practice almost simultaneously."

As board members engaged in animated discussions and began to file out of the board room, Jennifer thought to herself, "This is just the beginning!"

SUMMARY

Health IT is making it possible for healthcare organizations to provide faster and more accurate communications among a larger number of providers for a growing number of patients and conditions. Health IT systems often promote streamlined processes, thereby enabling organizations to compete on flexibility.

EHRs provide significant benefits, but there are challenges that must be considered. Cost is a major factor that needs to be considered when implementing an EHR, but organizations have shown that EHRs can provide significant savings when designed properly. The federal government is incentivizing the use of EHRs and regulating the sharing of health information. Interoperability and data analytics are increasing the power of health data to address health issues beyond the confines of a single health system. Because accurate, complete, and timely data are needed to optimally care for patients, data governance should be a priority in any healthcare organization.

Sharing of health information between organizations or across geographic areas is increasing patients' access to both primary and specialty care. Telemedicine offers improved connectivity, education, and support for both patients and their providers. This expansion of access and knowledge provides the needed flexibility to compete in an ever-changing healthcare environment.

Health IT supports the other competitive priorities (Figure 14.4). With reduced search time and greater and faster access to patient information, EHRs promote both delivery and flexibility. CPOE and e-prescribing reduce the intermediate steps and opportunities for errors involved in placing orders and sending prescriptions, thereby boosting delivery and quality. Furthermore, e-prescribing reduces the cost of paper waste. Telemedicine lowers access time (delivery) and improves quality through regular monitoring. Clinical DSSs facilitate decision making through access to large amounts of patient data and evidence-based practices (quality). Administrative support features facilitate and speed up the processes of billing, registration, discharge, and so on, which support delivery and cost through faster revenue collections. ICD-10 codes improve accuracy (quality), cut down on paperwork and waste (cost and delivery), and capture a greater range of healthcare services than was possible with code sets of earlier generations (flexibility). Interoperability fosters flexibility (Chapter 12) through an expansion of communication networks and decreases the problems associated with care fragmentation (quality). HIEs and healthcare analytics enable reliable data mining for faster (delivery) and improved patient care (quality), leading to lower hospitalization and readmission rates, which, in turn, reduce costs. In enabling the secure transmission of data among diverse systems, HIEs promote flexibility.

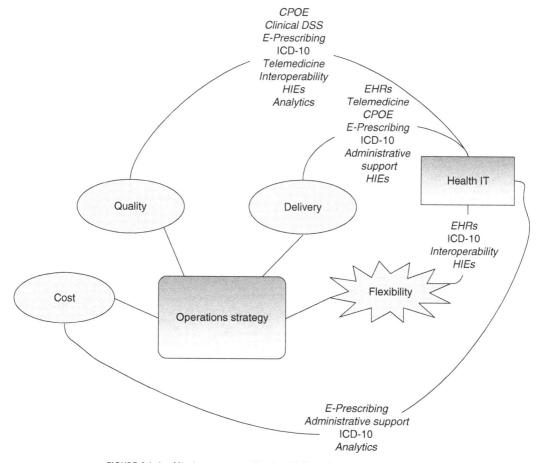

FIGURE 14.4 – Mind map connecting health IT to the competitive priorities.

KEY TERMS

Office of the National Coordinator for Health Information Technology (ONC)	IT governance
Electronic health record (EHR)	Health IT ecosystem
Meaningful Use	Health Insurance Portability and Accountability Act (HIPAA)
Computerized provider order entry (CPOE)	Health information exchange (HIE)
Alert	Health information organization (HIO)
Clinical decision support systems	Healthcare analytics
E-prescribing	Comparative effectiveness research
ICD-10 codes	Geographic hotspotting

WHAT DO YOU REMEMBER?

1. What is the connection between health IT and flexibility?
2. What is an EHR?
3. Name three benefits of adopting an EHR.
4. Name three barriers to adopting an EHR and give an example of each.
5. Why is it important to have providers enter orders for patients through an EHR?
6. What is a clinical DSS and how does it benefit patients?
7. What is telemedicine? Give three examples of situations in which telemedicine can improve care.
8. Why is IT governance important to oversee EHR activities? What are the three components of data quality?
9. Why do EHR implementations fail? Give specific examples as to why failure occurs.
10. Why is interoperability important in building an HIE?
11. Whom does HIPAA protect? How?

12. Why is it important to engage physicians in the design and implementation of EHRs?

13. How do healthcare analytics improve patient care at the individual level, group or disease level, and population level? Give examples.

THINK OUTSIDE THE BOOK!

1. How would you match patients across organizations through an HIE since you cannot use SSNs and each organization has a different way to identify individuals?

2. What are the benefits and barriers to implementing *ICD-10* coding? Do you think it helps improve healthcare delivery? Explain your answer.

3. What are other examples (not presented in this chapter) of how healthcare analytics can improve health at the individual, group, or population level?

REFERENCES

Accenture Solutions. (2013). *Clinical information systems of the future*. Dublin, Ireland. Retrieved from http://www.cas-ag.eu/SiteCollectionDocuments/PDF/Accenture-Clinical-Information-Systems-CIS-of-the-Future.pdf

The Advisory Board Company. (2014). *Daily briefing primer: Understanding meaningful use and its three stages*. Washington, DC: Author. Retrieved from https://www.advisory.com/daily-briefing/resources/primers/meaningful-use

Agency for Healthcare Research and Quality. (2012). *Barriers to HIT implementation*. Rockville, MD: Author. Retrieved from https://healthit.ahrq.gov/health-it-tools-and-resources/health-it-costs-and-benefits-database/barriers-hit-implementation

Blumenthal, D. (2010). Launching HITECH. *New England Journal of Medicine, 362*, 382–385.

Cortada, J. W., Gordon, D., & Leniban, B. (2012). *The value of analytics in healthcare: From insights to outcomes* [IBM Global Business Services, Executive Report]. Somers, NY: IBM Corporation.

Demster, B., Dooling, J., Kadlec, L., Torzewski, S., Walker, R., Warner, D., & Wiedemann, L. A. (2011). Limiting the use of the Social Security number in healthcare. *Journal of AHIMA, 82*(6), 52–56.

Department of Health & Human Services. (2006). *What does the HIPAA privacy rule do?* Washington, DC: Author. Retrieved from http://www.hhs.gov/ocr/privacy/hipaa/faq/privacy_rule_general_topics/187.html

Dugas, A. F., Jalalpour, M., Gel, Y., Levin, S., Torcaso, F., Igusa, T., & Rothman, R. E. (2013). Influenza forecasting with Google flu trends. *PLoS One, 8(2)*, e56176.

Embi, P. J., Yackel, T. R., Logan, J. R., Bosen, J. L., Cooney, T. G., & Gorman, P. N. (2004). Impacts of computerized physician documentation in a teaching hospital: Perceptions of faculty and resident physicians. *Journal of the American Medical Informatics Association, 11(4),* 300–309.

Fleshman, S. (2015, January 13). Why telemedicine's time has finally come. *Forbes.* Retrieved from http://www.forbes.com/sites/zinamoukheiber/2015/01/13/why-telemedicines-time-has-finally-come

Furukawa, M. F., King, J., Patel, V., Hsiao, C.-J., Adler-Milstein, J., & Jha, A. K. (2014). Despite substantial progress in EHR adoption, health information exchange and patient engagement remain low in office settings. *Health Affairs, 33(9),* 1672–1679. doi:10.1377/hlthaff.2014.0445

Garg, A. X., Adhikari, N. K., McDonald, H., Rosas-Arellano, M. P., Devereaux, P. J., Beyene, J., . . . Haynes, R. B. (2005). Effect of computerized clinical decision support systems on practitioner performance and patient outcomes. *Journal of the American Medical Association, 293(10),* 1223–1238.

Healthcare Information and Management Systems Society. (2014). *FAQ: Health Information Exchange (HIE).* Chicago, IL: Author. Retrieved from http://www.himss.org/library/health-information-exchange/FAQ

HealthIT.gov. (2015). Health IT legislation. Retrieved from http://www.healthit.gov/policy-researchers-implementers/health-it-legislation

Institute for Health Technology Transformation. (2013). Transforming health care through big data strategies for leveraging big data in the health care industry. Retrieved from http://ihealthtran.com/big-data-in-healthcare

Institute of Medicine. (2013). Appendix B. In M. Smith, R. Saunders, L. Stuckhardt, & J. M. McGinnis (Eds.), *Best care at a lower cost: The path to continuously learning health care in America* (p. 327). Washington, DC: National Academies Press. Retrieved from http://www.nap.edu/catalog/13444/best-care-at-lower-cost-the-path-to-continuously-learning

Kelemen, L. E., Lawrenson, K., Tyver, J., Qiyuan, L., Lee, J. M., Seo, J.-H., . . . Berchuck, A. (2015). Genome-wide significant risk associations for mucinous ovarian carcinoma. *Nature Genetics, 47,* 888–897.

Medicaid.gov. (2015). *ICD-10: Changes from ICD-9.* Baltimore, MD: Centers for Medicare & Medicaid Services. Retrieved from http://medicaid.gov/medicaid-chip-program-information/by-topics/data-and-systems/icd-coding/icd-10-changes-from-icd-9.html

NIH National Center for Research Resources. (2006). *Electronic health records overview.* McLean, VA: The MITRE Corporation.

Office of the National Coordinator for Health Information Technology. (2014a). Federal Health IT strategic plan (2015–2020). Retrieved from http://www.healthit.gov/policy-researchers-implementers/health-it-strategic-planning

Office of the National Coordinator for Health Information Technology. (2014b, October). Non-federal acute care hospital Health IT adoption. Retrieved from http://dashboard.healthit.gov/dashboards/hospital-health-it-adoption.php

Raghupathi, W., & Raghupathi, V. (2014). Big data analytics in healthcare: Promise and potential. *Health Information Science and Systems, 2*(3). Retrieved from http://www.hissjournal.com/content/2/1/3

Silow-Carroll, S., Edwards J. N., & Rodin, D. (2012). *Using electronic health records to improve quality and efficiency: The experience of leading hospitals* (Publication 1608). New York, NY: The Commonwealth Fund.

Smaltz, D. H., & Berner, E. S. (2007). *The executive's guide to electronic health records*. Chicago, IL: Executive Essentials, Health Administration Press.

Sox, H. C., & Greenfield, S. (2009). Comparative effectiveness research: A report from the Institute of Medicine. *Annuals of Internal Medicine, 151*(3), 203–205.

PART

VI

Connecting the
Concepts and
Reaping the Rewards

CHAPTER 15

ACCREDITATION, AWARDS, AND THE HIGHLY RELIABLE ORGANIZATION

BRADLEY PARK HOSPITAL 15.1

Francine Sutton, the chief nurse, knocks on Jennifer's office door. As she opens it, she sees that every wall is covered with value stream maps and Gantt charts. "Wow! You have been really busy," she comments.

"We have made a lot of progress and every clinic and ward has some quality-improvement project under way," Jennifer responded.

"All the staff are excited about Quality Day and are preparing their posters to show everyone what project they have been working on. The entire hospital and clinic seem to be energized. And Brent Gregg is reporting that the hospital finances are much improved."

"That is wonderful," Jennifer smiled. She was so proud of what she and her teams had accomplished, and now it showed in the financial reports. More patients were choosing Bradley Park Hospital (BPH), and the patient satisfaction numbers were all improving.

"How can I help you, Francine?" Jennifer asked.

"I came by to tell you that The Joint Commission will be visiting BPH soon and I wanted to be sure you were part of the planning process."

Jennifer looked puzzled. "Why would you want to include the quality team in the planning for accreditation?"

 Why would a hospital want the quality team to actively participate in the accreditation process?

INTRODUCTION AND LEARNING OBJECTIVES

Healthcare organizations must undergo accreditation and/or certification on a regular basis. Accreditation and certification validate an institution and may bring distinction for high standards. The standards for accreditation and certification are set by outside groups that encourage healthcare institutions to improve quality and maintain high standards for healthcare delivery. In some cases, accreditation status is necessary for payment. For example, as noted in Chapter 1, for payment from Medicare, healthcare providers must meet certain requirements and comply with regulations established by the Secretary of the Department of Health & Human Services. Awards, similarly, are ways that healthcare institutions can set themselves apart from others and show that they are exceptional. Achievement of this type adds luster to an institution's image, sets it apart from the competition, and is a focal point for employee pride.

In this chapter, we review the ways healthcare organizations and provider groups achieve accreditation and we describe the most notable healthcare award. We also discuss how organizations can become more consistent and reliable. By the end of the discussion, you will be able to:

1. **Describe why institutions undergo accreditation**
2. **Explain the difference between accreditation and certification**
3. **Articulate why the Malcolm Baldrige Award holds such prestige**
4. **Describe the criteria for the Malcolm Baldrige Award**
5. **Name five themes on which healthcare organizations with high levels of quality and safety focus**
6. **Learn the principles that make an organization highly reliable**
7. **Explain the importance of anticipation and containment for highly reliable organizations**
8. **Connect the mind maps from Chapters 2 through 14**

Accreditation

A process of validation in which healthcare organizations are evaluated. Outside entities set the standards by which healthcare organizations are measured. Often, accreditation is needed to ensure quality care prior to payment for services.

Joint Commission

A nonprofit organization that accredits and certifies more than 20,000 healthcare organizations in the United States.

ACCREDITATION

Accreditation is a rigorous and comprehensive process that examines the systems, processes, and performance of healthcare organizations. It is performed by impartial outside groups to ensure that business is being conducted in a way that meets national quality standards. In this section, we will look more closely at two accrediting bodies: The Joint Commission and the National Committee for Quality Assurance (NCQA).

The Joint Commission

In Chapter 1, the long history of The **Joint Commission** was recounted. Currently, this agency accredits and certifies more than 20,000 healthcare organizations in the United States. The Joint Commission accreditation or certification is recognized as symbolizing quality and an organizational commitment to meeting certain performance standards (The Joint Commission, 2015).

How Is Accreditation Achieved?

Joint Commission standards form the basis of an objective survey process that evaluates healthcare organizations. There are multiple chapters, but the most significant impact these areas of an organization (The Joint Commission, 2013):

- **Leadership and Human Resources**. These chapters focus on important functions that determine the culture of the organization and are essential to providing safe and high-quality care (Schyve, 2009). A healthcare organization must have the resources—human, financial, physical, and informational—to provide excellent care. It must have sufficient numbers of competent staff and care providers. Leaders must have the influence and control over the organization to provide these resources and create an environment of quality and safety.

- **Environment of Care**. The Environment of Care addresses the physical environment where healthcare delivery takes place. Buildings must be kept up to code, equipment must be calibrated and functioning properly, and the facility must be safe for patients and the staff. There are six functional areas that the organization must address with management plans. These areas are safety, security, hazardous materials and waste, fire safety, medical equipment, and utilities. In each of these areas, key topics, such as risk assessment, emergency response, performance monitoring, and staff development, must be addressed. These plans are not meant to be a checklist that is developed and then put on the shelf. The Environment of Care plan should be a way for an organization to constantly maintain a safe environment. The development of these plans can foster communication and transparency within an organization.

- **Life Safety**. This area focuses on fire safety. The buildings and operational activities must minimize fire hazards and provide a safety system in the case of fire. Facilities must be reviewed for occupancy and types of patients who may be in the facility. Because some patients, for example, those undergoing anesthesia, would not be able to care for themselves, organizations must carefully evaluate the services, treatments, and locations where individuals may need extra protection.

- **Emergency Management**. This section requires a comprehensive approach to planning, preparedness, testing, and other essential emergency management activities. There are six areas that must be considered. They are communications, resources and assets, safety and security, staff responsibilities, utilities, and patient clinical and support activities. Senior leadership within the organization must be involved and review the plans annually.

Under each of the functional areas, there are multiple standards that drill down to practices impacting patient care.

Healthcare organizations seeking accreditation must undergo an on-site review by Joint Commission trained survey teams every 3 years. (Note: Laboratories receive accreditation every 2 years.) The organizations do not receive notification of the survey date, but know that reaccreditation is between 18 and 39 months after the previous survey. The purposes of the survey are not only to evaluate the organization and facilitate reimbursement (Box 15.1), but also to provide the education and guidance that will help staff continue to improve performance (Sprague, 2005).

⊕ BOX 15.1 – DID YOU KNOW?

Other Accreditation Agencies for Medicare and Medicaid

To receive payment for services rendered to Medicare patients, healthcare providers must comply with regulations set out by the Secretary of the Department of Health & Human Services. Healthcare organizations can qualify for reimbursement in two major ways. They can receive accreditation from "deemed" entities—Joint Commission, American Osteopathic Association, and Det Norske Veritas—or they can apply directly to the Centers for Medicare & Medicaid Services to review whether they satisfy Medicare's Conditions of Participation. These reviews are carried out by state agencies (Lazarus & Chapman, 2013; Sprague, 2005).

Benefits of Accreditation

There is consistent evidence that accreditation programs improve healthcare organizations' care processes (Trentman, Sorung, & Frasco, 2005). But, in addition, there are benefits to the institution itself. Some of the benefits include:

- Help to organize and strengthen patient safety efforts
- Strengthen community confidence in care provided by the institution
- Provide education to enhance staff performance
- Build a framework for organizations to structure safety and quality efforts
- Provide a thorough and in-depth review of care processes

BRADLEY PARK HOSPITAL 15.2

Francine stood in front of the PowerPoint presentation and faced a room full of staff from all departments of BPH. "The Joint Commission survey process is a data-driven, patient-centered exercise that looks at the actual care processes going on in healthcare settings. Both our hospital and the clinics will be visited by surveyors in the next few months. The work that you have been doing to streamline care, increase patient satisfaction scores, and improve safety for our patients and staff will set us up well for the survey. I bet we will have many 'best practices' that we can show the surveyors. They are looking for continuous improvement in support of safe, high-quality care, and we have been focusing on that for the past year. I think if we can show them what we have been . . ."

A hand popped up. "When will they be coming?" a nurse from the back asked.

"Surveys are unannounced, but we know that they will be coming anytime within the next 6 months because our last survey was 30 months ago and hospitals like ours are surveyed between 18 and 36 months after the previous full survey," Francine responds.

She continues, "They use the tracer methodology where the surveyors follow the patient through the process. They will go wherever the patient goes and will ask each person who cares for the patient questions. You all have been working on improving the process and patient experience. I feel very confident that we will do well in the survey. The survey team may also teach us best practices from other organizations.

"We will be working with each area to be sure that all employees know their roles. Please let your supervisor know if you have any questions." Francine looked around for any more questions. She then turned to Jennifer, "Your work has really set us up for a good survey. We are all so appreciative." Jennifer smiled, "We will celebrate when it is all over!"

 In your opinion, what are the benefits of using the tracer methodology?

The Joint Commission accredits organizations that care for patients within their walls, such as hospitals and clinics. In contrast, the NCQA focuses on a different aspect of healthcare: insurance plans and provider groups.

National Committee for Quality Assurance

Founded in 1990, the **NCQA** is a private, 501(c)(3), not-for-profit organization dedicated to improving healthcare quality (NCQA, 2015) NCQA accredits health plans, provider groups, and health insurance organizations. The accreditation process is an on-site, rigorous review of more than 60 standards performed every 3 years. In addition, every year health plans must report on their performance. These performance reviews are tracked, and assessment scores, based on a set of clinical measures and consumer experience, are reported to the public.

When NCQA reviews a health plan, provider group, or health insurance company, it looks at structure, organization, and results in these areas:

- Quality management and improvement
- Utilization management
- Credentialing and recredentialing of providers
- Members' rights and responsibilities

National Committee for Quality Assurance (NCQA)
A nonprofit organization that accredits health plans, provider groups, and health insurance organizations.

- Standards for member connections
- Medicaid benefits and services
- Quality data (Healthcare Effectiveness Data and Information Set [HEDIS], Consumer Assessment of Healthcare Providers and Systems [CAHPS]) performance measures)

Any health plan sold on the health insurance exchanges as outlined by the Affordable Care Act (ACA) requires accreditation through NCQA, but many unaccredited plans are still sold through employers or in the private market. NCQA scores insurance plans on consumer satisfaction, preventive services provided, and treatment services. These scores are posted, and consumers can compare plans according to these parameters (Consumer Reports, 2014). As more data are made available, choosing a quality plan will become easier.

Certification

Designation by an authorized agency that verifies that a program meets the standards set.

Accreditation is an acknowledgment that a whole organization (e.g., a hospital) is complying with recognized standards of practice. In contrast, **certification** focuses on programs or functions (e.g., heart disease care; Box 15.2). Besides accreditation, The Joint Commission also grants certification of certain programs after evaluation. Another, highly regarded certification agency is the International Organization for Standardization (ISO).

🌐 BOX 15.2 – DID YOU KNOW?

The Difference in Accreditation, Certification, and Licensing

The terms "accreditation" and "certification" are often used interchangeably. However, they do not mean the same thing. **Accreditation** is voluntary and can be earned by an entire healthcare organization. **Certification** is also voluntary and is conferred on programs or services within or associated with a healthcare organization. **Licensure** is a nonvoluntary process in which a governmental agency permits an individual to engage in an occupation after demonstrating a certain level of competence (Rooney & van Ostenberg, 1999).

Designation	Who or What?	Voluntary	Agency
Accreditation	Organization	Yes	Nongovernmental
Certification	Program	Yes	Nongovernmental
Licensure	Individual	No	Governmental

CERTIFICATION
The International Organization for Standardization

The ISO, a nongovernmental agency counting over 160 member countries, established **ISO 9000 certification** in 1987. This certification originated in Europe as countries were coming together to form the

European Union. In order to facilitate the exchange of quality goods across borders, ISO 9000 established quality *management* standards, as opposed to *product* quality standards. Rather than dictating stringent product specifications, the standards established quality-assurance procedures in design, production, and delivery.

The purpose of ISO is to provide standards to companies and organizations wanting to ensure that their products and services consistently meet consumers' requirements and that the quality continuously improves. Embedding a quality management system within an organization increases productivity, reduces unnecessary costs, and ensures quality of processes and products (Perry Johnson Registrars, 2015). ISO certification applies to any organization, regardless of size or industry, and the ISO designation signals to customers that they will get a quality product.

In healthcare, ISO 9000 certification covers inpatient care management, general operating and administrative procedures, manufacturing methodologies, and medical product quality assurance (Box 15.3). It is based on seven principles that help build a quality management system for healthcare organizations (Table 15.1).

ISO 9000 Certification

Recognition by a non-governmental agency that international quality management standards have been met so that products and services consistently meet customer requirements.

⊕ BOX 15.3 – DID YOU KNOW?

ISO and Healthcare

The International Organization for Standardization published guidelines for the healthcare sector in 2001, and in 2008, Det Norske Veritas (DNV) became the third hospital accreditation organization to receive deeming authority (see Box 15.1). ISO 9001 is central to DNV's hospital accreditation program, which requires healthcare providers to demonstrate continuous quality improvement via implementation and certification of the international quality management system (QMS) standard (Lazarus & Chapman, 2013).

TABLE 15.1 – ISO's Seven Principles

Principle	Objective
1. Customer focus	Meeting and trying to exceed customers' needs
2. Leadership	Create unity of purpose, good communication, and strategy alignment
3. Involvement of people	Build a culture of motivated, committed workers at all levels
4. Process approach	Coordinate work processes and reduce variation to provide the most value to customers
5. Continuous improvement	Continuously examine and improve processes to lead to faster, more efficient, and higher quality operations
6. Evidence-based approach to decision making	Analyze and evaluate data to make informed decisions
7. Mutually beneficial relationships	Create a mutually beneficial relationship with suppliers to optimize resources and cost

Source: International Organization for Standardization (2015).

AWARDS

Unlike accreditation or certification, which indicates that specified standards are being met, a growing number of healthcare organizations are trying to differentiate themselves by seeking awards. Awards suggest that an institution is not just meeting the standards, but exceeding them in certain ways. There are numerous national, regional, and state awards in healthcare, but the Malcolm Baldrige Award is especially coveted.

Malcolm Baldrige Award

Malcolm Baldrige Award
One of the most prestigious awards in healthcare, which recognizes organizations that have implemented successful quality management systems.

As indicated, one of the most prestigious awards in healthcare is the **Malcolm Baldrige Award**. The U.S. Congress established this award in 1987 to recognize all types of companies that have implemented successful quality management systems (American Society for Quality, 2015). The award was named after a former Secretary of Commerce who was a proponent of quality management. The National Institute of Standards and Technology manages the award, and the president of the United States presents it annually. There are six categories of awards representing different segments of the economy, and an independent board judges the competition. Up to 18 awards are given yearly in the following six categories:

1. Manufacturing
2. Service
3. Small business
4. Education
5. Healthcare
6. Nonprofit

Organizations are judged based on the following criteria (Figure 15.1):

1. **Leadership**. The leaders do not just need to lead the organization well. The Baldrige Award goes beyond that and is interested in how the organization leads within the community.

2. **Strategy**. The organization must have a planning process that defines its direction and delineates how the strategy will be implemented. Strategic planning should lead to positive action, and the strategic plans should not just sit on the shelf.

3. **Customers and market focus**. The organization must show that it values its customers and builds strong and lasting relationships. These relationships are put in the context of the market as a whole. In healthcare, this means putting the patient at the center of its focus, but customers of various processes, such as physicians and other staff, are also valued.

4. **Measurement, analysis, and knowledge management**. The organization must be able to collect and use data to support its decisions, improve key processes, and manage performance.

The organization must turn data into information that can be used to drive its business.

5. **Workforce focus**. Organizations that value their human resources, train them, and empower them to do their jobs are more resilient and flexible. Workforce morale spills over into taking care of customers and organizational excellence. Organizations taking care of their people tend to perform better and maintain higher efficiency.

6. **Process management**. Operations management determines how well the organization is run. Excellent organizations are interested in identifying the processes that matter, designing them well, managing the variables, and continuously improving so that the outcomes are enhanced.

7. **Business/organizational performance results**. Organizations that focus on results have a broad portfolio of performance indicators: customer satisfaction, finance, human resources, supplier and partner performance, operations, governance and social responsibility, and competitiveness. Healthy organizations learn from comparing themselves to others and strive to adopt best practices.

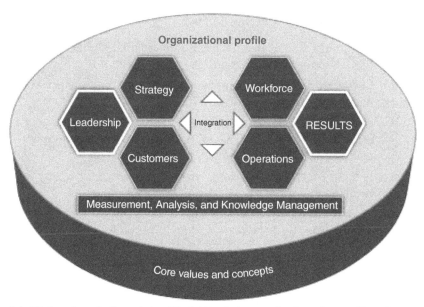

FIGURE 15.1 – Malcolm Baldrige Award framework.

Adapted with permission from Baldrige Performance Excellence Program (2015).

Note: This figure is used with permission of the Baldrige Performance Excellence Program. 2015–2016 Framework for Performance Excellence. A systems approach to improving your organization's performance. Gaithersburg, MD: U.S. Department of Commerce, National Institute of Standards and Technology. Obtain a full copy of the framework at http://www.nist.gov/baldrige/publications/Framework.cfm.

The framework for this award provides a set of criteria for organizational quality improvement that has become a model for the design of quality programs (Foster, Johnson, Nelson, & Batalden, 2007). Strategic plans focused on quality engender positive business results when senior leadership is committed, the organization takes a customer and market focus, and processes are driven through a culture of quality (Ghosh, Handfield, Kannan, & Tan, 2003).

Leadership

The first criterion of the Malcolm Baldrige Award is an evaluation of leadership. Let us explore this concept a bit further. Because lives are at stake, good leadership is especially critical to a healthcare organization's success. Joint Commission Resources likens a healthcare organization to a watch (Schyve, 2009). A watchmaker could gather the best components in the world and put them together, but the resulting watch would be unlikely to run. The individual components, although necessary, are not enough. It is how the components work together that creates a quality watch. In other words, healthcare organizations must be appreciated as a system, the components of which work together to provide high-quality care. Thus, when we talk of leadership in healthcare, it implies that the many leaders within the organization (the governing body, the chief executive and other senior leaders, and the leaders of the licensed independent practitioners) work well together. Distinctive leadership styles have been associated with high-performance organizations. In a study of 79 academic medical centers, Keroack and colleagues (2007) found that five themes were associated with measurable differences in patient-level measures of quality and safety. Those five themes were as follows:

1. **A shared sense of purpose**. Leaders articulated that "patients first" was the primary goal.

2. **Leadership style**. Leaders were passionate about quality and had an "authentic, hands-on" style.

3. **Accountability system for quality, safety, and service.** Strategic priorities and measures of success were developed and leaders were accountable for their achievement.

4. **A focus on results**. Leaders were relentless in their efforts to measure and improve their results.

5. **Collaboration.** Leaders recognized that contributions at every level within the organization were important.

Leaders are needed at all levels to transform healthcare organizations into safe and high-quality organizations. As institutions evolve, leaders must grow and change as well. Leaders do not have to know the answers to all of the questions, but instead, they need to create an environment where the right questions are asked. At times, it may be uncomfortable to ask or respond to hard questions, but it is important to take all questions seriously and try to answer them honestly (Table 15.2). Greater institutional tolerance and diversity of thought lead to higher performing organizations. The best leaders view every situation, no matter how challenging, as an opportunity to learn. If leaders are not willing to take a hard look inward and be willing to assess their own strengths and weaknesses, they will find it difficult to create an organizational culture where assessment is the norm.

TABLE 15.2 – Questions for a Leader to Ask Himself or Herself

- Are you committed to your own growth as you lead the organization?
- Are you creating an environment for the right, and frequently hard, questions that are being asked?
- Are you engaging in patient-centered and not ego-centered conversations?
- Are you embracing challenges that stretch your capacity as a leader?

Source: Hines, Luna, Lofthus, Marquardt, and Stelmokas (2008).

Different leadership groups that may be found within an organization are listed in the following sections. Although each of the leadership groups must work together as a team, each has a distinct role as it relates to quality. In small organizations, these groups may overlap, and a single individual may assume several roles.

The Governing Body

In Chapter 2, you may remember that when Mike Chambers took over as BPH's chief executive officer (CEO), one of his first actions was to discuss his plans with the board of directors. The commitment to patient safety and quality must start with the governing body or board of directors' level. Delivering quality healthcare is increasingly recognized as a corporate responsibility. Thus, in order to foster engagement and hold senior management accountable to the goals, the board must be involved in identifying quality goals. Boards must prioritize quality agendas and commit sufficient resources for the implementation of quality-improvement programs.

The Chief Executive and Other Senior Leaders

The CEO and senior leaders of an organization must take strong steps to create the expectation of quality. In Chapter 2, Mike Chambers, Brent Gregg, and the senior leadership team of BPH analyzed the hospital's operations and developed a strategic plan. The senior leadership team is responsible for the development and implementation of the strategic plan of the organization. This plan should include a clear focus on safety and teamwork among all staff. This group must prioritize projects, adopt quality measures to track, and set goals to accomplish (Table 15.3). This group sets the tone of the organization and should recognize and encourage leaders to listen, ask difficult questions, and provide the collaboration and openness necessary to achieve quality and safety.

TABLE 15.3 – Goals That All Leadership Groups Must Share

- To foster a culture of quality and safety
- To plan and provide services that meet patients' needs
- To secure a sufficient number of competent care providers
- To continuously evaluate and improve processes and outcomes

Source: Schyve (2009).

Strategy

By now, you probably realize that the organization of this text generally parallels the Malcolm Baldrige performance framework. In Chapter 2, you learned how to develop a business and operations strategy, taking into account the organization's strengths, weaknesses, opportunities, and threats (SWOT). Based on the SWOT analysis, a strategic path is chosen, and all of the functions within the organization—marketing, operations, finance, human resources, and information technology (IT)—must align their strategies with the business strategy. For operations (the focus of this book), building a strategic advantage means competing on the basis of quality, cost, delivery, and flexibility (Figure 15.2). Remember, however, that quality is the building block for overall excellence.

FIGURE 15.2 – Mind map of business, functional, and operations strategies.

Customers and Market Focus

The ultimate customers of the chain of interconnected processes are known collectively as the "market." They define the meaning of quality. In Chapter 4, you learned how to capture the voice of the customer (VOC). The VOC reflects the customers' opinions and perceptions regarding the service provided by the organization. In healthcare, the VOC often captures the following service characteristics: responsiveness, reliability, communication with providers, empathy, courtesy, ease of making an appointment, and tangible aspects of the service such as lighting, noise, cleanliness, and so on. The house of quality framework helps ensure that the VOC is translated into the voice of the process (VOP) and is measured through quality indicators along the three stages of the healthcare delivery system: structure (or input), process, and outcomes (or output). Many of the tools described in this text are designed to analyze a process and improve it so that the customer's needs and wants are met (Figure 15.3).

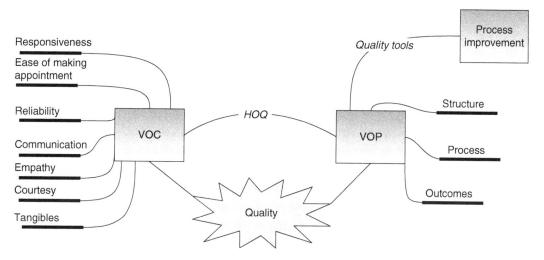

FIGURE 15.3 – Mind map of VOC and VOP.

Measurement, Analysis, and Knowledge Management

Chapters 4 to 7 introduced you to tools and methodologies that can be used to measure and analyze workflows and processes. These tools and methodologies are summarized in Appendix 15.1. Quality tools, statistical process control (SPC), process capability, process diagrams, 5w2h frameworks, process activity charts, and simulation help signal problems and identify opportunities for improvement. They are especially useful for systematically communicating to others within the organization what is needed to align activities with performance. When combined with total quality management (TQM), Lean/Six Sigma, and layout design methodologies, they help design or redesign processes that support quality (e.g., fewer errors), lower cost (e.g., less waste and variability), speed up delivery (e.g., more efficient layout), and enhance flexibility (e.g., greater skill repertoire).

Chapter 8 covered quantitative techniques (queuing theory and queuing simulation) aimed at finding optimal capacity (service) levels based on the demand (arrivals) placed on the process. In that chapter, you also learned how to manage bottlenecks using the Theory of Constraints (TOC). Such techniques support delivery through smoother flows, cost through appropriate staffing levels, quality through reduced wait times, and flexibility through capacity adjustments. The relationships between patient arrivals and providers' service times paved the way for efficient scheduling of staff (integer linear programming), jobs (sequencing rules), and patient appointments (Kaandorp and Koole's outpatient scheduling model) in Chapter 9.

The demand placed on a system determines not only the workforce capacity levels but also the inventory levels necessary to ensure a smooth flow, minimize service interruptions and waits, and control costs. In Chapter 10, you learned time series and associative models to produce accurate demand forecasts. These forecasts were used to determine both the quantity and timing of orders to replenish inventory (Chapter 11) while balancing the needs for adequate customer service and low costs. Chapter 12 further expanded on these concepts with a review of cost-accounting basics and a discussion of operations managers' influence on cost containment.

Chapter 14 focused on IT. All aspects of healthcare delivery generate abundant data. Their successful management improves patient safety, reduces waste, helps streamline operations, promotes fast or on-time delivery, and facilitates communication among diverse providers along the care continuum. Health IT can enable an organization to become more responsive to changes in customers' needs.

Improvement projects must be managed effectively. Chapter 3 provided a systematic approach to planning and steering projects to achieve the specific goals. The constraints on a project—cost, time, and resources—must be managed to achieve quality. Tools to help plan, schedule, and monitor projects can increase the likelihood that projects are completed on time and within budget (Figure 15.4).

Human Resource Focus

Although the focus of this book is operations management, and not human resources management, we did discuss in Chapter 2 how important it was for all the organizational functions—marketing, finance, IT, operations, and human resources—to align their strategies to support the overall organizational goals. Chapters 4 and 6 stressed the importance of creating a culture of quality and continuous improvement. For example, TQM, Lean, and Six Sigma stress employee respect and empowerment. Similarly, some of the process design principles in Chapter 7 emphasized employee autonomy and collaboration, whereas the drive to increase workforce flexibility in Chapter 13 called for job enlargement, cross-training, and job enrichment. Supervisors and leaders must learn from those actually doing the job and allow them to solve problems and improve processes when they see fit. Respect is a fundamental value in a continuously learning organization. Only when leaders and staff work together can an organization excel in all competitive priorities.

Process Management

Process management is the core of operations. Processes must be designed to support the organizational strategy. Starting in Chapter 2, you learned about the Institute of Medicine's call to design a system that makes it harder to do something wrong and easier to do something right. This idea paralleled Deming's point #3 (Chapter 4), which advocated productive systems geared toward prevention of errors

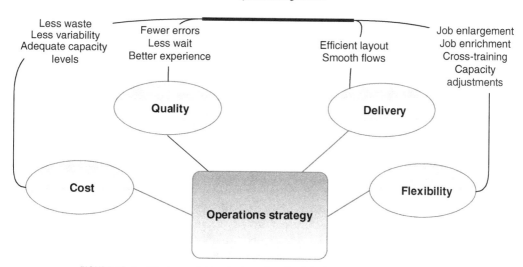

TOOLS

HOQ
Quality tools
SPC
Process capability
Process diagrams
5w2h frameworks
Process activity charts
Layout design tools
TQM
Lean/Six Sigma
Queuing models and simulation
TOC
Scheduling techniques
Forecasting techniques
Inventory models
Costing methods
Health IT
Project management

Less waste
Less variability
Adequate capacity
levels

Fewer errors
Less wait
Better experience

Efficient layout
Smooth flows

Job enlargement
Job enrichment
Cross-training
Capacity
adjustments

Quality

Delivery

Cost

Flexibility

Operations strategy

FIGURE 15.4 – Mind map linking tools and methodologies to competitive priorities.

rather than correction. Chapter 7 presented several process design principles, which built upon this concept as well as TQM and Lean/Six Sigma paradigms. The principles urge organizations to emphasize mistake-proofing, simplification, integration, collaboration, and reduction of variability to achieve excellence in quality, delivery, cost, and flexibility. They therefore serve as the basis for integrated supply chains, which are complex networks of interconnected processes (Chapter 11).

In the dynamic healthcare environment, processes cannot be static. Rather, they must evolve to continue to support changing strategies. Flexible processes can be adjusted to accommodate environmental changes and new market demands (range), with minimal penalties in terms of cost, time (mobility), and quality (uniformity); see Chapter 13. Although the concept of flexibility makes sense to most people in an organization, it is quite challenging to implement. Change is hard! Sometimes, even the simplest process modifications are met with harsh resistance (Box 15.4). Flexibility can only exist if the organizational culture embraces change and innovation at all levels (Figure 15.5).

⊕ BOX 15.4 – OM IN PRACTICE!

The Semmelweis Reflex

In the 1840s, a gifted physician named Ignaz Semmelweis worked in the Vienna General Hospital's first obstetrical clinic. The clinic was set up so that physicians delivered babies on some days of the week, and midwives delivered babies on the other days. Semmelweis was very observant. He noticed that patients cared for by the midwives had fewer deaths related to childbed fever compared to those cared for by the physicians. He also noted that physicians would come to the clinic from the autopsy suite and not wash their hands prior to delivery. Remember, this observation was prior to Pasteur's discovery in 1865 that germs caused disease. Semmelweis came up with the idea that doctors should wash their hands prior to delivering babies.

One would think that this would be considered a rational idea that was based on observation, right? Well, Semmelweis's suggestion was met with anger and dismissed by all his colleagues. In fact, Semmelweis was ridiculed by all for his suggestion. Why could the physicians not embrace this new concept? Was it because they did not want to appear "dirty" or thought Semmelweis was critical of the way they took care of their patients? No one really knows, but this response to new information is very common among all people. It is called the Semmelweis reflex, the rejection of the results of research and observable facts because it conflicts with established beliefs. It is not a person's personality or intelligence that causes this response, but rather the result of the deeply held beliefs of the person.

The Semmelweis reflex is a common occurrence during organizational change. Each of us is susceptible to this reflex. We need to recognize it and be sure that we are responding to change in a positive way.

Business/Organizational Performance Results

Chapter 2 introduced you to scorecards and dashboards to track performance metrics. Chapter 4 presented a quality dashboard; Chapters 7 and 9 covered delivery dashboards; Chapter 12 featured a cost dashboard; and Chapter 13 presented a flexibility dashboard. These dashboards roll up to an organizational scorecard where operational results can be quickly seen. Figure 15.6 displays the new dashboard for BPH. It reflects the improvements the organization has accumulated during its journey to operations excellence.

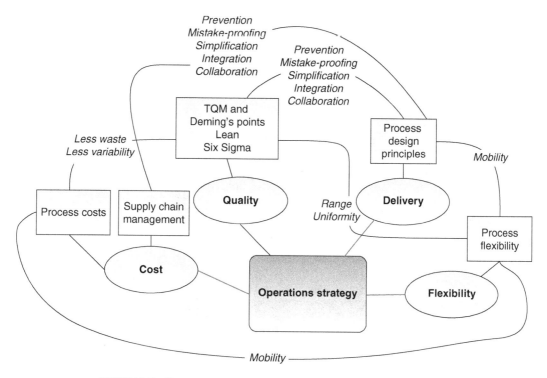

FIGURE 15.5 – Mind map linking process management to competitive priorities.

When quality is the driving force of an organization and the Malcolm Baldrige framework for performance excellence is achieved, business success follows (Ghosh et al., 2003). Deming taught that strong, visionary leadership is needed to drive organizational learning and cooperation (Deming, 1986). But leadership alone cannot lead to a quality organization. It takes a culture of quality and continuous improvement in all competitive priorities to achieve excellence in healthcare.

BRADLEY PARK HOSPITAL 15.3

Mike Chambers stood in front of a filled auditorium, a big smile on his face. "Congratulations, all of you! Bradley Park Hospital had a thorough survey by The Joint Commission, and they were impressed with your spirit, your dedication to quality patient care, and your love of Bradley Park. As with any survey, The Joint Commission found some things that we could improve upon, but overall, it was a huge success. Thank you."

As the animated crowd began to ask Mike questions, Jennifer, who was in the back corner with Don, Francine, and Eric, commented, "The work we have done over the past year has really paid off."

Don smiled, "You are so right. You deserve a lot of the credit, Jennifer."

"No one creates change alone. I was lucky to have many, many partners, including you three!"

Measures	FYTD Actual*	FY Target	Aug.	Sep.	Oct.	Nov.	Dec.
QUALITY							
Mortality index	1.05	0.95	1.30	1.00	0.95	0.92	0.90
Patient satisfaction	3.9	4.5	4.1	4.3	4.5	4.6	4.6
Hospital-acquired conditions per 1,000 discharges	137	135	137	135	130	130	125
All-cause, 30-day readmission rate (%)	10.92	< 11%	12	11	10	9	9
COST							
Cost per adjusted patient/day ($)	18,124	18,000	18,300	18,380	18,100	17,900	17,950
Productivity index (%)	93	97	95	97	97	95	97
Occupancy rate (%)	76	85	85	87	85	89	89
Supply cost per adjusted patient day ($)	2,568	2,500	2,600	2,400	2,450	2,390	2,450
Inventory turns	4.2	6	4	5	5	6	6
DELIVERY							
Average length of stay (ALOS)—inpatient	3.7	3.7	3.7	3.7	3.6	3.6	3.5
Extended stay >5 days	103	85	100	90	92	85	85
Extended stay >20 days	12.8	12	8	10	12	12	11
FLEXIBILITY							
Cross-trained nurses (%)	16.8	20	18	19	20	22	23
Bed turnover rate Admit/Discharge/Transfer percentage (%)	78.4	80	78	80	79	80	81
2-hour discharge rate (%)	47.1	75	50	60	70	73	75

FIGURE 15.6 – Updated strategic dashboard for operations.

☐ RED FLAG! Needs improvement.

*Metrics include January–December data (see Figure 2.6).

FYTD, fiscal year to date.

The crowd began to break up while continuing to talk excitedly. Mike walked over to Jennifer and Francine. "Hey, you two, can you come by my office in about an hour? I want to talk to you about where we go from here!"

Francine and Jennifer looked at each other with quizzical expressions, "Sure, Mike. See you then."

 Why does Mike Chambers want to see Francine and Jennifer? Because BPH has accomplished its goals, isn't it the end of the journey?

THE HIGHLY RELIABLE ORGANIZATION

Healthcare is a complex world with constant change and high risk. Doctors, nurses, and technicians work hard to deliver the best possible care. But in an environment of frequent and routine interruptions, patient variability, and occasionally emergent situations, it is difficult to consistently provide quality care or the "right care for the right patient at the right time—every time" (Clancy, 2009). As healthcare providers focus on improving quality and safety, they are turning to other industries that share characteristics of complexity and risk to learn how to avoid accidents. Industries, such as aviation, nuclear power, and the military, have studied past disasters to develop practices leading to improved safety. Weick and Sutcliffe (2007) demonstrated how the concepts of high reliability apply to healthcare and help prevent errors and avoid crises.

In Chapter 7, we looked at the concept of reliability, or the probability that each step will function effectively, without error, for a period of time. We will now explore how organizations can devise systems to adapt to unpredictable events and ensure safety and quality care. These are called **highly reliable organizations**.

Highly Reliable Organization (HRO)
An organization that devises systems to adapt to unpredictable events and to ensure safety and quality care.

Common Principles of Highly Reliable Organizations

Weick and Sutcliffe (2007) studied complex, high-risk organizations that coped well with sudden disasters and adapted in ways that prevented future catastrophes. They found that these institutions had a unique way of thinking and interacting. The culture of the organizations was constantly organizing and planning for the unexpected, as well as the expected. It was based on strong principles that were embraced at all levels and went beyond the process improvement concepts explained in Chapters 4 and 6 when we talked about TQM, Lean, and Six Sigma. The principles were as follows:

1. **Sensitivity to operations.** Leaders in HROs understand that employees involved in direct patient care understand best the state of the equipment and the adequacy of the processes to care for patients. TQM, Lean, and Six Sigma emphasized that those on the front lines must be involved in identifying quality processes. HROs adopt these principles and ensure that leaders and staff at all levels become aware of the risks to patients and work collectively to correct problems to improve the quality and safety of the care provided.

2. **Reluctance to simplify.** Lean and Six Sigma taught us that simplifying processes leads to improved quality and decreased variability. However, when analyzing a problem (not a process), it is important to understand the complexity of issues surrounding failures and not link the solution to a simple cause or set of simple causes. For example, assigning blame to a single staff member, inadequate training, poor communication, and so on may be easy, but the true reason for the failure will not be found and corrected unless (a) all possible causes, including the seemingly insignificant ones, have been identified and evaluated; and (b) the underlying causes of symptoms have been unearthed (Box 15.5).

⊕ BOX 15.5 – DID YOU KNOW?

O-Rings and the *Challenger* Accident

On January 28, 1986, the space shuttle *Challenger*, in its 10th flight, exploded 73 seconds after takeoff, killing the seven crew members inside. The entire event, captured on television, was horrifying to watch. What happened? Everyone wanted to know.

A Presidential Commission was convened and tasked with solving this mystery. And what was uncovered was no mystery at all. The point of failure should have been identified prior to the mission and corrected, but the complex situation was simplified to a point where the danger was ignored.

The failure that caused the *Challenger* explosion was an O-ring whose seal was breached, allowing pressurized burning gas from the solid rocket motor to reach the external fuel tank. Several factors, including the wear and tear of the aircraft after nine previous flights, the material used to make the O-rings, and the reaction of the joints as the shuttle launched, complicated the National Aeronautics and Space Administration (NASA) engineers' jobs. However, one factor, the temperature of the day, played a large role. The ambient temperature at Cape Canaveral, Florida, was 36° Fahrenheit. This was much colder than for any of the previous flights of the *Challenger*. Engineers had been concerned about the O-ring sealant at low temperatures, but this concern was not thought to be important enough to fix. Also, on that cold morning, the temperature or a possible O-ring failure was not factored into the calculations as the *Challenger* team was preparing for takeoff. The result of oversimplifying a complex and high-risk situation resulted in disaster (Presidential Commission on the Space Shuttle *Challenger* Accident, 1986).

---

3. **Preoccupation with failure.** Every organization has failures. HROs focus their attention on the little problems in order to prevent bigger mistakes. These small issues are viewed as symptomatic of underlying problems that need more attention. Through a systematic review and analysis of errors, big and small, HROs work to make their work environment more resilient (Box 15.6).

4. **Deference to expertise.** In every organization, there are people who are technical experts on processes or technology. The experts know how things work and the risks that patients face. Leaders of HROs must understand that these are the individuals who need to be drawn into the conversations if they want to build a culture of high reliability. Leaders (without the expertise) should not call the shots when circumstances call for those with specific expertise to direct the way.

⊕ BOX 15.6   OM IN PRACTICE!

Focus on Safe Medication Dispensing, Sentara Leigh Hospital

Employees of Sentara Leigh Hospital, a 250-bed community hospital in Norfolk, Virginia, observed that the areas within the nursing stations surrounding the medication-dispensing machines had become a place to congregate and talk. While nurses were waiting for their turn at the machine, people would chat, often to the person drawing up the doses.

These conversations created a distraction for those using the machines, which contributed to incorrect doses or incorrect stocking of the machine. Although no major medication error was identified, nurses using the medication-dispensing machines recognized that this practice could increase the possibility of medication errors and patient harm.

They convened those using the machines, discussed their concerns, and new practices were put into place. Machines were moved to areas away from the nursing workstations. A red-tile border surrounding the areas and signs indicating "NO INTERRUPTION ZONES" were added. All new personnel were introduced to the practices at orientation, and supervisors ensured compliance. No interruption during medication dispensing became the norm at this hospital, and patient safety was improved (Hines et al., 2008).

---

5. **Resilience.** There are always unexpected events. Leaders and staff in HROs are trained and prepared to respond when system failures occur. The capacity to recover quickly from unexpected events is called **resilience**. Resilient leaders design redundancy into their systems so that there will not be a single point of failure. Emergency situations are discussed, and the organization learns from errors. Planning efforts are organized so that all employees know their roles and have personalized plans of action so that they are not crippled when errors occur.

Resilience
The capacity to recover quickly from unexpected events.

The Importance of Mindfulness in HROs

The aforementioned five principles are interrelated and must be understood by everyone in the organization in order to have a collective "**mindfulness.**" Mindfulness is a rich awareness of detail that allows one to discover and correct errors that could escalate into a crisis. In HROs, everyone strives to see ways to improve the workings of the organization.

But mindfulness for the sake of mindfulness will not transform an organization to an HRO (Mayer, 2012). If errors are noticed, but not acted upon, healthcare delivery will not be safer. Mindfulness is as much about what people do when they see a mistake as noticing the mistake in the first place (Box 15.7).

Mindfulness
A rich awareness of detail that allows one to discover and correct errors that could escalate into a crisis.

BOX 15.7 – OM IN PRACTICE!

Lessons From an Aircraft Carrier

The navy has significantly reduced risk in their operations over the years by adopting the mind-set of highly reliable organizations. In his post, Dr. Muething described one example of how a culture of mindfulness improves safety. He was touring a naval aircraft carrier and watching the crew during a routine aircraft landing. A piece of paper floated up onto the deck, and a young trainee immediately responded by raising his hand. He understood how this could lead to distraction and danger. When other members of the crew saw his hand raised, they also raised their hands. The landing was aborted. The commander, when he heard of the trainee halting the landing, commended him and praised him by name. Safety is of utmost concern in HROs (Muething, 2011).

So what actually happened in the incident narrated in Box 15.7? A young recruit saw a piece of paper fly onto the flight deck. He saw the paper and could anticipate that something bad could happen as a result. Anticipation encompasses three of the five concepts of HROs:

1. **Preoccupation with failure.** The recruit was actively looking for signs that could indicate an error.

2. **Reluctance to simplify.** Foreign-object debris on the flight deck is a hazard. It can be sucked into jet engines and cause failure. The recruit saw the piece of paper and did not convince himself that the paper was too minor to cause problems.

3. **Sensitivity to operations.** The recruit understood how jet engines are able to draw foreign objects into them and how damage to engines and personnel can result.

Anticipation can also make healthcare safer. Imagine that instead of a young recruit on an aircraft carrier, you see a young nurse in the medical intensive care unit. She is helping a physician insert a central venous catheter, a catheter that is placed in a large vein and is at high risk for infection. The nurse, using the sterile technique, has set up all of the equipment needed for the catheter insertion. The doctor comes into the room and puts on sterile gloves. But the nurse notices that he has not washed his hands. Her mind is racing. She can anticipate that the error of not washing hands can result in a potentially life-threatening infection. In an HRO, she must speak up and stop the catheter from being placed. Anticipation is more than sensing early events that will lead to a problem; it also includes acting on observations to prevent the future event from occurring.

Anticipation is important, but errors do happen. Unexpected events or mistakes, no matter how carefully one tries to avoid them, occur.

HROs are able to respond appropriately when errors occur to contain the damage. The last two principles of HROs are related to containment:

1. **Deference to expertise.** In the last example, the physician must defer to the expertise of the nurse and respect her ability to see errors that will lead to infection. Even though the nurse did not have the same number of years of training, she did have the knowledge and experience to call out the error.

2. **Resilience.** The nurse and physician must regroup, absorb any strain, and preserve a professional relationship as they gather the necessary materials to restart the catheter insertion under sterile conditions. Both parties must also learn and grow from the episode.

HROs act mindfully to *manage* the unexpected. Note that we say "manage" and not "expect" the unexpected. Always expecting the unexpected is very stressful and signals that there is no expectation of stability within the organization. In managing the unexpected, HROs organize themselves to anticipate and notice aberrations and stop the development of errors. If they cannot halt mistakes, they focus on containment. If an event cannot be contained, HROs work to restore system functioning as soon as possible.

There are certain characteristics of an HRO that lead to "greatness." With healthcare being highly complex, with multiple simultaneous processes, numerous players, and unexpected events happening constantly, it is difficult to be highly reliable. Bad outcomes are a constant threat, even when you have caring and skilled personnel. Great healthcare organizations create structures that keep everyone attentive to risky processes and openly address problems. They make sure that small failures are tracked and corrected before they become large ones. Issues are addressed openly and are not passed off until the root cause is fully understood. Leadership resists the temptation to oversimplify issues and come to quick conclusions. Clinical operations remain the primary focus for everyone, and individuals at the "front lines" are involved in the analysis of the problem and the solution. Great organizations do not solely rely on hierarchy; they engage the technical experts to contribute to problem solving. Constant change, learning, and improvement create an environment that is resilient and can handle the shifting external challenges.

This book has been about a relentless pursuit of *quality*. But in the end, it is about being able to respond effectively and quickly to dramatic changes (*flexibility*). It is the "obsession" with quality that prepares the organization to be responsive (*delivery*), and the efficient use of resources (*cost*) that allows it to react to the most unanticipated changes. Focusing on the four competitive priorities and embracing the concepts of HROs will help you create a better healthcare organization.

CONNECTING THE CONCEPTS

With the challenges facing the U.S. healthcare system—spiraling costs, disappointing overall quality performance, limited patient access, complex regulatory environment, unfavorable population demographics, and workforce shortages—good operations management is more needed than ever. Operations management starts with a strategy that is aligned with the overall business strategy. The operations strategy is based on four competitive priorities—cost, quality, delivery, and flexibility—with quality being the foundation. By starting with the customers' needs, systems and processes can be designed to improve satisfaction, increase responsiveness, and reduce costly waste. You can also make operations more efficient with better layouts, better capacity planning and deployment, better inventory management, and fewer delays. Working in high-risk, complex healthcare organizations means you must also anticipate and contain the unexpected by following the principles of HROs.

All of the concepts presented in the book are interrelated. Mind maps representing these concepts can be put together into an interconnected whole, visually depicting that problems cannot always be approached in a linear fashion, and solutions must draw on many concepts simultaneously (Figure 15.7). As you pursue your career in operations management, we hope that you remember the success that the fictional characters of Bradley Park Hospital and Clinics achieved when they approached their problems methodically and understood that creating a culture of continuous improvement and learning is the key to reaching excellence.

BRADLEY PARK HOSPITAL 15.4

Mike welcomed Jennifer and Francine into his office. "Nice job on The Joint Commission survey. We could not have done it without you."

"And without all the other great people at Bradley Park," Jennifer added.

Mike continued, "I know you wonder why I asked you here. We have come such a long way this past year to build a quality culture. But I want to be sure that we don't end the work now and that we continue on the road to being a highly reliable organization."

"What is a reliable organization?" Francine asked.

"A highly reliable organization has systems in place that make them exceptionally consistent in accomplishing their goals and avoiding potentially catastrophic errors. Healthcare is complex, and errors can cause huge harm. I want BPH to be consistent in its processes, continuously improve its operations, and incessantly strive to be the safest hospital around. The airline industry has become much safer over the years because of its focus on reliability. The Joint Commission survey set us up to go further and ensure that we are always at the ready."

Jennifer spoke first, "I will look into what we need to do to become a reliable organization. If it builds on what we have done to date, and makes us even better, I am all for it."

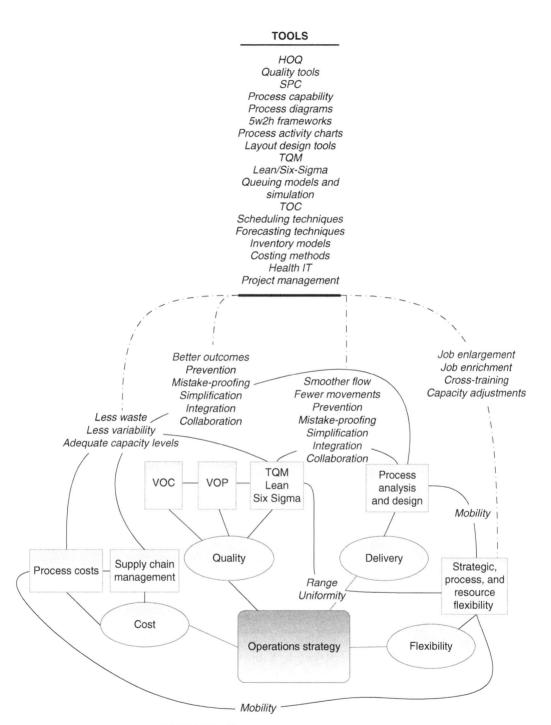

FIGURE 15.7 – Mind map connecting all concepts.

Francine added, "I am game for anything we can do to help us excel."
Mike concluded, "Thank you two for what you have done to date. I look forward to continuing the quality journey."

The end

KEY TERMS

Accreditation

Joint Commission

National Committee for Quality
Assurance (NCQA)

Certification

ISO 9000 certification

Malcolm Baldrige Award

Highly reliable organization
(HRO)

Resilience

Mindfulness

WHAT DO YOU REMEMBER?

1. Why would a hospital undergo accreditation by The Joint
    Commission? Name three benefits to the organization.

2. What is the difference between *accreditation* and *certification*?

3. What organizations are accredited by NCQA and why would this
    be important for consumers?

4. What is ISO 9000 and why was it established?

5. What is the Malcolm Baldrige Award and why is it considered
    prestigious?

6. What are the criteria for the Malcolm Baldrige Award?

7. What are five themes on which healthcare organizations should
    focus if they want to be excellent in patient-level measures of
    quality and safety?

8. Why is it important that the board of directors be engaged in the
    quest for quality?

9. What is an HRO? What are the five principles of HROs?

10. How can mindfulness prevent errors in the healthcare setting?
    Give one example.

BE A CONSULTANT FOR BPH

1. BPH is preparing for a Joint Commission survey. The Joint
    Commission uses a "tracer method," which follows the patient
    through the healthcare organization and looks at processes at each
    point along the way. How would you advise BPH to prepare for
    this type of survey?

2. What would it take for BPH to submit an application for the
    Malcolm Baldrige Award? Do you think they are ready?

3. As BPH starts to develop systems to become an HRO, how would
    you begin to incorporate the five principles of an HRO into the
    organization? Use the example of an upper level management

meeting that is discussing pharmacy errors and near misses over the past month. Give an example of how the five principles of HROs could be demonstrated in the meeting.

THINK OUTSIDE THE BOOK!

1. Why would the Centers for Medicare & Medicaid Services (CMS) allow an independent organization to survey healthcare organizations to ensure that they are complying with CMS standards?

2. Find two healthcare organizations that have received the Malcolm Baldrige Award to see whether the processes they followed prior to achieving this honor were similar or different. What is the underlying commonality that allowed the two organizations to be recognized for this award?

3. In Box 15.5, "O-Rings and the *Challenger* Accident," why were individuals hesitant to bring forward their concerns with O-ring failure? At the time, what were the potential cultural barriers at NASA that contributed to the disaster?

4. In the text, we gave examples of the HRO principles "reluctance to simplify" and "preoccupation of failure." Find a real-life example in which the HRO principles of "sensitivity to operations," "deference to expertise," and "resilience" were applied.

REFERENCES

American Society for Quality. (2015). Malcolm Baldrige National Quality Award (MBNQA). Retrieved from http://asq.org/learn-about-quality/malcolm-baldrige-award/overview/overview.html

Baldrige Performance Excellence Program. (2015). *2015–2016 framework for performance excellence: A systems approach to improving your organization's performance.* Gaithersburg, MD: U.S. Department of Commerce, National Institute of Standards and Technology.

Clancy, C. M. (2009). *What is health care quality and who decides* (Testimony before the Committee on Finance, Subcommittee on Health Care, United States Senate). Retrieved from http://www.hhs.gov/asl/testify/2009/03/t20090318b.html

Consumer Reports. (2014). *What's behind the health insurance rankings.* Yonkers, NY: Author. Retrieved from http://www.consumerreports.org/cro/2012/09/what-s-behind-the-health-insurance-rankings/index.htm

Deming, E. W. (1986). *Out of the crisis.* Cambridge, MA: Massachusetts Institute of Technology, Center for Advanced Engineering Study.

Foster, T. C., Johnson, J. K., Nelson, E. C., & Batalden, P. B. (2007). Using a Malcolm Baldrige framework to understand high performing clinical microsystems. *Quality and Safety in Healthcare, 16*(5), 334–341.

Ghosh, S., Handfield, R. B., Kannan, V. R., & Tan, K. (2003). A structural model analysis of the Malcolm Baldrige National Quality Award framework. *International Journal of Management and Decision Making* 4(4), 289–311.

Hines, S., Luna, K., Lofthus, J., Marquardt, M., & Stelmokas, D. (2008). *Becoming a high reliability organization: Operational advice for hospital leaders*. ([Prepared by the Lewin Group under Contract No. 290-04-0011] AHRQ Publication No. 08-0022, pp. 21–22). Rockville, MD: Agency for Healthcare Research and Quality.

International Organization for Standardization. (2015). *Quality management principles*. Geneva, Switzerland: Author.

Kaandorp, G. C., & Koole, G. (2007). Optimal outpatient appointment scheduling. *Health Care Management Science, 10*, 217–229.

Keroack, M. A., Youngberg, B. J., Cerese, J. L., Krsek, C., Prellwitz, L. W., & Trevelyan, E. W. (2007). Organizational factors associated with high performance in quality and safety in academic medical centers. *Academic Medicine, 82*(12), 1178–1186.

Lazarus, I. R., & Chapman, W. M. (2013, September 26). "ISO-style" healthcare: Designed to keep patients, practitioners, and management safe. *Becker's Hospital Review*. Retrieved from http://www.beckershospitalreview.com/hospital-management-administration/iso-style-healthcare-designed-to-keep-patients-practitioners-and-management-safe.html

Mayer, D. M. (2012). High reliability series: On collective mindfulness. Retrieved from https://educatetheyoung.wordpress.com/2012/07/25/high-reliability-series-on-collective-mindfulness

Muething, S. (2011). *Lessons from an aircraft carrier*. Cincinnati, OH: Cincinnati Children's Hospital Medical Center. Retrieved from Cincinnati Children's blog: http://cincinnatichildrensblog.org/hospital-operations/patient-safety/lessons-from-an-aircraft-carrier/#.VnTT8JpIhKo

National Committee for Quality Assurance. (2015). About NCQA. Retrieved from http://www.ncqa.org/AboutNCQA.aspx

Perry Johnson Registrars. (2015). Benefits of ISO 9000. Retrieved from http://www.pjr.com/standards/iso-90012008/benefits-of-iso-9000

Presidential Commission on the Space Shuttle *Challenger* Accident. (1986). *An accident rooted in history* [Report to the President, Chapter VI]. Retrieved from http://history.nasa.gov/rogersrep/v1ch6.htm

Rooney, A. L., & van Ostenberg, P. R. (1999). *Licensure, accreditation, and certification: Approaches to health services quality*. [Quality assurance methodology refinement series]. Bethesda, MD: USAID. Retrieved from http://pdf.usaid.gov/pdf_docs/Pnacf510.pdf

Schyve, P. M. (2009). *Leadership in healthcare organizations: A guide to Joint Commission leadership standards*. San Diego, CA: The Governance Institute. Retrieved from http://www.jointcommission.org/assets/1/18/WP_Leadership_Standards.pdf

Sprague, L. (2005). *Hospital oversight in medicare: Accreditation and deeming authority.* National Health Policy Forum (Issue Brief No. 802), 1–15. Retrieved from http://www.nhpf.org/library/issue-briefs/IB802_Accreditation_05-06-05.pdf

The Joint Commission. (2013). *Accreditation guide for hospitals.* Retrieved from http://www.jointcommission.org/assets/1/6/accreditation_guide_hospitals_2011.pdf

The Joint Commission. (2015). *Facts about joint commission standards.* Retrieved from http://www.jointcommission.org/facts_about_joint_commission_accreditation_standards

Trentman, T. L., Sorung, J., & Frasco, P. E. (2005). The impact of the Joint Commission for Accreditation of Healthcare Organizations pain initiative on perioperative opiate consumption and recovery room length of stay. *Anesthesia & Analgesia, 100*(1), 162–168.

Weick, K. E., & Sutcliffe, K. M. (2007). *Managing the unexpected: Resilient performance in an age of uncertainty* (2nd ed.). San Francisco, CA: Jossey-Bass.

APPENDIX 15.1—TOOL KIT

DOMAIN	TOOL	PURPOSE
Strategy	SWOT analysis	Approach used to identify the business's internal strengths (S) and weaknesses (W) and to evaluate the environmental opportunities (O) and threats (T). Its objective is to leverage the business's internal capabilities and benefit from market opportunities while mitigating external threats
	Balanced scorecard	Visual tool that provides a balanced view of organizational performance with key performance indicators
Project management	Project charter	Provides a road map for the project
	Traffic light flagging system	Communication tool that clearly depicts what projects (or tasks within the project) are on track (green), which ones are at risk of falling behind (yellow), and which ones are behind (red)
	Work breakdown structure	Hierarchical depiction of a project's components at various levels of detail that helps the planner identify all the work requirements of a project and organize them in a logical fashion
	Gantt chart	A chart showing the scheduling of activities and/or resources
	Network diagram	Diagram representing tasks required for completing the project and the minimum time to complete the task
	PERT	Planning and scheduling technique that takes into account uncertain times and helps determine the probability of completing a project by a certain date

(*continued*)

APPENDIX 15.1—TOOL KIT (*continued*)

DOMAIN	TOOL	PURPOSE
	CPM	An algorithm for scheduling a set of project activities. It is frequently used in conjunction with PERT
	Crashing	Method used to shorten the project's duration by reducing the time of one or more critical activities by adding more resources
Quality	House of quality (HOQ)	Matrix that clearly depicts the relationship between the VOC and the VOP
	Flowchart	Graphic representation of the sequential steps of a process
	Check sheet	Fact-finding tool that tracks occurrences and organizes the issues by category to identify critical problem areas
	Failure modes and effects analysis (FMEA)	Technique designed to identify potential failure points in a process and to assess the relative impact of these failures
	Spaghetti diagram	Diagram depicting traffic intensity and patterns within an area to help redesign layouts
	Cause-and-effect diagrams (fishbone diagram)	Diagram displaying potential sources of quality problems
	Pareto chart	Visual display of prioritized causes (or problems) based on the 80:20 rule
	Control chart	Chart depicting the behavior of a process through continuous tracking of performance with upper and lower control limits displayed
	Run chart	Chart that tracks values of an indicator over time to detect emerging patterns
	Plan–Do–Check–Act (PDCA) cycle	Continuous improvement cycle
SPC	Statistical process control charts (p, c, u, $\bar{X}$, R, s)	Charts depicting the behavior of a process over time through continuous tracking of performance with upper and lower control limits displayed (proportion defective in a sample, number of defects per unit, number of defects per unit when the area of opportunity fluctuates, sample means, sample ranges, sample standard deviations)
	Run test	Test used to detect patterns in a control chart divided into zones A, B, and C
Process capability	Process capability ratio	Metric used to determine whether a process in control has a distribution narrow enough to fit within specification limits
	Process capability index	Metric used to determine whether a process in control is properly centered with respect to a specified target value
Lean/Six Sigma	Value stream map	Diagram used in process modeling and analysis; it depicts a process flow from a Lean perspective, with areas needing improvement (*Kaizen*)

(continued)

APPENDIX 15.1—TOOL KIT (*continued*)

DOMAIN	TOOL	PURPOSE
	The 5 whys	Process used to identify the root cause(s) of a problem
	5S	Approach to make the use of the work space more effective and efficient
	Poka-yoke	System used to mistake-proof a process so that errors are identified before they happen
Process analysis and design	Flowchart	Diagram used in process modeling to visualize the movement of flow units in a process that displays the sequence of activities
	Swimlane diagram	Diagram used in process modeling to show the various participants in the sequence of process activities
	Simulation	Data analytical technique used in process modeling, analysis, and redesign that generates important process performance metrics that help assess current and alternative designs
	5w2h framework	Framework used in process analysis to understand the process by answering seven important questions and to identify improvement opportunities
	Process activity chart	Chart that displays all steps, categorizes them, and indicates whether they add value or not
	General process chart	Chart showing gains between the old and improved process designs
Layout	Line balancing	Technique used to produce equal task groupings when designing product layouts (repetitive processes)
	Block diagramming	Technique used to minimize the amount of load–distance when designing functional layouts
	Relationship diagramming	Technique used to satisfy qualitative requirements when designing functional layouts
Capacity and demand	Queuing analysis	Technique used to analyze queues and find optimal capacity levels
	Queuing simulation	Data analytical technique used to generate important queuing system performance metrics and evaluate current and alternative systems
	TOC	Methodology used to manage bottlenecks
Scheduling	Linear programming	Optimization model used to schedule labor resources according to a preset objective (e.g., minimize cost)
	Sequencing rules	Rules used to sequence the jobs to be performed in order to appear fair (FCFS), minimize congestion (SPT), minimize tardiness (EDD), minimize the number of tardy jobs (Moore's algorithm), etc.
	Kaandorp and Koole's (2007) optimal outpatient appointment scheduling model	Individual appointment-scheduling algorithm used to optimize waiting, tardiness, and idle time

(*continued*)

APPENDIX 15.1—TOOL KIT (continued)

DOMAIN	TOOL	PURPOSE
Forecasting	Time series models (naïve approach, simple moving average, weighted moving average, exponential smoothing, trend-adjusted exponential smoothing, and linear trend projection)	Forecasting techniques based on the assumption that the behavior or pattern of historical demand is likely to continue in the future
	Associative models (e.g., multiple linear regression)	Forecasting techniques that take into account the influence of several variables on demand
Inventory management	ABC analysis	Approach used to classify inventory items into three or more classes based on their annual dollar volume that helps design inventory systems appropriate for each classification
	Basic economic order quantity model	Inventory model used to determine the order size that will minimize the sum of annual holding and ordering costs
	Quantity discount model	Inventory model used to determine the order size that will minimize the sum of annual holding, ordering, and purchasing costs for different prices
	Reorder point model	Inventory model used to help determine the timing of an order based on inventory levels
Cost accounting	Cost-to-charge ratio (CCR) cost method	A method used to estimate the costs of services that uses charges as the basis to estimate and allocate costs
	Relative value units (RVU) cost method	A method used to estimate the costs of services that uses a standard estimate of the intensity and costs of work for services rendered
	Activity-based costing (ABC)	A method used to calculate costs by assigning costs to activities needed to provide a service and knowing the amount of activity that is consumed to provide the service
	Time-driven activity-based costing (TDABC)	A method used to measure the costs of services that uses a capacity cost rate to have a resource and then the time that capacity is consumed with a needed activity as the basis for determining costs

APPENDIX: STANDARD NORMAL DISTRIBUTION TABLE

z	.00	.01	.02	.03	.04	.05	.06	.07	.08	.09
.0	.5000	.5040	.5080	.5120	.5160	.5199	.5239	.5279	.5319	.5359
.1	.5398	.5438	.5478	.5517	.5557	.5596	.5636	.5675	.5714	.5753
.2	.5793	.5832	.5871	.5910	.5948	.5987	.6026	.6064	.6103	.6141
.3	.6179	.6217	.6255	.6293	.6331	.6368	.6406	.6443	.6480	.6517
.4	.6554	.6591	.6628	.6664	.6700	.6736	.6772	.6808	.6844	.6879
.5	.6915	.6950	.6985	.7019	.7054	.7088	.7123	.7157	.7190	.7224
.6	.7257	.7291	.7324	.7357	.7389	.7422	.7454	.7486	.7517	.7549
.7	.7580	.7611	.7642	.7673	.7704	.7734	.7764	.7794	.7823	.7852
.8	.7881	.7910	.7939	.7967	.7995	.8023	.8051	.8078	.8106	.8133
.9	.8159	.8186	.8212	.8238	.8264	.8289	.8315	.8340	.8365	.8389
1.0	.8413	.8438	.8461	.8485	.8508	.8531	.8554	.8577	.8599	.8621
1.1	.8643	.8665	.8686	.8708	.8729	.8749	.8770	.8790	.8810	.8830
1.2	.8849	.8869	.8888	.8907	.8925	.8944	.8962	.8980	.8997	.9015
1.3	.9032	.9049	.9066	.9082	.9099	.9115	.9131	.9147	.9162	.9177
1.4	.9192	.9207	.9222	.9236	.9251	.9265	.9279	.9292	.9306	.9319
1.5	.9332	.9345	.9357	.9370	.9382	.9394	.9406	.9418	.9429	.9441
1.6	.9452	.9463	.9474	.9484	.9495	.9505	.9515	.9525	.9535	.9545
1.7	.9554	.9564	.9573	.9582	.9591	.9599	.9608	.9616	.9625	.9633
1.8	.9641	.9649	.9656	.9664	.9671	.9678	.9686	.9693	.9699	.9706
1.9	.9713	.9719	.9726	.9732	.9738	.9744	.9750	.9756	.9761	.9767
2.0	.9772	.9778	.9783	.9788	.9793	.9798	.9803	.9808	.9812	.9817
2.1	.9821	.9826	.9830	.9834	.9838	.9842	.9846	.9850	.9854	.9857
2.2	.9861	.9864	.9868	.9871	.9875	.9878	.9881	.9884	.9887	.9890
2.3	.9893	.9896	.9898	.9901	.9904	.9906	.9909	.9911	.9913	.9916
2.4	.9918	.9920	.9922	.9925	.9927	.9929	.9931	.9932	.9934	.9936
2.5	.9938	.9940	.9941	.9943	.9945	.9946	.9948	.9949	.9951	.9952
2.6	.9953	.9955	.9956	.9957	.9959	.9960	.9961	.9962	.9963	.9964
2.7	.9965	.9966	.9967	.9968	.9969	.9970	.9971	.9972	.9973	.9974
2.8	.9974	.9975	.9976	.9977	.9977	.9978	.9979	.9979	.9980	.9981
2.9	.9981	.9982	.9982	.9983	.9984	.9984	.9985	.9985	.9986	.9986
3.0	.9987	.9987	.9987	.9988	.9988	.9989	.9989	.9989	.9990	.9990
3.1	.9990	.9991	.9991	.9991	.9992	.9992	.9992	.9992	.9993	.9993
3.2	.9993	.9993	.9994	.9994	.9994	.9994	.9994	.9995	.9995	.9995
3.3	.9995	.9995	.9995	.9996	.9996	.9996	.9996	.9996	.9996	.9997
3.4	.9997	.9997	.9997	.9997	.9997	.9997	.9997	.9997	.9997	.9998

INDEX

CPSIA information can be obtained
at www.ICGtesting.com
Printed in the USA
LVHW061739261219
641754LV00004B/40/P